Mentoring in Practice

A Reader

edited and introduced by

CAROL M. DOWNIE MSc RGN RM RNT

PRINCIPAL LECTURER, SCHOOL OF HEALTH AND SOCIAL CARE
UNIVERSITY OF GREENWICH

and

PHILIP BASFORD RGN RNT ARRC

MANAGEMENT AND TRAINING CONSULTANT, NTRG
VISITING LECTURER
UNIVERSITY OF GREENWICH

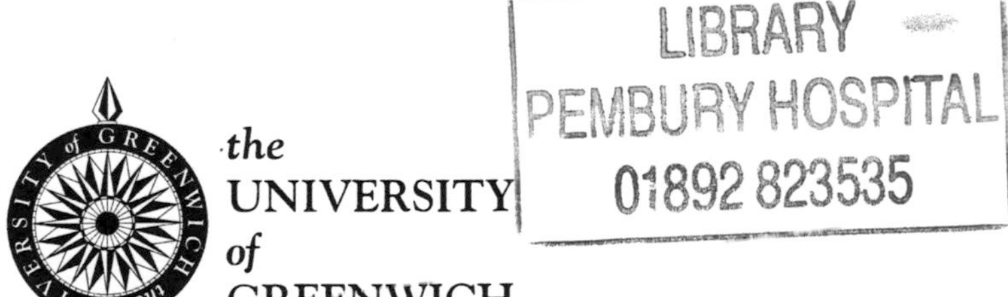

First published in 2003 and prepared for publication for internal university use only by:

Marketing Office
University of Greenwich
Riverside House
Beresford Street
London
SE18 6BU

ISBN 1 86166 194 0

Text design and layout by Angela Allwright. Cover design by Peter Birkett.

University of Greenwich, a charity and company limited by guarantee, registered in England (reg. no. 986729). Registered Office: Old Royal Naval College, Park Row, Greenwich, London SE10 9LS

55
56
133

Contents

Introduction

In the role of mentor, some of the skills individuals are expected to display are those of facilitation, assessing and evaluation. They also have to act as effective guides, supervisors and role models. In order to fulfil these roles and demonstrate the required skills, these individuals must also be able to plan effectively, be organised, be able to motivate and, perhaps most importantly, be able to demonstrate competent communication skills. From this, it is clear that the mentoring role is by no means a simple one and requires the development of a wide range of sometimes quite complex skills to enable the individual to be able to carry out the roles effectively.

Mentoring and the accompanying responsibilities are not something that most healthcare workers can easily avoid if they are to fulfil their professional responsibilities. The purposes of courses on developing the role of the mentor are to provide assistance in the development of theoretical knowledge and to allow an exploration of how this knowledge can be applied in the workplace.

This Reader is divided into four discreet sections which reflect the main content areas of most mentoring courses. The first section provides materials related to Adult Learning as it applies to the Mentoring Process and an attempt has been made to provide a range of sources on this topic which will complement any formal theoretical input received. As learners in healthcare are by definition adults, it would seem logical to explore this concept and gain a clearer understanding of the adult in a learning situation.

The second section seeks to explore the concept of the Mentor and Mentoring by providing a range of materials which examine the background to, current status of and the multi-faceted role of the mentor.

In section three, which focuses on the facilitation role of the mentor, the materials provided are designed to help in the exploration of a range of theories of learning and factors which influence the learning process, such as individual differences in learning styles, learning skills and experience. There is also an examination of the creation of an effective learning environment and how theoretical concepts and ideas can actually be applied in a practical setting. Very often students find theoretical concepts rather abstract and obscure and have great difficulty in identifying any meaningful relationship between the two. The extracts and articles provided will hopefully help in making this relationship clearer.

The final section covers Evaluation and Assessment, two key skills required of any mentor. Again a range of materials is provided to help demystify the theories of assessment and evaluation and allow an exploration of the roles of assessor and evaluator.

It would be unwise to consider that the contents of this book provide a definitive collection of articles and extracts, negating the need for further reading and investigation. It would be expected that it will merely provide a fairly secure foundation and that further investigation will be required to make your knowledge base more secure.

Carol Downie and Philip Basford
October 2003

Publisher's note

The contents of the readings in this anthology have been reproduced as they appear in the publications from which they are taken. In the majority of cases footnotes and bibliographic material are included, the exceptions being where they are of excessive length.

Adult Learning: Application in the Mentoring Process

The extracts and articles in this section are designed to give a reasonably balanced view of andragogy and experiential learning. Linked to formal theoretical input you should find these of value in developing your understanding of adult learning and the role you have to play, as a mentor, in facilitating the process. Much has been written about adult learning theory and to gain a more in-depth understanding of this aspect further reading and investigation will be necessary.

Malcolm Knowles (1990) is possibly one of the best known theorists in relation to adult learning and adult learner; it was he who developed the concept of andragogy. Andragogy is based on the assumption that adults differ in a range of ways from children in their approach to learning. As mentors generally deal with adults, it would seem reasonable for them to be familiar with Knowles' work and to have explored the concept of the adult learner.

Traditionally, education in healthcare was delivered using a predominantly pedagogical approach. That is to say that strategies used to teach were, in the main, teacher-led with the students playing a very passive, childlike role in the learning process. This has not entirely changed, nor perhaps is it appropriate that a pedagogical model is never used, but there are significant advances in ensuring facilitation strategies are suitable for the students involved in the learning process.

Milligan (1995) summarised the key elements of andragogy when he stated that it is:

> 'facilitation of adult learning that can best be achieved through a student centred approach that . . . . enhances student's self concept, promotes autonomy, self direction and critical thinking, reflects on experience and involves the learner in the diagnosis, planning, enacting and evaluation of their own learning needs.'

If one accepts that these elements are essential then it is incumbent on anyone involved in this process to develop their knowledge and skills in adult learning strategies in order for them to be better able to facilitate learners in the most appropriate and beneficial manner.

Those using this reader will almost entirely be involved in the facilitation of learning in the workplace where the vast amount of learning is experiential in nature. Experiential learning is viewed by Kolb (1984) as knowledge emerging through the transformation of experience. Kolb sees learning as a core process in human development and this development is gained through experience. Many of the elements of andragogy can be demonstrated within the Experiential Learning Cycle (Kolb, 1984), and it becomes clear that these two combined can offer a very useful means of assisting those in a learning situation to develop a range of skills that will equip them to function more effectively.

References

Knowles M (1984) *Andragogy in Action: Applying Modern Principles of Adult Learning*. Jossey-Bass, San Francisco.

Kolb D (1984) *Experiential Learning Cycle*. Prentice Hall, New Jersey.

Milligan F (1995) In defence of andragogy. *Nurse Education Today* 15: 22–27.

1. Introduction: The Art and Science of Helping Adults Learn

Malcolm S. Knowles

This is a very personal book — a collection of descriptions by people who have personally applied the andragogical model. It seems fitting, therefore, that I present my current thinking about adult learning as a personal account of my wanderings through the morass of learning theory; for, like the wanderings of Odysseus, mine were circuitous, not a direct flight. I see this chapter as a way of introducing newcomers to the world of andragogy with a route map, but those who are already familiar with this world may want to scan the chapter to note certain changes in my current views of adult education.

My first experiences with adult learners

My experience with adult education began in 1935. I had prepared in college for a career in the U.S. Foreign Service, but when I graduated I was informed by the State Department that only the most urgent vacancies were being filled and that only those who had passed their exams in 1932 were being considered. So I had to get a "holding" job for at least three years to support a new wife and hoped-for family. The job I got was as director of related training for the National Youth Administration (NYA) in Massachusetts. The NYA was a work-study program for unemployed youth between the ages of eighteen and twenty-five, with the mission of increasing their employability; I was put in charge of the study half of the program.

I had no formal qualifications for this job outside of leading some boys' clubs in a settlement house. Nonetheless, I sensed that a vocational training program for unemployed youth would have to be different from the prescriptive academic courses that I had taken, although I didn't know in what ways. I tried to find a book that would tell me how to conduct a program of this sort, and I couldn't find one. So I sought out people who were directing adult education programs — including the director of the Boston Institute for Adult Education, a director of adult education in a public school, and a couple of deans of evening colleges — and formed an advisory council to give me guidance. At their suggestion I made an informal survey of a sample of employers to find out what jobs were open and what skills they required. Then I organized courses to provide these skills, employed instructors, found locations for the courses to meet, and published a descriptive brochure. The response to the program was enthusiastic, and many of the youths (especially those between twenty-one and twenty-five years of age) began getting jobs. I loved what I was doing, but I didn't know that it had a name. Then, around 1937, someone asked me what I did. When I told him, he said, "Oh, you are an adult educator." So now I had an identity. He also told me that there was a national organization, the American Association for Adult Education, that was holding its annual conference in New York in several weeks. I attended the conference and was impressed with the people I met there and with their ideas about the differences between adult learners and school children. At that point I joined the association and notified the State Department that I had changed my career goals to adult education and was no longer available for the Foreign Service.

During my five years with the NYA, I observed that some teachers were more effective than others in working with young adults; and I began developing some generalizations — for instance, that the more effective teachers were more interested in their students as persons, were more informal in their manner, involved students more in participatory activities, and gave them more helpful support. But my understanding of the emerging theory of adult education came from two individuals and their books. The single most influential person in guiding my thinking was Eduard C. Lindeman, whose book *The Meaning of Adult Education* (1926) enlightened me about the unique characteristics of adults as learners and the need for methods and techniques for helping them learn. Lindeman was at that time director of educational projects for the Works Projects Administration and thus was in a sense my supervisor. We spent many hours together, discussing what adult education was all about, and I regarded him as my mentor. Dorothy Hewitt, director of the Boston Center for Adult Education, which provided informal courses to the citizens of Boston, was a member of my advisory council and showed me step by step how she planned and managed her program. The book she co-authored with Kirtley Mather, *Adult Education: A Dynamic for Democracy* (1937), served as my how-to-do-it manual. I still reread these two books periodically for inspiration and reinforcement. I marvel that these two early pioneers — especially Lindeman — had insights about adult learning that only recently have been verified by research.

In 1940 I was invited to become director of adult education at the Huntington Avenue YMCA in Boston, and I found myself in possession of a built-in laboratory for applying ideas I was picking up from people and publications and for experimenting with new ideas. *The Journal of Adult Education*, published by the American Association for Adult Education, and the *Adult Education Bulletin*, published by the Department of Adult Education of the National Education Association, were rich sources of information. Both of them frequently ran articles by "successful" teachers of adults ("successful" being defined as the ability to attract and retain students) describing how differently they treated adults from the way children and youth are traditionally treated in school and college. It is interesting to me now, in retrospect, that although there was general agreement among adult educators that adults are different from youth as learners, there was no comprehensive theory about these differences. The literature was largely philosophical and anecdotal and at most provided miscellaneous principles or guidelines.

Getting an academic foundation

In 1944 I enlisted in the U.S. Navy and during the next two years had more time to read and think than I had ever had before in my life. I devoured all the books in print about adult education and started trying to work out a comprehensive theory about it. In 1946 I became director of adult education at the Central YMCA in Chicago and enrolled in the graduate program in adult education at the University of Chicago for my master's and doctor's degrees. I was greatly influenced by the intellectual rigor and teaching style of my major professor, Cyril O. Houle. He related to his students as colleagues and demonstrated that principles of adult education could be applied even in a traditional university. At this time also, I experienced the challenge of being a truly self-directed learner in a seminar with Arthur Shedlin, an associate of Carl Rogers.

For my master's thesis, I decided that I would attempt to bring together all the insights, principles, and practices regarding the education of adults that I had garnered from the literature, from other adult educators, and from my own experience, as at least a first step in constructing a comprehensive theory of adult education. When I was about half way through it, Cyril Houle informed me that he had been talking with the editor of Association Press about projects his students were working on and that the editor had expressed an interest in seeing the outline and first couple of chapters of my thesis. As a result, my first book was published in 1950 under the title *Informal Adult Education.* I had been trying to identify the essence of adult education, the thing that made it different from traditional education; and the best I could come up with was "informal." I still had not developed a comprehensive, coherent, integrated theory. But it was a step in that direction.

Into the larger world of adult education

In 1951 I became executive director of the newly formed Adult Education Association of the U.S.A., and my line of vision shifted from individual learners in particular programs to the broad scope of the adult education movement. But three forces kept me thinking about the adult learner. One was my doctoral studies at the University of Chicago, through which I became familiar with the formal theories of learning. My strongest impression was that these theories had all been based on research on animals (mostly rodents, at that) and children, and I had trouble seeing their relevance to what I had observed about learning by adults. In fact, it dawned on me that the educational psychologists had not been studying learning at all, but reactions to teaching. The second force was the research that Cyril Houle was engaged in at the time regarding how "continuing learners" — people who have engaged in systematic learning on their own — go about learning. The results of his study were published in a monograph under the title *The Inquiring Mind* in 1961, and had the effect of redirecting subsequent research by adult education researchers, especially Allen Tough, to focus on the internal dynamics of learning in adults. The third force was my participation in the human relations laboratories of the National Training Laboratories (NTL) Institute of Behavioral Sciences in Bethel, Maine. From this experience I derived a deep understanding and appreciation of the forces affecting learning that are at work in groups and in larger social systems.

In 1960 I was invited to Boston University to start a new graduate program in adult education. During the next fourteen years, I had a laboratory where I could apply principles of adult learning in a university setting; I had time and motivation for doing research; and I had doctoral students to extend and deepen the research. During this period a theoretical framework regarding adult learning evolved. But I didn't have a label for it that would enable me to talk about it in parallel to the traditional pedagogical model. (Incidentally, "pedagogy" is derived from the Greek words *paid*, meaning "child," and *agogos*, meaning "leader of." So pedagogy literally means "the art and science of teaching children.)

I found the solution in the summer of 1967, when a Yugoslavian adult educator, Dusan Savicevic, attended my summer session course on adult learning and at the end of it exclaimed, "Malcolm, you are preaching and practicing andragogy." I responded, "Whatagogy?" because I had never heard the term before. He explained that European adult educators had coined the term as a parallel to pedagogy, to provide a label for the growing body of knowledge and technology in regard to adult learning, and that it was being defined as "the art and science of helping adults learn." It made sense to me to have a differentiating label, and I started using the term in 1968, in articles describing my theoretical framework for thinking about adult learning.

In 1970 I put it all together in a book, *The Modern Practice of Adult Education: Andragogy Versus Pedagogy*. The "versus" was in the title because at that point I saw the two models, pedagogy and andragogy, as dichotomous — one for children, the other for adults. During the next ten years, however, a number of teachers in elementary, secondary, and higher education who had somehow been exposed to the andragogical model told me that they had experimented with applying (or adapting) the model in their practice and had found that young people learned better, too, when the andragogical model was applied. On the other hand, many teachers and trainers working with adults cited circumstances — especially in basic skills training — where the pedagogical model seemed to be required. So the revised edition of the book, published in 1980, had the subtitle *From Pedagogy to Andragogy*.

Toward a theory of adult learning

During the two decades between 1960 and 1980, we gained more knowledge about the unique characteristics of adults as learners and their learning processes than had been accumulated in all previous history. Houle's seminal study in 1961 had stimulated a rash of research by adult educators (Boud, 1981; Boyd, Apps, and Associates, 1980; Cross, 1981; Houle, 1980; Howe, 1977; Knox, 1977; Long, Hiemstra, and Associates, 1980; Smith, 1982; Tough, 1967, 1979, 1982). But knowledge was flowing from other social science disciplines as well. Clinical psychologists and psychiatrists were learning about how to help people change their behavior (Bandura, 1969; Maslow, 1962, 1970, 1971; Rogers, 1951, 1961, 1969, 1980); and, since education also is concerned with behavioral change, their findings were relevant to adult learning. Developmental psychologists were discovering that there are predictable developmental stages during the adult years as well as through adolescence and that the transitions from one stage to another are one of the chief triggers of readiness to learn (Baltes, 1978; Erikson, 1959; Goulet and Baltes, 1970; Havighurst, 1970; Knox, 1977; Levinson, 1978; Lidz, 1968; Neugarten, 1964, 1968; Pressey and Kuhlen, 1957; Sheehy, 1974; Stevens-Long, 1979). Social psychologists were discovering how the conditions of our environment — such as color, population density, stress, social norms, social class, race, and group processes — affect learning (Barker, 1978; Birren, 1969; Bronfenbrenner, 1979; David and Wright, 1975; Deutsch and others, 1968, Lewin, 1951; Moos, 1976, 1979; Moos and Insel, 1974) and how change can be brought about in environments (Arends and Arends, 1977; Bennis,

Benne, and Chin, 1968; Eiben and Milleren, 1976; Greiner, 1971; Hornstein and others, 1971; Lippitt, 1969, 1973; Martorana and Kuhns, 1975; Zurcher, 1977). Sociologists were adding to our knowledge about how institutional policies and procedures (concerning, for instance, admissions, registration, financial matters, and reward systems) affect learning (Barrett, 1970; Boocock, 1972; Corwin, 1974; Etzioni, 1961, 1969).

Clearly, by 1970 — and certainly by 1980 — there was a substantial enough body of knowledge about adult learners and their learning to warrant attempts to organize it into a systematic framework of assumptions, principles, and strategies. This is what andragogy sets out to do. I don't know whether it is a theory; this is a controversial issue, which Cross (1981, pp. 220–228) discusses lucidly and objectively. I feel more comfortable thinking of it as a system of concepts that, in fact, incorporates pedagogy rather than opposing it — a notion that I will develop more fully later. First, I must clarify my current thinking about the pedagogical and andragogical models.

Traditional learning — the pedagogical model

The pedagogical model is the one we have all had the most experience with. In fact, it is the only way of thinking about education that most of us know, for it has dominated all of education — even adult education until recently — since schools started being organized in the seventh century. Stated in their purest and most extreme form, these are the assumptions about learners inherent in the pedagogical model:

1. *Regarding the concept of the learner (and therefore, through conditioning in prior school experience, the learner's self-concept):* The learner is, by definition, a dependent personality, for the pedagogical model assigns to the teacher full responsibility for making all the decisions about what should be learned, how and when it should be learned, and whether it has been learned. The only role for the learner, therefore, is that of submissively carrying out the teacher's directions.

2. *Regarding the role of the learner's experience:* Learners enter into an educational activity with little experience that is of much value as a resource for learning. It is the experience of the teacher, the textbook writer, and the audiovisual aids producer that counts. Accordingly, the backbone of pedagogical methodology is transmission techniques — lectures, assigned readings, and audiovisual presentations.

3. *Regarding readiness to learn:* Students become ready to learn what they are told that they have to learn in order to advance to the next grade level; readiness is largely a function of age.

4. *Regarding orientation to learning:* Students enter into an educational activity with a subject-centered orientation to learning; they see learning as a process of acquiring prescribed subject matter content. Consequently, the curriculum is organized according to content units and is sequenced according to the logic of the subject matter.

5. *Regarding motivation to learn:* Students are motivated primarily by external pressures from parents and teachers, competition for grades, the consequences of failure, and the like.

This may sound like a caricature, but think back to all the teachers you have had. Didn't most of them operate on the basis of these assumptions? Of course, there have always been great teachers who experimented with other assumptions, but in my experience they were few and far between. In fact, teachers have been under pressure from their systems to be loyal to these assumptions, often in the name of "academic standards."

A new approach to learning — the andragogical model

In contrast — and in equally pure and extreme form — the assumptions inherent in the andragogical model are these:

1. *Regarding the concept of the learner:* The learner is self-directing. In fact, the psychological definition of adult is "One who has arrived at a self-concept of being responsible for one's own life, of being self-directing." When we have arrived at that point, we develop a deep psychological need to be perceived by others, and treated by others, as capable of taking responsibility for ourselves. And when we find ourselves in situations where we feel that others are imposing their wills on us without our participating in making decisions affecting us, we experience a feeling, often subconsciously, of resentment and resistance.

This fact about adult learners presents adult educators with a special problem. For even though adults may be totally self-directing in every other aspect of their lives — as workers, spouses, parents, citizens, leisure-time users — the minute they walk into a situation labeled "education," "training," or any of their synonyms, they hark back to their conditioning in school, assume a role of dependency, and demand to be taught. However, if they really are treated like children, this conditioned expectation conflicts with their much deeper psychological need to be self-directing, and their energy is diverted away from learning to dealing with this internal conflict. As they have become aware of this problem, adult educators have been devising strategies for helping adults make the transition from being dependent learners to being self-directed learners. It has become increasingly widespread practice to include an orientation to self-directed learning at the beginning of an educational activity or program (see Knowles, 1975; [and selections 6 and 8 in Chapter Two; selections 1, 2, 3, and 8 in Chapter Three; selections 1 and 3 in Chapter Four]).

2. *Regarding the role of the learner's experience:* The andragogical model assumes that adults enter into an educational activity with both a greater volume and a different quality of experience from youth. The greater volume is self-evident; the longer we live, the more experience we accumulate, at least in normal lives. The difference in quality of experience occurs because adults perform different roles from young people, such as the roles of full-time worker, spouse, parent, and voting citizen.

This difference in experience has several consequences for education. First of all, it means that, for many kinds of learning, adults are themselves the richest resources for one another; hence the greater emphasis in adult education on such techniques — group discussion, simulation exercises, laboratory experiences, field experiences, problem-solving projects, and the like — that make use of the experiences of the learners. In addition, the differences in experience assure greater heterogeneity in groups of adults. The range of experience among a group of adults of various ages will be vastly greater than among a group of twelve-year-olds. Consequently, in adult education greater emphasis is placed on individualized learning plans, such as learning contracts (Knowles, 1975, 1980; [see also Chapter Two, selections 1, 6, and 8; Chapter Three, selections 1 and 5; Chapter Four, selection 3; Chapter Five, selections 1 and 3]). But there is a possible negative consequence as well. Because of their experience, adults often have developed habitual ways of thinking and acting, preconceptions about reality, prejudices, and defensiveness about their past ways of thinking and doing. To overcome this problem, adult educators are devising strategies for helping people become more open-minded (Benne, Bradford, and Lippitt, 1975; Davis and Scott, 1971; Ray, 1973).

There is a more subtle and perhaps even more potent consequence of adults' greater experience: it becomes increasingly the source of an adult's self-identity. Let me illustrate this point. If I had been asked when I was ten years old "Who are you?" I would have explained: "My name is Malcolm Knowles, the son of Dr. A. D. Knowles, a veterinarian; I belong to the Presbyterian Sunday School; I live at 415 Fourth Street, Missoula, Montana; and I attend school at the Roosevelt Grammar School on Sixth Street." My self-identity would be derived almost exclusively from external sources — the name I was given by my parents, my father's vocation, my religious affiliation, my residence, and my school. If I had been asked the same question at age forty, I would have given my name and then recounted the positions I had held with the NYA, the YMCA, the AEA, and so on. Like other adults, I would derive my self-identity from my experience. So if in an educational situation an adult's experience is ignored, not valued, not made use of, it is not just the experience that is being rejected; it is the person. Hence the great importance of using the experience of adult learners as a rich resource for learning. This principle is especially important in working with undereducated adults, who, after all, have little to sustain their dignity other than their experience.

3. *Regarding readiness to learn:* The andragogical model assumes that adults become ready to learn when they experience a need to know or do something in order to perform more effectively in some aspect of their lives. Chief sources of readiness are the developmental tasks associated with moving from one stage of development to another; but any change — birth of children, loss of job, divorce, death of a friend or relative, change of residence — is likely to trigger a readiness to learn. But we don't need to wait for readiness to develop naturally; there are things we can do to induce it, such as exposing learners to more effective role models, engaging them in career planning, and providing them with diagnostic experiences in which they can assess the gaps between where they are now and where they want and need to be (Knowles, 1980).

4. *Regarding orientation to learning:* Because adults are motivated to learn after they experience a need in their life situation, they enter an educational activity with a life-centered, task-centered, or problem-centered orientation to learning. For the most part, adults do not learn for the sake of learning; they learn in order to be able to perform a task, solve a problem, or live in a more satisfying way. The chief

implication of this assumption is the importance of organizing learning experiences (the curriculum) around life situations rather than according to subject matter units. For example, courses that might be titled "Composition I," "Composition II," and "Composition III" in a high school might better be titled "Writing Better Business Letters," "Writing for Pleasure and Profit," and "Improving Your Professional Communications" in an adult education program. I had a terrible time learning to use the computer on which I am writing this chapter because the instructional manual set out to teach me about computers rather than teaching me how to use the computer to compose a chapter.

Another implication is the importance of making clear at the outset of a learning experience what its relevance is to the learner's life tasks or problems. We have a dictum in adult education that one of the first tasks of a facilitator of learning is to develop "the need to know" what will be learned (see Freire, 1970; Knowles, 1980).

5. *Regarding motivation to learn:* Although it acknowledges that adults will respond to some external motivators — a better job, a salary increase, and the like — the andragogical model predicates that the more potent motivators are internal — self-esteem, recognition, better quality of life, greater self-confidence, self-actualization, and the like (Herzberg, 1966; Maslow, 1970). Program announcements are accordingly placing increasing emphasis on these kinds of outcomes.

Choosing which model to use

As I have said, I now regard the pedagogical and andragogical models as parallel, not antithetical. For centuries educators had only one model, the pedagogical model, to go on. Now we have two sets of assumptions about learners. In some situations, such as when learners of whatever age are entering a totally strange territory of content or are confronting a machine they have never seen before, they may be truly dependent on didactic instruction before they can take much initiative in their own learning; in such situations the pedagogical assumption of dependency is realistic, and pedagogical strategies would be appropriate. In many more instances, however, especially with adult learners, the andragogical assumptions would be realistic — particularly if the learners have had some orientation to self-directed learning — and andragogical strategies would be appropriate. There is growing evidence [see Chapter Seven, selections 1, 2, and 3] that the andragogical assumptions are realistic in many more situations than traditional schooling has recognized. For example, children are very self-directing in their learning *outside of school* and could also be more self-directed in school. Children and youth bring *some* experience with them into an educational activity, and this experience could be used as a resource for some kinds of learning. Children and youth also are more ready to learn when they experience a "need to know" than when they are told they have to learn, and we can expose them to life situations through which they will become aware of what they need to know. Finally, children and youth are naturally more motivated by intrinsic rewards than by external pressures; it is schools that have conditioned them to be otherwise [see Chapter Seven, selection 1].

Implications for program design

The pedagogical and andragogical models result in two very different approaches to the design and operation of educational programs. The basic format of the pedagogical model is a *content plan*, which requires the teacher to answer only four questions:

1. What content needs to be covered? The implication is that it is the teacher's responsibility to cover — in the classroom or through assigned reading — all the content that students need to learn. So the pedagogue constructs a long list of content items to be covered. (This requirement seems to me to place an unfair burden on the teacher to master all the content and to doom the students to be limited to the teacher's resources.)
2. How can this content be organized into manageable units, such as fifty-minute, three-hour, or one-week units? So the pedagogue clusters the content items into manageable units.
3. What would be the most logical sequence in which to present these units? It is the logic of the subject matter that determines the sequence, not the readiness of the learners or other psychological factors. So, in mathematical or scientific content programs, the sequence is typically from simple to complex; in history it is chronological.
4. What would be the most efficient means of transmitting this content? With highly informational content, the preferred means would probably be lecture or audiovisual presentations and assigned reading; if the content involves skill performance, it would probably be demonstration by the teacher and drill by the students.

In contrast, the basic format of the andragogical model is a *process design*. The andragogical model assigns a dual role to the facilitator of learning (a title preferred over "teacher"): first and primarily, the role of designer and manager of processes or procedures that will facilitate the acquisition of content by the learners; and only secondarily, the role of content resource. The andragogical model assumes that there are many resources other than the teacher, including peers, individuals with specialized knowledge and skill in the community, a wide variety of material and media resources, and field experiences. One of the principal responsibilities of the andragogue is to know about all these resources and to link learners with them.

An andragogical process design consists of seven elements:

1. *Climate setting*. What procedures would be most likely to produce a climate that is conducive to learning? In my estimation, a climate that is conducive to learning is a prerequisite to effective learning; and it seems tragic to me that so little attention is paid to climate in traditional education. I attach so much importance to climate setting that I devote about 10 per cent of the time available in an educational activity to this element, and most of the case descriptions [in this book] do, too. In planning procedures for climate setting, I give attention to two aspects of climate: physical environment and psychological atmosphere.

In regard to *physical environment*, the typical classroom setup, with chairs in rows and a lectern in front, is probably the least conducive to learning that the fertile human brain could invent. It announces to anyone entering the room that the name of the game here is one-way transmission, that the proper role of the student is to sit and listen to transmissions from the lectern. I make a point of getting to a meeting room before the participants arrive, and if it is set up like a classroom I move the lectern to a corner and put the chairs in one large circle or several small circles. My preference is to have the participants sitting around tables, five or six to a table. I also prefer meeting rooms that are bright and cheerful, with colorful decor.

Important as physical climate is, *psychological climate* is even more important. Here are the characteristics of a psychological climate that is conducive to learning as I see it:

- *A climate of mutual respect.* People are more open to learning when they feel respected. If they feel that they are being talked down to, ignored, or regarded as dumb, and that their experience is not valued, their energy is spent dealing with this feeling more than with learning.
- *A climate of collaborativeness.* Because of their conditioning in their earlier school experience, in which competition for grades and teachers' favor was the norm, adults tend to enter into any educational activity with a rivalrous attitude toward fellow participants. Since, for many kinds of learning in adult education, peers are the richest resources for learning, this competitiveness makes those resources inaccessible. For this reason the climate-setting exercise with which I open all my workshops and courses puts the participants into a sharing relationship from the outset.
- *A climate of mutual trust.* People learn from those they trust more than from those they mistrust. And here we who are put in the position of teacher or trainer of adults are at a disadvantage, for students in schools learn at an early age that on the whole teachers are not very trustworthy. For one thing, they have power over students; they are authorized to give grades, to determine who passes or fails, and otherwise to hand out punishments and rewards. For another thing, the institutions in which they work present them in their catalogues and program announcements as authority figures. And it is built into the bloodstreams of those who grew up in the Judeo-Christian democratic tradition that authority figures are to be mistrusted, at least until they are tested and their degree of trustworthiness determined. In my workshops I try to convey in various ways (for instance, by encouraging participants to make decisions and by lending them my books) that I trust participants and hope thereby to obtain their trust.
- *A climate of supportiveness.* People learn better when they feel supported rather than judged or threatened. I convey my desire to be supportive by accepting learners with an unqualified positive regard, matching any diagnosis of a weakness with a valuing of a strength, empathizing with their problems or worries, and defining my role as that of a helper. But I also organize them into peer-support groups and coach them on how to support one another.

- *A climate of openness and authenticity.* When people feel free to be open and natural, to say what they really think and feel, they are more likely to be willing to examine new ideas and risk new behaviors than when they feel the need to be defensive. In school we often have to pretend to know things that we don't or to think things that we don't or to feel things that we don't, and this interferes with learning. If the teacher or trainer demonstrates openness and authenticity in his or her own behavior, this will be the model that participants will adopt.
- *A climate of pleasure.* Learning should be one of the most pleasant and gratifying experiences in life; for, after all, it is the way people can become what they are capable of being — achieving their full potential. It should be an adventure, spiced with the excitement of discovery. It should be fun. I think it is tragic that so much of our previous educational experience has been a dull chore.
- *A climate of humanness.* Perhaps what I have been saying about climate can be summed up with the adjective "human." Learning is a very human activity. The more people feel that they are being treated as human beings, the more they are likely to learn. Among other things, this means providing for human comfort — good lighting and ventilation, comfortable chairs, availability of refreshments, designation of nonsmoking areas, frequent breaks, and the like. It also means providing a caring, accepting, respecting, helping social atmosphere.

[A climate-setting exercise designed to bring these characteristics into being is described in Chapter Four, selection 6, and other climate-setting strategies are described in Chapter Two, selection 8; Chapter Three, selections 7 and 8; and Chapter Eight, selection 2.]

2. *Involving learners in mutual planning.* What procedures can be used to get the participants to share in the planning? I sometimes have subgroups choose a representative to serve on a planning committee to meet with me to discuss where we should go next. Frequently I will present several optional possibilities for activities and ask the groups to discuss them and report their preferences. There is a basic law of human nature at work here: people tend to feel committed to any decision in proportion to the extent to which they have participated in making it; the reverse is even more true — people tend to feel uncommitted to any decision to the extent that they feel others are making it for them and imposing it on them.

3. *Involving participants in diagnosing their own needs for learning.* What procedures can be used for helping learners responsibly and realistically identify what they need to learn? One of the pervasive problems in this process is meshing the needs the learners are aware of (felt needs) with the needs their organizations or society has for them (ascribed needs). A variety of strategies are available, ranging from simple interest-finding checklists to elaborate performance assessment systems, with a balance between felt needs and ascribed needs being negotiated between the facilitator and the learners. I frequently use a model of competencies, which reflects both personal and organizational needs, so that the learners can identify the gaps between where they are now and where the model specifies they need to be (see Knowles, 1980, pp. 229–232, 256–261, 369, 371).

4. *Involving learners in formulating their learning objectives.* What procedures can be used to help learners translate their diagnosed needs into learning objectives? See the following section on learning contracts.

5. *Involving learners in designing learning plans.* What procedures can be used to help the learners identify resources and devise strategies for using these resources to accomplish their objectives? See the following section on learning contracts.

6. *Helping learners carry out their learning plans.* See the following section on learning contracts.

7. *Involving learners in evaluating. their learning.* Evaluation of the accomplishment of objectives by individual learners is treated in the following section. But evaluation is also concerned with judging the quality and worth of the total program. Assessing individuals' learning outcomes is a part of this larger evaluation, but more than this is involved in this process. This book is not the place to go into detail about the complex process of program evaluation, but I would be remiss if I neglected to call my readers' attention to the fact that a major turn in our very way of thinking about evaluation has been in progress in the last few years. This turn, away from almost exclusive emphasis on quantitative evaluation toward increasing emphasis on qualitative evaluation, is described in Cronbach and others, 1980; Guba and Lincoln, 1981; Kirkpatrick, 1975; and Patton, 1978, 1980, 1981, 1982.

Using learning contracts to provide structure

Learning contracts are an effective way to help learners structure their learning. Some people have difficulty with the term "contract" because of its legalistic flavor and substitute "learning plan" or "learning agreement" for it. But "learning contract" is the term most often found in the literature.

The procedure I use in helping learners design and execute learning contracts is as follows: (1) Each learner translates a diagnosed learning need into a learning objective that describes the terminal behavior to be achieved (which is appropriate for most basic skills learning) or the direction of improvement in ability (which is appropriate for more complex learnings). (2) The learner next identifies, with the facilitator's help, the most effective resources and strategies for accomplishing each objective. (3) The learner then specifies what evidence will be collected for indicating the extent to which each objective was accomplished. (4) Finally, the learner specifies how this evidence will be judged or validated. After the learners have completed a first draft of their contracts, they review the drafts with small groups of peers and get their reactions and suggestions. Then I review the contracts to make sure that the required objectives of the program are included, to suggest other resources, and to determine whether I can agree with the learners' proposals for collecting and validating evidence of accomplishment. Once I approve a contract, the learner proceeds to carry it out, with me always available as a consultant and resource. The resources specified in the contracts include group activities; information inputs by me or other specialists, peers, or individuals in the community; and independent study. When the contracts are fulfilled, the learners present me with their "portfolios of evidence," which often include papers, tapes, rating scales by judges or observers, and oral presentations. I indicate whether I accept the portfolio as fulfilling the contract or, if not, what additional evidence is required for my acceptance.

I use learning contracts in almost all of my practice. Students contract with me to meet the requirements of the university courses I teach. (Incidentally, even though there may be a number of unnegotiable requirements, the means by which students accomplish required objectives can be highly individualized.) Students going out on field experiences, such as practicums or internships, contract with me and the field supervisor — a three-way contract. I also use contracts in short-term workshops, but in these the learners leave the workshop with a contract specifying how they are going to continue to learn on their own. Finally, I use learning contracts in the in-service education programs I am involved in; many physicians, nurses, social workers, managers and supervisors, and educators are using learning contracts for their continuing personal and professional development.

More detailed descriptions of contract learning can be found in Knowles, 1975, pp. 25–28; 1978, pp. 127–128, 198–203; 1980, pp. 243–244, 381–389; [and in Chapter Two, selections 1, 6, and 8; Chapter Three, selections 1 and 5; and Chapter Five, selections 1 and 3, in this book].

Ways of using andragogy for education and training

The andragogical model has been widely adopted or adapted in a variety of programs — from individual courses at every level of education to total programs of in-service education, undergraduate education, graduate education, continuing education, human resources development, continuing professional education, technical training, remedial education, and religious education. It appears in almost every kind of institution, including elementary and secondary schools, community colleges, colleges and universities, business and industry, government agencies, health agencies, professional societies, churches, and voluntary organizations — in North America and around the world. "Andragogy" was so recently introduced into our literature (a decade and a half ago), though, that it does not yet appear in a dictionary. But it will before long.

As Cross (1981, pp. 227–228) states, "Whether andragogy can serve as the foundation for a unifying theory of adult education remains to be seen. At the very least, it identifies some characteristics of adult learners that deserve attention. It has been far more successful than most theory in getting the attention of practitioners, and it has been moderately successful in sparking debate; it has not been especially successful, however, in stimulating research to test the assumptions. Most important, perhaps, the visibility of andragogy has heightened awareness of the need for answers to three major questions: (1) Is it useful to distinguish the learning needs of adults from those of children? If so, are we talking about dichotomous differences or continuous differences? Or both? (2) What are we really seeking: Theories of learning? Theories of teaching? Both? (3) Do we have, or can we develop, an initial framework on which successive generations of scholars can build? Does andragogy lead to researchable questions that will advance knowledge in adult education?" Actually, a growing amount of research is being done, which I shall summarize in [the last chapter]. But I agree that andragogy's greatest impact has been in action.

References

Arends R I, Arends J H (1977) *Systems Change Strategies in Educational Settings.* Human Sciences Press, New York.

Baltes P D (ed.) (1978) *Life-Span Development and Behavior*, Vol 1. Academic Press, New York.

Bandura A (1969) *Principles of Behavior Modification.* Holt, Rinehart and Winston, New York.

Barker R G *et al.* (1978) *Habitats, Environments, and Human Behavior: Studies in Ecological Psychology and Eco-Behavioral Science.* Jossey-Bass, San Francisco.

Barrett J H (1970) *Individual Goals and Organizational Behavior.* Institute for Social Research, University of Michigan, Ann Arbor.

Benne K, Bradford L P, Lippitt R (1975) *The Laboratory Method of Changing and Learning.* Science and Behavior Books, Palo Alto.

Bennis W, Benne K, Chin R (1968) *The Planning of Change.* Holt, Rinehart and Winston, New York.

Birren F (1969) *Light, Color, and Environment.* Van Nostrand Reinhold, New York.

Boocock S S (1972) *An Introduction to the Sociology of Learning.* Houghton Mifflin, Boston.

Boud D (1981) *Developing Student Autonomy in Learning.* Nichols, New York.

Boyd R D, Apps J W *et al.* (1980) *Redefining the Discipline of Adult Education.* Jossey-Bass, San Francisco.

Bronfenbrenner U (1979) *The Ecology of Human Development.* Harvard University Press, Cambridge.

Corwin R G (1974) *Education in Crisis: A Sociological Analysis of Schools and Universities in Transition.* Wiley, New York.

Cronbach L J *et al.* (1980) *Toward Reform of Program Evaluation: Aims, Methods, and Institutional Arrangements.* Jossey-Bass, San Francisco.

Cross K P (1981) *Adults as Learners: Increasing Participation and Facilitating Learning.* Jossey-Bass, San Francisco.

David T G, Wright B D (eds) (1975) *Learning Environments.* University of Chicago Press, Chicago.

Davis G A, Scott J A (1971) *Training Creative Thinking.* Holt, Rinehart and Winston, New York.

Deutsch M *et al.* (1968) *Social Class, Race, and Psychological Development.* Holt, Rinehart and Winston, New York.

Eiben R, Milliren A (eds) (1976) *Educational Change: A Humanistic Approach.* University Associates, La Jolla.

Erikson E (1959) *Identity and the Life Cycle.* Psychological Issues Monograph 1. International Universities Press, New York.

Etzioni A (1961) *A Sociological Reader on Complex Organizations.* Free Press, New York.

Freire P (1970) *Pedagogy of the Oppressed.* Seabury Press, New York.

Goulet L R, Baltes P B (1970) *Life-Span Developmental Psychology.* Academic Press, New York.

Greiner L E (ed) (1971) *Organizational Change and Development.* Irwin, Homewood, IL.

Guba E G, Lincoln Y S (1981) *Effective Evaluation: Improving the Usefulness of Evaluation Results Through Responsive and Naturalistic Approaches.* Jossey-Bass, San Francisco.

Havighurst R (1970) *Developmental Tasks and Education,* 2nd edn. McKay, New York.

Herzberg F (1966) *Work and the Nature of Men.* World Publishing, Cleveland.

Hewitt D, Mather K F (1937) *Adult Education: A Dynamic for Democracy.* Appleton-Century-Crofts, New York.

Hornstein J A *et al.* (1961) *Social Intervention.* Free Press, New York.

Houle C O (1961) *The Inquiring Mind.* University of Wisconsin Press, Madison.

Houle C O (1980) *Continuing Learning in the Professions.* Jossey-Bass, San Francisco.

Howe M J A (ed.) (1977) *Adult Learning: Psychological Research and Applications.* Wiley, New York.

Kirkpatrick D L (1975) *Evaluating Training Programs.* American Society for Training and Development, Washington DC.

Knowles M S (1975) *Self-Directed Learning: A Guide for Learners and Teachers.* Follett, Chicago.

Knowles M S (1970) *The Modern Practice of Adult Education: From Pedagogy to Andragogy* 2nd edn. Follett, Chicago. (Originally published 1970.)

Knox A B (1977) *Adult Development and Learning: A Handbook on Individual Growth and Competence in the Adult Years.* Jossey-Bass, San Francisco.

Levinson D J (1978) *The Seasons of a Man's Life.* Knopf, New York.

Lewin K (1951) *Field Theory in Social Science.* Harper & Row, New York.

Lidz T (1968) *The Person: His Development Throughout the Life Cycle.* Basic Books, New York.

Lindeman E C (1926) *The Meaning of Adult Education.* New Republic Press, New York.

Lippitt G (1969) *Organizational Renewal.* Appleton-Century-Crofts, New York.

Lippitt G (1973) *Visualizing Change.* NTL National Learning Resources, Fairfax, VA.

Long H B, Hiemstra R *et al.* (1980) *Changing Approaches to Studying Adult Education.* Jossey-Bass, San Francisco.

Martorana S V, Kuhns E (1975) *Managing Academic Change: Interactive Forces and Leadership in Higher Education.* Jossey-Bass, San Francisco.

Maslow A (1962) *Toward a Psychology of Being.* Van Nostrand, New York.

Maslow A (1970) *Motivation and Personality.* Harper & Row, New York.

Maslow A (1971) *The Farther Reaches of Human Nature.* Viking Press, New York.

Moos R H (1976) *The Human Context: Environmental Determinants of Behavior.* Wiley-Interscience, New York.

Moos R H (1979) *Evaluating Educational Environments: Procedures, Measures, Findings and Policy Implications.* Jossey-Bass, San Francisco.

Moos R H, Insel P M (1974) *Issues in Social Ecology.* National Press Books, Palo Alto.

Neugarten B L (1964) *Personality in Middle and Later Life.* Lieber-Atherton, New York.

Neugarten B L (ed) (1968) *Middle Age and Aging*. University of Chicago Press, Chicago.

Patton M Q (1978) *Utilization-Focused Evaluation*. Sage, Beverly Hills.

Patton M Q (1980) *Utilization Evaluation*. Sage, Beverly Hills.

Patton M Q (1981) *Creative Evaluation*. Sage, Beverly Hills.

Patton M Q (1982) *Practical Evaluation*. Sage, Beverly Hills.

Pressy S L, Kuhlen R G (1957) *Psychological Development Through the Life Span*. Harper & Row, New York.

Ray W S (1973) *Simple Experiments in Psychology*. Behavioral Publications, New York.

Rogers C A (1951) *Client-Centered Therapy*. Houghton Mifflin, Boston.

Rogers C A (1961) *On Becoming a Person*. Houghton Mifflin, Boston.

Rogers C A (1969) *Freedom to Learn*. Merrill, Columbus, Ohio.

Rogers C A (1980) *A Way of Being*. Houghton Mifflin, Boston.

Sheehy G (1974) *Passages: Predictable Crises of Adult Life*. Dutton, New York.

Smith R M (1982 *Learning How to Learn*. Cambridge, New York.

Stevens-Long J (1979) *Adult Life: Developmental Processes*. Mayfield, Palo Alto.

Tough A M (1967) *Learning Without a Teacher*. Ontario Institute for Studies in Education, Toronto.

Tough A M (1979) *The Adult's Learning Projects*, 2nd edn. Ontario Institute for Studies in Education, Toronto. (Originally published 1971.)

Tough A M (1982) *Intentional Changes: A Fresh Approach to Helping People Change*. Follett, Chicago.

Zurcher L A (1977) *The Mutable Self: A Concept for Social Change*. Sage, Beverly Hills.

2. Adult Students

Who are they . . . ?

Alan Rogers

A profile

Much attention has been given in recent writings on adult education to the adult learner. Whole books have been devoted to the topic, and most general studies of adult education, based on the premise that all forms of teaching adults ought to be student-centred rather than teacher-centred, contain sections dealing with the way adults learn.

Drawing a profile

One feature of this discussion has been the compilation of lists of general characteristics of the adult student. Their aim is to help teachers of adults to become more conscious of what they are doing when they draw up a profile of their students, to test out the items specified to see which do not apply to their particular group and to identify other characteristics specific to their teaching context. One of the more helpful of these lists is that compiled by Harold Wiltshire (1977), but like so many it is limited in its application in that it is directed more towards the traditional student in non-vocational liberal adult education of an academic orientation than to basic education, practical skill-based courses or professional development programmes.

In many of these descriptions there are a number of myths about the adult student participant. Large generalisations are frequently made. It has been suggested at various times that adult students are people well beyond schooldays, full of a mixture of regret, determination, guilt and ambition, but dogged by lack of confidence and self-belief, harrassed by noise and diversions, facing problems of time and space to study, tiredness and opposition and mockery from spouses and friends. (These descriptions have all come from a number of recent writings purporting to describe the general principles on which adult education is predicated.) But clearly these do not describe all (or even perhaps many) adult students. Each such description needs to be drawn up with a proper regard to the individual group in question.

We all draw some picture of who our student participants are going to be. We do this as an integral part of the process of planning the programme and the course. Most of us can rely on past experience to help us, but new teachers of adults cannot do this; they may turn to other more experienced teachers to assist them, but even this is not always possible.

The process of compiling such a profile is often unconscious. We rarely make explicit the views we hold about the prospective learners, their abilities and motivations, what we can and cannot expect from them. Even in those programmes where the goals are negotiated with the potential learners, the teacher-planner still makes

Alan Rogers: 'Adult Students: Who are they . . .?' from *TEACHING ADULTS* (Open University Press, 1996; 2nd edn), pp. 51–73.

several assumptions: for example, that the participants want to join in, that they are willing to entertain the notion of change and that they are capable of engaging in the processes put before them.

We thus fall into unquestioned and possibly false presuppositions about our prospective student participants. We may on occasion assume that the learners are at the opposite extreme from our goals: that they possess no skills at all, if our goals relate to the acquisition of skills; that they are completely ignorant of the subject in hand, if our goals are knowledge-related; that they hold negative attitudes, if our goals are attitude change; that they have not yet begun to comprehend, if our goals are concerned with understanding; that they lack all forms of confidence, if our goal is confidence-building. None of this may be true. Indeed, it is most unlikely to be true. Those who come on a bird-watching course are already more likely than not to know something about the subject; those who attend car-maintenance classes will invariably have had some experience of a car; those who wish to learn about women in literature are most likely to have done some reading in this field already and will have views on the subject; those who come to family planning classes often know more than their teachers allow for. Unless we make conscious what we believe about our potential student participants, we are in danger of presupposing falsehoods.

Testing the profile

Having compiled a list of apparent characteristics of our potential learners, it is necessary to test these assumptions at the earliest possible moment. In some forms of teaching adults — correspondence courses, for example, or the educational programmes offered by the media, and the self-directed learning materials prepared by many agencies — the teacher-planners never meet the learners, so that the assumptions made cannot easily be assessed to see whether they are right or wrong. But in most other cases it will quickly become apparent whether we have judged correctly what the prospective student participants are able to do, what they are willing to do and what they want to do. Sometimes we will get it all wrong, so that there is nothing to be done after the first meeting with the participants other than to redesign the whole learning package. As with most skills of teaching, however, we can improve with practice; but even after long experience, because every group of adult learners is different, we must still test whether the presuppositions we have made about our student participants are correct or not, so that the programme of work can be revised or amplified as necessary.

Teachers are sometimes reluctant to do this in their first encounter with the student participants. It may be that they are hesitant to expose themselves from the start of their relationship with the learners, to give the impression that they are in any way uncertain. Or, having prepared something for the first meeting, they may be anxious to go ahead and give it. These teachers sometimes justify this on the grounds that the participants who have turned up want to have something 'meaty' at the first session so as to judge better the content, level and pace of learning involved in the course, that some prospective participants would find a first meeting devoted to a general discussion about the course an unsatisfying experience. Or the teacher accepts at face value the student participants' assessment of their own ignorance of the subject, their inability to contribute anything useful towards setting the goals and constructing the programme of work. There are many reasons for not opening up the assumptions we have made about the participants to challenge.

Despite all of this, it might be better to spend at least part of the first meeting with any group of adult student participants listening rather than talking, assessing whether the assumptions we have made about their interests and abilities are right or not. Even if we do not do this at the first meeting, the task will have to be done at some stage during the course. It should be done as early as possible so that there is no lengthy gap between bringing together their expectations as learners and our expectations as teachers.

The range is wide

In order to test out these presuppositions, we need to undertake the process consciously rather than subconsciously. It is useful to write down our description of the potential student participants, and here we run into the biggest problem of all. Most of us teach in groups, and the wide range of those who join such groups, even small groups, may hinder us from making realistic judgements about what we can in general expect from our student-learners.

Let us take one example as illustration. It is now thought that intelligence is not a fixed inherent ability that cannot be improved after the end of formal schooling, or a range of abilities that grow and decline along mathematical curves. Rather it is seen as being 'plastic'; it rises to peaks or falls into troughs throughout adulthood, largely governed by whether the activities engaged in and the environmental factors are stimulating and encouraging or whether they are damaging and inhibiting. Particularly the development of intelligence seems to be dependent as much on the amount of educational experience one has received and on the subsequent use of learning skills in one's occupations as it is on the basic learning ability developed when young. People who have had a good deal of education and who have been engaged in tasks calling for considerable and regular amounts of new learning will be 'more intelligent' at 50 than they were at 25; conversely, those who have been employed in occupations that have not required them to engage in new learning are likely not to have developed their intelligence to the same extent. Thus in any group of adults engaged in a learning programme, the range of learning ability, even among people of roughly the same age and same initial education, is likely to be considerably wider than in a comparable group of children.

Lifespan studies

It may be useful at this point to outline the general conclusions of what have been called 'lifespan studies' in relation to adult learning; for if learning is a process of personal changes made in adapting to changed situations and experiences, the study of different patterns of life is likely to throw light on such learning.

In the 1970s and 1980s, a general view of lifespan development emerged based on ideas about the major points of meaningful change that occur during adulthood. This was thought to give teachers a useful basis for this process of drawing a profile of their student participants. Although it is given less credence today, it is still worth reviewing this field. What follows is not intended to be a comprehensive guide to this area of study but an introduction. Teachers who want to pursue the subject further are referred to the books listed at the end of the chapter.

The terms 'growth', 'change' and 'development' are used in a variety of senses. Some educational writers see 'change' as quantitative accumulations to the content of thought, and 'development' as a qualitative transformation of one's thinking structures; but these distinctions omit any reference to intention and purpose. A more satisfactory definition sees 'change' as value-free, indicating an undirected process, whereas 'development' implies purposeful change, directed towards the achievement of some goal.

A number of writers see adult progression as growth, the gradual and natural increase of maturity. Others see it as development, i.e. goal achievement. For writers like Piaget and Kohlberg, the goal is one of 'rational autonomy'; for others there is the increasing sense of perspective as well. Viewed in goal-achievement terms, it is possible to determine stages of progress. On the other hand, some writers have rejected the concept of 'development' and replaced it with a more or less value-free view of change throughout adult life.

General considerations

It seems to be accepted that there are, for the adult, few (if any) age-related changes. Unlike the child and the adolescent, whose different stages are recognised (even if not universally agreed), adults change and develop more by experience and by the exercise of abilities than by mere age. There are physical changes that occur with increasing age, but none of these is related to any specific age, and the changes that take place differ for each individual.

Additionally there is in the West a strong emphasis on the physical elements in human make-up. Thus ageing is seen as a phenomenon to be resisted, something to be overcome rather than welcomed and valued for the wisdom and status it brings.

Adult development has several other dimensions. On the one hand, there are the changes that occur within each person as the years advance. On the other hand, there are those changes within the social and cultural context of the individual which call for new responses. We are dealing with a changing person in a changing world. Change, not stability, is the norm.

Among those many changes are variations in perspectives, including the view of the ageing process itself. Traditionally in Western societies, youth has been seen in positive terms while ageing has been regarded more negatively. But in recent years, views in relation to older persons have shown significant changes, with growing positive attitudes towards older age groups and rather more negative attitudes towards younger people, perhaps a result of the increasing number of older persons in society as a whole. In many developing countries on the other hand, influenced by Western cultural patterns, the reverse would seem to be happening, despite the increasing number of older persons in various forms of adult education. Society is not only imposing roles on individuals but is constantly reinterpreting those roles — and all these changes will call for learning on the part of every adult.

Ages of man and woman

Most of us are acquainted with Shakespeare's 'seven ages of man': the infant, the schoolboy, the lover, the soldier, the justice, the 'lean and slipper'd pantaloon', and finally second childhood. Since Shakespeare's time there have been many attempts to better this description of adult changes. Some are very general: Whitehead's successive phases of romance, precision and rationalizatlon, or Egan's romantic stage, philosophic stage and eirenic or fulfilled stage. Some still display the so-called 'plateau effect' of Shakespeare: growth, maturity and decline. The very title of the University of the Third Age perpetuates the outdated concept of a three-stage life consisting of growth, performance and 'completion'.

Recently it has been recognised that some of the earlier schemata relating to adult development were too closely tied to successive stages, and attempts have been made to break away from this. There is however still a tendency to see adults in too great an isolation from the social and physical environment in which they are located, to see society as static while the individual changes, to underestimate the effect of changes in social structures and values on the adult. Equally there is an underestimate of the effect that different educational and cultural backgrounds and different experiences can have on adults.

Dominant concerns

The most influential group of lifespan theories are those that see changes during the adult phase of life in terms of dominant concerns. Havighurst (1952) suggested that the individual passes through eight main stages; after the two periods of childhood and adolescence comes adulthood, a 'developmental period in about as complete a sense as childhood and adolescence are developmental periods'. From 18 to 30, adults are focusing their life; there is a concern for self-image. Self is a major preoccupation, not society (voting and civic duties are less frequent at this period). This is a period of experimentation, of settling into jobs and love affairs. Education tends to be turned to by some as an instrument for occupational advancement. From 30 to 40, adults are collecting their energies; this is a period of stability and relatively less introspection, less self-doubt. The job is now most important, with child-rearing a close second. Involvement in education now tends towards the expressive rather than the instrumental. The decade from 40 to 50 is a period of self-exertion and assertion. This is the peak of the life cycle. Public and civic activities are more prominent, whereas participation in educational programmes tends to decline. This stage is characterised by a turning out towards society from oneself, the family and the job. 'Action' is the means of dealing with the world, and this emphasis on action brings about the first consciousness of physical deterioration.

From 50 to 60, adults maintain their position and at the same time change roles; educational involvement is for expressive rather than instrumental purposes. There is increasing evidence of physical deterioration (sight and hearing), and larger amounts of energy have to be exerted to avoid losing ground. Often it is asserted that the adult is more passive and deferential, with a sagging sense of self-assurance. 'Thought' rather than 'action' is the means of dealing with the world, and there is more concentration on short-term rather than long-term achievements. The adult spends the years between 60 and 70 deciding whether and how to disengage. This is often the period of the death of friends and relatives, of less social concern, of less active preoccupations and more short-term gratifications. From 70 onwards is the period of making the most of disengagement. Healthy adults are not too preoccupied with the past, are self-accepting and relatively content with the outcomes of their life, but often the period is characterised by poor health, reduced means and dependence on others.

Havighurst's views, as set out above, are frequently cited by adult educators. They are almost the only ones that relate such changes directly to educational activities. But they are too simplistic, too rigidly tied to ages, and they are based on Western male-dominated concepts of a successful work career. Major changes in social structure have rendered such a neat analysis suspect.

These considerations have led to a more sequential approach without tying each stage too closely to ages. Neugarten (1977) speaks of adulthood as representing a 'movement from an active, combative, outer-world orientation to . . . an adaptive, conforming inner-world orientation'. Three stages are identified: a period of expressiveness, expansiveness and extroversion, of autonomy and competence (up to about the age of 30); an intermediate period of reorientation; and a third stage of change from active to passive modes of relating to the environment with greater introversion.

Tensions

Erikson (1965) sees the stages of human development in terms of different tensions. There is the general and continuing tension between 'the inner wishes . . . and the demands to conform to other people's standards and requirements', which all people experience and which leads to compromises if the adult is 'to maintain the integrity of his [*sic*] personality'. In addition there are a series of developmental tensions; in puberty and adolescence, there is the tension between identity and role confusion; in young adulthood, intimacy versus isolation; in adulthood, generativity versus stagnation; and in 'maturity', the integrity of the self versus despair. The educational implications of each stage are delineated: initial education for the child and adolescent, vocational education for the young adult, social and community education for the adult, and philosophical and creative education for the mature. Boshier (1989) similarly speaks of tensions (incongruence); he draws upon the work of Carl Rogers (1974) to depict the individual as having

> 'two problems; maintaining inner harmony with himself [*sic*] and with the environment. Incongruence is developed within the person (intra-self) and between the person and other-than-self experiences (self/other) . . . . The research of life-cycle psychologists supports the notion that younger [adults] manifest more intra-self and self/other incongruence than older, more mature [people].'
>
> (Boshier 1989: 147–50)

Time perspectives

Lifespan changes may be seen in terms of how time is viewed. Some writers have suggested that the child sees the future as far away; for the adolescent, the future is rosy; for the adult, time is finite, while the mature adult feels that time is running out. Friedman elaborated this version of the 'plateau' theory of lifespan changes, being particularly conscious that successive stages do not correlate with ages. He thus overlapped some stages:

- The *entry stage* (say 18–25): orientation is to the future — the future will be better than the present; change is good.
- *Career development* (say, 20–50): orientation is increasingly more to the present than to the future; away from interest in promotion towards an interest in the intrinsic value of work, together with participation and achievement in non-work areas.
- *Plateau* (say, 35–55): the main time-focus moves from the present to a feeling that time is running out; there is increasing neuroticism, especially among the lower socio-economic groups, who cope less well than professionals and managers (!).

After 55 comes a period of decline.

Sex and class factors

As these examples show, there is considerable sex and class bias in such analyses. This indicates the origin of most of the studies — amongst American white professional males, those who on the whole predominate in continuing education programmes in the United States. The sexual bias is surprising; all of these theories relate to male careers despite the fact that women predominate in most forms of non-vocational adult education. The women's movement has been seeking to redress the balance, exploring the cycle of adulthood for women. Similarly, it is likely that the lifespan stages and expectations of blacks are different from those listed above.

The class bias has received less attention. Almost all the above descriptions rely upon doubtful assumptions concerning the social and educational background of the participants; they relate to the educated, the professionally employed and the ambitious. One attempt to redress this balance towards the working class (by Guy Hunter, quoted in Stephens and Roderick, 1971) suggests that

> 'there is a rough sequence in a working life which the intellectual is too apt to forget. After the first period of school and pure technical training, the worker, for the ten years from 15 to 25, is pitchforked into practical life — finding and holding a job after marriage and founding a home on small resources . . . between 25 and 35, as the worker approaches a more responsible job, education should broaden his ideas of the nature of authority, of the social and human implications of any new job, of the deeper purposes of society. Once this broadening process has been started, it may well lead on into history, literature and art. It means at 21 bread and butter and the wage packet. At 30 it may include ideas of status, leisure, civic responsibility; and at 40 and thereafter it may deepen into a concept of the good life.'
>
> (p. 195)

Roles and crisis points

This attempt to draw up an alternative lifespan sequence to that of the male professional still assumes a working life. Long-term unemployment on a large scale and changes in attitudes to work and retirement have thrown doubt on much of the existing research. These changes and the patronising air that surrounds such efforts to define working-class life stages have led to a number of different approaches, some of which concentrate on the pattern of family life and/or lifestyles. Others seek not so much for the variations between separate groups of adults but for a comprehensive view of development common to all adults. A way forward is found in concentrating on the changing *roles* of the adult or on the crisis points that occur in the life of most adults of a particular generation, whether male or female, working class or middle class, black or white — although reactions to these new roles and crisis points vary considerably according to experience and the culture of the individual.

The most common roles and crisis points identified (Sheehy, 1976) usually relate to the first job, marriage, parenthood, the departure of children from the home, bereavement (especially the loss of parents and spouse), separation and divorce, loss of a job or other role, retirement and (less sequential and more occasional) moving house (a major period of stress in the lives of many people). Amongst these writers, a common crisis point is seen to occur somewhere about the age of 40 in both males and females.

Summary

The search for the stages of man or woman is still under way. From our point of view as teachers, it is wise to remember that adults age; and that, with ageing,

- physical changes occur, to a greater extent for some people than for others and in different ways;
- roles change, all calling for new learning, and there may on occasion be difficulties in adapting to new roles or to new perceptions of roles;
- various crisis points are passed, sometimes easily, sometimes with difficulty.

The mixed group that most teachers of adults face will not only possess a wide range of ability; they will also be at different ages and at different stages of development, and will in any case react in different ways to the very varied changes each one is experiencing in their own life.

General characteristics of adult student-learners

Despite the wide variations that exist between the members of our learning group, however, it is still possible to identify some of the common characteristics of adult student participants. What follows is my list; you may find it helpful to decide for yourself how far each of the categories is appropriate in your own circumstances. I have selected seven characteristics that seem to me to be true of the large majority of adult learners, whatever their situation or stage of development, although cultural settings may modify these to some extent:

- The student participants are adult by definition.
- They are in a continuing process of growth, not at the start of a process.
- They bring with them a package of experience and values.
- They come to education with intentions.
- They bring expectations about the learning process.
- They have competing interests.
- They already have their own set of patterns of learning.

1. They all are adults by definition

We have seen that adulthood is an ideal, never fully achieved. The concept implies movement, progress towards the fulfilment of the individual's potential, the development of balanced judgements about themselves and others, and increasing independence. Our student participants are people who are becoming more mature, and the way we teach adults should encourage this development in self-fulfilment, perspective and autonomy.

The most visible way in which the adult learners exercise their adulthood in relation to our programme of work is by voluntarily choosing to come to our classes. Adult student participants are not dependent in the way children are. Malcolm Knowles, who has written one of the more perceptive accounts of the subject (*The Adult Learner*, 1990), suggests that adulthood is attained at the point at which individuals perceive themselves to be essentially self-directing (although this may not be for many persons a single point). He points out that there is a natural process of maturation leading organically towards autonomy, but that this is limited by what the social culture permits. In many societies the culture does not encourage the development in some groups of people (women, for instance, especially married women, in many parts of the world) of those abilities needed for self-direction. Self-directedness then is often partial; it may not extend to all parts of life (including to education). Knowles points to the gap or tension that exists in these cases between the drive and the ability to be self-directing.

Some people will feel more strongly than others this compulsion, this urge to take control of their own lives, to be involved increasingly in the decision-making processes affecting their life choices. But it is there in virtually all adults nonetheless. The educational process for adults, to be effective, should coincide with this process of maturation. A situation that reverses the trend, treating the developing adult as a child, will find itself faced on most occasions with major blocks to learning. Our programme must adapt itself to this increasing sense of self-determination if it is to maximise learning.

Against this must be set the fact that some adults, re-entering education after some time away from school, expect to be treated as children. The expectations of 'being taught' are sometimes strong, and if these expectations are not met in some way or other, once again learning is hindered. Experience suggests however that even the most docile group of adult students, happy for much of the time to be passive learners as if they were back in school again, will at the right time rebel against their teachers when the affront to their adulthood becomes too great. It can be a great help to provoke such a situation when we feel the time has come to break up the more formal atmosphere and secure greater participation by the students in their own learning process.

2. They are all engaged in a continuing process of growth

Contrary to some assumptions, adult student participants have not stopped growing or developing. They are not at a static period in their lives, a plateau between the growth stages of youth and the declining stage of old age; they are still people on the move. Whatever our view about the way adults develop, the key issue is that growth and change are occurring in all aspects of our student participant's life — in the physical arena, in the intellectual sphere, in the emotions, in the world of relationships, in the patterns of cultural interests. This is true of all participants in all types of adult learning. The pace and direction of these changes vary from person to person; but that it is happening cannot be called into question.

The teacher should take this pattern of change seriously. The people we are trying to help to learn are not passive individuals; they are actively engaged in a dynamic process. And they are in the middle of this process, not at the start. They may be at the start of a new stage of the process, but this stage will draw upon past changes and will in turn contribute to the whole programme of development and growth. It is a process that, although continual, is not continuous; it usually proceeds in spurts, triggered off by new experiences (such as the adult class itself) or new perceptions.

We are normally aware of this process of change within ourselves; indeed, coping with teaching adults itself forms part of the changing pattern of our lives. But we are sometimes reluctant to accept that such a process occurs within the student participants, that they are in the midst of a series of changes when they come to us. It is not practical for us to know all our student participants intimately enough to assess accurately the position each of them has reached and the way by which they have got there. But we can be aware that the process is in every case still continuing. Sensitivity to this fact, and to the fact that the educational experience we offer forms part of this ongoing change process, helps a great deal in creating our responses to the varying demands the students make upon us.

3. They all bring a package of experience and values

Each of the learners brings a range of experience and knowledge more or less relevant to the task in hand. New students are not new people; they possess a set of values, established prejudices and attitudes in which they have a great deal of emotional investment. These are based on their past experience. Knowles (1990) suggests that, for children, experience is something that happens to them; for adults, experience serves to determine who they are, to create their sense of self-identity. When this experience is devalued or ignored by the teacher, this implies a rejection of the person, not just the experience.

This is true in all fields of teaching adults, even in the formal technical and higher educational programmes, but it becomes particularly important for the adult teacher in those contexts where personal growth forms the major objective of the educational programme. The tensions and concerns of both the learner and the teacher in these contexts have been particularly well described by John Wood in his 'Poem for Everyman' (1974).

Poem for Everyman[1]

I will present you
parts
of
my
self
slowly
if you are patient and tender.
I will open drawers
that mostly stay closed
and bring out places and people and things
sounds and smells, loves and frustrations, hopes and sadnesses,
bits and pieces of three decades of life
that have been grabbed off
in chunks
and found lying in my hands
they have eaten
their way into my memory
carved their way into my
heart
altogether — you or I will never see them —
they are me.
if you regard them lightly
deny that they are important
or worse, judge them
I will quietly, slowly
begin to wrap them up,
in small pieces of velvet,
like worn silver and gold jewelry,
tuck them away
in a small wooden chest of drawers

and close.

Such sentiments are not characteristic of all adult student participants. Far from being reticent, some are confident, and a few positively push their views and experiences at the group and at the teacher. But it is perhaps true of more adults in learning situations than we are aware of. The teacher of adults needs to be sensitive to the situation whenever it arises, and it often occurs in the most unlikely of settings and in every class, whether it is a closed group brought together for a specific training purpose, an open-recruitment general-interest course, a highly structured formal class or a community education or development group.

What are the implications of students' prior experience, knowledge and values for our approach to teaching?

First this 'package' determines what messages are received by the learner. The student participants see all new material they encounter through the lens of their existing experience and knowledge (just as the teacher does), and this may distort the messages. Constant feedback from the participants is essential if the teacher is to remain alive to exactly what the student is learning.

Secondly, in those cases where the student participants do not believe that they possess any relevant experience or knowledge, where they insist that they 'know nothing at all about the subject', it is possible to help them to become aware that they do in fact possess relevant material. For unless the new learning is related to this existing reservoir of experience and knowledge, it cannot be fully absorbed into the person; it will sit uneasily with the rest of the individual's make-up, it will be compartmentalised from the rest of their being and will thus not fully affect their attitudes and behaviour. It is not a difficult skill for the teacher to acquire to explore with the participants something of what they already know about the matter in hand: words and phrases relating to the subject of the course, collected from the participants and listed on a blackboard or otherwise, can demonstrate to them that they are able to contribute towards the programme of learning. It is usually necessary only for the teacher to make a beginning; once the process has begun, the participants will normally be able to continue the exploration for themselves and find new ways of relating the content of the course to different parts of their own experience and knowledge. The start of the process is the most difficult step for some of the student participants to take, but it is an essential one before deep and permanent learning can take place.

Thirdly, not all of this set of values, experience and knowledge is correct or helpful to the required learning. What is correct and helpful needs to be confirmed and reinforced; what is not correct needs unlearning. Experience of teaching adults reveals that there is often as much unlearning to be done as new learning, and because of the emotional investment in the existing patterns of experience and knowledge, the unlearning process is one of the more difficult tasks facing the teachers of adults.

Fourthly, this experience and knowledge (some of it unique to the individual participant and therefore new to the teacher) is a major resource for learning and can be harnessed into the work of the class to the enrichment of the whole group. Much new material can be drawn out from the student participants rather than be presented by the teacher to the taught. Theoretically, we should all start from where the student participants themselves are; but since we usually teach in groups this is not often possible except where the contract to learn has ensured that a more or less homogeneous group has been created. But the utilisation of the varied experience and knowledge of all the members of the group is essential not only to ensure effective learning at a personal level; it will help to bind together the group and make all of its members richer.

4. They usually come to education with set intentions

It is often argued that adult students come to adult education because of a sense of need. We shall look at this area of needs in adult education [in more detail later], but here we must note one or two points. First, it is not always strictly true that the members of our classes are motivated by needs; some job-related programmes, for instance, contain participants who have little or no sense of need. Perhaps it is more useful to talk of all adult student participants as having a set of 'intentions', which for many of them can imply the meeting of a felt need.

Secondly, for those who do come out of a want or need, it is on occasion a confused area. Sometimes the participant is imbued with a vague sense of unease and dissatisfaction. The reason for attending that they give to others and even on occasion to themselves is not the true reason; sometimes the reason is not related to learning at all but more towards social contact or getting out of the house or to please some third person (some research suggests that there is a high correlation between attending some forms of adult education and problems within the marriage relationship, to take but one example). Even when this sense of need is related to learning, there is at times an uncertainty as to what it is that they should be learning. R. D. Laing has expressed something of this in his poem 'Knots' (from the 1972 book of the same title):

Knots[2]

There is something I don't know
    that I am supposed to know.
I don't know *what* it is I don't know
    and yet am supposed to know,
and I feel I look stupid
    if I seem both not to know it
        and not know *what* it is I don't know.
Therefore I pretend I know it.
    This is nerve-racking
    since I don't know what I must pretend to know.
Therefore I pretend to know everything.

I feel you know what I am supposed to know
but you can't tell me what it is
because you don't know that I don't know what it is.

You may know what I don't know, but not
    that I don't know it,
and I can't tell you. So you will have to tell me everything.

At one end of the spectrum of student intentions then is the satisfying of some vague and ill-articulated sense of need. At the other end are those who are present out of a desire to solve a clearly identified problem or to undertake a particular learning task which they feel is required for the performance of their social or vocational roles — for example, to learn a language for their next holiday; to acquire mastery over a computer for job or leisure fulfilment; to understand the development processes of very young children to help them cope at home; or to come to a knowledge of one of the systems of government to enable them to play a more effective role in their local community. In the course of their own continuing development, these people find that they need a specific skill or knowledge or understanding to enable them to fit more easily into some existing or new situation. Even those who come to adult education classes in search of 'a piece of paper', a qualification, rather than new learning may be there for different motives. For some, it is the necessary preliminary to securing promotion or access to more education; for others, it is part of their pursuit of self-affirmation, a need to achieve a goal for themselves. A number come to seek reassurance, confirmation of their ability to achieve the goal. There is a wide range of such wants and intentions. These purposes, often perceived clearly, are almost always concrete and meaningful to their immediate concerns, though on occasion the learning is intended for longer-term future application.

These are the two extremes to this spectrum of adult intentions: those who come to achieve a particular piece of learning related to their present pattern of life, and those who come for social and/or personal reasons or out of some general indeterminate sense of urgency. In the middle are the many who come to learn a 'subject'. Here are those who wish to learn history or cooking or painting or bird-watching, material that is specific enough but not directly related to the solution of an immediate problem. For them it is a matter of interest, of adding to the richness of their present way of life.

Often no clear-cut distinction may be drawn between these three groups. Nevertheless, they may be more or less equated with what C. O. Houle, in his classic work *The Inquiring Mind* (1961), has identified as the three main orientations of the adult learner. In any adult learning situation, he claims, some of the student participants are *goal-oriented.* They wish to use education to achieve some external objective such as a certificate or promotion or to solve an immediate problem facing them. For them the learning experience tends to come to an end once the objective (often separate from the learning process) has been achieved.

A second group is described as *activity-oriented.* They like the atmosphere of the adult class, they find in the circumstances of the learning a meaning for themselves independent of the content or of the announced purpose of the activity. They attend because they get something out of the group apart from the subject-matter involved; it meets a range of needs that are mainly personal and/or social. These people frequently seek the continuance of the activity even though the content of the learning may well change; they may pass from one class to another, searching for satisfaction in the activity itself.

The third group is described as *learning-oriented.* They desire the knowledge or skill for its own sake. They pursue the subject out of interest and will continue to pursue it even without the assistance of a formal programme of adult learning (see Figure 1).

The implications for the teacher of the different intentions of each of these three groups (and of the many who occupy places on the spectrum between these three positions) are considerable. The responses of each group to the demands of the learning programme will vary. Those participants who are motivated to attend courses out of some sense of internal need may on occasion exhibit anxiety, sometimes mixed with hesitation and uncertainty; for the concept of need is threatening, demeaning both to oneself and to others. Such anxiety can be a useful thing — it can promote learning provided it is not too great. A gentle encouragement of the sense of need and particularly an attempt to focus it upon particular learning objectives that may help towards meeting the needs often bring about greater readiness to learn. The development of a clearer conception of the nature of the learning task and of the relevance of the material to the immediate concerns of the participant is an essential preliminary to the use of the learning programme to satisfy such needs. On the other hand, those whose motivation is to achieve some external goal (to pass an examination, for instance) will often reveal a great keenness. Here too, the clearer the awareness of purpose and of the relevance of the task to meet this purpose, the greater the motivation to learn.

Figure 1 Orientations of learning

Orientation	*Intentions*	*Learning process*	*Continuation at end of programme?*
Goal-oriented; end product	Achievement; problem-solving/ attainment	Learning most in certain specific areas	Process ceases on 'successful' completion of course
Learning-oriented	Interest in subject	Learning in all parts of subject-matter	Continued learning in same or related subject area
Activity-oriented	Social or personal growth needs; often indeterminate	Find in activities satisfactions to needs	A new situation or activity is sought

5. They bring certain expectations about education itself

Adult student participants come to their learning programmes with a range of expectations about the learning process, a series of attitudes towards education in general. These are usually based on their experience of schooling and of education since leaving school (if any). The conception of what education is and what it is for varies widely. Some people enjoyed their years in school; others did not. A number of our student participants assume that adult education will be like school. They expect to be taught everything by a teacher who 'knows everything'; they expect to be put back *in statu pupillari,* which is what education and learning imply for them. On the other hand, some are more confident, willing to engage for themselves directly with the material being handled. For some of them the joy of the adult class is that it is unlike school. Even for many of those who enjoyed their schooldays, the value of adult education is often that the contents and the methods employed are different from those experienced in the formal education system (Figure 2).

These expectations have different results on the attitudes of the participants towards the work of the group. Some tend more towards conformism, while others seek for a measure of independent learning. Some see, in the formal structure of an adult education class, support for themselves, feeling more at home with 'being taught' — though they may still be anxious as to whether their skills of learning are adequate for the purpose or not. They may feel that their ability to learn has declined since they were last in education (and this may be true; on occasion we may have to spend some time with our student participants boosting their confidence and, even in some advanced courses, strengthening their skills of formal learning). Some of those who have had experience of education over a longer time may look for a less formal structure or become impatient, wishing to push on faster; they feel able to deal with the material easily.

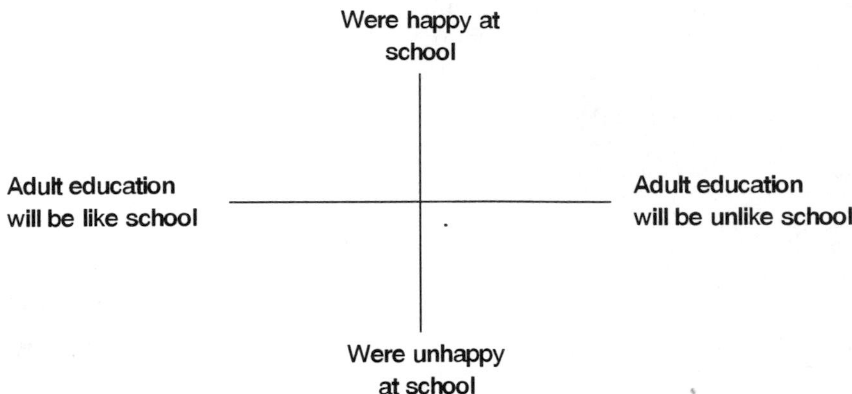

Figure 2 Orientations of learning

In particular, both kinds of student participant bring with them a set of *self-horizons* relating to the sort of material they can or cannot master. Most of us believe that there is some subject or other that we can never learn, that is just not compatible with our range of inherent abilities and interests. It is odd that so many voluntary adult students still find themselves in classes containing a good deal of material that from the start they are adamant they will never be able to learn. Students attend courses in religion and yet say they cannot cope with 'theology'; students join art classes with a firm belief that they can never learn to draw. Learning in parts of these fields is not for them; they confine themselves to the role of 'looker-on', as presumably they were at times in school. They may plead age, using this as an excuse to avoid causes of failing for other reasons. By contrast there will be those who see the entering of new areas as a challenge, difficult but not beyond the learning resources they can call upon.

We need to explore these views, about schooling, learning and what is expected in education, from an early stage in the learning programme. The worst thing we can do is treat all the participants alike, teaching one course to them all. The problem of the teacher of adults faced with a mixed group of student participants, encouraging those with low self-horizons and keeping the more self-reliant satisfied with their own progress, is one of constantly making choices between alternatives, of balancing between the needs of one sub-group and those of another while maintaining loyalty to the subject-matter of the course and the group as a whole.

6. They all have competing interests

Apart from those adults, still too few, who are for a relatively short period engaged in full-time courses, adult students are part-time. Education for them is a matter of secondary interest; it is not their prime concern. It is constantly overshadowed by the 'realities' of life: their job or lack of job, their family situation, their social life, other competing issues.

The adults who come to join us in the learning enterprise come from a complete social environment. They all have relationships such as parents, partners, workmates and friends, as well as being students. Adult learners should not be divorced from their background if their learning is to be relevant and thus effective. We need to take seriously the whole of the context within which our student participants live and where they use the new learning they have acquired. Students in other parts of the educational world may be taken out of their life situation to concentrate on their learning, but part-time adult learners continue to live within their world and to apply what they learn in that world.

Within that background there are factors supporting the learning endeavours as well as some militating against these same endeavours. Not all of the competing concerns that the participants bring with them to our programmes are hindrances. Some are supportive. Indeed, periods of intensive study can hardly be carried through without the identification of the support networks existing all around the adult learner, and it is to the advantage of both teacher and student participant to encourage the full exploitation of these supporting factors. This is particularly true where the class is a one-off episode, not backed up by other studies as it is at school or college. A short course, taken part-time and on its own, assumes in the life of many student participants rather less significance than it has for the teacher we must not be surprised if our students' attention is at times distracted towards the more urgent problems of the family's health, or the omission to fulfil some promised errand, or problems at work.

7. They all possess set patterns of learning

Adults are engaged in a continuing process of lifelong learning, and they have already acquired ways of coping with this. They often fail to see this as 'learning' in the educational sense, but it exists all the same. We shall look in more detail at the special features of the adult learning process, but here we must note two points: that each of the participants has developed such a style already; and that the styles that exist in our adult groups are varied.

Over the years, each of our adult student participants has developed their own strategies and patterns of learning, which they have found help them to learn most easily, most quickly and most effectively. Learning changes are not brought about without effort, and the process can be painful; it takes an investment of time and emotions, and, once done, no one wants to do it again. We all thus seek ways to ease the pain, shorten the time taken to master the necessary new material, and make the gains acquired more permanent. Experience has taught us what strategies we can adopt to achieve these ends.

Each of us learns in our own way, according to our particular aptitudes and experience. Some handle figures more easily than others. Some have fostered different methods for memorising facts (addresses, telephone numbers, etc.). Some need to see the written page in order to comprehend more fully rather than rely on the spoken word. Languages particularly throw up differences of approach in this respect. Some learners need a book and practise sounds from written words, finding it hard to react to spoken words, while others respond easily to oral tuition; both are valid methods of learning languages, and we should not try to force any learner into adopting a particular style because we prefer it to any other. We must thus remember that our student participants all have their own ways of dealing with learning needs, and opportunities to exercise these have to be created if new learning is to take place.

The pace of learning of each student participant also varies. In general, in those areas where the participants can call upon a good deal of experience — social relationships and roles, for instance — or where they may have direct experience of the subject-matter, they tend to learn fast, a good deal faster than young people, provided that the new material does not conflict with existing knowledge. But where they have less experience on which to fasten the new material — languages, for example, or computer studies — especially if it calls for extensive memorising, they tend to learn more slowly and have greater difficulty in mastering the material than their younger counterparts.

Such matters are central to our concerns as teachers. There is a wide range of learning styles within any group of adult learners, and we need to devise methods that give each of the participants full scope for exercising their own particular learning method, and as far as possible not impose our own upon them.

Implications for the teacher of adults

We can see, then, that teachers of adults, especially those who teach in groups, are faced with a difficult task from the start. Unless the group is narrowly conceived (as in some forms of industrial training), our student participants will consist of a wide variety of people all bringing their own advantages and disadvantages to the learning situation.

- Some are more adult than others; some are still searching in education for dependency, others for autonomy.
- All are growing and developing, but in different directions and at a different pace.
- Some bring a good deal of experience and knowledge, others bring less; and there are varying degrees of willingness to use this material to help the learning process.
- They have a wide range of intentions and needs, some specific, some more general and related to the subject-matter under discussion, and others unknown even to themselves.
- They are all at different points in the continuum between those who require to be taught everything and those who wish to find out everything for themselves; and they each have some consciousness of what they can and cannot do in the way of learning.
- They all have competing interests of greater importance than their learning.
- And they have all by now acquired their own ways of learning, which vary considerably the one from the other.

It is easy to view all of this in negative terms, to see most of what we have discussed as hindrances to learning. The pressure from competing interests, the worry and anxiety especially about their learning abilities, based as they often are on misconceptions as to what education involves, the problem of coping with unlearning and the attack on the personality that this can at times imply — all of these may seem to make the task of the teacher of adults particularly difficult. We must not be surprised if some of the student participants do not move as fast as we would wish them to; if they have difficulty in grasping some of the material that *we* find so easy and have so carefully constructed for them; if they show a lack of responsiveness to all our promptings to engage more wholeheartedly with the subject-matter of the class. We must not be put off if some of the learners require us to demonstrate or lecture when we would rather that they practise for themselves or discuss.

But there are many aspects of this discussion that give cause for hope. Within the group is a well of resources that we can use. Some of these can be quickly identified: the wealth of knowledge, skills and experience gathered together in one room; the fact that all the student participants, whether they know it or not, are already engaged in some form of learning; the awareness, however dim, of purpose and need; the greater use of reasoning powers, and the fact that adult students, when provoked, 'accept' the teacher's word less readily (those of us who prefer to demonstrate and to lecture, to perform rather than to watch, to listen to our own voice rather than to the voice of the learners, will not see this as a resource); the desire of many of the learners to apply what they learn one day to their lives the very next day and the fact that (unlike full-time students) they are in a position to do so. All these factors can be seen as combining to form a powerful aid to learning.

We need to try to identify both those factors that prevent us from being fully effective in the teaching-learning process and those resources that we can bring into play in order to overcome the obstacles. In adult education, our students are not there just to be taught; they are our greatest resource in the learning process.

Application
It should be important to you, as you look through this material, to relate it to your own experience. You may find it helpful to write down what assumptions you made about the potential student participants for the course you have chosen as your own, what characteristics they bring with them to your course. It may be possible for you, if you actually ran a course, to test this against the group that materialised so that you can assess how accurate your first thoughts were.

A second useful exercise at this stage is set out for yourself the range of helps and hindrances that you think your students will bring with them to the programme of study. Most of us do this without being fully conscious of it; to make it a deliberate process will help to bring into focus those whom we hope to help to learn.

Acknowledgements

1. From: Wood, John, *How Do You Feel? A Guide to Your Emotions.* Prentice-Hall, Inc.
2. Laing, R.D. *Knots.* Tavistock Publications Ltd, 1972.

Further reading

Allman P (1983) The nature and process of adult development. In: M Tight (ed.) *Education for Adults.* Croom Helm, Beckenham.

Chickering A W (1977) *Experience and Learning: An Introduction to Experiential Learning.* Change Magazine Press, New Rochelle, NY.

Chickering A W and Havighurst R W (1981) The life cycle. In: A W Chickering (ed.) *The Modern American College: Responding to the New Realities of Diverse Students and a Changing Society.* Jossey Bass, San Francisco.

Cross K P (1981) *Adults as Learners: Increasing Participation and Facilitating Learning.* Jossey-Bass, San Francisco.

Evans P (1975) *Motivation.* Methuen, London.

Giles K (1981) *Personal Change in Adults.* Open University Press, Milton Keynes.

Jarvis P (1987) *Adult Education in its Social Context.* Croom Helm, Beckenham.

Keeting M T (ed.) (1976) *Experiential Learning: Rationale Characteristics and Assessment.* Jossey-Bass, San Francisco.

Kidd J R (1973) *How Adults Learn.* Association Press, New York.

Knowles M S (1990) *The Adult Learner: A Neglected Species.* Gulf, Houston.

Knox A (1977) *Adult Development and Learning.* Jossey-Bass, San Francisco.

Levinson D (1978) *The Seasons of a Man's Life.* Knopf, New York.

Levinson D (1986) *The Season of a Woman's Life.* Knopf, New York.

Miller H L (1964) *Teaching and Learning in Adult Education.* Macmillan, London.

Pressey S, Kuhlen R (1957) *Psychological Development through the Lifespan.* Harper, New York.

Rayner E (1971) *Human Development: An Introduction to the Psychodynamics of Growth Maturity and Ageing.* Allen and Unwin, London.

Rogers J (1989) *Adults Learning.* Open University Press, Milton Keynes.

Sheehy C T (1976) *Passages: Predictable Crises of Adult Life.* Dutton, New York.

3. Teaching and Learning: A Climate of Change

Susan Major

We cannot teach another person directly, we can only facilitate his or her learning.

This paper stems from the author's experience on a Community Practitioner Teacher (CPT) course. It was in November 1988 that the course members were first exposed to various teaching and learning methods that had been developed around the experiential and student centred approaches. Experiential learning (EL) in particular may be argued as very different from most teaching and learning methods we are used to. This implies that traditional teaching and perhaps traditional nursing cannot be compatible with student centred and patient centred approaches. This ostensible incompatibility calls for a climate of change which will eventually shift the teaching and the practice from 'doing for' to 'doing with'.

It is evident that more educationalists have questioned the credibility of traditional methods of learning. The 'traditional' or expository teaching and learning has been described by Ausubel (1) as the 'presentation of the entire content of what is to be learned to the learner in its final form'. The learner plays a passive role, digesting the knowledge given to him by the teacher. Learning outcome is determined by what is accurate as defined and desired by the teacher.

On the other hand McEvoy (2) proposed that new models of learning should be adopted to make the learning process interesting, imaginative, and capable of critical reflection. This approach requires the student to be actively involved in the teaching and learning act, to determine for himself/herself the value of his/her experience and to share knowledge with colleagues.

This approach can also be argued to be central to experiential learning (EL).

It is difficult to attribute the EL model to any one pioneer, as in recent years numerous models of EL have been developed. Needles to say, definitions have been varied and wide. For instance, Rogers (3) defines EL as a learning experience with qualities of personal involvement. It takes into account both feeling and cognitive aspects of the person. Burnard (4) checked student nurses' perception of EL and found such definitives as:

- Learning through practice
- Learning without text book
- Learning without chalk and talk
- Warning through role play

Susan Major: 'Teaching and Learning: A Climate of Change' in *NURSING STANDARD* (1989), 4 (3), pp. 36–38.

The advent of EL

EL origins can be traced back to the 1940s. Perhaps Lewin's (5) work on action research and T groups (training groups) provided the foundation.

The 'T group' was discovered when Lewin, along with his colleagues, set up a training programme on group interactions. The programme centred around experiential activities such as discussion and role play. Staff and participants were treated equally, while their activities were observed by researchers. Normally, evening sessions gave Lewin and his staff an opportunity for feedback. However, by chance, three participants were allowed to join in on one such evening session. These participants concluded that they had learnt from the experience of sitting in. The staff also agreed that there was more insight and usefulness in such experiential reflections. This was the inception of the EL model, although further contributions to the EL model followed. The well known work of Kolb and Fry (6) is based on Lewin's ideas.

Kolb and Fry suggest that the basic perception of EL is misleadingly simple, that is change, growth and learning occur through a sequence of four logical stages of progression which can be summarised thus:

1. Concrete experience
2. Collating data and making observations about the experience
3. Analysing the data to formulate conclusions and feedback
4. Change in behaviour, to facilitate choice of new experience.

See Figure 1 for the EL cycle.

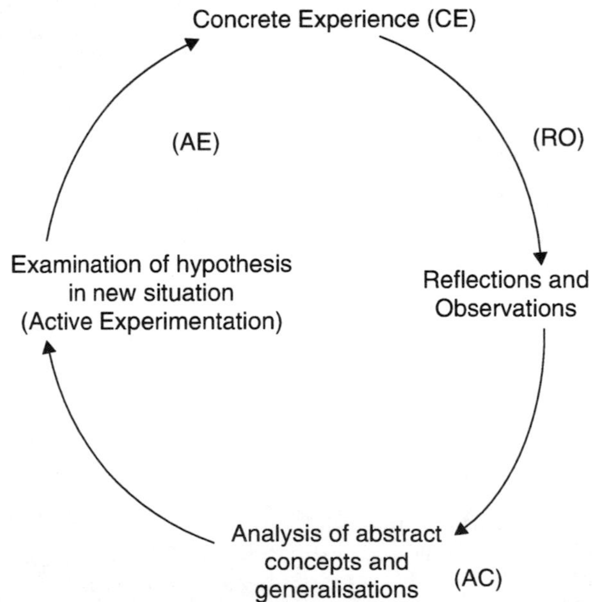

Figure 1 The EL Cycle: adapted from Kolb and Fry

According to Kolb and Fry, the development of EL starts with the concrete experience (CE) of here and now. This forms the foundations for stage two, reflecting and observing (RO). This subsequently leads to the abstract conceptualisation (AC) (stage three) from which a new naive experimentation (AE) may result (stage four).

Kolb and Fry out of their description of Lewin's work suggested that learning was helped in an environment where there is dialectic tensions and conflict between immediate concrete experience and analytic detachment. That is, by addressing the issues of the experience (CE) in open forum, where one can be challenged and aroused (RO), a cognitive awareness may result (AC). The creation of this cognitive awareness may be experimented with later (AE). Kolb and Fry further suggest that the acquisition of knowledge and skills are achieved through confrontation within the four angles of EL. To elaborate they identity four 'abilities' required by the student for effective learning. Concrete experience abilities, reflective observation abilities, abstract conceptual abilities and active experimentation abilities. However, the student will not learn unless he/she is able to judge the experience or mediate over it for meaning and form aims with reference to aspirations and calculations. Kolb and Fry see the students role as moving in fluctuating degrees from actor to observer, that is from specific involvement to the general analytic detachment. The role of the teacher becomes that of facilitator. The overall experience is the outcome of continually changing cognitive processes.

The EL process can be applied to any learning situation provided it is well understood, particularly by the teacher [or] facilitator.

The author has used counselling as an area of study to highlight the use of EL during a student's (mental health) field work placement. Student participation is increased by working through the themes of the nursing process. Emphasis is placed on the students' ability to learn. They are given the opportunity to reflect, process, interpret and apply meaning to their experience (RO–AE).

The EL stages can be seen as such:

Concrete Experience (CE): It is assumed that the student has been introduced to counselling during a theoretical block in college. In particular, they should be familiar with a model of counselling and be able to draw on the theoretical material implicit in the model. Selected reading, for instance Egan (7), Rogers (8) and Nelson-Jones (9), would be necessary. This experience provides the basis for reflection and observation.

Source of motivation

Reflection and observation: This stage may be seen as an introduction to EL activities. The student, in an attempt to get to know the team may engage in a group discussion where exchange of experiences and expression of attitudes and opinions can be voiced. Boydell (10) indicates that learning is achieved through the interaction and association with people who eventually become a source of motivation. Furthermore, he points out that the advancement and possession of knowledge, and its interpretation, depends on the strength of interpersonal relationships maintained with other well motivated people.

Abstract conceptualisation (AC): Out of the students' ability or inability to reflect and observe their past experiences (inductive reasoning), should come the desire to develop a knowledge/theoretical base (deductive reasoning) to provide a foundation for future practice. Learning will take place through further reading, student led case presentations with key areas of counselling skills being identified for discussion, role play, video tape recordings, psycho drama and so on. For instance, the CPT (facilitator) may invite the student (actor) to role play a situation that may illustrate communication techniques for example, reflecting:

Client (student): Do you think I should leave my job?

Counsellor (CPT): Do you think you should leave your job?

Active Experimentation (AE): The student will be invited to 'take on' a client for counselling sessions under the direct supervision of his/her CPT. For the purpose of this paper, the client contact will enable the student to follow the sequence of the learning cycle, nursing process and the counselling cycle (Figure 2).

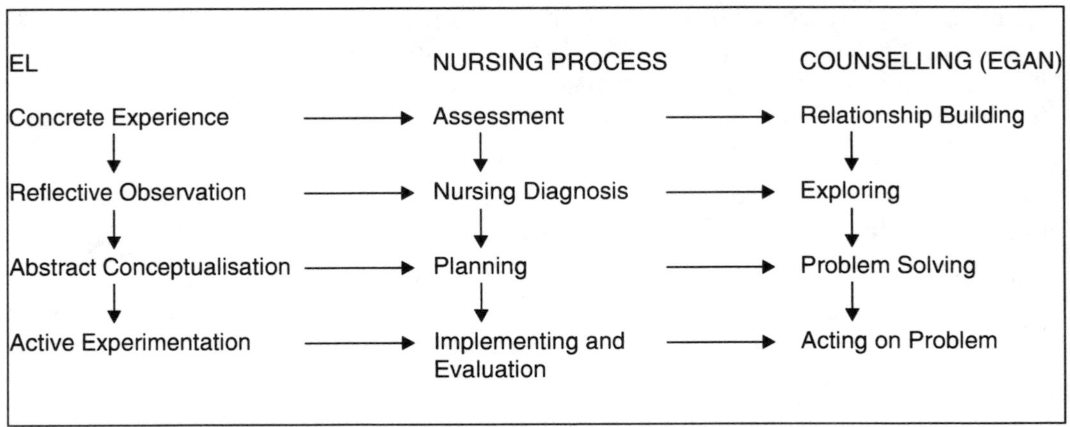

Figure 2 Comparative stages between EL, the nursing process and counselling
Source: SF Major (1989) unpublished.

Elaborating, the concrete experience (CE) will be viewed in two parts. Firstly as experience before the placement and secondly as the initial contact with the client (assessment), where trust, warmth and respect (relationship building) may develop.

The reflecting and observing (RO) will take place between the client and counsellor (student). They may identify (nursing diagnosis) and explore the problems that arise out of the assessment and plan further interventions.

The ability to draw conclusions (AC) can be seen as problem solving with the client formulating ideas that may resolve conflicts.

The active experimentation (AE) assumes that the client is now able to act upon the problems and examine the change that has occurred, hence evaluation.

It is not uncommon for nurses who undertake post basic courses based on experimental philosophies to feel apprehensive at the prospect of being responsible for their own learning. After all, so many have been previously taught using traditional expository teaching methods. But how does EL differ from the traditional approaches?

Traditional models assume that:

- the teacher is the expert, with a reservoir of knowledge that is tapped by the student.
- the possession of expertise can make claims to primacy, that is the teacher not only has a hierarchial authority, but is seen as a total resource, deemed necessary for the learning process to be achieved.
- students may interpret learning as memorising, that is they merely retain knowledge until it is required for external evaluation.

By contrast, EL assumes that:

- the teacher is a facilitator of learning, with attitudinal resources that help initiate a relationship between himself and the learner.
- learning is self-initiated, students are expected to take on responsibility for their own learning.
- learning is a meaningful experience. It allows students to develop their own level of inquiry, sanction and be critical of their own experience.
- the learner is seen as a 'whole' person, with both the psychological and intellectual components being identified for learning to take place.

These assumptions are not exhaustive, but serve to highlight some of the fundamental differences between traditional and experiential learning.

It can be argued that the advent of the 1982 Mental Nursing Syllabus, the shift from training to education, the proposals of Project 2000 aimed at producing a knowledgeable doer and the profession's desire to advocate continuous assessment in clinical practice, can only be truly realised under a climate of change. Central to this climate of change is questioning the hidden values and assumptions about teaching and learning. More importantly, clinical facilitators (supervisors) should realise they cannot teach another person direct but can only encourage and motivate his/her learning. It is, therefore, the facilitators task to create a climate conducive to experiential learning and other problem-solving approaches.

Conclusion

The purpose of this paper has been to emphasise the shift from traditional learning/ teaching methods to experiential means. The EL self directed approach has been questioned by nurses who see it as too radical a shift from the expository teaching methods. Maybe the traditional teacher and the traditional nurse feels more comfortable controlling his/her student and patient. In either case, a real shift to experiential learning and patient centred care can only be realised when the anxiety if not compulsion 'to do for' is replaced by the desire 'to do with'. EL requires 'doing with' and doing with enhances meaningful learning, problem-solving potential, and intrinsic motivation for professional development.

References

1. Ausubel D P (1968) *Educational Psychology: A Cognitive View.* Holt, Rinehart and Winston, New York.
2. McEvoy P (1989) A new model for learning. *Senior Nurse* 9 (2).
3. Rogers C R (1969) *Freedom to Learn.* Merrill, Colombus, Ohio.
4. Burnard P (1989) Psychatric nursing students perception of EL. *Nursing Times* Jan 14.
5. Lewin K (1948) *Resolving Social Conflicts: Selected Papers on Group Dynamics,* 22: 491. Harper PA, New York.
6. Kolb D A, Fry R (1975) Towards an applied theory of experiential learning. In: G L Cooper (ed.) *Theories of Group Processes.* John Wiley, London.
7. Egan G (1986) *The Skilled Helper.* Brooks/Cole, California.
8. Rogers C R (1951) *Client Centered Therapy.* Constable, London.
9. Nelson-Jones R (1982) *The Theory and Practice of Counselling Psychology.* Cassell, London.
10. Boydell T (1976) *Experiental Learning.* Manchester Monograph 5. Dept. Adult Education, University of Manchester.

4. An Adult Learning Framework for Clinical Education

Lindy McAllister

Chapter overview

Some factors which make clinical education such an important and vital part of the preparation of health, education and welfare professionals are explored in this chapter. The chapter considers how clinical education offers unique opportunities to work with student learning styles and to promote deep approaches to learning which result in the development of clinical knowledge/clinical reasoning and the ability to work in complex and changing environments. It considers the goals of clinical education in terms of generic attributes, competence and capability, and discusses reasons why we fail to achieve those goals. The importance of the semantics used in talking about who we are and what we do as clinical educators is considered.

The chapter outlines a philosophical and theoretical approach to clinical education grounded in adult learning, which is more congruent with the broader goals of clinical education. Adult learning theory and approaches are reviewed, and factors which make clinical education a unique context for the application of these theories and approaches are highlighted. Processes of teaching and learning – autonomy, self-directedness, interdependence and peer learning – which are congruent with adult learning are outlined. The characteristics of clinical educators operating effectively within an adult learning framework are discussed.

Learning in clinical settings

This is a book which focuses on students' learning, not teachers' instructing or 'supervisors' supervising. It is about the education of students who will one day be our professional peers, colleagues and co-learners in the clinical settings in which we work. It is a book about clinical education – education for the realities of professional practice in the changing health, education and welfare sectors (see Case Study 1).

Lindy McAllister: 'An Adult Learning Framework for Clinical Education' from Lindy McAllister, Michelle Lincoln, Sharynne McLeod and Diana Maloney (eds) *FACILITATING LEARNING IN CLINICAL SETTINGS* (Stanley Thornes, 1997), pp. 1–26.

Case Study 1

Sally is an Australian speech therapy student who has just arrived in a developing country in Asia to begin a nine-week period as a volunteer on a project to establish a community-based rehabilitation (CBR) early intervention programme. She will work under the guidance of an Australian paediatrician, who has volunteered for a three-year period to establish community health services in this remote rural area. Sally will work closely on the project with local CBR workers. She doesn't know what will be expected of her by the local or international staff. Because she knows we have a great interest in her and the project, Sally will send us weekly postcards from the project. Her first postcard appears below (see Postcard 1).

Postcard 1

Dear All

Well here I am in ... [the local regional centre]. It was an amazing 11 hour bus trip here from the capital, along narrow roads perched on the edge of the mountain. When I could bear to look down, I could see the flooded rice paddies and the raging rivers – very beautiful. The town has about 5,000 people and I'm staying in the mission guest house half an hour walk from town. The area is very lush at this time of the year and I'm told I'll often walk to work in the heavy monsoonal rain. I was able to buy in the local markets a suitable outfit for work here – light cotton top to the knees, long sleeves, matching trousers. Wait till you see the photos! I start work tomorrow. The Community Based Rehabilitation (CBI) project has been running for about three months. There are four team members all of whom have received six weeks of CBR training in rehab., OT, physio., social work and 2 days on speech therapy (mainly hearing impairment). This is going to be an interesting experience!

love Sally

As we read Postcard 1 from Sally, we shared her excitement and her anxiety. We talked a lot about the personal and professional growth we had witnessed in Sally and how much of a contribution we could claim in that growth. As her clinical educators over the past four and a half years had we provided her with a clinical education that would enable her to meet the challenges she now described? We would look forward to the story which unfolds in the ensuing weekly postcards.

Naming ourselves and defining what we do

In this book we name the process in which we are engaged as *clinical education;* hence we name ourselves as *clinical educators.* We take a broad view of clinical education, which we define as:

a teaching and learning process which is student focused and may be student-led, which occurs in the context of client care. It involves the translation of theory into the development of clinical knowledge and practical skills, with the incorporation of the affective domain needed for sensitive and ethical client care. Clinical education occurs in an environment supportive of the development of clinical reasoning skills, professional socialization and life-long learning.

Our definition encompasses the acquisition of the knowledge, skills and attributes needed to become a competent professional as well as a competent clinician. Education for professional socialization, the development of moral and ethical positions, and the promotion of the attributes of a life-long learner are deemed to be just as important as the development of clinical skills. Our emphasis is on education towards certain goals, not the instruction in certain techniques or supervision of skill acquisition, nor transmission of prescribed information. We believe that the latter are approaches to teaching and learning which do not fit with the current goals of professional preparation. We will return to a discussion of these goals in a later section.

We believe that this naming of ourselves and the work in which we are engaged is vital for clarity of purpose and clarity of communication. In stating our position, we allow an exploration of the meaning attached to our work, and the philosophical and theoretical foundations of our work.

The semantics of clinical education

The process of preparing students for work in the health, education and welfare sectors has many names: clinical instruction, fieldwork education, supervision, clinical teaching and clinical education to name a few. Similarly, we find in the literature ourselves referred to as clinical instructors, clinical tutors, clinical supervisors, clinical teachers and clinical or fieldwork educators. These terms are often used interchangeably as if they had the same meaning. We suggest that there is confusion and limitation inherent in the ways currently used in the literature to name and define what we do. Getting the semantics right is important with regard to the perceptions we and others have about the scope and value of our work.

Some of the confusion derives from the historical usage of the terms. Cross (1994) has commented on the change in terminology in physiotherapy clinical education in the United Kingdom. She traces the development of clinicians' roles from the 1960s to the 1990s, from clinical instructor to clinical educator. She describes the *clinical instructor* as a clinician working in a fairly circumscribed environment, who with almost 'amateurish enthusiasm' drilled students to reproduce traditional procedures.

As student numbers increased and curricula broadened in the 1970s, the role became one of *clinical supervisor* of the activities of several students, ensuring that they did not disrupt the normal running of the department. There is an element of controlling and limiting students inherent in this description. The 1980s brought increased professional autonomy and university-based education programmes. 'Training' was transformed into 'education' (Cross, 1994, p. 610). *Clinical teachers* placed a greater emphasis on individual student development.

The enormous changes in the health, education and welfare sectors in the 1990s have required that clinicians develop expertise in a wide range of personal, interpersonal and management skills, in addition to core discipline skills (Cross, 1994). Cross suggests that 'physiotherapy educators ... have a responsibility to equip students fully to take up the cause of quality physiotherapy in the future' (p. 610). The role is now one of *clinical educator,* developing in students a breadth of personal, interpersonal and management skills.

Cross makes it clear that the terms used were linked to expectations and roles of the time. These expectations and roles have changed for all professions. The professions have a broader view of who they are and what they do. Terminology must change to reflect these broader visions, roles and expectations.

A definition offered by the *Shorter Oxford English Dictionary* (Onions, 1992) for education is of relevance to our argument. *Education is* defined as 'the process of nourishing or rearing; the process of bringing up' and 'culture or development of powers, formation of [intellectual or moral] character'. This definition strikes the right note with us. It suggests that we are *educating* for the future, sometimes for as yet ill-defined goals in changing professional contexts. It suggests that the education in which we engage is systematic, but also nourishing and developing of the character of future professionals.

The story of Sally powerfully illustrates what it means to be a clinical educator rather than an instructor, supervisor or teacher (see Case Studies 2 and 3).

Case Study 2

It has taken Sally five years to near completion of our four-year speech therapy degree programme. In the early years of the programme she failed academic and clinical subjects. Sally had difficulty applying theory to practice, developing intervention plans and implementing these proficiently with her clients. ln part this was because she had a weak theoretical background, in part because she was chronically disorganized. However, Sally had good interpersonal skills and was helpful and considerate to her fellow students and staff of the clinic. Her clients liked her. The willingness with which Sally accepted and acted on feedback and repeated failed subjects demonstrated her commitment to becoming a good therapist.

We, her clinical educators, respected her and believed in her potential to achieve her goal. It would have been easier for us to have continually shown her what to do and told her how to do it. We could have acted always as instructors. Or we could have supervised all her activities and controlled every learning opportunity. Instead we let her learn from her mistakes provided those mistakes did not compromise client care. We had a clear vision of what it meant to us to be educators, operating within an adult learning framework. We helped Sally identify what she already knew and needed to know next, in order to improve. We helped her to identify resources she could utilize to improve her knowledge and skills. We encouraged her to work with her peers to develop her knowledge and

Case Study 2 cont.

skills, and encouraged her peers to give her feedback about the confusion her disorganization engendered in the clinic.

As clinical educators committed to an adult learning approach, we chose not to stop at the stage of developing clinical skills. We respected Sally and affirmed her personal and professional growth and encouraged her to develop further her professional identity. In other words, we functioned as *educators*. We nourished her character and promoted her professional socialization. As her competence grew, we treated her more like a colleague, sharing the responsibility for decision-making about her learning experiences and goals. We encouraged her to pursue her interest in working in the developing world, and acted as sounding boards as she considered various strategies which would enable her to rearrange her programme to take time out to go to the CBR project in Asia and which would enable her to arrive well prepared.

Case Study 3

Throughout the negotiations with us about rearranging her final semester's commitments and gathering materials to take with her to the CBR project, Sally showed great maturity, confidence and organizational skill. In conversations she showed that she had considered various possible needs the project might have and tapped into our network of colleagues with CBR and WHO (World Health Organization) experience. She spoke to colleagues about what she might expect culturally, what information, materials and skills might be most appropriate for a CBR project of this type. She interviewed fellow students from other disciplines who had recently returned from CBR project work in India. She photocopied and organized a wide array of information and read widely outside her own discipline area. All this she accomplished while completing coursework and working part-time to fund her trip and living expenses in Asia. We felt like we were interacting with a peer within a rewarding educational relationship.

Cross (1994) notes that educational relationships such as these have a different balance of power to instructing, supervising or teaching relationships. There is power sharing, based on approachability, disclosure and respect. Cross (1994) suggests that 'the linkage between these three elements holds the potential to empower the clinician-student relationship in a way which supports students in their early attempts to develop basic management skills' (p. 611). Sally has finally developed personal and professional management skills. We believe that she has grown into a competent clinician and a life-long learner, as her first postcard suggests.

Sally's story illustrates the importance of clinical education to the development of professionals. The next section discusses this topic in more detail.

The importance of clinical education

Clinical education is a vital and irreplaceable component in preparing students for the reality of their professional role (Grahn, 1989; Williams and Webb, 1994).

Clinical education is about the real world of professional practice, where learning is holistic and involves transfer, reorganization, application, synthesis and evaluation of previously acquired knowledge, along with the acquisition of new knowledge and skills. Clinical education enables the development of skills best learned in the clinical setting, such as clinical decision-making and problem-solving. The clinical setting promotes the integration of theoretical and skills-based components of the curricula, and efficient reorganization of knowledge, so that it may be applied to the problem-solving and clinical decision-making required in real-life client care. The following sections explore aspects of learning in the clinical setting.

The development of clinical knowledge, clinical reasoning and clinical know-how

Lectures, tutorials, seminars, lab or practical sessions all have an important place in the development of cognitive, technical and affective skills which underpin clinical and professional practice. However, outside the clinical setting this knowledge remains at an abstract theoretical level. Polyani (1958) calls this *explicit knowledge* – the objective, public, written knowledge of the world, the type of fact-laden theory which students bring unintegrated to the clinic, unsure of what it might mean and how to apply it.

Students also need to be able to develop *tacit knowledge* about the reality of their professional role, based on experience. Tacit knowledge is demonstrated in action. It becomes the personal practical knowledge (Brown and McIntyre, 1993) of skilled clinicians. The distinction between explicit and tacit knowledge is similar to the distinction between knowing what and knowing how. Knowing how is the clinical knowledge needed for competent professional work.

Benner (1984) has outlined the stages of learners in their movement from novice to expert status. Not all clinicians become expert, and expert status is not a realistic goal for clinical education programmes aiming to produce entry level graduates. However, aspects of expert practice are goals of clinical education which can only be achieved in clinical settings. Skilled professionals develop through thoughtful reflection on their practice rather than longevity or amount of practice (Oldmeadow, 1996). By engaging in reflective practice (Schön, 1987), professionals become competent in what he calls the 'grey areas' of professional practice, those situations which require creative thinking or problem-solving. Highly skilled professionals develop a sense of what is salient in any situation and recognize patterns. They develop common-sense understanding of their clients and contexts, and skilled know-how. These attributes can only be developed in meaningful, real-life, ongoing interactions with clients – in other words, in the clinical setting.

The promotion of deep approaches to learning

This real-life client care also creates a meaningfulness to learning activities, which is intrinsically motivating to students (Scanlan, 1978). This intrinsic motivation is one of the features distinguishing students engaged in deep approaches to learning as opposed to surface approaches to learning (Marton and Säljö, 1984). Deep approaches to learning are found in students who are affectively engaged in searching for personal meaning and understanding (their own personal practical knowledge), seeing the whole picture or person – not just the isolated features or disembodied problems – drawing on their personal experience to make sense of new ideas and experiences, and relating evidence to conclusions. These deep approaches to learning are in marked contrast to surface approaches exhibited by students who seek only to memorize and reproduce information or skills, see only the discrete 'bits', expect the educator to be in control of their learning, and are largely motivated by the external imperative to pass an assessment or gain their qualification. In other words, they are self-focused rather than client-focused.

Professional preparation programmes aspire to engage all students in deep learning, to ensure quality of client care, as well as quality of student learning. Certainly, the clinical education setting has been shown effectively to facilitate deep learning (Coles, 1989; 1990). However, some students even in the clinical setting may remain what Ramsden (1984; 1988) and Entwistle and Waterson (1988) have referred to as strategic learners, those that use their personal organization skills to select the 'right' information and approaches needed to pass assessment tasks and achieve high marks. This strategic learning tends to occur in overloaded competitive learning environments. Care needs to be taken to ensure that the clinical education environment is conducive to deep learning. This topic will be explored in more depth later in this chapter.

Utilizing and broadening students' learning styles

Clinical settings and professional practice require many different skills from clinicians. Clinics are busy, task-focused places; things have to get done, often by yesterday. Meeting client needs requires the ability to think on one's feet, sometimes to make decisions quickly or expediently, sometimes with much thought and reflection. Some aspects of clinical practice or clinical management require a thorough understanding of the latest theories and issues. Different people will rise to each of these occasions differently, depending on their learning style.

(a) Describing learning styles

A learning style is conceptualized as the 'preference or habitual strategy used by an individual to process information for problem solving' (Katz and Heimann, 1991, p. 239). Researchers have investigated individual differences in learning styles and there is wide acceptance that individuals do develop consistent and distinctive styles to resolve conflict and analyze experience, or in other words, to learn.

The work of Kolb (1976; 1981; 1984; 1986) has been particularly influential in learning styles research. Kolb proposed a four-category model to facilitate the understanding and investigation of human learning styles and tested the Learning Style Inventory (LSI) as a brief self-descriptive inventory to categorize reported learning preferences. Analysis of an individual's responses reveals a preference for one of four styles:

- A person who reports that he or she learns most from abstract conceptualization and reflective observation is classified as an *assimilator*.
- A person who reports that he or she learns most from concrete experience and reflective observation is classified as a *diverger*.
- A person who reports that he or she learns most from abstract conceptualization of events and active experimentation is classified as a *converger*.
- A person who reports that they learn most from concrete experience and active experimentation is classified as an *accommodator*.

Honey and Mumford (1986) developed a Learning Styles Questionnaire (LSQ) which has much in common with Kolb's (1981) Learning Style Inventory (LSI). The LSQ determines individuals' preference between four primary learning styles: reflector, theorist, activist and pragmatist, each of which are different from Kolb's (1981, 1984) reported learning styles. According to Honey and Mumford (1986)

- A *reflector* learns by listening to different perspectives before coming to a conclusion. He or she likes to observe and reflect on experiences. A reflector would be classified as an assimilator or a diverger by Kolb (1984) depending on his or her preference for abstract or concrete conceptualization.
- An *activist* thrives on the challenge of new experiences and learns by active experimentation. Kolb (1984) would classify this learner as an accommodator or a converger depending again on his or her preference for abstract or concrete material.
- A *theorist* analyzes and synthesizes observations into theories, attempting to make pieces of information form a whole.
- *A pragmatist* prefers to experiment with new ideas, theories and techniques and is interested in the practicality and application of information.

People who report that they utilize three or four of Honey and Mumford's learning styles are referred to as 'all rounders'. Learners may also have combinations of two learning styles (for example, activist-reflector).

(b) The learning styles of health science students

Kolb (1984) suggested that learning style is shaped by four forces: early educational experiences, educational specialization, professional career choice and current job role. Predominant learning styles are apparent for people pursuing health science careers (for example, Katz and Heimann, 1991; Lovie-Kitchin, Coonan, Sanderson and Thompson 1989; McLeod, Lincoln, McAllister, Maloney, Purcell and Eadie, 1995; Vittetoe and Hooker, 1983; Wells and Higgs, 1990). Careers such as medicine consist predominantly of people who display a *converger* learning style, whereas careers such as occupational therapy consist of people who predominantly display an *accommodator* learning style (Kolb, 1984). McLeod *et al.* (1995) found that second- and third-year speech therapy students were predominantly *activists*.

(c) Application of learning styles in clinical education

Learning styles are of interest to clinical educators for two reasons. Firstly, it is thought that by matching learning opportunities to students' reported learning styles more successful and efficient learning will occur (Vittetoe and Hooker, 1983; Svincki and Dixon, 1987). Secondly, it is thought that students who can effectively utilize a variety of learning styles will be able to adapt successfully to any learning situation (Honey and Mumford, 1989; Dixon, 1985). Consequently clinical educators may utilize learning styles either to maximize student learning or to challenge students to adapt their styles to the demands of the learning situation. Identification of learning styles may enable clinical educators to be more sensitive to the differences students bring to their learning experiences. Clinical education experiences can be challenging or comfortable depending on whether or not the learning experience matches students' personal learning styles. Clinical educators can decide whether they wish to support students by providing learning opportunities which utilize their dominant learning styles, or to challenge students by encouraging them to explore learning opportunities using other than their dominant learning styles.

An understanding of their learning style may help students become deep learners, adept at creating their own personal practical knowledge and clinical know-how, as well as the skills necessary for clinical practice. Working with students' learning styles may help them better achieve the goals of clinical education.

Goals of clinical education

The settings and demands of professional practice are changing. So too should the missions of the professional preparation programmes and the goals of clinical education change. Higgs, Glendinning, Dunsford and Panter (1991) surveyed allied health professional education programmes and developed the list of goals for clinical education which is shown below. It is important to note that clinical skills and knowledge relevant to the student's discipline are but two of the 15 goals listed. There is an increasing emphasis on generic goals for clinical education to enable graduates to work in complex, changing environments.

Goals of clinical education for the health science professions
(Higgs *et al.*, 1991)

- Understanding of health, illness and the health care system
- Awareness of own attitudes, values and responses to health and illness
- Ability to cope effectively with the demands of the professional role
- Understanding of the interrelated roles of the health care team
- Clinical competencies relevant to the student's discipline, including clinical reasoning skills, psychomotor competencies, and interpersonal and communication skills
- Ability to provide a sound rationale for interventions/actions
- Skills in the education of relevant people (for example, patients, clients, the community, staff)
- Self-management skills (for example, time and workload management)
- Ability to process, record and use data effectively
- Ability to evaluate critically and develop own performance
- Ability to review and investigate the quality of clinical practice
- Professional accountability commitment to clients/self/employers
- Commitment to maintain and develop professional competence
- Skills necessary for lifelong professional learning
- Ability to respond to changing community health care needs

Preparing students for complex, changing work environments

Higgs *et al.* (1991) and Engel (1995) have highlighted that graduates of health science education programmes are expected not only to be competent in the practice of their discipline – that is, to be able to apply the basic sciences and applied sciences to the care and management of clients, and to be adept and professional in their interactions with colleagues and clients – they are also expected to develop competence in what Schön (1987) describes as the 'indeterminate zones of practice' (p.11), those grey areas of 'uncertainty, uniqueness, and value conflict [which] escape the canons of technical rationality' (p. 6). Such situations arise in most professions. For example, in clients whose life-span is limited and where the costs of support services and intervention are high, professionals may face ethical dilemmas in addressing concerns of offering intervention to enhance the quality of remaining life. Clinical education which seeks to promote competence in these grey areas must build on different theories of teaching and learning to those used in instruction and supervision for competent, clear-cut, discipline-specific practice. Schön argues for the development of the reflective practitioner.

More recently, Engel (1995, p. 29) developed a similar position in his discussion of the need for a 'capability approach' to medical education. He outlined two major tasks for medical schools. He suggested that medical schools should continue to help students acquire the discipline specific competences required to fulfil the responsibilities expected of new graduates under supervision. In addition, he suggested medical schools should seek to provide a general education that focuses on the generally applicable competences, in which he includes the abilities to adapt to change and participate in change, to communicate for a range of purposes (for example, obtain and give information, negotiate, consult and counsel), to collaborate in groups or teams, and to be self-directed life-long learners who can apply critical reasoning and a scientific approach to decision-making in unfamiliar situations.

Facilitating students' development of generic attributes

In addition to being prepared to function in complex and uncertain environments, university graduates are expected to develop generic attributes which enable them to function in less uncertain but more diverse settings and roles. These attributes include a variety of knowledge skills, thinking skills, personal skills, attributes and values, and professional and technical skills. There is a lively debate about generic attributes, their relationship to professional competences and the competence movement in general, particularly in the United Kingdom. The place of competences in higher education has been criticized. However, Gonzci (1994) argues that it is possible to develop competency standards for professions which are holistic and integrate cognitive, affective and technical aspects of professional work. It is this holistic integrated view of competence which has been embraced by the professions in Australia for example, and which has allowed the integration of professional competency standards into the university professional preparation programmes.

Facilitating capability in students through clinical education

Stephenson (1996) has moved the debate about competence forward with his discussion of capability, which he defines as 'an all-round human quality, and integration of knowledge, skills and personal qualities used effectively and appropriately in response to varied, familiar and unfamiliar circumstances'. He suggests that capability is having justified confidence in one's ability to 'take appropriate and effective action, communicate effectively, collaborate with others and learn from experiences in changing circumstances'.

The work of Schön and Stephenson highlights the need for clinical education to emphasize personal qualities and capability for professional practice in uncertain and changing environments. In this book, we would argue that clinical education is ideally and uniquely suited to achieve the development of capability.

With the knowledge explosion in all disciplines, graduates are expected to be critical consumers of information and life-long learners who maintain competence in their discipline, expand and test their own knowledge and skills, and contribute to the expansion of knowledge in the field. Professional practice in the clinical setting requires professionals to be life-long learners (Lincoln and McAllister, 1993). Appropriate clinical education has the potential to set students on the path of life-long learning.

Life-long learning

The ability to be a life-long learner is a valued attribute and essential component of capability. Candy (1994) has discussed the development of life-long learning through undergraduate education. He has profiled the qualities or characteristics of life-long learners, an adaptation of which appears on page 56.

It is essential to be a life-long learner who is aware of one's learning style and approaches to learning, who has the ability to access learning resources, and who self-directs and self-evaluates one's learning. The ability to collaborate with other professionals in learning, and in service delivery is vital. This collaboration could be called *interdependence,* a concept which will be elaborated in a later section. Employers value such attributes and the changing nature of professional practice demands it.

As Cross (1994) has noted, the goals of clinical education have grown from a training and instruction focus on the drilling of prescribed procedures to include an emphasis on the development of generic attributes essential to professional competence, capability and life-long learning.

Profile of the attributes of a life-long learner (Candy, 1994)

- *An inquiring mind:*
  - a love of learning
  - a sense of curiosity and question asking
  - a critical spirit
  - comprehension monitoring and self-evaluation
- *Helicopter vision:*
  - a sense of the interconnectedness of fields
  - an awareness of how knowledge is created in at least one field of study, and an understanding of the methodological and substantive limitations in that field
- *Information literacy:*
  - knowledge of major current resources available in at least one field of study
  - ability to frame researchable questions in at least one field of study
  - ability to locate, evaluate, manage and use information in a range of contexts
  - ability to retrieve information using a variety of media
  - ability to decode information in a variety of forms: written, statistical, graphs, charts, diagrams and tables
  - critical evaluation of information
- *A* sense *of personal agency:*
  - a positive concept of oneself as capable and autonomous
  - self-organization skills (time management, goal-setting, etc.)
- *A repertoire of learning skills:*
  - knowledge of one's own strengths, weaknesses and preferred learning style
  - range of strategies for learning in whatever context one finds oneself
  - an understanding of the differences between surface and deep learning.

Are we achieving the goals of clinical education?

The goals for clinical education outlined in previous sections are not new. Over a decade ago, Stritter, Baker and Shahady (1986) outlined their learning vector model which has as goals independent learning and autonomy. Most contemporary clinical education programmes would espouse similar goals and values. One indicator that these values were being enacted and goals achieved would be the nature of the interactions between clinical educators and their students. Such interactions should exemplify the promotion of the broader goals of clinical education

However, the literature suggests that interactions between clinical educators and students are often counterproductive to the pursuit of the goals of interdependence, autonomy, self-direction and self-evaluation. Research into the communications between clinical educators and students reveals a consistent picture of clinical educators dominating interactions, doing most of the initiating, talking, information-provision and problem-solving (Anderson, 1988). Students take a passive, responsive role even though they say they would like to take greater responsibility for directing the interaction and problem-solving themselves (Kenny & McAllister, 1993). The research literature suggests this pattern to be resistant to change and unresponsive to growth and change in the student (Anderson, 1988).

Another indicator that the goals of clinical education were being met would lie in the content of educational sessions conducted with students in clinical settings. Grahn (1989) studied clinical education situations in radiation therapy and concluded that they were 'capricious endeavours. Anything, good or bad, could be the outcome' (p. 27).

We suggest two of many possible reasons for these incongruities between the goals and processes of clinical education. The interactions with students described above are those of *instructors* acting out of a philosophy of instructing for limited skills, rather than of *educators* facilitating learning and educating for broader goals. Further, it is suggested that clinical education lacks a theory of education which would promote the attainment of the broader goals of clinical education outlined previously. A review of the clinical education literature (Kenny, 1996) revealed, with a few exceptions, a marked lack of any explicit reference to a theory of clinical education. Opacich (1995) alluded to a similar belief in her critique of the lack of a philosophy of clinical education in occupational therapy.

One notable exception to atheoretical discussions of clinical education is the work of Stengelhofen (1993). She does discuss the differences between adult learning (andragogy) and pedagogy and the characteristics of adult learners. Stengelhofen then goes on to discuss the implications of these for the roles clinical educators can adopt with students.

We believe that adult learning theory is congruent with the goals of clinical education and argue that widespread adoption might enable clinical education more successfully to meet the goals to which it aspires. The following section briefly reviews key elements of the adult learning literature.

Adult learning

Knowles (1970), in discussing the search for a theory of adult learning, introduced into the English language literature on adult learning the term *andragogy* which he defined as the art and science of helping adults learn. Today this term is used to refer more broadly to an approach to teaching and learning for any age group, which is student-centred and which fosters learner autonomy. This is in contrast to traditional notions of pedagogy, which was initially used to refer to the didactic teaching of children but is now commonly used to indicate teacher-directed learning.

Characteristics of adult learners

There are a number of key assumptions about the characteristics of adult learners upon which Knowles (1980) bases his model of andragogy. These assumptions are that as adults mature:

- they become more self-directing, although they may choose dependence on the teacher in some circumstances
- their life experiences become a rich resource for learning and they tend to learn better through experiential means
- their learning needs are more often determined by life circumstances at the time, for example the need to acquire job-related skills
- their learning becomes more problem-centred for immediate performance in life circumstances.

Although subsequent investigators have refined Knowles' original concepts, there tends to be general agreement in the literature regarding the characteristics of adult learners. Brookfield (1986) concludes that autonomy in the learning programme and the use of one's life experience as a learning resource are the two characteristics of adult learning most frequently reported in the literature on adult learning.

Principles of adult learning

Brookfield (1986, p. 31) summarizes the work of several authors who have attempted to specify the principles of adult learning, as follows:

> 'adults learn throughout their lives, with the negotiations of the transitional stages in the life-span being the immediate causes and motives for much of this learning. They exhibit diverse learning styles – strategies for coding information, cognitive procedures, mental sets – and learn in different ways, at different times, for different purposes. As a rule, however, they like their learning activities to be problem centred and to be meaningful to their life situation, and they want learning outcomes to have immediacy of application. The past experiences of adults effect their current learning, sometimes serving as an enhancement, sometimes as a hindrance. Effective learning is also linked to the adult's subscription to a self-concept of himself or herself as a learner. Finally, adults exhibit a tendency toward self-directedness in their learning.'

The implications for clinical education of these characteristics of adult learners and principles of adult learning will be elaborated throughout this book.

Clinical education: a unique opportunity for adult learning

It can be argued that clinical education is an ideal context in which to adopt an adult learning approach. Clinical education is by its very nature experiential: it involves obtaining experience in working with clients in real contexts. These clients bring to the health, education or welfare setting real problems which they wish to solve. Clients' needs provide the immediacy for problem-solving and clinical decision-making, and the motivation needed for successful learning by adult learners. To be successful, students need to engage in deep learning, as discussed earlier in this chapter. Students learning to be clinicians engage in problem-solving with their clients, their clinical educators and their peers, as they seek to solve the presented problems. They draw not only on what they know, their previous clinical and classroom experiences but also past life experiences. As students are motivated by the need to solve real and immediate problems presented in the clinical and professional environments, they are likely to reflect on their actions and decisions, either during the client contact or after it. Students in clinical settings have a real need to make the most of the experience in which they find themselves. The reality of the clinical environment is highly congruent with adult learning theory.

We suggest that adult learning theory provides a strong theoretical foundation for clinical education. The characteristics of adult learners are those demonstrated in students engaged in clinical experiences. The principles of adult learning lend themselves to application in the clinical setting. The characteristics of effective facilitators are congruent with those characteristics needed for effective clinical educators. The goals of adult learning and clinical education are similar in that they both emphasize the need for self-directedness and autonomy. The following section will explore further some of the common themes which arise in adult learning and clinical education. It will discuss ways in which adult learning principles can be incorporated into clinical education programmes to promote the attainment of the goals of clinical education outlined earlier in this chapter.

Autonomy and self-directedness

Autonomy and self-directedness are both processes of learning as well as desired goals of learning. Candy (1991) states that 'a person may be regarded as autonomous to the extent that he or she conceives of goals and plans, exercises freedom of choice, uses the capacity for rational reflection, has willpower to follow through, exercises self-restraint and self-discipline, views himself or herself as autonomous' (p. 125). Four dimensions of self-direction are elaborated by Candy (1991): personal autonomy, self-management in learning, the independent pursuit of learning, and student control of instruction. The implications which these dimensions have for managing clinical education programmes are explored below.

(a) Constraints to autonomy and self-directedness

It is apparent that a clinical education programme wishing to promote the goals of autonomy and self-directedness will need to consider carefully issues of student control, freedom, independence and interdependence within the learning programme. Legal and ethical concerns related to client care dictate that students can not have full control of their learning programme. Their clinical educators are ultimately legally responsible for client care. The gatekeeping function held by universities for the professions also means that clinical education programmes have some basic curricula to be covered and assessed, and need to be able to certify competence in their graduates. There is a potential dilemma for programmes and clinical educators in seeking to enact adult learning principles of student freedom to direct their learning whilst maintaining legally and societally determined controls.

Some guidance on dealing with this dilemma comes from the work of Torbert (1978) on the paradoxical concept of *liberating structures.* Torbert argues that structure for a learning programme comes from its organization and the leadership exercised in implementing the learning programme. The nature of the constraints built into a programme structure can paradoxically free students to achieve more than they could have otherwise. These concepts of liberating programmes, and paradoxical structure and freedom are important in the implications they hold for clinical education programmes and clinical educators.

In applying these concepts Higgs (1993) sees freedom and control as occurring on a continuum. At one end lies clinical educator dominance and control, at the other *a laissez-faire* approach by the clinical educator and control by the student. The balance of these two would be *controlled freedom,* such as that which can occur in *liberating programme structures* defined by Higgs (1993) as 'the dynamic framework ... a complex whole in which numerous environmental, task, social and individual dimensions need to operate congruently to optimize learning opportunities and outcomes' (p. 126).

Higgs recognizes that students need to be ready to undertake the learning task at hand, a concept which she refers to as *learner task maturity*. Students need to be prepared and supported in their readiness for a task. The clinical educator needs to structure tasks and control students' access to tasks relative to their readiness for the tasks, in order to enhance the likelihood that the freedom they will have within the task leads to successful learning and, in the context of clinical education, to client care. The clinical educator in a liberating programme structure functions as a manager of the student's learning programme.

Interdependence

The promotion of autonomy and self-directedness as goals and processes of a clinical education programme does not imply total independence. That is, independence does not imply that students learn in isolation from each other, and are unable to learn from the experiences of others. Autonomy and self-directedness occur in a social context. True autonomy requires emotional maturity. Students should not continually need approval and reassurance. They should also be technically independent, able to carry on with a task and cope with problems which may arise in a mature, professional way. They should not have to run for help immediately, but should be able to analyze the problem and discuss the decisions they made and the strategies they implemented in later consultations with their clinical educators. Simultaneously, students must operate interdependently, contributing to the social (in this case the clinical and professional) structure in which they find themselves, as well as receiving from it.

This concept of interdependence is vital in clinical education and clinical practice. It provides the key to assuring the ethical and legal demands placed on clinical educators and clinical practitioners with respect to client care are met. Students who have moved through dependence to independence in the task or client problem at hand can be expected to function interdependently with their clinical educators. We interpret this to mean that such students should keep their clinical educators informed of their plans and outcomes, even though these may be developed and executed independently of the clinical educator.

Boud (1988) argues that students pass thorough stages of development from dependence to counterdependence to independence and finally to interdependence. He suggests that in this final stage, students are engaged in mature relationships within their world, interrelating with their world rather than being apart from it. We would suggest that on reaching this stage, students are demonstrating the outcomes of the professional socialization process. The stages through which students move on their way to achieving interdependence, as outlined by Boud, are not unlike those of Anderson's (1988) continuum of supervision. We would expect that students functioning interdependently would use their clinical educators as a resource and sounding board for discussion or problem-solving, just as they would use their peers in this way. Evidence of these behaviours is a hallmark of student growth.

Peer learning

Health, education and welfare professionals rarely work alone. Their work settings almost always call upon them to work as part of a departmental or multidisciplinary team. Lincoln and McAllister (1993) noted that the major way in which professionals continue to learn, that is to function as life-long learners, is to learn with and from their peers. Therefore, it makes sense to establish the process of peer learning in the clinical education setting. Working with peers is in fact one of the hallmarks of experiential and self-directed programmes, and a goal of clinical education.

The collaborative models of clinical education highlight the need for effective peer learning. The ability to learn from and with peers is a characteristic of adult learners (Lincoln and McAllister, 1993). Members of a peer group bring to the group different life and prior clinical learning experiences. Sharing these, participating in each other's ongoing learning, assisting each other with reflection during and after experiences can significantly enhance peers' learning. It can also help reduce the anxiety associated with clinical education (Clan, Carter and McAllister, 1994). Clinical educators who actively utilize the resources that peers bring to a group and create a learning environment in which peer learning can occur are using adult learning theory in their approach to facilitating student learning.

(a) Benefits of peer learning

The benefits of peer learning can be enormous for the clinical educator and the clinic, as well as for the students. Clinical educators who regularly use peer teaching or collaborative learning report reduced stress for themselves in that they have fewer competing demands in managing students' clinical education programmes, they have more free time to attend to the non-client aspects of their job and they do not have to play social host to solo students in their facility (Callan, O'Neill and McAllister, 1994).

Economic benefits to the facility have also been identified. Ladyshewsky and Healey (1990), in a Canadian study of physiotherapy students, reported greater efficiency in the planning and orientation phases of students' placements, greater input into problem-solving and more time available for improving the quality of client care. Perhaps more importantly for clinic administrators, after the settling-in phase of a block clinical placement, two senior students were able to carry a caseload greater than that of a solo clinician. This finding has recently been replicated with a study by Ladyshewsky and Barrie (1996) with speech therapy students in Australia.

(b) Pitfalls in peer learning situations

The benefits of peer learning or collaborative learning accrue only through careful management of clinical placements by clinical educators. Best and Rose (1996) have identified some of the challenges in this approach which need to managed. They include the risk of comparison of one student with another, competition between students, personality clashes, dealing with students functioning at different levels, assurance of client safety, dealing with a shortage of client numbers or appropriate clients for student learning, limited physical space for students to work or students working in different areas of the facility. We know from experience that careful planning, skilled monitoring and treating students like adult learners can overcome most of these challenges.

Learning from experience

Clinical education programmes are by their nature experiential. Students actively engage in experiences with clients, their families and other professionals. These experiences can be enormously satisfying, or very bewildering; they can engender in students great highs and lows of emotional reaction to all aspects and individuals in the clinical setting. Students will almost always report that they learned a lot in clinic. However, learning does not accrue only from experience. What is also required for learning to occur is reflection.

Boud, Keogh and Walker (1985) proposed a model for reflection *following* experience. The key elements of the model are 'returning to the experience', 'attending to feelings' and 're-evaluation of the experience' leading to new learning. Boud and Walker (1990) have also explored possibilities for promoting reflection *during* experience.

The work of Boud and his colleagues has been widely applied in the development of reflective curricula in many professional education programmes. Another major catalyst to the development of reflective curricula has been Schön's (1983, 1987) work on reflective practitioners and their education. Schön's views that reflection on practice is what allows practitioners to work in uncertain and changing environments, the 'grey area' of professional practice as he calls them, have been discussed earlier in this chapter.

This section has outlined a theoretical and philosophical framework for clinical education grounded in adult learning theory. We have suggested that the principles of adult learning and the characteristics of adult learners are highly congruent with the characteristics of students in clinical education settings and with the nature of clinical education. There also needs to be congruence between the characteristics of facilitators of adult learning and the characteristics of clinical educators.

Characteristics of effective clinical educators operating in an adult learning framework

Heron (1989) has discussed the characteristics of facilitators in adult learning programmes. Many of these characteristics have also been identified by clinical educators and students alike as facilitative of learning in clinical settings.

Communication and interpersonal skills

The characteristics of clinical educators consistently identified in the literature as most valued by students are communication and interpersonal skills (Emery, 1984; Cupit, 1988; Jarski, Kulig and Olsen, 1990; Neville & French, 1991; Onuoha, 1994; Williams and Webb, 1994). These were rated higher or more frequently mentioned than professional competence or teaching skills. This is the case whether the studies used questionnaire-based methods of data collection with quantitative analysis, or the critical incident technique with subsequent qualitative data analysis, such as was used by Williams and Webb (1994).

Neville and French (1991) listed the following personal attributes desirable for clinical tutors: friendly, helpful, forthcoming with information and approachable. The physiotherapy students surveyed by Cupit (1988) listed as their top three desirable attributes for clinical supervisors: an awareness of the student as a person and future colleague; being inspiring and enthusiastic about work, teaching and student learning; and being encouraging and emotionally supportive. The next two attributes on the list were being a good professional role model and an ability to draw on and extend student knowledge. Even when discussing educative skills, communication and interpersonal skills are given priority. For example, when listing the qualities of effective clinical teachers (as named by Irby, 1978), the qualities listed under group instruction skills are to do with rapport, respect, listening and answering, and questioning skills. To be effective facilitators of student learning, clinical educators need to develop their interpersonal and communication skills.

This value on communication skills and interpersonal skills accorded by both students and clinical educators is of interest, given that Pickering (1984) found that feelings were rarely discussed in interactions between students and clinical educators. The clinical educators in Pickering's study made journal entries in which feelings were noted, and the work by Chan, Carter and McAllister (1994) highlighted the anxiety that students feel about their interactions with clinical educators (as well as about their work with clients). Yet these feelings about relationships with clinical educators, the clinical education process and assessment are apparently rarely raised by either party for discussion.

The work of Boud, Keogh and Walker (1985) and Mandy (1989) stresses the need to deal with feelings in the clinical education process. Clearly this is an area warranting attention from clinical educators who wish to facilitate student learning within an adult learning environment. Providing negative (as well as positive) feedback and assessing students in ways which are congruent with adult learning principles are difficult tasks for clinical educators.

Professional and teaching skills

Although the studies discussed in the previous section highlighted the value of communication and interpersonal skills, that is not to imply that students do not also value sound professional and teaching skills. The studies by Onuoha (1994) and Williams and Webb (1994) found that students do value these skills when they are utilized within an adult learning approach, and enacted through the use of good interpersonal and communication skills. Williams and Webb found that students appreciated the characteristics of clinical educators which encouraged active participation in the learning process. The fact that there was a difference in value placed on andragogic skills by students and clinical educators lead Onuoha to suggest that clinical educators need to be educated themselves on teaching and learning within an andragogic (adult learning) framework.

Summary

This chapter has discussed the nature and goals of clinical education. It has suggested that clinical education lacks a theory and a philosophy, and argued that the adoption of adult learning theory and approaches may make the broader goals of clinical education more achievable. The congruence between adult learning and clinical education processes has been discussed. The final section has highlighted the value placed on facilitating clinical learning within an adult learning framework by students and clinical educators, and the need for more education of clinical educators.

References

American Speech and Hearing Association (1978) Current status of supervision of speech-language pathology and audiology. Special Report. *Asha* 20: 478–486.

Anderson J L (1988) *The Supervisory Process in Speech-language Pathology and Audiology.* College Hill Press, Boston.

Benner P (1984) *From Novice to Expert: Excellence and Power in Clinical Nursing Practice.* Addison-Wesley, Menlo Park.

Best D, Rose M (1996) *Quality Supervision, Theory and Practice for Clinical Supervisors.* W. B. Saunders, London.

Boud D (1988) Moving towards autonomy. In: D Boud (ed.) *Developing Student Autonomy in Learning.* Kogan Page, London.

Boud D, Keogh R, Walker D (1985) Promoting reflection in learning: A model. In: D Boud, R Keogh, D Walker (eds) *Reflection: Turning Experience into Learning,* pp. 18–40. Kogan Page, London.

Boud D, Walker D (1990) Making the most of experience. *Studies in Continuing Education,* 12 (2): 61–80.

Brookfield S D (1986) *Understanding and Facilitating Adult Learning.* Open University Press, Milton Keynes.

Brown S, McIntyre D (1993) *Making Sense of Teaching.* Open University Press, Milton Keynes.

Callan C, O'Neill D, McAllister L (1994) Adventures in two to one supervision: Two students can be better than one. *SUPERvision* 18: 15–16.

Candy P (1991) *Self-direction for Lifelong Learning: A Comprehensive Guide to Theory and Practice.* Jossey-Bass, San Francisco.

Candy P (1994) *Developing Lifelong Learners Through Undergraduate Education.* Commissioned Report No. 28. National Board of Employment, Education and Training. Australian Government Printing Service, Canberra.

Chan J, Carter S, McAllister L (1994) Sources of anxiety related to clinical education in undergraduate speech-language pathology students. *Australian Journal of Human Communication Disorders* 22: 57–73.

Coles C (1989) The role of context in elaborated learning. In: J Balla, M Gibson, A Chang (eds) *Learning in Medical School: A Model for the Clinical Professions.* Hong Kong University Press, Hong Kong.

Coles C (1990) Elaborated learning in undergraduate medical education. *Medical Education* 24: 14–22.

Cross V (1994) From clinical supervisor to clinical educator: Too much to ask? *Physiotherapy* 80 (9): 609–611.

Cupit R (1988) Student stress: An approach to coping at the interface between clinical and preclinical. *Australian Journal of Physiotherapy* 34: 215–219.

Dixon N M (1985) The implementation of learning style information. *Lifelong Learning* 913: 16–20.

Emery M (1984) Effectiveness of the clinical instructor: Students' perspectives. *Physical Therapy* 64: 1079–1082.

Engel C E (1995) Medical education in the 21st century: The need for a capability approach. *Capability* 1: 23–30.

Entwistle N, Waterson S (1988) Approaches to studying and levels of processing in university students. *British Journal of Educational Psychology* 58: 258–265.

Gonzci A (1994) Competency based assessment in the professions in Australia. *Assessment in Education* 1: 27–44.

Goodyear R, Bernaud J (1992) *Fundamentals of Clinical Supervision.* Allyn & Bacon, Massachusetts.

Grahn G (1989) Educational situations in clinical settings. *Radiography Today* 55: 26–27.

Heron J (1989) *The Facilitators' Handbook.* Kogan Page, London.

Higgs J (1993) The teacher in self-directed learning: Manager or co-manager. In: N Graves (ed.) *Learner Managed Learning: Practice, Theory and Policy.* World Education Fellowship.

Higgs J, Glendinning M, Dunsford F, Panter J (1991) Goals and components of clinical education in the allied health professions. *Proceedings of the World Confederation for Physical Therapy: 11th International Conference.* World Confederation for Physical Therapy, London.

Honey P, Mumford A (1986) *The Manual of Learning Styles,* 2nd edn. author, Berkshire.

Honey P, Mumford A (1989) *Capitalising on Your Learning Style.* King of Prussia, Organisation Design and Development Inc, Pennsylvania.

Irby D M (1978) Clinical teacher effectiveness in medicine. *Journal of Medical Education* 58: 808–815.

Jarski R, Kulig K, Olsen R (1990) Clinical teaching in physical therapy: Student and teacher perceptions. *Physical Therapy* 70: 173–178.

Katz N, Heimann N (1991) Learning styles of students and practitioners in five health professions. *The Occupational Therapy Journal of Research* 11: 238–245.

Kenny B, McAllister L (1993) An investigation of typical and self-evaluation supervisory conferences in speech pathology. *Proceedings of the Annual Conference of the Australian Association of Speech and Hearing, Darwin, Australia.*

Kenny B (1996) An investigation of students' self-evaluation skills in supervisory conferences. Unpublished master's thesis. University of Sydney, Sydney, New South Wales, Australia.

Knowles M (1970) *The Modern Practice of Adult Education: Andragogy Versus Pedagogy.* Association Press, New York.

Knowles M (1980) *The Modern Practice of Adult Education: From Pedagogy to Andragogy.* Cambridge, The Adult Education Co, New York.

Kolb D (1976) *Learning Styles Inventory: Technical Manual.* McBer & Co, Boston.

Kolb D (1981) Learning styles and disciplinary differences. In: A W Chickering *et al. The Modern American College*, pp. 232–255. Jossey-Bass, San Francisco.

Kolb D (1984) *Experiential Learning: Experience as the Source of Learning and Development.* Prentice Hall, Englewood Cliffs, NJ.

Kolb D (1986) *Learning Style Inventory: Technical Manual.* McBer & Co, Boston.

Ladyshewsky R, Barrie S (1996) Measuring quality and cost of clinical education. Paper presented at the Annual Conference of the Higher Education Research Development Society of Australia, Perth, July.

Ladyshewsky R, Healey E (1990) *The 2:1 Teaching Model in Clinical Education: A Manual for Clinical Instructors.* University of Toronto, Department of Rehabilitation Medicine, Toronto.

Laschinger H, Boss M (1983) Learning styles of nursing students and career choices. *Journal of Advanced Nursing* 9: 375–380.

Lincoln M, McAllister L (1993) Facilitating peer learning in clinical education. *Medical Teacher* 15: 17–25.

Lovie-Kitchin J, Coonan I, Sanderson R, Thompson B (1989) Learning styles across health sciences courses. *Higher Education Research and Development* 8: 27–37.

Mandy S (1989) Facilitating student learning in clinical education. *Australian Journal of Human Communication Disorders* 17: 83–93.

Marton F, Säljö R (1984) Approaches to learning. In: F Marton, D Hounsell, N Entwhistle (eds) *The Experience of Learning.* Scottish Academic Press, Edinburgh.

McLeod S, Lincoln M, McAllister L, Maloney D, Purcell A, Eadie P (1995) A longitudinal investigation of the learning styles of speech pathology students. *Australian Journal of Human Communication Disorders* 23: 13–25.

Neville S, French S (1991) Clinical education: Students and clinical tutors' views. *Physiotherapy* 77: 351–353.

Oldmeadow L (1996) Developing clinical competence: A mastery pathway. *Australian Physiotherapy* 42 (1): 37–44.

Onions C T (ed) (1992) *The Shorter Oxford English Dictionary on Historical Principles*, 3rd edn. Oxford University Press, Oxford.

Onuoha A (1994) Effective clinical teaching behaviours from the perspective of students, supervisors and teachers. *Physiotherapy* 80: 208–214.

Opacich K (1995) Is an educational philosophy missing from the fieldwork solution? *American Journal of Occupational Therapy* 49: 160–164.

Pickering M (1984) Interpersonal communication in speech-language pathology supervisory conferences: A qualitative study. *Journal of Speech and Hearing Disorders* 49: 189–195.

Polyani M (1958) *Personal Knowledge.* Routledge and Kegan Paul, London.

Ramsden P (1984) The context of learning. In: F Marton, D Hounsell, N Entwhistle (eds) *The Experience of Learning*. Scottish Academic Press, Edinburgh.

Ramsden P (1988) *Improving Learning: New Perspectives*. Kogan Page, London.

Romanini J, Higgs J (1991) The teacher as manager in continuing and professional education. *Studies in Continuing Education* 13: 41–52.

Scanlan C L (1978) Integrating didactic and clinical education – high patient contact. In: C W Ford (ed.) *Clinical Education for the Allied Health Professions*. C. V. Mosby, St Louis.

Schön D (1983) *The Reflective Practitioner: How Professionals Think in Action*. Temple-Smith, London.

Schön D (1987) *Educating the Reflective Practitioner*. Jossey-Bass, San Francisco.

Stengelhofen J (1993) *Teaching Students in Clinical Settings*. Chapman & Hall, London.

Stephenson J (1996) *Beyond Competence to Capability and the Learning Society*. International Programme of Seminars and Workshops on Higher Education. University of Sydney, April.

Stritter F T, Baker R M, Shahady E J (1986) Clinical instruction. In: W C McGaghie, J J Frey (eds) *Handbook for the Academic Physician*, pp. 99–124. Springer Verlag, New York.

Svincki M D, Dixon N M (1987) The Kolb model modified for classroom activities. *College Teaching* 35: 141–146.

Torbert W R (1978) Educating toward shared purpose, self-direction and quality work: The theory and practice of liberating structure. *Journal of Higher Education* 49: 109–135.

Vittetoe M C, Hooker E (1983) Learning style preferences of allied health practitioners in a teacher education programme. *Journal of Allied Health* February: 48–55.

Wells D, Higgs Z A (1990) Learning styles and learning preferences of first and fourth semester baccalaureate degree nursing students. *Journal of Nursing Education* 29: 385–390.

White R, Ewan C (eds) (1991) *Clinical Teaching in Nursing*. Chapman & Hall, London.

Williams P L, Webb C (1994) Clinical supervision skills: A delphi and critical incident technique study. *Medical Teacher* 16: 139–155.

5. Empowering Versus Enabling in Academia

Karen Espeland and Linda Shanta

The literature endorses empowered nurses as essential to changing not only the nursing profession but also the current health care system. Nurse educators have embraced the concept of empowering students. However, faculty frequently enable students rather than empower them in both clinical and classroom settings. This article describes the difference between enabling and empowering. Collegiality, communication, accountability, and autonomy are components of a model used to compare empowering versus enabling in the academic setting. Nurse educators will become aware of behaviors that sabotage the empowerment of students. Strategies designed to facilitate students' development of empowering behaviors will be provided throughout the article.

Since the late 1980s, the nursing literature has called for a curriculum revolution to liberate and empower faculty and students. It is only recently that some authors have begun to voice the reality of the revolution in terms of the challenges faced by faculty, especially at the undergraduate level. Diekelmann (1993) found that faculty feel pressure to find a way to present the massive amount of content necessary to facilitate passing of the licensing examination. Other issues confronted by nurse educators include an industry that judges graduates not as much by what they know but by their efficiency. The burden of transmitting the knowledge and skills required by the technologically driven health care industry in a short time is faced every day by nursing faculty. In addition, the pressure to meet the needs of nontraditional students may cause faculty to reduce their expectations of students. The purpose of this article is to describe empowering versus enabling in academia, identify the main elements of empowering and enabling in nursing curricula, and address how faculty can avoid enabling students and actually empower them.

Empowering

Empowering is a popular concept noted in the literature of many disciplines, including social work, psychology, and education (Hawley McWhirter, 1991). Empowering and empowerment are noted in nursing literature as well. Empowerment has been defined as "the interpersonal process of providing the resources, tools, and environment to develop, build, and increase ability and effectiveness of others to set and reach goals for individual and social ends" (Hokanson-Hawks, 1992, p. 610).

The argument for empowering nurses and nursing students that emerged in the literature review included the importance of increasing the professional stature and recognition of nurses, as well as enhancing nursing students' feelings and behaviors

Karen Espeland and Linda Shanta: 'Empowering Versus Enabling in Academia' in *JOURNAL OF NURSING EDUCATION* (2001), 40 (8), pp. 342–346.

associated with a professional identity. Glass (1998) related three components for empowering nurses, "...the raising of consciousness, the development of a strong positive esteem, and the political skills needed to negotiate and change the healthcare system" (p. 134). Empowering strategies have been identified as essential in preparing nurses to be change agents in the rapidly changing world of health care. The literature exemplifies additional benefits of the empowerment process including enhancement of nurses' ability to meet clients' needs and improvement of nurses' own professional concept (Clay, 1992; Coulter, 1990; Davis, 1991). Another benefit of the empowerment process, which is of primary importance, is the increase noted in nurses' ability to solve problems effectively and, thus, improve the quality of care provided to clients (Gorman and Clark, 1986).

Nursing faculty have responded to the urging of nurse authors and leaders to humanize their curricula. The literature suggests that faculty should be the facilitator of learning, rather than instructor and evaluator (Coulter, 1990). In theory, this concept aligns closely with the basic philosophy of many nurses (i.e., interacting, sharing, making decisions through consensus).

However, the manner in which nurses are trained and educated can be rigid and controlling, keeping students entrenched in a hierarchy (Carlson-Catalano, 1992; Clare, 1993a). Admittedly, the task of transmitting large amounts of information in a short time frame narrows the focus of the educational process and discourages critical thinking and autonomy among students (Gorrell and Langenbach, 1994), and the constraints driven by industry can be used as a ready justification to support the status quo. Such justification is short sighted at best because learning then becomes mechanical and technical, thus encouraging conformity, passivity, and subordination.

In an attempt to redesign and revolutionize nursing education, faculty may be tempted to reduce expectations and eliminate evaluations to gain student consensus. However, nursing is a practice profession that demands a high level of knowledge and safe practice. Nurse educators feel an overwhelming responsibility to transmit information and teach skills to ensure a safe level of practice from students and ultimately graduates of the programs. A dichotomy seems to exist between the education requirements necessitated by industry and the humanistic type of curricula supported by the nursing literature.

The empowerment process seems to enhance nurses' ability to meet clients' needs and improve their professional concept (Clay, 1992). Nurse educators' attempt to change the manner of educating to a more empowering system sometimes may be misdirected, at best, and may sabotage the essence of the empowerment process, at worst (Clare, 1993b). Essentially, the empowerment process will allow students to take control of their own lives. In a professional sense, the goal of empowering students is to help them develop autonomy and accountability for professional practice. Faculty who try to humanize the manner in which nurses are educated by reducing expectations or by shouldering some of the responsibility for learning that rightfully belongs to students may in fact send a message of doubt and lack of confidence in students' ability to reach the goal of autonomy.

Enabling

What is an enabling system in nursing education, and how does it manifest itself? Enabling has been defined as "behaviors by others that perpetuates dependent behaviors" (Haber, Krainovich-Miller, McMahon and PriceHoskins, 1997, p. 516). The term enabling is found in addiction literature (Haber *et al.*, 1997) and is by no means positive in this sense, as it may be in many other contexts (e.g., her expertise enabled her to establish a consulting firm). In the field of alcohol and drug dependence, enabling refers to allowing or encouraging a bad situation (e.g., alcohol or drug dependence) to continue or grow worse.

Enabling is a component of codependency. According to Malloy and Berkery (1993), historically codependency was a term used to describe behavior of a person, usually a woman, that enabled a spouse or significant other to continue a destructive path, most often that of alcoholism. Currently, the concept of codependency has broadened, and it has developed into a national buzzword. The most simple and concise definition was developed by Beatie (1987) who defined a codependent person as one who has let someone else's behavior affect him or her and who is obsessed with controlling other people's behavior. According to Fontaine and Fletcher (1995), codependent behaviors focus on control, making excuses for others' behaviors, inability to trust self, and feelings of inadequacy and insecurity. Codependent people have a strong need to assume responsibility, take care of others' needs, and rescue others from the consequences of their behaviors.

According to Schaef (1987), codependency is built on an abnormal thought process. Many codependent behaviors (e.g., caring for, nurturing, assisting, supporting) often are associated with women and especially nurses. Snow and Willard (1989) estimated that 80% of the nurses they observed had problems with codependency. According to Schaef (1986), codependency is a woman's issue and a nursing issue.

How do codependent faculty enable students? Faculty who enter academia with unresolved codependency issues may have difficulty empowering students in the classroom and in nursing practice, unless they make significant changes in their teaching strategies to empower, instead of enable, students (Caffrey and Caffrey, 1994).

Enabling in academia can be reinforced by well-meaning faculty who unwittingly allow or encourage students' irresponsible behavior, shielding them from the consequences of their actions or fostering dependence on faculty as the final authority, thus inhibiting the critical thinking aspect of learning. The faculty behaviors described encourage or support situations that are potentially destructive. According to Caffrey and Caffrey (1994), in codependent relationships both participants are involved in attempts to control one another, and neither participant is empowered in a way that fosters self-actualization. It is unlikely that faculty consciously would undermine students' sense of responsibility. However, sometimes faculty develop patterns that are more enabling than empowering.

Implications for nursing education

Worrell, McGinn, Black, Holloway and Ney (1996) proposed a model for empowerment. The model suggests that the critical elements of empowerment rely not only on the process of being empowered but also on the outcome of empowerment. The model lists four critical elements:

- Collegiality, which is a relationship based on cooperative interactions and mutual respect for individuality.
- Communication, which is the effective transmission of information and its meaning among individuals.
- Autonomy, which is the ability to be independent, self-directing, and self-governing.
- Accountability, which is an assumption of responsibility and answering for the outcomes of one's actions.

This model will be used to differentiate empowering versus enabling in teaching strategies, faculty-student interactions, and nursing practice experiences.

Collegiality

Interactions occur among nurse educators and students on many levels during the education process. In the empowerment model, interactions among students and nurse educators take the form of collegiality and as a community of learners, rather than from a position of authoritarian to subordinate or as a caretaking relationship.

Faculty who enable students will take care of them, rather than foster independence. Their highest priority is pleasing the students. According to Subby (1987), codependent individuals adapt by adjusting their behavior to accommodate others no matter how unreasonable the expectation. Codependent people obtain their feelings of self-worth from other people, which is described by Schaef (1987) as external referencing.

In an enabling model, if students are happy, the faculty is happy, and if students are discontent, the faculty is discontent. Faculty who are student pleasers want others to like them. They will tell students what they want to hear whether it is accurate or not, which sends students mixed messages about professional values. The faculty's self-esteem may be tied to satisfying others, and therefore, they may have difficulty making decisions that are unpopular (Caffrey and Caffrey, 1994). Faculty may have an overinvestment in student grades and the need to be a friend or parent to students.

In contrast, when faculty seek to empower students, honest feedback is given to students to encourage growth. The students learn the benefit of peer feedback and the value of professional colleagues.

Methods that increase collegiality include altering the role of the educator from that of the giver of information to that of coach (i.e., coaching students through the cognitive process of analysis) (Bevis and Watson, 1989). Coaching will expand nurses' potential for understanding and modifying an environment and can be extended as an analytic strategy to use the nursing process. Coaching can be an effective means to provide frequent, positive, and constructive feedback.

Passing information from those who possess it to those who desire it is important to the collegial role. Professionals who mentor or sponsor students increase collegiality and facilitate students in growing from novices to experts. DeMarco (1993) studied mentorship from a feminist perspective. Mentors are defined as "individuals who are in relationships with the expressed desire of assisting others in a particular goal or objective" (pp. 1242–1243). Within the mentoring relationship information is used to help students gain the "inside" information from experts within the profession. Mentorship also may be found among peers. Students may attain high levels of trust, respect, and desire to assist their peers in their quest for personal and professional growth (Glass and Walter, 1998).

Faculty can facilitate this opportunity for mutual growth among students by validating students' attempts to develop relationships characterized by shared meaning, control, and responsibility. Faculty members provide positive role modeling for decision-making strategies in not only classroom and clinical settings but also in the manner in which they interact with their own peers, modeling constructive coping within collegial relationships. Nurse educators can help students develop this collegial relationship with educators, peers, and preceptors by providing support for growth within the profession (Hezekiah, 1993). Glass (1998) recommended mentoring throughout the nursing profession. She further stated that it is a strong political survival skill (Glass, 1998).

Communication

Communication is the process of exchanging thoughts or information in a reciprocal relationship between faculty and students. Communication may be verbal or nonverbal by writing, gestures, facial expressions, or body behavior. The way in which educators interact with students may either empower or enable.

Communication in an enabling environment focuses on faculty providing the information, without the opportunity for student exchange (Caffrey and Caffrey, 1994). Faculty who enable students use this type of communication in the clinical setting as well as in the classroom. Faculty who select a noninteractive lecture format for their teaching strategy may be selecting an enabling form of communication in the classroom. Faculty who organize and decide the information that is important for student learning, without student input, eliminate chances for students to ask for clarification or feedback (Clare, 1993a).

In essence, faculty assume control for all of the learning. Student participation, critical thinking, and ultimately synthesis are not encouraged, and dependence on faculty is encouraged. This style of communication is passive, and the paternalistic message received by students is one requiring robotic conformity. For example, in the nursing practice setting, students who are taught to follow computerized care plans may infer that the faculty are all knowing. These students may suffer diminished ability to be creative and use critical thinking skills, and consequently, may have lower levels of self-confidence.

By communicating with students as valued members of the nursing community, the nucleus for leadership, collegiality, and self-respect is implanted (Carlson-Catalano, 1992). Creating an environment in which students feel free to express opinions to faculty is essential for an empowering experience (Worrell *et al.*, 1996). However, for communication to be empowering between faculty and students, the communication must be based on mutual respect and honesty.

Glass (1998) asserted that honesty and strong belief in each individual's worth were key to collaborative communication. Faculty feedback to students should be presented in a straightforward and honest manner. Students should be encouraged to validate and clarify the feedback message with faculty, which allows students to share the benefits, as well as the responsibility, of the information exchange. Strategies to assist students to develop the skills necessary for professional communication need to permeate curricula and be evident in the manner in which faculty communicate with their students and peers. When faculty model clear communication techniques, with respectful messages for their students and peers, students learn to communicate respectfully and maintain responsibility for the information they exchange.

Autonomy

Autonomy should be an outcome of the education process and demonstrates shared responsibility for learning. Autonomy can be achieved through the development and use of problem-solving skills (Hokanson-Hawks, 1992). Faculty who enable students do not encourage or facilitate students' development of problem-solving skills in the classroom, clinical setting, and occasionally their personal lives. This decreases students' self-esteem, possibly furthering their self-concept of inadequacy, rather than increasing their self-esteem and enhancing their autonomy (Clare, 1993b). In a codependent environment, there is little opportunity for personal growth because the system demands compliance and lack of autonomy (Caffrey and Caffrey, 1994).

Faculty who enable, rather than empower, students have poorly defined boundaries themselves and do not encourage students to become independent professionals. According to Pilette, Berck and Achber (1995), the boundaries of a relationship, particularly a professional therapeutic relationship, are complex and sometimes unclear. Codependent individuals have difficulty recognizing and setting boundaries, and they either take on the feelings of other people or blame others for the way they feel.

Zerwekh and Michaels (1989) stated that allowing others to have their own thoughts and the ability to think independently of others indicates one's intellectual boundary is intact. Faculty with ill-defined intellectual boundaries may over-help students in nursing practice or their personal lives (Pilette *et al.*, 1995). Paradoxically, faculty also may look only for weakness in students so they can feel needed. According to Caffrey and Caffrey (1994), codependent caring is motivated by false feelings of duty or responsibility for others and is fueled by fear of rejection, abandonment, failure, or conflict, which leads to feelings of shame, guilt, anger, or jealousy. Faculty who enable students frequently may be late for faculty meetings because they are helping students when tutors or the college counseling center could handle these situations more appropriately.

Faculty seeking to empower students can model autonomy by maintaining flexible but intact boundaries. For example, faculty express their own autonomy by maintaining time schedules assertively and guarding their privacy in the office for reflective and analytical thinking. Sharing authority and responsibility traditionally held by instructors results in autonomy and emancipation (i.e., "power to" versus "power over") (Hedin, 1989). Faculty can help students with problem solving without taking over by providing frequent feedback and guidance during the process. In this way, students become more comfortable with their own independence, while avoiding total faculty intervention or control. Reinforcing positive behaviors and decision making increases the likelihood that students will repeat positive behavior and feel empowered. Faculty increasingly function as facilitators and assume the observer or participatory role, creating a shift to a more egalitarian relationship (Clare, 1993a).

Accountability

Accountability is the final concept discussed by Worrell *et al.* (1996). Although accountability is last to be discussed, it is perhaps the most important to true empowerment. Accountability, a significant value in the nursing profession, is the assumption of responsibility for one's own learning. An empowering relationship between faculty and students encourages accountability in students and allows the emergence of political skills necessary for effecting change within the health care system (Glass, 1998).

Instead of helping students take control of their own lives, faculty who enable students make excuses for the students' lack of preparation for nursing practice experiences or for incomplete written assignments. By accepting use of the excuse that students have so many obligations at home or at their place of employment, faculty take accountability away from students. According to Glass (1998), positive self-esteem is necessary for empowerment. Student self-esteem may suffer when faculty do not hold students accountable for their decisions and actions. Faculty who shield students from accountability not only inhibit opportunities for the students to grow but convey a lack of confidence in the students' ability, further promoting students' negative self-concept.

Faculty who do not require students to be culpable for deadlines on written assignments or attendance at clinical practice may hinder students' development of accountability. Students are deprived of opportunities to assume responsibility, which reduces or restricts the emergence of professional and political skills. Sometimes faculty take care of students to shield them from the challenges of developing problem-solving skills.

Codependent faculty are often overcommitted and overworked. They feel driven to offer unsolicited advice or act on behalf of students who are capable of acting for themselves (Pilette *et al.*, 1995). They want to be needed by students and regularly will solve problems for students. Caretaker behaviors can result in faculty never having time to complete their own projects because they constantly are meeting student requests. They feel guilty when they require students to find their own answers or when a student fails an examination. Caretaking causes faculty to feel exhausted, stressed, overworked, and out of control (Caffrey and Caffrey, 1994).

Using deliberate strategies designed to facilitate students' development of introspection, problem-solving skills, and assertiveness, professional accountability will emerge (Davis, 1991). Students should learn problem-solving models in which problems are identified, possible solutions are delineated, and the best solution is selected. The faculty's role in problem solving should be only to provide feedback and guidance as students analyze problems and develop possible solutions. Accountability through empowering demands affirmation of one's own strength and sharing that strength with others (Mason, Costello-Nickitas, Scanlan and Magnuson, 1991).

When evaluation is shifted from what faculty do to students to how students assess their own learning, the locus of control is shifted to within the students (Mason *et al.*, 1991). The final compelling consequence of accountability is improved care for individual clients (Clay, 1992). Self-confident nurses who have well-developed problem-solving skills and the ability to adapt quickly to changing situations and technology will provide substantially better care and guidance to clients.

Conclusion

As faculty encourage students to participate in their education, learning has the potential to become more exciting and rewarding. Students who participate are more likely to feel personally empowered. As students share their experiences with one another, an enhanced sense of empowerment may result. Students accepting responsibility for themselves is key to the outcome of empowerment. Faculty alone cannot empower students. Students must fully commit to the empowerment process. However, faculty can take every opportunity to encourage students to become active participants in their learning. Faculty who are facilitators and advocates can empower students to become active participants in all phases of their education and professional lives.

References

Beatie M (1987) *Co-dependent No More.* Hazelden Foundation, Minneapolis.

Bevis E O, Watson J (1989) *Toward a Caring Curriculum: A New Pedagogy for Nursing.* National League for Nursing, New York.

Caffrey R, Caffrey P (1994) Nursing: caring or codependent? *Nursing Forum* 29 (1): 12–17.

Carlson-Catalano J (1992) Empowering nurses for professional practice. *Nurse Outlook* 40: 139–142.

Clare J (1993a) A challenge to the rhetoric of emancipation: Recreating a professional culture. *Journal of Advanced Nursing* 18: 1033–1038.

Clare J (1993b) Change the curriculum-or transform the conditions of practice? *Nursing Education Today* 13: 282–286.

Clay T (1992) Education and empowerment: Securing nursing's future. *International Nurse* 39 (1): 15–19.

Coulter M A (1990) A review of two theories of learning and their application in the practice of nurse education. *Nurse Education Today* 10: 333–338.

Davis P S (1991) The meaning of change to individuals within a college of nursing education. *Journal of Advanced Nursing* 16 (1): 108–115.

DeMarco R (1993) Mentorship: A feminist critique of current research. *Journal of Advanced Nursing* 18: 1242–1250.

Diekelmann N L (1993) Behavioral pedagogy: A Heideggerian hermeneutical analysis of the lived experiences of students and teachers in baccalaureate nursing education. *Journal of Nursing Education* 32: 245–250.

Fontaine K, Fletcher J S (1995) *Essentials of Mental Health Nursing*, 3rd edn. Addison-Wesley, Redwood City, CA.

Glass N (1998) Becoming de-silenced and reclaiming voice: Women nurses speak out. In: I I Keleher, P McInerney (eds) *Nursing Matters*, pp. 127–137. Harcourt Brace and Company, Melbourne.

Glass N, Walter R (1998) Exploring women's experiences: The critical relationship between nursing education, peer mentoring, and female friendship. *Contemporary Nurse* 7: 511.

Gorman S, Clark N (1986) Power and effective practice. *Nurse Outlook* 34: 129–135.

Gorrell B J, Langenbach M (1994) Curriculum issues related to nurse turnover. *Journal of Nursing Education* 33: 101–106.

Haber J, Krainovich-Miller B, McMahon A. Price-Hoskins P (1997) *Comprehensive Psychiatric Nursing*, 5th edn. Mosby, St. Louis.

Hawley McWhirter R (1991) Empowerment in counseling. *Journal of Counseling and Development* 69: 222–227.

Hedin B (1989) *Expert Clinical Teaching. Curriculum Revolution: Reconceptualizing Nurse Education* (NLN Publication No. 15-2280). National League for Nursing, New York.

Hezekiah J (1993) Feminist pedagogy: A framework for nursing education? *Journal of Nursing Education* 32: 53–57.

Hokanson-Hawks J (1992) Empowerment in nursing education: Concept analysis and application to philosophy, learning and instruction. *Journal of Advanced Nursing* 17: 609–618.

Malloy G, Berkery A (1993) Co-dependency and feminist perspective. *Journal of Psychosocial Nursing and Mental Health Services* 31 (4): 15–19.

Mason D J, Costello-Nickitas D M, Scanlan J M, Magnuson B A (1991) Empowering nurses for politically astute change in the workplace. *The Journal of Continuing Education in Nursing* 22: 5–10.

Pilette C P, Berck C, Achber L (1995) Therapeutic management of helping boundaries. *Journal of Psychosocial Nursing and Mental Health Nursing* 33 (1): 40–47.

Schaef A W (1986) *Co-dependence Misunderstood-mistreated.* Harper & Row, San Francisco.

Schaef A W (1987) *When Society Becomes an Addict.* Harper & Row, San Francisco.

Snow C, Willard D (1989) *I'm Dying to Take Care of You": Nurses and Co-dependency, Breaking the Cycle.* Professional Counselor Books, Redmond, WA.

Subby R (1987) *Lost in the Shuffle: The Co-dependent Reality.* Health Communications, Pompano Beach, Florida.

Worrell J, McGinn A, Black E, Holloway N, Ney P (1996) The RN-BSN student: Developing a model of empowerment. *Journal of Nursing Education* 35: 127–130.

Zerwekh J, Michaels B (1989) Co-dependency: Assessment and recovery. *Nursing Clinics of North America* 24: 109–120.

6. Mentoring: Towards a Professional Friendship

Coral Gardiner

Mentoring is a rapidly growing area covering the fields of education, business and community. At a fundamental level, mentoring provides individuals with a relationship which builds from a foundation of friendship. This paper looks at the possible role of 'friendship' informal mentoring systems. It analyses the elements and components of friendship and offers a model of 'professional friendship' within the formal mentoring context. The model represents what a mentoring relationship might be at a generic level and the paper argues for a model of 'professional friendship' to be integral to quality mentoring.

Introduction

Mentoring is a helping strategy to assist with the professional and personal development of an individual on a one-to-one basis through a special relationship. What distinguishes mentoring as a special relationship and how it differs from other helping strategies is described by Clutterbuck (1991),

> 'Mentoring involves primarily listening with empathy, sharing experience and learning (usually mutually), professional friendship, developing insight through reflection, being a sounding board, 'encouraging.'

Clutterbuck also suggests that a number of key mentor activities may be seen as indicators of successful mentoring.

> 'Key mentor activities include, using coaching behaviours, using counselling behaviours, challenging assumptions/being a critical friend, opening doors, being a role model.'

It is not a great step forward to suggest that a number of these activities could be said to be linked to 'friendship' in a successful mentoring relationship. It is how this very informal concept of 'friendship' can be applied within the context of formal mentoring systems that is explored here.

Why should friendship be defined within the formal mentoring system?

There are three main reasons for this, the first being, that there is no common interpretation of what 'friendship' could mean within the formal mentoring context. Secondly, research has found 'friendship' to be a significant element in more than half of mentor/mentee relationships surveyed (Gardiner, 1996). The third reason is that in formal mentoring systems, the relationship processes can be measured and tested.

Coral Gardiner: 'Mentoring: Towards a Professional Friendship' in *MENTORING AND TUTORING* (1998), 6 (1/2), pp. 77–84.

This is due to the structure of formalised systems usually facilitating easier access to participants.

In the booklet published by Channel Four Television to accompany a programme to celebrate Adult Learners week in May 1995, it is documented that a mentor helps during the mentee's transition as a long-term guide, counsellor and 'friend'. There are other references to the mentor as 'friend', for example, Reg Hamilton (1993) calls the mentor a 'non-judgemental friend'. BP Chemicals cited by Clutterbuck (1991) describe the ideal mentor as:

> 'a professional employee with substantial work experience whose role is to counsel and befriend the new recruit.'

Clutterbuck refers to the case study by saying that the mentor must be ready to:

> 'extend friendship to the protege and be willing to let the relationship extend beyond the normal limits of the business relationship'.

Other references to 'friendship' in the relationship include Gordon Shea (1992) who states that the mentor is a 'friend able to offer support' and Parsloe (1994) refers to the mentor as 'friend' within the formal, commercial and educational contexts.

A model of friendship in the mentoring relationship

- *The Contract*

All relationships hold to contracts, albeit in the main implied or negotiated and understood. We can find this process being described in mentoring as the setting of ground rules or boundaries. The mentoring contract relates to the personal, professional, ethical and moral boundaries of the relationship. At this contract setting stage, goals will be established and set. At different phases in the relationship the contract can be revisited and amended. If mentoring can be said to be about learning and change then the contract is critical to the developmental processes of moving on.

It is possible to isolate a number of processes which attach to the concept of friendship in this contractual context.

- *Reliability*

For a friendship to develop each party should be able to expect the other to be reliable in their attitude and practice. This is particularly important in developing a position of trust. The processes used to develop the contract, which include defining and objective setting, may result in some small actions being taken. These will provide the opportunity for mentor and mentee to demonstrate reliability to each other.

- *Openness*

In mentoring friendships, 'openness' can be taken to mean open to 'learning' and open to 'change'. In relation to learning, the friendship allows for professional and personal growth which requires openness for the learning and change to occur. Learning about 'self' is implied within the mentoring friendship context. Growth is an outcome of the learning process which by necessity involves change because it brings about the 'new states of the person' (Rogers, 1961). Critical to the success of a good mentoring relationship is that both parties enter into 'openness'.

- *Sharing*

Sharing as a characteristic of 'friendship' is about the sharing of experiences, knowledge, thoughts and feelings. In the mentoring friendship this is a contributory factor to the openness of the learning process.

- *Respect*

Respect in friendship is about treating or regarding the other party with deference, esteem and honour. To show respect as a friend or mentor would be the demonstration of consideration of the other party. This may be visible through paying attention by active listening and non-verbal signalling as well as by verbalising the regard.

- *Genuineness*

Carl Rogers (1961) derived the 'Client Centred Counselling' theory which, from its time and its cultural setting emphasises personal growth through a special kind of human relationship. He stated that helping relationships are characterised by what he calls 'genuineness', which he conceives as a transparency of approach in which 'my real feelings' are displayed. In the context of the mentoring friendship this is about showing the other party who you really are in an 'authentic' sense.

- *Warmth*

Rogers (1961) defines warmth as an 'acceptance of prizing the other person as a separate individual'. Warmth in the mentoring friendship may be expressed through facial expression and verbal and non-verbal language and communication. In the context of the friendship model, the demonstration of warmth from the mentor to the mentee or vice versa may act as a form of reassurance of acceptance. The demonstration of warmth to the other person can contribute to the quality of the friendship relationship. In this way, warmth can help to nurture the self-esteem of the receiver.

- *Honour*

This is the old-fashioned notion that one party would never do any thing which may hurt the other in, a deliberate manner. This implies that the relationship only involves honourable intention. Honour is linked to respect, by respecting the person with a will to avoid causing pain through suspicion or mistrust.

- *Support*

The reason for a friendship lasting over time may be based on the level, type and amount of support offered and received. As one of the purposes of a mentoring relationship is to help, the visibility of support is critical. The relationship may well depend on it and be the reason for its existence and continuance. In a mentoring relationship, Clutterbuck (1991) suggests that support offered by mentors is emotional, intellectual and practical. As the relationship is a two-way process it may be found to be reciprocated and thus contribute to the longevity of the friendship.

• *Non-judgemental*

Hamilton (1993) suggested that the mentoring relationship is one of 'non-judgemental friendship'. This implies that if we are to judge our friends we could be creating a barrier to the support and help which is needed. This is an important element of the mentoring friendship model because without it trust could be weakened, undermined or lost.

• *Empathy*

According to Rogers (1961) empathy is 'a sensitive ability to see the other's world as he sees it'. He also suggests that:

> 'If I can provide a certain type of relationship, the other person will discover within himself the capacity to use that relationship for growth and change, and personal development will occur.'

Rogers' view was that it was possible to have the ability to accept another individual for who and what they are at that moment. He called this ability 'unconditional acceptance/regard' of the person. This set of theoretical constructs is known as 'the person centred approach' and has been adopted as an underpinning philosophy in some fields of work with 'friendship' mentoring relationships (B.E.A.T, 1995). Alongside of this are implied other characteristics associated with friendship such as being non-judgemental and non-directive. These elements of acceptance make empathy easier to attain.

• *Challenging*

Where the parties in the friendship feel able to challenge each other they are helping to develop within the relationship a greater sense of openness, honesty and thus trust. This process helps to facilitate the learning, changing and moving-on processes. Because the relationship is valued and meaningful the challenging is received in a non-threatening way.

• *Non-directive*

It is important to recognise that neither the mentor nor mentee should be coming from a position of power nor to try to develop power over the other in the relationship. If the mentor or mentee demonstrates a directive approach they are working against the process of empowerment which is the goal of the mentee. On this basis the friendship model allows the mentee to make their own decisions and to take responsibility for their own actions.

• *Loyalty*

Loyalty is often valued in relationships and is often implied within the contract. In the mentoring friendship it refers to an allegiance to the supporter or supported. Subsumed within this quality may be others such as dependability, reliability and trustworthiness.

• *Advocacy*

Advocacy is the active support of another. This should not be understood to apply to the mentor only. The two-way nature of the mentoring relationship means that the mentee may choose to reciprocate support. The point here is that support can come in many forms, for example to offer backing to a decision made, or to give encouragement to the mentor.

• *Congruence*

As an expression of a friendship mentoring relationship, congruence occurs when the elements of friendship combine together in agreement. This situation allows for the growth and building of a harmonious compatibility between mentor and mentee.

• *Understanding*

To have understanding within the friendship requires tolerance and patience. The gaining of understanding can be encouraged through developing empathy. In its literal interpretation, 'understanding' means to know and comprehend the nature or meaning of the other party. This can be made easier by the person centred approach allowing the parties to accept each other with warmth and ease. In turn this helps the mentor/mentee to begin to understand things from the other's perspective. The understanding is always from the person's own experience which in itself may be similar to the other party's experiences.

• *Honesty*

This is another characteristic of a quality mentoring friendship relationship. It allows a two-way commitment to grow as honesty is necessary for the development of trust. Also, it is characterised by openness within the relationship.

• *Rapport*

This is meant not just as the development of an initial rapport for the good of a relationship but also for its maintenance. If rapport becomes lost there may be no reason to continue the friendship. Without rapport, openness, trust and other elements of the relationship may wither. Maintenance of rapport is important to the development of trust and encourages the parties to be both relaxed and responsive in the relationship. The building of rapport involves elements of trust, focus, empathy congruence and empowerment (Clutterbuck, 1991).

• *Active listening*

This is a particularly valued element of the friendship model and is demonstrated by showing interest. The interest is seen to be through the use of words, non-verbal communication such as body language, facial expression and eye contact. It is likely to be the most used and practised activity in the relationship.

• *Awareness of need*

As part of the original contract of friendship the parties will make each aware of their needs. This is so that each party can assess in the first instance whether or not these needs are likely to be fulfilled. On this basis the relationship may or may not proceed. When the needs cease to be met there will be a natural diminishing of the relationship as it loses its sense of purpose.

• *Shared values*

Matching of mentors to mentees can be problematical but where it is possible to match their values, failure in the relationship is less likely. The sharing of values can be a positive motivator in the relationship because they can facilitate trust. Empathy occurs more easily as does the encouragement of honesty and openness. It is argued that sharing values adds to the confidence and belief in one another, because sharing something which is so important to self worth increases perceived self worth.

• *Trust*

Trust within any relationship can be implied but is often expected as an outcome. If trust does not develop it is unlikely that any of the other complementary elements of a friendship mentoring relationship will appear. Trust in this context can be taken to mean the trusting of self as well as of others.

• *Confidentiality*

Inside the formal mentoring system confidentiality can be known as 'institutional confidentiality' as opposed to the absolute confidentiality which may be expected in informal relationships. Within the formal mentoring friendship relationship, confidentiality involves trust, openness and honesty. Its boundaries or interpretations should always be made clear at the contract making stage. Confidentiality which is agreed within these boundaries would and should not be expected to be broken.

• *Intuition*

Positive mentoring relationships based on friendships can develop intuitively as can other types of relationships. For this to occur the parties are likely to have developed the relationship to know each other deeply and have a high degree of integrity and trust.

• *Caring*

In friendships 'caring' is the demonstrating of regard, concern and consideration and is an integral part of a good mentoring friendship relationship.

What are the types of friendship in mentoring relationships?

It is clear that the processes outlined above are rarely discreet in themselves, but often highly interrelated. Their successful application represents success in a friendship mentoring relationship when associated with an appropriate contact setting. But the use of a relatively informal friendship model within a formal mentoring context will clearly be beset with tensions. The most obvious of these tensions is whether the model is developed as one of 'personal friendship' or 'professional friendship'.

• *Personal friendship*

Mattoon (1991) expresses personal friendship as a relationship of one's own choosing and this can be taken to mean within a formal mentoring system based on mutual liking and affection. She suggests that such relationships are based on common interest and a limited number of them will develop to deep mutual appreciation and trust. Mattoon also says that as we begin to move away from our family we may seek to find contemporaries or elders who become our teachers and mentors where this is outside of a formal mentoring system:

> 'Later we may find mentors who teach and encourage us in establishing ourselves as adults... A teacher/mentor may pass out of one's life when that function is needed no longer, or that person may become a friend'.

Whilst Mattoon describes the possibility of mentors becoming friends she does not go so far as to argue that mentoring relationships might be based on friendship, as the model discussed in this paper proposes.

Mattoon's research focused only on informal relationships. How in this context are the relationships identified and evaluated? Where are the boundaries for the personal, professional, ethical and moral considerations? Personal friendship implies that the relationship may be subjective and this can lead to value judgements being formed. Subjectivity in mentoring relationships is potentially threatening as it can lead to the devolution of power by one party. It is argued that personal relationships within formal mentoring schemes allow the boundaries of the contract to become relatively fluid without the express permission of the parties.

- *Professional friendship*

Kalbfleisch and Keyton (1995) compared women's mentoring relationships with their friendships in formal mentoring situations within employment and informal friendship relations. They found that the friendships were perceived as having higher levels of formality and composure than their mentoring counter relations. The mentoring relationships were seen as being more emotionally open. These findings suggest that the female mentoring relationships may be more relaxed and casual than previously thought. No research has yet demonstrated that this may also be the case with their male counter parts but if the elements of friendship outlined above are indeed common to all friendship relationships (as the literature suggests), then the possibilities are that the findings would reflect the same for male mentoring relationships and their friendships, as Kalbfleisch and Keyton found to be the case for women. Also of interest in the women's research were the few differences overall between mentoring and friendship, again indicating that the underlying nature of mentoring relationships and friendships may not be that different. Both types of relationships were characterised by positive feelings, emotional intimacy, meeting relational needs and providing satisfying outcomes. In concluding, it was suggested that an important aspect of the mentoring relationship was the need within it for 'friendship'. The research found that for women to gain empowerment in the workplace it was useful to adopt a friendship model in their professional mentoring relationships. What currently characterises the mentoring relationship in a formal structure is its implied objectivity. To be objective in a mentoring relationship the mentor needs to be able to stand outside of themselves and the other party. A professional friendship model could be expected to provide impartiality or 'professional objectivity'. In this case the position is similar to professions which are designed to protect the confidential nature of some special relationships, such as clergy-parishioner, doctor-patient or, in some cases, counsellor-client. These professions expect professional judgement and thus fairness to be used. Professional friendship is found in the legal profession where the solicitor acts as an advocate and 'professional friend'. The service received from a 'professional friend' in this context is of a high quality standard and is presented with relative objectivity. In the context of professional friendship in mentoring relationships the mentor can be expected to be able to act in a fair, even handed way.

Conclusion

The professional friendship model in a formal mentoring system offers the participants the possibility of greater stability in the relationship than in the more, largely informal contractual, mentoring relationship. The 'professional friend' mentoring model provides a special relationship which is outside of the usual relationship norms and is therefore unique. It has special purposes and goals which relate to the contract setting. The characteristics of this special type of relationship are offered as interrelated elements of friendship utilised within the context of professional objectivity. The components of coaching and counselling behaviours as used by mentors are inclusive to the friendship model and include listening, giving recognition, trusting and challenging. As a professional friend the mentor is able to act as a sounding board, door-opener and role model by utilising the interrelated components of the professional friendship model. In short, the model offers an enhancement of the quality of a mentoring relationship but remains within a formal context.

References

Clutterbuck D (1991) *Everyone Needs a Mentor: Fostering Talent at Work.* Institute of Personnel Management, London.

Clutterbuck D (1995) *Consenting Adults, Making the Most of Mentoring.* Channel Four Television, London.

Gardiner C (1996) *Mentoring: A Study of the Concept, Theory and Practice in the Educational Field.* MA dissertation. University of Central England.

Hamilton R (1993) *Mentoring.* The Industrial Society, London.

Kalbfleisch P, Keyton J (1995) *Gender, Power and Communication in Human Relationships.* Lawrence Erlbaum Associates, Hillsdale, New Jersey.

Mattoon A, Wilmer H (eds) (1991) *Closeness in Personal and Professional Relationships.* Shambhala Publications Inc., Massachusetts.

Megginson D and Clutterbuck D (1995) *Mentoring in Action, A Practical Guide for Managers,* Chapter 2. Copyright B.E.A.T. Kogan Page, London.

Parsloe E (1994) *Coaching, Mentoring and Assessing, A Practical Guide to Developing Competence.* Kogan Page, London.

Rogers C (1961) *A Therapist's View of Psychotherapy: On Becoming a Person.* Constable, London.

Shea G (1992) *Mentoring: A Guide to the Basics.* Kogan Page, London.

7. Creating a Climate for Critical Thinking in the Preceptorship Experience

Florence Myrick and Olive J. Yonge

The impact of the learning climate on students' ability to think critically during preceptorship cannot be underestimated. The success of students in learning to think critically rests largely with the tone set by preceptors and staff (Myrick 1998). Students must be led gently into the active role of discussing, dialoguing, and problem solving (Meyers 1986). They watch very carefully how respectfully preceptors and staff field their comments, quickly notice nonverbal cues that indicate how open, approachable and supportive the preceptors and the staff are to their questions and contributions, and then discern how valued they are as colleagues. When preceptors genuinely value, support, and work with students in the practice setting and staff accept them as part of the team, a climate that is conducive to learning and critical thinking is established. This is due to the fact that students feel safe enough to question, to challenge and be challenged, and to be creative in their problem solving. The purpose of this paper is threefold: a) to identify key factors in the preceptorship experience that contribute to the creation of a climate that is conductive to critical thinking; b) to provide important insights into the role of the preceptor and the staff within that context; and c) to discuss how nursing faculty can more actively contribute to ensuring that such a learning climate is achieved in the preceptorship experience.

Introduction

> I think they [students] do worse if they feel intimidated and they're not allowed to make mistakes. If they're really uptight with you and you're coming down hard on them they're not going to learn. All they're worried about is making mistakes and they're just going to learn how to survive. I have learned that fear is not a good motivator for anybody. (Words of a preceptor found in Myrick 1998, p. 52).

Over time much has been documented regarding the importance of the learning environment or climate as it impacts both positively and negatively on students (Brookfield 1986, 1987; Flynn 1997; Friere 1997; Mezirow 1990). Most experts concur that the most effective climate in the promotion of learning and critical thinking is the one that reflects support, is devoid of threat, fosters openness, inquiry and trust, and avoids competitive performance judgements (Manley 1997). If students are constantly in fear of making an error, they become limited in their ability to think critically and to develop experientially (Öhrling and Hallberg 2000, Pt. 1; Reilly and Oermann 1992).

The creation of a positive learning climate has always been a challenge for nurse educators and subsequently this challenge has been passed on to preceptors as they

Florence Myrick and Olive J. Yonge: 'Creating a Climate for Critical Thinking in the Preceptorship Experience' in *NURSE EDUCATION TODAY* (2001), 21, pp. 461–467.

assume a major responsibility for clinical teaching. A grounded theory research project focusing on the development and promotion of the critical thinking skills of basic baccalaureate nursing students via nurse preceptors had *the climate* emerge as a primary theme. This paper identifies key factors in the preceptorship experience that contribute to the creation of a climate conducive to the enabling of critical thinking, provides insights into the role of preceptors and staff, and discusses how nursing faculty can more actively contribute to ensuring such a learning climate for the preceptorship experience.

Research method

The grounded theory research project was guided by two questions: 1) how do preceptors and preceptees perceive critical thinking and the process that is entailed therein; and 2) how are preceptees fostered to think critically while being preceptored in the practice setting? After receiving ethical approval, six preceptees and six preceptors were interviewed and observed in a tertiary care agency. The students were in the fourth and final year of the basic baccalaureate nursing program in a 14-week intensive clinical course. Analysis began with the first interview and followed the stages of open to theoretical and finally selective coding. Memos and field notes were maintained throughout the process. For purposes of the study, critical thinking was acknowledged to be 'a nonlinear, recursive process in which a person forms a judgment about what to believe or what to do in a given context' (Facione and Facione 1996, p. 131).

Definitions

Preceptor

A nurse who teaches a student nurse, from a baccalaureate nursing programme, clinical nursing skills for various lengths of time. The word preceptor means 'to tutor' and should not be confused with the functions of a mentor or apprentice.

Preceptee

A student in a baccalaureate nursing programme who learns the skills of nursing by being assigned a registered nurse (preceptor) in the practice setting. A student is usually assigned to one preceptor but on occasion may be assigned to more than one.

Findings: key climatic factors

Two climatic factors prevail to influence the development and promotion of critical thinking in the preceptorship experience: the *preceptor* and the *staff*. While the preceptor plays the pivotal role in the process of enabling students to think critically in the practice setting, it is the staff with whom the students must interact on a daily basis who also play a crucial role. Ultimately, it is the preceptor and the staff who directly impact on how the students develop experientially and whether they become enabled to think critically.

The preceptor

The climate in the preceptorship experience is influenced significantly by the preceptor. While the learning climate needs to be provocative, stimulating and disciplined, it should also be a 'humanistic one which is authentic, supportive and caring' (Reilly and Oermann 1992, p. 45). Sensitivity and caring about individual students does not imply preclusion of an acceptable level of performance or clinical competence, but rather that the preceptor is committed to helping the student achieve desired goals and objectives (Reilly and Oermann 1992). It also implies that students' perspectives are encouraged and supported as a preparatory measure for success in their future professional practice. Specifically, the preceptor's ability to *value,* to *work with,* and to *support* the student is essential for providing a climate that is conducive to the promotion of critical thinking in the practice setting (Myrick 1998).

Valuing the students

Brookfield (1987) indicates that when individuals are encouraged to think critically, they must be *valued* for their selves. Valuing is a characteristic that is shared by preceptors who are effective in enabling students to think critically, a characteristic that is in turn reflected in their approachability, openness and respect for students' perspectives. Of particular significance in the process are the preceptors' recognition of the fact that the students wish to be acknowledged and valued as colleagues. Though new to the setting, they are 'nonetheless important and equal human beings with ideas and opinions of their own' (Manley 1997, p. 14). Valuing means respecting students as persons and demonstrating positive regard for them.

Valuing is reflected by preceptors who demonstrate confidence in students' capabilities and who acknowledge that they bring their own individual experiences and qualities to their preceptee role. Through their words and actions preceptors reflect respect for the individuality of students, which in turn encourages critical thinking (Brookfield 1987). If students do not feel valued, their ability to think critically may be impaired, for they need to feel comfortable asking questions. They need to know that the preceptors will be there if they need them (Manley 1997). The worst thing preceptors can do is 'suggest, by a verbal response or some kind of body language (smirk, sigh, quizzically raised eyebrow)' (Brookfield 1987, p. 72) that their comments or questions or other forms of contribution are somehow substandard. Such behaviour can easily threaten students' self-concepts, heighten their sense of vulnerability, and instantaneously render them voiceless, which inhibits their ability to think critically in any situation, especially when as beginners their sense of self is still so fragile (Myrick 1998). As one student noted, 'you spend so much time walking around on egg shells that you're not thinking up to your capacity' (Myrick 1998, p. 61). Preceptors who enable students to think critically do so by helping them to meet their goals without seeking to control or dominate them. One preceptor described students as 'like a flower, they just open up, it's beautiful' (Myrick 1998, p. 62). According to Brookfield (1987), 'there is an uneasy tightrope to be walked in developing critical thinking in others' (p. 73). Preceptorship is thus a balancing act between valuing both the integrity and the individuality of the students while ensuring that they are sufficiently challenged in their practice experience.

The process of working with *the student*

Generally speaking, the role of the preceptor is to 'bridge the gap between the reality of the workplace and the idealism of an academic environment without compromising professional ideals' (O'Mara 1997, p. 57). Above all else, open and honest communication can contribute to the creation of a positive preceptorship relationship. Intrinsic to that communication is the preceptor's ability for *working with* or collaborating with, as opposed to dictating to the student throughout the practice experience. Dictating to the student is an approach that encourages development of hierarchical relationships and discourages egalitarian ones. Indeed, the process of 'working with' reflects a reciprocal relationship between preceptor and student involving active collaboration aimed at achieving the goals and objectives of the learning experience. The perspectives of the preceptor and the student are equally worthwhile and valid. The major advantage of the preceptorship experience is that it is a one-to-one relationship in which preceptors and students work together to assess what learning is required and to design experiences to achieve that learning.

Authentic collaboration occurs after preceptors have spent considerable time earning students' trust and by acting democratically and respectfully toward them (Brookfield 1995). Trust in another person is a most fragile commodity which requires knowing individuals over a period of time and experiencing their honesty mirrored in actions that reflect their consistency and dependability (Morrow 1984). Students who trust their preceptors are more inclined to discover and to seek out new experiences, to question their own decision-making and actions, and ultimately to think critically about their nursing care situations. Preceptors who communicate confidence in students' abilities to achieve in clinical practice, who take students seriously and who treat them as adults, demonstrate that they can be trusted. Preceptors who do not impose or force their viewpoints, demonstrate the ability to work with students in a truly collegial manner, a behaviour which forms the basis of true collaboration and the process of working with students. As a great 20th century philosopher suggests, 'if the relation between the teacher and the taught is genuine...there is never a place in it for the authority of the know-it-all' (Heidegger 1968, p. 15).

It is in the process of working with students that preceptors enable them to become responsible and accountable for their own decisions, to think critically about those decisions, and to achieve an acceptable comfort level in reaching those decisions. Through such a process, students gain the experience required for evolving into practising nurses. They learn to think on their feet and deal appropriately with the day-to-day clinical situations that require sound, clinical, decision-making grounded in critical thinking.

Integral to clinical practice is the evaluation process which entails the acquisition of information by preceptors for making judgements about the students' performance. The climate in which this takes place is an important determinant of student performance (Reilly and Oermann 1992). A climate which reflects mutual trust and respect between preceptors and students is fundamental for evaluation to be viewed as a means of growth and this growth is valued by the students. In the true spirit of working with one another, feedback from the preceptors can be viewed by students as a learning opportunity or a means by which to discover new experiences that ultimately further their clinical competencies and promote their critical thinking ability (Öhrling and Hallberg 2000, Pt. 2). Thus, evaluation within this context is not perceived as a punitive process that addresses only the negative aspects of their performance (Reilly and Oermann 1992).

When preceptors are working with students, the students come to see themselves as participants and not merely as subordinates needing direction. They come to accept that they have answers and/or are capable of discovering them, and that they do not need to wait for preceptors to tell them what to do and how to think (Hedin and Donovan 1989). Trust on the part of the students is as important as trust on the part of the preceptors. Indeed, it is an essential component in the process of working with one another. Students gain their preceptors' trust by demonstrating initiative in ensuring that the learning objectives are clearly conveyed and met, by taking responsibility for communicating effectively with preceptors, and by being accountable for their professional behaviour (McGregor 1999).

In the process of working with students, the ability of preceptors to empathize is also an important asset (Myrick 1998). Empathy implies that preceptors can view a situation from students' perspectives, that they can see experiences through the eyes of students. Projecting empathy toward students indicates that preceptors are giving full attention to students' concerns and really understand what students wish to have understood. This signifies to students that they are important and worth their preceptors' time, which is critical because 'there is no way that giving time and attention can be faked' (Gazda *et al.* 1982).

Supporting the students

A practice setting replete with learning experiences yet devoid of support can discourage students and result in the loss of many opportunities for growth (Reilly & Oermann 1992; DeJong and Bechtel 1999). Preceptors play a major role in influencing the nature of the practice setting and in influencing the degree to which students are supported in their learning experience and are enabled to think critically. As one student noted, 'I think it makes it even easier' cause all the staff like her [preceptor], so I mean they like her and I'm kind of an extension of her so that's what I find. Like everybody's been super nice' (Myrick 1998, p. 72).

The impact of preceptor support on the student cannot be underestimated. Even when their preceptors are unavailable and students are assigned to other staff nurses, preceptor support continues to be integral to the learning experience. The support demonstrated by preceptors has a significant impact on students' abilities to think critically and to perform competently. In essence, support provides a safety net in a setting that at times can be overwhelming to the neophyte nurse (Myrick 1998). Preceptors who are aware of the subtle dynamics occurring in the practice setting exert great influence on the preceptorship experience by modifying the environment enough for students to reach an acceptable comfort level, a factor which is essential to the development and promotion of critical thinking (Farnkopt 1983; Sedlak 1999). Preceptors can raise the awareness level of those staff members who are insensitive to the dynamics involved and facilitate staff consciousness by presenting a positive role model of cordiality, acceptance and hospitality to students (Farnkopt 1983).

Preceptors who support students are those who, rather than encouraging dependence and reliance on preceptor approval, foster independence with learning and self-reliance (Robinson *et al.* 1999). According to Reilly and Oermann (1992), in the practice setting 'students need freedom to explore, question and dissent because without this, critical thinking is inhibited' (p. 118). Supportive preceptors are those who accept differences among students' approaches to solving clinical problems, promote independent learning, continue to hold students accountable for their actions and finally who meet commitments to their nursing care. Students assume responsibility for providing quality care and for completing the patient assignments for which they are held accountable. Prior to the preceptorship experience, students are held accountable through preclinical preparation time, which gives them the time and the opportunity to acquire the necessary knowledge and skills for safe, competent practice (O'Mara 1997). Preceptorship may offer students their first experience of situations in which they cannot prepare for all challenges in advance, thus preparation is defined differently. While students bring knowledge to the practice setting, they must process patient information quickly and use sound judgement to make immediate or on the spot clinical decisions. This can be a daunting prospect for students unless they are working with preceptors who are supportive, and who provide a 'healthy measure of support in all stages of their attempt to become critical thinkers' (Brookfield 1987, p. 74). In the process of enabling students to think critically, it is as important for the preceptors to know when to provide them with unconditional support as it is to know when to challenge them. Ultimately, it is the simultaneous challenging of the students' mode of thinking while providing structure and support for their ideas that enables them to think critically (Brookfield 1987).

Roles

The role of staff

The staff in the practice setting and their *acceptance* of students as part of the team impacts significantly on students' experiences and on their ability to think critically (Myrick 1998). While the preceptor is the primary influence in preceptorship, others in the setting, from the nurse unit manager to the staff nurse, from the physician to the physiotherapist, from the housekeeper to the ward clerk, all impact on the learning climate in the practice setting. All subsequently enhance or impede student experience ultimately affecting their ability to think critically.

One factor deemed essential for the success of students in meeting their learning goals and objectives in the practice setting is the staff attitude (Myrick 1998). A new face on a nursing unit can alarm members of the nursing and ancillary staffs. New faces often imply new or different ideas and change. This can be threatening to established staff. Student input, while intended to be helpful, can be construed by the staff as critical or intrusive. Resulting defensiveness can spell disaster for students. Fortunately, the majority of nurses enjoy the opportunity to work with student nurses (Farnkopt 1983).

According to Manley (1997), 'the environment that is most effective in enhancing learning has available learning resources' (p. 33). A large component of those resources include staff with whom the students must work and staff who also possess expertise which can contribute to students' experiences. A major factor that impinges on that experience is the relationship between the staff and the preceptor, and how they interact with one another. Preceptors' relationship with their fellow nurses and the other health care professionals often directly affects the students. Recently a student recounted her experiences:

> I think I lucked out. My preceptor is a good nurse. She's liked by the staff and they know she's competent . . . I guess 'cause the staff respect her and it actually amazingly rubs off on me. Because she's treated me like a colleague, it seems like the people she's friends with treat me like a colleague too (Myrick 1998, p. 87).

Staff acceptance and support cannot be underestimated. It is a significant factor in enabling students to think critically (Myrick 1998). It is in the practice setting that students begin to operationalize the theories that have been in the forefront of their classroom experiences. Although they may have been taught new and alternative ways of interpreting and analysing nursing situations in the familiarity of the classroom and laboratory setting, it is in the unfamiliarity and sometimes overwhelming milieu of the practice setting, or real world of nursing, that they acquire the ability to apply that way of thinking to the patient situations. It is in the practice setting that they must adjust to and accommodate to the idiosyncrasies of staff. If staff are not accepting, this can become a formidable and not infrequently insurmountable challenge.

The role of faculty

The role of nursing faculty cannot continue to remain on the periphery of clinical teaching, where it has been for the past decade (Laforêt-Fliesser *et al.* 1999). Indeed, the teaching expertise of nursing faculty is indispensable to the success of student learning, not only in the classroom but in the practice setting as well. In assuming a more active role in the implementation of preceptorship, nursing faculty can monitor the development and promotion of the critical thinking ability of nursing students while they are under the tutelage of preceptors. In assuming a more active role, nursing faculty can provide preceptors with the benefit of their expertise to ensure the frequent use of appropriate strategies that directly enable the critical thinking ability of basic baccalaureate nursing students as they carry out their nursing care.

Faculty need to consider seriously the development of routine assessment or appraisal of the individual nursing units to which students are assigned. Such assessment should include, but not be limited to, determining relevant clinical experiences available for achievement of student and/or course objectives, careful consideration and/or scrutiny of staff receptiveness to student placements, and continuous monitoring of the experience by faculty through regular meetings with preceptors, students and staff in the practice setting. Such an arrangement would provide not only knowledge of the preceptorship relationship, but would also afford the faculty a first-hand impression of staff and student interaction.

Faculty also have a role in supporting the preceptor. Currently, it is not known how best to support preceptors (Laforet-Fliesser *et al.* 1999), although Dibert and Goldenberg (1995) concluded that preceptors were more likely to be committed to their role if they were supported and rewarded. The Dibert and Goldenberg (1995) study was replicated by Usher *et al.* (1999), and they found that support from administrators and team mates was vital if a preceptor was to be effective. Faculty need to be part of this support network by determining what would be 'supportive' to preceptors and aligning themselves with administration and nurses on the floor. For example, if monthly meetings with all preceptors in a particular service as suggested by Roberson (1992) would be perceived as supportive, then faculty should assist in organizing these meetings.

Future research questions

1. What additional factors contribute to the impact of the learning environment on the critical thinking ability of nursing students? Within this context, what is the role of the clinical setting, the presence of other health professionals, gender, educational level and time pressures in the clinical setting?
2. How do faculty role model and teach about the learning environment with regard to the promotion of critical thinking for students and preceptors?
3. What specific strategies do preceptors use to demonstrate the process of valuing, supporting and working with the student in the preceptorship experience?
4. How does the existing power difference that is inherent in the preceptorship relationship impact on the learning climate?

Summary and conclusion

In summary, the impact of the learning climate on the ability of students to think critically in the practice setting is a pivotal one (Myrick 1998). Much success in leading students to think critically rests with the tone set by preceptors and staff. It is important that students be introduced gently to the active role of discussing, dialoguing, and problem solving (Meyers 1986). They watch very carefully to see how respectfully preceptors and staff field their comments and quickly detect nonverbal cues that indicate how open, approachable and supportive the preceptors and the staff are to their questions and contributions, as well as how valued they are as colleagues.

When preceptors genuinely *value, support, and work* with students in the practice setting, and when staff *accept* them as part of the team, together they set the stage for a climate that is conducive to learning, a climate which promotes critical thinking by making students feel safe enough to question, to challenge and be challenged, and to problem-solve creatively. The goal of baccalaureate nursing education to provide critical thinkers requires nothing less than the fostering of such a climate in the practice setting.

References

Brookfield S D (1986) The facilitator's role in adult learning. In: *Understanding and Facilitating Adult Learning: A Comprehensive Analysis of Principles and Effective Practices*, pp. 123–165. Jossey-Bass, San Francisco.

Brookfield S D (1987) *Developing Critical Thinkers. Challenging Adults to Explore Alternative Ways of Thinking and Acting*. Jossey-Bass, San Francisco.

Brookfield S D (1995) *Becoming a Critically Reflective Teacher*. Jossey-Bass, San Francisco.

Delong T H, Bechtel G A (1999) Enhancing relationships between nursing faculty and clinical preceptors. *Journal for Nurses in Staff Development* 15 (4): 148–151.

Dibert C, Goldenberg D (1995) Preceptors' perceptions of benefits, rewards, support and commitment to the preceptor role. *Journal of Advanced Nursing* 21: 1144–1151.

Facione N C, Facione P A (1996) Externalizing the critical thinking knowledge development and clinical judgment. *Nursing Outlook* 44 (3): 129–136.

Famkopf F T (1983) Criteria for evaluating a clinical setting for a preceptor. In: S Stuart-Siddall, J M Haberlin (eds). *Preceptorships in Nursing Education,* pp. 157–164. Aspen, Rockville.

Flynn J P (ed.) (1997) *The Role of the Preceptor. A Guide for Nurse Educators.* Springer, New York.

Friere P (1997) *Pedagogy of the Oppressed.* (New revised 20th anniversary edn.) Continuum, New York.

Gazda G M, Childers W C, Walters R P (1982) *Interpersonal Communication. A Handbook for Health Professionals.* Aspen, Rockville.

Hedin B A, Donovan J (1989) A feminist perspective on nursing education. *Nurse Educator* 14 (4): 8–13.

Heidigger M (1968) *What is Called Thinking?* (J Glenn Gray, trans.) Harper, New York (Original work published 1954).

Laforet-Fliesser, Ward-Griffin C, Beyon C (1999) Self-efficacy of preceptors in the community: a partnership between service and education. *Nurse Education Today* 19: 41–52.

Manley M J (1997) Adult learning concepts important to precepting. In: J P Flynn (ed.) *The Role of the Preceptor. A Guide for Nurse Educators and Clinicians*, pp. 15–47. Springer, New York.

McGregor R J (1999) A precepted experience for senior nursing students. *Nurse Educator* 24 (3): 13–16.

Meyers C (1986) *Teaching Students to Think Critically.* Jossey-Bass, San Francisco.

Mezirow J (1990) *Fostering Critical Reflection in Adulthood: A Guide to Transformative and Emancipatory Learning.* Jossey-Bass, San Francisco.

Morrow K L (1984) *Preceptorship in Nursing Staff Development.* Aspen, Rockville.

Myrick F (1998) *Preceptorship and Critical Thinking in Nursing Education.* Unpublished doctoral dissertation. The University of Alberta, Edmonton.

Öhrling K, Hallberg I R (2000) Student nurses' lived experience of preceptorship. Part 1 – in relation to learning. *International Journal of Nursing Studies* 37: 13–23.

Öhrling K, Hallberg I R (2000) Student nurses' lived experience of preceptorship. Part 2 – the preceptor – preceptee relationship. *International Journal of Nursing Studies* 37: 25–36.

O'Mara A M (1997) A model preceptor program for student nurses In: J P Flynn (ed.) *The Role of the Preceptor. A Guide for Nurse Educators and Clinicians*, pp. 47–45. Springer, New York.

Reilly D E, Oermann M H (1992) *Clinical Teaching in Nursing Education,* 2nd edn. National League for Nursing, New York.

Roberson J (1992) Providing support for preceptors in a community hospital. *Journal of Nursing Staff Development* January/February: 11–13.

Robinson A, McInerney F, Sherring M, Marlow A (1999) Developing a collaborative preceptor program involving registered nurses, student nurses and faculty. *Australian Journal of Advanced Nursing* 17 (1): 13–21.

Sedlak C A (1999) Differences in critical thinking of nontraditional and traditional nursing students. *Nurse Educator* 24 (6): 38–45.

Usher K, Nolan C, Reser P, Owens J, Tollefson (1999) An exploration of the preceptor role: Preceptors' perceptions of benefits, rewards, supports and commitment to the preceptor role. *Journal of Advanced Nursing* 29 (2): 506–514.

Exploring the Concept of Mentoring

This section seeks to provide you with a range of texts and articles which should provide you with a greater insight into the concept of mentoring in the workplace. Taylor and Stephenson (1996) have suggested that there are no definitive answers to the questions 'what is mentoring?' or even to the one that is most pressing for most mentors, 'what do I have to do if I am a mentor?' It is undoubtedly true that mentoring is a complex, multi-faceted role that does need careful examination before you can be sure you at least have some understanding of what it is all about. Many definitions of mentoring have been devised and here are two that you might wish to consider.

> "Mentoring involves a process whereby an experienced, highly regarded, empathic person guides another individual in the development and re-examination of their own ideas, learning and personal and professional development." (SCOPME, 1998).
>
> "The mentor relationship is explicitly a personal one to one relationship. One in which two people relate to each other with the explicit purpose of the one assisting the other to learn" (Jarvis P and Gibson S, 1997)

Mentors come in the shape of parents or relatives, teachers, older friends, colleagues and line-managers. Mentoring relationships develop naturally and spontaneously as well as through deliberate action. Discussions with people who are considering becoming mentors almost always reveal that the motivation can be traced back to a helpful relationship in their own past. This means that, in a sense, you know a great deal about mentoring. Such reflections, and a sense of 'ordinariness' of mentoring, are an important resource on which mentoring can draw, especially if there is little time and space for reflection in the conditions of modern, working life.

However, mentoring is about using a lot of skills you already possess and a lot of qualities you have developed through time and experience. Your mentoring relationship will help you develop a fuller awareness of yourself. Mentoring presents a challenge to know yourself well enough to help and support another person and at the same time is a valuable way to develop self knowledge.

Morton-Cooper and Palmer (2000) suggest that the mentor fulfils a support role in three key areas; functional, personal and relational. To be effective in a functional role mentors must provide individuals with teaching, coaching, role modelling, counselling support, advice, sponsorship, guidance and resources. From a personal perspective, the mentor has a critical role in helping the individual develop and grow by promoting such things as self confidence, confidence building, creativity, fulfilment of potential and risk taking. All these qualities are essential for the effective qualified healthcare professional. Finally, and very often overlooked when considering mentor roles, are the relational responsibilities that a mentor has. A mentor needs to facilitate interpersonal relations, social relations, networking, sharing and trust.

References

Jarvis P, Gibson S (1997) *The Teacher Practitioner and Mentor in Nursing, Midwifery, Health Visiting and the Social Services*. Stanley Thornes, Cheltenham.

Morton-Cooper A, Palmer A. (2000) *Mentoring, Preceptorship and Clinical Supervision*. Blackwell Science, London.

SCOPME (1998) An enquiry into mentoring supporting doctors and dentists at work. Standing Committee on Post Graduate Medical and Dental Education.

Taylor and Stephenson (1996) What is mentoring. In: M Mawer (1996) *Mentoring in Physical Education: Issues and Insights*. Falmer Press, London.

8. Mentoring in Practice

Alison Morton-Cooper and Anne Palmer

'Come to the edge', he said.
They said, 'We are afraid'.
'Come to the edge', he said.
They came.
He pushed them . . .
and they flew!

Giullaume Apollinaire

Introduction

The complex, intriguing concept of mentoring continues to tax authors and researchers from a variety of different disciplines as they explore the role of mentors in a range of settings that includes the health, education and business arenas. From its origins in classical Greece through business interpretations of the 1970s with adaptations in education and nursing during the 1980s, much has been written about the subject and a multitude of different approaches taken (Merriam, 1993; Fish, 1995; Weightman, 1996; Jarvis and Gibson, 1997).

Mentoring has become a high profile topic in business, women's magazines, the press and nursing, and it is beginning to find its place in current teacher preparation, the police service and the medical profession (Smith and West-Burnham, 1993; Tomlinson, 1995; Freeman, 1997). Mentoring has associations with the personal and professional development of individuals in a wide variety of organisational settings. It is also seen as a necessary factor for career socialisation, advancement and success. Claims have been made that mentors:

- Make good leaders (Zaleznik, 1977; Pelletier and Duffield, 1994)
- Are required for success in business (Collins and Scott, 1978; Segerman-Peck, 1991)
- Are needed for executive success (Roche, 1979; Conway, 1996)
- Lead to scholarliness (May *et al.*, 1982; Sands *et al.*, 1991)
- Are a key to the future of nursing professionalism (Cooper, 1990)
- Can help in tackling social exclusion (Community Care, 1998).

This chapter aims to introduce the mentor and mentoring through an exploration of the differing interpretations for this interesting role and unique relationship in business, education and health care. A conceptual view will be offered in attempts to discover the nature of mentoring via an analysis of the functions, roles and

Alison Morton-Cooper and Anne Palmer: 'Mentoring in Practice' from *MENTORING, PRECEPTORSHIP AND CLINICAL SUPERVISION* (Blackwell Science, 2000), pp. 35–88.

relationships that identify this significant and dynamic, professional support relationship.

What is mentoring?

Mentoring continues to be in vogue and everyone has a mentor or is beginning to want one; however the question remains – is the concept clearly understood? What is a mentor, how do they function, and what are the complexities of the mentoring processes involved? These are questions that need to be addressed if appropriate and viable mentoring systems are to be developed and evaluated. As recently reported, there remains 'considerable semantic and conceptual variability about what mentoring is and does, and what a mentor is and does (SCOPME, 1998, p.5). To separate the myths from the mystique of mentoring is crucial, and we have to consider the origins, influences, approaches, terminology and the variety of different contexts in which mentoring has become visible.

Origins

The term 'mentor' is derived from the Classics, as identified in Homer's *Odyssey* where Mentor, the trusted son of Alimus, was appointed by Ulysses to be tutor-adviser to his son, Telemachus, and guardian of his estates while he was away fighting the Trojan wars. Mentor became more than a guardian, teacher and adviser as he had considerable influence and personal responsibility for the development of the young Telemachus. However, whether Mentor fulfilled his responsibilities diligently and was successful in the role is in doubt, as Homer further informs us that the goddess Athena assumed the disguise of Mentor to act as adviser to the youth. Safire (1980) suggests it was all a trick and that Homer was sending a warning to look out for mentors! It could be, however, that the poet was drawing attention to the complex nature of the relationship, suggesting that there was more to the role than being an older, wiser, adviser of first impressions. There are other scholars who suggest it was all a myth and that Homer's work has been badly misinterpreted in the literature (Playdon, 1998).

It was common in ancient Greece for young males to be partnered with older, experienced males who were often relatives or friends of the family. It was expected that the youths would learn from and emulate the values of their assigned 'mentor'. The term mentor became synonymous with wise, faithful guardian and teacher (Hamilton, 1981).

Roman generals had mentors by their side on the field of battle to advise them, and there are links with mentorship in the master craftsman–apprenticeship unions of mediaeval times. Guild masters were not only responsible for the teaching of particular crafts but also for their apprentices' social, religious and personal habits.

Few references to mentoring appear in the literature until a resurgence of interest was generated by Levinson's seminal study of adult development (Levinson *et al.*, 1978). The mentor was identified as normally older, of greater experience and more senior in the world that the young man was entering. This mentor was viewed as a transitional, exemplar figure in a young male's development. This was built on in business, education and nursing with the result that mentors and mentoring have been firing the imagination of many occupational groups and professions in recent years (Vance, 1982; Monaghan and Lunt, 1992).

Mentoring terms

The literature is full of various labels for the mentor and mentee (individuals involved) and mentoring or mentorship (the process). The identified labels within a structured, mentoring programme appear to reflect the organisational culture, management style, philosophy or mission of a particular organisation. In health care individuals who are being mentored are described as mentees or students. Murray and Owen (1991) document popular labels in other organisational settings as 'apprentice', 'aspirant', 'advisee', 'counselee', 'trainee', 'protégé' and 'candidate'. Less popular terms are 'follower', 'subordinate', 'applicant', 'hopeful', 'seeker' and we would add 'pupil', 'ward', 'novice', 'novitiate' and 'initiate', which could be considered limiting and judgmental in the mentoring context.

Influences

Moves towards providing organisational support systems that place importance on personal growth and development have roots in a variety of different movements of the 1970s and 1980s. The emergence of management theory and the role of management as a distinct discipline have played a part. However, the major influences appear to have been the human resource development initiatives of the 1970s (Eng, 1986) and the acceptance of freedom-to-learn approaches and adult learning theories of Rogers (1983), Kolb (1984) and Knowles (1984). The resulting shift in organisational and educational philosophies has led to the search for effective strategies that are directed towards making the most of human potential and stimulating learning in practice. The emphasis on being self-directed and *owning* the learning experience has increased responsibility for self learning, self awareness and problem solving, which arises from the acceptance of the theoretical assumptions of adult development and maturation. This involves acknowledging that adults can:

- Move from a state of dependence to become self directed – able to take responsibility for their own actions, self development and lifelong learning.

- Accumulate experiences – being able to build a biography of experience that can be drawn on to test and evaluate new experiences. This leads to the search for new learning opportunities, resulting in abilities to learn, change and provide a rich resource for themselves and others.
- Have an orientation towards personal developmental and professional roles, demonstrating a willingness to learn and seek guidance as necessary.
- Change from needing to acquire knowledge and being subject-centred to becoming more performance-centred, resulting in the application of experience and the development of sound critical thinking abilities.

Underpinning these assumptions is the notion that individual growth is perceived as a process of becoming, and not as a process of being shaped or cloned. It is important to realise that self experience and self discovery are important facets of learning (Rogers, 1983). Adults have built-in motivations to learn, and a need to gain in self-confidence, self-esteem and self-awareness. These are important attributes for any occupational or professional group but are crucial for those caring for the health needs of others. Self-awareness is also an important and necessary prerequisite for 'appreciating self and the situation of others' (Bernard, 1988, p. 229). This is a vital component of personal growth and development and it fits well with the 'process of becoming' as a continual journey of self discovery. Assistance, offered by a confident, self-secure, experienced guide and enabler in the form of a mentor, can aid the keen, inexperienced traveller.

The raison d'être *of mentoring*

Mentoring is an exciting complex phenomenon that is natural or artificially contrived to benefit individuals within a sharing partnership (Palmer, 1987). In the true classical sense it is much more than the experienced guiding the inexperienced: mentoring is dynamic and exciting, in part because of its kaleidoscopic nature and also because it is a relatively complex concept, made more intricate by the various connotations placed on it. It is a good example of a transcendental semantic signifier – taken in this context to mean that mentoring can be viewed from many different perspectives and is open to a variety of interpretations depending on its differing applications and settings.

Mentoring concerns the building of a dynamic relationship in which the personal characteristics, philosophies and priorities of the individual members interact to influence, in turn, the nature, direction and duration of the resulting, eventual partnership. What lies at the heart of the process is the shared, encouraging and supportive elements that are based on mutual attraction and common values. It is these aspects that facilitate the personal development and career/professional socialisation for the mentee – leading to eventual reciprocal benefits for both parties.

A mentoring relationship is one that is enabling and cultivating, a relationship that assists in empowering an individual within the working environment. A mentor is not a prerequisite for advancement or success as such events regularly occur without access to this type of significant helper. It is important to recognise that mentors do not have magic abilities or powers to fashion great individuals (Melds, 1991). They do, however, enable individuals to discover and use their own talents, encouraging and nurturing the unique contributions of their mentees, to help them be successful in their own right.

Mentoring is concerned with making the most of human potential and significantly is becoming more widely recognised in health care at a time of political change and with moves away from competitive, market approaches towards collaborative practices (DoH, 1997). As part of an identified support framework of other more recognisable roles and staff development programmes, mentoring fits well with humanistic management, education and training initiatives. This involves adult approaches and learning experiences supported by the principles of self-development, self-directedness, mutual understanding and negotiation.

However, in the British health service and the general and higher education systems, currently concerned with diminishing resources, efficiency and value for money, mentoring mechanisms of a more formalised nature may rest more easily within the prevailing ethos. For the clinical manager, educator, lecturer, staff developer or researcher, mentoring presents an intriguing challenge when considering the what, how and where of practical application.

Mentoring challenges

On examining mentoring it rapidly becomes apparent that the views from a variety of perspectives, and the lack of clarity of purposes and functions of the mentor, are not assisted by anecdotal reports, lack of empirical evidence and confusion with other professional support roles. What remains crucial in today's climate is a need to come to terms with the nature of new support roles and then to apply them appropriately. This is important with regard to the types of approaches that are available and may be required.

Important questions to be considered include who needs, wants or will benefit from such new roles? Making informed decisions about what systems are required and how they should be planned, implemented, evaluated and resourced will enable managers, educators and those from staff development units to make adequate preparations to assist staff to come to terms with new support roles, structures and frameworks.

It would be easy to step into the 'quagmire of definitions' envisaged by Hagerty (1986). It is far better to clarify the roles that already exist and to consider the nature of the classical mentor as interpreted by Levinson *et al.* (1978). This leads to the discovery of the richness of the relationship and facilitates an explanation of the various mentoring approaches that exist. Informed decisions and choices can then be made regarding the development of sound mentoring frameworks to complement the other organisational support systems that are available.

The classical mentor

In reviewing mentoring it soon becomes apparent that common elements underpin the different perspectives, cultures and approaches. Vance (1982) helps to clarify the situation by drawing attention to the earlier suggestions arising from business studies, that mentoring is not defined in the identification of formal roles but in the character of the relationship and the function it serves. Business, education and nursing applications of mentoring may initially appear different in terminology, focus and approachs; however, certain common elements emerge. These can be identified as:

- The character of the relationship is that of enabling and empowerment
- The mentor offers a repertoire of helper functions (or assisting functions) to facilitate guidance and provide support
- The mentor role comprises an interplay of personal, functional and relational aspects
- Individual purposes and helper functions are mutually set by the individuals involved
- Helper functions are mutually determined by the individuals

- Individuals choose each other and there are identifiable stages in the relationship.

Character of the relationship

In classical mentoring the central focus of the partnership concerns the mutual trust of two adult individuals attracted by the possibility of what has been described as a mentor signal (George and Kummerow, 1981). The two parties are drawn together naturally by their personal characteristics, attributes and common values. They demonstrate a willingness to spend time together, to learn from each other and to share each other's experiences.

In the early stages of the relationship the mentee may appear initially dependent or reliant on the mentor in terms of the intensity of the support offered. As the relationship develops there will be changes in the intensity as the needs and priorities of the mentee change. This results in an intimacy to the relationship made possible by mutual relevance and closeness and a reciprocal partnership develops into one that is dynamic, emotionally intense and beneficial to each party.

Recognition of the partnership, and better understanding of his/her own needs, allows the mentee to become proactive in triggering the specific support or assistance required. The mentee can begin to be self-selecting with regard to the helper functions required and can begin to make informed decisions about personal development.

Testing, taking risks, making mistakes and the freedom to be creative take place within the mutual understanding that the mentee is valued and supported. Safety mechanisms exist in the form of the wide range of helper functions offered the mentor. The mentee becomes gradually more self-aware, gains in confidence and begins to achieve the capacity to 'go it alone'. It is at this stage that he/she may look for another mentor or become a mentor to someone else.

In this manner the classical mentor facilitates personal growth and development and assists with career progression, while guiding the mentee through the clinical, educational, social and political networks of the working culture. The elements of mentoring that set it apart from other more specific relationships and give it its multidimensional and dynamic nature are the:

- Repertoire of helper functions
- Mutuality and reciprocal sharing
- Duration, identified stages and transitional nature of the relationship.

These required elements match with Darling's (1984) vital ingredients for mentoring, which she identifies as attraction, action and effect.

Repertoire of helper functions

Within work, individuals may develop relationships that are specific in nature such as role modelling, teaching or counselling. These relationships are clearly defined and are considered functionally specific. If a deeper association develops with mutual attraction, and the wide range of helper functions is offered, then the relationship becomes dynamic, reciprocal and emotionally intense, and true, classical mentoring occurs (Palmer, 1987, p. 36). The emotional aspect arises from an intimacy that is made possible by the closeness and understanding of those involved. The helper functions of mentoring are:

- Adviser
- Coach
- Counsellor
- Guide/networker
- Role model
- Sponsor
- Teacher
- Resource facilitator

Adviser

Support and advice is offered in both career and social terms. The advice given demonstrates an awareness of the mentee's merits and abilities within the organisation's requirements. This process aids in building the self-image and confidence of the mentee.

Coach

In mentoring, the coaching function concerns the mutual setting of guidelines with the mentor offering advice and constructive feedback. The mentee can then test such feedback in differing practice situations. The mutual exchange between the individuals allows feedback to be analysed and refined for future action.

Counsellor

The role of counsellor facilitates self-development of the mentee in his/her own terms as psychological support systems are made available. The mentor acts as a listener and sounding-board to facilitate self-awareness and encourage independence.

Guide/networker

As a supportive guide, the mentor introduces the mentee to the helpful contacts and power groups within the organisation. Networking is an extension of guiding as the mentor facilitates introductions to the values and customs of the organisation, including socialisation to the mentor's own occupational, professional and social groups.

Role model

A role model provides an observable image for imitation, demonstrating skills and qualities for the mentee to emulate.

Sponsor

The sponsor influences and facilitates entry to the organisational and professional cultures. The mentor influences career development by providing introductions, promoting the mentee and making recommendations for advancement.

Teacher

The teacher function involves sharing knowledge through experience and critical inquiry, facilitating learning opportunities, and focusing on individual needs and learning styles to promote ownership and responsibility for continuing professional education. Such activities and reflection on experience assist personal development, in order to fulfil intellectual and practical potential.

Resource facilitator

The mentor acts as an experienced practitioner and colleague sharing experiences and information, as well as providing access to resources. This forms the preceptor-type, resource element within the range of helper functions.

Personal, functional and relational factors

The personal and relational factors are concerned with individual growth, self-development, self-awareness and personal fulfilment. Knowing that there is someone out there willing to offer support and encouragement and 'in their corner' enables the mentee to come to terms with his/her role in the organisation or professional setting. The mentor offers personal, functional and relational assistance to provide a comprehensive framework of support that goes beyond those of the more usual teaching and advisory roles in clinical practice. Within such a framework the mentee can begin to constructively question his/her own abilities and can gain in confidence, be creative and endeavour to take risks. The inter-relationship of these personal, functional and relational factors is identified in Table 1.

Table 1 The support framework of personal, functional and relational factors within mentoring

	Mentor Role	
Personal	Functional	Relational
promoting	*providing*	*facilitating*
self development confidence building creativity fulfilment of potential risk taking	teaching coaching role modelling counselling support advice sponsorship guidance resources	interpersonal relations social relations networking sharing trust

Mutual setting of individual purposes and functions

Jointly attracted by each other's qualities and attributes, in classical mentoring the mentor and mentee are free to develop the relationship in the manner of their choosing. The emphasis is on informality, and the needs of the individuals concerned form the character and nature of the resulting relationship. The mentee can feel safe in selecting particular helper functions that are required in his/her own terms, while moving from initial dependency in the relationship to becoming independent and his/her own person.

In classical mentoring informal assessment may exist in the tentative, early phases of the partnership but only in the form of evaluating each other's experiences, abilities, approachability and willingness to find time for each other. It is our considered opinion that formal assessment and documentation procedures have no place in this type of mentoring.

Mentor language, functions and organisational culture

In classical mentoring, it is important to recognise that the nature and terms of the relationship are set informally by the people involved. The nature of the relationship is determined by the qualities and characteristics of the people drawn together through the sharing of common values or attitudes to form an initial attraction and bonding. The processes which evolve are formulated by both parties, naturally occurring and informal within the specific organisational culture. The expectations and any issues that arise will relate to what the mentor and mentee may deem as important in gaining the 'tribal wisdom' of an organisation (Darling, 1984) or obtaining the 'DNA of a profession' (Palmer, 1992).

The expectations include the need for active participation and developmental outcomes tailored to the needs of the mentee to provide a sharing, collaborative partnership that benefits both individuals and the organisation or relevant occupational group or profession.

The nature of the relationship will be affected by the organisational culture that consists of the values, norms and beliefs of the structures and systems that give an organisation its own identity (Handy, 1985; Cray and Mallory, 1998). In classical mentoring the relationship is inherently of their own making and not artificially contrived. Modifications to classical mentoring in order to fulfil a variety of differing individual and organisational requirements have led to the application of more formal approaches. The true elements of classical mentoring (mutuality, repertoire of helper functions, duration) may well be evident but there will be adaptations and a differing emphasis placed on career support, socialisation and the criteria for success.

In more formal forms of mentoring such as contract (Monaghan and Lunt, 1992) or facilitated mentoring (Murray and Owen, 1991), mentor terminology and helper functions are determined by the organisational culture (refer to Table 2 for an explanation of approaches). Contract mentoring concerns the adaptation of classical mentoring and its resulting application within structured programmes of support. The people involved are obliged to achieve the identified aims, purposes and outcomes of a recognised programme of development and support. The relevant aims, purposes and outcomes may or may not be negotiable, depending on the degree of formality of the programme. Individuals can be assigned to each other (forced matching) or may be able to make a choice from a selected group of mentors, known as the 'mentor pool'. These issues will be explored later in the chapter.

Table 2 Mentoring approaches

Type	Nature
1. True mentoring relationships	
(i) Classical mentoring – informal. (Primary mentoring) A natural, chosen relationship. Purposes and functions are determined by the individuals involved. An enabling relationship in personal, emotional, organisational and professional terms.	• Self-selection of individuals, persuasive influences; attraction with a shared wish to work together. • No defined programme. • Less specific purposes and functions as set by the individuals, circumstances and context. • No explicit financial rewards for mentor. • Probable duration, 2–15 years.
(ii) Contract mentoring – formal. (Facilitated mentoring/secondary mentoring) An artificial relationship created for a specific purpose, that is essentially determined by the organisation. Some elements of mentor function, with focus on specific helper functions.	Programmes are identified by: • Clear purposes, functions, defined aims or outcomes. • Selected individuals with assigned mentors, forced matching or choice of mentors from mentor pool. • Explicit material rewards; possibilities of financial incentives for mentors. • Probable duration, 1–2 years.
2. Pseudo-mentoring relationships (Quasi mentoring/partial mentoring/ sequential mentoring) Mentoring approaches in appearance only – as offered by academic involvement in thesis preparation, orientation and induction programmes.	• Focus on specific tasks or organisational issues of short lived duration. • Guidance from several mentors, for short periods. • Relationships do not demonstrate the comprehensive enabling elements of the true classical model. • Specified clinical placements. • Probable duration, 6 weeks to one year.

The nature of the process may have superficial similarities within different organisations or within differing occupational groups, but how the process is explained and understood may take on a variety of appearances. Often formulated for organisational requirements as part of staff development programmes, the use of different terminology and the change in emphasis for the helper functions give rise to the different approaches of mentoring that are evident within differing cultures.

Classical mentoring and contract mentoring can be considered as true mentoring as both contain the vital elements essential to mentoring: the helper functions, mutuality and sharing and identified stages/duration. Pseudo-mentoring or quasi-mentoring approaches have probably arisen due to the initial lack of understanding of the roles, purposes, processes and formal application of mentoring.

Early applications tended to confuse mentoring with the support provided by preceptors, academic counsellors and personal tutors. Mentoring was also used for the singular purposes of orientation and induction, where the richness of the relationship is wasted and more functional enabling roles such as preceptorship would suffice. (An elaboration of pseudo-mentoring is given in Table 2.)

Organisational applications in business and education

In business, the emphasis is for the mentor to function as a sponsor, guide or networker within a competitive culture that is often male dominated (Demarco, 1993). The main focus has been on career guidance, executive nurturing and managerial support, with informal or formal, planned programmes of contract/facilitated mentoring (Murray and Owen, 1991). Mentoring in business organisations is considered to have a place in developing potential managers and executives, as well as having a strategic role in managing change and implementing new work practices (Slipais, 1993; Conway, 1996).

In the USA, business interest in mentoring systems stimulated education policy makers and educators to consider such approaches for student preparation, teachers and school administrators (Klopf and Harrison, 1981; Fagan and Walter, 1982). The focus for mentor function was essentially that of teacher and role model with educational aims that were adapted from those of business to reduce the accent on financial rewards. Education has become more concerned with the process of learning, resulting in roles for educators that stimulate adult learning and reflection, altering the balance of power towards the learning needs of the student.

In general education in the UK, the focus for mentoring programmes was initially conceived for educational and pastoral support in probationary periods. Scant further interest was taken in the concept, despite the recommendations of the James Committee (James Report, 1972). Later in the 1970s the Advisory Committee on the Supply and Training of Teachers (ACSTT) set up a subcommittee, chaired by Professor Haycocks, which subsequently produced three influential reports. The second subcommittee report on the training of adult education and part-time further education teachers (ACSTT II), which became more popularly known as Haycocks II, reported in March 1978.

One of the report's recommendations centred on the provision of a local team of mentors to play a part in offering a role as classroom counsellors in teacher training. Holt (1982, p. 153), in valuing such a proposal for 'on-course, in-house support', identified difficulties in implementation because of cost, mentor training and the effectiveness of the supervisory role in the classroom.

Beyond initial school education, the envisaged changes had implications for general staff development, providing 'training for the trainers' and for those involved in further education (Cantor and Roberts, 1986, p.192). Current interest has once again arisen due to the changes in initial teacher training programmes and the increase in school-based training as part of initial teacher training (Department for Education, 1992; Boydell and Bines, 1994; Tomlinson, 1995). Student teachers are located in educational placements and are expected to learn 'on the job', with support from a qualified teacher acting as a mentor.

In primary education, mentoring for student teachers has tended to take the form of collaborative relationships which facilitate openness, the sharing of feelings and professional issues (Boydell, 1994). Mentoring has continued to gain momentum in secondary education with the introduction of school-based initial teacher training/education schemes. As a result an interesting discourse has been and is taking place, with the sharing of widely differing interpretations and applications for the mentor in general and higher education (Standing, 1999).

Glover *et al.* (1994) with evidence from a wide scale study on mentoring have uncovered what they consider are the three determinants that affect the mentoring process. These are identified as the subject mentor, the subject department and the staff of the school, and it is suggested that the balance of these three factors has the greatest effect on the mentoring relationship and student experience. A rational and useful explanation for the development and current explosion of mentor interpretations in education is offered by Brooks and Sikes (1997), who trace the application of the various emerging models which complement the 'classical' approach. Such models are identifiable as the three types offered here.

(1) The apprenticeship model and the mentor as skilled crafts person

Practical applications:

- Pupil–apprentice and teacher-master roles
- Learning by observing, 'sitting by Nellie'
- For initial teacher training mode (O'Hear, 1988).

There have been some adaptions to this model and there is recognition for the change in language from apprenticeship to that of 'modelling' (McIntyre, 1994). This it would appear provides a useful and supportive relationship when identified circumstances dictate the need for security at the start of a course.

(2) The competence-based model and the mentor as trainer

Practical applications:

- Training and induction with the role of the trainer as an instructor and coach who demonstrates and assists the student to achieve a set of competencies, as identified by the Department for Education (1992, para 2.1). Parsloe (1995) explains the coaching role well and makes helpful links with the development of competencies.

(3) The reflective practitioner model and mentor as critical friend and co-enquirer

Practical applications:

- Promoting collaboration and partnership in the learning process
- The notion of challenge to promote professional growth.

This mode of mentoring in general secondary education initiates learning from experience, with reflection, 'in and on action', to assist new teachers with the complexities of their teaching role and the 'swampy lowlands of professional practice' (Schon, 1988). This type of mentoring relationship fits well with the notion of quality mentoring forwarded by Fish (1995) who makes links with the need for reflective practice as well as a healthy balance of the process and skills required to be a competent and 'quality mentor'.

Application to health care

In British health care, supportive role developments have been many and varied with occupational groups such as social workers and occupational therapists devising structured, sound, clinical enabling relationships that develop therapeutic competence (Hawkins and Shohet, 1989; CCETSW, 1992). Such relationships and supervisory support roles assist training and facilitate assessment in practical placements, as well as support advanced practice. Modifications of therapeutically determined supervisory roles allow learning support to be provided by practising field work teachers, supervisors and community trainers. Those in physiotherapy and the complementary therapies such as acupuncture also recognise a need for students to experience professional work, enabling them to re-examine practice effectively through investigation, analysis and professional support (Pratt, 1989; MacPherson, 1997).

Supervision appears to be the identified learning support role for the therapies and social work disciplines, particularly for those on training programmes, while mentors have responsibility for supporting the qualified worker (Rumsey, 1995). In radiography and medicine, mentoring is steadily being explored (Barr *et al.*, 1993; Bould, 1996).

Despite comprehensive activity in North America, in the UK only a few mentor programmes for senior managers have been instigated (Muller, 1984; Holloran, 1993). For the most part in the National Health Service at present, mentoring is 'provided' for student nurses and student midwives and 'faculty mentors' were recommended for medical students (Callans *et al.*, 1987). In British nursing and midwifery, mentoring issues have been further complicated by the confusion over the role and functions of other support roles – preceptor and clinical supervisors.

It is well documented that the terms mentor and preceptor were brought to the consciousness of most British nurses via the educational language and curriculum developments of the 1990s. The nursing originators who set the scene for the take up of the concept in the UK were mainly North American authors, consultants and researchers, notably Vance (1982), Darling (1984) and Puetz (1985). Most admit to having drawn on the experiences of the business and commercial arenas where the empirical evidence has involved mostly male experiences in the world of work and has concentrated on leadership development.

Nursing, midwifery and the other health care professions remain primarily female and transferring empirical and anecdotal evidence from different cultures can further complicate understanding and application. There are fundamental differences of product process ethos between business and service organisations like the health service which has imperatives for setting social objectives and 'managing for social result' (Weil, 1992; Morley, 1995). In nursing, important mentoring issues of cross gender approaches and some female nurses' lack of apparent abilities to network, share and support emerging leaders have been readily addressed (Hamilton 1981;

Hardy 1984). There is evidence that nurses are gaining in assertiveness and increased political acumen in other countries but in Britain gender remains a key factor in how nurses value their health care contribution (Davies, 1995).

The word 'mentor' first appeared in the curriculum preparation documents produced by one of the statutory bodies, the English National Board (ENB, 1987, 1988). New roles were rapidly created and new name badges worn with some pride and a great deal of puzzlement for both qualified staff and students alike. The use of the term preceptor, again with its origins in North America, had appeared earlier in the nursing index for 1975 and in popular nursing press reports, where a scheme was developed within one health authority (Raichura and Riley, 1985).

The use of preceptors has once again been brought to notice by the stated intentions of the Post-Registration Education and Practice initiatives (PREP), which explore the requirements for continual updating, post-registration support and the development of appropriate portfolios of practice achievements (UKCC, 1995). Critical examination by British authors and researchers has continually highlighted the need to use preceptors appropriately in the clinical setting (Morley, 1990; Barlow, 1991) and it has been noticeable that nursing authors switched emphasis from discussing the merits of mentorship to comparing and contrasting both roles and how they could best be used (Armitage and Burnard, 1991; Ashton and Richardson, 1992).

Clarity about the nature of the different roles has not been helped by early articles that attempted to describe mentoring but with the benefit of hindsight were describing preceptorship programmes or pseudo-mentoring approaches. Morley (1990) concluded that current role definition is probably inappropriate and nursing would be better advised to use the term 'preceptor', a role more oriented and suited to practice. What is important in the current debate in nursing is that mentoring, preceptorship and the emerging professional support role of clinical supervision, should all be seen to have equal value for development and support in whichever setting they are applied.

Mentoring in medicine is steadily gaining credence and, after a late start in comparison with the other health care groups, has begun to identify suitable guidance for the role of mentoring within continuing medical education. Recognition has been forthcoming for a number of years concerning the need for support in all branches of medicine and the importance for effective continuing education (SCOPME, 1997; Freeman, 1998).

However, it is only relatively recently that mentoring has been viewed as a pivotal relationship in supporting the various grades of doctor. Mentoring in general practice schemes has highlighted the tensions and dilemmas between providing pastoral support or educational support (Alliott, 1996) and a range of mentoring activities have been identified including that of the 'holistic' mentor (Freeman, 1997). The holistic mentor is thought to bind together the classical components of mentoring which the author and researcher considers are continuing professional education, personal support and professional development (Freeman, 1997, p. 457).

A new study offers clarity of definition and sound conclusions are reached to assist the implementation of mentoring in medicine and dentistry. Mentoring, it is suggested, involves 'a process whereby an experienced, highly regarded, empathetic person (the mentor) guides another individual in the development and re-examination of their own ideas, learning and personal and professional development' (SCOPME, 1998, p. 12). If mentoring is to become a successful, worthwhile activity the authors of the report conclude that there is a need for:

- Dissemination of mentoring's potential benefits, risks, aims and processes
- Promotion of opportunities for mentoring, but it should not be imposed
- Identification of mentoring as a priority for newly appointed career grade doctors and dentists
- Development and evaluation of preparation programmes for those volunteering to become mentors
- Clarity of initiatives developed locally and nationally
- View of mentoring as a positive, enabling experience separate and distinct from organisational systems of monitoring or performance review.

Mentoring is coming of age in the medical profession, having learnt from the early confusions and pseudo-mentoring approaches still being agonised over in nursing. However, small pockets of mentoring initiatives will have to be nurtured and traditional cultures of 'difficult rites of passage' will have to be addressed, if the full potential of this enabling relationship is to be realised in both secondary and primary health care.

Choice and mentoring stages

Individual selection is a vital process of classical mentoring as the relationship is dependent on the joint, dynamic, sharing characteristics of both parties for its nature and success. Matching characteristics and a 'coming together' are naturally implied in the mentor signal and common attraction that ignites the relationship. Enjoyment of each other's company and a willingness to spend time together may signal the start to this informal mentoring process. Styles of approach and the individual preferences of both parties play their part in how the 'personal fit' is best made (Klopf and Harrison, 1981).

Phases or stages to the relationship are variously described and documented and these are commonly identified as the initiation, development and termination phases (Campbell-Heider, 1986; Earnshaw, 1995). Others suggest that there are four phases and clarify these as: initiation, training and termination with the establishment of lasting peer friendship as a follow-up to an amicable ending (Hunt and Michael, 1983).

In nursing, Hawkins and Thibodeau (1989) specify invitational, questioning, informational/working and termination stages. Common to many of the deliberations on the phases or stages is the fact that the relationship is transitional and there is always a recognisable start, middle and end to any mentoring relationship.

Initiation

The start or initiation concerns the 'locking on' of individuals who are brought together by common characteristics, abilities or recognition of shared values. This involves the selection and 'getting to know you' period of the relationship. Working in close proximity, having access to each other and being able to observe each other's actions in a variety of work situations, influences the initial attraction and assists the 'coming together' phase.

Working phase

The working or training phase of the process is where the main focus for individual growth and development lies. The dynamics of the mentoring relationship are maintained by the interactions of both individuals and the increasing trust and closeness that begins to develop. The mentee may commence this phase by being heavily reliant on the mentor's greater experience, awareness of the networks and wide variety of influential contacts.

The mentee is faced with the repertoire of helper functions that the experienced mentor has to offer and the choice of assistance may initially be erratic and left to chance. As this phase develops, mutual trust and sharing become evident and the mentee is more readily able to choose the specific helper functions that are best suited to his/her needs. This is a very active phase and the intensity of the relationship moves to that of common understanding and solid partnership. The mentee gradually becomes more independent and is eventually able to trigger or request the specific helper functions required.

Through the mutual sharing of experiences and needs, the mentee is able to make informed decisions and become self-selecting within the relationship. Figure 1 shows the mentoring phases with relevant activities and degree of attachment. The transitional nature of the relationship sets the scene for the mentee to have the confidence to be creative and to experiment with risk-taking ventures that further encourage growth and development.

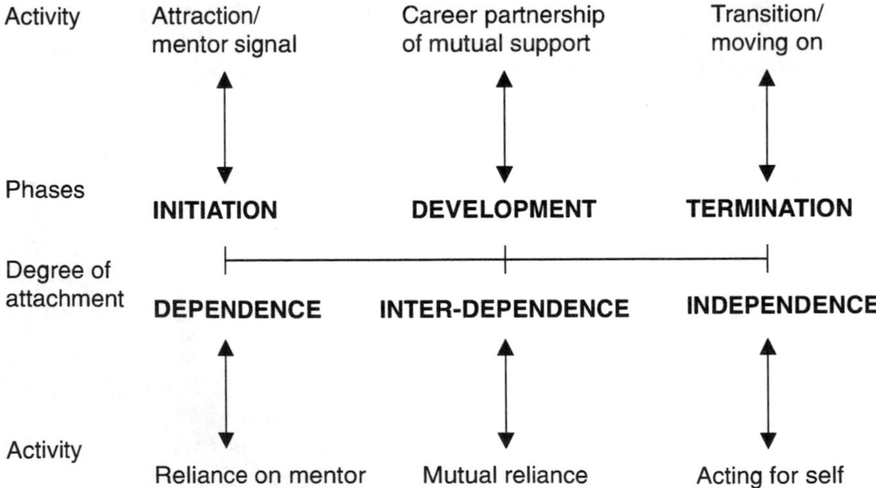

Figure 1 Matching phases of mentoring with activities and degree of attachment

The need to test and take risks arises within the understanding that the mentee is valued and supported and that there are safety measures available should mistakes occur. The mentee becomes increasingly more confident to go it alone and the relationship moves towards the terminating phase.

Termination phase

The mentee has begun to act on his/her own initiative and is now in a position to begin to act independently. The termination phase can end positively as supportive friendship or negatively where there is conflict or emotional tension and general dissatisfaction (Blotnick, 1984; Wheatley and Hirsch, 1984). The ending can be precipitated by changing career interests, a need to find another mentor or to take on the challenges of mentoring others, or the emergence of toxic mentoring. (This is explored more fully in the benefits and limitations of mentoring dealt with later in this chapter.)

If the process has been beneficial with the identified needs being met, the two individuals may maintain their friendship and the mentee may move on to mentor others. This may be due in part to the need for another association that involves sharing or a desire for a degree of emotional intensity that is not always readily available within other working relationships.

Attributes, qualities and abilities of an effective mentor

Just as there is no single definition for a mentor, there is no single personality type that is synonymous with being or becoming an effective mentor. But it is evident that successful mentors are reported as employing a range of enabling strategies and skills within mentoring relationships (Fields, 1991; Anderson and Shannon, 1995). In considering who should mentor it is important to consider the behaviours, qualities and characteristics of those who will be deemed suitable to provide this supportive role for others. The intention is not to be prescriptive but to present some idea of what is meant by positive strategies in order to assist managers, educators and practitioners in making a sound selection. This will aid the deliberations about who is best fitted to support others and who requires help in attaining appropriate qualities, and it will perhaps identify those who should never be placed in a position to support or mentor others.

In this chapter, a common theme in the discussion is the use of the term 'enabling' – epitomising the positive aspects of human relationships that foster growth and development in others. 'Enabling' refers to the ability to make things happen and in recent years it has become associated with the other positive development concepts of facilitation and empowerment. The working world would be vastly different if organisations were staffed and managed solely by people with these enabling qualities. The richness, complexity and challenges of the working culture are, however, diversified by the fact that human beings are capable of displaying both enabling and disabling qualities.

Disabling traits

In examining the nature of support roles it is necessary to reflect on the less positive aspects of human nature that can have a detrimental effect on others. Having identified individuals in management systems who are disruptive, Heirs and Farrell (1986) categorise these individuals who through their thought processes and actions typify aspects of disabling behaviour. The 'destructive minds' are categorised by the following features:

The rigid mind:

- Concrete thinkers, dealing with only black and white concepts
- Stereotyped, with preconceived ideas that are difficult to change
- Set values, which lack imagination or creativity
- In authority, stifle others, suspicious and resistant to new ideas
- Safe and secure in bureaucratic surroundings.

The rigid mind: stifles originality, ignores change and encourages complacency.

The ego mind:

- Self interested and self important
- Uninterested in others and keen to always get their own way
- Unable to share
- Destroys team cohesiveness and spirit
- Works well as an outsider or entrepreneur.

The ego mind: destroys objectivity and makes 'thinking collaboration' impossible.

The machiavellian mind:

- Devious, calculating and manipulative
- Obsessed by internal politics and politicking (Heirs and Farrell, 1986, p.182)
- Interested in power and power plays.

The machiavellian mind turns all thinkers into bureaucratic connivers and all thinking into political thinking.

Heirs and Farrell suggest that we should learn to manage these individuals and attempt to understand how they operate. However, if this is not possible then Heirs and Farrell advise avoiding them, taking care that they do not 'infect' your thinking (Heirs and Farrell, 1986, p.86).

Vera Darling (1986), in taking a slightly different perspective, offers a 'galaxy of toxic mentors', developed from interviewing nurses. Four distinct types of disabler are observed and these she refers to as the avoiders, dumpers, blockers and destroyer/criticisers. This informal classification and the associated subgroups are presented in overview in Table 3. The apparent behaviours have similarities to those presented by the 'destructive minds' and these are clearly not the qualities expected of an enabler or those we would wish to identify as effective in supporting others. They present as those clearly at the other end of a continuum of positive supporting strategies.

Table 3 The galaxy of toxic mentors

Type	Features
Dumpers	Not available or accessible Throw people into new roles Leave them to 'sink or swim' strategies
Blockers	Avoid meeting others' needs by: refusing requests ('the Refuser') controlling through withholding information ('the Withholder') arresting development by over supervising ('the Hoverer')
Destroyer/Criticisers	Set out to destroy others by: subtle attacks to undermine confidence ('the Underminer') open approaches of verbal attack and argument to deliberately destroy confidence ('the Belittler') constant put-downs and questioning of abilities ('the Nagger')

Source: Darling (1985)

Rather than present a continuum of positive support with polarisations of enabling and disabling traits, which gives the appearance of being relatively simple and of one dimension, another positive attribute, facilitation, can be added to the equation, along with that of another negative trait, such as manipulation. The resulting perspectives demonstrate the rich diversities of enabling and disabling characteristics that can occur. This is demonstrated in Figure 2, where the positive qualities of enabling are in opposition to those of the negative disabling. These in turn are counter-balanced by the positive nature of facilitation and the negativity of manipulation.

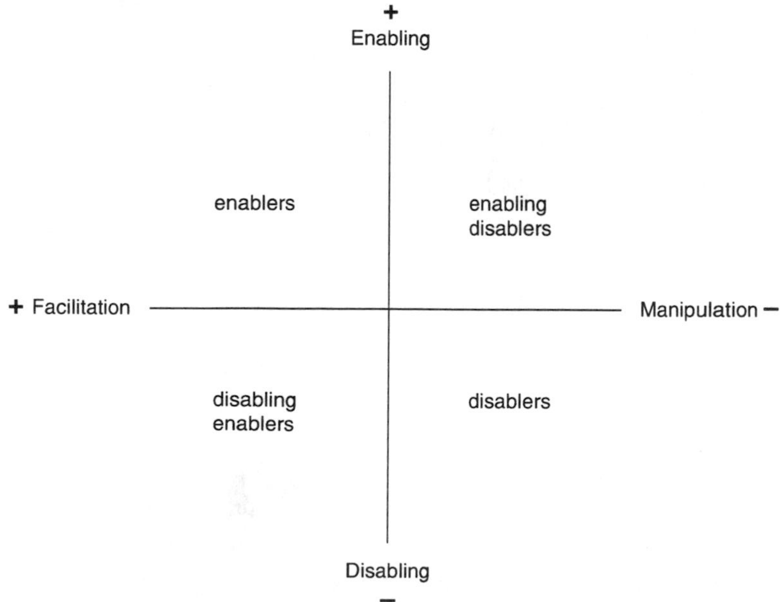

Figure 2 Enabling–disabling traits

This completes the four quadrants, and the entities of the enablers, disablers and those that fall between – the enabling manipulator (enabling-disabler) and disabling facilitator (disabling-enabler) – emerge. Although it is relatively easy to spot the true enablers and disablers within an organisation, it is not always so easy to identify the negative and detrimental effects of those who are enabling-disablers or disabling-enablers. Often these individuals present with a much more subtle approach, and it may take some time to realise that a relationship that appears as initially sound is, in fact, disabling and having a negative effect.

The disablers fit with Darling's description of dumpers and blockers while the enabling-disablers and disabling-enablers are easily recognisable within the category of destroyers and criticisers. By creating tensions and disruptions they can cause others to move departments or change jobs; conversely, enablers may create too comfortable an existence that is reassuring and seducing. That is not to say that these behaviours are tolerated, rather that an understanding of how they operate can help us work with, manage and draw those who demonstrate disabling traits towards the beneficial effects of a supportive relationship.

Enabling traits

Having dealt with the negative aspects we can now focus on the more positive elements. An enabler is someone who appears as an open, honest communicator, a person who feels positive about him/herself and about his/her value to the organisation and to others within it. Enablers are people-centred and because they feel worthy and can value themselves, they are in turn able to recognise the value of others. An enabling individual is:

- Accessible to those around him/her
- Responsive to others' needs
- Easy to trust
- Comfortable with him/herself and his/her abilities
- Able to command mutual respect.

Other authors list a comprehensive range of characteristics or qualities that appear to be best suited to mentoring as a long-term, close working relationship. Holloway and Whyte (1994, p. 16) identify a checklist for the ideal mentor which includes the attributes of 'relevant job related experience; well developed interpersonal skills; an ability to relate; a desire to assist; an open mind; a flexible attitude and a recognition of their own need for support'.

Extensive lists and tables of the essential ingredients needed to function as an effective mentor can be drawn together within a framework of three important personal attributes. We suggest that these are competence, demonstrating personal confidence, and having a commitment to the development of others. In possessing these personal attributes the mentor has the qualities and abilities to extend a working relationship beyond that of ordinary limits to ensure that mentoring occurs and is effective for all concerned.

Competence

The mentor has competence:

- Arising from having appropriate knowledge and experience to be effective in their work within the organisation and able to command respect from others
- To build on the mentee's strengths and offer constructive feedback on his/her limitations
- In the skills associated with the repertoire of helper functions, such as interpersonal relations, communication, counselling, instructing and coaching, skills that are more value if exercised and up to date
- In providing a reliable source of information and availability of resources
- To promote good judgement.

Confidence

The mentor has confidence to:

- Have and share a network of valuable personal contacts
- Be imaginative
- Demonstrate initiative, take risks and have personal power with charisma that is used appropriately
- Allow the mentee to develop within his/her own terms
- Seek new challenges and initiatives
- Be successful at what he/she does, providing status and prestige
- Lead and offer clear direction
- Recognise and share credit for achievements
- Be able to deal with another's personal problems, challenges and triumphs.

Commitment

The mentor is committed to:

- Staff development
- Being people orientated and having a keen interest in seeing others develop and advance
- Investing time, energy and effort within a different type of working relationship
- Sharing personal experiences, knowledge and skills
- Personal motivation and a desire to motivate others.

Competence, confidence and commitment ensure that the mentor can be flexible, proactive and responsive, to balance the requisites of a long-term, intimate working relationship with an understanding of its transitional nature and eventual conclusion.

It is also important that the mentor is self-aware with a clear sense of his/her own strengths and limitations, enabling assistance in another's personal growth and development. Positive qualities of flexibility, approachability, accessibility, political astuteness, patience, perseverance and a sense of humour are also essential for effective mentorship. These are sound qualities that ensure that mentors are relatively at ease with themselves, do not take themselves too seriously and can with competence, confidence and commitment be generous towards others, playing their part as an effective enabler and leader. By recognising the differing qualities, needs and aspirations of those around us, we can begin to assist them to value their strengths in becoming part of the team and providing support to others. In summary (modified from the first edition of this book), a mentor has the following characteristics:

Core enabling characteristics – a mentor:

- Motivates individuals to set their own agenda for working and learning
- Provides safe opportunities for critical reflection
- Advises, counsels and guides on personal, professional and career matters
- Assists the mentee to learn through their successes and failures
- Is an effective role model
- Recognises and supports the mentee's strengths
- Develops capabilities by offering constructive feedback.

Specific enabling characteristics – a mentor:

- Is supportive and encouraging
- Helps identify resources for learning and career socialisation
- Is challenging and acts as a critical friend
- Encourages creativity and risk taking in learning and working
- Assists the mentee to critically reflect on his/her personal and professional capabilities.

Qualities for attracting a mentor

Mentoring always concerns two interested parties, with the abilities to form and sustain a working relationship. Although the qualities and skills that a mentor possesses are vital to the nature and effectiveness of the ensuing relationship, the qualities of a mentee also come into play when considering the unfolding of the resulting relationship. The essential ingredients and basic roles to be undertaken are also influenced by the qualities, skills and characteristics of the mentee. Indeed there are those who suggest that there are identifiable strategies that can be employed in attracting a mentor (Zey, 1984, p. 175; Holloway and Whyte, 1994). Qualities that endeavour to make a mentee potentially 'attractive' to a mentor include:

Standing out of the crowd:

- Achieving high visibility
- Having a positive attitude to work or career
- Willing to take risks
- Commitment to own development.

Demonstrating the potential to succeed:

- Willingness to learn and assist the mentor to achieve goals
- Having initiative and motivation
- Ambitious and conscientious
- Receptive to coaching, advice and support.

Adult intimacy capabilities:

- Having a positive self esteem
- Able to make a personal contribution
- Loyal to individuals and the organisation
- Enlightened and enthusiastic
- Making oneself accessible
- Able to make a personal contribution
- Willingness to develop a relationship with the mentor.

Benefits and limitations of mentoring

The benefits

Evidence in the literature suggests that the positive effects are mutually split to benefit the mentor, mentee and organisation (Zey, 1984; Cooper, 1990; Freeman 1997). The strengths and benefits of mentoring arise from the attraction, sharing and developing properties of the relationship. The beneficial effects can be related to degrees of satisfaction for those involved:

- *The mentor:* personal satisfaction and professional development from aiding and abetting another's development
- *The mentee:* professional identity and increased job satisfaction with the possibilities of advancement and success as they become socialised to the organisation
- *The organisation:* a satisfied and motivated workforce with positive outcomes for customers and clients.

Other benefits concern leadership development as the qualities and abilities associated with effective mentoring are synonymous with good leadership. Mentoring can assist in developing leaders, with mentees looked on as emerging leaders, cultivated for their flexibility, adaptability, sound. judgement and creativity within an organisation. If mentoring is appropriately recognised as part of the organisational culture, working relationships are very likely to be more open and effective. Such openness improves communication and encourages a greater degree of collegiality and general sharing approaches.

Finally, thoughts should be directed towards the possible constraining factors that may inhibit mentoring from occurring, even if formal programmes of contract mentoring are organised.

The limitations

The limitations to mentoring are perhaps best described by the use of the term toxic mentoring, identified by Darling (1986) and discussed earlier in this chapter. Toxic mentoring concerns the disabling elements and strategies that may be employed by an ineffective mentor and these should be avoided at all cost.

The essence of toxicity arises from a dysfunctional relationship that is not built on mutual trust, shared values or reciprocity. In a toxic relationship the mentee is directed not facilitated, and ultimately disabled rather than enabled or supported. Toxic mentoring can take the form of an exploitative, manipulative relationship, the 'Queen bee, worker-drone syndrome' illustrated by Hawkins and Thibodeau (1989). The features of toxic mentoring are:

- The mentor uses the mentee and does not promote the mentee's ideas, taking any credit due
- Some recognition of a partnership but the mentor uses the mentee's abilities to further their own career and standing in the organisation
- The power in the relationship may remain with the mentor, resulting in mentee manipulation, over-protection, increased dependency, and lack of development
- Control and excessive direction causing the mentee to conform to an identical set image of the mentor, resulting in cloning
- Elitism and mutual seclusion causing the mentee to withdraw from other relationships and become dependent on the mentor.

Strategies for avoiding toxic mentors

(1) Self select a classical mentor or if offered a mentor programme, choose a mentor who is interested and who you can work with

(2) Do not choose an individual who is a disabler

(3) Examine the relationship regularly for signs of toxicity – cloning, dependency, mentor self-interest, manipulation or exploitation

(4) Monitor personal development and prepare a sound, appropriate end to the relationship

(5) Be prepared to eject from a mentor who is showing signs of toxicity

(6) Ensure that the person chosen as a mentor is successful and 'going places' in the organisation.

Recognition of the benefits and limitations of mentoring facilitates a better understanding of what mentoring is all about and allows a healthy dialogue to commence regarding the salient issues that may arise.

Constraints to mentoring

Although personnel newly appointed to an organisation may have the necessary personal qualities for becoming a mentor, they are unlikely to have the networking contacts to provide for effective mentoring. As they settle to the organisation culture they will initially lack power, experience and possibly influence within the organisation. Research by Earnshaw (1995, p. 278) found stress was a problem for staff nurses who were expected to be mentors to students while they were 'trying to establish themselves professionally'.

Other constraints to effective mentoring – particularly classical mentoring – are working cultures where there is a rigid hierarchy or where disabling strategies prevail and there is subsequently a lack of collegiality and trust. Clutterbuck (1985) further identifies problems in organisations where heavy politics are evident, staff turnover is high and morale is poor, all acting as deterrents to effective mentoring.

Mentoring limitations of working cultures where women make up the majority of the workforce, and how this affects the existence of mentoring, are well documented by writers exploring the nature of mentoring (May *et al.,* 1982, p.27; Hardy, 1984). It is important to note that in nursing, midwifery and other professional groups where the majority of the working population is female, there remain issues of gender and professional identification to be taken into account (Davies, 1995).

Women's working image and self-esteem along with the training and education of women in professional groups, and their socialisation into vocational work, have to be further explored and researched. Whilst there is evidence for constraints, such as women having to make it alone and having little time or effort left to support others, there is growing evidence that women do indeed identify with the need to support and bring others along as they make their way though corporate and professional environments, (Segerman-Peck, 1991; Conway, 1996).

Others suggest that women do help and support each other, even if they do not formally recognise this assistance as mentoring (Vance, 1979). Although not always recognising or fully appreciating the networking qualities of the processes involved, Sheehy (1976, p. 34), reported that 'women who haven't had a mentor relationship miss it, even if they don't know what to call it'. The confusion about mentoring over the years has added to the difficulties of role recognition and this comment could now apply equally well to men.

However, when considering women and mentoring, it is important to appreciate the issues of language, organisational context and sexual stereotyping in formulating, reflecting and reinforcing ideologies of gender (Demarco, 1993; Parsons, 1993). Formal mentoring programmes constructed from business orientated models may indeed offer a foundation for design but should be adapted to readily encompass the working needs of women in health care.

Contemplating such issues leads us to the need to consider the effective development and implementation of mentoring programmes that capture the richness of the relationship. It is now appropriate that we consider mentoring in action. The early part of this chapter focused particularly on the nature of the classical mentor and how this has been translated through history and by differing organisational challenges and demands. In considering the application of mentoring in practice it is necessary to contemplate the more structured systems and processes that exist in the form of formal or contract (facilitated) mentoring.

Formal mentoring: devising a mentor programme

In setting up a mentor programme, with the notion of providing formal or contract mentoring in the workplace with formal mentors or contract mentors, it is important to appreciate the complexities involved. Whether the decision is made to build your own programme or buy in a 'ready made, adapted to fit your needs programme' the groundwork has to be thorough and the intentions clear if the venture is to be a success. For diagrammatic representation of a workable model for practice see Figure 3, which presents an overview; Figure 4 illustrates the processes involved.

Design deliberations should include:

- The type of mentoring approaches to be employed
- Resource allocation
- Mentor-mentee preparation and support
- Effective evaluation.

Resources and approaches

Resources and approaches will depend on the requirements of the organisation, what is available and the commitment of senior staff for this type of support development. A general shift towards an appreciation that a learning culture is good for staff, customers and business has led to manufacturers providing increased resources for staff development (Ball, 1992). Those interested in developing mentoring programmes within the health service can draw on the experiences of these other organisations to convince managers that effective investment in sound programmes will have an impact on staff with the ultimate aim of improving patient/client care. There is increasing evidence that mentoring is effective as part of a recognisable staff development programme and benefits working relationships (Kelly, 1992; Mumford, 1998).

Sensible resource decisions also require consideration of the types of approaches to be used. It is uneconomical to devise intricate formal mentoring structures with extensive mentor preparation if what is required is staff induction and orientation. Of course these elements can be incorporated into the contract mentoring role, but it will not be cost effective if the process required is someone to introduce new staff or acclimatise those who are returning to work. Practical induction and orientation processes can be readily incorporated into existing management roles.

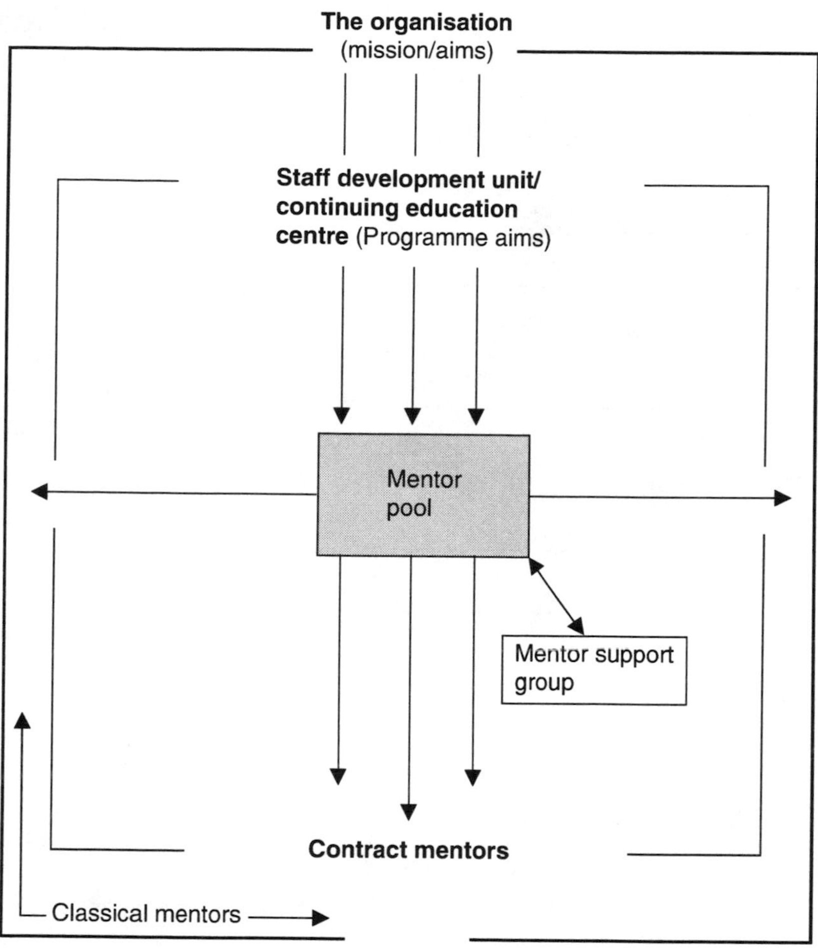

Figure 3 Mentoring – an overview of a workable model in practice

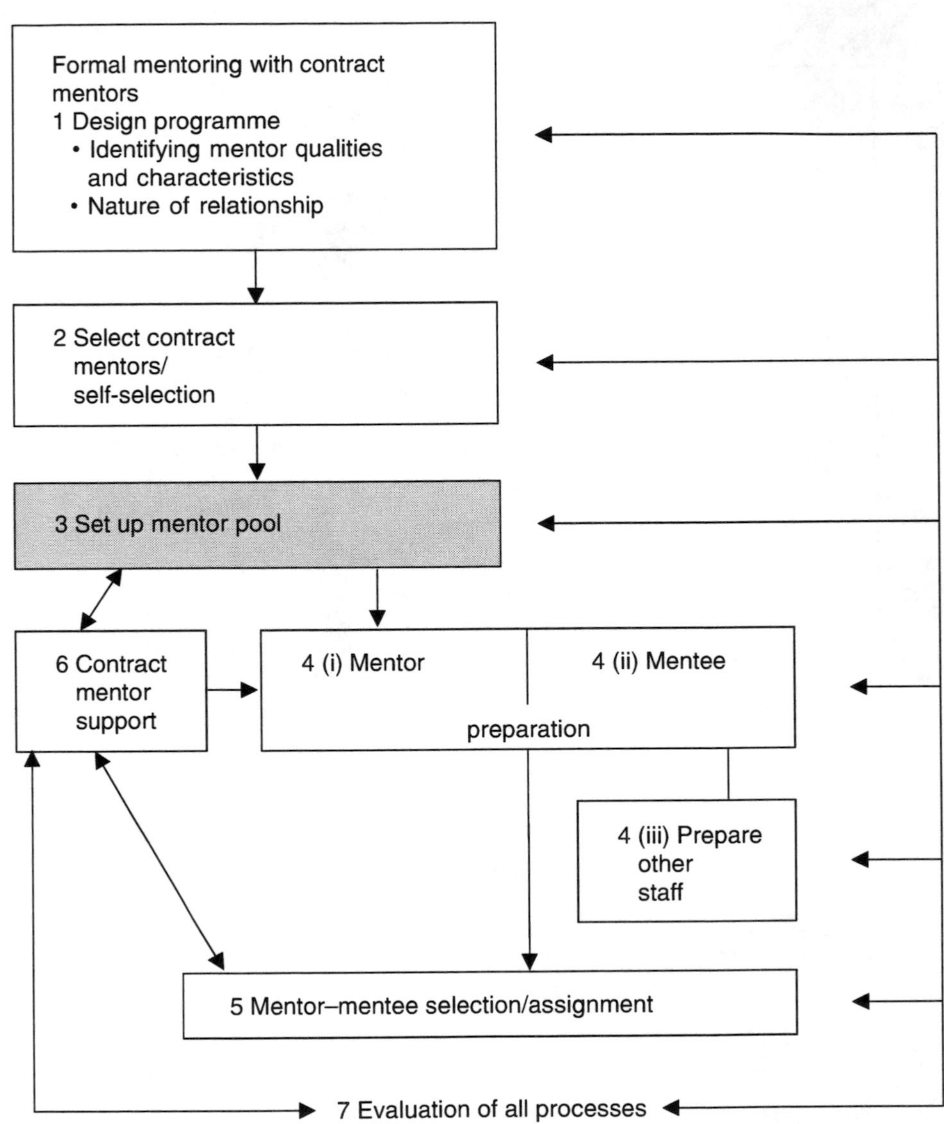

Figure 4 A workable model for practice: processes involved

Effective economies can be made by shared learning opportunities or by including mentor preparation in other programmes that focus on interpersonal, facilitation and enabling skills. Mentors, preceptors and clinical supervisors can be prepared together for part of a common programme, as long as the similar elements and differences are made very clear. This should work well in aiding understanding of each other's role. It will help to start the 'mutual respect and sharing philosophies' necessary to underpin such developments and to prevent the possibility of a 'hierarchy of roles' developing.

It is worth mentioning prepared mentor packages at this point as there are a variety of models available. We describe these as:

- *The Takeaway* – ready-made off the shelf; just add to your organisation or department
- *The Savile Row* – made-to-measure and tailored to your organisation's individual needs
- *The Pick and Mix* – selected from ready-made models and adapted to your individual preference.

When considering bought in, prepared or tailored mentoring packages there are important questions to consider:

(1) Are they flexible for the organisation's needs? Does the programme match with the mission, aims, philosophies, value systems and organisational culture?

(2) How are the mentors' roles and functions perceived? How does this fit in with existing support and development roles that already exist in the organisation?

(3) What are the cost implications of buying and then running the programme?

(4) Is programme evaluation included and how does it operate?

(5) Can a sound, cost-effective programme be prepared within the organisation or is consultation required?

Mentor-mentee preparation and support

This remains a developing area with the type, duration of preparation and resulting support networks for the mentors appearing as extremely varied. A range of formal programmes exists which can be seen to relate to a continuum, from those closely aligned to the characteristics of classical mentoring (Hernandez-Piloto Brito, 1992) to more formal functional structures where contracts are set and mentors assigned and monitored (Anworth, 1992) (see Figure 5): the continuum of informality and formality. Preparing mentors remains a contentious subject and is an aspect of the process that would benefit from further research and perhaps case studies to illuminate the processes involved in adequate preparation. Fish (1995, p. 30), in identifying mentor education for what she calls 'quality' mentors in education, makes the point that preparation should include consideration of rights and responsibilities; awareness of partnership agreements and contractual obligations; and an understanding of articulating theory and practice, as well as the development of practice skills to assist the mentor. with forming an effective relationship. She suggests that this gives the mentors a sense that they have a 'new competence'.

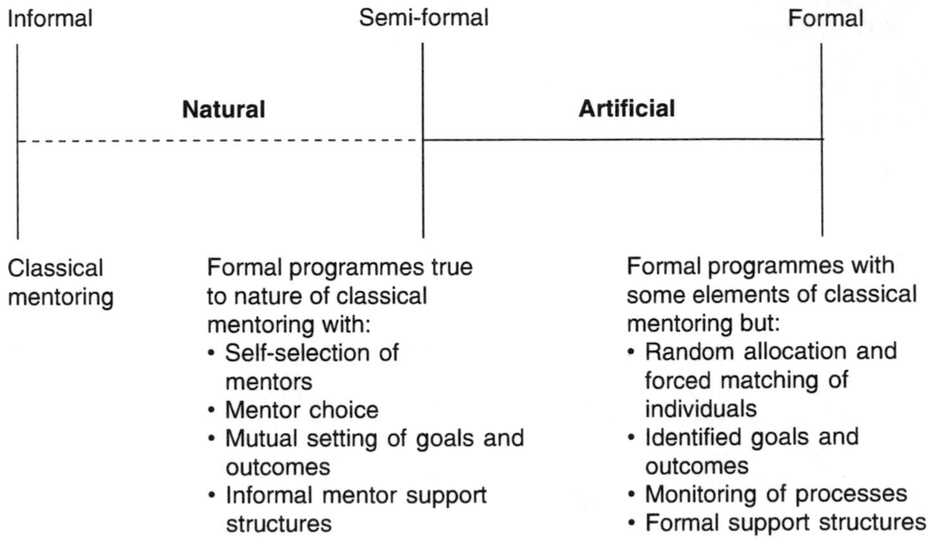

Figure 5 Mentoring: the continuum of informality and formality

In social work practice where mentoring is applied at the post qualifying level and is linked to the Advanced Award in Social Work, training for mentors is advocated and guidelines identified for the type of experience and qualifications required of those preparing for this essentially educational role. What separates this from other mentor training is the inclusion of the need to provide evidence from practice of anti-racist, anti-oppressive and anti-discriminatory practice. This goes further than other mentor programmes, where potential mentors have to demonstrate commitment to adult learning and continuing professional education, as well as capabilities of personal awareness, effective communication skills and sound abilities to relate to others.

The business organisation approach, where the mentor may have a more clearly defined role in relation to managing change and developing leaders and executives, offers useful case studies for mentor preparation. Slipais (1993) identifies a development process that combines in-house training, experience as an instructor, refresher sessions and formal advanced preparation which should include training skills, task analysis, communication skills, problem solving and decision-making (Slipais, 1993, pp. 134–5).

Other authors identify certificated preparation for mentorship and a variety of preparation approaches that range from the residential to day release or in-service programmes (Wilkin, 1992). In identifying a programme for preparing 'holistic mentors', Freeman (1998, p. 54) describes a scheme with introductory workshops to enable would be mentors 'to work freely and confidently at their task, maximising potential for their own professional task'. In preparing mentors using a collaborative learning approach, the GP mentors were encouraged through a series of reflective workshops to explore their understanding of role and develop effective enabling skills.

Despite the passing years and greater awareness of mentoring generally, the other main contentious issues remain those of mentor selection and mentor-mentee matching.

Mentor selection

As can be seen from the discussions on classical mentoring, it is important that the mentor is capable of the qualities, characteristics and skills inherent within an enabling role. Mentors are required to feel competent, confident and committed to taking part. Failures in the past of not building and maintaining relationships probably resulted from forced matching or random allocation of individual participants. This was true particularly, for example, in British nursing education, where staff irrespective of their experience or expertise were given mentoring responsibilities for a number of students at a time.

The statement 'appropriately qualified and experienced individual' appears to have become a popular way of identifying possible mentors and it is important to identify what is meant by such a broad statement. The term 'qualified' has formal and informal connotations in this context. It may be interpreted to mean that an individual has completed a recognisable training or education programme, or in its broadest sense it may relate to the capabilities of the mentor in terms of the personal qualities that they possess.

It is for the programme developers, educators, administrators and managers within a particular setting to clarify what is meant by 'appropriately qualified and experienced', and to state what they require from mentors. Clearly identified aims and a selected target audience for the preparation programme, with an appropriate definition of the characteristics and capabilities of the mentor, will assist successful implementation (Wilson, 1998).

The mentor pool

To assist in making informed selections a mentor pool may be needed and this should be identified early in the programme deliberations. A mentor pool is a group of people with appropriate qualities, abilities and experience to take on the rigours and complexities of mentoring. Ideally, this pool should consist of volunteers who are aware of the nature of mentoring (by personal experience or identified criteria), and who are prepared to become committed to a formal programme and its aims.

Setting identified criteria and 'trawling' for mentors can take a variety of forms: some programmes have involved marketing techniques (Hernandez-Piloto Brito, 1992); others ask for volunteers, or prospective mentors are chosen/volunteered by their managers. Being chosen or volunteered has potential drawbacks, minimised if consultation and negotiation take place between all those involved. Being volunteered for mentor selection particularly increases the risks of toxic mentoring, mismatching of individuals and personality clashes (Palmer, 1986).

Mentor-mentee matching

Mentor-mentee matching will remain contentious until there is sufficient evidence to demonstrate whether freedom to choose or forced matching of mentors provides the best method for assigning mentees. Access to a mentor pool allows individuals to make some form of selection, and this process is assisted if the members of the pool prepare brief mentor-biographies of professional and personal experiences. These identify their main interests, work experiences and the helper functions they can offer a potential mentee.

Time will need to be set aside within the programme for facilitated sessions where the mentors and mentees can meet for introductions, the sharing of relevant biographies and setting guidelines for the relationship. The informal meetings that arise from these initial discussions can then be left to the individuals concerned to arrange, supported if necessary by an identified mentor coordinator or facilitator.

Effective criteria, appropriate selection and time allocated for 'making the match' should ensure that freedom to choose does indeed occur. Issues of mentor-mentee ratios can tax the uninitiated; however, taking into consideration the time, effort and commitment required, it is suggested that a mentor should not have more than two mentees at any one time.

It is also important to build workshop sessions into a programme, to follow up on any mentors who may be disappointed in not being selected. This may be important with the development of such a new initiative and where mentors may well be selected or proposed by their managers. Until the parameters have been tested and flexibly set, it may be the case that people will be asked to attend a mentor course, by managers and administrators, in order to gain enabling skills – rather in the traditional manner of being sent on communication courses to learn how to communicate! It needs to be stressed to all concerned that this is not the aim of mentor programmes.

This should become less of a problem as mentoring becomes a better understood concept and as selection criteria are more adequately addressed. Complementary, enabling programmes can be devised and worked into a framework of continuing professional education that will feed into appropriate support role programmes to inform other staff who may be involved only indirectly.

The programme

The essence of mentor preparation involves an exploration of the nature of mentoring, the processes, benefits and limitations. Programme aims, strategies, content and outcomes will vary considerably depending on the needs of the organisation and the personnel involved. It is important that the programme has clear, well-defined outcomes as it should facilitate:

- An understanding of support within continuing professional development
- The clarification of new roles and support frameworks
- Opportunities to enhance enabling skills in relation to the helper functions

- Feedback on individual performance
- Opportunities for shared learning
- Networks of personal support and guidance
- Understanding of toxic strategies and possible role conflict
- An understanding of how mentoring fits within the organisation.

Many care workers and professionals in the health field already have preparation containing elements of this type of programme. What needs to be stressed, however, is the need to refocus on certain attitudes and skills to include coaching, consultation and feedback that may not be readily apparent in other continuing professional education programmes. It is also crucial to the effectiveness of such a programme that the aims, teaching, facilitating and support strategies should be congruent with the open, enabling philosophy of this type of relationship. It is also important that programme aims or philosophies match those of the organisation, as previously discussed.

There is no universally agreed length of programme and some mentor preparation has been included in statutory teaching and assessing courses. This usually involves the allotment of two hours or an afternoon to discover the complexities of mentoring. Tuck (1993) very briefly outlines a two day training course for mentors and their 'clients' that relates reflective activities to curriculum skills and the interpersonal skills of mentoring. Other programmes have been devised to incorporate a series of workshop days to facilitate a better understanding; however, suggestions have been made that a basic training of five days is appropriate to provide more time for the actual processes (Wright, 1990; Kelly *et al.,* 1991; Palmer, 1998).

Evidence has emerged regarding the implementation and evaluation of mentoring programmes and formal mentoring approaches based on assigning contract mentors. *The Mentor's Task: Main Activities and Standards,* prepared by the Oxford Brookes University and Oxford Health Authority, is documented in Heslop and Lathlean (1991, p.113).

An investigation into the development and running of an initial teacher training (ITT course mentor programme is analysed by Corbett and Wright (1993). Their two year, school-based ITT programme involved asking head teachers to select a teacher to act as a mentor for those on the course. Mentors were offered financial reward and some freeing of their time by one half day per week supply cover. Certain issues surfaced as the study progressed, including:

- The crucial role of the head teacher in setting the mentor culture
- The teacher's development was linked to the development of the mentor
- Certain groups of individuals appeared better suited to provide the mentor role; these were identified as those new to teaching and those with more experience but with no senior management responsibilities
- Effective skills and approaches concerned areas of organisation, communication, counselling, supporting, monitoring, collaboration and problem solving

- A willingness to learn, develop and engage in learning were viewed as necessary attributes for mentor selection. Mentors needed to recognise change in their mentees, and to allow them to establish their own capabilities and responses
- Mentor training was found to be a restrictive term and mentor development better advised. Development should include broad range activities such as attending conferences, manager support, accredited study and informal mentor networks.

Respecting that it is not advisable to generalise from one study, it is interesting to note that this analysis goes some way towards validating previous deliberations. It offers evidence for the type of considerations and decisions to be made for those planning similar mentoring schemes. Regular follow-up sessions should be accommodated within each scheme to explore emerging issues as the mentoring relationships develop, and to provide support for each mentor.

Supporting the mentor

By providing effective preparation and in acknowledging the need for mentor support, mentors are able to make contact with each other and share the challenges that arise. Depending on the degree of formality of the structured programme on offer, they can build and develop their own networks. Highly experienced individuals of the calibre required to be effective mentors will already, as discussed earlier, have made themselves a niche in the organisation.

The need for recognisable and more structured methods of support for mentors has mainly arisen due to the indiscriminate use of this concept in some clinical areas. In classical mentoring, support should be negotiable and informal and the appropriate mechanisms developed by the mentors themselves. While formal mentoring may be more structured in approach, it is still the participating individuals who decide on the nature of the relationship and how it runs its course. This will allow them the freedom to identify and explore salient issues within a clear remit of respecting the confidentiality of the mentoring relationships.

Excessive formal structure with monitoring and feedback reflects traditional rigidity that is inappropriate for this type of enabling relationship or programme. Taking a rigid approach may deflect some of the intricate interactions from the mentor-mentee partnership and raise concerns regarding the maintenance of confidentiality and mutuality.

Evaluation

Evaluation plays an important part in professional practice and is an essential element in any new design process (Palmer and Wilson, 1997). Its importance in constructing formal mentoring programmes is significant because of the lack of empirical evidence and the confusion and contentious nature of the concept (McIntyre *et al.,* 1993; Maggs, 1994). Information obtained from sound evaluation techniques will aid future mentoring deliberations and developments.

A combination of quantitative and qualitative evaluation approaches is useful to illuminate the complexities of making formal programmes work in practice settings. Such studies should be set within the context of a realistic assessment of the resources available. This is elaborated by Puetz (1992) in her discussion of evaluation and staff development issues. A checklist for designing an evaluation of a programme has been formulated by Murray and Owen (1991, p. 172). In considering the appropriate approaches to be used, it is recommended that both the value to the individual and to the organisation should be included in any evaluation deliberations. For a very helpful discourse on evaluation and the issues that may arise, see Carter (1993).

Whatever evaluation methods are decided on, it is a useful technique when exploring this complexity of the relationship to record the experiences of those involved, and this is where qualitative research approaches can be beneficial in further illuminating the mentoring relationship in depth. Collecting narratives and asking individuals to record their reactions, expectations and feelings can only further our understanding of what remains a fascinating relationship. As Demarco (1993) urges, we should become conscious of our biases towards this type of relationship and explore the 'lived experience'.

The case studies that follow are offered to add to the richness of the discussion and encourage further reflection about this significant professional support role.

Reflection: mentoring case studies

These case studies are not intended to be fully representative, but to provide an outline of different types of mentoring relationships. Indeed, in two of the studies presented concerns are raised and mentoring does not appear to have occurred in the richness that is so often reported. Many informal and formal mentoring relationships are positive and develop (through the stages identified previously in this chapter) to become very useful and enabling for those involved. Presenting these practical applications allows some of the issues surrounding mentoring in practice to be highlighted and reflected on.

As you read through the studies you might like to identify relevant issues that you feel are important in relation to what has been discussed in this chapter and your own experiences of mentoring. If you identify a significant relationship that had or has the elements of classical or contract mentoring, you could ask yourself the following questions, recording your deliberations in your portfolio/reflective journal or whatever you use to capture your experiences and reflections:

- What personal qualities did the person have that attracted you to him/her?
- How did they help or support?
- Why did you want to work with, or learn from him/her?

Reflection: What is emerging from this information and how will it help you build significant relationships in the future?

The new community midwife nurse

Chris is a very experienced community midwife in her early 30s. She is keen, quick thinking and considered by those around her as a good manager, being well liked and respected by both peers and the women she is responsible for. She enjoys teaching and, 'seeing those around me settle in, obtain midwifery experience and get on'.

When Pauline, a new community midwife joins the district, Chris elects to orientate her and the two of them 'hit it off immediately'. Pauline is a mature woman who has returned to community midwifery, 'after taking time out to have the children'. Despite the obvious age gap, Chris senses 'something of myself in Pauline's attitudes and responses to her work with the mothers and babies.

They get on well together during Pauline's orientation period, with Chris interested in sharing her experience of the busy district. When work loads and team commitments allow, the two spend time discussing their cases and experiences. Pauline is quick to learn, respects Chris' judgment and shows a willingness to become involved in all aspects of midwifery in the community. They remain good working companions and although Pauline appears eager to meet more often, they manage to meet only infrequently because of the changing nature of community care and differing shift patterns. Chris makes time but gradually meeting together becomes a rare event. Chris is disappointed that the opportunities to share good practice and discuss 'our ideas for the future of midwifery have become less and less, as we pass like two ships in the night'.

Newly qualified and moving on

Sue is 26 years old and a student midwife. Her most recent post was as a registered nurse on a renal surgical ward at the hospital that she trained in. As a third year she did well on this particular placement and found she liked and respected the ward sister, Carol Williams. On qualifying she asked to go back there to staff and 'to learn, about looking after patients with renal problems and ward organisation'.

Sister Williams was much older than Sue and nearing retirement but had lost none of her keenness for caring for patients and making them comfortable in hospital. She was always the first to arrive on an early shift and the last to leave on a late one, despite having a family and social commitments. As Sue explains, 'She was part of the old school and I admired her for her personal abilities and nursing skills; she was always willing to share her experiences and spend time with me'. During the first year the sound, easy-going relationship continued. Sue was quick to learn and Sister Williams, whilst not singling her out from the other team members for extra support, encouraged and spent time with her. Sue felt trusted to 'run things when Sister wasn't there', and she grew in self-confidence and became more competent in her abilities to handle difficult situations.

Towards the end of the second year, Sue began to get restless as her friends and colleagues discussed different courses and plans for travelling. She shared her thoughts with Sister who had always been ready to listen and counsel in the past. However it was different this time and 'I soon became aware that she didn't want to know about me moving on or doing my midwifery which is what I had always planned to do'. Sue went ahead and applied and was accepted for a midwifery programme in the autumn. She was unprepared for Sister's negative response to the news, and despite maintaining a semblance of cordiality whilst working together for the remainder of her notice, Sue and Sister never really spoke again. Sue left the ward without saying goodbye, 'as Sister changed her day off and didn't attend my leaving party'.

Mature and keen to care

Peter is a physiotherapy student. He has had numerous jobs and spent the last few years as an air traffic controller. He decided to become a physiotherapist after caring for a relation following a road traffic accident. He is one of only three mature students on his course and the only male student. He is enjoying the course and gets on well with his peers, although he sometimes gets 'frustrated by their lack of life experience and flippant attitudes to serious concerns'. He is doing well academically and as the course has a formal mentor scheme he is assigned a mentor for his first clinical placement, which he is looking forward to.

Elizabeth is a bright, articulate, eager to teach individual who is younger than Peter. She volunteered for the hospital mentor scheme and enjoys 'the one-to-one relationship with a colleague, teaching and advising them and seeing them develop as they come to terms with what is expected of them as a student and finally a qualified physiotherapist'. Initially Peter and Elizabeth appear to 'hit it off', but gradually Elizabeth becomes aware that Peter does not readily seek her company. He appears to meet with her reluctantly, and only when she suggests they get together to discuss his progress in the clinical placements and on the course. Over several months, with little progress in the relationship and tensions on both sides, Peter asks his personal tutor if he can change mentors and choose his own this time.

The teacher and mentoring comparisons

Amy is a teacher and she has had 'two significant mentoring relationships', as she puts it, in her career as a teacher. She is currently a faculty head in a department for children with special needs, having moved from Expressive Arts recently. When she started as a young teacher she formed a mutually supportive relationship with the head of her department. They got on well, sharing the same views on teaching and had a similar sense of humour. They worked very well together and Amy found that Jan helped her settle into her new teaching role, as well as helping her to learn about how the school worked. In the early stages of the relationship Amy found that she relied on Jan for her considerable expertise and extensive knowledge. In return Amy would share her ideas and was happy to take on the projects that Jan put her way.

When Jan left to take up a senior teacher's post in a neighbouring community college, it was mutually agreed that Amy would move to the same college as there was a vacant post at a higher incentive allowance. To Amy it seemed 'a sensible option and there was also the possibility of promotion and of course Jan was going too'. After a successful interview, Amy joined the Expressive Arts Faculty.

In the new college Amy settled in well and her relationship with Jan 'continued much as before'. However after several months Amy became aware that Jan, who initially shared ideas and appeared keen to promote their joint work and projects, was changing. In the new setting Jan 'was now taking my ideas and putting them forward as her own; she even presented a paper at an INSET day that I had written, without acknowledging me. I felt I was doing all the hard work, but kept in the background'. Amy attempted to talk this over with Jan with little effect.

Amy left to head a faculty in a different school at the beginning of the new term. She now feels settled and is experiencing a much more positive working relationship with a deputy head, that is supportive and enabling. 'I feel I'm developing in an equal power relationship, able to be me and getting credited with what I do best.' She feels she can be creative, share her ideas and has something to offer her new mentor and faculty.

Classical mentoring: positive returns

Karen was a young occupational therapist when she first joined the faculty of health sciences at a new London University. She had always enjoyed the clinical aspects of occupational therapy (OT) but had always been drawn to teaching, 'interested in sharing her knowledge and clinical expertise'. She completed a postgraduate certificate in education at the university and then joined the staff, as a lecturer. Karen is an outgoing, affable person who has a keen sense of fun and a deep commitment to her chosen profession.

Following the first year in her lecturing post she remained undecided about a career in higher education and felt 'the loss of my clinical identity; I missed the patients, clients and team work'. She found working with the students rewarding but experienced difficulties in settling into what was a 'rather traditional department with old fashioned approaches to teaching and learning at a time when educational methods were advancing'.

Karen's attempts at introducing problem-based learning to one of her courses were met with resistance by other members of the department. She was feeling unsettled when a chance, informal meeting with the head of the department, Edwina, altered her perspective. Edwina was a visionary, extremely capable with an encouraging, honest manner and she did not take herself too seriously despite her position and stature in the OT world. Edwina spoke of the changes and the dilemmas that were occurring as new approaches and methods were considered in OT. She spoke of her commitment to developing education initiatives that would benefit the students and their patients and assist staff to come to terms with the challenges in education and health. This 'sounded like a blueprint for a better future and I could identify with that', Karen remembers afterwards.

Following their initial meeting Edwina invited Karen to join a faculty working party to develop a new curriculum. Over a period Karen found herself more and more involved in the affairs of the department and taking increasing responsibility for new projects. This led to more settled feelings and 'a renewed sense of purpose; I felt as if a new wider world had opened up and I felt very much a part of it'.

The relationship with Edwina was developing positively and Karen found she could discuss issues with her and on the occasions 'when I put my foot in it and got things wrong, I was assisted to see the error of my ways without being made to feel insignificant; I could be creative and take some risks but as time went on the risks and mistakes reduced as Edwina and I became tuned in'. When the principal lecturer's post was advertised Karen felt confident to apply and despite strong external opposition, impressed the panel with her abilities.

Following this senior appointment she found herself working more closely with Edwina, observing her style of management and leadership qualities at first hand. As their relationship developed, and was openly acknowledged as that of classical mentoring, Karen began to specifically choose the assistance she needed. 'At first I wanted anything Edwina had to offer, it was exciting and stimulating, but as time went on I felt confident to make choices. I asked to be sponsored for a course and I began to know instinctively when I needed counselling or just wanted advice.' With Edwina's support, Karen joined the College of OT as a regional council member. She began to play a part in exploring wider concerns of the profession: 'Edwina opened up a new world to me by asking me to join committees and ultimately, as our respect and trust grew, I began to take her place at certain meetings.' Karen found that they worked out ideas together in a relationship where challenges and tensions could be met head on and strategies devised for success.

After seven years Karen knew it was time to move on: 'I felt capable of taking a leadership role for myself.' Together they explored the possibilities of future job prospects and Karen felt that at the start Edwina was rather reticent at the thought of her moving on: 'She would mention a post, leave the job description on my desk and say don't think about it too long'. Talking over the proposed move together made it more real and Karen's reflections of this period suggest that it was a time of excitement at the prospects of new horizons but sadness as a chapter closed in her working life. 'I felt I was getting ahead now and Edwina admitted that sometimes she felt she was following in my footprints instead of leading the way.'

Finally, after Edwina and Karen discovered the same post in separate advertisements, they knew this was the time to move on. Karen successfully applied for the head of school's post at a northern university. She is now a nationally respected figure representing OT at the highest levels. Edwina has now retired but they remain in regular contact and have become firm friends who still like nothing better than 'getting together to discuss OT issues and the changes that lie ahead'.

Case studies: the issues

Sue and Sister Williams built up a good relationship that started when Sue went originally to the ward in her final year of her education programme. They had a mutual interest in their chosen speciality and common commitments to patient care and ward management. What starts for Sue as admiration and role modelling is extended to a more rounded, enabling relationship as Sister gives time to her and shares her clinical expertise. Sue is willing to learn and with her motivation and interest in the ward, she becomes a worthwhile partner in caring for the patients. It is readily apparent that mutual admiration and respect has developed.

Problems occur when Sue wishes to move on. Sister is possessive and not ready to let go. She is nearing retirement and possibly fears the changes that will result when Sue leaves. She has also invested time and effort into the relationship, and careful negotiation and a gradual separation are required in this type of situation. Although it may appear in classical mentoring, mentor possessiveness is a more common criticism offered by mentees in more formal mentoring programmes. Feelings of being trapped can occur when the mentee is submissive and unable to remove themselves from what they see as a claustrophobic situation. In both types of mentoring, making both individuals fully aware of the processes and phases of mentoring can go some way towards preventing this difficulty and allowing endings to be more positive. As it is, Sue was unable to resolve the situation and was unprepared for Sister William's distancing behaviour; the relationship ends negatively without the rewards of maintaining contact and friendship.

Pauline is returning to midwifery in the community and although having to face new challenges she is a mature individual. She may well know her own mind at this time of her life or indeed may not recognise the need for support at this stage. Chris and Pauline are mutually attracted, and seemingly get on and work well together. Chris is apparently sending out mentor signals but these are not being picked up by Pauline as she settles into the rigours of busy midwifery life. Work commitments, lack of regular contact and different shift systems are inhibiting the natural processes of mentoring. Although Chris has been helpful in orientating Pauline and assisting her to settle in her new post, there is no time to build on the mutual attraction and respect that has initially occurred. Chris appears ready to mentor and it is highly probable that she will continue to send out signals that will be eventually taken up when an appropriate individual and right circumstances prevail.

Peter is a mature student and has been assigned a mentor, in this case a younger female who is keen to help him in his first placement. Peter may be well aware of his needs and we do not know how he has been prepared for the mentoring experience. Sound preparation, with time allotted to get properly acquainted, assist potential mentees to set realistic expectations.

Peter's case raises issues of cross-gender mentoring and although not identified in this chapter, there are other implications when contract mentoring involves individuals from differing cultures and ethnic groups. Cross-gender mentoring is extensively covered in business and can be associated with sexual liaisons either actual or implied by others, who may well be motivated by favouritism or jealousy. The possibility of sexual tensions and attractions between individuals of different or the same sex should be acknowledged in initial mentor orientation, and the outcomes and complications discussed openly.

Risks of personality clashes can occur when mentors are assigned and a mismatch of personalities occurs. From the author's own research and personal experience, if an assigned mentor is not seen to be meeting the needs of the assigned mentee and if there is any dissatisfaction or hostility, then the mentee will seek a more appropriate individual and set up informal mentoring networks elsewhere. These often run parallel to those planned and directed by the staff educators. We do not know what preparation Peter has had or his expectations for this type of relationship, but he draws our attention to issues of choice in selecting a mentor. It is also important to consider Elizabeth's preparation and experience of mentoring; she may have only been assigned younger or female students previously.

Amy and Jan's case illustrates potential power relationships in mentoring which may evoke similar reactions and endings to those between Sue and Sister Williams. In this situation, Jan with her charisma and winning ways could be seen as enticing the initially submissive Amy. In negative terms, Jan is using her to further her own development and career. Mutuality has ceased and the power balance has shifted towards that of meeting the needs of a powerful, controlling mentor.

Amy, in changing jobs, moves the focus from that of her own needs and development to that of maintaining Jan's credibility in the new college. This study presents us with an example of the 'queen bee/worker drone syndrome': if one party remains submissive and readily supplies the 'queen bee', the two can advance through the hierarchy together until circumstances cause them to fall out or drift apart. In this example, Amy is able to recognise what is happening and is very capable in acting quickly to get herself out of the situation. She is then able to commence a new relationship with the deputy head in the new college. This relationship is much more aligned to that of true classical mentoring. Amy experiences none of the toxicity of the previous encounter and is able to feel confident in sharing in more collaborative surroundings.

The last case demonstrates the positive aspects of classical mentoring in terms of the natural nature of the collaboration – the mutual rewards and the longevity as the two individuals start to trust, share and respect each other. This is similar in essence to the supportive and enabling relationship that Amy, in the previous case, has begun at her new school. Karen's commitment and need for change are recognised by her senior colleague. A relationship develops that assists Karen to sort out her feelings about her career, to become involved in departmental initiatives and to rehearse areas of learning that facilitate an awareness of her own abilities.

In the early stages of the relationship Karen notes the need for any type of support and is not discerning in selecting what she requires. However, as the mutual trust, honesty, communication and respect build, she becomes more confident to choose the assistance she requires. Karen is well aware of the risks she takes and the development that occurs. The personal guidance offered is such that she maintains her self-esteem and confidence, as well as being encouraged to learn from less positive events. Karen is able to develop her own professional identity constructively, eventually leading to her taking a significant leadership role in her chosen profession. Edwina in her retirement, can feel satisfied that she played a part in Karen's success and that she has left her profession in capable hands.

These cases have demonstrated a range of issues and I am sure that you will have identified others within the examples given and from contemplation of your own experiences. It is only by illuminating mentoring in its many forms and by understanding how it works in practice, that we will be able to provide adequate programmes of preparation in the future. A clearer understanding of this intriguing subject will go some way towards removing the scepticism and negative effects that may arise from using the concept inappropriately and with little thought. Effective programmes and better understanding will also assist in encouraging those qualified practitioners wanting to become mentors to view mentoring as a recognition of their qualities, approachability and professionalism and not as a 'right'.

References

Alliott R J (1966) Facilitating mentoring in general practice. *British Medical Journal.* Career focus series. 28 September, 1996.

Anworth P (1992) Mentors, not assessors. *Nurse Education Today* 12 (4): 299–302.

Anderson E M, Shannon A L (1995) Towards a conceptualization of mentoring. In: T Kerry, A S Shelton Mayes (eds) *Issues in Mentoring.* Routledge, London.

Armitage P, Burnard P (1991) Mentors or preceptors? Narrowing the theory-practice gap. *Nurse Education Today* 11 (3): 225–229.

Ashton P, Richardson G (1992) Preceptorship and PREPP. *British Journal of Nursing* 1 (3): 143–146.

Ball C (1992) The learning society. *Royal Society of Arts Journal* May: 380–394.

Barlow S (1991) Impossible dream. *Nursing Times* 87 (1): 53–54.

Blotnick S R (1984) With friends like these. *Savvy* 10: 45–52.

Bould J (1996) *Getting it Right: Mentoring in Medicine. The Practical Guide.* University of Leeds. CCDU, Training & Consultancy.

Boydell D (1994) Relationships and feelings: the affective dimension to mentoring in primary school. *Mentoring and Tutoring* 2 (2): 37–44.

Boydell D, Bines H (1994) Beginning teaching: the role of the mentor. *Education* 22: 29–33.

Brooks V, Sikes P (1997) *The Good Mentor Guide. Initial Teacher Education in Secondary* Schools. Open University Press, Buckingham.

Burnard P (1988) Self evaluation methods in nurse education. *Nurse Education Today* 8: 229–233.

Calkins E X, Arnold L M, Willoughby T L (1987) Perceptions of the role of a faculty supervisor or 'mentor' at two medical schools. *Assessment and Evaluation in Higher Education* 12 (3): 202–208.

Campbell-Heider N (1986) Do nurses need mentors? *IMAGE: Journal of Nursing Scholarship* 18 (3): 110–113.

Cantor L M, Roberts I F (1986) *Further Education Today. A Critical Review*, 3rd edn. Routledge, Kegan Paul, London.

Carter E M A (1993) Measuring the returns. In: B J Coldwell, E M A Carter (eds) *The Return, of the Mentor. Strategies for Workplace Learning.* Falmer Press, London.

CCETSW (1992) *The Requirements for Post Qualifying Education & Training in the Personal Social Services: A Framework for Continuing Professional Development.* Paper 31 revised education. Central Council for Education & Training in Social Work, London.

Clutterbuck D (1985) *Everybody Needs A Mentor – How To Further Talent Within An Organisation.* The Institute of Personnel Management, London.

Collins E G C, Scott P (1978) Everybody who makes it has a mentor. *Harvard Business Review* July/August: 89–102.

Community Care (1998) Social exclusion – stand by me. *Community Care* 29 January–4 February: 18–19.

Conway C (1996) Strategic role of mentoring. *Professional Manager* September.

Cooper M D (1990) Mentorship: the key to the future of professionalism in nursing. *Journal of Perinatal Neonatal Nursing* 4 (3): 71–77.

Corbett P, Wright D (1993) Issues in the selection and training of mentors for school-based primary teacher training. In: D McIntyre, H Hagger, M Wilkin (eds) *Mentoring: Perspectives on School-based Teacher Education*, pp. 220–233. Kogan Page, London.

Cray D, Mallory G R (1998) *Making Sense of Managing Culture.* Thomson Business Press, London.

Darling L A W (1984) What do nurses want in a mentor? *Journal of Nursing Administration* 14 (10): 42–44.

Darling L A W (1986) What to do about toxic mentors. *Nurse Educator* 11 (2): 29–30.

Davies C (1995) *Gender and the Professional Predicament in Nursing.* Open University Press, Buckingham.

Demarco R (1993) Mentorship: a feminist critique of current research. *Journal of Advanced Nursing* 18 (1): 1242–1250.

Department for Education (1992) *New Criteria and Proceeds for Accreditation of Courses of Initial Teacher Training.* Circular 9/92. HMSO, London.

DoH (1997) *The New NHS: Modern – Dependable.* Department of Health, London.

Earnshaw G J (1995) Mentorship: the student's views. *Nurse Education Today* 15: 274–279.

ENB (1987) *Institutional and Course Approval/Reapproval Process, Information Required – Criteria and Guidelines,* 1987/28/MAT. English National Board, London.

ENB (1988) *Institutional and Course Approval/Reapproval Process, Information Required – Criteria and Guidelines.* 1988/39/APS. English National Board, London.

Eng S P (1986) Mentoring in principalship education. In: M A Owen, M Murray (eds) *Beyond the Myths and Magic of Mentoring. How to Facilitate an Effective Mentor Program.* Jossey-Bass, Oxford.

Fagan M M, Walter G (1982) Mentoring among teachers. *Journal of Educational Research* 76 (2): 113–118.

Fields W L (1991) Mentoring in nursing: a historical approach. *Nursing Outlook* Nov/Dec: 257–261.

Fish D (1995) *Quality Mentoring for Student Teachers. A Principled Approach to Practice.* D. Fullan Publishers, London.

Freeman R (1997) Mentoring in general practice. *Education for General Practice* 7: 112–17.

Freeman R (1998) *Mentoring in GP Practice.* Heinneman Butterworth, London.

George P, Kummerow J (1981) Mentoring for career women. *Training* 18 (2): 44, 46–49.

Glover D, Gough G, Johnson M, Mardle G, Taylor M (1994) Towards a taxonomy of mentoring. *Mentoring and Tutoring* 2 (2): 25–30.

Hagerty B (1986) A second look at mentors: do you really need one to succeed in nursing? *Nursing Outlook* 34 (1): 16–19, 24.

Hamilton M S (1981) Mentorhood, a key to nursing leadership. *Nursing Leadership* 4 (1): 4–13.

Handy C (1985) *Understanding Organisations.* Penguin Business, Harmondsworth.

Hardy L K (1984) The emergence of nurse leaders: in case of, in spite of, not because of. *International Nursing Review* 31 (1): 11–15.

Hawkins J W, Thibodeau J A (1989) *The Nurse Practitioner and Clinical Nurse Specialist. Current Practice Issues,* 2nd edn. The Tiresias Press Inc., New York.

Hawkins P, Shohet R (1989) *Supervision in the Helping Professions.* Open University Press, Buckingham.

Heirs B, Farrell P (1986) *The Professional Decision Thinker – Our New Management Priority*, 2nd edn. Garden City Press, Hertfordshire.

Hernandez-Pilot Brito H (1992) Nurses in action. An innovative approach to mentoring. *Journal of Nursing Administration* 22 (5): 23–28.

Heslop A, Lathlean J (1991) Teaching and learning. In: J Lathlean, J Corner (eds) *Becoming a Staff Nurse – A Guide to the Role of the Newly Registered Nurse*. Prentice Hall, London.

Holloran S D (1993) Mentoring. The experience of nursing service executives. *Journal of Advanced Nursing* 23 (2): 49–54.

Holloway A, Whyte C (1994) *Mentoring: The Definitive Handbook*. Development Processes (Publications)/Swansea College, Swansea.

Holt R (1982) An alternative to mentorship. *Adult Education* 55 (2): 152–156.

Hunt D, Michael C (1983) Mentorship. A career training development tool. *Academy of Management Review* 3: 475–485.

James Report (1972) *Teacher Education and Training*. HMS0, London.

Jarvis P, Gibson S (1997) *The Teacher-practitioner and Mentor in Nursing, Midwifery, Health Visiting and Social Services*. Stanley Thornes, Cheltenham.

Kelly K J (1992) *Nursing Staff Development. Current Competence Future Focus*. J B Lippincott, Philadelphia.

Kelly M, Beck T, Thomas J (1991) More than a supporting act. *The Times Educational Supplement* 8 November.

Klopf G J, Harrison J (1981) Moving up the career ladder, the case for mentors. *Principal* 61 (1): 41–43.

Knowles M S (1984) *Andragogy in Action: Applying Modern Principles of Adult Learning*. Jossey-Bass, San Francisco.

Kolb D A (1984) *Experiential Learning*. Prentice Hall, New Jersey.

Levinson D J, Darrow C N, Klein D B, Levinson M H, McKee B (1978) *The Season's of a Man's Life*. Knopf, New York.

MacPherson H (1997) Great talents ripen late. Continuing education in the acupuncture profession. *The European Journal of Oriental Medicine* 1 (6): 35–39.

McIntyre D (1994) Classrooms as learning environments for beginning teachers. In: M Wilkin, D Sankey (eds) *Collaboration and Transition in Initial Teacher Training*. Kogan Page, London.

McIntyre D, Hagger H, Wilkin M (1993) *Mentoring. Perspectives on School-based Teacher Education*. Kogan Page, London.

Maggs C (1994) Mentorship in nursing and midwifery education: issues for research. *Nurse Education Today* 14: 22–29.

May K M, Meleis A I, Winstead-Fry P (1982) Mentorship for scholarliness, opportunities and dilemmas. *Nursing Outlook* 30 (Jan): 22–28.

Merriam S (1993) Mentors and proteges; a critical review of the literature. *Adult Education Quarterly* 33 (3): 161–173.

Monaghan J, Lunt N (1992) Mentoring: person, process, practice and problems. *The British Journal Of Educational Studies*, xxxx (3): 239–217.

Morley K M F (1990) Mentorship, is it a case of the emperor's new clothes or a rose by any other name. *Nurse Education Today* 10 (1): 66–69.

Morley L (1995) Theorising empowerment in the UK public services. *Empowerment in Organisations* 3 (3): 35–41.

Muller S (1984) Physicians for the 21st century. Report of the project panel on general professional education of the physician's preparation for medicine. *Journal* of *Medical Education* 59: 2.

Mumford A (1998) Choosing development methods. *Organisations & People* 5 (2): 32–37.

Murray M, Owen M A (1991) *Beyond the Myths and Magic of Mentoring. How to Facilitate an Effective Mentor Program.* Jossey-Bass, Oxford.

O'Hear A (1988) *Who Teaches the Teachers?* Social Affairs Unit, London.

Palmer E A (1987) *The Nature of the Mentor.* Unpublished thesis. South Bank Polytechnic, London.

Palmer A (1986) *Evaluation Notes 11 for Enrolled Nurse Conversion.* Unpublished project report. St. Mary's School of Nursing, London.

Palmer A (1992) *The Role of the Mentor in Critical Care.* Conference Paper, 7th Annual Conference, The British Association of Critical Care Nurses, September, Manchester University.

Palmer A (1998) *GP Mentoring and Practice Development.* London Inner Zone Education initiative, Academic Support Plan. Centre for Community Care and Primary Health, University of Westminster, London.

Palmer A, Wilson A (1997) *The Evaluation of 'Innovative Practice Projects'.* An evaluative study of 125 projects implemented within 34 NHS Trusts to support the 'New Deal' objectives. South Thames NHS Executive, London.

Parsloe E (1995) *Coaching, Mentoring and Assessing. A Practical Guide to Developing Competencies,* revised edition. Kogan Page, London.

Parsons S F (1993) Feminist challenges to curriculum design. In: M Thorpe, R Edwardes, A Hanson (eds) *Culture and Processes of Adult Learning.* Routledge, London.

Pelletier D, Duffield C (1994) Is there enough mentoring in nursing? *Australian Journal of Advanced Nursing* 11 (4): 6–11.

Playdon Z (1998) Mentor the myth. In: *An Enquiry into Mentoring. Supporting Doctors and Dentists at Work,* Annex 3, Appendix 1, pp. 32–35. SCOPME, London.

Pratt J W (1989) Towards a philosophy of physiotherapy. *Physiotherapy* 75 (2): 114–120.

Puetz B E (1985) Learn the ropes from a mentor. *Nursing Success Today* 2 (6): 11–13.

Puetz B E (1992) Evaluation: essential skill for the staff development specialists. In: K J Kelly (ed.) *Nursing Staff Development: Current Competence, Future Focus,* pp. 183–201. J B Lippincott, Philadelphia.

Raichura L, Riley M (1985) Introducing nurse preceptors. *Nursing Times* 20 November: 40–42.

Roche G R (1979) Much ado about mentors. *Harvard Business Review* 56 (Jan/Feb): 14–18.

Rogers C (1983) *Freedom to Learn* for *the Eighties.* Charles E Merrill, Columbus, Ohio.

Rumsey H (1995) *Mentors in Post Qualifying Education. An Interprofessional Perspective.* CCETSW, London.

Safire W (1980) On language. *New York Times Magazine,* November. Reported in: J Kummerow, P George *Mentoring for Career Women. Training* 18 (2): 44, 46–49.

Sands R G, Parsons L A, Duane J (1991) Faculty mentoring faculty in a public university. *Journal of Higher Education* 62 (2): 175–193.

Schon D (1988) *Educating the Reflective Practitioner. Towards a New Design for Teaching and Learning in the Professions.* Jossey-Bass, London.

SCOPME (1997) *Multiprofessional Working and Learning: Sharing the Educational Challenge.* Standing Committee on Postgraduate Medical & Dental Education, London.

SCOPME (1998) *An Enquiry into Mentoring. Supporting Doctors and Dentists Work.* Standing Committee on Postgraduate Medical & Dental Education, London.

Segerman-Peck L (1991) *Networking & Mentoring.* Judy Piatkus Publishers, London.

Sheehy G (1976) The mentor connection and the secret link in the successful woman's life. *New York Magazine* 8: 33–39.

Slipais S (1993) Coaching in a competency-based training system: The experience of the power brewing company. In: E M A Carter, B J Caldwell (eds) *The Return of the Mentor. Strategies for Workplace Learning.* Falmer Press, London.

Smith P, West-Burnharn J (1993) *Mentoring in the Effective School.* Longman, Harlow.

Tomlinson P (1995) *Understanding Mentoring. Refective Strategies for School-based Teacher-Preparation.* Open University Press, Buckingham.

Tuck R (1993) The nature of mentoring. *The New Academic* Autumn: 25–26.

UKCI (1995) *PREP and You: Maintaining your Registration, Standards for Education Following Registration,* pp. 183–201. UKCC, London.

Vance C N (1979) Women leaders: modern day heroines or societal deviants? *MACE, Journal of Nursing Scholarship* 11 (2): 40–41.

Vance C (1982) The mentor connection. *The Journal of Nursing Administration* 12 (4): 7–13.

Weightman J (1996) *Managing People in the Health Service.* Institute of Personnel and Development, Cromwell Press, Wiltshire.

Weil S (1992) Learning to change. In: *Managing Fundamental Change: Shaping New Purposes and Roles in Public Services.* Report of a one day conference organised by the Office for Public Management, June 1992.

Wheatley M, Hirsch M S (1984) Five ways to leave your mentor. *MS Magazine* September: 106–108.

Wilkin M (ed.) (1992) *Mentoring in Schools.* Kogan Page, London.

Wilson A (1998) *An Evaluation of the London Inner Zone Education Projects.* Centre for Community Care & Primary Health, University of Westminster, London.

Wright C M (1990) An innovation in a diploma programme: the future potential of mentorship in nursing. *Nurse Education Today* 10: 355–359.

Zaleznik A (1977) Manager leaders, are they different? *Harvard Business Review* 55 (3): 67–78.

Zey M G (1984) *The Mentor Connection.* Dow Jones Irwin, Homewood, IL.

9. Mentoring in Action

David Megginson and David Clutterbuck

Introduction

In this book you will find an introduction to the state of the art of mentoring as revealed by the literature and by our experiences of working with mentors, learners and mentoring schemes. There then follows a series of case studies of contrasting schemes, and a number of stories of individual mentoring relationships. Because mentoring is such a private relationship it is unusual to get this kind of insight into what goes on face to face, so these one-to-one accounts offer many new insights. Finally, all this material is drawn together to build a picture of mentoring in the future, which will act as a guide for learners, mentors and scheme organizers.

In this chapter we examine the state of mentoring and notice how it is flourishing in a hundred guises. We examine why this is so. What are the conditions in organizations, individuals and careers that make mentoring so popular? We ask what mentoring is, and aim to discover the irreducible core of experiences that is labelled mentoring.

What is mentoring?

Our preferred definition of mentoring is that it is:

> off-line help by one person to another in making significant transitions in knowledge, work or thinking.

There is a lot in these few words, so we will highlight some of the features of our definition that point up the particular nature of the mentoring process.

First we see mentoring as off-line; that is it is not normally the job of a line manager. A mentor is usually more senior or experienced than the learner, but there are also cases of peer mentoring that work very successfully. On occasion in formal schemes and more often in natural, spontaneous or informal mentoring relationships, the mentor is also the line manager. Where we find line managers successfully acting as mentors, they seem to have a highly developed capacity to separate out the two functions. The line responsibility is often about pressure for immediate results. The mentoring relationship tends more towards giving time and space for taking a wider view. Skilled mentors make these distinctions clear, even if they do not always formally say: 'This is now a mentoring session'. The message becomes clear as the meeting progresses.

Something that makes mentoring exchanges different, whatever role the mentor has, is also captured in our definition: mentoring is about support in significant transitions. There is a Latin tag about the law not being concerned with trivia, and the same could be said for mentoring. Put another way, the mentor has a role to help the learner grasp the wider significance of whatever is happening, where at first it might appear trifling or insignificant.

David Megginson and David Clutterbuck: 'Mentoring in Action' from *MENTORING IN ACTION: A PRACTICAL GUIDE FOR MANAGERS* (Kogan Page, 1999), pp. 13–39.

A final feature of our definition is that mentoring is about one person helping one other. There is an example in this book of a scheme, described by Michael Green, which uses group mentors. We leave it to our readers to decide whether this falls within the boundary of what they consider mentoring to be. The case is useful, because it is on the edge of the field and challenges us to consider our view on this matter.

The state of the art

At the 1994 European Mentoring Centre/Sheffield Business School Mentoring Research Conference (Megginson, Clutterbuck and Whitaker, 1994) we noted that it was clear that the field of mentoring is both well established and wide open for growth and innovation in the areas of practice and theory. The power of mentoring to change mind-sets was seen as well established. This confirmed the research that had been carried out in the previous few years that mentoring had been increasing in significance for developers and for people seeking development.

The *Developing the Developers* research (Boydell *et al.*, 1991) asked 633 developers which developmental approaches of over 80 they intended to use in the future. Mentoring was chosen more frequently than all the other methods except for team building. Coaching was placed third. This was confirmed by an Industrial Society (1992) survey the next year, which also placed mentoring above coaching.

Research that has been carried out in the UK has indicated that the British approach to mentoring differs from that in the USA. In an article by Gibb and Megginson (1993) we reported that in America mentoring focused upon career and psychosocial functions. In Britain, by contrast, learning was becoming more important as a focus, and, for some, the emphasis on the mentor sponsoring someone's career was seen as not legitimate.

These findings are summarized below. The American agenda addressed the following issues that enhanced career advancement:

- ☐ *sponsorship* – for career advancement
- ☐ *exposure and visibility* – bringing the learner to others' attention
- ☐ *coaching* – helping performance on the job
- ☐ *protection* – the opposite side of the coin from sponsorship
- ☐ *challenging assignments.*

The American research also showed that there was a strong psychosocial element in mentoring there, including:

- ☐ *role modelling* – demonstrating how to handle themselves in the organization or the role
- ☐ *acceptance and confirmation* – personal support
- ☐ *counselling* – dealing with personal issues which may or may not relate directly to work
- ☐ *friendship* – building on the personal dimension of the relationship.

The British experience, which is reinforced by the studies in this book, was somewhat different. Although some of the features of American mentoring were present, there was also a different agenda. The four roles we identified were:

- ☐ improve performance
- ☐ career development
- ☐ counsellor
- ☐ sharing knowledge.

Each of these roles had a British slant on it which differentiated it from the American experience. Improving performance, which relates to the 'coaching' in the American list, was either the most important or the least important of the roles in the British schemes surveyed. This suggests that a polarization was taking place – some schemes are about the current job and improving performance, others take a wider, career and learning-focused view. It could be argued that schemes focusing solely upon performance improvement are not really mentoring at all, but our experience was that the schemes in Britain did not do this, and even those that put performance first also addressed the rest of the British agenda. So, mentoring is multi-faceted.

Career development in Britain is not a matter of sponsorship giving a disproportionate advantage to the learner over their peers who were not being mentored. It is more about giving the learner an opportunity to think through their career direction and to make choices and pursue options on their own behalf. In Britain, there seems to be a caution about mentoring favouring the learner too much, and steps are taken to prevent this happening, or alternatively of allowing everyone to have the opportunity to have a mentor. Sponsorship is, however, widely seen to be justified when the mentoring is designed to compensate for disadvantage in employment caused by race, gender, age or a record of offending. There are a number of heartening examples in this book of the mentor unashamedly sponsoring such disadvantaged individuals to good effect in a way that it would be churlish to take exception to.

The counselling role tends in Britain to focus more upon work issues than upon personal aspects of the life of the learner. Clearly, as a relationship deepens the two tend to become harder to separate. However, the greater social distance between people in Britain, and the reticence about entering into counselling relationships, means that this role is more circumscribed in Britain than in America.

Finally, sharing knowledge was a growing issue in mentoring relationships in Britain, whereas it did not appear on the agenda in the studies of American mentoring that had been undertaken ten years earlier. In the British schemes, sharing knowledge was virtually never the main role of the mentor but it was often the second most important one of the four. This seems to have come about because many mentoring schemes in Britain have grown out of support for learners attending a part-time course of study.

The EMC/SBS conference referred to earlier also served to remind us that there was a need to *reinstate the learner* at the top of the agenda. In recent years, with the development of new applications of mentoring and schemes for delivering them, structural issues have been foremost in the concerns of both practitioners and researchers. When individuals *have* been considered, the emphasis has been on the mentors. The need to consider their selection and training has been paramount. However, at the conference, we recognised the importance, for both theorists and practitioners, of *shifting the focus onto the learner*.

The centrality of the learner in the relationship is confirmed by some research carried out in Motorola by Richard Caruso (1992). He concluded that, in the well-established scheme in Motorola, mentoring was seen as a dispersed, mentee-driven activity. By this he meant that mentees, in practice, made choices of who they would seek help from, and typically selected from a range of choices, which might include several mentors. This finding has been confirmed in research by Caroline Altounyan (1995), who has examined the sources of support taken up by part-time personnel management students. She found that students used formal and self-chosen informal mentors as well as their line managers, tutors and other students on the course.

Measuring the effects of mentoring

Recent work with a number of organizations by the European Mentoring Centre indicates that there are a few basic elements to measuring mentoring, as shown below:

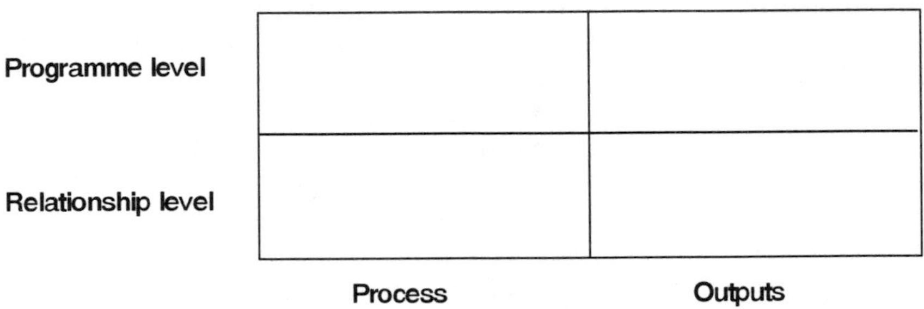

Relatively few schemes carry out systematic evaluation, but we believe this is an important part of maintaining the credibility of mentoring and relating it to business benefit.

Measuring *relationship processes* asks questions such as:

- ☐ have mentor and mentee established a close rapport?
- ☐ does the relationship have a clear objective, committed to by both parties?
- ☐ are meetings sufficiently frequent?
- ☐ are they sufficiently to the point?
- ☐ are they valued by mentor and mentee?
- ☐ are both mentor and mentee learning?

Measuring *relationship outputs* focuses on more quantitative data. For example, hard measures might be:

- ☐ how many of our learning milestones did we reach?
- ☐ has the mentee improved key scores on his or her performance appraisal?

Soft measures could be:

- ☐ does the mentee feel more confident in his or her ability to tackle new challenges?
- ☐ does the line manager feel that mentoring is helping the mentee make progress?

Clearly, the ability to achieve quantifiable measurements at the relationship level will depend to a considerable extent upon the clarity of the objectives of the programme.

Measuring *programme processes* may be a matter of simply aggregating the experiences of mentoring pairs. But it may also involve questions such as:

- ☐ were the selection criteria adequate?
- ☐ what proportion of relationships succeeded and failed?
- ☐ do mentors feel they had sufficient training?
- ☐ what skills deficiencies do mentees perceive in their mentors?
- ☐ is the programme support sufficient?

Measuring *programme outputs.* Again, these might be *hard,* eg:

- ☐ decrease in turnover of graduates/junior managers
- ☐ achievement of improved appraisal scores on key competencies
- ☐ number of mentees considered suitable for promotion after a set period.

Or *soft,* eg:

- ☐ proportion of mentors/mentees who believe they have achieved significant progress through the relationship
- ☐ perception of mentor's direct reports on the improvement in his or her dealings with them.

Applications areas

Mentoring is spreading rapidly outside the business areas too. A remarkable diversity of schemes can be seen in schools and universities, among fledgling entrepreneurs, disadvantaged minorities and even among recently released prisoners. Mentoring is so flexible an approach that it can help almost any group of people with difficult transitions to make.

In business and the public sector, there are mentoring schemes for:

- ☐ *Graduate recruits.* The most common form of business mentoring, graduate induction's popularity stems from its efficacy in attracting and keeping a valuable human resource.
- ☐ *Junior managers and supervisors,* especially where these have missed out on formal training.

- *People moving into head office from the field.* To help people withstand the culture shock of moving to Somerset House, the Inland Revenue provides 'old hands' or mentors, who can reassure the newcomer that the stresses and strains will diminish.
- *Disadvantaged groups,* such as women who have reached the glass ceiling. Volvo and Ireland's Aer Rianta are among companies with this kind of scheme.
- *Local citizens in developing countries,* where the government is keen to promote its citizens into jobs currently held by ex-patriates.
- *Newly qualified professionals,* such as members of the Institute of Personnel and Development (IPD) who may receive as mentor someone who is highly experienced from another company.
- *People about to take up major job challenges,* for example, Store Managers (designate) at Asda.
- *Top management.* An increasing proportion of CEOs and directors are seeking help from mentors. These tend to be people outside the organization, for obvious reasons.

In education, mentors are frequently assigned to:

- *Student teachers,* especially in their final year of tuition and first year after graduation.
- *University students 'at risk' and disadvantaged schoolchildren.* Students from disadvantaged backgrounds have a higher dropout rate that can be countered by effective mentoring.
- *Gifted schoolchildren* schemes in the USA match retired engineers, musicians and other people with expertise with youngsters who have similar talent. The relationship encourages the child to persist with its studies and practise.
- *New head teachers* in many areas of the country are entitled to a mentor for the first year or two of their new job.
- *New lecturers* in universities. At Sheffield Hallam University all new lecturers are offered a mentor, an experienced lecturer who has volunteered to share their experience and has been trained to do so.

In the community, mentoring schemes are used to:

- *Help mentally and physically handicapped people into employment,* for example, the Rathbone Trust.
- *Keep young people on probation out of trouble.*
- *Support people starting small businesses,* by linking them with a big company mentor. The entrepreneurs not only get the benefit of the mentor's experience, but access to free, in-depth guidance from the mentor's colleagues.

Why business is taking to mentoring

A number of trends have combined to raise the profile of mentoring in business. Among them is *the changing role of training and development.* The question 'How do we add value?' has increasing importance for the training and development (T&D) function. Frequently whittled down to a half or less of its size a decade ago, T&D is expected to do more with less. Inevitably, that reinforces the requirement to push responsibility for developing talent and career management on to the line and to the individual employee. T&D's role becomes increasingly one of co-ordination, resourcing and helping line managers develop others.

Mentoring meets a strong current need because line managers frequently have great difficulty coping with broader development issues. Coaching people to improve their skill at current tasks is relatively easy, if the manager is prepared to put aside the required quality time. But development often requires a different perspective – an ability to put aside the current task and examine future possibilities. At its best, it also requires a relationship of trust which is very difficult to achieve in a judgemental relationship – yet line managers are under pressure to be judgemental, both to maintain discipline and to carry out performance appraisals, with their inherent undertones of punishment and reward. The mentor, as an off-line friend with no such impediments, provides an ideal second opinion.

T&D is also under considerable pressure to show results. Because well-constructed mentoring programmes automatically set quantifiable objectives, they help T&D demonstrate its contribution to the business. It is no coincidence that the programme objectives for many mentoring projects echo the language of the company's key corporate objectives.

Mentoring is also attractive to T&D because it requires a relatively low input from the T&D budget for mentor and learner training, and for programme administration. Most of the cost is borne by the line, in terms of the time spent by mentor and learner. There is also a pay-off for T&D in the fact that mentoring provides a two-for-one benefit – so much so that in some organizations mentoring has been sold to top management primarily on the basis of the learning for *mentors*.

Why mentoring now?

There seem to us to be a number of factors that converge to make mentoring a method of the times. The ones that stand out are:

- ☐ the reduction in the capacity of personnel and training departments
- ☐ pressures on the role of the line manager
- ☐ the move towards learning companies
- ☐ new perspectives on careers
- ☐ changing professional requirements.

The capacity of training departments

The reduction in the size of personnel and training departments (for example, recently British Telecom announced a halving of its personnel department) means that they have less *internal* resource to provide for the direct development of individuals. In many organizations they also have less budget for running internal events or for sending people off on expensive external courses. The pressure on time seems to continue to increase. In the past 30 years, courses have shrunk from a fortnight to a week, to a couple of days, to a day or even less in many organizations today. There is also a sharper demand from power-holders in organizations for an increase in the relevance and immediacy of application of learning. Additionally, there is a widespread demand from people in organizations that learning be related to the organization's strategy.

The combined effect of all these factors is that the human resource management/development departments are less significant players in the direct provision of learning opportunities.

Pressure on the contribution of the line manager

This raises the question of who is to fill the role that was previously held by the full-time T&D people. In many organizations greater pressure is being put upon line managers to develop their own staff. They are asked to move towards the role of teacher, educator, developer or coach. The advantages of this proposed solution are that the cost of line managers doing these activities is effectively hidden, as they do it in the time that they would have been working for the organization anyway, so there are no identifiable costs associated with this work. There are opportunity costs, in terms of their being unable to do other things while they are developing their staff. People who are keen on this solution say that even these opportunity costs are negligible, as acting as a developer of your people saves time that would otherwise be spent on controlling staff or correcting the errors and answering the queries of staff who were less able to function effectively in a relatively autonomous role.

However, many organizations are finding that line managers are overburdened. The increasing rate of stress and excessive hours among managers is well documented. There is ample evidence that the formal requirement on managers to develop their staff, such as the carrying out of staff appraisal or development review, is often not done at all or only done with extreme reluctance, under pressure and late. It is our experience that this does not arise so much from incompetence or unwillingness on the part of line managers as from an unbearable pressure of other demands on their time. Delayering has led to an increase in the number of direct reports that they have. Other systems of support that would be needed to enable them to discharge their developmental duties have not been put in place. In particular, management information systems that are user friendly and available to managers and all their staff are the exception rather than the rule in today's organizations. This defect is particularly marked in the public sector, but the lack of information systems is also widespread in private sector organizations.

All this means that line managers are often unable to carry out the developer's role to the full. Additionally, in many organizations, the role of the line manager has a heavy requirement for control. Middle managers are appointed to make sure that the ship is kept tight and there is no leakage of resources through inefficiency, slackness or fraud. Whatever the wishes of individual managers in these circumstances, there will be strong pressures for development to be set on one side.

Finally, in many organizations, with project-based management or matrix structures, it is becoming increasingly hard to work out who is anyone's line manager anyway!

Multiple bosses or diffused leadership roles are often pointed to as a weakness of matrix-type organizations. However, it is worth pointing out that proponents of this form have, from the early 1970s, insisted that it is only viable in an organization culture where there is a high level of interpersonal skill. Staff need to be able to manage upwards and to negotiate a constructive accommodation of the conflicting demands for their time and attention. There are suggestions that the matrix form is on the decline, and some companies such as Shell have indeed diluted their matrix, although they have not in any sense abandoned it – they are far too complex to manage without it. However, there is also a large number of major organizations that are moving more strongly towards a matrix structure, and Ford is an example of this trend.

In matrix organizations, the diffusion of responsibility is often accompanied by a very rapid set of movements of staff and bosses from project to project, location to location.

In these circumstances, the mentor can provide a useful contribution, giving individuals time to concentrate single-mindedly on their own development, but in a way that is deeply informed about the needs, urgencies and pressures of the organization. In an era of rapid change they can also provide a continuity, which may be lacking as line managers are changed and new projects come on stream. They can do this in part because mentoring is an occasional role, and, even if the learner and mentor are moved apart, they can still continue the relationship. Later in this book you will find a number of examples where this continuity has been afforded and has provided a source of stability in an otherwise uncomfortably fluid situation.

Some organizations have no stable line management structure for most of their employees. At Perot Systems, for example, most people work on projects. Over the course of a year, they may work for several project leaders, sometimes for more than one at a time. An off-line mentor provides a point of stability, someone to whom they can turn for authoritative advice. These mentors also, unusually, take responsibility for performance appraisal. Rather than sit in judgement, they collect and collate observations from the mentee's colleagues and project managers and feed this back in a supportive, developmental manner.

The move towards learning companies

One of the main drivers in the quest for the learning company and the competitive advantage that learning can bring is the encouragement of individual responsibility. This responsibility is for taking the initiative around the work itself – not waiting to be told but getting on with what needs doing. As a conspicuously successful young civil servant said to one of us 'It is easier to apologise after than to seek permission before'.

Creating a learning company involves individuals taking responsibility not only for their work but also for their learning. They have to wean themselves from the dependence on the organization to doing development for them. For many people this will not come easy and it may need to be a staged process. Traditionally, full-time training and development people were charged with responsibility of others. In recent years there has been a call for line managers to become more involved. This process can be welcomed as progress, but line managers too have limits in terms of role and availability. The next stage in the weaning process could be seen as having the mentor support the individual, in a more hands-off way than the line manager might, but this is not the end of the chain. In a functioning learning company, there would be little need for appointed mentors because individuals would be running with the responsibility for doing it themselves. They may well have mentors as part of their network of growth, but they would manage the choosing, contracting and progressing of the relationship.

Schematically, the progression we have described looks like this:

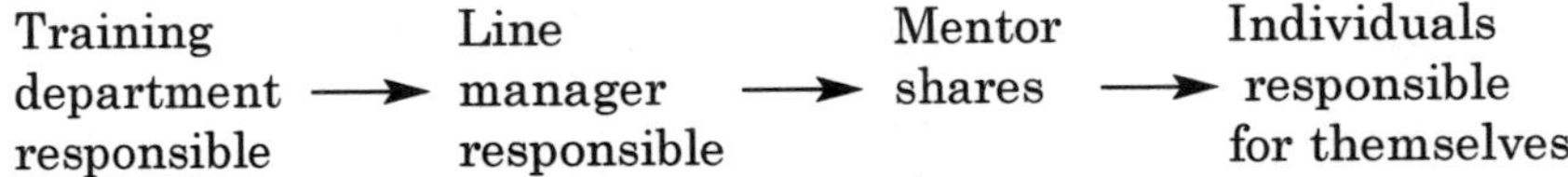

The research in Motorola emphasises this importance of the learner in selecting the network of those who will help.

The ability of the mentor to help people gain insights is critical here. Insights may be personal (what motivates them; their strengths and weaknesses; how other people see them); or systematic (how things work here; what's the best way to get things done in these circumstances); or political (eg the nature and shape of organizational alliances). A model of the learning process we have developed elsewhere suggests that it is a cycle:

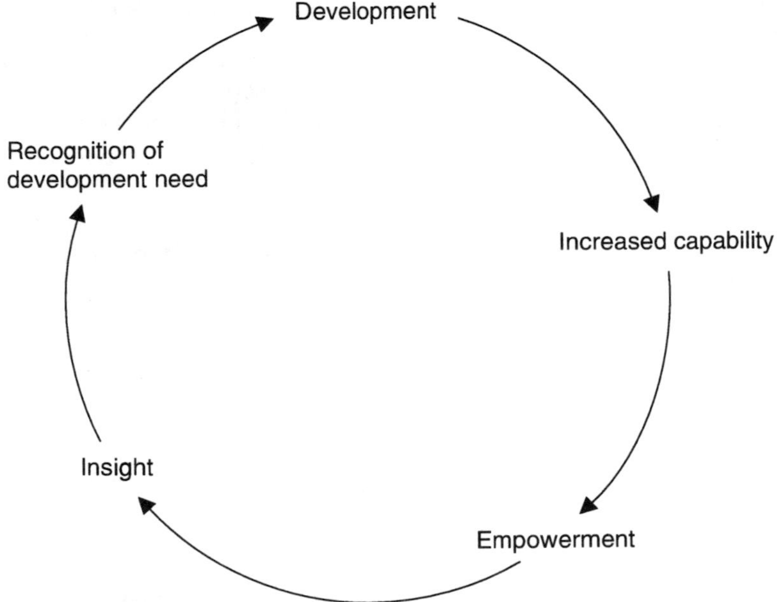

This cycle works equally for individuals, teams and whole organizations.

The new career paradigm

There are two points we wish to make about the new patterns for careers:

- careers in flattened and unstable modern organizations are less like a smooth escalator going up and more like a maze with blind alleys, secret gardens and underground tunnels
- there is still a need for people to move through to take leadership positions in organizations and there are now new routes to the top.

The career maze. In contemporary organizations each individual has more pressure on them to manage their own career. It has become a truism that companies can no longer offer even their core employees the promise of permanent employment. What is on offer at best is a promise to enhance employability. With less layers to rise through, more people will plateau earlier than in the past and will spend longer on one level. Many organizations used to hold out the promise of promotion almost as a substitute for taking seriously the development of individuals. This carrot is no longer so readily available.

The metaphor of the secret garden characterizes one feature of new careers. If people will not be moving up they need to be helped to find a place where they can experience adventure, challenge and growth without necessarily having a bigger job title.

There are also, as we suggested, underground tunnels. The trap doors that open into these tunnels are the envelopes left on the desk containing the P45 form to take to the unemployment benefit office. If organizations cannot guarantee employment then there is a moral and practical obligation to support the development of individual contributors so that they can sleep at nights in the knowledge that if they lose their job they are well equipped to handle the situation and find themselves something satisfying and rewarding to do.

Recent research by one of the authors has focused on the changes in routes to the top. The conclusions support the view that personalized assistance with career planning is increasingly a necessity. As people are obliged to work out their own paths through the maze, it helps to have a friendly sounding board, who can ideally take a broader perspective of the opportunities likely to open up within the organization.

Changing professional requirements

The British emphasis on the learning role of the mentor is encouraged by the pressure from National Vocational Qualifications and professional bodies moving towards competence-based development and accreditation of prior learning.

At the same time, professions such as personnel management increasingly recognize that achieving paper qualifications does not necessarily make someone confident and competent to practise. For the first few years, it helps greatly for them to have a more experienced practitioner, who can help them relate the theoretical to the practical and focus on broader career opportunities than just those on offer with their current employer.

What is a mentor?

We turn our attention now to the individual mentor and learner and the nature, skills and dynamics of their relationship.

One way of answering the question 'What is a mentor?' is by way of formal definition. Another is by the use of images. The image of the old, bearded, wise man in the Odyssey looking after the young prince, Telemachus, is quite well known. What is less well known is that Mentor in Homer's story is actually a form taken by the goddess Athene, thus neatly setting to one side any gender related image about mentors. Furthermore, when Odysseus returns from his wandering and he and his son Telemachus are faced with their final challenge, Athene, the mentor, did not:

> throw all her powers in, to give him victory, but continued to put the strength and courage of both Odysseus and Telemachus on trial, while she herself withdrew, taking the shape of a swallow and darting aloft to perch on the smoky beam of the hall. (Homer, 1964, p. 22)

The power of this image is that it puts mentors where they need to be, out of the action, looking on and encouraging, rather than taking over and doing the work for the learner. This is closer to the emerging British view of the role than some of the older images fostered in the USA.

An image of what mentoring is not comes from Caroline Altounyan's (1995) work where she talks of another Greek myth, about Procrustes. He lived in a cave and invited visitors in for a sumptuous banquet, with lots of wine. At the end of the evening he invited his tired and emotional visitors to stay the night. This is where the story gets nasty. If a visitor was too short for the bed, then Procrustes would put them on a rack to stretch them till they fitted better. If they were too long, then he chopped off the bits hanging over the end.

This image has two aspects. First, mentoring offers a rich banquet, and there are many different aspects of life and work that can be focused upon. Secondly, it is not our task, as mentors, to cut people down to the size that our preferences or the organization specification requires. Mentoring is too rich and individual for that: it is not a Procrustean bed.

Participants at the EMC/SBS mentoring research conference were asked to draw their own images of mentoring. From the range they drew, strong messages came about mentoring being about:

- ☐ big ears, small mouth
- ☐ finding the tune that the learner wants to play
- ☐ harmonizing the various contributors
- ☐ being in the delivery room, supporting new growth
- ☐ an upward, widening spiral
- ☐ seeing life as a tree, with roots as deep as the branches are high
- ☐ a 'Nellie', sitting alongside

- ☐ a laser beam
- ☐ a hand, a book and a boot
- ☐ a pebble in a still pool sending out ripples that extend in space and time.

All these images offer directions for us in considering what mentors might do. Often being connected to a visual image makes them more memorable too. These images all attest to the depth of the mentor's contribution. Having a mentor is an important developmental opportunity, not a fashion accessory.

Instructor, coach and mentor: some key distinctions

We can also become clearer about what mentoring is by attending to what it is not. The mentor stands distinct from either a coach or an instructor.

Instructors focus on the task, and their time perspective is a day or two. They show and tell, and give supervised practice: ownership of the relationship is with the instructor and they attempt to eliminate ambiguity.

The coach shifts the focus to the results of the job, and extends the time span of attention to months rather than days. They explore the problem with the learner and set up opportunities for the learner to try out new skills: ownership is shared and puzzling out ambiguity is seen as a challenge.

By contrast, mentors focus on the individual learner developing through their career or life. They act as friends willing to play the part of adversary in challenging assumptions, they listen and question to encourage the learner to widen their own view: they are happy for the ownership and direction of the relationship to lie with the learner and they accept ambiguity as an exciting part of life, providing the learner with the openings for change and autonomy.

The mentoring process

What do mentors do? Most successful mentoring relationships go through four phases. We describe these as:

1. establishing rapport (initiation)
2. direction setting (getting established)
3. progress making (development)
4. moving on (finalizing/maintenance).

Each of the phases has its own tasks, dynamics and skill requirements. We outline these below.

Mentoring works best when it is learner driven, so we are not attempting here to be prescriptive, and we expect that some relationships will take quite different paths driven by different urgencies. However, what follows describes the progress of a typical mentoring relationship.

Establishing rapport

Tasks. During this phase the mentor and the learner will:

- ☐ work out whether they can get on and respect each other
- ☐ exchange views on what the relationship is and is not
- ☐ agree a formal contract
- ☐ agree a way of working together
- ☐ set up a way of calling meetings, frequency, duration, location
- ☐ set up other contacts.

Dynamics. This phase can be characterised by:

- ☐ impatience to get going
- ☐ tentativeness and unwillingness to commit
- ☐ politeness
- ☐ testing out and challenging.

Skill requirements. In this phase the mentor may need to:

- ☐ suspend judgement
- ☐ be open to hints and unarticulated wishes or concerns
- ☐ be clear about what needs establishing and open about what can be left out
- ☐ establish a formal contract
- ☐ agree a way of working together
- ☐ set up details of future meetings
- ☐ achieve rapport.

Direction setting

Tasks. The mentor and the learner will:

- ☐ learn about the learner's style of learning
- ☐ think through the implications of their style for how they will work together
- ☐ diagnose needs
- ☐ determine learner's goals and initial needs
- ☐ set objective measures
- ☐ identify priority areas for work
- ☐ keep open space
- ☐ clarify focus of their work
- ☐ begin work.

Dynamics. Characteristic issues may include:

- ☐ over-inclination to shut down on possibilities
- ☐ unwillingness to set goals
- ☐ reluctance to open up possibilities for diagnosis.

Skill requirements. In addition to those mentioned earlier there will be:

- ☐ using and interpreting diagnostic frameworks and tools
- ☐ encouraging thinking through of implications of diagnoses
- ☐ setting up opportunities for diagnosis to be informed by third parties
- ☐ adopt developmental approach to goal setting for the learner
- ☐ help the selection of the initial area for work
- ☐ give feedback/set objectives/plan
- ☐ have clarity about the next step.

Progress making

Tasks. The mentor and the learner will:

- ☐ create a forum for progressing the learner's issues
- ☐ use each other's expertise as agreed
- ☐ establish a means for reviewing progress and adapting the process in the light of this review
- ☐ identify new issues and ways of working that are required
- ☐ be ready for the evolution of the relationship.

Dynamics. This phase will typically include:

- ☐ period of sustained productive activity
- ☐ dealing with a change in the relationship or the learner's circumstances
- ☐ reviewing and adapting the relationship
- ☐ preparing for moving on.

Skill requirements. This phase also requires:

- ☐ monitoring progress of learner
- ☐ relationship review and renegotiation
- ☐ recognizing achievements/objectives attained
- ☐ timing and managing the evolution of the relationship.

Moving on

Tasks. Now the mentor and the learner will:

- ☐ allow the relationship to end or evolve
- ☐ move to maintenance
- ☐ review what can be taken and used in other contexts.

Dynamics. This phase may include:

- ☐ dealing with rupture and loss
- ☐ major renegotiation and continuation ·
- ☐ evaluation and generalization.

Skills requirement. In this phase there may be a need to:

- ☐ address own and other's feelings of loss
- ☐ develop next phase and/or
- ☐ orchestrate a good ending
- ☐ think through and generalize learning
- ☐ establish friendship.

Determine the focus

It is worth bearing in mind that the presenting issue that the learner identifies may be only the first step towards the exploration of some deeper issue that they will not want to raise at first, or may not even be consciously aware of. This framework, therefore, serves to set out an agenda of possibilities for future attention. The issues that the learner might want to discuss could be:

- ☐ focused on the organization's strategy and process
- ☐ focused on their role
- ☐ focused on a big task or project
- ☐ focused on particular skills
- ☐ focused upon development needs and career direction
- ☐ open – acting as sounding board.

An indication of which area a learner wishes to focus upon will come from the issues that they raised during the initiation and direction-setting stage. Some examples of the ways these issues are expressed are given below:

Organizational strategy and process

- ☐ I want to explore the organization's strategy
- ☐ I want to look at how we are organized

- ☐ I want to address how we are managed, eg quality issues, corporate responsibility, customer/supplier relations
- ☐ I want to improve the way we communicate in the organization
- ☐ I want to review how we work together and the performance of teams and individuals
- ☐ I want to get clearer about the environment we are working in and the competition we face.

Role

- ☐ I want to clarify what difference my new role makes to what I do
- ☐ I want to expand the possibilities of what I can do
- ☐ I want to resolve conflicts with other roles.

Big task or project

- ☐ I want to think through the benefits of this task/project
- ☐ I want to think through the formal and informal relationships I have and need in a major project
- ☐ I want to run my ideas for a major project in front of a dispassionate outsider
- ☐ I want to monitor my contribution to a major project.

Skills

- ☐ I want to get clear about what my strengths and weaknesses are
- ☐ I want to examine my own skills
- ☐ I want to build up specific skills, eg communication, decision-making, presentation.

Development needs and career

- ☐ I want to develop a plan for my own development in my current role
- ☐ I want to look beyond my current role
- ☐ I want to clarify what I am here to do, my purpose
- ☐ I want to look at how I can learn better from what happens
- ☐ I want to learn from my successes and failures.

Open space

- ☐ I want a sounding board
- ☐ I want time for me, and I am happy to see what comes up and run with it.

The focus can change over the life of a mentoring relationship, and this framework can provide guidance for mentors and learners seeking to keep an eye on the way the relationship is evolving.

Mutuality

Various authors on mentoring have made passing reference to the fact that mentors also learn, but there has been relatively little analysis of *what* and *how* they learn from the relationship. This is a theme that has preoccupied one of the authors for some time and is the subject of on-going research. Sufficient feedback has been gathered to provide some straightforward observations, however. Mentors gain from their mentees:

- ☐ Insights into new areas of skill/technology. (Younger people are frequently much more adept at using computer functions, for example.)
- ☐ An opportunity to evaluate critically the intuitive processes they use. To explain their thinking to the mentee they often have to articulate subconscious processes and open them up for critical discussion and reflection.
- ☐ The benefit of matching experience-based advice against what happens when the mentee follows it.
- ☐ A stimulus to review their own knowledge and learning of topics that come up for discussion.
- ☐ Clues to hidden issues that their own direct reports will not broach with them. As one group of learners in cross-cultural mentoring relationships put it: 'the mentor will learn about the little things that frustrate us and recognize that he may be frustrating his own people'.

There are benefits for the mentor outside the learning framework. Surveys conducted by the authors have invariably identified 'satisfaction in seeing someone else grow' as the principal benefit mentors perceive. This psychosocial gratification is reinforced if the learner acknowledges the debt.

As the relationship matures, the mentor may find that the giving of support becomes increasingly mutual. The partners use each other as sounding boards. In the cross-cultural case referred to above, mentors began to ask their learners questions such as: 'How do you think a Malay audience would react to this?'

A code of ethics for mentoring

The rapid spread of applications of mentoring has increasingly raised the issue of proper conduct by mentor and learner. Some generic guidelines have always been present in formal business mentoring schemes – for example, the importance of strict confidentiality and for the learner to avoid misusing the mentor's authority. Less clear, however, are issues such as:

- ☐ Where are the boundaries of what can be discussed?
- ☐ To what extent should the mentor attempt to drive the learner towards a particular action or decision?
- ☐ In a conflict of interest between the mentor and the learner, where should the mentor's priorities lie?

Mentoring Directors, an organization specializing in the provision of external mentors for senior executives, has developed a code of practice for its mentors, and we expect this practice to spread. At the very least, it will provide a useful starting point for discussion in organizations wishing to establish their own guidelines.

Summary

Two trends are happening simultaneously in mentoring. One is that the application of the technique is spreading well beyond the business/professional boundaries, creating exciting new opportunities to learn from schemes that begin from very different perspectives. The other is that the focus for innovation in research and application of business mentoring has shifted from North America to the UK and Europe.

As a result, a whole range of issues and options has opened up, stimulating an explosion of research and experimentation. Some of the experiments are reported in the cases in this book – but these represent only a small proportion of the innovation going on.

References

Altounyan C (1996) *Putting Mentors in their Place: the Role of Workplace Support in Professional Education*, MSc HRM Dissertation. Sheffield Business School, Sheffield.

Boydell T, Leary M, Megginson, Pedler M (1991) *Developing the Developers*. AMED, London.

Caruso R E (1992) *Mentoring and the Business Environment: Asset or Liability?* Dartmouth, Aldershot.

Gibb S, Megginson D (1993) Inside corporate mentoring schemes: a new agenda of concerns. *Personnel Review* 22 (1): 40–54.

Homer (trans. E V Rieu) (1964) *The Odyssey*. Penguin, Harmondsworth.

Industrial Society (1992) *Training Report* No. 4. Industrial Society, London.

Megginson D, Clutterbuck D, Whitaker V (1994) Conclusions from the conference, *Proceedings of the EMC/SBS Mentoring Research Conference*, European Mentoring Centre, UK.

10. The Roles of the Teacher Practitioner and Mentor

Peter Jarvis and Sheila Gibson

This chapter explores:

- *The concepts of field of practice and practical knowledge*
- *The mentor*
- *The teacher*
- *Straddling two professionalisms*
- *The teacher practitioner within professional education and training.*

Introduction

Contemporary society is one in which the practical is being increasingly emphasized, almost at the expense of the theoretical which is being reduced in some instances to 'the merely academic'. While this is not a position adopted in this book, the significance of the practical is emphasized and its relationship to the theoretical is explored in considerable detail, since this underlies the theory of the role of the teacher practitioner and the mentor. However, nursing, midwifery and health visiting have always emphasized the practical side of their work, having introduced such roles as clinical tutor, practical work teacher and fieldwork teacher long before many other occupations and professions had even considered the idea, although the concept of apprenticeship (*apprendre* (Fr.) = to learn) was jettisoned before it was thoroughly explored.

The title teacher practitioner is, in a sense, an umbrella term for all of these other roles which emerged in the early 1980s, encompassing the designated roles of a practitioner with a teaching responsibility in nursing, midwifery and health visiting. More recently the words have been reversed, with the appearance of practitioner teacher. Lecturer practitioner has assumed some currency since the preparation for these professions has been relocated in higher education. Nevertheless, the term teacher practitioner is used throughout this book since the meaning of the term lecturer is much more restricted than that of teacher. The use of the word lecturer in this context, however, probably reflects the higher status of a lecturer in higher education compared with that of the school teacher – although university teacher is the traditional term for one who lectures in a university. The fact that the job title changes periodically to reflect the contemporary social situation is interesting, although it can lead to some confusion.

Irrespective of the term, teacher practitioners are practitioners who have a teaching role, working in a practical setting and combining their practice with teaching the practical component of a professional role. While it might be justifiably claimed that

Peter Jarvis and Sheila Gibson: 'The Roles of the Teacher Practitioner and Mentor' from *THE TEACHER PRACTITIONER AND MENTOR IN NURSING, MIDWIFERY, HEALTH VISITING AND THE SOCIAL SERVICES* (Stanley Thornes, 1997; 2nd edn), pp. 1–17.

every qualified professional has this duty, and the English National Board (ENB) requires all teachers in these professional groups to work within a practice setting for one day per week (ENB, 1993: 2.13, para 3.2), there are certain roles where the duty is particularly specified by reason of the designation and specification of the post.

In precisely the same way, another term has come to the fore in recent years, mentor, and this is also frequently used in a similar manner to teacher practitioner (see Morton-Cooper and Palmer, 1993), although its usage varies with different occupational groupings. It is similar to the teacher practitioner in as much as the mentor is usually a highly qualified professional who enters a one-to-one relationship of teaching and learning with junior colleagues in order to help them perform their role better or develop and mature as human beings.

While some of these different occupational roles are referred to in this introduction, such as clinical tutor and practical work teacher, the role of the teacher practitioner is to 'plan and provide a learning environment in the context of the specialist area of practice' (ENB, 1993: 4.35. Para 1.1).

While community mental handicap nurses (CMHNs), community psychiatric nurses (CPNs), district nurses (DNs), registered health visitors (RHVs) and occupational health nurses (OHNs) are required to study and pass a community practice teacher course comprising theory-practice components relating to teaching, learning and assessment before assuming the role of practitioner teacher, this is not the case for all teacher practitioners. Since 1992, as a result of a Joint Practice Teacher Initiative, the Community Practice Teacher Course has had to include a common core element agreed between the ENB and the Central Council for the Education and Training of Social Workers (CCETSW) and the College of Occupational Therapists (COT) (ENB, 1993: 4.35, para 1.2).

During the 1970s, according to Kadushin (1976 pp2–3) a greater emphasis was placed on the preparation of professionally trained social workers for supervision, consultation, administration and planning. According to her (Kadushin, 1976 p125):

> Educational supervision is the second principal responsibility of the supervisor. Educational supervision is concerned with teaching the worker what he needs to know in order to do his job and helping him to learn . . .

This trend has continued throughout the 1980s and 1990s and it has become more formalized in the UK and USA.

Yet this teaching role has been strangely neglected by many other professions and occupations, learners being treated rather like apprentices, observing the masters at work and seeking to emulate their practice. Some branches of nursing have been much more far-sighted than this, creating both a practical teaching role and providing opportunity for some experienced practitioners to be prepared for it. The extent to which the training is adequate remains largely unresearched, although Battle and Salter (1981 p20) discovered that the practical work teachers that they interviewed were mainly satisfied with their preparation. However, there is a need for more research into the preparation of teacher practitioners in a variety of situations.

Mentors, on the other hand, have not always been trained for their role and, while some branches of nursing have used the term mentor in relation to the initial preparation of student nurses and, on occasions, for post registration students, its use is much wider in other occupations. Many professional groups have used the term to refer to a senior colleague who is given, or has assumed, some responsibility to help newly qualified employees establish themselves in the profession or the company. Occasionally, the term has also been used to describe a supervisory role.

Thus it may be seen that both teacher practitioners and mentors have a dual role: as practitioners and as teachers. But the roles may be full-time in themselves: nursing and social work are certainly full-time and so may teaching adults be a full-time occupation. Significantly the ENB requires institutions to count teachers as 0.8 full-time-equivalent in order to enable them to practise (ENB, 1993 pp2–3, para 3.2). Even so many of these teachers still have difficulty in finding time to practise their discipline on the wards or in the community, simply because of the heavy demands of their teaching role. It is also significant that school teacher trainers are also increasingly being asked to have recent and relevant school experience. Nevertheless, the roles of teacher, practitioner and mentor are very significant ones, since they are at the interface of theory and practice.

Neither the teacher practitioner's role, nor that of the mentor, are merely amalgams of the two roles that describe teacher and practitioner, they are important specialist functions in their own right. The roles of the teacher practitioner and mentor, consequently constitute the focus of this opening chapter, whilst subsequent ones develop the educational theory underlying the teaching aspect of the roles. Neither is any attempt made in this short text to discuss the occupational roles specific to the branch of nursing or social work within which the teacher practitioners and mentors may function.

The concepts of the field of practice and practical knowledge

A field of practice is, as the term implies, a site in which a specialist occupation is conducted. It constitutes a focus for the practice of an occupation or a profession. By contrast, a field of study is the focus of a special area of research, and in studying an occupation a field of practice for the practitioner becomes a field of study for the researcher.

Since both nursing and social work are practical professions, it seems obvious to refer to the field of nursing practice and the field of social work practice. However, professions are rarely single or simple entities, but rather they comprise a number of different strands undertaking similar work in the same or different locations. Consequently, it is more accurate to see nursing spanning a number of different fields of practice and social work doing the same. The fields within nursing and social work all overlap which suggests that there is some commonality about them, although there are whole elements of practice which are discrete, as Figure 1 illustrates.

Even more significantly, some of the fields of practice of nursing may overlap with those of social work and so the occupational picture becomes even more complex. Such overlap within and between occupations reflects the fragmented world of late modern society.

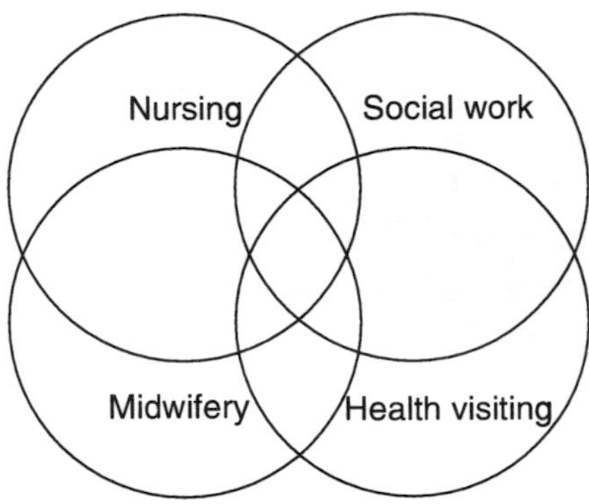

Figure 1 Overlapping fields of practice

Each occupation, however, has its own expertise and its own body of knowledge, so that it is easier to concentrate upon only one occupation in order to explore the idea of practical knowledge. Before this is undertaken, however, it is necessary to examine the idea of knowledge itself and its relation to skill. Precisely what is knowledge? How can people be sure that what they know corresponds with the 'real' world out there? How can they be sure that that knowledge is true? These are but some of the major questions that confront any philosopher analyzing knowledge itself. They cannot all be answered here since this is not the purpose of this book, but these are some of the questions that need to be explored if practical knowledge is to be understood.

Sheffler (1965) sought to respond to the questions about knowledge as truth propositions when he distinguished between three ways of verifying knowledge: rational-logical, empirical and pragmatic. Rational-logical knowledge is that which is used when a mathematical problem is solved, since the logical rules have been followed and a conclusion has been reached. Empirical knowledge is that which people gain through their senses. Pragmatic knowledge is experimental and individuals have it when they know that something they know actually works for them in practice – in this sense it is scientific. If that knowledge is not capable of producing the types of results that are expected, then it is rejected and new knowledge sought that works. Herein lies the idea of the human being as scientist, seeking always to understand and experiment upon social reality (Kelly, 1963). It should be noted that in the postmodern literature (for example, Lyotard, 1984) pragmatism is regarded as the sole legitimator of knowledge, reflecting the previous discussion which indicated the movement towards a greater emphasis on practice and less on theory.

However, this idea of experimentation is also quite crucial to understanding something of the relationship between personal knowledge and action – perhaps, between theory and practice. It is always a probability situation. Heller (1984 p166) suggests that the 'pragmatic relationship denotes the direct unity of theory and practice'. People almost always act upon the probability that the action will achieve the desired results, and they act with 'sufficient ground' (Heller, 1984 p169), that is to say that they have some knowledge that enables them to act in a certain way and that they believe that their action will have specific results, or else they will not so act. Pragmatic knowledge is a form of scientific knowledge that should underlie a great deal of all professional practitioners' actions. Because they know it works, it is necessarily conservative in nature – why should individuals change their behaviour when they know that what they are doing works? It is no good the theoretician trying to convince them that they are wrong, because they have proved to themselves that what they know works. However, they cannot necessarily control all the circumstances within which their actions occur, hence every situation is one of probability.

This is a weakness in Habermas' (1972) formulation of technical-cognitive knowledge. It will .be recalled that Habermas also has three forms of knowledge or, as he calls them, processes of enquiry: the technical-cognitive, the historical-hermeneutic and the emancipatory. The technical-cognitive form is about practical knowledge and he (1972 p309) regards this as having 'control over objectified processes'. Whilst this control may well refer to the human action itself, the possession of knowledge does not necessarily mean that those who possess it have control over the outcomes of the practical acts that stem from its utilization. It means only that they understand them.

It was Ryle who raised this question of practical knowledge in a seminal study in 1949. He (1963) distinguished between *knowledge how* and *knowledge that* and suggested that in everyday life 'we are more concerned with people's competences than with their cognitive repertoires' (1963 p28). Here he was attacking the intellectual emphasis upon cognitive knowledge, and yet he oversimplified the problem by adopting a behaviourist solution, and he suggested that when 'I am doing something intelligently . . . I am doing one thing and not two' (1963 p32). Here Ryle has actually confused three things: the skill, the knowledge how to perform the action, and the monitoring of the action. Ryle also implicitly raised two sets of inter-related problems: firstly, he implied that 'knowing how' and 'being able' are synonymous, which is incorrect; secondly, he demonstrates quite clearly that when people perform an action they cannot necessarily always articulate the theory underlying the action.

Sheffler (1965) also points out that knowing how and being able are not synonymous concepts. He provides the illustration of a person who might know how to drive a car but be prevented from doing so for a variety of reasons, for example, having a broken leg. There are contingencies that cannot always be controlled. The difference between having the knowledge and being able to perform the skill still remains crucial to this discussion. However, this illustration does not probe deeply enough and another question emerges – when people say 'I know how to . . .' are they really using a term that has a cognitive orientation at all? Would it not be more correct to claim that 'I am able to . . .'? In other words, the possession of a skill does not necessarily always mean that people have all, or much, of the *knowledge how*, although there may well be other occasions when they actually have or have had that knowledge. There are no doubt times when a skill is learned and only as it is being acquired do the actors gain any *knowledge how* and as they realize that there are alternative procedures that they might practise, they learn the *knowledge that* the different procedures will produce different outcomes, etc.

While Ryle's distinction between *knowing how* and *knowing that* is important, there is another dimension which he omitted – *knowing why* something is valid or not. Being able to understand why certain outcomes are likely to occur as a result of specific actions is a very important aspect of practical knowledge. Consequently, it might be argued that practical knowledge has at least three different forms of conscious knowledge. Practical knowledge is one element of theory – it is the theory *of* practice.

Having clarified the distinction between skill and elaborated on knowledge it is now possible to return to the idea of a field of practice and Figure 2 illustrates the inter-relationship between the practice and the practical knowledge that is required to perform the role.

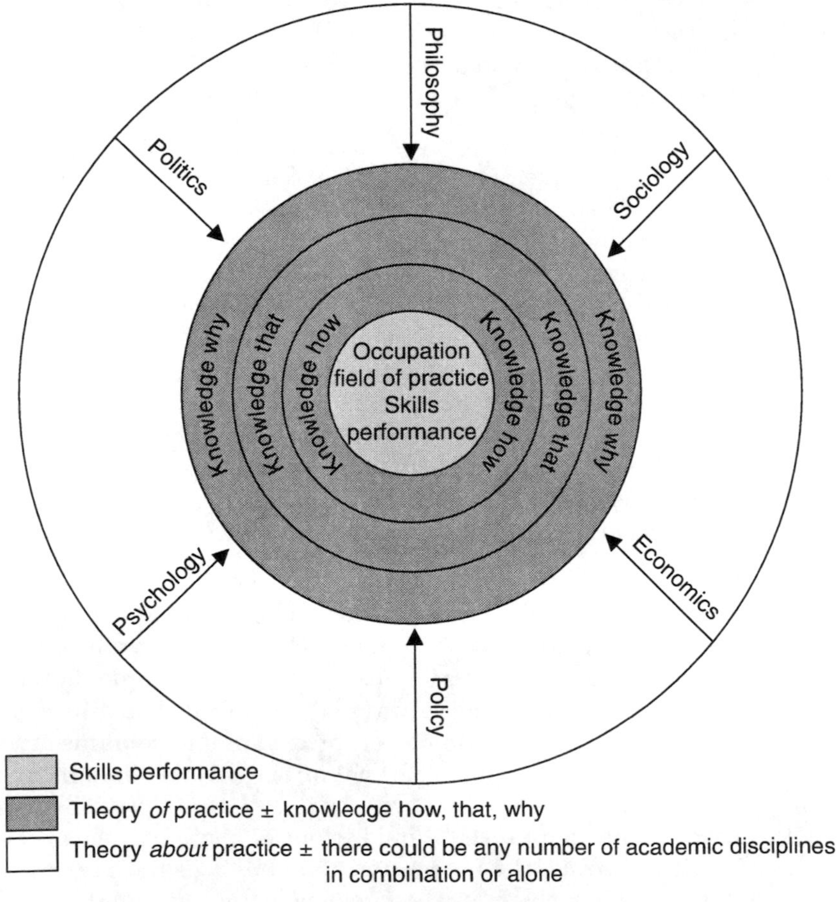

Figure 2 **Knowledge and skills: theory and practice**

It can be seen that all these three forms of knowledge are driven by practice. They are all pragmatic, in Sheffler's sense, and the expert practitioners have a considerable body of knowledge which relates to their own experience of practice, but there are occasions when they have habitualized their actions to such an extent that, even if they ever knew the underlying theory about certain aspects of their practice, they cannot specify precisely what it is. Additionally, they might also find it difficult to explain to others precisely how they perform certain procedures, etc. In a recent study about practical knowledge and expertise, Nyiri (1988 pp20–1) writes:

> One becomes an expert not simply by absorbing explicit knowledge of the type found in textbooks, but through experience, that is, through repeated trials, 'failing, succeeding, wasting time and effort . . . getting to feel the problem, learning to go by the book and when to break the rules'. Human experts thereby gradually absorb 'a repertory of working rules of thumb, or "heuristics", that, combined with book knowledge, make them expert practitioners'. This practical, heuristic knowledge, as attempts to simulate it on the machine have shown, is 'hardest to get at because experts – or anyone else – rarely have the self-awareness to recognize what it is. So it must be mined out of their heads painstakingly, one jewel at a time'. (All quotes from Feigenbaum and McCorduck, 1984.)

Ryle may well be correct when he suggested that some of the original rules are forgotten through constant practice, but Nyiri is suggesting another element – that, through continuous experimentation, new knowledge is gradually absorbed from experience which might never have been articulated. Practical knowledge, then, is hidden in the practitioner, or as Polyani (1967) suggests, it has become tacit knowledge, i.e. knowledge that cannot necessarily be expressed in words. The nature of that knowledge is also pragmatic, i.e. it is accepted because it is known to work. But, because it is known to work, practitioners are loathe to change it, and so it is essentially conservative.

It is therefore maintained here that practical knowledge has two interrelated aspects: conscious cognitive knowledge, having at least three dimensions, and tacit knowledge. Learning tacit knowledge is a process that has been discussed elsewhere (Jarvis, 1994), although there will be more references to it later in this book.

The significant thing about this body of practical knowledge is that it is totally inter-disciplinary, there is no pure philosophy, no sociology, etc. It consists of its own constitution of different 'bits' of applied knowledge from different disciplines. Practical nursing knowledge differs from practical social work knowledge simply because it requires different skills and different mixes of applied philosophy, sociology, psychology, etc. However, there can be a sociological, or a philosophical, or an economic, etc. study of each field of practice but when the studies are located in the disciplines rather than in practice, they are driven by the internal logic of the discipline rather than the vicissitudes of practice. These studies constitute the second feature of theory: this is theory *about* practice.

The teacher practitioner and the mentor both exist to help the students, the new recruits or the junior colleagues to acquire some of this practical knowledge. Having begun to explore the nature of practical knowledge, it is now necessary to look at the role of the mentor.

The mentor

Mentorship has suddenly assumed a respectability in professional education, and beyond, and those who use it often try to differentiate it from the image of the apprentice master, the teacher practitioner, etc. Indeed, there have been a number of attempts to define the term. Fish and Purr (1991 p47), for instance, say that 'nurses who supervize the clinical practice' are called mentors, and they briefly go on to highlight the relationship between the mentor and the student. Sloan and Slevin (1991 p20) suggest that, while there is no real agreement in the literature:

> as new entrants progress through the early experiences, they require considerable personal support **(mentorship)** and directive teaching-learning **(preceptorship)**. Later they require more space, and the clinician's role is more of a **facilitator** – providing tuition at a more advanced level, being available on request, acting as a critic and a 'stimulator' of reflection in practice. (underlining in the original)

The passage then goes on to discuss yet another function, that of the role model. Obviously, these are all different functions in the teaching and learning process in practice and, if they were agreed upon as all being relevant, it would be possible for one, or more than one, person to perform the various functions, stipulated here, and elsewhere. To have a variety of role players, however, as different occupational categories, would perhaps be excessive, so that these may merely reflect the different roles that one person might play. Such a person might be a teacher practitioner, a manager or a supervisor of professional practice – or even a mentor!

Both Fish and Purr and Sloan and Slevin seem to relate mentoring to professional practice only, whereas Carruthers (1993 p11) suggests that there is another form of mentoring which is as much concerned with personal development as with the professional development.

Defining the concept of mentor has run into several of the difficulties implicit in the above discussion, as Hagerty (1986) demonstrated when she claimed that the literature confuses the person, the process and the activities. But this is no less true of a word like 'teacher' and so the problems surrounding the concept of mentorship are not insurmountable, even though any resolution will not necessarily gain universal support. The concept of mentorship is now discussed, followed by an examination of the mentor's functions.

The concept of mentorship

There seems to be almost universal agreement that mentoring involves a relationship with the learner. Consequently, it is possible to begin to define the mentor relationship as *one in which two people relate to each other with the explicit purpose of the one assisting the other to learn.* The fact is that this relationship is explicitly a personal one-to-one relationship, and this is the crucial difference between the roles of mentor and teacher, although this does not necessarily apply in the case of the teacher practitioner; in mentoring the relationship comes closer to that of counsellors with those whom they counsel. However, the function of the relationship lies in mentors assisting the learners (or mentees, or protégés, to learn and to perform their role more effectively, or to develop themselves. Frequently, this may involve direct teaching although there are many occasions when the mentor is not the teacher, but may be a facilitator of reflective practice or an opener of doors that lead to other learning opportunities, etc. This concentration on the nature of a relationship appears to be another crucial difference between mentoring and teaching. However, it must be recognized that relationship lies at the heart of all social living and not something particular to the roles being discussed here.

Murray (1991 p5) points out that there are two schools of thought about mentoring: the one suggests that it can be structured or facilitated, while the other maintains that it can only happen when the 'chemistry' between the two people is right. However, these are not automatically exclusive, since a facilitated relationship might actually develop into one where the chemistry appears to be right for the relationship to continue and to deepen. Clearly, in education and training, structured or facilitated mentoring is called for and this creates a form of mentorship which is very similar to being a teacher practitioner but, unlike being a teacher practitioner, mentoring is not something that can just be turned on and off with the passing of every short module, etc. This has already been discovered in nursing when, as Barlow (1991) reports, short-term mentorship did not seem appropriate for clinical practice with students. Indeed, these mentors were often new staff nurses who would no doubt have benefitted from being mentored themselves. It is also for this reason that some branches of nursing have referred to this structured form of mentoring as preceptorship, which has been defined as 'a registered nurse who has been specially prepared to guide and direct student learning during clinical placements'.

It is the relationship which is important in mentoring – in Buber's (1959) words, it is an I-Thou relationship.

But who is the mentor? On occasions the mentor can be the teacher, but on others the mentor may be an adviser, a senior colleague or an expert. Occasionally, it can be the manager – but it might be difficult to enter such a relationship with an immediately junior colleague, so that where there is a facilitated mentor relationship the mentor is often at least two rungs higher than the protégé.

The functions of the mentor

It is clear from this discussion that mentoring is not regarded here in the same light as coaching (Schon, 1987) or supervising in clinical practice, or even personal tutoring (Barlow, 1991). However, there is a sense in which the personal tutor can become a mentor with students, as Daloz (1986) demonstrates in liberal adult education where adults are returning to college to study. But if the mentor is to play a role in education and the professions, especially after the mentee has graduated, then the personal tutor may not be able to perform it and, in some cases, the ex-students may not want it. Hence, it seems that Murray's (1991) distinction between facilitated and unstructured mentoring becomes even more important. During studentship, some form of mentor role might be performed by the personal tutor, especially one who is acknowledged to be concerned about excellence in practice. Mentorship might also be facilitated for junior qualified staff, in the way that Murray indicates. She (1991 p58) records a top level executive as saying:

> 'I'm always mentoring, both formally and informally. My role is to help my subordinates make decisions. I let them bounce ideas off me and I give my input. But ultimately, I want them to make decisions. If I were making all the decisions for them, I wouldn't need them, would I? So taking on what you call an "additional protégé" is no great hardship for me in terms of time. It's what I do anyway.'

Here the distinction between acting formally and informally is important – perhaps the informal mentoring relationship, which just emerges or emerges after the formal relationship has been created, is at the heart of mentoring.

In his excellent book on mentoring, Daloz (1986 pp215–35) suggests some of the major things that good mentors do in the situations of mentoring adult students, and he does so under three headings – support, challenge and provide a vision. Each of these are sub-divided into a number of different functions:

- *Support* – listening, providing structure, expressing positive expectations, sharing ourselves, making it special
- *Challenge* – setting tasks, engaging in discussion, heating up dichotomies, constructing hypotheses, setting high standards
- *Vision* – modelling, keeping tradition, offering a map, suggesting new language, providing a mirror.

Morton-Cooper and Palmer (1993 pp62–4) also suggest a number of different functions of the mentor; they specify eight: adviser; coach, counsellor; guide/networker; role model; sponsor; teacher; resource facilitator.

In a sense, in these instances, the role of the mentor is to help the protégés to reflect on their practice, to learn from their experiences and to improve their practice and to develop themselves, so that they might exercise even more expertise and maturity. In mentoring, this is done through an in-depth relationship whether it is structured or informal, a primary experience, Buber's educative relationship. Indeed, it is the relationship that makes mentorship so important – not just to professional practice. It is then not only in practice that the mentee gains, it is also a life-enriching relationship – but should the mentor also gain from such a relationship?

> But connections achieve . . . only in so far as they make the existence of the connected into *being for each other*, not merely being with each other. My continued being 'makes sense' only in as far as there are others who go on needing me. Beckoning to me, making me attentive to their plight, filling me with the feeling of responsibility for them, they make me unique, irreplaceable, indispensable individual that I am: the entity whose disappearance would make a hole in the universe, create that void . . . Unless 'I am *for*, I am not. (Bauman, 1992a p40)

Being open to others is at the heart of human being, but if the mentor smothers the mentee, then the fears expressed by Burnard are justified. Mentorship is about exercising this human characteristic in genuine dialogue, so that ultimately both develop and feel needed through the relationship.

The teacher

Malcolm Knowles (1980 p26) claims that many people perform a teaching role and, indeed, they do. However, they do not all have to be teacher trained in order to teach, since anybody who facilitates another's learning may be regarded as an educator. Mentors may be more rarely trained for mentoring but they might certainly be regarded as teachers or facilitators of others' learning. Even so, in the case of the teacher practitioner, the role is much more specific, since it involves inducting the student into the work situation, which may be located in a ward, a community setting, a department in a school or college, etc. Yet it is more than merely a process of induction, it is an active teaching role in an interpersonal situation. Two points arise from this – they are both roles of educators of adults (although mentoring can occur with children) and they are of an interpersonal nature.

There is an increasingly significant body of knowledge emerging about the art of teaching adults and a considerable amount of research results are beginning to appear about individualized learning, so that it is important for teacher practitioners and mentors to be aware of this work. Unfortunately, the body of literature on the art and science of teaching adults in an interpersonal, one-to-one situation is still small although it is growing (for example, Megginson and Clutterbuck, 1995).

While mentors and teacher practitioners may not always regard themselves as teachers of adults and may not regard their occupation as adult educators, they actually straddle the expertise of two professions – their own and that of educators of adults. But the concept of profession has never been agreed upon by scholars and so it is wiser here to separate occupational structures (profession) from occupational attitudes (professionalism), and it is much more significant to enquire whether teacher practitioners are professional teachers than to ask whether they are members of two professions. The teacher practitioners should be experts in teaching adults in an interpersonal situation; they should have both the knowledge and skill to undertake this role with competence. Additionally, since the body of knowledge in the education of adults is expanding rapidly, they should be endeavouring to keep abreast with all of these developments, so that they can offer their learners the most expert service. Hence, teacher practitioners should be both professional teachers and professional practitioners in order to perform their role: this combination of professionalisms is the essence of their role.

Such an argument also holds good for those mentors who facilitate and structure learning, whose role is *de facto* that of teacher practitioner even though they may be called mentors.

Straddling two professionalisms

The teacher practitioner and those mentors are, therefore, in a most interesting position, they straddle two professionalisms and should be experts in both. Such a role has its own responsibilities, rewards and problems. They should keep abreast of new knowledge and skills in their practice, but at the same time they are required to be aware of new educational knowledge and to be skilful in the manner by which they facilitate the learning of their students. But there is only a limited amount of time for reading and studying, and few people are prepared or are able to devote all their leisure (if they have any!) to work preparation, so that they are frequently confronted with a dilemma – wherein do they place their energies? This problem is exacerbated when they have heavy workloads, as is increasingly happening in the Health and Social Services, since they are still expected to continue their professional practice as well as to teach the learners. In the ward situation, it might sometimes be possible for the clinical nurse having a teaching role to assume it quite specifically for some time, whilst colleagues concentrate more on their clinical roles. But this type of division of labour cannot occur so easily in the community where, for instance, practice teachers are independent professional practitioners. Students may, therefore, be viewed as additional burdens to an already overloaded practice.

Straddling two professional roles has, however, a great many rewards as well as additional responsibilities: it can, for instance, result in job satisfaction at two levels, that of caring for patients/clients and that of helping students and junior colleagues to improve their own practice. This latter aspect has the additional bonus of knowing that the teacher practitioners' own standards of role performance can be maintained and perpetuated, in part, since they can learn from their students and junior colleagues as well as teach them. Yet it must be recognized that, however rewarding the work, straddling two professional roles is both a difficult and demanding task for those who undertake it and it is one that teacher practitioners will inevitably perform in different ways.

Some teacher practitioners may discover that they prefer professional practice and get more satisfaction from its performance, others may find more pleasure from conducting their teaching role and assisting learners to become more competent practitioners, while a third group may gain satisfaction from combining both teaching and practising. Some teacher practitioners might ultimately resign from their teaching role in order to concentrate on professional practice. Many others, for example, ward managers, have little choice and are required to perform both of these roles, plus their managerial one. However, if teacher practitioners and occasionally nurse teachers are available to assist ward managers, some of the latter may find great satisfaction in mentoring, etc.

The teacher practitioner's role straddles two entirely different professionalisms, yet it is a specific role. It is, in many ways, amongst the most significant in any occupation since it combines theory, practice and the teaching of practice. Nursing and to some extent social work, unlike many professions, have recognized the importance of the role and have offered some form of preparation for it. The teacher practitioner's role is not only highly skilled but also very significant because it lies at the interfaces of theory and practice and occupational preparation and practice.

The teacher practitioner within professional education and training

Teacher practitioners are practitioners and so they are also teachers of professional skills. Their own professional experience means that they have built up their own repertoire of expertise, but they have to be aware that they do not assume their expertise in such a way that they cannot teach it. What should make them different from the expert discussed earlier is that they are aware of the way that skills are performed and are able to teach learners how to perform them.

In students' minds it is easy for theory and practice to become divorced: it is quite common to hear learners, returning to a school or college after a period of professional practical experience, exclaim how much they had enjoyed their practice but how irrelevant the theoretical knowledge appears. A variety of reasons may exist for this, including:

- Practice is obviously very relevant to what the students are looking for and so theory seems distant from it.
- Theory tends to be abstract, generalized and impersonal whereas practice appears concrete, specific and personal.
- Theory is sometimes taught in an uninteresting fashion and not applied to the actual occupational experience.
- Teachers of theory may be far removed from practice and immersed in it for its own sake.
- Modular systems of training may not be in operation and the theory may not be immediately applicable to the students' current work situation.
- The theory taught is discipline-based rather than practice-based and, while it is necessary to have some discipline-based understanding, it is more important to have a good grasp of practical knowledge from the outset.
- Teachers might come from the disciplines rather than from practice, and this is increasingly likely as nursing and social work education becomes more closely integrated into higher education.

None of these reasons is an excuse for poor teaching but they are offered as examples of reasons why students may feel that the two are so far apart.

Yet a great deal of curriculum knowledge, i.e. theoretical knowledge, is included in the curriculum by the different professions's ruling bodies. However, there is often a lack of sophisticated understanding between the two types of theory – theory *of* practice and theory *about* practice, the former being practice-driven and the latter driven from the demands of the cognate disciplines themselves. It is important that this difference is fully recognized in curriculum planning. It is at this interface of practice and practical knowledge that the teacher practitioners and mentors perform much of their roles. It is not just a matter of helping the students and the new entrants to the profession to utilize the practical knowledge that they have been taught, it is also a matter of helping them become reflective practitioners and to learn from their own practice so that they can begin to construct and enlarge their own bodies of practical knowledge.

Teaching theory has often been equated with 'education' while the teaching of practical skills has usually been called 'training'. Education has been regarded as a high status process and training as low status. However, with the emergence of the idea of practical knowledge, this distinction is becoming blurred, and it has been argued elsewhere (Jarvis, 1983a; Pring, 1993) that this distinction is over-simplistic and that training may also be educational. Indeed, with the growth of the idea of continuing education, and the development of such new degree courses as practitioner doctorates, this crude separation between education and training should be regarded as something historical and, especially in vocational education, the two should be combined since practice and practical knowledge are pragmatically related and cannot be separated.

The preparation of professionals should always be regarded as an educational process, even when they are learning skills. However, there are sociological studies that examine the reasons why theoretical knowledge has high status and practical knowledge has low status (for example, Young, 1971), and the fact that this actually occurs does mean that teacher practitioners, despite their very significant role, usually have lower status than the lecturer of theory in higher education. At the same time, their role is significant in professional preparation and, as was pointed out earlier, they often become role models for the new recruits to the profession. In addition, they are most frequently the assessors of students' performances so that they also become the gate-keepers to the profession; assessment is a subject to which further reference is made later in the book and so it will not be discussed further here.

Teacher practitioners and mentors, therefore, occupy a significant place in the preparation and development of recruits to, and junior staff in, the profession: without such roles the education, training and professional and personal development of students and staff would be impoverished beyond measure.

Conclusion

This chapter has examined the roles of the mentor and the teacher practitioner, highlighting some of its significant features and illustrating some of its satisfaction and challenges. Their role is of a dual nature, practising and teaching, in which there are inherent conflicts and tremendous opportunities. However, the concern of this book is the performance of the educational and developmental elements of the roles and so the focus of the remainder of the book is on these processes, rather than the actual professional performance of the practitioners.

11. Mentoring – Rhetoric and Reality

Gary Stidder and Sid Hayes

This study looks at the impact of the recent changes in teacher training at an East Sussex Secondary School where teachers have responsibility for mentoring initial teacher trainees (ITTs). While this has provided an opportunity to become more involved in the preparation of new teachers, a chance to change focus and, to a certain extent, increase job satisfaction, the speed of change has presented some practical difficulties and problems in implementing and fulfilling the role. Specific reference is made to Physical Education as the nature of the work in this area can pose unusual problems. The 'partnership' between the school and the Higher Education Institution is examined to ascertain the extent to which mentors feel that they are being adequately supported.

The information gained was collected through informal interviews with colleagues in school and Higher Education Institutions. This information has been analysed and forms the basis for some recommendations for 'partnerships' in initial teacher training.

Introduction

Regulations introduced in 1992 and 1993 (DFE, 1992 and DFE, 1993) require students studying a B.A. QTS (Qualified Teacher Status) to spend thirty two weeks in schools throughout their four years of study. This represents twenty five percent of the course in total, while PGCE students spend twenty four weeks out of thirty six in schools representing sixty six percent of their time. Since these recommendations demand more classroom experience for ITT it raises the question of who ultimately will provide the professional support for their training. While Higher Education Institutions (HEIs) certainly have some part to play there has been a significant increase in the role the school must assume in the overall professional development of the trainee teacher. Whilst these changes have altered the way in which teachers are trained, Beels and Powell (1994) point out that there are no rules to define mentorship and set it within a statutory framework unlike, for instance, the regulatory framework surrounding appraisal. To date there has been limited published research in the area of partnerships between schools and HEIs and even less on the development of the mentor system. The purpose of this study is to assess the impact which these changes are having on the working experiences of physical education teachers and their partners in HE.

Defining mentoring

The origins of mentorship can be traced back to ancient Greece (in Homer's Odyssey). The professional origins come from the corporate world and over the past two decades it has become a prominent feature of many professions including teaching (Kerry and

Gary Stidder and Sid Hayes: 'Mentoring – Rhetoric and Reality' in *MENTORING AND TUTORING* (1998), 5.3, pp. 57–64.

Mayes, 1994). The term has been the subject of much debate and has stimulated discussion among educationalists and a multitude of different approaches have been taken (Merriam, 1983).

While mentoring has become a topical issue in education, there still seems to be very little progress in establishing its meaning. Morton-Cooper and Palmer (1993), for example, agree that mentoring is in vogue but question whether the concept is clearly understood. Beels and Powell (1994) have stated that defining mentoring is particularly difficult because no two organisations are the same.

Jaques (1992) sees a mentor as being instructor, teacher, counsellor and assessor rather than simply a craft expert to be copied by the novice. Morton-Cooper and Palmer (1993) believe that, although expertise is a relative term not everyone will want to equate expertness with seniority. Mawer (1996) agrees that in essence the mentor (in schools) may need to view him/herself not only as a professional guide, facilitator and assessor but also a bit of a personal/pastoral tutor and counsellor. However, at the same time he warns of the temptation to 'clone' a copy of themselves in the trainee.

From their observations and interviews with mentors and student teachers Yeomans and Sampson (1994) argued that some general principles of mentoring were beginning to emerge. These included personal, professional and structural support in the form of counselling, educating, planning and training. Beels and Powell (1994) found some common threads and suggest that the fundamental roles of mentoring should include teacher development, school induction support, pastoral support, being a sponsor and an assessor of teacher competence.

Mentoring still remains an area open to interpretation. The mixture of opinions and viewpoints should be seen as opportunities to begin to formulate a working practice for mentors in order to dispel some of the existing confusion and to reassure teachers involved in the training of ITTs. Taylor and Stephenson (1996) have agreed that there are no definitive answers to the question what is mentoring? or even to the one that is more pressing for most mentors – What do I have to do if I am a mentor? Therefore, it can only be concluded that student teachers will continue to have different experiences until a working code of practice is formulated.

Methodology

In the absence of a clear conceptual lead, one of the tasks of this study was to formulate, for the local situation, a working definition of the process of mentoring and the role of mentors in schools. For the purpose of this enquiry, mentoring is viewed as a form of professional and personal support in which the supporting teacher (mentor), trainee and the HEI staff work closely together in order to improve and develop their understanding of teaching and the school environment and enable the trainee to incorporate this knowledge within his/her emerging professional expertise. The research focuses on the partnerships between a physical education department of a university in the south east of England and an urban secondary school in East Sussex. The authors believe this school to be a typical secondary school which is co-educational from the age of 11–16 with 900 pupils on roll from a variety of social backgrounds. Nevertheless we recognise that the limited focus of the fieldwork limits the extent to which we can generalise our findings. The study focused on the demands that mentoring has placed on teachers. Data was obtained through observation and unstructured interviews based on opportunistic and spontaneous conversations (See Burgess, 1988). These included brief discussions in the staff room, conversations over lunch, exchanges of ideas at staff meetings and social gatherings. The intention was to find out how teachers experienced the role of mentoring.

Time

At the East Sussex Secondary School the teachers who already carry out a range of responsibilities, usually in middle management, are trusted with the job of mentoring Initial Teacher Trainees. Phillips, Latham and Hudson (1996) found that, without exception, mentors perceive their role to be largely under-resourced in terms of time. Thane (1996) has remarked 'that since teachers are employed to teach, then it must follow that their other responsibilities must not take up too much of their time' (p 12). In some cases, more time is spent trying to fulfil these other responsibilities than actually teaching children. One senior teacher commented that, 'There is no core activity in teaching anymore.' Curriculum planning, lesson preparation, marking, budgeting, reporting, pastoral duties, parents evenings, health and safety audits, setting exams and special needs are but a few demands on teachers' time. Physical Education is unique because whilst PE specialists share all these responsibilities the demands of extra curriculum duties make their time even more precious. It is recognised that a situation where mentors teach full time and fit their mentoring duties in around the edges does not permit staff development to flourish (Fullan, 1993) and structures within schools may account for much of this time deficiency, for as one teacher said 'If things don't get done because of time then I think that I am being poorly managed.' Therefore, those responsible for running schools and liaising with HEI's must consider the allocation of time to mentors if effective training is to take place.

This raises a number of questions about the quality of training that students are receiving. Phillips, Latham and Hudson (1996) believe that 'the responsibility has swung too far towards the schools and that they are being asked to do far more than they can possibly deliver given that their prime responsibility is to their pupils and the National Curriculum' (p.127).

Teachers' priorities rest primarily with their pupils; it is reasonable therefore to suggest that in situations where mentors are not afforded sufficient time to provide the support necessary trainees are neglected and this can have a profound effect on their learning experience. Hardy (1996) is in no doubt that if mentors are going to have an impact on trainees' development they will need time during the day to deal with their concerns. Yau (1996) found that trainees in need of help would often perceive their mentors as being too busy to interrupt or bother, believing the teachers' schedule to be more important. This is particularly worrying as trainees may tend to seek advice elsewhere or even worse, keep their concerns to themselves. The whole mentoring process, in these circumstances, becomes what Taylor and Stephenson (1996) describe as 'A messy and fuzzy series of overlaps and blurred edges' (p 30).

Phillips, Latham and Hudson (1996) suggested that mentors believe that there should be more conscious awareness of a mentor's normal teaching load. Alternatively Tait (1996) has said that it is the responsibility of those that plan school-based courses to take into consideration the context and time-consuming nature of teachers' work in schools. If mentoring is to be successful in schools and trainees are to develop their skills, those responsible for their preparation must have the time available to give appropriate support. There is also a further consideration that warrants some attention – that of burn out. This is particularly relevant where schools are in close vicinity to the teacher training institution as is the case in this study. The high demand for local schools means that requests for student places could mean the mentor being involved in this process for thirty two weeks of the school year. To date there is little research carried out on the effects that many years of mentoring may have.

Teachers are only too aware of the lack of quality contact time that they have with their trainee teachers and question whether they are fulfilling their role as a mentor, as well as their ability to offer support, guidance, assessment and induction to trainees in order to develop their teaching plans and competencies (University of Brighton, 1994). Other teachers in this study have also expressed self doubt and experienced a lack of confidence in performing the role of mentor which is supported by the following statement from a practising mentor, 'because there is no quality assurance built into the structure there is no real way of knowing that what you are doing is right.' Yau (1996) highlights this point:

> In the short term the trainee will ultimately pass or fail – be successful or unsuccessful in gaining teaching status. The mentors are not assessed in the same way and so evidence of the rate at which they are developing as mentors is unclear and not evaluated or appraised synonymously with that of the student. (p. 118)

Evidence from the study suggests that the whole scheme is grossly under-resourced and relies heavily on goodwill. School managers can never guarantee to safeguard any time during the school year for any sound post lesson evaluation (Brawdy and Byra, 1995) and teachers invariably are diverted to cover for absences. One teacher commented 'I have to speak to my students during my free lessons but five out of seven 'frees' have been taken already this week.' Brooks (1994) warns that the demands on staff nominated for this role are extensive and cannot be limited to sessions of free time set aside for the purpose. Mentoring PE students can be particularly demanding because a commitment to extra-curricula clubs, activities and teams in a school where sport provides much of its kudos makes post-school, let alone post-lesson, evaluation next to impossible. Therefore, it is not surprising that PE trainees have expressed concern at receiving feedback in the corridor or changing room while children were about (Yau, 1996). Taylor and Stephenson (1996) found that the pressures on teachers today meant that other responsibilities took precedence over trainees needs in that meetings were either postponed or cancelled. But under the current system mentors have said that they have very little choice.

Implications for training

The concerns of mentors in this study tended to focus on the lack of time available to fulfil mentoring duties. This in turn has had an effect on the standard of training that trainee teachers are receiving. The training of mentors was also a central issue for as one teacher commented 'I don't feel adequately prepared for the role. Attending a one day course is not sufficient.' Almond (1996) reinforces this view: 'The transfer of responsibility from University to schools means that teachers have to expand their repertoire.' Greater input from this particular teacher training institution would hopefully alleviate some of the stresses without undermining the mentors' role. At present there does not appear to be any clear cut procedures for selecting mentors. There are no definitive job descriptions, incentives or prescriptions. The training offered does not always increase teachers' understanding of mentoring.

Assessment issues and role conflict

The impact of teachers becoming more involved with the preparation and assessment of future professionals has placed extra demands and pressures on mentors. Being at the forefront of the assessment procedure, as is the case in this partnership, has many implications for both trainee and teacher. There can be a conflict between the role of personal and pastoral supporter, referred to in much of the literature (Jaques, 1992, Morton-Cooper and Palmer, 1993, Yeomans and Sampson, 1994, Mawer, 1995 for example), and that of assessor. At present, in this specific partnership, the mentor passes or fails the trainee. To ask the mentors to take sole responsibility for passing or failing a trainee teacher can place an unnecessary burden solely on the mentor. There is perhaps an opportunity here for the Higher Education institution to offer more support. Joint responsibility would relieve the pressure somewhat as well as acting as a moderation process for the mentor and trainee. This would also go some way towards ensuring quality and consistency of the assessment of trainee competencies as highlighted in the TTA framework for the assessment of quality and standards in initial teacher training (1997). If the spirit of partnership is to be embraced, joint ownership of 'unpalatable' decisions is essential. After all it is the mentor who will have to deal with the consequences of such dilemmas on a day-to-day basis. Teachers in this study felt that being 'judge and jury' placed mentors under too much pressure particularly in situations where student teachers were experiencing difficulties or where there was a clash of personalities. Much of the recent research has identified this as a particular problem. Hardy (1996 p 70)) found that 'trainees would keep quiet about their feelings and comply reluctantly in order to pass their teaching practice.' Phillips, Latham and Hudson (1996) discovered that because students perceived their mentors to hold the key to their qualification they tended to conceal their mistakes because they wished to create a good impression.

There is a further consideration that is worth noting at this point. If a trainee teacher is to be classified as a 'fail' this creates a dilemma for the mentor who has been a significant player in the trainee's development. Will the mentor then begin to question his/her ability as a mentor? Will an in-experienced mentor be tempted to pass a trainee to avoid any self criticism? These are burdensome considerations for mentors who although established professionals may be subject to self-doubt and close scrutiny.

Conclusions

The issues of time allocation, training and role conflict may partly explain why some teachers, in this study, had misgivings about taking on the role. These were typical comments 'I don't want to become a jack of all trades and a master of none' and 'You have to be careful that the quality of your work does not get diluted.' Burn-out should not be under-estimated. One teacher in the study spoke of overload and warned of 'biting off more than you can chew.' Thane (1996) succinctly states that stress, exhaustion and running to stand still are endemic in education today. This would seem to support the findings of Yau (1996) where there was a reluctance, or at least a passive resistance amongst teachers to take on the role of mentor as they perceived it to be yet another responsibility which got in the way of their real work and one that afforded neither status, financial reward nor career development. Other recent research (Mawer, 1996) found that there were anxieties among teachers about taking on the role without adequate time and funding and many were apprehensive about what had to be achieved.

A joint decision with the link tutor from the Higher Education institution on assessment issues would perhaps relieve such pressure and contribute positively to the mentors' practical role as well as peace of mind. This would further develop the whole training process by involving the link tutor in the assessment process. Quality assurance could be enhanced if the tutor was able to act as a moderator between the schools serviced by the Higher Education representative. This could contribute to the mentors' development as they could receive feedback on how other schools were assessing trainees. This moderation could also be an opportunity to develop the mentors' role by encouraging them to move the trainee towards a co-enquirer into aspects of educational practice. This may help to remove some of the feelings of isolation that mentors feel when training teachers. Ultimately all parties, mentors, link tutors and most importantly, trainee teachers could benefit from joint ownership of assessment decisions.

Teachers in this study have expressed a need for effective training in observing, assessing and reporting the progress of ITTs. Thane (1996, p13) has suggested that schools should employ specialists. The business analogy used in supporting his argument is an interesting one: 'No-one expects British Aerospace to be staffed entirely by engineers or Boots by pharmacists so why should teachers hold all the jobs in schools? 'Employing professional full time mentors, who may have little or no teaching commitment during the week may be idealistic and would certainly have implications for funding, but is nevertheless an interesting idea.

The new framework for the assessment of quality and standards in Initial Teacher Training will hopefully address some of these issues. It is hoped that the criteria will help to collect and audit qualitative information as well as review new priorities and set new targets for improvement in ITT (University of Brighton Newsletter 11/96). Furthermore, a series of mentor conferences are planned in order to help subject mentors share ideas, develop skills, consider new initiatives, provide HEI's with feedback about current practice and contribute to the development of partnerships. These undertakings have gone some way in reassuring mentors that their concerns are now being addressed. Clearly the issues of time, support for the job from both the school and the HEI along with the moderation of trainee assessment are still of paramount importance and need to be addressed further. One final question: to what extent do teachers wish to share in the responsibility for the training of entrants into the profession within the present structures? Clearly the constraints mentioned earlier can limit their effectiveness as mentors.

Bibliography

Almond L (1996) Mentors need more than tips. *Times Educational Supplement* 22 November.

Beelp C, Powell D (1994) *Mentoring with Newly Qualified Teachers. The Practical Guide.* CCDU, University of Leeds.

Brawdy P, Byra M (1995) The physical educator supervision of pre-service teachers during an early field teaching practice. *The Physical Education* 52 (3): 147–158.

Brook V (1994) In: C Beels, D Powell *Mentoring with Newly Qualified Teachers. The Practical Guide*, p. 13. CCDU, University of Leeds.

Burgess R (1988) Conversations with a purpose. The ethnographic interview in educational research. *Studies in Qualitative Methodology* 1: 137–155.

DFE (1992) *Initial Teacher Training* (Secondary Phase). Circular 9/92. HMSO, London.

DFE (1993) *Initial Teacher Training* (Secondary Phase). Circular 14/93. HMSO, London.

Fullam M (1993) *Change Forces.* Falmer Press, London.

Glover D, Mardle G (1995) *The Management of Mentoring: Policy Issues.* Kogan Page, London.

Hardy C (1996) Trainees concerns, experiences and needs: implications for mentoring in physical education, In: M Mawer *Mentoring in Physical Education*, pp. 59–72. Falmer Press, London.

Jaques K (1992) Mentoring in initial teacher education. *Cambridge Journal of Education* 22 (3): 337–351.

Kerry T, Mayes A S (1995) *Issues in Mentoring.* Routledge, London.

Mawer M (1995) *The Effective Teaching of Physical Education.* Longman, London.

Merriam S (1983) Mentors and proteges. *Adult Education Quarterly* 33 (3): 161–173.

Morton-Cooper A, Palmer A (1993) *Mentoring and Partnership.* Blackwell, Oxford.

Phillips R, Latham A M, Hudson J (1996) Physical education mentors needs. In: M Mawer *Mentoring in Physical Education: Issues and Insights*, pp. 123–140. Falmer Press, London.

Sampson J, Yeomans R (1994) *Analysing the Work of Mentors.* Falmer Press, London.

Tait E (1996) An account of Laura's first term on a school based placement. In: M Mawer *Mentoring in Physical Education: Issues and Insights*, pp. 73–88. Falmer Press, London.

Taylor M, Stephenson J (1996) What is mentoring. In: M Mawer *Mentoring in Physical Education: Issues and Insights.* Falmer Press, London.

Thane P (1996) Circles of confusion. *Teaching Today*, NASUWT Termly Review, Autumn (15): 12–13.

TTA (1997) *Standards for the Award of Qualified Teacher Status.* Teacher Training Agency, London.

University of Brighton (1994) *Partnerships in Education Handbook.* University of Brighton.

University of Brighton (1996) *Newsletter* (3) November.

Yau C K (1996) Trainees views of mentoring in physical education. In: M Mawer *Mentoring in Physical Education: Issues and Insights*, pp. 108–119. Falmer Press, London.

12. The Mentoring Dilemma: Guidance and/or Direction?

Brian Gay and Joan Stephenson

How effective is your mentoring programme? How does the nature of a mentoring programme influence outcomes? By looking beneath the process and practice, an examination, analysis and classification of the nature of current real-life mentoring practice is made and a template for the identification of your own project is presented.

Introduction

In this paper we will look at a number of areas within education where mentoring is used as one of a range of development strategies. This will include an overview of practice in mentoring in general, analysing concepts and practices of mentor-like behaviour from historical to present day real-life examples. Reference will be made to specific projects within our respective universities. In reviewing these areas of application it is inevitable that the concept of life-long learning be explored and that the implications of the mentoring process for the development of a learning organisation be acknowledged. A range of models of mentoring practice will be suggested, along with a framework for possible categorization of specific schemes. They are set within a social and political perspective and hypotheses raised about the 'fitness for purpose' of the identified categories of mentoring. Readers will be invited to consider their own experience and intended outcomes. Benefits to the players in the process will be discussed as will the issues and tensions that seem to be surfacing as the practice of mentoring becomes more firmly embedded within the British educational system.

The national context and our place in it

It has been recognised for some time that for the concept of life-long learning to become a reality it is necessary to get people to learn. The implementation and successful achievement of the National Targets for Education and Training have, as a prerequisite, the engagement of individuals with the process of learning and development. So the practice of 'Compact' arrangements between employers and school, schools and colleges of higher and further education, and schools and community groups, and the use of mentoring as a tool to engage young students actively in the process of learning, have become well established. There are now a number of networks across the United Kingdom, each of which is approaching what is essentially the same issue, though on occasions from slightly different directions. For some 21 years now, the Pimlico Project has been placing students from the Science Faculty of Imperial College in schools in East London. This Pimlico connection is now manifested nationally by over 180 institutions of higher and further education in what is called the BP/Community Service Volunteers Learning

Brian Gay and Joan Stephenson: 'The Mentoring Dilemma: Guidance and/or Direction?' in *MENTORING AND TUTORING* (1998), 6. 1/2, pp. 43–54.

Together Project. This is an example of where student tutoring, as it is more generally known, can begin to move into what we recognise as mentoring. The project itself involves students voluntarily giving up some of their free time to undertake work in a classroom situation over a period of some 10–15 weeks. At the University of the West of England, the project lasts for 15 weeks and each student is expected to donate 2 hours a week to this activity.

Students can be working with groups of pupils on a particular project or with individual pupils who have specific learning difficulties. As a major provider of initial education for teachers, De Montfort University chose to be involved in peer tutoring with pupils in a local Special School. This school caters for children with a range of mental and physical learning difficulties across the 5 to 18 age range. Although the pupil-teacher ratio is superior to that in a normal school, there is still considerable need for increased adult involvement in one-to-one work. It was felt that for pupils to spend some of this time with role models not far removed from their own age group would be beneficial. Given the special needs of the children, the staff at school were concerned that they should be able to rely on a basic understanding of child development and communication skills, for this their first venture into mentoring. It was therefore decided to ask for volunteers from the 4-year Bachelor of Education Courses. Students with scientific and IT skills were especially needed to complement the skills of school staff and to raise the profile of these subjects in the eyes of the school pupils. Students spent one morning a week over the university year (30 weeks), working with individual children in their own classrooms. Evaluations have shown perceived benefits for both children and students. Although initially the student-tutor took a quasi-teacher role, over time this has developed into an 'older friend' basis, confidences and discussion has moved outside the subject knowledge 'zone', and most children bring up personal concerns and requests for advice with their 'mentors' that are not addressed to their teachers. This area of possible sensitivity has been dealt with by the introduction of 'forums', where issues of note are shared between the adults concerned and confidentiality is guaranteed.

Since the age range of pupils encountered by students from both universities can be anything from 5 to 18, we feel it is encumbent on us as institutions to make sure that our students undergo a reasonably thorough training to prepare them for the world they are about to enter.

In April of 1995 BP hosted an international conference on student mentoring and tutoring which brought together over 250 delegates from more than 23 nations (Goodlad, 1995). The purpose of this conference was to seek to explore the ways in which student tutoring is developing and how in fact mentoring as a specific dimension within student tutoring can be effectively applied. It was so successful a forum for the exchange of ideas, experiences and proposals for development, that a second meeting was arranged.

Alongside such activities, we have the National Mentoring Network which, at its annual conference, brings together practitioners in the mentoring field who are primarily involved in Compact arrangements within their local education authority.[1] This network, which has on its steering committee representatives of government departments, Compact consortia, international corporations and higher education institutions, aims to promote best practice within the mentoring arena as it can be applied in Compact arrangements. The network has a published directory of members and outlines within that directory their areas of application. Parallel to this we also find the National Mentoring Consortium. This is a particular organisation, the focus of which is to address mentoring for ethnic minority groups within higher education. It seeks to match students with individuals in corporate organisations who can provide support and guidance during the course of an individual's undergraduate programme. Perhaps one of the best publicised areas of application here is that of Business in the Community with its *Roots and Wings* initiatives. In this venture, individuals are seconded from business to administer programmes across the United Kingdom where school children are linked with mentors from the community within which their school is located.

The European Mentoring Association, another umbrella organisation, seeks to expand the dissemination of practice in mentoring across the countries of Europe and includes, within its glossary of members' interests, the possibility of putting like-minded practitioners in touch with one another.

All this activity in the practice of mentoring has led to a variety of research projects carried out by members of higher education institutions, by research units in corporate business and by professional consultants who are bought in to study the effects and outcomes of mentoring programmes in a variety of contexts. The Mentoring Network of the Society for Research in Higher Education (SRHE) has a membership made up of people who are actively involved in the research and development of the mentoring process in all its aspects. Its register of members' activities reflects the wide range of settings in which mentoring or mentor-like activity is found.

Why mentoring?

A common theme running through the programmes that have been mentioned is the attempt to engage under-represented or under-achieving individuals in the process of learning. The belief is that the use of mentoring within this area would allow individuals better to develop their potential and therefore their contribution to society as a whole (Gay, 1994). The same can be said of those schemes, operated by both our universities, where a more knowledgeable person is placed in a mentor-like relationship with another, to guide him/her through an induction period which is in essence an enculturation to a role, ethos or set of rules for survival. An instance of this is the help and guidance given to a new lecturer by another member of the department, in the planning, resourcing and teaching of course material. In the same vein, on the affective side the easing of the newcomer into the ethos of faculty life and 'back-door' methods of obtaining resources and recognition. This all done without any judgmental or appraisal motivation. In the life of students this role is sometimes of a similar altruistic nature, and can have the mentor's role being taken by a member of staff, whose primary interest is the emotional, personal and academic well-being of the student, divorced from any disciplinary or assessment function, or a student of advanced position in the learning process. Increasingly, however, this mentoring role is being combined with a judgmental purpose, namely that of seeing not only that the students make the right academic and personal choices and practices for their own individual good and fulfilment, but that the needs of the university i.e. for students' success in a more highly rated area and award level, are met. Payment by results and differential funding of subjects in universities by central government, has encouraged and could further accelerate this trend.

In addition to all the incidences of mentoring outlined above, there is also the growing fashionableness of mentoring as a means of training for a job. Apprenticeship, but of a particular kind, has gained much ground in government eyes, as a cheap way of training a work force. An example of an idea now abandoned by the former Secretary of State for Education and Employment[2] will illustrate the less acceptable motives of this.

The United Kingdom, in common with many other developed countries, has many disaffected teenagers who resort to disturbance and petty crime. Many of these children are below 16, which is the statutory school leaving age. They truant from school, because, it is said, the academically-based education system does not appeal to this section of society. In an attempt to remove these young persons from the streets and temptation, it was announced that from the age of 14 they would spend half of the week in a workplace, where they would be 'mentored' by a worker there. There was an outcry, both from the children who saw themselves as being used as cheap labour and from the workers who were to be used as social agents with no training, support or remuneration. The educationalists and mentoring practitioners also had much to say and the directive was quietly dropped.

Within professional training schemes for teachers, the government have also required providers to include mentoring by practising teachers within the programme of training, and other public sector professionally-trained employees are also increasingly having some form of mentoring activity included with their preparation.

Investment and pay-out

If we look at the schemes above in some detail, questions have to be raised about the return that is achieved for the investment that is made (Freedman, 1993). This seems a rather market-driven approach to the activity. Nevertheless it is a question that does have to be raised. If we examine some of the mentoring programmes that are currently underway in America, in much the same arenas as here, we find that this question has been asked and some very clear answers are coming forward. The most clear lesson that can be learned is that if one wishes to ignite and develop the desire for learning within individuals, then what is necessary is not more of the same but something that is different.

In what way do we mean this? In the majority of the types of mentoring that we have been talking about so far, the activity is supplemental to the main teaching activities that are surrounding the individual learners. Mentoring as a supplemental activity to those mainstream strategies has at its disposal the opportunity to be more flexible. Evidence from America suggests that if one is able to identify the preferred learning styles of individuals and provide materials and opportunities for learning in those styles, then initial learning is engaged more readily and accelerates more rapidly. Mentoring, because of its opportunities for flexibility and variability in dealing with individuals, can therefore provide learning opportunities alongside mainstream teaching, which do not conflict with the objectives of the school curriculum. A teacher actively involved with 30 plus pupils in the classroom teaching a prescribed curriculum, has little opportunity to engage in such an individualised approach. As an interesting aside, it is worthy of note that this focus upon preferred learning styles is being exploited by the world of management education and development. For example, International Learning Systems have, on the basis of their own research, indicated that cost-effective management training is provided only where the preferred learning styles of individuals are identified. They then work with *Fortune 500* companies, with cohorts of managers of an identified style, in such a way as to achieve cost effectively the objectives of the training programme. In the world of universities competing for part-time paying higher-degree students, preferred learning styles are being taken into account as a factor in recruitment in such schemes as De Montfort University's Master's degree by assessment, in as much as they provide feedback to their individual protégés on how they are performing relative to a particular standard. The mentor therefore needs knowledge of those standards in order to be able to advise the protégé wisely. The role of the mentor in summative assessment, as illustrated in teacher education and nurse training, is completely different. Here they are not the key holders to resources for learning but door keepers to further progress within the learning situation. Their perception of the student's progress or achievement is paramount and not infrequently includes a definition of practice that is not shared by the student and which the student, for a variety of constraining reasons largely connected with power, is not able to contradict (Stephenson, 1995). When we add to this the consideration that in teaching the 'good practice' the mentor is to pass on is that defined by Her Majesty's Inspectors[3] this raises questions about how open the learning methods in the achievement of objectives are permitted to be. To clone the model of 'good practice' and the ways of achieving it, is surely prescriptive as to approach, methods and content and a far cry from the flexibility of preferred learning styles discussed before. All Education Schools in United Kingdom Universities are faced with this dilemma.

We can cross-reference this to practice within current post-experience programmes where mentors are often provided as a condition of programme entry by a sponsoring organisation. These mentors have the responsibility for providing opportunities, exposure to learning situations and support and guidance, a similar prescription to that of teacher and nurse mentors, they do not however have the responsibility for assessment. The issue here is, are we in fact seeing the activity of mentoring being moved, as a consequence of the imposition of pressure from stakeholders, from a developmental into a directive mode of operation?

If we identify some of the relationships that we can see in developmental situations we can then go on to identify some of the contextual sources of pressure that can be brought to bear upon that activity.

If we look at the four sets of relationships that we have in Figure 1, then in terms of the therapist/client dimension here, the situation is non-judgemental, open-ended in terms of time, and supportive yet questioning in its application. In the master/disciple relationship, perhaps most clearly identified in the area of Zen Buddhism, we have the situation where a master walks at the pace of the disciple's individual needs and does so in such a way that is non-judgemental yet clear in terms of stages of development. The medieval craftsman took on board an apprentice. The apprentice was tied to the master craftsman for a significant period of time for the development of a particular area of skill. When the craftsman was of the opinion that the apprentice had reached a significant level of development and was proficient in his trade, he would allow the apprentice to present himself to a panel of peers of the craftsman in order to demonstrate his skill and knowledge and it was for them to judge the individual as now being or not being a craftsman himself.

CHARACTERISTICS OF RELATIONSHIPS
(expressed as verbal nouns)

1.	**MENTOR – PROTÉGÉ (MP)**	
ADVISING		COACHING
GUIDING		SUPPORTING
TEACHING		AFFIRMING
2.	**MASTER – DISCIPLE (MD)**	
EXPLORING		TEACHING
REVEALING		AFFIRMING
GUIDING		CONFIRMING
3.	**CRAFTSMAN – APPRENTICE (CA)**	
EXPLORING		SUPPORTING
TEACHING		DIRECTING
TRAINING		AFFIRMING
4.	**THERAPIST – CLIENT (TC)**	
EXPLORING		SUPPORTING
REVEALING		AFFIRMING
	CENTRAL DYNAMIC	
DEPENDENCY	____________________	INDEPENDENCE

Figure 1 4 possible models

Looking at the mentor/protégé relationship, we have to ask ourselves does it or should it conform to any or some of the previous models? What the three previous models have in common is what Baker-Miller (1986) refers to as temporary inequality. By this she means that the purpose of the relationship between the partners is one in which whatever gap exists between the client/disciple/apprentice and the therapist/master/craftsman is a gap that is temporary in nature and that is to be filled. The object therefore is for the individual to pass by the position that the teacher currently holds. This is to happen irrespective of whatever shaping and acculturation which naturally takes place. We need to bear in mind that the development of a individual always takes place within a context and that part of that context may be focused upon shaping an individual in terms of their extra socialisation into appropriate characteristics. This leads us towards a situation that can be summarised in the following diagram, Figure 2 where not only. the nature of the relationships but the intentions and outcomes of the project can be shown to have the potential to be governed by and to govern the nature of the process taking place.

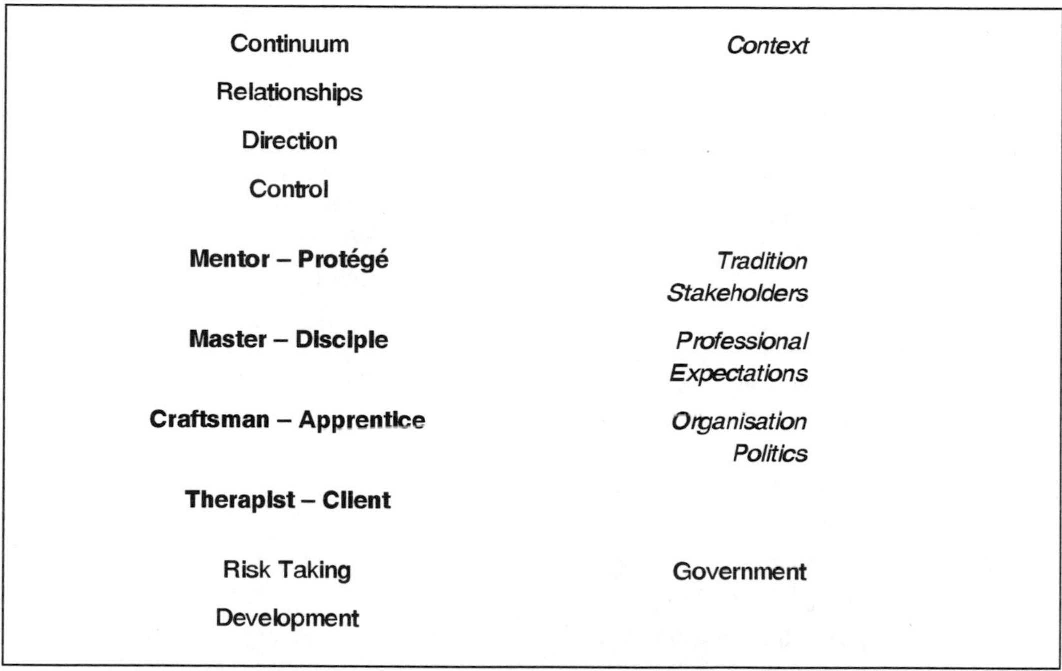

Figure 2 Relationship context and continuum: towards an analytical framework (Gay and Stephenson, 1996)

We would suggest that not only an analysis but an evaluation of the purposes and outcomes of mentoring as a learning vehicle are long overdue. In order to do this an audit of practice and fitness for purpose set against stated and hidden objectives of the individual, personnel, organisation and social climate needs to take place.

Bearing in mind the points raised with regard to both the context and the perceived purpose of the mentoring activity it is possible to view a range of potential forms of interaction. Each of these forms would reflect the relative power distribution within the relationship and therefore the degree of prescription or risk taking evidenced in the mentoring process. This range is capable of expression in the following diagram, Figure 3 which could be considered as an attempt to construct a conceptual framework within which the relationships previously described, and indeed any form of mentoring or coaching activity, could be evaluated. Fitness for purpose, so long as purpose is clearly defined, might then lend itself to critical and self-critical reflection and evaluation.

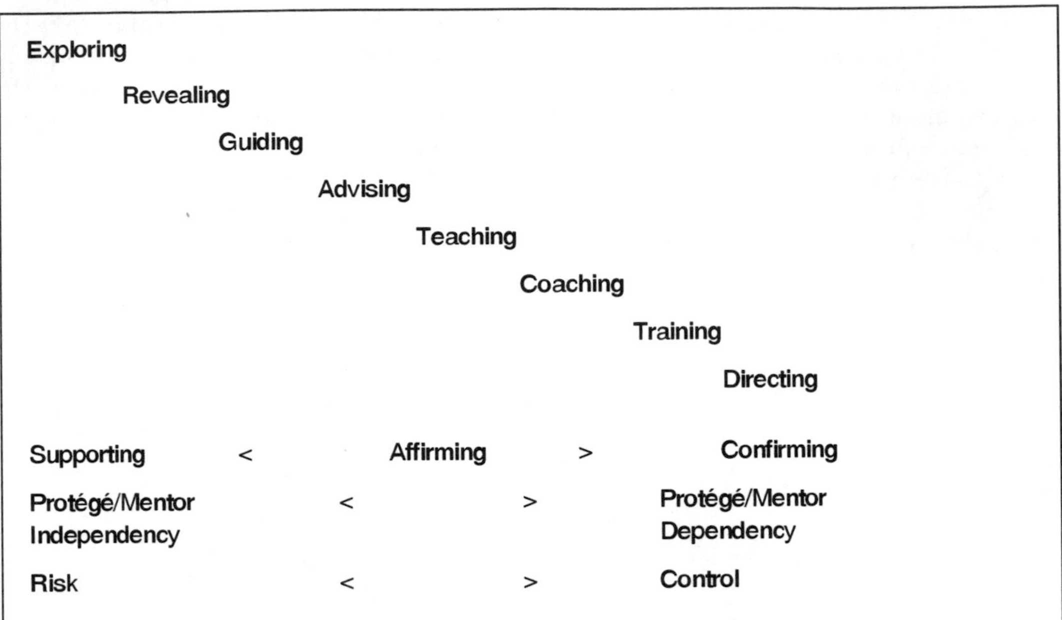

Figure 3 Towards a framework for evaluation
(first presented at the International Mentoring Conference, San Antonio 1996)
(Gay and Stephenson, 1996)

At this point we can now look at two definitions of mentoring, one over 20 years old, the other more recent; they point up to some extent the issues raised here and the sort of tensions that we have to address. The first definition is that of Levinson *et al.* (1978) in their seminal book:

> The mentor relationship is one of the most complex, and developmentally important, a man can have in early adulthood. The mentor is ordinarily several years older, a person of great experience and seniority in the world the young man is entering. No word currently in use is adequate to convey the nature of the relationship we have in mind here. Words such as 'counsellor' or 'guru' suggest the more subtle meanings, but they have other connotations that would be misleading. The term 'mentor' is generally used in a much narrower sense, to mean teacher, adviser or sponsor. As we use the term it means all these things, and more (97).

The second definition is that of Murray and Owen (1991):

> Facilitated mentoring is a structure and series of processes designed to create effective mentoring relationships, guide the desired behaviour change of those involved and evaluate the results for the protégés, the mentors and the organisation (5).

Whatever the field of application, the practice of mentoring is coming under increasing pressure. It is being toasted as the answer to so many of our problems, and is feted as a means for more confidently moving into the future. These claims need to be based on evidence from the empirical evaluation of practice. What we need to be constantly aware of, however, is the ways in which a practice that had its origins in the developmental relationship of one individual with another is now being structured, directed and redefined to satisfy institutional as well as individual needs.

Notes

1. Local Education Authorities, commonly known as LEAs, are responsible for the provision of state schooling within their geographical area. These are generally the same as the 'counties' into which the United Kingdom is split for local government purposes. However larger conurbations often have an administrative system of their own, separate from the rest of the county in which they are situated.
2. Under the United Kingdom system of parliamentary democracy, the party in power, the Government, headed by the Prime Minister, has a cabinet of senior politicians chosen by him or her, to head areas of government; they are collectively known as 'cabinet ministers' and individually as Secretary for State.
3. Her Majesty's Inspectors (HMIs), are the body of people employed to check upon the quality in schools, which they do by spending time in a school investigating all aspects of work, administration and resources. They are controlled by OFSTED (Office for Standards in Education) and work to a prescribed set of articles.

References

Baker Miller J (1986) *Towards a New Psychology of Women*, 2nd edn. Beacon Press, Boston.

Freedman M (1993) *The Kindness of Strangers: Adult Mentors, Urban Youth and the New Voluntarism*. Jossey-Bass, San Francisco.

Gay B (1994) What is Mentoring? *Education and Training* 36 (5): 4–7.

Gay B, Stephenson J (1196) A coat of many colours: mentoring in higher education – a British perspective. *Proceedings of the International Mentoring Association*, San Antonio, Texas.

Goodlad S (1995) (ed.) *Students as Tutors and Mentors*. Kogan Page/BP, London.

Levinson D J, Darrow C, Klein E, Levinson M, Mckee B (1978) *The Seasons of a Man's Life*. Ballantine, New York.

Murray M, Owen M A (1991) *Beyond the Myths and Magic of Mentoring*. Jossey-Bass, San Francisco.

Oxford Polytechnic/Department of Employment (1992) *Work-Based Learning Contracts*. HMSO, London.

Stephenson J (1995) Significant others – the primary student view of practice in schools. *Education Studies* 21 (3): 323–335.

Yeomans R, Sampson J (1994). The role of the mentor. In: R Yeomans, J Sampson (eds) *Mentorship in the Primary School*, Falmer Press, London.

13. Are Mentors Ready to Make a Difference? A Survey of Mentors' Attitudes Towards Nurse Education

David Pulsford, Kath Boit and Sharon Owen

This paper reports on a survey of practitioners who act as mentors to student nurses from a Higher Education Institution in Northern England. The aims of the survey were to gain a profile of mentors, and to seek their views regarding their degree of support in undertaking the mentoring role, and their experience of mentors' update sessions. Respondents were experienced as mentors. As a group, they felt supported by their work colleagues, but fewer felt that they had adequate support from the HEI or their managers. Respondents wanted more time for mentoring activities, closer links with the HEI before, during and after practice placements, and more user friendly assessment documentation. Respondents did not report difficulty in spending enough time working with students, although this is a frequent complaint of students. Mentors update sessions were often not attended, either through staff shortages, or through lack of information.

Introduction

The face of nurse education is changing, as Higher Education Institutions (HEIs) implement the recommendations of Chapter Four of *Making a Difference* (Department of Health 1999) and *Fitness for Practice* (UKCC 1999) within their pre-registration nursing courses. Two key principles of these documents are, firstly the greater prominence to be given to practice-based learning, and the acquisition of nursing skills, and secondly, the enhancement of partnership between HEIs and health care providers in the provision of nurse education. Practitioners who take on the role of practice-based mentors will have a central part to play in ensuring the success of new pre-registration courses developed to implement *Making a Difference* and *Fitness for Practice.* They will need to have a positive approach towards mentoring students, and to feel supported in their role.

This paper reports on a survey of mentors of student nurses within a number of NHS Trusts which offer placements to student nurses from a College of Higher Education in the North of England (referred to in this paper as the HEI). The survey was carried out as part of a project undertaken by the HEI in partnership with local NHS Trusts and PCTs to implement the recommendations of Chapter Four of *Making a Difference* within the HEI's catchment area. This project involved revising the HEI's pre-registration nursing programmes, taking measures to enhance access to nurse education, and implementing initiatives to enhance partnership between the HEI and local health care providers. The intention of the survey was to provide information as to the views and perspectives of practitioners regarding nurse education, in order to judge their readiness for the significant role in practice-based

David Pulsford, Kath Boit and Sharon Owen: 'Are Mentors Ready to Make a Difference? A Survey of Mentors' Attitudes Towards Nurse Education' in *NURSE EDUCATION TODAY* (2002), 22, pp. 439–446.

learning implied by the changes proposed within *Making a Difference,* and to identify areas where partnership between the HEI and grass roots practitioners may be strengthened.

The concept of mentorship

The literature has reported confusion as to the roles of practitioners in nurse education, and the terminology used to describe those roles (Andrews & Wallis 1999, Neary 2000, Watson 1999). The terms mentor, assessor and supervisor have all been employed, and the distinct activities that each term implies have often become blurred together. Recently, the UKCC has issued advisory standards, which indicate that *mentor* should be the term of choice, and set out the roles and responsibilities of a mentor (UKCC 2000). Mentors should involve themselves in:

- Providing constructive support to students,
- Assisting in integrating learning from practice and educational settings,
- Developing opportunities for students to undertake experiences to meet their learning needs,
- Maintaining a learning environment,
- Acting as a role model,
- Assessing the student in practice,
- Improving practice,
- Contributing to course development.

All student nurses from the HEI are allocated a mentor on each practice placement who undertakes the above roles as appropriate. Each practice placement also has a designated link tutor: a member of the lecturing staff who is responsible for visiting students on placement within their link areas, and liaising with practice-based mentors regarding the students for whom they are responsible.

Literature review: mentorship in pre-registration nurse education

The idea of mentorship took hold in pre-registration nurse education with the introduction of Project 2000 in the late 1980s (Andrews and Wallis 1999). Prior to then, students were employees, who mainly learnt their trade through being part of the complement of the clinical area. In the last ten years, a number of research studies have explored mentorship, from the perspective of students, and from the viewpoint of mentors themselves. Overall, the literature concludes that good mentors are appreciated by students, and can assist their learning (Neary *et al.* 1996), particularly in the earlier stages of pre-registration courses (Gray and Smith 2000). The personal qualities of the mentor, and the nature of the relationship between the mentor and student are central to the success of mentorship. Good mentors feel genuine concern for students as individuals, and want to be mentors (Gray and Smith 2000). A positive mentor/student relationship is one based on partnership, consistency and mutual respect (Cahill 1996, Andrews and Wallis 1999). Poor mentors on the other hand, according to Gray and Smith (2000), break promises, lack knowledge and expertise and have poor teaching skills. They tend to either overprotect their students, or 'throw them in at the deep end', and delegate unwanted jobs to them.

There is a correlation between morale in the clinical area, and the quality of mentorship. Where staff work together and are motivated and satisfied, students feel more supported, while in areas with low morale and dissatisfaction, students are seen as an imposition (Wilson-Barnett *et al.* 1995). Those nurses perceived by students as poor mentors tend to dislike their job, and may be unpopular with their work colleagues (Gray and Smith 2000).

One theme in the literature is the extent to which practitioners regard mentorship as integral to their job as Registered Nurses, or as a separate, additional responsibility. Those practitioners who see mentorship as being a fundamental part of their job are less disturbed by the time impositions of mentoring students (Atkins and Williams 1995). On the other hand, students report that teaching is sometimes separated from care giving, and perceived as something to be done after the 'work' of patient care has been completed – and only if there is enough time (Cahill 1996).

Time is universally regarded as the biggest constraint on effective mentoring (Atkins and Williams 1995, Wilson-Barnett *et al.* 1995, Watson 1999, Phillips *et al.* 2000). Many mentors experience competing demands on their time, and mentoring students often has to give way to the priorities of patient care. Mentors report giving up their own time to meet their responsibilities towards their students (Atkins and Williams 1995, Phillips *et al.* 2000).

A frequent complaint by students is the lack of continuity in their experiences of mentorship. Several studies have reported that contact between students and mentors is often limited, either through mentors being away from work during the student's placement, or through working on opposite shifts (Cahill 1996, Alderman 1998, Phillips *et al.* 2000, Lloyd Jones *et al.* 2001). Students attribute this phenomenon to competing demands on mentors' time, poor planning and managerial support, or lack of interest on the part of mentors (Cahill 1996). Phillips *et al.* (2000) concluded that the validity and reliability of mentors' assessment of students' competence in practice was being compromised by the lack of time that mentors spent working with and observing the students for whom they were responsible.

Another issue is the degree of support that mentors feel they have in undertaking the mentorship role. Sources of support are work colleagues, managers and lecturing staff from HEIs. Staff who support each other are more able to support students (Wilson-Barnett *et al.* 1995). Work colleagues are regarded as important people with whom mentors can discuss problems about students, and colleagues can also assist materially, by helping with workloads (Atkins and Williams 1995). Assistance is sought from managers in matters such as facilitating working on the same shifts as students, and freeing up sufficient time for mentorship activities (Cahill 1996, Watson 1999). Support from lecturers should take the form of clarifying expectations, and giving feedback to mentors as to their performance in that role (Atkins and Williams 1995). One aspect of support that does not appear to have been covered in the literature is the provision by HEIs of annual updating sessions for mentors. It is an English National Board standard that all mentors attend an annual update, facilitated by HEIs, in order to keep abreast of issues in nurse education, discuss mentoring issues with lecturers and their peers, and maintain their competence in undertaking the mentoring role (ENB 1997). The present study gathers information as to mentors' experiences of annual updates, and their views as to how updating may be best facilitated.

Aims of the study

- To gain an overview of practitioners who act as mentors for pre-registration nursing students within the catchment area covered by the HEI.
- To gain information as to mentors' perceived levels of support in undertaking the mentoring role, and factors that would enable them to carry out that role more effectively.
- To ascertain mentors' experiences of annual update sessions, and their views as to how updating may be best facilitated.

Method

A questionnaire was devised, with the assistance of the audit departments of two local NHS Trusts, and following a piloting exercise was distributed by post to 400 mentors from the list of approved mentors held by the HEI. The survey was carried out in April and May 2001. Recipients were selected by choosing at random one mentor from every second clinical placement area from an overall list of placements. This was done to attempt to ensure representation from all the Trusts and PCTs within the HEI's catchment area, and from all Branches of nursing. The questionnaire sought quantitative data regarding the study's aims, and also qualitative data in response to the question, What would make your role as a mentor easier and/or more fulfilling?

A total of 198 questionnaires were returned; a response rate of just under 50%.

Findings

Profile of mentors

Respondents were asked how long they had acted as mentors, and how many students they had mentored in the past year. Figure 1 provides a breakdown of the length of time respondents had been mentors.

The mean number of students for whom respondents had acted as mentors during the past year was 3.3 students. The mode was 2 students, and the range was 0–20 students.

Support for undertaking role of mentor

Figure 2 details mentors' views as to the level of ongoing support they receive from the HEl, their managers, and their colleagues.

Mentors' updates

Figures 3–5 give information as to respondents' experiences of annual mentors' update sessions. Figure 3 details how long ago respondents last attended an update session.

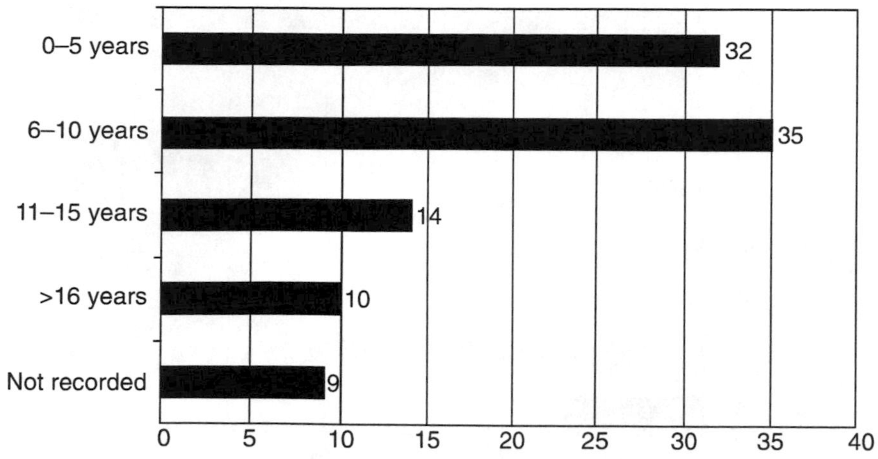

Figure 1 Length of time as a mentor (%)

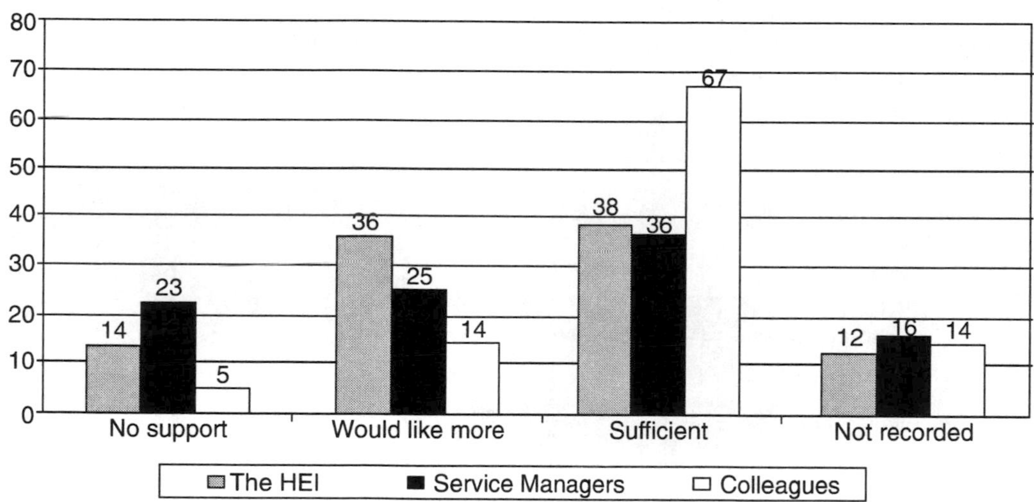

Figure 2 Support for undertaking role of mentor (%)

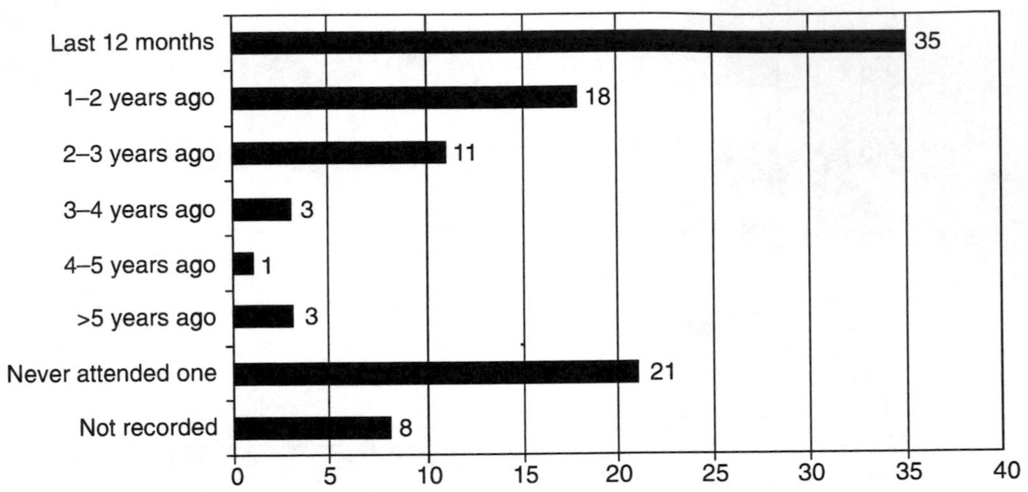

Figure 3 Last mentor's update (%)

Figure 4 details reasons for non-attendance, or why respondents do not attend more regularly. Figure 5 gives respondents' views as to how they would prefer to receive formal updating information and support.

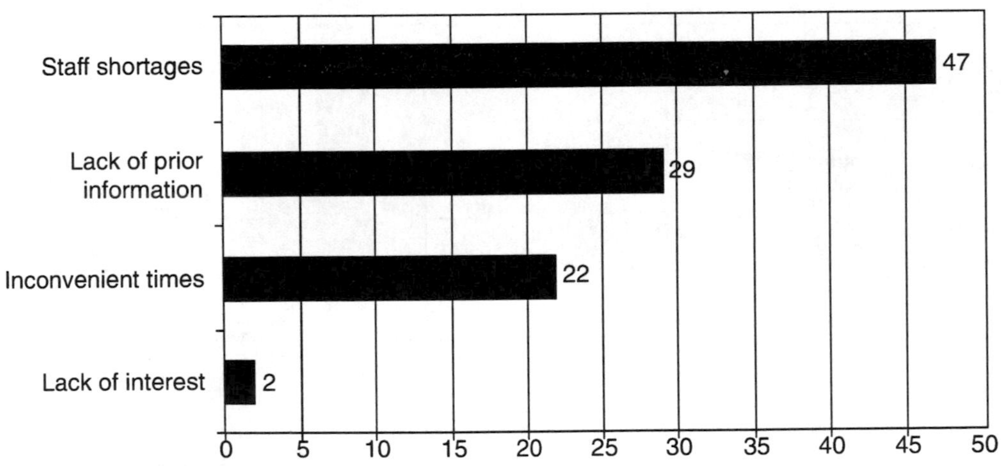

Figure 4 Factors preventing mentor's update attendance (%)

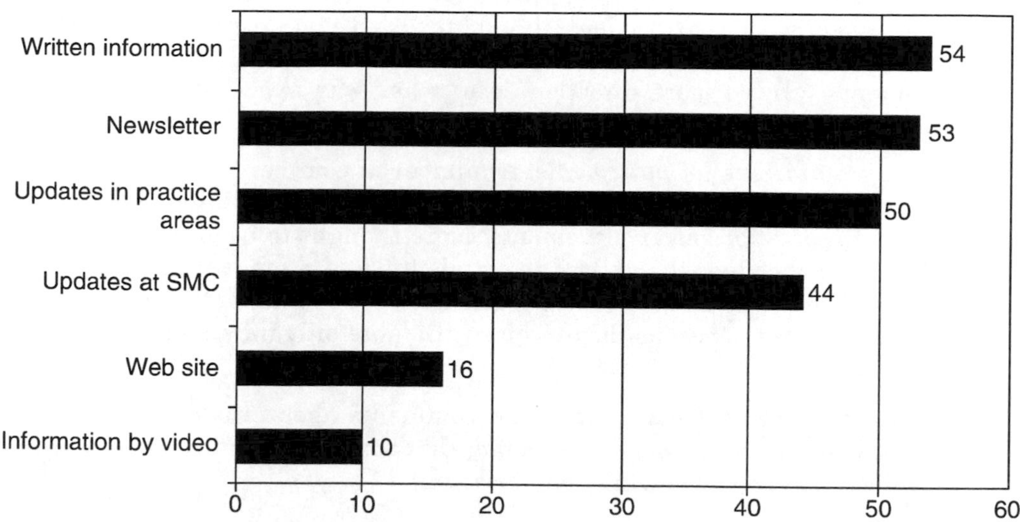

Figure 5 Preferred means of mentor updating (%) includes mutiple answers

Factors that would enhance mentors' ability to provide practice-based learning for student nurses

Respondents were asked to provide qualitative responses to the question: What would make your role as a mentor easier and/or more fulfilling? Responses were sorted into themes by the authors of the survey. The following main themes emerged:

- *Time for undertaking mentoring role:* A large number of respondents reported problems with finding the time to spend with students. Several would prefer supernumerary time, or additional staff cover to allow for spending more time with students. Smaller numbers sought time for doing the paperwork associated with mentoring students, or for gathering information. A couple of respondents stated that they carried out aspects of the mentoring role in their own time.

- *Management support:* Some respondents looked for more management support, in terms of recognition of the demands of the mentoring role, and guidance as to how to prioritise mentoring students, in relation to other professional demands placed on practitioners.

- *Partnership with the HEI:* A number of respondents commented on aspects of the links between practice areas and the HEI. Respondents wanted more information from the HEI about students' placements prior to the commencement of placements, and in particular, more feedback from the HEI as to students' progress, and their evaluations of placement experiences. Some respondents felt that link tutor visits should be more frequent or extensive, and some wanted more contact with the HEI as a whole, rather than contact being focussed on the link tutors. Only one respondent felt that lecturers should be more involved in actual clinical practice.

- *Practice learning documentation:* Several respondents sought enhancements to the documentation that students brought with them to practice placements. There was a desire for less paperwork, or more 'user-friendly' documents. A few respondents wanted more direction as to what was expected of students and themselves during a particular placement.
- *More appropriate use of placements:* A number of comments related to the way that particular clinical areas were used for placements. Respondents wanted students to come for longer placements; more thought to be given to the nature of the placement area when allocating students, and a more even throughput of students. There was also a sense of some mentors feeling on the peripheries of the students' experience, as they received students only infrequently, or for very short periods.
- *Students' motivation:* There were a few comments about students' commitment and motivation, with respondents feeling that some students needed to be more motivated and pro-active whilst on placement.
- *Extra pay:* A small number of mentors would have liked more pay for taking on the mentoring role.

Discussion

This survey reveals a profile of experienced mentors within the HEI's catchment area, with around 60% of respondents having been mentors for more than five years. This may reflect the semi-rural area covered by the HEI; an inner-city area may have a greater turnover of staff. The involvement of respondents with students is very variable. While the majority of mentors work with two or three students per year, some mentors work with much larger numbers. Others work with very few students, and one theme of the survey is of some practitioners who are recognised as mentors, but who are currently on the periphery of local nurse education provision.

The data regarding support for the mentoring role reveals a mixed picture. The majority of respondents felt supported by their work colleagues. This is encouraging, as peer support is a factor in enhancing mentors' ability to work effectively with students (Wilson-Barnett *et al.* 1995). On the other hand, little more than a third of respondents felt they had sufficient support from the HEI, or from their managers. Indeed, a quarter felt that their managers gave them no support. This perceived lack of support may lead to low morale and motivation among mentors, to the detriment of students (Wilson-Barnett *et al.* 1995).

The qualitative information supplied by respondents indicates areas in which greater support is felt to be necessary. This survey supports previous research in identifying time for undertaking mentoring activities as being a significant factor (Atkins and Williams 1995, Wilson-Barnett *et al.* 1995, Watson 1999, Phillips *et al.* 2000). Respondents looked to managers for assistance in managing the demands on time of multiple roles, including mentoring. Several felt that dedicated time should be allocated within the working day to mentoring activities.

Respondents wanted more linkage with the HEI at all stages of the placement allocation process. They expressed the need for more information prior to a student arriving on a placement; greater involvement from link tutors during placements, and, in particular, more feedback following placements, as to the students' evaluation of their experience, and their thoughts about their mentor. This also matches findings from previous research (Atkins and Williams 1995).

Respondents also wanted clearer and more user-friendly assessment documentation. The HEI has attempted to meet this need through developing revised documentation for its new pre-registration nursing courses. The new documentation was developed by a working group which included a cross-section of practitioners, allowing mentors a direct say in the nature of the documents that they will have to complete with students during placements.

There were some issues that the mentors in this survey did not highlight. No respondents expressed difficulty over spending enough time actually working with students to whom they were allocated. This contrasts with the view expressed by students in previous research (and expressed anecdotally by students at the HEI) that mentors did not spend enough time with them (Cahill 1996, Alderman 1998, Phillips *et al.* 2000, Lloyd Jones *et al.* 2001). We may speculate that there is a mismatch between students' and mentors' views as to what constitutes adequate time spent working together.

Another issue that was barely mentioned was that of lecturers from the HEI working alongside students and mentors in the clinical area. It is an English National Board standard that lecturers spend up to 20% of their time in clinical practice (ENB 1997), and the HEI is working towards meeting this standard. However, only one respondent wrote that lecturers working in practice settings would enhance their own ability to mentor students.

The data on mentors' update sessions revealed that fewer than half of respondents had attended an update session in the past year, and 20% had never attended an annual update. The single biggest reason for this was cited as staff shortages, indicating that practitioners prioritised the adequate staffing of clinical areas over attendance at mentors' updates. A significant subsidiary reason was lack of information about the provision of updates. Partnership between HEIs and health care providers implies effective channels of communication between the partners. The communication systems between the HEI and practice placements in this study are revealed as inadequate.

Respondents appeared committed to the principle of updating; only 2% citing lack of interest as a reason for non-attendance.

Respondents looked for greater flexibility in the provision of updating, with a slight preference for written information, and sessions held within practice areas, rather than at the HEI. The literature suggests another way of enhancing update sessions. Mentors in previous research have expressed a desire for peer support groups for mentors (Atkins & Williams 1995). Mentors updates organised as forums for mutual support and exchange of ideas between mentors may be more useful than straightforward information giving sessions.

Conclusions

This study provides a snapshot of mentors of pre-registration nursing students, in the period leading up to the implementation of the recommendations of Chapter Four of *Making a Difference* at one HEI in Northern England. It complements previous research into the experience of mentorship, and reaches similar conclusions to earlier studies, suggesting that there are ongoing issues around mentorship that remain unresolved. The current study reveals a picture of an experienced body of mentors, who carry out their role despite the competing demands on their time, and their perception that they could be better supported by the HEI and their own managers. The survey hints at a mismatch between the concerns of mentors and those of students, in that mentors do not seem to share students' dissatisfaction with the amount of time they spend working together. Mentors want more from lecturing staff, in terms of information, support and feedback, but do not express a need for greater clinical involvement from lecturers. While respondents are committed to the notion of updating their knowledge and competence regarding mentoring, update sessions have to compete with more pressing demands on their time. Finally, if the notion of greater partnership in nurse education argued for in *Making a Difference is* to become a reality, HEIs and health care providers must work to enhance communication channels between each other.

Acknowledgements

The authors would like to acknowledge the advice and assistance of the Audit Departments of Morecambe Bay Hospitals, and North Cumbria Hospitals NHS Trusts.

References

Alderman C (1998) Clinical placements. *Nursing Standard* 12: 22–24.

Andrews M, Wallis M (1999) Mentorship in nursing: a literature review. *Journal of Advanced Nursing* 29 (1): 201–207.

Atkins S, Williams A (1995) Registered nurses' experiences of mentoring undergraduate nursing students. *Journal of Advanced Nursing* 21 (5): 1006–1015.

Cahill H A (1996) A qualitative analysis of student nurses' experiences of mentorship. *Journal of Advanced Nursing* 24 (4): 791–799.

Department of Health (1999) *Making a Difference: Strengthening the Nursing, Midwifery and Health Visiting Contribution to Health and Health Care.* Department of Health, London.

English National Board for Nursing, Midwifery and Health Visiting (1997) *Standards for Approval of Higher Education Institutions and Programmes.* English National Board, London.

Gray M A, Smith L N (2000) The qualities of an effective mentor from the student nurse's perspective: findings from a longitudinal qualitative study. *Journal of Advanced Nursing* 32 (6): 1542–1549.

Lloyd Jones M, Walters S, Akehurst R (2001) The implications of contact with the mentor for pre-registration nursing and midwifery students. *Journal of Advanced Nursing* 35 (2): 151–160.

Neary M, Phillips R, Davies B (1996) The introduction of mentorship to Project 2000 in Wales. *Nursing Standard* 10: 37–39.

Neary M (2000) Supporting students' learning and professional development through the process of continuous assessment and mentorship. *Nurse Education Today* 20 (6): 463–474.

Phillips T, Schostak J, Tyler J, Allen L (2000) Practice and assessment: an evaluation of the assessment of practice at diploma, degree and post-graduate level in pre- and post-registration nursing and midwifery education. *English National Board Research Highlight* No. 43.

United Kingdom Central Council for Nursing, Midwifery & Health Visiting (1999) *Fitness for Practice: Report of the Commission into Nurse Education.* United Kingdom Central Council, London.

United Kingdom Central Council for Nursing, Midwifery & Health Visiting (2000) *Standards for the Preparation of Teachers of Nursing, Midwifery and Health Visiting.* United Kingdom Central Council, London.

Watson N A, (1999) Mentoring today – the students' views. An investigative case study of pre-registration nursing students' experiences and perceptions of mentoring in one theory/practice module of the Common Foundation Programme on a Project 2000 course. *Journal of Advanced Nursing* 29 (1): 254–262.

Wilson-Barnett J, Butterworth T, White E, Twinn S, Davies S, Riley L (1995) Clinical support and the Project 2000 nursing student: factors influencing this process. *Journal of Advanced Nursing* 21 (6): 1152–1158.

14. First-person Mentoring

Bob Garvey, Geof Alred and Richard Smith

Introduction

This article is addressed to anyone who is in the process of becoming interested in mentoring. It offers a distinctive view of being a mentor and attempts to anticipate the questions and concerns of anyone who suspects that mentoring has something to offer them, especially as a mentor but also as a mentee. It is for those who would like to know more about mentoring, or who have recently become involved in what is an increasingly common feature of the workplace. In particular, we are answering the questions: what is mentoring like? how am I likely to experience being a mentor? what will I get out of it?

Much of what is written about mentoring, as about most areas of human resource development, is written from the "external", pseudo-objective, perspective. It describes, explains and analyses. This is the conventional academic mode. The difference signalled by our title is that we are attempting to enter the first-person perspective: to draw on our personal experiences of mentoring and being mentored.

In a sense this is to move outside the "objective" framework for academic writing but this is our intention because we prefer a more subjective approach and lean towards the view that objectivity is "a figment of our minds; it does not exist in nature"[1, p. 42]. We believe that is appropriate in writing about an activity which, being relentlessly affective, is best communicated when the writer gets "on the inside". We are *for* mentoring, and not simply wanting to study it, or write about it[2]. We have been mentors and we have trained mentors; we are committed to mentoring both on experiential and theoretical grounds[3].

Talk of "being committed to" mentoring might suggest subjectivity in a pernicious sense, as if for example the whole business came down solely to your own capacities as an individual. This does not have to be the case. What we often think of as the personal qualities of the mentor – integrity, judgement, wisdom and self-knowledge – are, to some degree at least, functions of the organization. The company can make it more or less possible to be a good mentor, for example, by the provision of proper support, by acknowledging the importance of mentoring in appraisal and other procedures, and in a variety of other ways: basically by taking the whole thing seriously. This is not to deny that people have personal qualities which they bring to the activity, but rather to recognize that these do not flourish in a vacuum.

If your organization is thinking about mentoring it is probably one that values its employees and recognizes that the success of the organization rests ultimately on the commitment and talents of all the workforce. Within the diversity of organizations, such recognition can be more or less explicit.

Bob Garvey, Geof Alred and Richard Smith: 'First-person Mentoring' in *CAREER DEVELOPMENT INTERNATIONAL* (1996), 1 (5), pp. 10–14.

In some organizations there have always been mentors who know intuitively the value of relating in a certain way to another, usually younger, member of staff for the good of the individual and the organization. In recent times this recognition has been articulated more fully and mentoring is linked explicitly with an organization's viability, whether that is seen as a matter of competitive advantage, quality of service, corporate longevity or some other criterion.

So, if you are considering mentoring, either because it appeals to you or because you have been asked to, we offer the following thoughts on what you might want to know more about, and on how you might respond to the prospect of continuing a tradition that is at least 3,000 years old, beginning with the original mentor, friend and adviser of Telemachus, Odysseus's son in Homer's epic poem.

I'm not sure what's involved

You may be unclear what mentoring means in your organization, and you may feel uncertain about your own suitability for the role. Do you have the experience and the qualities required? You may find yourself asking "What am I supposed to do?"

It is likely that you have had some experience of being mentored in your past, even though you may not have thought of it as mentoring at the time, and it is helpful to reflect on this. Who were your mentors, who were the significant older persons who brought you on at crucial periods in your career or your life in general?

When we have asked this question of managers, there is seldom anyone who cannot think of a helpful relationship they have had that seems to fit the idea of mentoring. It sometimes takes a little time to come to an answer and the range of answers is wide. Mentors come in the shape of parents or relatives, teachers, older friends, colleagues and line managers. Mentoring relationships develop naturally and spontaneously, as well as through deliberate action.

Discussions with people who are considering becoming mentors in their organization almost always reveal that the motivation can be traced back to a helpful relationship in their own past. This means that in a sense you know a great deal about mentoring. It is not significantly different from aspects of many kinds of friendship, from parenting or from relationships with younger siblings. Such recollections, and a sense of the ordinariness of mentoring, are an important resource on which the mentor can draw, especially where there is little time and space for reflection in the conditions of modern working life.

You would probably feel flattered

When you are asked, or encouraged to volunteer, to be a mentor, you are likely to feel flattered. Being asked to be a mentor is a form of recognition that another individual has faith in you and feels that you have something valuable to offer. There are two sides to this. One is a sense of the weight of responsibility: someone has entrusted you with their hopes and aspirations, confidences, and even their deepest feelings. The other side is that this can be profoundly affirming of you and your sense of yourself. There is reassurance and satisfaction in having your experience, maturity, career success and contribution to the organization positively valued in this way.

You need not bear responsibility in this on your own. If your organization is a "mentoring organization", that is one rather like the learning company as defined by Pedler *et al.*[4] – one which "facilitates the learning of all its members and continuously transforms itself" – there will be support available to you. Where the organization properly understands the nature and benefits of mentoring and related people-developing' activities, support for you as a mentor is more likely to be forthcoming and, in accepting the responsibility, you are entering an environment in which the business of mentoring is understood. The support may be available in the form of your own mentor. This is one way in which your organization can extend a people-focused philosophy by widening support networks.

You may be a little sceptical

It may be that what your organization means by mentoring is not what you understand, or what we understand, by mentoring. Mentoring is sometimes used for activities as diverse as coaching for particular tasks, sponsoring high-fliers or identifying candidates for redundancy and early retirement. There may be occasions when you become aware of the tensions between the needs of the organization and the needs of the individuals whom you are mentoring.

If your view of mentoring is at odds with the view which your organization takes, you may believe that you can nevertheless contribute to the development of an individual and in this way help to improve the quality of relationships within the organization. You may also find that you have gained an ally in another part of the organization which, in itself, can be beneficial. The notion of the "mentoring organization" is perhaps an ideal, and if you are in an organization that falls short of this ideal, as most organizations do, this should not discourage you from becoming a mentor. When it is successful, mentoring is one way in which organizational climate can be improved.

You will know your organization

Your knowledge of your organization is of crucial importance to your mentoring relationship. You will understand the politics and the language of the organization and where the power lies. You will be able to make this knowledge available to your mentee to help him or her find their way around the organization You will feel committed to the organization. This is not just a commitment to its profitability or mission statement but to its long-term health and well-being, the factors that make this a company worth working for. Here we are not saying that a good mentor is a "company man" or "company woman". The wider perspective, a commitment to underlying ethical values, is good for the mentor and the mentee; it is also good for the company, as others have argued[5].

You will look for the aspects of your organization that support mentoring

The dominant style of management in your organization will influence the nature and scale of the mentoring you do. Some of your managers may wish to quantify and measure mentoring and may ask, "What are the outcomes? What will the pay-off be for the organization that invests in mentoring?" and you may feel uneasy about this. Such questions typically look only to the immediate future. The perspective of mentoring, by contrast, is long term.

Mentoring is a natural activity of the human life-cycle and while there are clear short-term benefits to the individuals and the organization (reduced stress, less absenteeism and improved learning: cf. Clutterbuck[6] and Garvey[7], mentoring relationships often have a long-term impact on people. The experience often becomes a reference point throughout a person's life. The apparently hard-nosed, realistic questions about outcomes are often one more symptom of the short-termism endemic in British industry and public life generally[8], and are not central to valuing mentoring.

If your organization wishes to set targets for mentoring and manage it like an appraisal system this need not inhibit the relationship you develop with your mentee. You may find that your commitment and enthusiasm for mentoring as a developmental activity influences other people quite naturally and that interest spreads. You will know that mentoring is essentially a powerful and important relationship because you are participating in it and, as we mentioned earlier, because you remember and value different kinds of mentoring that you have enjoyed yourself. And you will wish to share your understanding of mentoring with others in order to foster the growth of your colleagues and your organization.

Are you concerned about time commitment?

Many organizations are creating a "time pressure culture"[7, p. 16] and yours may be the same. People compete for "who puts in the longest day" and this behaviour creates tensions. In this environment you may feel that you do not have enough time to mentor somebody.

You may feel that it is appropriate sometimes to hold mentoring sessions after work, in the pub on the way home, for example. Yet if mentoring is important to your organization and your people, the implication is that it should be as central a part of "real work" as any other activity.

Mentoring is not a luxury, it is not a marginal activity or an indulgence. It sits comfortably with ideas of coaching, counselling and professional development in general and there are points of connection between mentoring and performance management. By the same token mentoring cannot be all-consuming. It is there to meet the needs of the organization and its employees, and is just one among the many ways in which those needs are met.

Do you think that you need new skills to be a mentor?

You may feel you have to acquire new skills. Many consultants would have us believe that this is an essential prerequisite of being a mentor. Again there is both truth and falsity in this. The truth is that skills can help. To remember, for example, the importance to effective listening, of eye-contact and "congruent body-language", or of asking open questions, summarizing and reflecting, is helpful. It is equally true that you will be drawing on qualities and capacities that you have always had. These abilities are not predominantly technical skills of an esoteric sort that have to be acquired from new. They are capacities which you use in your ordinary daily life.

Thinking of them as skills carries the risk that we regard them as new things which we need to acquire, and this brings the possibility that when mentoring is formalized, it is experienced not as the confirmation that it can be but as an implied threat that we shall be found wanting.

During a period of involvement with an LEA programme of mentor training in secondary schools, we came to know a senior teacher, for example, who had been, unofficially, an outstanding mentor to new teachers for many years. Government reforms of training and induction into the profession, however, meant the introduction of a formal mentoring scheme. Becoming a "proper" mentor made this man feel that he would have to go away to be trained:

> I don't think I've got the skills for it – I hope there will be some proper training so I can make a decent job of being a mentor ... some courses I can go on to learn what to do.

Here the tendency of our world to label all human qualities as "skills" (parenting skills, human relationship skills...) has proved destructive to the mentor's confidence and obscured his self-knowledge. These effects are the opposite of what is potentially on offer to the prospective mentor. Your mentoring relationship, by definition, will help you to develop a fuller awareness of your self. Mentoring simultaneously presents a challenge to know yourself well enough to help and support another person and at the same time is a valuable way to develop self-knowledge. Talk of skills may at times be a useful shorthand but it does not adequately express the demands, process or benefits of mentoring.

The challenge to know yourself also means that you will be taking your own learning and developmental needs seriously as through this you will be recognizing the importance of development for your mentee and others in the organization in turn. Through your learning about learning you will be able to support your mentee effectively through application of this understanding.

You are likely to gain a great sense of satisfaction

You are unlikely to be in it for your own career advancement. Mentoring is not a rung in any career ladder. It nevertheless has the potential to benefit your career because it will help you to stand back and see where you are and where you are going; to think afresh about your priorities. Helping your mentee can become a source of great satisfaction as you observe him or her progressing and growing in confidence and stature. And as in any serious relationship, the benefits cannot be wholly predicted. There are examples of mentoring relationships maturing into long-standing friendships. Mentoring is one way to satisfy the deep-seated desire to "leave an impression on the world", which is recognized as a characteristic of mature adulthood[9].

What mentors do

There is surprisingly little research into what actually happens in a mentoring relationship. From our own experience these are some of the more common activities:

- *Mentors tell stories.* They tell stories about the organization, about their past, how they coped with a particular situation, what somebody did once and what their actions led to, and they will not be afraid of being anecdotal and figurative.

- *Mentors listen.* They can resist the temptation to think that listening is only ever preliminary to offering advice or suggesting courses of action. Listening is often the most effective help a mentor can offer.
- *Mentors allow the mentee to tell stories.* They recognize that sometimes people's meanings can only be reached in roundabout ways. The mentor gives space for the mentee to find his or her own way to a personal truth, clarifying his or her priorities and aspirations.
- *Mentors are generous with their time.* A mentor knows that it is important to allow sufficient time and to meet regularly.
- *Mentors lead.* They will take the initiative in organizing meetings and, at times, provide a framework and focus for discussion. They recognize when the mentee will benefit from a directive approach. They will not dominate.
- *Mentors are professional.* They recognize that the relationship exists for professional purposes, and as the mentee develops they help the relationship come to a natural end.

Conclusion

> Being a mentor has been a way in which I've been able to bring together different parts of my life. As I've got older it's been good to feel that I have more, not less, to offer to the younger generation. It's helped me discover and value things about myself and to see them as part of what I have to contribute at work. I hadn't thought this way before – it was as if my personal life was separate and private, and work was about professional things, and the two parts had to be kept apart and couldn't feed each other...

When we talk to mentors, we find, as in this quote, that they speak as much about the benefits to themselves as about what they feel they have been able to offer to mentees. They have often been surprised, particularly about the way in which personal and professional benefits have seemed to come together. In putting the interests of others, their mentees, first they have found considerable benefits for themselves.

What has been crucial, though, has been the extent to which mentors have felt themselves supported and valued – especially where they had the good fortune to have enjoyed in the past, or currently to be enjoying, the support of those who stood as mentors to them. It is as if mentoring has awakened and fed their personal qualities – openness, trust, tact and so on – and the mentor is then able to draw on this to support his or her own mentoring activity. In mentoring these personal qualities are always foremost and the first person perspective is inescapable.

References

1. Skolimowski H (1992) *Living Philosophy: Ecophilosophy as a Tree of Life.* Arkana, London.
2. Carr W (1995) *For Education: Towards Critical Educational Inquiry.* Open University Press, Buckingham.

3. Reason P (ed.) (1994) *Participation in Human Inquiry*. Sage, London.

4. Pedler M, Burgoyne J, Boydell T (1991) *The Learning Company – A Strategy for Sustainable Development*. McGraw-Hill, New York.

5. Handy C (1995) *Consult* November/December: 16–17.

6. Clutterbuck D (1992) *Everyone Needs a Mentor*. Institute of Personnel Management, London.

7. Garvey B (1995) Healthy Signs for Mentoring. *Education + Training* 37 (5): 12–19.

8. Hutton W (1995) *The State We're In*. Jonathan Cape, London.

9. Erikson E (1965) *Childhood and Society*. Penguin, Harmondsworth.

15. Three Decisions about Nurse Mentoring

M. Cameron-Jones and P. O'Hara

The literature of the 1980s and 1990s records enormous interest in mentoring. However, this interest is accompanied by anxiety in many professions that the role of the mentor is not becoming more clearly defined and has rarely been the subject of informative research. This paper reports a research study on the mentor role. The study was carried out with 87 nurse mentors and 39 student nurses. The nurse mentors and the students agree on the essential core of the mentor role. Beyond that, however, the two parties differ in their view. The mentors, in addition to the core of the role, emphasize its supportive aspects. In contrast, the students predict that, in addition to the core of the role, mentors will in future emphasize its challenging aspects. These findings are interpreted in the paper, which ends with a logical analysis of the three decisions facing nursing managers who respond to the findings reported in the paper.

Introduction: the original person called Mentor

The original story which made 'mentor' eponymous is well known. Homer told it in The Odyssey. He described how Odysseus, because he was leaving his family in order to go and fight in the Trojan wars, entrusted the upbringing of his son to a faithful friend. The son was called Telemachus. The friend was called Mentor. When the wars were over and Odysseus did not come home, Telemachus went to search for him. Mentor went with Telemachus to guide and advise him during his journey. Mentor was a senior person, being older than Telemachus. He also acquired the reputation of being a wise person. This was because Athene, the goddess of wisdom, used to disguise herself as Mentor whenever she gave advice to Telemachus. Athene even disguised her voice so that when she spoke to Telemachus she sounded like Mentor as well as looking like him.

This story is the first piece of literature on mentoring. It gives us the familiar, traditional picture of a mentor as a senior and wise person who in a friendly way supports the person being mentored.

Background to the research study

The modern literature on mentoring increased enormously in the 1980s. This is shown by the fact that Jacobi (1991) was able to report that in the 10 years between 1978 and 1988 the number of references in the ERIC database which included 'mentor' as a key word had increased from 10 to 95. The literature of the 1990s continued this growth. It reports the development of numerous mentoring arrangements, including many for the mentoring of nurses at various levels (Little 1990; Caldwell and Carter 1993; Morton-Cooper and Palmer 1993; Conway 1994; Yassin 1994). Despite this high level of interest in mentoring and its development,

M. Cameron-Jones and P. O'Hara: 'Three Decisions about Nurse Mentoring' in *JOURNAL OF NURSING MANAGEMENT* (1996), 4, pp. 225–230.

however, many writers are uneasy because the role of the mentor is not very clear and there is little reliable research about it. In 1988, Noe (1988) reported that 'few empirical studies of mentoring relationships have been conducted' and concluded that 'further, systematic study' was necessary in the field of mentoring. Healy and Welchert (1990) warn that although 'the promise of mentoring' seems to be great no clear definition of mentoring is generally agreed. Burnard (1990) concludes that, the overall picture of mentoring 'seems to be a confused one', and notes that there have been many calls for the development of mentors even though people are unsure what the mentor role exactly is. Also, Marriott (1991) states that, 'The dearth of research into mentorship in Britain is all the more remarkable in view of its increasing use here'.

The present study provides research about mentoring in Britain. It focuses on the debate about what mentors ought to be like. Much of that debate in various professions has centred on whether mentors should continue to emphasise the traditional idea of the mentor as a supportive friend to the person they are mentoring, as the original Mentor did in Homer's story, or whether the modern mentor role should now expand to incorporate more challenging methods of mentoring. Writing about this debate, Boydell (1994) is anxious that the supportive, befriending aspects of mentoring might be swamped as the modern practice of mentoring becomes increasingly challenging. In contrast, Watt (1995) notes that the way in which mentors define their role should take into account what the people being mentored expect their mentors to do. According to this argument, if the people being mentored expect their mentors to be challenging in their approach, the mentor role should adapt accordingly. The debate around this issue, however, continues unresolved and managers continue to face decisions about the best way to facilitate nurse mentoring in their own institutions. Should nursing managers continue to facilitate mentoring as a predominantly supportive activity as it traditionally was in the past? Or should they encourage an expansion in the role, so that the modern mentor role incorporates challenging aspects as well? At the moment, the debate continues to run on and there is very little solid evidence on which to base such management decisions. The present study, however, does provide firm evidence.

The research study

Famously, Darling (1985) published in the United States an analysis of the nurse mentor role. Darling's analysis is well known and widely respected. However, Darling published it in the 1980s which was several years before the present study began. In addition, Darling's analysis derived from her work in the United States of America. It was important therefore to ensure that the version of it to be used for the research reported in this paper would be a valid and comprehensive analysis of the mentor role as practised in the 1990s in the United Kingdom.

Accordingly, an adapted version of Darling's analysis was produced for the present study. Where Darling's analysis had listed 14 aspects of the mentor role, the new analysis lists 18 such aspects (see Figure 1). The four additional aspects of the role were included after consultation with a panel of 15 nursing managers and 15 nurse mentors. Items described by two-thirds of the members of each of these panels as 'advisable to include' in the new analysis were added to Darling's original analysis.

(They are items 15–18. They are shown in Figure 1.) The attendant definitions for these and the other items were then generated and refined as necessary. The new analysis was then finally piloted in its entirety with 12 mentors practising in hospital and community settings. It (see Figure 1) lists 18 aspects of the mentor role and defines the meaning of each aspect by giving quotations of how a student who is being mentored might describe it.

Aspects of the role	Examples of what student(s) might say:
Model	"I have learned from his/her ability to..."; "I have watched the way he/she..."
Envisioner	"he/she gave me a picture of what being a nurse can be like"; "showed me possibilities"
Energizer	"enthusiastic, gingered me up"; "was dynamic"
Investor	"he/she put a lot into my training"; "saw my capabilities and put effort into improving me"; "saw something in me"
Supporter	"willing to listen and help"; "available to me if I got discouraged and wondered if I was doing the right thing"
Standard-Prodder	"very clear what he/she wanted from me"; "kept prodding me"; "made sure I kept up to the mark"
Coach	"said "Lets see how you could have done it better"; "pushed me to improve"; "helped me evaluate myself"
Feedback-Giver	"gave me a lot of positive and negative feedback"; "let me know what I was doing was right and not so right"
Eye-Opener	"helped me understand the patients/clients"; "explained the reasons why he/she did things in a certain way"
Door-Opener	"included me in ward/practice life generally"; "put me in touch with people who were helpful/important"
Idea-Bouncer	"bouncing things off him/her brought them into focus"; "we would discuss nursing issues and professional ideas"
Problem-Solver	"helped me think through"; "helped me work out what to do about problems"
Career-Counsellor	"I could go to him/her when I was trying to think out where I wanted to go, what I wanted to do in the future"
Challenger	"made me really look at my decisions and grow up a bit"; "he'd/she'd challenge me and I'd be forced to prove my point"
Friend	"he/she befriended me"; "was personally kind to me"
Assessor	"he/she gave me assessments"; "let me know where I stood, compared with where I should have been"
Intermediary	"he/she oiled the wheels with the college/department"; "helped my relationships with other people in the practice/on the ward"
Tutor	"he/she talked to me about the different parts of my course"; "discussed my reading"

Figure 1 The mentor role analysis

The research study proper was then carried out with nurse mentors and student nurses, using the analysis given in Figure 1.

The research on nurse mentors

The research on nurse mentors used an instrument which incorporated the role analysis given in Figure 1. Each mentor completed his or her own instrument independently. Eighty-seven nurse mentors were invited to take part in this stage of the study and all agreed.

The instructions attached to the analysis asked each mentor to say how much emphasis he/she in practice put on each role-aspect. The scale was given as 1–5, with 5 indicating the highest amount of emphasis and so on down to 1 which indicated the lowest amount of emphasis.

The research on student nurses who had experience of being mentored

The study with the student nurses used the same analysis of the mentor role as had been used by the nurse mentors (see Figure 1), i.e. the students were presented with the same 18-item role analysis as had been developed for the mentors. The student's instrument, however, had different instructions about what to do with the analysis. Those instructions asked the students what they thought nurse mentors of the future would be likely to do 'to make sure that students are well equipped for their role in the century ahead'. To indicate this, students chose six role aspects to be labelled as 'E' (with 'E' meaning that this role aspect was Essential in nurse mentors of the future), and six role aspects to be labelled as 'L' (with 'L' meaning that this role aspect was Least important for nurse mentors in the future). Each student completed his or her own instrument independently.

Thirty-nine final-year nursing students (out of a graduating class of 40) took part in this stage of the study.

The findings of the research study

Table 1 shows the emphasis given to each aspect of the mentor role by the 87 practising nurse mentors. They had put most emphasis on being a supporter to the students they mentored and least emphasis on being a challenger of the students.

Table 2 shows the students' ideas about which aspects of the mentor role would be important in the future. They said that in future it will be most important for a mentor to be a supporter of students and least important to be an intermediary.

Comparison of Tables 1 and 2 shows a high degree of similarity between the mentors' and the students' ideas. The similarity can be seen simply by inspection of the two tables, but it is also made clear by the fact that the two rank orders correlate quite highly (Spearman's $\rho = +0.56$, $P = 0.02$). Further, when one examines the mentors' 'top six' aspects of the mentor role and compares them with the 'top six' identified by the students, it can be seen that three of the items are identical. These three items can be thought of as representing therefore the essential core of the mentor role. The three items which make up that core are supporter, feedback-giver and model.

Table 1 What the 87 nurse mentors emphasized. (The mentors put most emphasis on being a supporter, least on being a challenger)

Aspect of the mentor role	Mean score (min = 1, max = 5)	Rank order
Supporter	4.24	1
Eye-opener	4.12	2
Door-opener	4.01	3
Feedback-giver	3.78	4
Model	3.75	5
Friend	3.67	6
Investor	3.64	7
Problem-solver	3.61	8
Coach	3.60	9
Assessor	3.56	10
Idea-bouncer	3.52	11.5
Standard-prodder	3.52	11.5
Envisioner	3.48	13.5
Energizer	3.48	13.5
Intermediary	3.44	15
Tutor	3.39	16
Career-counsellor	3.24	17
Challenger	3.05	18

Table 2 The predictions of 39 student nurses about which aspects of the mentor role will be 'essential' in nurse mentors of the future and which will be 'least important' in nurse mentors of the future. The final column in the table shows the rank order of what students see as important for the future

Aspect of the mentor role	The number of students saying this will be 'essential' in nurse mentors of the future	The number of students saying this will be 'least important' in nurse mentors of the future	Rank order of overall importance for the future
Supporter	26	3	1
Feedback-giver	25	7	2
Problem-solver	18	6	3
Assessor	16	7	4
Model	19	11	5
Energizer	19	13	6
Friend	18	13	7
Standard-prodder	14	10	8
Investor	14	14	9
Career-counsellor	9	13	10
Door-opener	8	13	11
Coach	10	17	12
Eye-opener	9	17	13.5
Idea-bouncer	5	13	13.5
Challenger	2	12	15
Envisioner	9	21	16
Tutor	4	18	17
Intermediary	0	17	18

However, beyond the core of the role, the mentors and the students emphasise different aspects of it. The mentors say that they give precedence to being an eye-opener, door-opener and friend. The students, on the other hand, believe that mentors in the future should give precedence to being a problem-solver assessor and energizer.

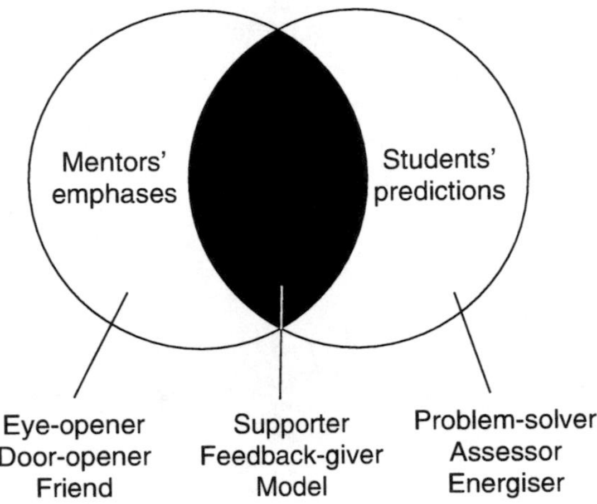

Figure 2 The mentor role now and in the future
Diagram to show aspects of the role which nurse mentors emphasize at present and aspects of the role which students predict will be important in the future. The mentors and the students agree about three aspects of the role (supporter, feedback-giver and model) but differ in their views thereafter.

The similarities and differences between the mentors and the students are shown in Figure 2. It is helpful, when interpreting Figure 2, to go back to Figure 1 to see the definitions of the various aspects of the mentor role. The definitions which make up the core of the mentor role, as shown in Figure 2, are: supporter – defined as 'willing to listen and help', 'available to me if I got discouraged and wondered if I was doing the right thing'; feedback-giver – defined as 'gave me a lot of positive and negative feedback', 'let me know what I was doing was right and not so right'; and model – defined as 'I have learned from his/her ability to...', 'I have watched the way he/she...'.

Reading these definitions, it is scarcely surprising that so many of the people who write about the mentoring of nurses believe so strongly in the power of mentoring to promote professional growth. Nurse mentors who support their students, give them feedback and act as models for them in the practice workplace must be investing in the profession some of the most powerful and influential training which students receive in the whole of their career. Small wonder that advocates of mentoring believe in it so strongly and are so little downcast by the lack of firm research about it.

On the other hand, Figure 2 also gives food for thought about how managers might best prepare for nurse mentoring in future. Thus, the mentors and the students, while agreeing on the core of the role, do differ in their views of what is important beyond that core. In their top priorities mentors give a high place to the roles of eye-opener, door-opener and friend. In contrast students give a high place to the roles of problem-solver, assessor and energizer. By returning to the definitions of these which are given in Figure 1 one can see the key to this difference of view between the mentors and the students. The key to it is that while present-day nurse mentors are faithful to the idea of mentoring as a predominantly supportive activity, the students, when they look to the future, anticipate an extension of the mentor role to incorporate more challenging aspects. Thus, the mentors' priorities of eye-opener, door-opener and friend ('helped me understand', 'included me', 'befriended me') reflect the traditional supportive 'friendly face' of mentoring. In contrast, the students predict the need for mentors in future to act as problem-solver, assessor and energizer. The definitions of these aspects of the role ('helped me think', 'gave me assessments', 'enthusiastic, gingered me up') show students anticipating that nurse mentors in future will use more challenging approaches.

Discussion of the implications for nursing managers

This paper has reported a research study which involved 87 nurse mentors, 39 student nurses and an 18-item analysis of the nurse mentor role. In consequence, it gathered a large amount of detailed evidence. Emerging clearly from the fine detail of the evidence, however, are the study's main findings. The study shows that nurse mentors and nurse students agree on what the core of the mentor role is. Beyond that core, nurse mentors continue to present a traditional, supportive view of mentoring whereas students predict that mentoring in future will develop its more challenging characteristics. These findings are interesting. They suggest that present-day nurse mentors are faithful to the supportive, friendly definition of their role which has a long and respected history stretching back to Homer. Their students, however, in predicting that the mentor role will soon incorporate more challenging approaches, are in tune with the demanding organizational cultures increasingly encountered by health professionals in modern times.

Logically, three kinds of responses might be made by nursing managers who read these research findings. The three are outlined below in the form of three decisions facing managers, and are labelled (a) (b) and (c) in the diagram below:

Diagram

Three decisions about nurse mentoring which might be made by nursing managers, and the thinking underpinning each decision

(a)	Do nothing	What mentors and mentees in my organization think about the mentor role at present and in future is a matter for the individuals concerned. These things are not something on which managers need to form a view.

(b)	Endorse a supportive view of mentoring	Mentoring is traditionally a supportive, befriending activity. Nursing managers should endorse mentor practice which continues to be faithful to that traditional definition.
(c)	Guide development of the mentor role so that it incorporates more challenging approaches in the future.	The roles of health professionals and the cultures in which they work are changing everywhere. The role of the nurse mentor must change with them to reflect the climate of challenge in which we live.

The literature as a whole, as well as the particular piece of research being reported in this paper, suggests that decision (c) is the most demanding one. It would involve mentors changing not only the ways in which they present themselves to their mentees but, more deeply, the ways in which they construe the mentor-mentee relationship in its entirety. Such depth of change calls for understanding and sensitivity from the nurse managers who encourage it and wish to see it happen.

Conclusion

This paper began by noting that there is an enormous literature about mentoring. Most of it is in favour of mentoring but little of it contains informative research evidence on which to base management decisions about nurse mentoring in Britain. The present study provides such research, and on its basis it is possible, as a matter of logic, to outline three decisions which a nursing manager might take in response to the evidence now available. The three decisions are mutually exclusive and the one selected by any individual nursing manager will of course be affected by his or her responsibilities and the kind of organization in which he or she is working. The best decision therefore is not obviously the same for every manager. Each individual manager's choice, however, will have ramifications for nurse mentoring in the organization concerned for many years to come, and is accordingly a matter of important consequence.

Acknowledgement

The study reported in this paper is part of a project funded by the Scottish Home and Health Department. We are very grateful to the funders of the work and to all the nurse mentors and student nurses who participated in it.

References

Boydell D (1994) Relationships and feelings: the affective dimension to mentoring in the primary school. *Mentoring and Tutoring* 2: 37–44.

Burnard P (1990) The student experience: adult learning and mentorship revisited. *Nurse Education Today* 10: 349–354.

Caldwell B J, Carter E M A (1993) *The Return of the Mentor: Strategies for Workplace Learning.* Falmer Press, London.

Conway C (1994) *Mentoring Managers in Organisations.* Ashridge Management Research Group, Berkamsted.

Darling L A W (1985) What do nurses want in a mentor? *Nurse Educator* January: 18–20.

Healy C C, Welchert A J (1990) Mentoring relations: a definition to advance research and practice. *Educational Researcher* 19: 17–21.

Jacobi M. (1991) Mentoring and undergraduate success. A literature review. *Review of Educational Research* 61: 505–532.

Little J W (1990) The mentor phenomenon and the social organisation in teaching. *Review of Research in Education* 16: 297–351.

Marriott A (1991) The support, supervision and instruction of nurse learners in clinical areas: a literature review. *Nurse Education Today* 11: 261–269.

Morton-Cooper A, Palmer A (1993) *Mentoring and Preceptorsbip, A Guide to Support Roles in Clinical Practice.* Blackwell Science, London.

Noe R A (1988) An investigation of the determinants of successful assigned mentoring relationships. *Personnel Psychology* 41: 457–479.

Watt D (1995) The roles of the mentor and link tutor in primary school teacher training. *Mentoring and Tutoring* 3: 13–18.

Yassin T (1994) Exacerbation of a perennial problem? The theory-practice gap and changes in nurse education. *Professional Nurse*: 183–187.

16. Clinical Staff as Mentors in Pre-registration Undergraduate Nursing Education: Students' Perceptions of the Mentors' Roles and Responsibilities

Filomena L. W. Chow and Lorna K. P. Suen

This paper reports part of a multiple-phase action research initiated by a university nursing department in Hong Kong. Local hospitals were invited to collaborate in a joint mentoring programme which recruited clinical staff to mentor pre-registration nursing students during clinical placement. Interviews based on the five roles – assisting, befriending, guiding, advising and counselling, as outlined by the English National Board, were conducted to explore students' views of the mentor's roles. Findings showed that students in general agreed that the five roles depicted were necessary roles of the mentors. They saw the roles of assisting and guiding as most crucial, while the befriending role was useful to facilitate their settling into the ward. The advising and counselling roles were seen as less important. It was concluded that students tended to be more instrumental in viewing their mentor's behaviours; activities that have a direct effect on their learning arc considered as more important, while other factors which have a less immediate or less direct effect on their learning, are seen as of lower priority.

Introduction

Facilitating student learning in the field of nursing by using staff from the clinical setting has been widely employed (Atkins and Williams 1995, Burnard 1988). This concept of mentorship was first introduced in the academic and business worlds of North America. Mentorship is an important and emerging tool for preparation of professionals, as mentioned by various researchers (Laurent 1988, Levinson *et al.* 1978, Roche 1979). The idea of mentorship has been widely used within the clinical setting during the last two decades. With the implementation of Project 2000 in the National Health Service, the United Kingdom witnessed the transfer of clinical supervision by teaching staff from schools of nursing to mentors actually working in the ward. This was in order to help smooth the transition from student to professional (Bracken 1989, Hunt and Michael 1983, Phillips *et al.* 1996, Gray and Smith 1999). The mentor-student relationship is arranged formally by the teaching institution, with students being assigned to mentors for periods of time, corresponding to their clinical placement (Foy and Waltho 1989). In this case the emphasis is on facilitation of learning (Burnard 1988) and preparation for the uptake of the professional role (Watson 1999).

Filomena L. W. Chow and Lorna K. P. Suen: 'Clinical Staff as Mentors in Pre-registration Undergraduate Nursing Education: Students' Perceptions of the Mentors' Roles and Responsibilities' in *NURSE EDUCATION TODAY* (2001), 21, pp. 350–358.

Despite the fact that mentoring is considered as a key concept in the successful preparation of professionals, it was not until recent years that clinical placements for the nursing undergraduates in the baccalaureate program in Hong Kong began to be supervised by clinical staff. Only at the initial stage of the introduction of the first full time pre-registration nursing degree program in Hong Kong, from 1991 to 1993, were a few full time clinical staff recruited from the hospital setting as clinical teachers to join the academics in doing clinical teaching on a temporary full-time basis. In the last triennium, from 1996–1999, there was a cut in the funds in the tertiary education sector. It was then envisaged by the Nursing Department that it would be more economical for the university to recruit mentors from the clinical setting than to employ full-time academic staff for students' clinical supervision. As a result, one of the universities in Hong Kong initiated and developed an 'Honorary Clinical Instructors' scheme in 1996–1997, whereby a joint effort between the academic institution and the participating hospitals in the supervision of the pre-registration baccalaureate nursing students was called for. According to this scheme, the clinical staff who were appointed as 'Honorary Clinical Instructors' would be recruited as mentors for undergraduate students, providing clinical supervision and mentoring to students in the assigned units throughout the semester. These appointed clinical staff remained full time employees of the hospital, held regular nursing duties in the units they were committed to, but at the same time would take two students under their supervision during their span of duty. In the process of developing these clinical staff as mentors for the pre-registration baccalaureate nursing students, it was important for the department to explore what the roles and responsibilities of these mentors should be, and what the students' perceptions of the mentor's roles were? This paper is a report of the study which explored the students perceptions of the roles and responsibilities of the clinical staff as mentors in the Hong Kong context.

Literature review

The literature generally agrees that mentor experiences are valuable resources for student learning (Ferguson 1996, Watson 1999). Undoubtedly, clinical supervision by academic staff from the tertiary institution helps strengthen students' theoretical knowledge; nevertheless, research has shown that students benefit differently from different mentoring experiences. Clinical staff as mentors will have the most up-to-date information on the practices in the clinical areas related to students' placement (Davis and Barham 1989, Hunt and Michael 1983, Marriott 1991, Spouse 1996). In addition, when the students see their mentors in action the role modelling will be more explicit for the students. The one-to-one relationship between clinically skilled nurses and students helps the student to obtain clinical knowledge, skills and judgements (Ferguson 1996). Mentors are seen as facilitators helping to socialize students to the nursing profession, easing transition to the workplace, and increasing clinical competence (Rittman 1992, Voignier and Freeman 1992). In addition, Ferguson (1996) sees the mentors having duties such as an evaluator of student performance, student advocate, role model and counsellor to the student.

In the United Kingdom, the English National Board defined mentors as:

> . . . appropriately qualified and experienced first level practitioners who by example and facilitation guide, assist and support students in

> learning new skills, adopting new behaviours and acquiring new attitudes. . . . Mentors are there to assist, befriend, guide, advise and counsel students (ENB in Woodrow 1994, p. 812).

Here, the roles of the mentors are clearly stated, but these roles have not been explored in the Hong Kong context. Even in the UK, where mentorship is widely used within the Project 2000, and many authors had proposed models or frameworks for mentoring activities, no one model is seen as appropriate universally, and the choice mostly depends upon the mentor's familiarity with a particular framework (Andrews and Wallis 1999). In addition, no explorations on precisely how the mentors function in the mentoring roles, as suggested by the ENB, are available.

Relating to how students were being supervised, Morgan and Knox (1987) studied the characteristics of 'best' and 'worst' clinical teachers/supervisors in the clinical setting. The study was repeated among a group of Greek nursing students and clinical teachers (Kotzabassaki *et al.* 1997). Both these studies found that being a good role model and encouraging a climate of mutual respect are among the best characteristics of clinical teacher's, but neither study clearly examined the multiple roles of the mentors.

Other researchers have examined the concept of mentoring from different perspectives. Hagerty (1986) explored the concept of mentoring from the organizational framework, defining the structural roles of mentors and exploring the importance of the interpersonal aspect of mentoring. Darling (1984) explored the absolute requirements for successful mentoring relationships, stating the importance of a long and intense relationship. Davis and Barham (1989) and Bracken (1989) provided useful guidelines to the implementation of mentorship schemes, and Woodrow (1994), having explored the perceptions of mentorship from a broader sense, makes recommendations for managing the possible pitfalls arising from a mentoring relationship. Spouse (1996), after analysing the student-mentor relationship, suggests that mentorship could be developed into a model of student-centred learning. None of these studies, however, examined the roles and responsibilities of a mentor from the students' perspective, nor were the potential cultural dimensions that might affect the students' expectations examined.

In view of the above, the project team proposed to examine the mentoring roles in a local context where the Chinese culture dominates. The ENB definition was used as a framework for exploring the student's expectations of the mentor's roles. The students' understandings of the 'assisting', 'befriending', 'guiding', 'advising' and 'counselling' responsibilities were sought. A list of the mentors' expected behaviours were then formulated, and after adjustments from the faculty staff, this served to inform potential mentors of the students' expectations. Additionally the findings were compared with the ENB definition, to discover if there were any significant cultural differences in the interpretations of these roles.

Methodology

This study is part of a multiple-phase action research project, which involved using a qualitative design in the initial phase to seek views from students on the roles and responsibilities of a mentor. The informants were pre-registration nursing undergraduates who had been exposed to the new mentoring scheme. Students were invited to attend informal interviews. A qualitative approach was used as this allowed the research team to amass useful qualitative data which were not available from previous research. The researchers used a semi-structured interview to elicit information from students on their perceptions of the roles of a mentor. An interview guide was developed based upon the definitions as proposed by the ENB. The use of a semi-structured interview guide helped the interviewers to remain focused on the issue, and at the same time allowed room for the researchers to make clarifications whenever necessary throughout the interviewing process. This allowed the interviewers to explore individual student's perceptions and experiences.

This study was conducted at the end of the first semester in the academic year 1996–1997 when some of the students in the second and third year of their 4-year programme had had 4 months' mentoring experience of the newly introduced scheme. Students were recruited on a voluntary basis. The interviewed group represented around 40% ($n = 22$) of the sample population. This sample size was considered to be representative enough to provide the project team with a fairly comprehensive range of experiences and reflections of the students' perceptions of the roles of the mentor, and was at the same time a manageable sample size for a qualitative study. Each interview was audio-recorded for data analysis. Supplementary interview notes were also taken.

To ensure ethical clearance, all students who participated in the study were fully informed about the nature and purpose of the study, and emphasis was made on the voluntariness of the participation. Refusal or withdrawal from the study would not affect their undergraduate study in any way. Informed consent was obtained and consent forms were signed prior to the interview. Also, permission to audio-record the interview was obtained. Names were not to be disclosed during the interview or in the reporting to ensure confidentiality of the participants, and codes for content analysis were used when necessary. The participants were informed that any identifying materials such as the audiotapes would be kept locked in appropriate facilities, and would be destroyed after the completion of the report writing. Anonymity and confidentiality in treatment of the data and reporting were strictly observed.

Data analysis

Taped recordings of the semi-structured interview were transcribed verbatim in Chinese. Students' descriptions of expected mentors behaviours were first extracted from the transcriptions and became the raw data for further analysis. These statements were then clustered under the five categories of mentors' roles as suggested by the ENB. The statements were compared to each other for similarities and differences. Statements with the same theme were then subsumed under one statement. Negative statements were grouped under a positive statement under the same theme so that when the list of expected mentors' behaviours was used for subsequent mentor preparation workshops, a positive impression would be conveyed. In this process, inter-rater reliability was established by involving at least two members of the research team. Each transcript was reviewed to identify significant statements, then the project team agreed on the summary statements, considering their adequacy in fully describing the students perceptions and expectations of mentors behaviours. These statements were also verified against the original transcripts for validation. At the end, a list of expected mentor activities was formulated (Table 1). This list was then translated into English for subsequent uses in later phases of the study. Backward translation of the list was carried out to ensure that the original meanings in the Chinese version were preserved.

Findings and discussion

Twenty-two students from the undergraduate nursing program (12 from year two and 10 from year 3) were interviewed *on* a voluntary basis. The first and the fourth year students were not included, as these two groups did not have clinical staff as mentors in the initial development of the mentoring scheme.

When students were asked to define the roles of a mentor, diverse perceptions were observed. For example, some students perceived the mentor's most important role was as a facilitator for learning during clinical placement, a role model for students to follow, and a person to help them to explore more learning opportunities during their clinical placement. But others saw the personality and characteristics of a mentor as the key to successful clinical placement, with nearly all students agreeing that the five roles as defined by the ENB were essential functions of a mentor. However, most students could not clearly differentiate between the activities of the five roles, and opinions on expected behaviours were sometimes replicated among the different roles they described. For example, students perceived that one of the assisting roles of the mentor was to give positive and negative feedback on their performance, while this was placed under the advising role by some other students. Therefore, the students' descriptions of the activities of the five mentor roles were reorganized according to the categories as stated in the ENB. For brevity and clarity, the details of the findings are presented in Table 1, which lists all the students' perceptions of an effective mentor's behaviours. Most of the statements are worded in a positive tone, and those behaviours that matched with the ENB descriptions are marked with asterisk(s)*.

While students gave both positive and negative comments on their perceptions of the performance of mentors, it is worth noting that students were more likely to start off with perceptions of what they thought the mentors should not do, rather than what the mentors should do. For example, they talked about mentors not calling them by their names, which in the summary list was subsumed under a positive statement 'My mentor always calls me by my name' (Table 1, Item 14). Nevertheless, the students came up with more positive comments as the interview progressed. Two speculations here might account for this observation. First, it maybe that students believed that the interviews provided a forum for them to express their feelings, especially those who considered their mentoring experience as negative. These students might then have expressed more positive perceptions once their initial feelings were accepted. Secondly, in the Chinese culture, it is more likely that when comments are sought, they will be negative ones. This may be due to the fact that some Chinese are thought to be 'humble' and consider themselves as 'unworthy', and therefore less forthcoming with positive comments about themselves and others. Praising someone may render the person arrogant and pompous and therefore is generally not the norm to be positive when comments are sought. This may be related to the Confucian idea of self reflection, where one should examine ones faults and then identify areas and strategies for improvement, and this sometimes extends to expectations of others.

Table 1 Summary statements of students' perceptions of the mentors' roles

Assisting role:

1. My mentor always organizes learning opportunities for me.*
2. My mentor helps me to adapt into the setting of the clinical placement.
3. My mentor helps me to fulfil my clinical learning objectives by giving me appropriate job assignments.
4. My mentor helps me to develop the identified psychomotor skills.
5. I can learn the ways of interaction with the client from my mentor.
6. My mentor exposes me to new ideas and concepts.
7. My mentor assigns me tasks by taking into account my level of ability.
8. My mentor facilitates the communication between the patient and me.
9. My mentor pushes me to reach high standards of excellence.*
10. My mentor acts as a role model to me in his/her caring attitude towards patients.

Befriending role:

11. My mentor introduces me to the ward staff/team.*
12. My mentor orientates me to the clinical environment.*
13. My mentor helps me to cultivate a sense of belonging in the clinical setting.
14. My mentor always calls me by my name.
15. My mentor has a warm and friendly attitude.
16. My mentor has a strong motivation to teach.
17. My mentor is concerned with my occupational safety during placement.
18. My mentor has trust in what I am doing.*
19. My mentor does not give too much pressure to me during his/her supervision.*
20. I have the feeling of being respected by my mentor.*

Guiding role:

21. My mentor communicates an image, goal or vision of the professional world that is meaningful to me.*
22. My mentor emphasizes the holistic approach of patient care.
23. My mentor supplements my performance by providing specific guidance related to the skills practised.*
24. My mentor can give hints and guidance whenever necessary.*
25. I am guided to perform the future role of a registered nurse by my mentor.
26. My mentor helps me to put theory into practice.

Advising role:

27. My mentor provides feedback on my clinical performance.*
28. My mentor stimulates me to critical thinking.*
29. My mentor helps me to explore issues more deeply.*
30. My mentor discusses with me the ways of improving my practices in next performance.
31. My mentor suggests to me alternative ways of performing the same task.
32. My mentor helps me to understand the reason behind the way I practice.
33. My mentor corrects my mistakes related to my performance immediately under 'unsafe' conditions/environments.
34. My mentor provides me with chances to express my opinion on my performance.
35. My mentor recommends sources of references to me.**

Table 1 Summary statements of students' perceptions of the mentors' roles

Counselling role:
36. My mentor provides me with emotional encouragement.*
37. My mentor helps me to examine career interests.
38. My mentor enhances my confidence in practice.
39. There is a mutual understanding relationship between my mentor and me.
40. My mentor shares his/her own experiences with me.**
41. I am willing to share my learning experiences with my mentor.*
42. My mentor expresses his/her concerns on my learning needs.**
43. My mentor helps me to examine long-range plans on career issues.

*Items that are also listed by the ENB under the same role.
**Items that are listed by the ENB but under a different role.

When comparing the list of the summary statements from the local students to that by the ENB, it is interesting to note that students in Hong Kong are more dependent on their mentors in providing opportunities in a 'safe' environment for them to learn. Examples of statements which showed a strong student dependency on the mentor's provision included: 'My mentor helps me to fulfil my clinical learning objectives by giving me appropriate job assignments'; 'My mentor assigns me tasks by taking into account my level of ability'; 'my mentor is concerned with my occupational safety during placement'. In reality, it would be expected that a tertiary student take the initiative to negotiate his/her own learning objectives and opportunities, yet the students explicitly stated that they considered it the mentor's role to provide opportunities for learning. This may be due to the fact that the local educational system does not always encourage students to be creative and take responsibility in designing their own learning. Some students prefer to feel safe and be 'spoon-fed', being told what to learn and to secure a passing score. The situation is particularly aggravated when students are in an unfamiliar environment and do not feel they have a grasp of the situation.

In the subsequent section; further discussion is made on the students' perceptions of the five mentoring roles. The sequence of the roles listed is according to the degree of importance as perceived by the students.

The assisting role

The students saw the role of assisting as the most important role of mentor. Most students agreed that the assisting roles of mentors are 'organizing learning opportunities' and 'facilitating learning in the clinical setting'. They also agreed that mentors met their expectations in fulfilling this role.

According to the students, mentors from the clinical setting were superior to the academic staff in fulfilling the assisting role. This could be due to the fact that mentors had a better understanding of the client's condition, and were more familiar with the clinical practices that were current in the unit, and thus would be able to assist the students in performing the clinical tasks with greater ease and with better skills. In addition, most students saw the mentors as effective persons to help them bridge the theory-practice gap. Through clinical practice and visualizing their mentors providing nursing care and management to the patient, the students reported that they could implement theory in practice with greater confidence and clarity.

On the negative side, students did state that some of the mentors did not arrange nursing assignments appropriate to their learning objectives or level of study. Upon further exploration, it was noted that there were two reasons for these comments. First, some of the mentors were not aware of the different learning objectives that students of different levels might have. Secondly, some of the students were not familar with the clinical setting and consequently did not have a full understanding of the nature of the work and routines in different units, so in turn had unrealistic expectations of job assigments. For example, while ward policies might allow students in general units to perform injections, it might not be the routine for students to perform the same task in specialised areas, such as the neonatal unit. Similar situations also happened in the Common Foundation Programme on a Project 2000 course in the UK, where nursing students felt that some mentors would involve them only in basic nursing care or, in some cases, no clinical practice whatever (Watson 1999). Certainly, this calls for more open communication between the mentor and the student, and at the same time the university could play an important role in facilitating such communication. Moreover, a clinical map suggested by Kersbergen and Hrobsky (1996) may be considered so as to enable the mentors and the students to meet identified learning objectives and achieve clinical outcomes in a timely fashion.

Guiding and advising roles

The guiding and advising roles were seen as the next most important roles among the five listed. However, students did not see the guiding role as distinctly different from the advising role. Most students depicted behaviours such as 'giving me advice as what to do in specific situations' as advising, 'help to develop my future role as a nurse' as guiding. Most students perceived that evaluation and providing feedback were important behaviours when advising, and in particular pointed out that these activities should be done in confidence and in a 'safe' environment, so that they did not feel humiliated by the experience.

When students were asked if their mentors had stimulated their critical thinking abilities, which was considered by the students as an advising activity, most students did not agree. Most students believed that the reasons for this lack of stimulation in their critical thinking had been that their mentors were task oriented, had a mind set of completing the 'ward routine' as a priority and were usually very busy. There was also a concern among students that the mentors sometimes might encounter a conflict in their dual roles as a mentor and as a member of the ward team, because the mentors would have a full patient load and at the same time had their mentoring duties to fulfil. In these situations, the students reported frustration that their learning opportunities were not being provided adequately for by their mentors who had been under pressure with the competing demands of a teacher and a carer. Another possible reason why some students perceived that mentors did not fulfil the advising role fully was that these mentors had not received training; neither had they been encouraged to develop critical thought during their own student years. Their training as nurses had been apprenticeship-based, and the work setting forced them to be task-oriented, therefore they had not been educated to 'ask' questions, nor to challenge accepted practices. Frustrations thus occurred when the university undergraduates started to ask questions and the mentors might feel threatened. This could lead to a tension in the mentor-mentee relationship, which further jeopardised the mentor's guiding and advising roles. In a small scale study conducted by Atkins and Williams (1995), the authors also concluded that mentors should be formally prepared before taking up the role of clinical teaching.

The befriending role

It is interesting to note that students did not see the befriending role as all that important, but asserted that it was important for the mentor to have a friendly and warm personality. Generally, students found many mentors did not achieve the befriending role adequately. Most students prepared themselves to be a team member of the ward and had tried to develop a sense of belonging to the wards, but were treated as 'guests' by the mentors or the ward team. In extreme cases, some students said that they were not called by their names in the clinical setting, but rather called 'the students from the university'. This made the students feel that they were outsiders, and were categorized as a distinct group, separated from the norm. This might be due to the fact that some students were not looked after by just one mentor, but by several during the clinical placement. As people take time to accept each other, and rapport needs time to develop and is reinforced through a long-term working relationship, hence it might be difficult for the mentor to treat the new students as team members within a short period of time. In addition, the duration of clinical placement for the university students was relatively short, usually lasting for around 6–8 weeks, and such an arrangement did not provide sufficient time for the mentors and students to develop a strong rapport and interdependent relationship, considering the students only worked with the mentors for two duties per week. Many authors (Andrew and Wallis 1999, Watson 1999) also pointed out that when the contact between mentor and student is minimal, the mentoring process is seen as less effective and this makes it difficult for the mentors to exercise their roles realistically. It was also agreed that greater managerial support from above is necessary, so that mentors could work on the same shifts as the students they are looking after as far as possible (Watson 1999).

Fortunately, positive situations were also reported whereby the mentors were known to be very open, supportive and made an effort to include the students in a variety of activities apart from the clinical supervision in the ward setting (for example, having tea breaks and lunch together). The reporting from the students suggested that having an open, warm and friendly personality was a definite asset to help a mentor establish a befriending role. It is also interesting to note that in a replication study conducted by Kotzabassaki *et al.* (1997), the most distinguishing characteristics between 'best' and 'worst' clinical teachers for students and faculty were being a good role model and encouraging a climate of mutual respect.

The counselling role

The role that was considered to be least important and not very well taken up by the mentors was the counselling role. Students reflected that this would be an important role, particularly when they encountered job stress in the ward setting. Counselling from the mentors would help them tremendously to deal with emotionally demanding situations. Other behaviours that were considered to be counselling behaviours were sharing personal experiences with the students, and showing concern for the learning needs of students. Very few respondents mentioned that they expected their mentors to counsel or advise them on their long-term career goals. The short clinical attachment did not allow the mentor-mentee relationship to have enough time to establish a strong rapport for the counselling role to be initiated. Most of the students claimed that they would return to the faculty staff for counselling should they see a need in this area. Earnshaw (1995) also noticed that some nursing students might even prefer the newly appointed registered nurses as their mentors, as they felt closest to them in a hierarchical sense and that the mentors would be more understanding of the needs of the students.

On the whole, students saw the assisting, and guiding roles as most important, and were able to list several behaviours relating to these roles. They viewed the befriending role as a significant factor contributing to success in the mentor-mentee relationship, which also facilitated the teaching-learning process. The advising and counselling roles were not seen as being as important as the other roles, however. They were still regarded as necessary roles which should ideally be properly fulfilled. Respondents did not see a direct consequence for the clinical attachment if these two roles were not satisfied. It was also noted that the students' perceptions of the mentor's role were mainly instrumental. Behaviours that they saw as having a direct impact on their clinical learning were considered as more important, for example, behaviours relating to guiding and assisting, whereas the behaviours which have a less direct effect on their ward learning were seen as of less importance, for example, counselling and advising. While being new to the environment, all students saw the befriending role as beneficial as it helped them to settle down in the ward.

Conclusions

Nursing is a practice-based profession. In order to assist students in taking up their professional role, nursing departments in tertiary institutions are recognizing the value of recruiting clinical staff to provide supervision for students. In developing a clinical mentoring program for nursing students, it is important to explore the students' expectations of the mentors' roles and responsibilities and make these known to mentors. While the mentors' roles can be described by the five aspects as stated by the ENB – assisting, befriending, guiding, advising and counselling – it is worth noting that the kinds of behaviours students expected of these roles varied from student to student. Before success in the relationship can be anticipated, both faculty and the mentors need to be informed of the students' expectations through open communication. Conversely, students should have a more realistic interpretation of the mentors' roles and responsibilities.

Acknowledgements

This project was funded by a Teaching and Learning Development Grant from The Hong Kong Polytechnic University. Appreciation goes to Miss Josephine Hung an ex-member of the project team, to the research assistants who contributed to the data collection and analysis, and to the students who volunteered to participate in the study.

References

Andrews M, Wallis M (1999) Mentorship in nursing: a literature review. *Journal of Advanced Nursing* 29 (1): 201–207.

Atkins S, Williams A (1995) Registered nurses' experiences of mentoring undergraduate nursing students. *Journal of Advanced Nursing* 21: 1006–1015.

Bracken E (1989) The implications of mentorship in nursing career development. *Senior Nurse* 19 (5): 15–16.

Burnard P (1988) A supporting act. *Nursing Times* 84 (46): 27–28.

Darling A W (1984) What do nurses want in a mentor? *The Journal of Nursing Administration* October: 42–44.

Davis L L, Barham P D (1989) Get the most from your preceptorship program. *Nursing Outlook* July/August: 167–171.

Earnshaw G (1995) Mentorship: the students' view. *Nurse Education Today* 15: 274–279.

Ferguson L M (1996) Preceptor's need for faculty support. *Journal of Nursing Staff Development* March/April: 73–80.

Foy H, Waltho B J (1989) The mentor system: Are learner nurses benefiting? *Senior Nurse* 9 (5): 24–25.

Gray M, Smith L (1999) The professional socialisation of diploma of higher education in nursing students (Project 2000): a longitudinal qualitative study. *Journal of Advanced Nursing* 29 (3): 639–647.

Hagerty B (1986) A second look at mentors. *Nursing Outlook* 34 (1): 16–19, 24.

Hunt D M, Michael C (1983) Mentorship: a career training and developing tool. *Academy of Management Review* 8 (3): 475–485.

Kersbergen A L, Hrobsky P E (1996) Use of clinical maps guides in precepted clinical experiences. *Nurse Educator* 21 (6): 19–22.

Kotzabassaki S, Panou M, Dimou F, Karabagh A, Koutsopoulou B, Ikonomou U (1997) Nursing students' and faculty's perceptions of the characteristics of 'best' and 'worst' clinical teachers: a replication study. *Journal of Advanced Nursing* 26 (4): 817–824.

Laurent C (1988) Mentors: on hand to help. *Nursing Times* 84 (46): 29–30.

Levinson D J, Darrow C M, Klein E G, Levinson M H, Mckee B (1978) *The Seasons of a Man's Life*. A A Knopf, New York.

Morgan J, Knox J E (1987) Characteristics of 'best' and 'worst' clinical teachers as perceived by university nursing faculty and students. *Journal of Advanced Nursing* 16 (10): 25–30.

Marriot A (1991) The support, supervision and instruction of nurse learners in clinical areas: a literature review. *Nurse Education Today* 11: 261–269.

Phillips R M, Davies W B, Neary M (1996) The practitioner-teacher: a study in the introduction of mentors in the preregistration nurse education program in Wales. *Journal of Advanced Nursing* 23: 1037–1044.

Rittman M R (1992) Preceptor development programs: An interpretative approach. *Journal of Nursing Education* 31 (8): 367–370.

Roche G R (1979) Much ado about mentors. *Harvard Business Review* 57 (1): 17–28.

Spouse J (1996) The effective mentor: a model for student-centred learning. *Nursing Times* 92 (13): 32–35.

Voignier R R, Freeman L H (1992) Helping staff help students. *Journal of Nursing Staff Development* 8 (4): 165–169.

Watson N A (1999) Mentoring today – the student's views. An investigative case study of pre-registration nursing students' experiences and perceptions of mentoring in one theory/practice module of the Common Foundation Programme on a Project 2000 course. *Journal of Advanced Nursing* 29 (1): 254–262.

Woodrow P (1994) Mentorship: perception and pitfalls for nursing practice. *Journal of Advanced Nursing* 19: 812–818.

Facilitating Learning in Practice

The concept of facilitation is being used increasingly in educational contexts, with many involved in the education process advocating a change from the traditional, formal teacher/student relationship to that of a more dynamic and interactive partnership between facilitator and student. The more traditional approach is based on a hierarchical model with the teacher having the position of power because of his/her knowledge and experience, and is still very prevalent in both academic and workplace learning environments.

Facilitation, on the other hand, promotes the ideals of sharing and partnership in the learning process where both student and facilitator are working together on a relatively equal basis to maximise the learning experience. Carl Rogers (1969) is recognised as one of the principal proponents of the concept of facilitation. Rogers sees anyone involved in promoting learning as a facilitator, a provider of resources for learning and someone who shares his/her feelings as well as knowledge with students. Thus the prerequisites for an effective facilitator are awareness of self, being oneself in the learning environment, accepting and trusting students, and empathy (Quinn, 2000).

Facilitating learning in a formal classroom setting is somewhat different to doing so in a workplace learning environment. The basic qualities of genuineness, trust and empathic understanding suggested by Rogers are required whatever the environment, but the learning experiences are bound to be less structured and more opportunistic than those involved in a formally designed programme of study.

Nicklin and Kenworthy (2000) suggest that the challenge to practice-based facilitation of learning is to *"enthral the student with the quality of practice demonstrated by skilled practitioners who have themselves reached the level of discrimination."* In this context dissemination means that the individual has reached the stage in their own development where they are in a position to influence others (Steinaker and Bell, 1979). Clearly, in order for facilitators to reach this stage they require a sound knowledge base in relation to teaching and learning strategies and must have developed the practical skills to be able to implement these strategies appropriately and effectively. Each work area is a unique, ever changing and dynamic learning environment for both students and trained staff alike. It is important that as facilitators of learning you are aware of this environmental uniqueness.

Reflective practice has been practised by some for many years but has only relatively recently been formalised with the emergence of a theoretical foundation and a range of supporting literature. Reflection is now recognised by the healthcare professions as a required competency, and as such, facilitators of learning require to have a sound understanding of what reflection is and its benefits to the learning process.

The overall goal of facilitating reflection is to foster both an intellectual and action oriented approach to learning, encouraging analytical reflection as a precursor to action and change (Glen *et al.* 1995). In order to promote reflective practice in others it is first essential to ensure that you yourself fully understand the concept and have the appropriate skills to reflect effectively on your own practice. Learning to reflect and learning from those reflections is a very individual process. Some people are more naturally reflective than others but reflection is a skill that can be learned, practised and refined by anyone. If you also take into consideration the uniqueness of each individual student in relation to such things as learning skills, learning style and past experiences, you may then start to realise the importance of the role of planning for the facilitator.

The focus of the extracts in this section is therefore on the facilitation of learning in the practice, and a range of strategies is explored and their application to practice explained and analysed.

References

Boud D *et al.* (1985) *Reflection: Turning Experience into Learning.* Kogan Page, London.

Glen S *et al.* (1995) Reflecting on reflection: a personal encounter. *Nurse Education Today* 15 (1): 61–68.

Quinn F M (2000) *The Principles and Practice of Nurse Education.* Chapman and Hall, London.

Rogers C (1994) *Feedom to Learn*, 3rd edn. Merrill, Columbus, Ohio.

Nicklin P, Kenworthy N (2000) *Teaching and Assessing in Nursing Practice*, 2nd edn. Scutari Press, London.

Schon D (1990) *Educating the Reflective Practitioner.* Jossey-Bass, San Francisco.

Steinaker N, Bell M (1979) *The Experiential Taxonomy. A New Approach to Teaching and Learning.* Academic Press, London.

17. Setting the Scene for Learning Styles

Peter Honey and Alan Mumford

Introduction

This guide is for all trainers, educators and development advisers – in fact for anyone who has an interest in helping people learn (for convenience we will use the term helper). It gives you all the background you need to help people use and understand the learning styles questionnaire. The questionnaire itself is in the new learner's booklet entitled *Learning Styles Questionnaire (80-item version)*, together with all the data an individual learner needs to interpret, understand and act on the results.

Learning is such a fundamental process that many people take it for granted, conveniently assuming that by the time they are adults they have learned how to learn and need no further assistance with the process. Thus teachers concentrate on teaching and assume students are skilled at such learning activities as listening, note taking, researching, essay writing and revising. Trainers too often assume that learners are empty buckets waiting to be filled by whatever training method the trainer favours. The fact that the buckets are different shapes and sizes is conveniently overlooked.

Yet it is patently clear that people vary, not just in their learning skills but also in their learning styles. Why otherwise might two people – matched for age, intelligence and need – react so differently when exposed to the same learning opportunity? One person emerges enthusiastic, able to articulate and implement what has been learned, yet the other claims it was a waste of time and that nothing has been learned.

This guide aims to show that the reason for this divergence stems from unspoken preferences about how to learn. Perhaps the learning opportunity involved being 'thrown in at the deep end' with minimal guidance – this might suit one person's style but not the other, who might prefer to learn by being thoroughly briefed before 'having a go'.

The term 'learning styles' is used as a description of the attitudes and behaviours that determine an individual's preferred way of learning. Most people are unaware of their learning style preferences. They just know vaguely that they feel more comfortable with, and learn more from, some activities than others. Helpers often realise people learn differently, but may not be sure how and why. In this guide we show how learning styles can be identified and how this can benefit both helper and learner.

The case for helping people to be more effective learners ought to be self-evident, yet many trainers still give insufficient recognition to it. It is perhaps the most important of all the life skills since the way in which people learn affects everything else. We

Peter Honey and Alan Mumford: 'Setting the Scene for Learning Styles' from *THE LEARNING STYLES HELPER'S GUIDE* (2000), pp. 6–13. Published by Peter Honey, Ardingly House, 10 Linden Avenue, Maidenhead, Berks SL6 6HB.

live in the post industrial 'information' age where information has a shorter shelf-life and where transformational changes are less predictable and occur more rapidly than ever before. Clearly learning is the key, not just to surviving, but to thriving on all these changes. So this guide gives help on the crucial issue of learning to learn, thus enabling people to continue to learn throughout life.

What is learning?

Learning has happened when people can demonstrate that they know something they didn't know before (insights and realisations as well as facts) and/or when they can do something they couldn't do before (skills).

We learn in two substantially different ways. Sometimes we are 'taught' through formal structured activities such as lectures, case studies and books. We also learn informally from our experiences, often in an unconscious, ill-defined way. Formal learning dedicated to the acquisition of knowledge is both more familiar and more straightforward than experiential learning. It is more familiar, not because we necessarily do it more often, but because most people associate the word 'learning' with the acquisition of facts rather more than with the messier process of learning from day-to-day experiences. As we shall see, learning style preferences have implications for all types of learning.

The range of influences on learning

The history of developing ways to help people learn how to be more effective is relatively short, perhaps fifty years in the UK and a little longer in the USA. One of the constant features in that history has been the discovery of a succession of what were claimed to be uniquely appropriate 'methods'. Lectures were abandoned and replaced by case studies. Books about human relations techniques were replaced by T Groups. 'Sheep-dip' training schemes gave way to individual commitment and self-development. The problem of ineffective learning remains, because all these 'solutions' dealt too exclusively with delivery methods and not sufficiently with differences in individual approaches to learning.

This guide is about the contribution that can be made to effective learning by understanding, and using, individual styles of learning. We are, however, clear that we are describing one of several major ingredients that need to be present before effective learning occurs. We are not adding another innovation and claiming that without it nothing useful will be done; we are saying that with attention to individual learning styles much more effective learning can take place.

In order to emphasise the importance of placing learning styles in the total learning context, it is worth remembering the large number of factors that influence the extent of learning. The following diagram shows just some of the many influences on what is learned or not learned.

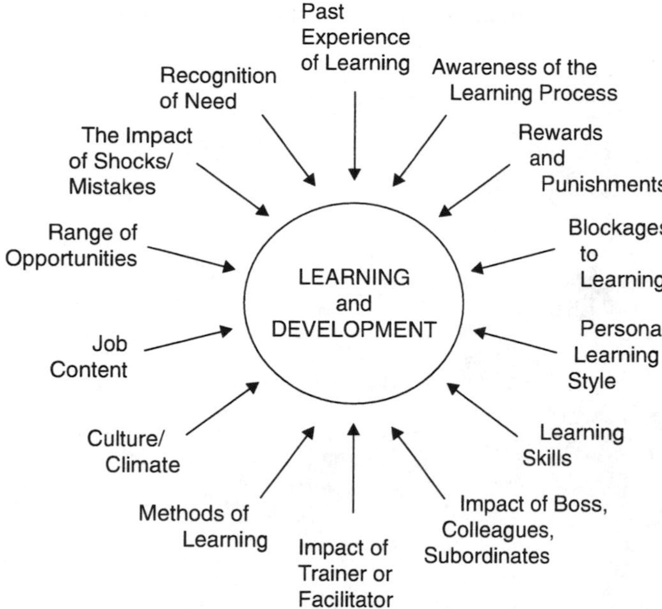

This helps to put this guide into its proper perspective, since it can be seen that it focuses on just one of the range of influences: personal learning style. However, the learning cycle and learning styles are particularly important for the helper because they fall within an area that the helper can directly influence.

Learning as a continuous process

Learning is a lifelong process. It never makes sense to say we have learned all there is to learn or that our learning is complete. The continuous process is rather like the coils in a spring or a never-ending spiral.

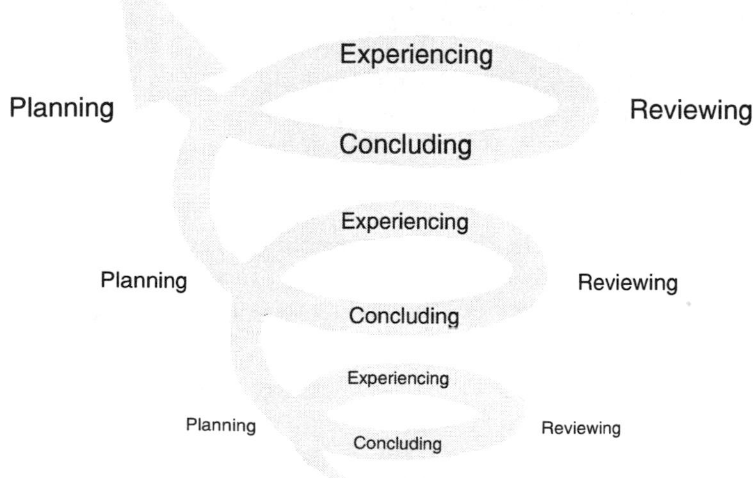

Each coil of the spring, or loop in the spiral, has four distinct stages:

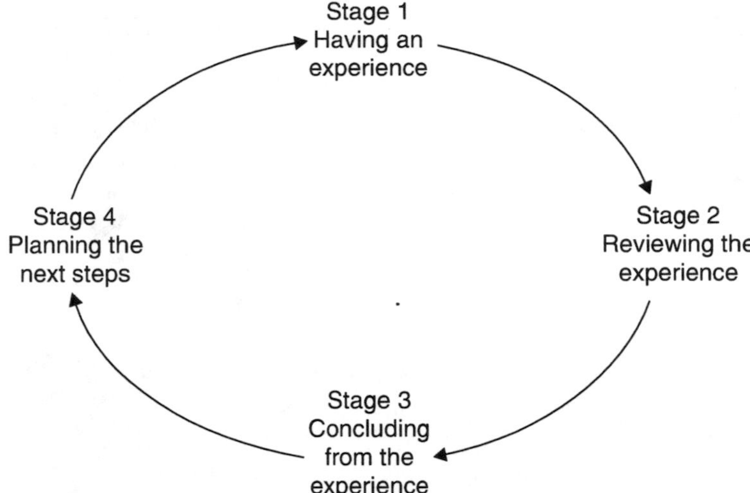

Our description of the stages in the learning cycle originated from the work of David Kolb. Kolb uses different words to describe the stages of the cycle and four learning styles. The similarities between his model and ours are greater than the differences. However, since we first published the *Learning Styles Questionnaire* (in 1982) many users have found it enjoys a greater face validity with learners, mainly because – unlike Kolb – we refrain from asking direct questions about how people learn.

A learner can start anywhere on the cycle because each stage feeds into the next. A person could, for example, start at stage 2 by acquiring some information and pondering it before reaching some conclusions, stage 3, and deciding how to apply it, stage 4. On the other hand, someone could start at stage 4 with a technique they plan to incorporate into their *modus operandi.* Using the technique would then be at stage 1 in the cycle before reviewing how it worked out, stage 2, reaching conclusions stage 3, and modifying the technique in the light of the experience, stage 4.

This continuous, iterative process is so fundamental that it underpins many other approaches. The scientific method is one example. Many problem solving/decision making processes also map onto the stages in the learning cycle as do the methods of continuous improvement in Total Quality Management.

Ways of distorting the learning cycle

The four stages – experiencing, reviewing, concluding and planning – are mutually supportive. None is fully effective as a learning procedure on its own. Each stage plays an equally important part in the total process (though the time spent on each may vary considerably).

Most people, however, develop preferences that give them a liking for certain stages over others. The preferences lead to a distortion of the learning process so that greater emphasis is placed on some stages to the detriment of others. Here are some typical examples:

- Preferences for experiencing to the extent that people develop an addiction for activities and rush around constantly on the go. This results in plenty of experiences and the assumption that having experiences is synonymous with learning from them.
- Preferences for reviewing such that people shy away from first-hand experiences and postpone reaching conclusions for as long as possible whilst more information is gathered. This results in an 'analysis to paralysis' tendency with plenty of pondering but little action.
- Preferences for concluding such that people have a compulsion to reach an answer quickly. This results in a tendency to jump to conclusions by circumventing the review stage, where uncertainty and ambiguity are higher (conclusions, even if they are dubious, are comforting things to have).
- Preferences for seizing on an expedient course of action and implementing it with inadequate preparation. This results in a tendency to go for 'quick fixes' by over-emphasising the planning and experiencing stages to the detriment of reviewing and concluding.

Learning styles

Learning styles are the key to understanding these different preferences. Learning styles, in common with any other style, have in themselves been learned as people repeat strategies and tactics they find to be successful and discontinue those that are not. In this way preferences for certain behaviour patterns develop and become habitual. These styles tend to be strengthened as people gravitate towards careers that are compatible with their preferred *modus operandi.*

Here are descriptions of the four learning styles.

Activists

Activists involve themselves fully and without bias in new experiences. They enjoy the here and now and are happy to be dominated by immediate experiences. They are open-minded, not sceptical, and this tends to make them enthusiastic about anything new. Their philosophy is *"I'll try anything once"*. They tend to act first and consider the consequences afterwards. Their days are filled with activity. They tackle problems by brainstorming. As soon as the excitement from one activity has died down they are busy looking for the next. They tend to thrive on the challenge of new experiences but are bored with implementation and longer term consolidation. They are gregarious people constantly involving themselves with others but, in doing so, they seek to centre all activities on themselves.

Reflectors

Reflectors like to stand back to ponder experiences and observe them from many different perspectives. They collect data, both first hand and from others, and prefer to think about it thoroughly before coming to any conclusion. The thorough collection and analysis of data about experiences and events is what counts, so they tend to postpone reaching definitive conclusions for as long as possible. Their philosophy is to be cautious. They are thoughtful people who like to consider all possible angles and implications before making a move. They prefer to take a back seat in meetings and discussions. They enjoy observing other people in action. They listen to others and get the drift of the discussion before making their own points. They tend to adopt a low profile and have a slightly distant, tolerant, unruffled air about them. When they act it is part of a wide picture which includes the past as well as the present and others' observations as well as their own.

Theorists

Theorists adapt and integrate observations into complex but logically sound theories. They think problems through in a vertical, step-by-step, logical way. They assimilate disparate facts into coherent theories. They tend to be perfectionists who won't rest easy until things are tidy and fit into a rational scheme. They like to analyse and synthesise. They are keen on basic assumptions, principles, theories, models and 'systems thinking'. Their philosophy prizes rationality and logic, *"if it's logical it's good"*. Questions they frequently ask are "Does it make sense?", "How does this fit with that?", "What are the basic assumptions?" They tend to be detached, analytical and dedicated to rational objectivity rather than anything subjective or ambiguous. Their approach to problems is consistently logical. This is their 'mental set' and they rigidly reject anything that doesn't fit with it. They prefer to maximise certainty and feel uncomfortable with subjective judgements, lateral thinking and anything flippant.

Pragmatists

Pragmatists are keen on trying out ideas, theories and techniques to see if they work in practice. They positively search out new ideas and take the first opportunity to experiment with applications. They are the sort of people who return from management courses brimming with new ideas that they want to try out in practice. They like to get on with things and act quickly and confidently on ideas that attract them. They tend to be impatient with ruminating and open-ended discussions. They are essentially practical, down-to-earth people who like making practical decisions and solving problems. They respond to problems and opportunities as a challenge. Their philosophy is "*There is always a better way*" and "*if it works it's good*".

The links between styles and the stages in the cycle

Each style 'connects' with a stage on the continuous learning cycle. People with Activist preferences, with their 'I'll try anything once' approach, are well equipped for Experiencing. People with Reflector preferences, with their predilection for mulling over data, are well equipped for Reviewing. People with Theorist preferences, with their need to tidy up and have 'answers', are well equipped for Concluding. Finally, people with Pragmatist preferences, with their liking for things practical, are well equipped for Planning. The diagram overleaf shows the learning styles positioned around the learning cycle.

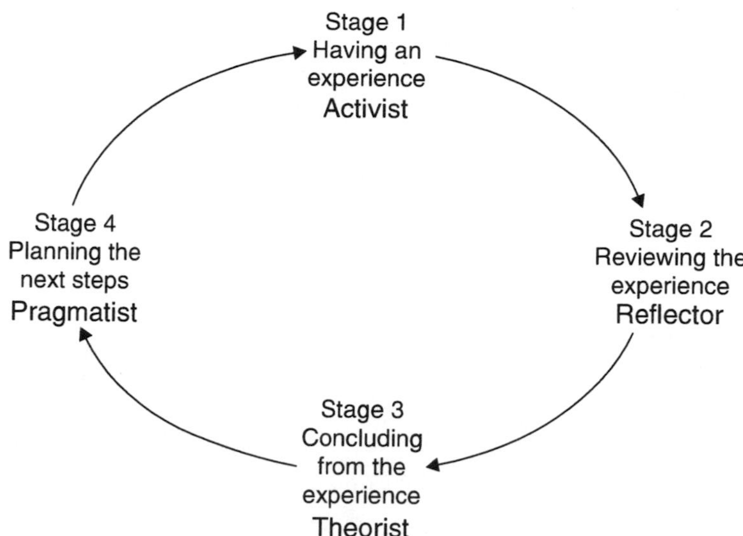

This guide

This guide is practical rather than theoretical. It shows how learning activities can be designed to encompass the full cycle. It also confirms that people are more effective learners once they are aware of their learning style preferences. The questionnaire results provide a starting point, not a finishing point, because knowledge of learning styles is only useful if it is applied rather than merely recorded. In the sections that follow, we describe how this can be done. The most significant uses explored in this guide are:

- Increased awareness of the match between learning activities and different styles
- A better choice by helpers and learners of those activities, leading to more effective and more economical learning provision. Avoidance of inappropriate learning experiences is both good in itself and less likely to lead to the 'Shakespeare effect', where unfortunate early experiences put young people off for life
- Identification of ways in which a person's less effective learning processes and skills can be improved
- Advice on how your different learning styles as a helper influence the way you help others to learn.

18. Preparing Professionals for the Demands of Practice

Donald A. Schön

The crisis of confidence in professional knowledge

In the varied topography of professional practice, there is a high, hard ground overlooking a swamp. On the high ground, manageable problems lend themselves to solution through the application of research-based theory and technique. In the swampy lowland, messy, confusing problems defy technical solution. The irony of this situation is that the problems of the high ground tend to be relatively unimportant to individuals or society at large, however great their technical interest may be, while in the swamp lie the problems of greatest human concern. The practitioner must choose. Shall he remain on the high ground where he can solve relatively unimportant problems according to prevailing standards of rigor, or shall he descend to the swamp of important problems and nonrigorous inquiry?

This dilemma has two sources: first, the prevailing idea of rigorous professional knowledge, based on technical rationality, and second, awareness of indeterminate, swampy zones of practice that lie beyond its canons.

Technical rationality is an epistemology of practice derived from positivist philosophy, built into the very foundations of the modern research university (Shils, 1978). Technical rationality holds that practitioners are instrumental problem solvers who elect technical means best suited to particular purposes. Rigorous professional practitioners solve well-formed instrumental problems by applying theory and technique derived from systematic, preferably scientific knowledge. Medicine, law, and business — Nathan Glazer's "major professions" (Glazer, 1974) — figure in this view as exemplars of professional practice.

But, as we have come to see with increasing clarity over the last twenty or so years, the problems of real-world practice do not present themselves to practitioners as well-formed structures. Indeed, they tend not to present themselves as problems at all but as messy, indeterminate situations. Civil engineers, for example, know how to build roads suited to the conditions of particular sites and specifications. They draw on their knowledge of soil conditions, materials, and construction technologies to define grades, surfaces, and dimensions. When they must decide *what* road to build, however, or whether to build it at all, their problem is not solvable by the application of technical knowledge, not even by the sophisticated techniques of decision theory. They face a complex and ill-defined mélange of topographical, financial, economic, environmental, and political factors. If they are to get a well-formed problem matched to their familiar theories and techniques, they must *construct* it from the materials

---

of a situation that is, to use John Dewey's (1938) term, "problematic." And the problem of problem setting is not well formed.

When a practitioner sets a problem, he chooses and names the things he will notice. In his road-building situation, the civil engineer may see drainage, soil stability, and ease of maintenance; he may not see the differential effects of the road on the economies of the towns that lie along its route. Through complementary acts of naming and framing, the practitioner selects things for attention and organizes them, guided by an appreciation of the situation that gives it coherence and sets a direction for action. So problem setting is an ontological process — in Nelson Goodman's (1978) memorable word, a form of worldmaking.

Depending on our disciplinary backgrounds, organizational roles, past histories, interests, and political/economic perspectives, we frame problematic situations in different ways. A nutritionist, for example, may convert a vague worry about malnourishment among children in developing countries into the problem of selecting an optimal diet. But agronomists may frame the problem in terms of food production; epidemiologists may frame it in terms of diseases that increase the demand for nutrients or prevent their absorption; demographers tend to see it in terms of a rate of population growth that has outstripped agricultural activity; engineers, in terms of inadequate food storage and distribution; economists, in terms of insufficient purchasing power or the inequitable distribution of land or wealth. In the field of malnourishment, professional identities and political/economic perspectives determine how people see a problematic situation, and debates about malnourishment revolve around the construction of a problem to be solved. Debates involve conflicting frames, not easily resolvable — if resolvable at all — by appeal to data. Those who hold conflicting frames pay attention to different facts and make different sense of the facts they notice. It is not by technical problem solving that we convert problematic situations to well-formed problems; rather, it is through naming and framing that technical problem solving becomes possible.

Often, a problematic situation presents itself as a unique case. A physician recognizes a constellation of symptoms that she cannot associate with a known disease. A mechanical engineer encounters a structure for which he cannot, with the tools at his disposal, make a determinate analysis. A teacher of arithmetic, listening to a child's question, becomes aware of a kind of confusion and, at the same time, a kind of intuitive understanding, for which she has no readily available response. Because the unique case falls outside the categories of existing theory and technique, the practitioner cannot treat it as an instrumental problem to be solved by applying one of the rules in her store of professional knowledge. The case is not "in the book." If she is to deal with it competently, she must do so by a kind of improvisation, inventing and testing in the situation strategies of her own devising.

Some problematic situations are situations of conflict among values. Medical technologies such as kidney dialysis or tomography have created demands that stretch the nation's willingness to invest in medical services. How should physicians respond to the conflicting requirements of efficiency, equity, and quality of care? Engineering technologies, powerful and elegant when judged from a narrowly technical perspective, turn out to have unintended and unpredicted side effects that degrade the environment, generate unacceptable risk, or create excessive demands on scarce resources. How, in their actual designing, should engineers take such factors into account? When agronomists recommend efficient methods of soil cultivation that favor the use of large landholdings, they may undermine the viability of the small family farm on which peasant economies depend. How should their practice reflect their recognition of the risk? In such cases, competent practitioners must not only solve technical problems by selecting the means appropriate to clear and self-consistent ends; they must also reconcile, integrate, or choose among conflicting appreciations of a situation so as to construct a coherent problem worth solving.

Often, situations are problematic in several ways at once. A hydrologist, employed to advise officials of a water supply system about capital investment and pricing, may find the hydrological system unique. He may also experience uncertainty because he has no satisfactory model of the system. In addition, he may discover that his client is unwilling to listen to his attempts to describe the situation's uniqueness and uncertainty, insisting on an expert answer that specifies one right way. He will be caught, then, in a thicket of conflicting requirements: a wish to keep his job, a feeling of professional pride in his ability to give usable advice, and a keen sense of his obligation to keep his claims to certainty within the bounds of his actual understanding.

These indeterminate zones of practice — uncertainty, uniqueness, and value conflict — escape the canons of technical rationality. When a problematic situation is uncertain, technical problem solving depends on the prior construction of a well-formed problem — which is not itself a technical task. When a practitioner recognizes a situation as unique, she cannot handle it solely by applying theories or techniques derived from her store of professional knowledge. And in situations of value conflict, there are no clear and self-consistent ends to guide the technical selection of means.

It is just these indeterminate zones of practice, however, that practitioners and critical observers of the professions have come to see with increasing clarity over the past two decades as central to professional practice. And the growing awareness of them has figured prominently in recent controversies about the performance of the professions and their proper place in our society.

When professionals fail to recognize or respond to value conflicts, when they violate their own ethical standards, fall short of self-created expectations for expert performance, or seem blind to public problems they have helped to create, they are increasingly subject to expressions of disapproval and dissatisfaction. Radical critics like Ivan Illich (1970) take them to task for misappropriating and monopolizing knowledge, blithely disregarding social injustices, and mystifying their expertise. Professionals themselves argue that it is impossible to meet heightened societal expectations for their performance in an environment that combines increasing turbulence with increasing regulation of professional activity. They emphasize their lack of control over the larger systems for which they are unfairly held responsible. At the same time, they call attention to the mismatch between traditional divisions of labor and the shifting complexities of present-day society. They call for reforms in professional norms and structures.

In spite of these different emphases, public, radical, and professional critics voice a common complaint: that the most important areas of professional practice now lie beyond the conventional boundaries of professional competence.

The late Everett Hughes, a pioneering sociologist of the professions, once observed that the professions have struck a bargain with society. In return for access to their extraordinary knowledge in matters of great human importance, society has granted them a mandate for social control in their fields of specialization, a high degree of autonomy in their practice, and a license to determine who shall assume the mantle of professional authority (Hughes, 1959). But in the current climate of criticism, controversy, and dissatisfaction, the bargain is coming unstuck. When the professions' claim to extraordinary knowledge is so much in question, why should we continue to grant them extraordinary rights and privileges?

The crisis of confidence in professional education

The crisis of confidence in professional knowledge corresponds to a similar crisis in professional education. If professions are blamed for ineffectiveness and impropriety, their schools are blamed for failing to teach the rudiments of effective and ethical practice. Chief Justice Warren Burger criticizes the law schools, for example, because trial lawyers are not good at their jobs. In the present climate of dissatisfaction with public schools, schools of education are taken to task. Business schools become targets of criticism when their M.B.A.'s are seen as having failed to exercise responsible stewardship or rise adequately to the Japanese challenge. Schools of engineering lose credibility because they are seen as producing narrowly trained technicians deficient in capacity for design and wisdom to deal with dilemmas of technological development.

Underlying such criticisms is a version of the rigor-or-relevance dilemma. What aspiring practitioners need most to learn, professional schools seem least able to teach. And the schools' version of the dilemma is rooted, like the practitioners', in an underlying and largely unexamined epistemology of professional practice — a model of professional knowledge institutionally embedded in curriculum and arrangements for research and practice.

The professional schools of the modern research university are premised on technical rationality. Their normative curriculum, first adopted in the early decades of the twentieth century as the professions sought to gain prestige by establishing their schools in universities, still embodies the idea that practical competence becomes professional when its instrumental problem solving is grounded in systematic, preferably scientific knowledge. So the normative professional curriculum presents first the relevant basic science, then the relevant applied science, and finally, a practicum in which students are presumed to learn to apply research-based knowledge to the problems of everyday practice (Schein, 1973). And the prevailing view of the proper relationship between professional schools and schools of science and scholarship still conforms to the bargain enunciated many years ago by Thorstein Veblen (1918/1962): from the "lower" technical schools, their unsolved problems; from the "higher" schools, their useful knowledge.

As professional schools have sought to attain higher levels of academic rigor and status, they have oriented themselves toward an ideal most vividly represented by a particular view of medical education: physicians are thought to be trained as biotechnical problem solvers by immersion, first in medical science and then in supervised clinical practice where they learn to apply research-based techniques to diagnosis, treatment, and prevention. In this view of medical education, and its extension in the normative curriculum of other professional schools, there is a hierarchy of knowledge:

Basic science
Applied science
Technical skills of day-to-day practice

The greater one's proximity to basic science, as a rule, the higher one's academic status. General, theoretical, propositional knowledge enjoys a privileged position. Even in the professions least equipped with a secure foundation of systematic professional knowledge — Nathan Glazer's (1974) "minor professions," such as social work, city planning, and education — yearning for the rigor of science-based knowledge and the power of science-based technique leads the schools to import scholars from neighboring departments of social science. And the relative status of the various professions is largely correlated with the extent to which they are able to present themselves as rigorous practitioners of a science-based professional knowledge and embody in their schools a version of the normative professional curriculum.

But, in the throes of external attack and internal self-doubt, the university-based schools of the professions are becoming increasingly aware of troubles in certain foundational assumptions on which they have traditionally depended for their credibility and legitimacy. They have assumed that academic research yields useful professional knowledge and that the professional knowledge taught in the schools prepares students for the demands of real-world practice. Both assumptions are coming increasingly into question.

In recent years there has been a growing perception that researchers, who are supposed to feed the professional schools with useful knowledge, have less and less to say that practitioners find useful. Teachers complain that cognitive psychologists have little of practical utility to teach them. Business managers and even some business school professors express a "nagging doubt that some research is getting too academic and that [we] may be neglecting to teach managers how to put into effect the strategies which they develop" (Lynton, 1984, p. 14). Policy makers and politicians express similar doubts about the utility of political science. Martin Rein and Sheldon White (1980) have recently observed that research not only is separate from professional practice but has been increasingly captured by its own agenda, divergent from the needs and interests of professional practitioners. And Joseph Gusfield (1979, pp. 22), addressing himself to sociology's failure to provide a firm and useful grounding for public policy, has written a passage that could have a much more general application: "The bright hope had been that sociology, by the logic of its theories and the power of its empirical findings, would provide insights and generalizations enabling governments to frame policies and professionals to engineer programs that could solve the exigent problems of the society and helping intellectuals to direct understanding and criticism. Our record has not been very good. In area after area — gerontology, crime, mental health, race relations, poverty — we have become doubtful that the technology claimed is adequate to the demand. . . . It is not that conflicting interests lead groups to ignore social science. It is rather that our belief in the legitimacy of our knowledge is itself in doubt."

At the same time, professional educators have voiced with increasing frequency their worries about the gap between the schools' prevailing conception of professional knowledge and the actual competencies required of practitioners in the field. An eminent professor of engineering, commenting on the neglect of engineering design in schools devoted to engineering science, observed nearly twenty years ago that, if the art of engineering design were known and constant, it could be taught — but it is not constant (Brooks, 1967). Another dean of an engineering school said, at about the same time, that "we know how to teach people how to build ships but not how to figure out what ships to build" (Alfred Kyle, personal communication, 1974). The dean of a well-known school of management observed a decade ago that "we need most to teach students how to make decisions under conditions of uncertainty, but this is just what we don't know how to teach" (William Pownes, personal communication, 1972). Law professors have been discussing for some time the need to teach "lawyering" and, especially, the competences to resolve disputes by other means than litigation. A major school of medicine is undertaking a pilot program one of whose goals is to help students learn to function competently in clinical situations where there are no right answers or standard procedures. In all these examples, educators express their dissatisfactions with a professional curriculum that cannot prepare students for competence in the indeterminate zones of practice.

Awareness of these two gaps, each contributing to and exacerbating the other, undermines the confidence of professional educators in their ability to fulfill their mandate. Nevertheless, many professional schools — certainly those of medicine, law, and business — continue to attract large numbers of students in search of the traditional rewards of status, security, and affluence. Self-doubt coexists with pressure to provide traditional services to students who seek traditional rewards.

Thoughtful practitioners of professional education have tended to see these problems in very different ways. Some, in the fields of medicine, management, and engineering, have focused attention on difficulties created for professional education by the rapidly changing and proliferating mass of knowledge relevant to professional practice. They see the problem as one of "keeping up with" and "integrating" into the professional curriculum the stream of potentially useful research results. Others, in law or architecture, for example, have focused on aspects of practice for which traditional professional education provides no formal preparation. They recommend such marginal additions to the standard curriculum as courses in professional ethics or professional/client relationships. Still others see the problem as a loosening of earlier standards of professional rigor and probity; they want to tighten up the curriculum in order to restore it to its former level of excellence.

These are patchwork approaches to problems seen as peripheral. But another group of critics, including some students, practitioners, and educators, raises a deeper question. Can the prevailing concepts of professional education ever yield a curriculum adequate to the complex, unstable, uncertain, and conflictual worlds of practice? A recent example of this school of thought is a book by Ernst Lynton (1985) that links the troubles of the professional schools to a multidimensional crisis of the university and calls for a fundamental reexamination of the nature and conduct of university education. Such commentaries trace the gaps between professional school and workplace, research and practice, to a flawed conception of professional competence and its relationship to scientific and scholarly research. In this view, if there is a crisis of confidence in the professions and their schools, it is rooted in the prevailing epistemology of practice.

Turning the problem upside down

It is striking that uneasiness about professional knowledge persists even though some practitioners do very well in the indeterminate zones whose importance we are learning to recognize. Some engineers are good at engineering design. Some lawyers are good at lawyering, competent at the skills of negotiation, mediation, and client relations that lie beyond the conventional boundaries of legal knowledge. Some business managers are manifestly better than others at making sense of confusing situations; and some policy makers are significantly endowed with the ability to work out useful integrations of conflicting views and interests.

Few critics of professional practice would deny these things, but few would take them as a source of insight into the crises of professional knowledge and education. The difficulty is not that critics fail to recognize some professional performances as superior to others — on this point there is surprisingly general agreement — but that they cannot assimilate what they recognize to their dominant model of professional knowledge. So outstanding practitioners are not said to have more professional knowledge than others but more "wisdom," "talent," "intuition," or "artistry."

Unfortunately, such terms as these serve not to open up inquiry but to close it off. They are used as junk categories, attaching names to phenomena that elude conventional strategies of explanation. So the dilemma of rigor or relevance here reasserts itself. On the basis of an underlying and largely unexamined epistemology of practice, we distance ourselves from the kinds of performance we need most to understand.

The question of the relationship between practice competence and professional knowledge needs to be turned upside down. We should start not by asking how to make better use of research-based knowledge but by asking what we can learn from a careful examination of artistry, that is, the competence by which practitioners actually handle indeterminate zones of practice — however that competence may relate to technical rationality.

This is the perspective of the present book, which starts from the following premises:

- Inherent in the practice of the professionals we recognize as unusually competent is a core of artistry.
- Artistry is an exercise of intelligence, a kind of knowing, though different in crucial respects from our standard model of professional knowledge. It is not inherently mysterious; it is rigorous in its own terms; and we can learn a great

deal about it — within what limits, we should treat as an open question — by carefully studying the performance of unusually competent performers.

- In the terrain of professional practice, applied science and research-based technique occupy a critically important though limited territory, bounded on several sides by artistry. There are an art of problem framing, an art of implementation, and an art of improvisation — all necessary to mediate the use in practice of applied science and technique.

Not only the question of the relationship between competent practice and professional knowledge but also the question of professional education needs to be turned upside down. Just as we should inquire into the manifestations of professional artistry, so we should also examine the various ways in which people actually acquire it.

When, in the early decades of this century, the professions began to appropriate the prestige of the university by placing their schools within it, "professionalization" meant the replacement of artistry by systematic, preferably scientific, knowledge. As awareness of the crisis of confidence in professional knowledge has grown, however, educators have begun once again to see artistry as an essential component of professional competence, to ask whether the professional schools can or should do anything about it and, if so, how education for artistry can be made coherent with the professional curriculum's core of applied science and technique.

The debates surrounding these questions have taken different forms in different professions and schools. In an engineering curriculum organized mainly around engineering science, for example, how should students learn engineering design? How should students of such policy sciences as economics, decision theory, operations research, and statistical analysis learn the political and administrative skills of policy implementation?

Legal education has traditionally aimed at preparing students to "think like a lawyer." Law schools pioneered in the use of Christopher Langdell's case method to help students learn how to make legal arguments, clarify legal issues by adversarial process, and choose from among plausible judicial precedents the one most relevant to a particular question of legal interpretation. For some years, however, faculty members in some of the most eminent law schools have argued the need to develop competences that go beyond thinking like a lawyer — for example, skills in trial work, client relations, negotiation, advocacy, and legal ethics. In medical education, new programs have been devised to address the problems of preparing students not only for the biotechnical demands of clinical practice but also for family practice, management of the chronically ill, and the psychosocial dimensions of illness. Critics internal and external to the business schools now question the adequacy of the hallowed case method to the specific demands of management in particular industries as well as to the more general demands of responsible stewardship and management under conditions of uncertainty. In such fields as these, a professional curriculum organized around preparation for presumably generic competences of problem solving and decision making has begun to seem radically incomplete.

In some fields, the question of professional artistry has come up in the context of continuing education. Educators ask how mature professionals can be helped to renew themselves so as to avoid "burnout," how they can be helped to build their repertoires of skills and understandings on a continuing basis. Teacher education is an interesting example. Public awareness of the problems of schools has tended over the past thirty years to move in and out of focus, crystallizing from time to time around such issues as the quality of teaching and the in-service education of teachers. Teachers, who often resent becoming targets of blame for the perceived failures of public education, tend nevertheless to advocate their own versions of the need for professional development and renewal. Critics inside and outside the schools have argued in recent years that we must foster and reward development of the craft of teaching.

Where the core curriculum of professional education is relatively diffuse, unstable, and insecure, as in Nathan Glazer's "minor professions," the problem of education for artistry tends to take a different form. In social work, city planning, divinity, and educational administration, for example, educators tend to ask more open-endedly what competences ought to be acquired, through what methods, and in what domains of practice and even to wonder aloud whether what needs most to be learned can best be learned in a professional school. Here education for artistry becomes embroiled in the larger question of the legitimacy of professional education.

As we consider the artistry of extraordinary practitioners and explore the ways they actually acquire it, we are led inevitably to certain deviant traditions of education for practice — traditions that stand outside or alongside the normative curricula of the schools.

There are deviant traditions in the professional schools themselves. In medical schools and schools modeled at least in part on medicine, one often finds a dual curriculum. When interns and residents under the guidance of senior clinicians work with real patients on the wards, they learn more than application of medical science taught in the classroom. There is at least an implicit recognition that research-based models of diagnosis and treatment cannot be made to work until the students acquire an art that falls outside the models; and on this view, widely held by practicing physicians, the medical practicum is as much concerned with acquiring a quasi-autonomous art of clinical practice as with learning to apply research-based theory.

Beyond the confines of professional schools, there are other deviant traditions of education for practice. There are apprenticeships in industry and crafts. There is athletics coaching. And, perhaps most important, there are the conservatories of music and dance and the studios of the visual and plastic arts. The artistry of painters, sculptors, musicians, dancers, and designers bears a strong family resemblance to the artistry of extraordinary lawyers, physicians, managers, and teachers. It is no accident that professionals often refer to an "art" of teaching or management and use the term *artist* to refer to practitioners unusually adept at handling situations of uncertainty, uniqueness, and conflict.

In education for the fine arts, we find people learning to design, perform, and produce by engaging in design, performance, and production. Everything is practicum. Professional knowledge, in the sense of the propositional contents of applied science and scholarship, occupies a marginal place — if it is present at all — at the edges of the curriculum. Emphasis is placed on learning by doing, which John Dewey described long ago as the "primary or initial subject matter": "Recognition of the natural course of development . . . always sets out with situations which involve learning by doing. Arts and occupations form the initial stage of the curriculum, corresponding as they do to knowing how to go about the accomplishment of ends" (Dewey, 1974, p.364).

Students learn by practicing the making or performing at which they seek to become adept, and they are helped to do so by senior practitioners who — again, in Dewey's terms — initiate them into the traditions of practice: "The customs, methods, and *working* standards of the calling constitute a 'tradition,' and . . . initiation into the tradition is the means by which the powers of learners are released and directed" (1974, p.151).

The student cannot be *taught* what he needs to know, but he can be *coached*: "He has to *see* on his own behalf and in his own way the relations between means and methods employed and results achieved. Nobody else can see for him, and he can't see just by being 'told,' although the right kind of telling may guide his seeing and thus help him see what he needs to see" (1974, p.151).

Often, there is a powerful sense of mystery and magic in the atmosphere — the magic of great performers, the mystery of talent that falls capriciously, like divine grace, now on one individual, now on another. There are the great performers who symbolize it and the child prodigies whose occasional appearance gives evidence of its continual renewal. In this rather magical environment, the function of coaching is controversial. In the absence of talent, some coaches believe, there is little to be done; and if there is talent in abundance, it is best to keep out of the student's way. Others believe that talented students can learn, by a kind of contagion, from exposure to master practitioners. And still others frame learning by doing as a disciplined initiation into the setting and solving of problems of production and performance.

Perhaps, then, learning *all* forms of professional artistry depends, at least in part, on conditions similar to those created in the studios and conservatories: freedom to learn by doing in a setting relatively low in risk, with access to coaches who initiate students into the "traditions of the calling" and help them, by "the right kind of telling," to see on their own behalf and in their own way what they need most to see. We ought, then, to study the experience of learning by doing and the artistry of good coaching. We should base our study on the working assumption that both processes are intelligent and — within limits to be discovered — intelligible. And we ought to search for examples wherever we can find them — in the dual curricula of the schools, the apprenticeships and practicums that aspiring practitioners find or create for themselves, and the deviant traditions of studio and conservatory.

References

Brooks H (1967) Dilemmas of engineering education. *IEEE Spectrum*: 89–91.

Dewey J (1938) *Logic: The Theory of Inquiry*. Holt, Rinehart and Winston, New York.

Dewey J (1974) R D Archambault (ed.) *John Dewey on Education: Selected Writings*. University of Chicago Press, Chicago.

Glazer N (1974) The schools of the minor professions. *Minerva* 12 (3): 346–363.

Goodman N (1978) *Ways of World Making*. Hackett, Indianapolis.

Gusfield J (1979) 'Buddy, can you paradigm?' The crisis of theory in the welfare state. *Pacific Sociological Review* 22 (1): 3–22.

Hughes E (1959) The study of occupations. In: R K Merton, L Broom, L S Cottrell, Jr (eds) *Sociology Today*. Basic Books, New York.

Lynton E (1984) Universities in Crisis. Unpublished memorandum. Boston.

Lynton E (1985) *The Missing Connection Between Business and the Universities*. McGraw-Hill, New York.

Rein M, White S (1980) Knowledge for Practice: The Study of Knowledge in Context for the Practice of Social Work. Working paper. Division for Study and Research in Education, Massachusetts Institute of Technology.

Schein E (1973) *Professional Education*. McGraw-Hill, New York.

Shils E (1978) The order of learning in the United States from 1865 to 1920: The ascendancy of the universities. *Minerva* 16 (2): 159–195.

Veblen T (1962) *The Higher Learning in America*. Hill and Wang, New York. (Originally published 1918.)

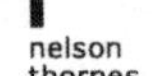

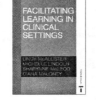

Clinical Supervision and Mentorship in Nursing
- Second Edition

Tony Butterworth is Dean and Professor of Community Nursing, University of Manchester, UK. J Faugier is Director of National Nursing Leadership Project, Manchester, UK. P Burnard is Vice Dean in the School of Nursing Studies, University of Wales College of Medicine, UK

This well established text has contributed to clinical supervision becoming a part of nursing practice. It brings together important contributions from a variety of settings and presents research findings on supervision in practice.

- Offers support to supervisors and supervisees through practical ideas.
- Practitioners from a wide range of nursing disciplines use real-life examples of nursing supervision.
- Provides examples of supervision in different nursing fields.

0 7487 3304 3 | 1998 | Available on inspection | 248pp | £19.00

"A worthwhile text which sets out to address a subject area which has been peripheral but is now firmly established in the curriculum."

Nurse Lecturer and Module Co-ordinator, University of Abertay Dundee

Facilitating Learning in Clinical Settings

*Edited by **L McAllister, M Lincoln, S McLeod,** and **D Maloney**, University of Sydney, Australia*

The book links theory and practice across a range of health care disciplines. Using a case study which runs throughout, it enhances personal and professional growth in independent learning.

- Practical strategies given for students and clinical educators.
- Theoretically sound experimental learning is integrated throughout.

0 7487 3316 7 | 1997 | Available on inspection | 320pp | £21.75

"Covers the important concepts in clinical education in a well-written, and well-structured format that integrates theory and practice."

Journal of Language and Communication Disorders

The Teacher Practitioner and Mentor in Nursing, Midwifery, Health Visiting and the Social Services - Second Edition

***P Jarvis** and **S Gibson**, University of Surrey, UK*

This widely used text defines the role of the teacher, mentor and practitioner and discusses the importance of relationships within the education process.

- Particular emphasis is given to reflective practice and the quality of the learning experience.
- Full consideration is given to assessment of knowledge and skills, covering topics such as profiling and portfolios, credit transfer, and assessment of prior learning.

0 7487 3338 8 | 1997 | Available on inspection | 184pp | £15.50

19. Barriers to Reflection on Experience

David Boud and David Walker

Having given quite explicit guidelines to our co-authors, we were confronted with the task of writing our chapter within the framework which we had provided. We had said to the others, 'write yourselves into your chapters, don't just treat experience as if it happened to other people. Tell the story of how you came to adopt your present perspective on learning from experience.'

Our plan was quite straightforward. We would use as our organizing theme an account of, and reflection on, our work together over the past decade. We decided to take our earlier model of reflection on learning (Boud *et al.* 1985) and work through it focusing on our collaborative activities. We would do this as a real exercise and we would follow wherever our reflections led us. This meant going back through our experience of collaboration, drawing out what we considered to be significant (*return to experience*); working with any feelings that had come out of it, that might help or hinder our reflection (*attending to feelings*); and then going on to reappraise the experience in the light of what had arisen (*re-evaluation*). This final stage involved singling out an aspect of the experience and relating it to previous experience and learning (*association*), integrating the new experience with previous learning (*integration*), testing its validity (validation) and making it our own (*appropriation*). We proceeded along these lines.

However, having done it, we were confronted with an unexpected experience in the light of the reactions of several colleagues to the draft that we had produced. They failed to see connections that were obvious to us. We reflected further. These reflections brought home to us the unpredictable nature of the process of learning from experience, led us to new ways of viewing our own experience, and clarified for us what was involved in using our model for reflection. We have incorporated this new learning into our chapter.

Return to experience

We met for the first time through being allocated to the same table in a workshop on self-directed learning which Malcolm Knowles conducted near Sydney in 1978. We had both heard of his work, had some sympathy for his outlook on learning and wanted to meet the famous man in person. Little of the workshop remains in mind, except for the tremendous impact of Knowles as workshop leader — he provided clear leadership, but essentially trusted us to look after our own learning. Perhaps it was this which prompted us into conversation, perhaps we would have talked about learning whatever the quality of the workshop. Regardless of causes, our continuing relationship emerged from our mutual interest in the role of experience in learning.

We visited each other's workplaces and discovered that our specific educational practices had more in common than we would ever have imagined; one of us was an

David Boud and David Walker: 'Barriers to Reflection on Experience' from David Boud, Ruth Cohen and David Walker (eds) *USING EXPERIENCE FOR LEARNING* (Open University Press, 1993), pp. 73–86.

academic with an interest in improving teaching in universities and the other was a priest who was committed to bringing spirituality into organized religion. Our involvement in the Australian Consortium on Experiential Education (ACEE) — a Sydney-based group of teachers and trainers involved in helping others learn through their experience — maintained our focus on the importance of experience, and developed our confidence in its central role in learning.

However, it was some time before we started to collaborate. The impetus was a move, within ACEE, to explore how experience leads to learning. Members of the organization conducted workshops in which were demonstrated various approaches to teaching and training. They provided a range of different experiences, techniques and strategies. However, organizing frameworks which transcended the particularities of any given method were absent and there was little explanation of how best to draw learning effectively from experience. While the workshops were highly stimulating, they ultimately left us feeling unsatisfied.

This dissatisfaction, together with our belief that we were engaged in very worthwhile activities, stimulated a group of us to undertake a more systematic study of factors which are important in facilitating learning from experience. The key factor which we identified for closer exploration was that of learners reflecting on their experience. Different descriptions were used for what we termed reflection: debriefing, processing, journal keeping, each with a characteristic flavour, but we took all to have a common core in which learners examined their experience and worked with it in some way leading to the possibility of new learning.

The outcome of the study was a book which described a variety of techniques relating to reflection. Together with our late colleague Rosemary Keogh, our role was to provide the conceptual glue which held the collection together. Little did we know at the beginning how difficult our task would be. None of the existing frameworks provided a satisfactory structure in which to place the rich and interesting techniques of experiential learning which were so ably described by others.

After many meetings in a smoke-filled corner of the government building in which Rosemary worked, and after many drafts and false starts, we finally arrived at a model with which we all felt comfortable. It didn't include everything which we had originally hoped for, but it did satisfy our basic criterion of simplicity and it did point to key ideas about which we were enthusiastic. In our efforts to understand experience further, we had moved from a focus on the experience itself, to working with that experience through systematic reflection.

While it took us twenty-three pages to describe (Boud *et al.* 1985), the essence of the model was that there were three key factors in reflecting on experience. The first was a return to the experience, in which the learner recalled the experience, in a descriptive way as it had apparently occurred, without judgement or evaluation. The second was to attend to feelings that arose out of the return to the experience. Obstructive feelings needed to be worked with so that reflection could take place constructively, and supportive feelings needed to be fostered to assist the process of reflection. The third factor was the re-evaluation of the experience, in which learners linked with this experience elements from their past experience (*association*), integrated this new experience with existing learning (*integration*), tested it in some way (*validation*) and made it their own (*appropriation*).

This model pointed to enough important features of reflection to enable us to help learners make a useful start on reflecting on their past experience. The framework was a generic one which could be readily translated into specific circumstances, e.g. in debriefing group activities, in keeping a learning journal or, as we are doing in this chapter, providing the structure for reviewing an entire sequence of activities. However, this did not seem enough. The model referred to a particular circumstance of reflection — what happens after the event — but what should occur at other times?

The stimulus and opportunity for the additional work needed to develop our ideas further came with the Second International Conference on Experiential Learning, held in Sydney in 1989. The ACEE was the joint sponsor and we became heavily involved in the organizing committee. Our work associated with the conference led us to focus again on the experience itself, to explore further the elements that were important within a learning event. We realized that we had not yet taken sufficient account of learners' prior experience, and their intent, on what and how they learn. These needed to be related to our reflection model. We saw, too, the need to focus on the opportunities which occur for reflection while the learner is still engaged in an activity. Our experience at the conference of trying to implement our views about experiential learning, alongside others which we felt to be incompatible, highlighted for us that reflection happens in the midst of action, not only in the calm light of recollection at leisure! We were also well aware of the fact that our model did not fully capture what we ourselves regarded as important in our own learning: the surprise of meeting the unexpected, the change of direction required as we confronted difficulties, and the importance of advance preparation to help address at least some of the challenges which may arise.

We devised a number of activities for conference participants to help them focus on their intents and their expectations of the conference. These included pre-conference correspondence, daily sheets of simple reflective exercises related to each stage of the conference (entering and departing from the experience, noticing and acting within it), a workshop which examined the framework we were using, and a final keynote workshop to help conference participants reflect on their learning from the week. These activities brought together our ideas and their personal experience of the conference. While we did not achieve all that we had hoped, we received enough encouragement from the participants who appreciated what we were doing to enable us to persist in the direction we were taking.

Following the conference, we entered a tortuous period in which we took some time to focus on the next stage of our research. In retrospect, we realize that we needed time to recover emotionally from the conference, but rather than fully debrief the experience we spent meeting after meeting with a whiteboard and pen trying to pick out ideas from among the feelings. At many points we felt that we had reached an understanding only to find that what seemed so clear when we talked, not surprisingly, did not translate into writing. While we were searching for expression of our thoughts, we received an invitation from Deakin University to write a monograph for a distance education course they were designing about adult learning in the workplace. We proposed that we would write about our current thinking and they accepted. As it turned out, we were not able to write a monograph for students without including other material, thus reducing the space for our new thinking. So we worked in parallel on the monograph (Boud and Walker, 1991) and a paper (Boud and Walker, 1990).

Our reflection in the midst of this action focused enough on our feelings from the conference for us to reach beyond them and begin building our thinking anew. We reminded ourselves that what had brought us together was an interest in the role of experience in learning. We had begun to collaborate around the issue of reflection after the experience, and this had led us back to explore further the nature of experience. We had begun with a model for reflection, but now we were being drawn into a model of experience which included much more than reflection after the event.

We took up again two important concepts: *personal foundation of experience* and *intent*. We singled out two further aspects of experience which we had begun to work with earlier, but which now became the focus of our attention: *noticing* and *intervening*. We saw these two activities as part of the dynamics of reflection-in-action, which led us to apply our previous research on 'reflection after the event' to 'reflection which takes place during the event', and which is an important constituent of it. We also became more aware at this time of the need to prepare for the experience. We summarized our work diagrammatically (see Figure 1).

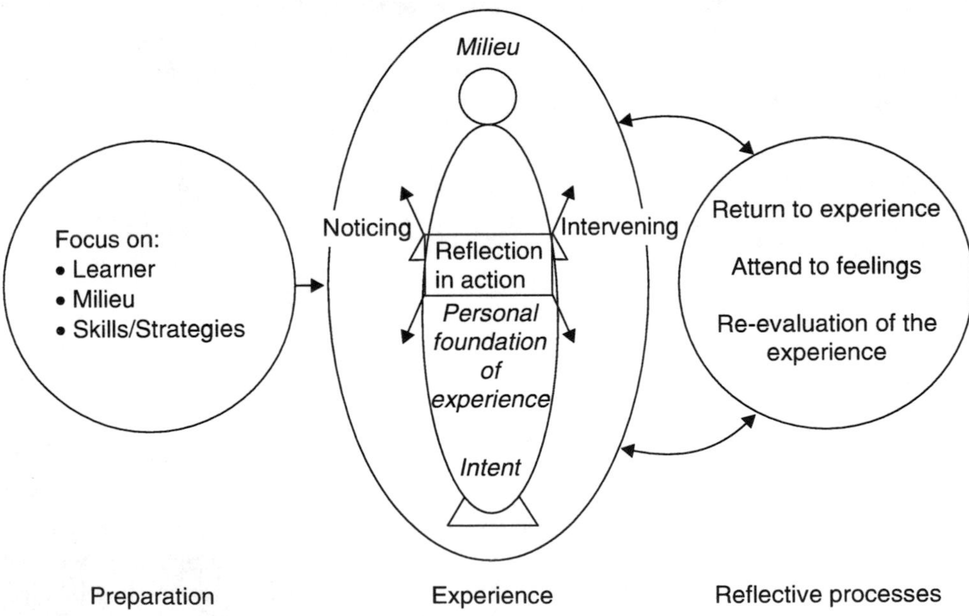

Figure 1 Model of reflection processes in learning from experience

We have written thus far mostly about the development of our concepts and the events which have been a catalyst to that development. However, there was also a very definite feeling dimension to this collaborative experience. It was a mixture of excitement and frustration, certainty and doubt, unity and discord. We experienced high excitement and certainty when we reached stages where we could look at what we had achieved and say, 'damn it, this really does make sense. It doesn't matter what anyone else thinks, what we have here is worthwhile just for us.' This often came after periods of doubt and what felt like wallowing in uncertainty. There was frustration as we tried to articulate our perceptions. Yet we had to make a statement and stick to it. We had to persist and not let our feelings of inadequacy hold us back. In our efforts, we were encouraged by feedback which made us feel at one with the on-going research being conducted by our colleagues. However, at times, there was a discordant note as comments and actions of colleagues made us feel somewhat apart from the mainstream.

As we looked back over our work together, we understood that we had tried to explore how to facilitate learning, and were offering our thoughts on how this could be done. However, there remained a discord. We recognized a tension between what we have understood and were satisfied with, and what is left out of our portrayal of the process of learning from experience.

In focusing on positive action around reflection, both after and in the midst of action, we had not explored sufficiently the many negative aspects which impede learning. It became glaringly obvious that we had not directly addressed the issues of barriers which inhibit working with experience. We had confronted our own barriers to learning as a result of our experience at the conference, but even then we had not been able to name them as barriers, even though we had experienced a strong sense of being blocked. We knew that barriers are strong and that many are not easily susceptible to removal or being circumvented. Some have indeed served an important purpose in our lives, for example, in protecting us from the degree of pain we would have had to face if we [had] not held back from jumping into a difficult situation from the deep end. It was this focus on barriers to learning, both conceptual and emotional, that emerged from our return to the experience of working together. However, before focusing on them further, we needed to proceed with the next stage of our model. These barriers became the focus of our further reflection.

Attending to feelings

The excitement and sense of achievement, which has been predominant, remains strong. We have fostered these supportive feelings by sharing our research with others, and attending to their feedback. Our mutual acknowledgment of the feeling provides further strength and helps the positive mutual interaction. Conversely, we have experienced a sense of frustration as to the adequacy of our expression. Are we presenting our ideas well and taking account of all the issues relevant to them? We sometimes doubt that we can do justice to our research within the space limitations of a chapter. There is the feeling, too, of academic caution, which sometimes can bring a paralysis that prevents publication. However, our challenge to — and support for — each other helps to overcome these obstructions, and the desire to go on being creative is an effective antidote to them.

Building on the positive is an important part of our dynamic. At times, there was a shared feeling of 'pumping up' the mental adrenalin to generate enough enthusiasm and achievement to carry us through the often tedious task of writing it down in a way which would make sense to ourselves and, hopefully, other readers. This building of momentum was only noticeable in retrospect, but always included a clear sensation of the need to get far enough in one of our meetings to carry us through to the next.

Re-evaluation of the experience

Association

After we reviewed our experience together and explored the feeling dimension, we moved into a new phase. We turned to the whiteboard and spent an absorbing few hours engaged in an exercise which we have often used in our workshops. In the centre of the blank space, we wrote 'BARRIERS TO WORKING WITH EXPERIENCE' and sat back and pondered on that theme. At times we wrote furiously, at others we waited for associations to strike us as we trawled our consciousness and waited for our intuition to provide inspiration. As we wrote, we thought and discussed and attempted to articulate to each other what we were trying to express. We made no attempt to fit the fragments together and find patterns, just to associate whatever was in our consciousness relating to barriers to working with experience.

At the end, the board was packed with words, phrases and fragments of ideas, too messy and dense to reproduce here. However, to give the flavour, we list in Table 1 some of the associations which emerged from our own experience, and that of others, about barriers to working with experience. Although we had not only been thinking of ourselves during the generation phase, as we transcribed them and read through them individually, we recalled examples of each of them in our own lives: 'you're not allowed do that' (translated as: someone from your class/with your accent must be excluded from these privileges); 'I'm not bright enough to go to university'; 'I'm too frightened to try that again', etc.

Table 1 Our brainstormed list of barriers to working with experience

- Presuppositions about what is and is not possible for us to do.
- Not being in touch with one's own assumptions and what one is able to do.
- Past negative experiences.
- Expectations of others: society, peer group, figures of authority, family.
- Threats to the self, one's world view, or to ways of behaving.
- Lack of self-awareness of one's place in the world.
- Inadequate preparation.
- Hostile or impoverished environments.
- Lack of opportunity to step aside from tasks.
- Lack of time.
- External pressures and demands.
- Lack of support from others.

- Lack of skills: in noticing, intervening.
- Intent which is unclear or unfocused.
- Established patterns of thought and behaviour.
- Inability to conceive of the possibility of learning from experience: 'this is not learning', 'this is not possible'.
- Stereotypes about how we learn.
- Obstructive feelings: lack of confidence or self-esteem, fear of failure or the response of others, unexpressed grief about lost opportunities.

We were somewhat overwhelmed by the number and diversity of blocks to learning we had identified. Nevertheless, we were satisfied that we were beginning to come to grips with a very important issue to us and we pressed on to see if any *integration* of all this was possible.

Integration

In meetings following our session with the whiteboard, we played with the ideas generated and struggled to articulate some of the patterns which were emerging for us concerning barriers to learning. We returned again to some of our earlier thinking and came to a working definition: barriers are those factors which inhibit or block learners' preparedness for the experience, their active engagement in it, and their ability to reflect rationally on it with a view to learning from it. With this definition in mind, it was possible to bring together our ideas under a number of headings: understanding barriers to learning; their origins; their interaction with each other; how to deal with them; and how to work with them.

Understanding barriers to learning

Our working definition points to the fact that barriers can inhibit learning at each stage of our understanding of the learning process: the preparation, the experience itself and the reflection on it (Boud and Walker, 1990). In preparation they can inhibit learning by reducing the learning potential of the experience, by limiting the learner's awareness of the learning environment, failing to focus existing knowledge and skills in relationship to it, and creating a vague or ill-defined intent for entering the experience. Within the experience, they can limit the essential processes of noticing and intervening, thereby having an adverse affect on the learner's engagement in it. They can paralyse the reflection processes within the experience, and after it, so that the experience becomes non-reflective and is robbed of much of its learning potential. After the experience, these barriers can raise emotional factors which made reflection impossible or limit it; they can isolate and impoverish the new experience by making it difficult to relate the new experience to past experience; they can make it difficult to integrate new learning with past knowledge, and to make judgements and draw conclusions from it. They can also make it difficult for the learner to appropriate the new learning.

Looking at the barriers in terms of their origins in relation to the learner, some barriers are external impositions while others stem from ourselves. External barriers can come from people, the learning environment, the larger personal situation and context of the learner, and social forces, such as stereotyping, cultural expectations, classism and so on. Internal barriers stem from the unique personal experience of the learner. They can include previous negative experiences, accepted presuppositions about what the learner can do or about what learning can take place, a lack of awareness of one's assumptions, the emotional state of the learner, established patterns of behaviour.

Classifying types of barriers in terms of whether they are external or internal to the learner raises the important point of the interaction between them. Many of the supposedly external barriers only begin to have real force when we take them on ourselves and think and act as if they were true. Often self-imposed censorship is more pernicious than anything imposed by others. The power that external forces have is in proportion to the degree to which we appropriate them. There is a strong dynamic whereby learners are tricked, or trick themselves, into thinking barriers are external when they are not — 'no-one from my background could possibly aspire to a job like that'.

A second realization was that personal distress mixed with the mostly unconscious oppressive behaviour of others underlies many of the barriers we identified. Although we experience barriers as internal — 'I can't possibly do that' or 'I don't want to do that' — they often arise from external influences which impacted on us at an earlier time and which left us feeling disempowered or de-skilled or inhibited. When we were treated as working-class boys who 'should' have low expectations of life, rather than as the particular individuals whom we were, we internalized the external oppression and censored our own aspirations.

Our own experience led us to the view that barriers to learning revolve around the individual learner, even when the key factors involved appear to be social or cultural. While some influences may impinge on many people, in the final instance, a barrier is only a barrier when a particular learner is impeded in learning. What may seem to be endemic, may not apply in a given case. This means that the real battleground for working with these barriers is the learner; the learner is the locus within which we need to situate barriers to learning. While it is in this individual context that barriers are revealed, and it is here that often one must address them, we cannot deny that social intervention on a broader front aimed at addressing endemic discriminatory practices is also necessary to achieve a learning society.

Discovering barriers to learning

We were not content to leave our considerations of barriers there. We wanted to make learning more effective, to change it, not just to understand it. We wanted to know how to help learners (ourselves included) work with the barriers and find ways of eliminating or circumventing them. Facilitation of learning is essentially about helping learners deal with their barriers to learning. Helping them to conceive of a barrier to learning as susceptible to influence rather than an inherent deficiency can be a personally empowering step. However, a key element in facilitation is raising awareness of the existence of barriers, and their origin and nature.

How does one notice a barrier? Comparing one's thoughts, feelings and behaviour with those of others can indicate that we are experiencing differently, which can prompt us to ask why. The feedback of others can also help us recognize inadequacies in our ability to work with experience, as can working through a common experience with a group. Exposure to others is one of the best ways of becoming aware of barriers to learning from experience. Hearing them tell their story, and telling our story to them, can help us to see ourselves and how we experience and learn.

Sometimes, it is necessary to cease being involved in a certain type of activity in order to become aware that it may not be fruitful in terms of learning. Action not only reinforces presuppositions, but sometimes obscures the assumptions from which it flows. Action of a different kind, exposure to new experiences, reaching beyond the confines of a limited set of experiences, can expose limitations, highlight barriers to learning, and give us a new appreciation of our learning capacities.

Our own personal awareness, our instinctive feelings, can also alert us to barriers. Heeding our own comfort level within a given situation can bring us to an awareness of our abilities, or lack of them, to work with experience as a source of learning. Being in touch with oneself within the experience is an important way to appreciate one's potential, or lack of it, to learn from the experience.

Working with barriers

Some barriers stem from the perception of the learner, and a transformation of that perception can lead to their diminishing or disappearing. Others, however, are more deep-seated. The barrier has been learned and the ability to respond has been impaired. Sometimes, this is an emotional impairment which has occluded the learner's capacity to learn anew. This can often require the learner to re-visit past experiences and examine them from their current, more powerful perspective. At times, more intensive therapeutic assistance may be required, which goes beyond the scope of the educational facilitator.

It is important to recognize whether the barriers can be altered or transformed with ease or with difficulty. Four useful steps emerged from our considerations on how to work with barriers. The first is to acknowledge that they may exist. An acceptance of their presence is the beginning of working with them. Secondly, having acknowledged them, they need to be named (Griffin, 1987). The more clearly we understand them and can describe them, the more easily we will be able to work with them. This clarifying and naming can come from our own reflection and experience or from the help and experience of others.

The third step is to identify how the barriers operate by examining their origins. A useful concept in this regard is that of critical reflection, which presupposes that our experience is substantially influenced by presuppositions we bring to it. These exist prior to experience as part of our personal foundation of experience. The forces that shape these presuppositions and fix us into certain patterns of behaviour, thought or feeling sometimes need to be recognized and challenged. Critical reflection is a useful instrument for recognizing these forces, both those which come from our own personal story and those which come from the social, cultural context in which we have developed. The enlightenment that comes through critical reflection helps us to understand the origins of barriers to learning from experience, and offers us new opportunities to overcome them, by clarifying how they operate and what needs to be done to counter them. As we reflected on this step, we became aware that the very model of reflection which is being illustrated in this chapter can have an important role to play in critical reflection.

The fourth step is to work with the barriers. Working with them can involve strategies which are confrontational or transformative. Re-examining past experiences from a current, more powerful situation, or reframing old experiences or concepts in the light of new understanding can lead to their transformation (Minsky, 1982; Bolman and Deal, 1991). The recognition of one's powerlessness or lack of awareness in past situations puts them in a new perspective and transforms our understanding and appropriation of them. Sometimes, confrontational strategies are appropriate. This involves taking a stance which contradicts the influence of the barrier in every respect. For example, a barrier which causes a learner to believe that they cannot do something, when there is no apparent external limitation present, can be contradicted by the learner acting as if they could undertake the task and dealing with the feelings that this stance provokes. One can find ways of contradicting former patterns of behaviour and substitute them for the former ways. One can enter into forbidding experiences with new awareness and knowledge and work through the issues as one is experiencing them.

Validation

Much needs to be done now to validate these ideas in terms of our own experience. To what extent does it help us make sense of our own experiences, the barriers we have encountered to learning and the way which we have been effective in dealing with these barriers in our own lives? We have done this implicitly to some extent in constructing the thinking we describe above, but we now need to extend this to other examples, ones we were not thinking of before. These thoughts also need to be checked against the experience of others. This occurred as others read this account in draft form and their comments helped to clarify and explicate our thinking about barriers.

One of the most significant points that emerged from our integration was the application of our reflection model to using critical reflection in dealing with barriers. It became the immediate focus of our research, and we set to working on a paper in which we relate our model of reflection to the exercise of critical reflection (Walker and Boud, 1992).

Appropriation

We cannot tell in advance what knowledge we will make our own. Having a theoretical framework in itself does not remove the barriers. The next step is to accept the challenge which our reflection has posed for us. Explaining a problem does not mean that we have dealt with it. We feel than we have made some progress, but this needs to be consolidated and made our own. What we have appropriated about barriers to learning from experience we will only be able to be identify in retrospect.

Second thoughts

We had shown a draft of the preceding sections to two of our colleagues. To our surprise, they found a massive discontinuity between the experience of collaboration we had described and the reflections on barriers which followed. They saw a huge leap from the account of the experience to the later reflection, which seemed unconnected, both in style and content, to the recount of the experience which led to them. Our immediate reaction was to protest that this couldn't possibly be the case — our experience was seamless, we moved from one section to the other without being at all conscious that we were doing anything other than continuing the natural course of our reflection. Our considered response led us to reconsider what we believed about learning from experience.

Re-reading our text, it was clear that the reference to barriers had emerged rather abruptly and unexpectedly from what had gone before. Yet we knew that it had come directly from our experience. In describing our experience, we had not captured something important. How on earth did we get from the stage of feeling good about writing together to that of confronting major barriers to learning from experience? It clearly did not come directly from our experience as we described it. What had led us to move from the reflection on our collaborative experience to a focus on barriers? As we reflected further, several possibilities emerged.

Our work together had been an exploration of learning about learning from experience, and a focus on the essential elements of it which could be developed to enhance learning. In presenting those elements of learning from experience, we tended to emphasize their positive contribution to learning. However, what we had presented could also have implications for impediments to learning. The focus on barriers which emerged was simply a development of our original thoughts, a consideration of our key points from a different point of view, i.e. how learning can be impaired. We needed to develop this aspect of our thoughts to appreciate the full significance of the elements we had been emphasizing. As we reflected in this way, the movement from our previous work to a consideration of barriers did not seem quite so abrupt. However, it did not explain why we had made the transition from one to the other. We searched further for some explanation.

A possible explanation for this related to the work in which we were concurrently engaged on critical reflection. We had received an earlier response to our model which had questioned its application to critical reflection. This had led us to begin to explore this area and, while working on this chapter, we were simultaneously working on the paper on critical reflection for the Third International Conference on Experiential Learning held at Pondicherry in India (Walker and Boud, 1992). It was an application of our model to critical reflection. We investigated the sources of the critical reflection movement, and found that they were very much concerned with the assumptions and presuppositions which limited the experiences of people and constrained their freedom. We could see how our current preoccupation with such limits and constraints could cause us to move from the positive aspects of the work we had been reflecting on for this chapter, to explore how learning from experience could be limited or impeded.

Two important realizations emerged from these reflections. The first was that our present preoccupations had deeply influenced our reflection on past experience. They had caused us to view our experience in a new light and open up areas that previously we had not noticed, or at least did not consider important enough to explore. This whole experience gave us another view about how our model for reflection could be used, and how, in using it, one needs to be aware of one's present situation and preoccupations.

This experience also brought home to us that our lived experience can never be fully transmitted to another person, even when we go to great lengths to describe that experience. Sometimes, important dynamics operate which seem so commonplace to us that we do not include them in our descriptions. Indeed, we may not even be aware that they exist. There are many stories we can tell about our experience. All may be 'true' to the teller, but they each reflect some part of the whole. Some will resonate more with the reader than others as they touch their sensibilities and have meaning for them. The more the reader learns, the more they can build a fuller picture; but this picture is always partial, large chunks are obscured and many meanings can be drawn from it.

Conclusion

This reflection on our collaborative work in the light of our model has been a more enriching experience than we had anticipated. It has given new meaning to our past experience and aspects of it that we had hitherto overlooked. It has enabled us to apply the model we had developed, and given us new ways of seeing how it can be used. Above all, it has given us some fascinating insights into the ways in which we create our own version of experience.

We had thought that we could end this chapter by making some useful remarks about barriers to learning and the importance of reflection. But we can no longer do this in the way we had anticipated. What we can say is that learning from experience is far more indirect than we often pretend it to be. It can be prompted by systematic reflection, but it can also be powerfully prompted by discrepancies or dilemmas which we are 'forced' to confront. It can be helped by 'naming' the process and admitting that there is an event which is unresolved. Other people can provide an invaluable means of identifying the discrepancy or dilemma; they can often see what may be obvious, but which is too close for us to notice. By supportively drawing it to our attention, they can help us learn from experience, even when they do not see themselves in that role.

Much as it can be convenient to break up our experience, to name the parts and to work intensively on some aspects of it, we have come now to recognize the importance of what some of our colleagues elsewhere in this book are emphasizing. Whatever else we do, we must always consider the whole. We must treat the whole of our experience as relevant and not be too surprised when connections are made which, previously, we had been unable to see. Much as we may enjoy the intellectual chase, we cannot neglect our full experience in the process. To do so is to fool ourselves into treating learning from experience as a simple rational process.

References

Bolman L, Deal T (1991) *Reframing Organisations.* Jossey-Bass, San Francisco.

Boud D, Walker D (1990) Making the most of experience. *Studies in Continuing Education* 12 (2): 61–80.

Boud D, Walker D (1991) *Experience and Learning: Reflection at Work.* Deakin University Press, Geelong, Victoria.

Boud D, Keogh R, Walker D (1985) Promoting reflection in learning: A model. In: D J Boud, R Keogh, D Walker (eds) *Reflection: Turning Experience into Learning,* pp. 18–40. Kogan Page, London.

Griffin V (1987) Naming the processes. In: D J Boud, V Griffin (eds) *Appreciating Adults Learning From the Learners' Perspective,* pp. 209–221. Kogan Page, London.

Minsky M (1982) *The Society of Mind.* Picador, London.

Walker D, Boud D (1992) Facilitating critical reflection: Opportunities and issues for group learning. In: *Proceedings of the Third International Conference on Experiential Learning,* pp. 43–57. Union Territory Administration, Pondicherry, India.

20. The Nature of Learning
What is it . . . ?
Alan Rogers

Introduction

Some readers may understandably be tempted to give this chapter a miss. The world of educational psychology is full of division and uncertainty, and it is not always clear how a consideration of the various learning theories can help us as teachers of adults in the practice of our craft.

Nevertheless, it is always useful to stand back from what we are doing and look at it in terms of general principles. On the one hand, it is surely necessary that the overall theories should be pressed into service to assist concretely the teaching process; there is otherwise little point in all the speculation. This is beginning to happen: although relatively few of those who research into learning processes have devoted time and space to considering the relevance of their studies to the activity of teaching, there is a small but growing interest in the application of this type of theory to practice.

From the point of view of the teacher of adults, then, an examination of theory is important. For how we view learning affects how we teach. Teaching is concerned with the promotion of learning, and we therefore need to understand what it is that we are promoting. In particular, part of our task is to help our adult student participants to 'learn how to learn', or rather to learn how to learn more effectively. To be able to do this properly, we need to be aware of what is involved in the process of learning.

The distinctiveness of adult learning

And here we run immediately into an issue which has been debated widely among educators particularly. For the first question that needs to be addressed is whether the differences which characterise adult learning are so great that they call for a different view of learning from that applicable to younger age groups. The issue is whether the learning — and thus the education built upon it — that occurs throughout the whole of life in both youth and adulthood is essentially the same or whether adult learning — and thus the education of adults — is distinctive. Is there any justification for discussing *adult* education at all or are we just talking about education in general and 'good' (i.e. effective) education in particular?

In many ways this is the most crucial question facing teachers of adults. We have to decide whether we believe that teaching adults is different from teaching children or younger persons or not; whether the same strategies by which we were taught as young people, and which we may already be using in other settings, are appropriate for the groups of adults now under our supervision. It is not just a question as to whether the adult student participant — the mother, the worker on the farm or in

---

Alan Rogers: 'The Nature of Learning: What is it . . .?' from *TEACHING ADULTS* (Open University Press, 1996; 2nd edn), pp. 74–93.

the factory, shop or office, the trainee or manager, the churchgoer, the local resident, the interested member of the public, the keen sportsman or -woman — whether they all *expect* all education to be the same, whether they expect or wish to be taught in the same way they were taught at school or college. The question is rather how we as teachers of adults see our student participants.

Those who teach adults are divided in their approach to this question. Many — indeed, I think an increasing number — argue that there is only one activity, 'education', and that adult education is essentially the same as teaching younger persons. The education of adults is for them merely one branch of the whole field. But others point out that within this field of education, we already draw distinctions; we distinguish between the various branches.in one way or another. The education of primary children, of secondary pupils and of students in further, advanced or higher education all call upon different teaching–learning processes. We may at times use similar methods with all of these groups, but the basic approach in each case is varied. We cannot teach an 18-year-old in the same way as an 8-year-old. We assume that each level of student can cope with distinct learning tasks and that they are motivated to learn most efficiently through the adoption of teaching–learning styles appropriate to the stage of development they have reached.

We have in part then answered the question. Even if there is only one general activity, education, there are variations between groups of learners. The question thus becomes: in what ways does the teaching of adults differ from the teaching of younger students? It is the difference in degree that is at issue.

At the same time, by concentrating on various strategies appropriate to different levels of student learners, taking into account their motivations, their experience, skills of learning and the development of their capabilities, we have immediately created another problem. For we have noticed that adults are enormously varied, far more varied than any school class or college year. Some have much wider ranges of (relevant and irrelevant) experience to draw upon than others; and among those with a wide range of experience, some are apparently more willing and more able to learn from this experience than others (some studies of soldiers returning from active campaigning have shown this). The range of motivations will be very wide indeed. And some adults have been away from education for a long time and in some cases have never developed the range of their formal educational skills greatly, while others have continued to use on a regular basis and in a structured way the talents for learning they have acquired. Do we treat the former like primary and/or secondary pupils and the latter in a more 'advanced' way, using sophisticated techniques of learning and more complex conceptual materials? Or is there a common way in which all adults learn that can form the basis for our adult teaching?

Both of these seem to be true. It is necessary to adapt our methods of teaching adults to the range of educational skills they possess. Those with the least developed skills, either because they never fully mastered them during their initial education or because the formal learning skills they once possessed have fallen into disarray, will need to be helped in building up these skills as well as coping with the task of the moment. Those who are accustomed to learning may often be left with the activity to work at on their own. Both formal and non-formal strategies may be appropriate at different times, with different groups and at different stages of each learning task. But at the same time, there are ways in which the learning processes of adults in general are distinctive, and we will best serve our student participants if we can understand these processes and build our educational programmes upon them.

This is a huge field, fraught with dangers and complexities. Whole books have been written about learning theories or about small parts of one particular theory. The language is often abstruse, and there is no agreement as to the 'true' models; polemics fly. Particularly there is a call by some writers today for a complete transformation of the relations between teacher and taught, and between all members of the learning group (including the teacher) and knowledge, authority and expertise. There is no general consensus yet among adult educationalists, although there are signs of some growing together. To attempt to sum all this up within the compass of two chapters may seem to be courting disaster.

To assist you with finding your way through this section, it may be helpful to set out here its structure. It will look in turn at the following topics:

- what do we mean by 'learning'?
- when do we learn?
- adult learning: the natural 'learning episode';
- why do we learn?
- how do we learn?
- learning styles;
- and finally, the implications of this discussion for the teacher of adults.

What is learning?

In common parlance the word 'learning' carries at least two meanings. There is first a general one of some kind of change, often in knowledge but also in behaviour. 'I met Mr X today and learned that he had lost his job.' 'Today a new bus timetable was introduced. A spokesman for the council said that he believed the public would soon learn to use the new routes.' But there is also a more intense sense of the verb 'to learn' meaning to memorise, learn by heart: 'Take this poem home and learn it.'

We may leave on one side the meaning of the word as 'memorising' and concentrate instead on the 'learning as change' meaning. To say that 'learning is change' is too simple. First, not all change is learning. The changes brought about by ageing or other physical processes can hardly be described as 'learning changes', though they may in their turn bring about learning changes. Secondly, some forms of learning are confirmation rather than changes of existing patterns of knowledge and behaviour. Since the knowledge is more strongly held or the behaviour more intensely engaged in after the learning has taken place, it can still perhaps be said that learning is change, but on these occasions the changes are directed more towards reinforcement than to alteration of patterns of knowledge and behaviour.

Learning as change takes two main forms. There are those more or less automatic responses to new information, perceptions or experiences that result in change; and secondly there are those structured purposeful changes aimed at achieving mastery. There is a difference in meaning between the use of the word in contexts such as: 'He burned his fingers. He learned not to do that again', and 'I had some trouble with the machine but I learned how to manage it.' The second implies both purpose and effort which the first, being unintended and involuntary, lacks.

What we usually mean by 'learning' are those more or less permanent changes brought about voluntarily in one's patterns of acting, thinking and/or feeling. There is a widely held (and even more widely practised) view of learning which says that it is the receipt of knowledge and skills from outside. But recent work on learning indicates that

- learning is active, not the passive receipt of knowledge and skills;
- learning is personal, individual: we can learn from and in association with others, but in the end, all learning changes are made individually;
- learning is voluntary, we do it ourselves; it is not compulsory.

There are then two models of learning, traditional and modern:

Traditional / input	*Modern / action*
passive	active
receipt	search
fill a deficit	seek for satisfaction
responsive to outside stimulus	initiated by inner drive
keywords: 'give, impart'	keywords: 'discover, create'
transfer of knowledge/skills	problem-solving
need for teacher	self-learning

Areas of change (learning domains)

There have been several attempts to describe the different areas of learning change. Many of these are overlaid with philosophical assumptions about human nature and the nature of knowledge that are difficult to test. Sometimes they are seen to be hierarchical — that is, some areas of learning are viewed as being of a higher order than others, though not necessarily dependent on prior learning.

The main and traditional distinction has of course been between learning knowledge and learning skills; but others have elaborated on this. Several have pointed to the need to include the learning of attitudes as a third area of learning. In the field of learning objectives, knowledge, skills and attitudes (KSA) is a well-worn path. Bloom (1965) drew a clear distinction between learning in the cognitive domain and learning in the affective domain. Kurt Lewin (1935) suggested that learning changes occur in skills, in cognitive patterns (knowledge and understanding), in motivation and interest, and in ideology (fundamental beliefs). Gagné (1972) identified five 'domains' of learning:

- *motor skills* which require practice;

- *verbal information* — facts, principles and generalisations which, when organised into larger bodies of information, become knowledge: 'the major requirement for learning and retaining verbal information appears to be its presentation within an organised, meaningful context';
- *intellectual skills* — the skills of using knowledge; those 'discriminations, concepts and rules' that characterise both elementary and more advanced cognitive learning in a way that motor skills and verbal information do not;
- *cognitive strategies* — the way knowledge is used; the way the individual learns, remembers and thinks; the self-managed skills needed to define and solve problems. These require practice and are constantly being refined;
- and *attitudes*.

Learning then takes place in a number of different spheres. We may categorise these using the mnemonic KUSAB:

1. We may learn new *knowledge* as we collect information that is largely memorised.
2. Such knowledge may be held uncomprehendingly. We thus need to learn to relate our new material in ways that lead to new *understanding*, that process of organising and reorganising knowledge to create new patterns of relationships.
3. We may learn new *skills* or develop existing skills further; not just physical skills, our ability to do certain things, but also skills of thinking and of learning, skills of coping and solving problems and survival strategies.
4. Further, since we can learn new knowledge, new understanding and new skills without necessarily changing our attitudes, the learning of *attitudes* is a distinct sphere of learning.
5. Finally, it is possible for learning changes to be brought about in all four of these areas without accompanying alterations in our way of life, our pattern of behaviour. It is therefore necessary to learn to apply our newly learned material to what we do and how we live, to carry out our new learning into changed ways of *behaving*: what some people would call to learn 'wisdom', in short.

The way these five areas of learning change relate to each other is complex. Changes in attitude rely to a large extent on changes in knowledge and understanding, and behavioural changes can hardly take place without accompanying changes in one or more of the other areas. But the relationship between changes in knowledge and attitude or between new knowledge and changed behaviour is idiosyncratic and uncertain. When new knowledge (e.g. 'smoking can damage your health') meets contrary behaviour (the habit of smoking), one of a number of different reactions may occur. The information may be decried, ignored or rejected ('It's all very exaggerated', or 'I know but I don't care'); the new knowledge may be accepted but rationalised away by other knowledge ('Less than 30 per cent of smokers die of cancer caused by smoking and I'll be one of the lucky ones', or 'It is more dangerous to cross the roads than to smoke'); or the new knowledge can be accepted and the way of life adapted to fit in with it. The way any individual reacts to learning changes in any one domain seems to depend on personality and situational factors.

From the teacher's point of view, it is useful to keep the distinctions between these different areas of learning in mind during the preparation of the learning programme. We will find it helpful to ask ourselves whether our teaching is *primarily* in the area of skills or knowledge or understanding or attitudes or behaviour. For this will influence the practices we adopt in the programme of learning. Most of our teaching will cover several different areas of learning, probably all of them. It is doubtful whether they can be kept apart. Nevertheless, while bearing in mind that teaching which concentrates primarily on one of these areas (e.g. skills) inevitably involves learning in other areas (knowledge, understanding, attitudes and behaviour) as well, we need to ask ourselves precisely what sort of learning change we and our student participants are attempting to deal with at this particular stage of the learning programme.

When do we learn?

Learning is not of course confined to the classroom.

It is strange how many people who know a lot about adult education and lifelong learning use language very loosely. They talk about 'motivating people to learn', they urge that we need 'to get people into learning' — by which they mean that they wish to persuade people to come to classes, thereby implying that there is no learning going on outside of the classes. They use the word 'learners' to mean those people who are in the classes, as if those who are not inside their classes are not learners. 'Learning' and 'education' thus very frequently get mixed up. Even experienced adult educators use the term 'lifelong learning' and speak about adult education as existing 'to provide opportunities for lifelong learning' when they really mean 'lifelong education', that the function of adult education is to provide structured programmes of directed learning, often classes, which are open to people of any age. They do not realise that 'lifelong learning' is simply that, learning which goes on more or less all the time without any help from adult educators, that 'opportunities for lifelong learning' exist around us every day and in everything we do. But as we have already seen, there is a distinction to be drawn between learning and education. All education must involve learning; but not all learning is education.

We do therefore need to stress very clearly that learning is quite independent of the classroom. People are learning all the time, whatever they are doing.

Learning is part of living

Learning comes from experience. It is closely related to the way in which individuals develop in relation to their social and physical environment. And since experience is continuous, so too learning is continuous. It occurs throughout life, from start to finish. Nearly everything we do has been learned and is constantly being relearned.

And this means that learning is individual. It is not a collective activity. 'Each individual is processing the experience uniquely for personal use. . . . In learning, the individual is the agent, even though the agent may be subject to the social pressures of the group' (Brookfield, 1983: 1–4). Learning is affected and may even to some extent be controlled by society or other collectives, but the learning activity itself — introducing learning changes — is personal.

Learning desires

Learning, then, is natural, as natural as breathing. It is the continual process of adapting to the various changes which we all face, changes in our social and cultural contexts, changes in our own social roles, the daily tasks we perform, our own personal growth and development.

But it goes deeper than this. Within every individual there is a bundle of learning desires. In part they spring from the drive towards adulthood which we have already seen, the urge towards more maturity, the search for meaning, the drive towards more responsibility and autonomy. In part they spring from half-finished earlier learning activities. In part they spring from our own interests and experiences, an earlier spoken or written word or a glimpse of something having aroused unsatisfied curiosity.

Some of these learning desires are very pressing, arising from or reinforced by urgent matters. But most of them lie dormant, overlaid by more immediate concerns, awaiting either a suitable learning opportunity or an increased sense of need to bring them to life (this is the 'I've always wanted to learn something about this or that' syndrome). For some people, these desires for more learning have been damaged or buried deep by other experiences (often by formal education, especially at secondary levels where discovery learning methods are sometimes less frequently used than at primary level), but they still exist and can in appropriate circumstances be awakened.

Intentional and unintentional learning

Much of our learning — perhaps most of it — is unintended. A good deal is very casual: it comes from chance happenings (roadside posters, snatches of overheard conversation, newspaper reading or television watching, meeting people: 'adventitious learning [which] springs from accidental encounters with unintentional sources' (Lucas, 1983: 2–3). There are however some 'sources of learning' [who] intend learning to take place — through mass campaigns, advertisements, political persuasion, social propaganda, etc. — even though the learner has no intention of engaging in learning.

But beyond this, there are occasions when we engage in some more purposeful learning activity, some structured process of mastering a situation — learning to deal with a new piece of equipment, for instance, or to adjust to new bus timetables or to cope with a new baby. At certain times throughout their lives, all adults will bend their energies and attention to achieving some learning task directed towards a set goal. Some of these occasions may call for formal methods of learning (learning to drive a car is probably the biggest formal programme of teaching adults in many countries) but with most of them we cope more informally (see Figure 1).

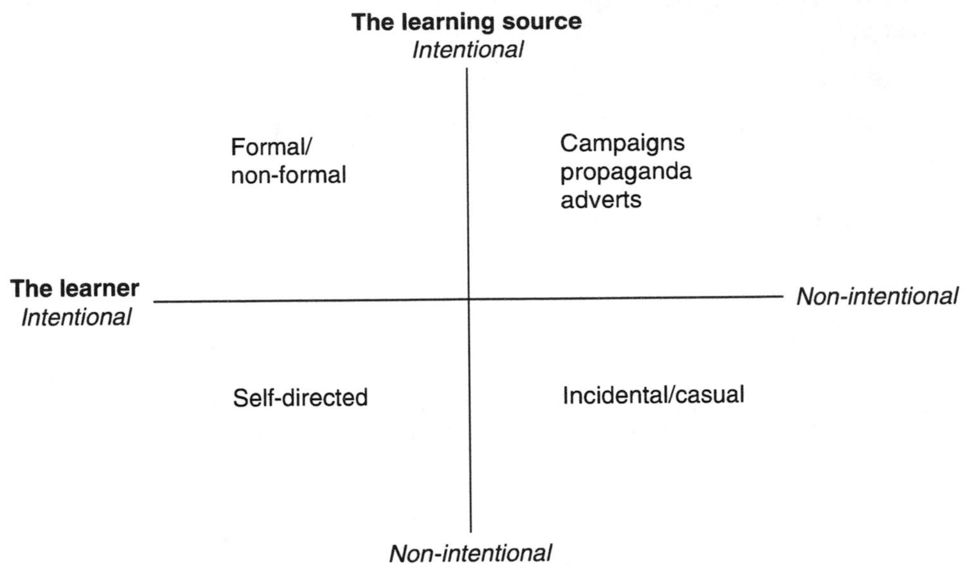

Figure 1 Learning matrix

Learning episodes

Such 'learning episodes', as we may call these intended purposeful learning activities, are usually voluntary and are always purposeful. Some of course come from external requirements: a new task set for us by our employers for, example, or changes in legislation which call for changes in our working practices; learning called for by some of the welcome or unwelcome changes that may come in our personal circumstances, and so on. Many an adult has had to learn about new financial matters through divorce or separation. But the majority are undertaken voluntarily and with some measure of enthusiasm and commitment. And they are always purposeful: they are designed to achieve a particular goal which the learners set for themselves. Learning episodes are therefore distinct from the incidental and unintended learning which characterises the majority of our learning experiences.

Such learning episodes arise from a perceived need or challenge — from those changes in our social relationships, in our occupations (however widely defined that term may be used), in our personal development or in preparation for further learning which we wish to pursue. It is therefore clear that such learning episodes are closely related to the lifespan development of each one of us, however that lifespan development is defined.

Learning objectives or 'clearing up messes'?

These learning episodes are voluntary, intentional, purposeful; the adult learner is seen to be active, struggling with reality, rather than responsive to stimuli. And this would seem to suggest that they are directed by clearly perceived learning objectives.

To some extent, this is true. When we set out to learn to meet some need or to increase our expertise in some field of interest, there will be occasions when we will be able to focus our efforts on defined learning objectives, when we can see what it is that we are trying to achieve. When deciding to learn to drive a car, for example, we can set for ourselves a clear goal, and we can see relatively plainly whether we are making progress towards the achievement of this goal. We can clear our mind of all that will block the way and set out to achieve the mastery we require of ourselves.

But in other cases, the situation is not so clear. Ackoff (1978) (talking about managers) has pointed out that we are often in a more confused situation: we

> 'are not confronted with problems that are independent of each other but with dynamic situations that consist of complex systems of changing problems that interact with each other. I call such situations 'messes'. Problems are extracted from 'messes' by analysis; they are to messes as atoms are to tables and chairs . . . [We] do not solve problems, [we] manage messes.'

This would seem to be particularly true of many learning episodes which we undertake throughout our lives — for example, coping with a new baby. Our task in these cases is not straightforward, simply meeting a need. Rather, it is to unravel a tangle, to sort out a mess.

In these circumstances, how and what we learn depends on how we define the situation we are facing. We analyse the issue, determine what the problem looks like so far as we can see it, and try to solve it. How we do that depends on how much and what kind of experience we can bring to the 'mess'. That will determine the way we look at the problem and the language in which we express it. Learning is a haphazard process of trial and error and we often get it wrong. As Donald Schön puts it in regard to his chosen professionals:

> 'Problems must be constructed from the materials of problematic situations which are puzzling, troubling and uncertain . . . [We] are frequently embroiled in conflicts of values, goals, purposes and interests . . . the effective use of specialised knowledge to well-defined tasks depends on a prior structuring of situations that are complex and uncertain.'
>
> (Schön, 1983)

Learning episodes and the teaching of adults

These structured and purposeful learning episodes may be undertaken by the learners on their own or they may invoke the assistance of some helper. And it is here that they can be seen to be of considerable significance for teachers of adults. For our purpose is to create one or a number of such learning episodes for our adult student participants.

Not only this but, since they are intended and purposeful, these natural learning episodes reveal more about the sort of learning opportunity that we as teachers of adults seek to construct than do the more ubiquitous, haphazard and largely unintentional learning activities that spring from the constant interaction of the individual with the environment. The way adults learn purposefully on their own will tell us much about the way they will learn in our programmes.

Some adult educators are hesitant about using these natural learning episodes as the basis for building a theory of adult learning. They point out that each of us engages with the environment in ways limited by our experience and existing learning abilities, and that this social environment itself controls our learning. They suggest that what is needed is to break free from such restraints. Nevertheless, these episodes show us something of the way adults learn and the special features of adult learning as distinct from the processes of schooling. They can form a guide as we construct learning opportunities for those who come to our programmes.

Characteristics of learning episodes

There are three characteristics about these self-directed learning activities that are relevant to our discussion.

First, *they are usually episodic in character, not continuous.* They come in short bursts of relatively intensive activity, absorbing the attention, and they usually come to an end as soon as the immediate purpose has been felt to be achieved. There are some, particularly in the self-fulfilment area, that spring from long-term interests (gardening, for instance, or following trends in modern or classical music); but even within these overall patterns of persistent learning, there come more intensive short-term episodes of learning directed towards the achievement of some immediate goal. We cannot keep this sort of pressure up for long; we need to be motivated by an achievable purpose; and when that is over, there may come a rest or a slower pace of learning before the next episode occurs. (How far this episodic character is part of our way of life in a modern Western society rather than an inherent adult process is not clear, but it would seem to be of more general application than confined to just one form of social structure and culture.)

Secondly, *the goal that is set is usually some concrete task, some immediate problem that seems important.* Such learning episodes, self-directed or otherwise, are in general aimed at the solution of a particular problem. The situations they are designed to meet are concrete rather than theoretical. We need to decorate this room, to master the relationship between these stamps, to cope with this particular change in the family circle, to understand a new procedure at home or at work, and so on. Even when the learning is part of a long-term and developing interest (chess, say, or cooking), the individual episode of learning is directed towards a particular goal to be achieved.

There are several implications flowing from this:

- We do not on the whole approach any situation academically. To decorate a room, we do not study design as such. To cope with a family issue, we do not take a course on interpersonal relations or psychology — although we might well consult books on the subject. We are not concerned so much with a subject as to resolve a one-off concrete situation.
- This means that the learning task is rarely pursued in a systematic way. It is limited learning, limited to the task in hand. Adult learners do not often pull down a textbook and start at the beginning, with a general introduction to the field of study, nor do they pursue it from A to Z in sequence to the end. It is only with those who have had extensive experience of formal education, who have

developed and maintained advanced study skills, that a systematic exploration of a field of knowledge becomes at all common. This is a replication in private of the formal systems of learning that characterise schooling and is thus confined to relatively few, and to a few occasions in their lives. They too will also engage in the more limited goal-oriented episodes of learning at other times. Most of us most of the time use only those parts of any subject that help us to meet our immediate task.

- The learners do not start with the simple and move on to the more difficult. They tackle the problem with which they have to deal at the level at which it occurs in their lives. They cope with quite difficult language and terms from the start so long as these are of direct relevance to the learning process.
- The learners do not on the whole draw on compartmentalised knowledge such as was learned at school, history separated from geography or maths from physics. They bring all that they know from all sorts of fields to bear upon the particular instance. Such an academic compartmentalised approach may occur on occasion, especially in the self-directed learning activities [noted above]; but even here there is often a particular need to be met that leads to the use of knowledge from different fields of study rather than a restricted compartmentalised approach to knowledge.
- Such episodes are aimed at immediate rather than future application. There are, it is true, some learning episodes which are intended as a preparation before embarking on a course of action: religious preparation classes, pre-marriage groups, holiday language courses, pre-retirement programmes are examples of these. But on the whole, most learning episodes are undertaken in the process of doing a particular task or meeting a situation. The material, as it is mastered, is applied at once. We learn how to use a new washing machine by using it; we learn a new bus timetable as we use the service; we learn how to cope with a baby by coping with a baby.

Thirdly, since most of these learning episodes are directed towards specific goals, *there is relatively little interest in overall principles.* Few attempts are made by the learner to draw general conclusions from the particular instance being learned. Once the immediate situation has been resolved, the goal attained or the problem solved, the adult learner normally brings the process of investigation to a close, storing away the learning gained for another day. What is stored is the way to cope with the particular situation, not general principles. Learning to use a new washing machine will be concentrated on the specific instrument in hand, not on washing machines in general. The learning needed to cope with a new bus timetable will deal not with the entire transport system but with the one or two routes needed to make a particular journey. Learning a new craft or industrial technique will be confined to what is needed for the moment, not to wider applications. All of these situations may arouse in our minds wider issues of obsolescence and modern technology, or public and private transport provision or the demands of new processes as a whole; but these will occur mainly as spasmodic thoughts and grumbles, usually quickly pushed away and forgotten. The efforts are centred on the immediate and the particular, not on the long-term and the general.

Why do we engage in these learning episodes?

There is a very large literature which suggests that all learning (certainly all purposeful learning) comes from a sense of need.

> 'Learning is something which takes place within the learner and is personal to him [*sic*]; it is an essential part of his development, for it is always the whole person who is learning. Learning takes place when an individual feels a need, puts forth an effort to meet that need, and experiences satisfaction with the result of his effort.'
>
> (Leagans, 1971)

There is much truth in this, and the awakening of a sense of need has been identified by most writers on adult learning as a precondition of effective learning. But we have to tread carefully here. Not all purposeful learning comes from a sense of need; some for example comes from an increased interest.

'Needs', then, is a dangerous concept in adult education. It often leads to an assumption that 'I know what you need to learn even though you don't know what you need.' 'Needs' are externally identified; 'wants' are internally identified. Purposeful adult learning, the kind of voluntary learning episodes we have been talking about above, come from identified wants rather than externally set needs. It is a search for satisfaction in some sense or other.

Motivation and learning

Much has been written about motivation in relation to the education and training of adults. In many forms of adult education and extension in developing countries, it forms the keystone of the training programme. But in the West, rather less consideration has been given to it in practice. In most forms of adult education (except perhaps those industrial and professional development programmes where some of the participants may be seen to be reluctant participants), we tend to rely on the fact that adult student learners come to us of their own free will, that they are already interested in the subject, that they are already motivated to learn. We forget that initial motivation to learn may be weak and can die; alternatively that it can be strengthened and directed into new channels. This is the task of the teacher of adults — and as such we need to understand motivation.

Motivation is usually defined as those factors that energise and direct behavioural patterns organised around a goal. It is frequently seen as a force within the individual that moves him or her to act in a certain way. Motivation in learning is that compulsion which keeps a person within the learning situation and encourages him or her to learn.

Motivation is seen as being dependent on either *intrinsic* or *extrinsic* factors. Extrinsic factors consist of those external incentives or pressures such as attendance requirements, external punishments or examinations to which many learners in formal settings are subjected. These, if internalised, create an intention to engage in the learning programme. Intrinsic factors consist of that series of inner pressures and/or rational decisions which create a desire for learning changes.

Most adult learning episodes are already dependent on intrinsic motivational factors; but not all of them are. It has been argued that intrinsic factors are stronger and more enduring than extrinsic factors. But even within intrinsic motivation, there is a hierarchy of factors. For example, a desire to please some other person or loyalty to a group which may keep a person within a learning programme even when bored with the subject are seen as intrinsic motives of a lower order than a desire to complete a particular task in itself.

There are three main groups of ideas behind the development of a theory of motivation. The first says that motivation is an inner drive to fulfil various needs. The second says that motivation can be learned. And the third claims that motivation relates to goals set or accepted by oneself.

Needs-related motivation

Many people see motivation as internal urges and drives based on needs. All individuals vary in the composition of these needs and their intensity. At their simplest instinctual level, they may be the avoidance of pain and the search for pleasure, or the Freudian drives related to life, death, sex and aggression; but all such instincts can be modified by learning.

Most theorists see a motive as a learned drive directed towards a goal, often regarded as a search for the reduction of tension or conflict. Boshier (1989) and others see this as having two main dimensions: the reduction in inner conflicts between different parts of the self and different experiences (intra-resolution); and the reduction of conflicts and tensions between the self and the external social and physical environment (extra-resolution). The individual is seeking for harmony, for peace. Such directed drives may be aroused and sustained, as we have seen, by incentives (external factors) and by goals set or accepted by the individual (internal factors).

Some writers have distinguished between needs (seen to be physical) and drives (psychological). More often however the distinction is drawn between primary needs (viscerogenic, related to bodily functions) and secondary needs (psychogenic). The latter come into play only when primary needs are to a large extent met.

Two major writers, Carl Rogers (1974) and Abraham Maslow (1968), have helped us to see learning as the main process of meeting the compulsions of inner urges and drives rather than responding to stimuli or meeting the demands of new knowledge. Whether viewed as goal-seeking (based on limited and specific goals set by themselves) or ideal-seeking (related to objectives set by the value system the learners have come to accept and hold), both argue that the learner is impelled to seek out learning changes from within rather than by outside imperatives. Rogers viewed this as a series of drives towards adulthood — autonomy, responsibility, self-direction — though it is now clear that the precise forms which such drives take are culturally bound, varying from society to society. Maslow concentrated on the urge to satisfy in part or in whole a hierarchy of needs.

Abraham Maslow is recognised as the apostle of the 'needs' school of thought. He distinguished basic drives from temporary needs, and established a hierarchy which is often quoted (Figure 2); and he developed a theory of 'pre-potency' — that one need must be largely satisfied before the next need can come into full play.

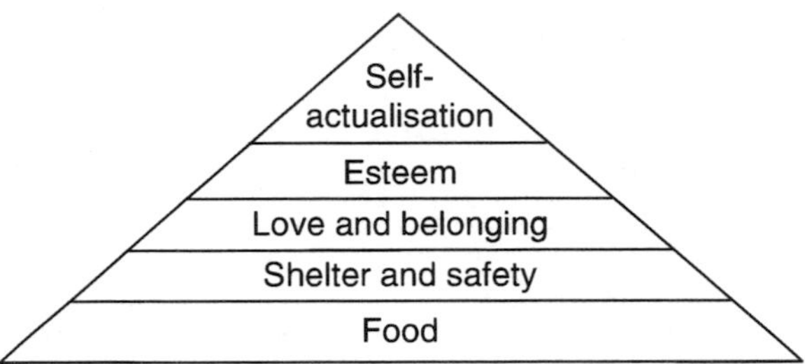

Figure 2 Maslow's hierarchy of needs

Maslow argued that all people are driven through the first four stages of basic needs. As each lower need is in part met, the next higher level of need is triggered. Several levels of need can be in operation at the same time. The highest level of need, self-actualisation, may not be reached by some individuals on more than an occasional basis. This level consists of a need to create, to appreciate, to know and to understand. (Maslow indicated in his teaching a further level of need above self-actualisation: self-transcendence, a need to express tangibly concern for others, but this hardly appears in his writings.)

Maslow's concern for self-actualisation accounts for the increasing popularity of the many adult education programmes of today designed to enhance the students' understanding of the 'self' — programmes like learner-generated 'life histories' or autobiographies, and the programmes of creative writing aimed at increasing self-confidence and self-expression.

From the point of view of the teacher of adults, Maslow's work will be a reminder that within any group of adult learners there will be a wide variety of needs, and within each individual student participant there will be a different mixture of needs. This mixture will be constantly changing as the learning proceeds and as the individual's life situation changes. This is why predetermined and uniform learning outcomes can never be achieved in adult learning programmes, why each adult learner will take away from any learning situation what he or she will require, why adult learning is unique to each learner and uncertain.

But Maslow's hierarchy of needs fails us as adult educators precisely at the point we need it most. It offers us an analysis of the *preconditions* to the type of learning we are most interested in: the self-evident truth that the prior personal and social needs (food, security, personal relationships and a sense of esteem) must be satisfied, at least in part, before motivation for the more creative, evaluative and self-fulfilling kinds of learning will be aroused. But it also reminds us that when some of our student participants come to our programmes from a desire for social relationships or to gain some sense of esteem, as many do, they are being driven by needs that must be met at least partially before further learning can take place.

Maslow also suggests that if the lower levels of needs are satisfied in part, the motivation to self-actualisation will be automatically triggered because it is inherent within each person. If it is not so triggered, this is because one of the lower levels of need has been inadequately met. This is by no means certain: and in any case, it does not explain the motivation towards different forms of self-actualisation which occurs between individuals.

To explain this, we need to turn to other work on motivation. We have already noted Carl Rogers's view of the drive towards adulthood — towards maturity and autonomy. Houle (1961) sees motivation as more complex, as being related to the goal-orientation or process-orientation or subject-orientation that comprises the inherent learning drives of the individual. A different picture is that of a spectrum consisting at one end of those who are 'high-achievement oriented' (not just ambitious, though it includes them: this group embraces those who seek to play chess or do crosswords or make bread or breed pigeons better than their neighbours) and at the other end those who are anxious about failure. The former experience has been called an 'approach motivation', a drive towards engaging in some activity or other, while the latter experience an 'avoidance motivation'. Success encourages the former, and failure does not put them off easily, it can become a further challenge; whereas both success (generally regarded as a 'flash in a pan' that will not necessarily be repeated) and failure alike encourage the latter to withdraw.

The danger with this — as with so many such schemes of categorisation — is that of assigning individual student learners to particular categories; for such 'personality types' can themselves become a hindrance to learning, a demotivaton. The very designation itself may prescribe the way in which people will behave and will certainly determine the way we view other people. There is some value in knowing that such factors are at work; but they are not determinants but explanations of what is happening.

Learned motivation

Such achievement orientation suggests that motivation can be learned. It is thus seen by some as the fruit of the reward-and-punishment systems that people have been exposed to during the course of their prior development. If this is true, then perhaps motivation may be altered by a new system of approvals and disapprovals, by specific training activities accompanied by a change of the learning environment to emphasise achievement rather than failure. Exactly what the factors are that lead to motivation being learned is not clear. Stimulus–response theories may help here; success and pleasure in early educational experiences seem to play a part. It is pointed out, for example, how many of those who liked their schooling and were a success in educational environments return to participate in adult education activities of both a formal and non-formal kind, while although others use the lack of education to rationalise their lack of success, relatively few are motivated by this lack to return to education. But the issues remain unclear.

Motivation and goals

The third group of ideas centre themselves round the concept that motivation is related to the goals set and accepted by the participants for themselves. It has been noted that motivation is highest among those who are most concerned with the process involved, who are satisfying their goals in each task, whereas those who have their sights set on goals which are further away (to pass an examination or to get a better job after the course is over) have a lower level of motivation. Motivation then seems to be related to the nearness of achieving the desired goal.

The importance of this to the teacher is that the student participants need to see clearly the immediate goals, to accept them for themselves, to believe them to be achievable and to be able to see some progress towards their attainment, if their motivation to learn is to be kept at the highest possible level. But there is a further factor here: confidence. Individuals will be more positively motivated if they are confident that they can not only cope with the learning situation but alter it to meet their own needs.

The learning situation

For it is important for us to realise that motivation relates as much to the situation in which the learning episode is taking place as to the individual. So far most of the theories of motivation have regarded the learner as a person divorced from any particular setting. But all learning is located within a particular time and place; and we know from the work of Herzberg (1972) and others that this setting influences motivation as much as the internal drives and avoidances.

Herzberg's work related to industrial activities; but it is of direct relevance to learning. He developed the concept of 'motivators' and what he called 'hygiene' factors (demotivators). He saw 'motivators' as those factors which make the participants 'feel good' about their work — a sense of achievement, recognition, responsibility, advancement and personal growth. Most of these are internal factors; and when they are present, the participants have a positive attitude towards their tasks. These feelings however are not on the whole long-lasting, they need to be continually reinforced. But they spring directly from the work in hand.

In contrast, the 'hygiene' factors that create a sense of dissatisfaction normally spring from external factors in the context of the activity — from inappropnate direction or methods, inadequate working conditions, unsatisfactory relationships within the group and so on. These tend to be longer-lasting in their nature.

These two sets of factors are not the plus and minus of the motivational situation. The presence of motivators and the reduction of hygiene factors are both necessary to achieve positive motivation. Removing the hygiene factors alone without increasing the presence of motivators will not help the task, and similarly strengthening the motivators without removing the demotivators will not increase effectiveness.

It is thus clear that motivation factors in learning lie as much within the learning situation as within the individual student participants themselves. In this context, the teacher of adults plays a vital role. Motivation is as often in the eye of the beholder as is beauty. We need to be reminded of McGregor's Theory X and Theory Y: that the teacher may assume that all learners have an inherent dislike of work and will avoid it if they can (Theory X), that they wish to escape from responsibility, that they have a static range of abilities that nothing within the learning situation will improve, that it is the function of the teacher to direct them to the work of learning (McGregor, 1960).

Theory X	*Theory Y*
The average human being has an inherent dislike of work and will avoid it if he/she can.	The expenditure of physical and mental effort in work is as natural as play and rest.
Because of this, most people need to be coerced, controlled, directed and threatened with punishment to get them to put enough effort to contribute to organisational goals.	External control and threats of punishment are not the only means to encourage them to make an effort to contribute to organisational goals. People will engage in self-direction and self-control to achieve objectives to which they are committed through the rewards which the achievement itself brings.
The average person prefers to be directed, wishes to avoid any responsibility, has relatively little ambition, and wants security above all.	The average person, under the right conditions, learns not only to accept but to seek responsibility. The capacity to exercise a fairly high degree of imagination, ingenuity and creativity in the solution of organisational problems is widely, not narrowly, distributed. In most societies, the intellectual potential of the average person is not fully utilised.

In this case, in the way of all self-fulfilling prophecies, we as teachers become part of the extrinsic factors influencing motivation; we become a hygiene factor ourselves, a demotivator. Or (Theory Y) we can assume that learning changes are natural to all human beings and certainly are the expressed desire of our student-learners; that they are willing to accept responsibility for their own learning; that it is external factors such as the educational system itself and the existing patterns of work in society rather than internal factors that are inhibiting the student participants from exercising their imagination, creativity and ingenuity; that all students are capable of breaking out. In this case, the teacher will become a 'motivator' in the learning environment. Motivation then depends as much on the attitudes of the teacher as on the attitudes of the students.

The implication of all of this for the teacher of adults is varied. Although it is useful to look at needs and at other views of initial motivation, it is probably best for the teacher not to rely solely on this original impetus but to seek to build up new kinds of drive in relation to the subject-matter itself. An emphasis on the extrinsic factors of motivation rather than the intrinsic will not lead to a durable level of motivation towards achieving the learning task. Although many adults are motivated by such concerns, it would seem that, particularly for adults, a stress on attendance, examinations and discipline is not an appropriate way to heighten or build new forms of motivation, although other forms of incentive may be helpful in some circumstances.

Further reading

Belbin E, Belbin R M (1972) *Problems in Adult Retraining.* Heinemann, London.

Bloom B S (1965) *Taxonomy of Educational Objectives.* Longman, London.

Gagné R M (1972) Domains of learning. *Interchange* 3 (1): 1–8.

Gagné R M (1975) *The Conditions of Learning.* Holt, Rinehart and Winston, New York.

Habermas, J. (1978) *Knowledge and Human Interest.* Heinemann, London.

Lenz E (1982) *The Art of Teaching Adults.* Holt, Rinehart and Winston, New York.

Lovell R B (1980) *Adult Learning.* Croom Helm, Beckenham.

Maslow A H (1968) *Towards a Psychology of Being.* Van Nostrand, New York.

Rogers A (1992) *Adults Learning for Development.* Cassell, London, and Education for Development, Reading.

Rogers A (1993) Adult learning maps and the teaching process. *Studies in the Education of Adults* 22 (2): 199–220.

Schön D A (1983) *The Reflective Practitioner: How Professionals Think in Action.* Basic Books, New York.

Smith R M (1983) *Helping Adults Learn How to Learn.* Jossey-Bass, San Francisco.

Smith R M (1984) *Learning How to Learn: Applied Theory For Adults.* Open University Press, Milton Keynes.

Squires G (1987) *The Curriculum Beyond School.* Hodder and Stoughton, London.

21. Learning Theories Made Easy: Behaviourism

Gilean McKenna

The last few years have witnessed many developments in nurse education, particularly as links with higher education are strengthened. The clinical environment, however, remains a key area for learning, and practitioners continue to make a huge contribution to the education of both pre- and post-registration students. In order to maximise opportunities, a knowledge of learning theories is useful. This is the first of three articles explaining the different theories of learning. This week the behaviourist theories are described. The following weeks will discuss cognitive and humanist perspectives. The series of three articles uses a creative approach to explain the theories, and to highlight their relevance for teaching in clinical practice.

The Director of Nurse Education (DNE) at the St Elsewhere Academy of Nursing is trying a create the ultimate programme of nursing education. In order to ensure that the very highest standards of teaching and learning are achieved, she has decided to employ a theorist of learning.

The job has been advertised and three very different candidates, representing the schools of behaviourism, cognitivism and humanism, have been shortlisted for interview.

The first person to present a case was from the school of behaviourism. This man believed learning to be a change in observable behaviour, which occurred when a link or connection was made between two events — that is, a stimulus and a response. By manipulation of this link the behaviour could be altered. To support his argument for the behaviourist theory of learning, the candidate produced evidence from many early, noted psychologists.

Watson (1878–1958) observed the behaviour of animals and children, and concluded that the more frequently a stimulus–response (S–R) link occurred, the more likely it was to be established as learned behaviour.

To add to this concept, Guthrie's theory of contiguity was discussed. This theory stated that if a stimulus occurred at the same time as a response, the response would be repeated when the stimulus subsequently occurred again — that is, following repeated pairings, the stimulus and response would be linked together. For example, it may be desirable to pair handwashing and aseptic procedures together.

The next piece of work to be presented was by the Russian physiologist, Pavlov (1849–1936), who broke new ground with his theory of classical conditioning.

While experimenting with salivation in dogs, he linked one stimulus — meat powder, to a second stimulus — a bell sound, to produce a response of salivation. After

Gilean McKenna: 'Learning Theories Made Easy: Behaviourism' in *NURSING STANDARD* (1995), 9 (29), pp. 29–31.

conditioning, the dogs would salivate to the sound of a bell (conditioned stimulus), even in the absence of the meat powder (unconditioned stimulus). On this occasion the salivation is called a conditioned response. Pavlov found that once a response had been conditioned, it could then be produced by other stimuli, similar to the conditioned response. He called it generalisation.

The DNE looked puzzled. 'That may well be true, but what have salivating dogs got to do with the education of student nurses?'

The candidate smiled and proceeded to explain that, as parts of nursing and nurse education may be of a highly emotional nature, there is a place for classical conditioning in nurse education.

He referred to Woolfolk and Nicolich (1) who suggested that emotional responses to particular situations were learned, in part through classical conditioning. He continued by quoting Bernard Lovell: 'It is the kind of learning that underlies the acquisition of the emotional component of our attitudes' (2).

He added that an emotional response to an experience can be either positive or negative. A bad experience may well produce a physiological response of fear or anxiety.

For example, if a student is forced to participate in a role-play for a particular teacher, and is then humiliated for the performance, an anxiety response (sweaty palms, palpitations, dry mouth) may be evoked when role-play is next suggested in that class. Generalisation of this conditioned response may be exhibited if the student becomes anxious at the suggestion of role-play in another class.

Extinguishing fear/anxiety

Another use of classical conditioning in education is to extinguish already established fear/anxiety responses. If, for example, a student has had a bad experience giving an injection and now trembles at the thought of having to give one, the teacher must help him/her overcome the fear.

The performance may be broken down into small steps, perhaps starting with watching a video of injection techniques, or touching and handling syringes. As each step is achieved without the expected negative outcome, the student will gradually lose the fear anxiety/response associated with injections.

'All right,' said the DNE. 'I accept that classical conditioning has a place in nurse education, but it is rather limited. What else have you got to offer?' The man then rummaged in his briefcase and produced a rather large folder. His eyes lit up as he began to recite the findings of Thorndike and of Skinner.

Thorndike (1874–1949), through his theories of trial and error learning, suggested that learning occurred when a specific response became linked to a specific stimulus, by a process of trial and error, until the successful link was found. Unlike Watson, who was mainly concerned with the simultaneous presence of a stimulus and response, Thorndike emphasised the importance of the end effect of the response, suggesting that a positive outcome to a response would result in that response being repeated.

This belief was reflected in Thorndike's law of effect, which stated that satisfying results serve to strengthen or reinforce S–R links. Dissatisfying outcomes did not necessarily extinguish the response, but did cause alternative responses to be found by 'trial and error'. Watson's work was supported, however, by Thorndike's law of exercise which stated that S–R links were strengthened by repeatedly occurring together, provided that positive reinforcement normally occurred.

The DNE summarised by saying: 'So in nursing education, although repetition and practice are very useful, it is knowledge of results that is crucial.' The man smiled in agreement and continued.

Like Thorndike, Skinner believed that it was the end result of behaviour that governed its repetition but rather than being a random response to a stimulus, he viewed behaviour as a deliberate action that was influenced by a positive or negative outcome, or reinforcement. From this principle Skinner formulated 'operant conditioning', which stated that behaviour was directed by its consequences, in order to bring about certain desirable objectives.

'I see, a little like Freud's belief that we go through life seeking pleasure and avoiding pain,' added the DNE.

Encouraged by this, the candidate continued to explain the effect of antecedents and consequences on behaviour.

Depending on the consequences, the repetition of behaviour can be increased or decreased. Positive or negative reinforcements are used to encourage the repetition of behaviour, and punishment can be used to eliminate or decrease a behaviour. Hence, behaviour can be controlled by its consequences.

Some behaviours may have to be achieved gradually, each step being shaped by its consequence, until the desired behaviour is elicited. To maintain the behaviour the reinforcements must continue.

The DNE butted in: 'So you are saying that, as soon as the reinforcement stops, so will the behaviour? That's no good. The teachers can't spend all their time reinforcing the students' every move.'

After a quick rustle of papers, the candidate produced a schedule of reinforcement, illustrating that frequent reinforcement is important when a new behaviour is being learnt, but that intermittent reinforcement is much more effective in maintaining that behaviour.

For example, when a student nurse is learning an aseptic dressing technique, the teacher may give praise for each step — preparing the patient, handwashing and so on — thus shaping behaviour until the complete procedure is able to be performed.

Then the praise should be given only for the complete, correct performance and become increasingly intermittent, in order to maintain the behaviour.

Cueing

The other way that teachers can influence behaviour is by giving information or cues prior to the behaviour being performed. Cueing is an example of how antecedents can be influenced positively, and serve to remind the learner of the appropriate or expected behaviour (for example, when the teacher mentions handwashing to a learner before he/she starts an aseptic procedure, or gives precise guidelines or criteria for a case-study).

Evidence of operant conditioning is also found in various forms of self-directed learning. Linear programmes and computerised study packs involve students with a sequence of questions. If students answer correctly, they are informed, that is, reinforced, and are able to move on to the next question. If they answer wrongly, they are also informed, given an explanation, and offered the chance to answer again until the correct answer is selected.

Bernard Lovell (2) suggested that Skinner's operant conditioning was the most significant single contribution to the theory of learning.

The DNE was clearly still not convinced. 'I can see that operant conditioning does have its uses,' she said. 'But isn't it very reliant on the student emitting some sort of behaviour first, before all these reinforcements can be used, and isn't all this a rather slow process?'

The candidate then reached for his final offering — the work of neobehaviourist Albert Bandura (3) and his theory of social learning or vicarious conditioning. This theory involves the observed behaviour of others and the consequences of those behaviours. If the consequences are perceived to be desirable, the behaviour may be copied or modelled. If the consequences are seen to be undesirable, the behaviour may be avoided. Hence, learning can occur vicariously, through the experience of others.

This theory differs from those previously discussed because learning may occur instantly. It also acknowledges the thinking process in that behaviour is influenced by the meaning attached to it and the perceived consequences.

The DNE appeared to be impressed. 'Yes, I can see that this is highly significant to nursing education, particularly as the behaviour, attitudes, and values of teachers or other role-models may be copied by the learners.'

The man nodded in agreement. He concluded by explaining that this is particularly significant in the clinical area, where any behaviour that is seen to be rewarded, for example, by patient satisfaction or peer admiration, is likely to be copied. When the copied behaviour is of a high standard, the role-modelling is highly effective and positive.

There may be dangers, however, when questionable practices are copied as there is limited discrimination between 'good' and 'bad' behaviour, and only perceived desirable or undesirable outcomes which result from the behaviour.

The DNE pondered for a few seconds: 'Thank you, I can see that there are some uses for classical, operant, and vicarious conditioning in nursing education. However, I'm not sure I like the idea of the students being motivated mostly by reinforcement, rather than learning by self-motivation. I want my nurses to think, and not just respond.'

'I'll be in touch when I have interviewed the other candidates for the post.'

References

1. Woolfolk A E, Nicolich L M (1980) *Educational Psychology for Teachers.* Prentice-Hall, Englewood Cliffs, NJ.

2. Bernard Lovell R (1987) *Adult Learning.* Croom Helm, London.

3. Bandura A L (1977) *Social Learning Theory.* Prentice-Hall, Englewood Cliffs, NJ.

22. Learning Theories Made Easy: Cognitivism

Gilean McKenna

This is the second of three articles explaining theories of learning with particular relevance to clinical areas. In the story so far, the Director of Nurse Education at the St Elsewhere Academy of Nursing is trying to create the ultimate programme of nursing education. In order to ensure that the very highest standards of teaching and learning are achieved, the DNE has decided to employ a theorist of learning. Last week she interviewed the candidate representing the school of behaviourism. This week, the candidate from the school of cognitivism makes his presentation.

The DNE welcomed the candidate into her office and began the interview. 'In your application you claim to have the ideal theory for the 21st century. You say that your theory will produce a truly educated nurse, who is knowledgeable, questioning, research-minded and able to problem-solve. Please tell me more.'

The young man leaned forward in his chair and began to explain enthusiastically that his theory was not like the behaviourist view, in which learning involves little thinking and is observed to be a change in behaviour. In contrast, the cognitive psychologists believe that learning is an internal purposive process concerned with thinking, perception, organisation and insight.

He referred to Woolfolk and Nicolich (1), who suggested that this type of learning could not be observed directly as it involved a change in the capability of the individual to respond. The learner was actively involved with problem-solving, seeking out new information, and drawing on past experience in order to gain understanding.

He began to state his case by explaining the significance of Gestalt psychology to the origins of cognitive learning theories.

Referring to Child (2), he described Gestalt, a German word that means pattern or form, and the work of the early Gestalt psychologists — Wertheimer (1880–1943), Kohler (1887–1967), and Koffka (1886–1941).

These men were initially concerned with the study of perception and their work emphasised the ability of the individual to organise and integrate what is perceived into an overall pattern or Gestalt.

Wertheimer believed that breaking down behaviour into constituent parts obscured the full meaning of the total behaviour. From this stemmed the Gestalt phrase: 'The whole is greater than the sum of its parts.'

Gilean McKenna: 'Learning Theories Made Easy: Cognitivism' in *NURSING STANDARD* (1995), 9 (30), pp. 25–28.

Wertheimer believed that perceptions were organised by the individual, using the principle of 'pragnanz', into as simple a structure or form as possible, in order that meaning could be imposed. Pragnanz was made up of four laws of perception — similarity, proximity, closure and continuity. Referring to Quinn (3), the candidate continued to explain how Koffka believed that these laws of perception could also be used as laws of learning, and from this grew the Gestalt theory of learning by insight.

Insightful learning occurs when a problem is suddenly solved by the restructuring of the component parts into new relationships, so they are perceived as a whole. Kohler demonstrated insightful learning in 1925, using a chimpanzee in a cage with some bananas suspended out of reach. The chimpanzee also had some boxes which, if stacked, could be used to reach the bananas. After various futile attempts, the chimpanzee suddenly perceived the relationship between stacking the boxes and reaching the bananas. This insight to the solution of the problem could be transferred and repeated in similar future situations. Thus learning had occurred.

Previous knowledge

The DNE grinned and said excitedly: 'Yes, I see. So this could apply to the situation where students cannot initially make any sense of the squiggles that make up an ECG rhythm strip. Then, when the students understand cardiac conduction, and relate the activity of the heart during the cardiac cycle to the ECG readings, they are able to understand the significance of the P wave and the QRS complex . . . But, hang on a minute, doesn't all this require previous knowledge?'

Pleased with this response, the candidate reached for his copy of Child (2) to explain that, rather than using mechanical repetition of stimulus-response bonds, insightful learning depends on the adaptation of past experience or existing knowledge to form new insights.

'Yes that is true, but how can nurse teachers use this in education?'

The candidate explained that a nurse teacher may use the principles of pragnanz to structure sessions so they are seen as a whole rather than as isolated facts.

For example, if a session on the structure and function of the respiratory tract is linked to a disorder such as bronchitis and to the activities of daily living, the students will then perceive the anatomy and physiology, the disordered condition, and the effect on the patient as a whole, rather than three unrelated units.

The use of problem-solving techniques may allow learners to undergo an insightful process. For example, rather than telling students about the nursing care of a patient with bronchitis, the teacher can explain the disordered physiology. The students can then work out what problems the patient may experience and identify the appropriate nursing care, relating all this to the physiology and to the patients they have nursed with this condition.

Bruner's theory of learning through discovery was introduced next. Bruner (4) suggested that the ultimate aim of teaching was to instill a general understanding of the structure of a subject.

He believed learning to be an active process, stimulated by curiosity. The knowledge is constructed by relating the incoming information to a previously acquired frame of reference. The frame of reference is a system of representation that gives meaning and organisation to knowledge and experience. There are three modes in Bruner's 'system of representation' — *enactive, iconic* and *symbolic*:

- The *enactive* mode of representation consists a habitual set of actions, known without the use of imagery or words, that are appropriate for achieving a certain result. This often applies to motor skills.
- The *iconic* mode is based on imagery, and used for knowledge, represented by images that 'stand' for a concept, but do not fully define it.
- The *symbolic* mode is the transformation of the iconic imagery into a symbolic system — usually language.

Although these three stages develop during childhood in the order presented, they extend more or less intact throughout adult life.

The DNE was becoming a little impatient. 'Will you please get to the point. What is the use of these icons and things to nursing education?'

The candidate quickly responded with an example of blood pressure recording. When a student initially learns the motor skill of measuring blood pressure, but has no concept at all of the significance of that recording, it will be an enactive representation. Later, as the student begins to grasp the concept of 'blood pressure', it may be in the image of a pump (the heart), connected to a series of narrowing and widening tubes (the blood vessels), with blood circulating around the body. This will be iconic representation. Eventually the student will reach the symbolic mode, being able to define blood pressure and describe the significance of cardiac output and peripheral resistance.

The DNE nodded approvingly. 'I see, so if a learner is having trouble grasping a concept, the teacher could help by using imagery or making analogies to everyday things that are understood — like comparing the effects of vasoconstriction to someone standing on the garden hose.'

The candidate nodded and proceeded to explain that as well as describing a hierarchical structure of learning — that is action, image, and symbol — Bruner also suggests there is a coding system that makes up the pattern of enactive, iconic and symbolic representations.

This coding system allows the thousands of perceived facts to be grouped and related to each other. This allows learners to go beyond the information given and formulate new ideas by deducing additional information from previously learned principles stored in the system.

For example, if given the specific information that hypovolaemic shock is caused by a reduced circulating volume, a learner with a sound understanding of the concept of blood pressure and its control will be able to deduce that this will lead to a reduced cardiac output and result in a decreased blood pressure and increased heart rate.

Learning by discovery

Sequence is important and sessions should be structured to make use of relevant existing knowledge. Bruner (4) advocates the use of a spiral curriculum, in which all important concepts and subjects are introduced in a simple form at a very early stage of the programme, and then built upon with more complex ideas.

The candidate then referred to the work of Bigge (5) to discuss the advantages of Bruner's theory of learning by discovery.

- Once a situation is mastered, the individual alters the way in which new situations are approached in the search for information, so the student learns how to learn.
- The student is encouraged to discover the value of intuitive guesses, and try out his/her own hypotheses.
- The student's ability and confidence in problem-solving will increase as he/she acquires understanding of basic concepts and the ability to transfer knowledge.
- There is increased self-motivation and accountability for learning.
- Curiosity is aroused and the student is encouraged to adopt a questioning, research-minded approach.

The DNE smiled smugly. 'That might well be so, but according to my friend Mr Myles (6), this approach to learning may be difficult to structure in large groups of mixed ability learners, and it can be very time consuming, as well as expensive getting lots of fancy equipment; not to mention that a few 'bright sparks' might be doing all the discovering, leaving the rest feeling bewildered. What else have you got to offer me?'

The candidate described the work of Ausubel (7), which suggests that students learn more efficiently when they are presented with material in an organised, sequenced form that can be assimilated to their previous knowledge. This is the basis of the theory of reception or assimilation.

Ausubel (7) believes that learning is a deductive process that should move from an initial understanding of general concepts, to an understanding of specifics. This is unlike Bruner (4) who suggests that learning occurs inductively, using specifics to discover general concepts.

He advocates a method of expository teaching in order to enhance 'meaningful learning'. This method of teaching is very closely linked to the students' previous knowledge, and involves high levels of interaction between the teacher and the students. Meaningful learning is suggested to be more efficient than rote learning, which is unlikely to be retained because it is not connected with existing knowledge.

Ausubel (7) describes a sequence of learning that considers the students' existing knowledge and the processes by which they are most likely to assimilate new material into their existing conceptual structures. This is achieved by the use of an advance organiser, followed by the subordinate content. Quinn (3) describes an 'advance organiser' as a concept that is introduced in advance of the new material in order to provide an anchoring structure for it. This conceptual statement may be in the form of prose or a diagrammatic flow-chart.

For example, when teaching about pressure sores, a broad statement can introduce the session, such as: 'Pressure sores are known as decubitus ulcers. They are skin ulcers which occur over bony prominences, due mainly to restricted mobility. They can be prevented by the principle of relieving pressure.' This can then be followed by the subordinate content such as the pathophysiology, aetiology and nursing care.

To emphasise this point, the candidate then quoted Bernard-Lovell, stating: 'The principle function of the advance organiser is to provide a scaffolding of ideas to bridge the gap between what the student already knows and what he/she needs to know before he/she can learn the new material in a meaningful fashion' (8).

The candidate continued by outlining the advantages of Ausubel's approach to teaching. First, it activates the relevant knowledge the student already has, and second, it enhances the assimilation of new knowledge into the established conceptual structure, which increases retention and makes rote learning unnecessary.

'Yes,' said the DNE, rubbing her chin thoughtfully. 'I suppose these advance organisers do help create the right learning set, and assist the student to focus on the relevant aspects of a session. In fact, I think they could even be a little more stimulating than the usual objectives that we churn out before a session. You don't seem very fond of rote learning, but I do believe that it has a place — how else do students recall the cranial nerves? Have you got any proof of the efficiency of this reception learning in nursing education?'

The candidate shook his head, but quickly pointed out the work of Woolfolk and Nicolich (1), which suggests that Ausubel's approach is particularly suitable when teaching the relationship between concepts, or for introducing novel or difficult material. It is also very appropriate for adult learners, who have a lot of previous knowledge and are able to manipulate ideas.

Information processing

Moving on, the candidate next introduced the work of Robert Gagné (9), concerning the information-processing model of learning based on the study of memory. An analogy is often made between a computer and the human mind, as both go through a similar process of gathering information from incoming stimuli, organising the information, that is, encoding it, retaining it, and, when needed, retrieving it.

The candidate explained that, although the other cognitive theorists acknowledge the importance of existing knowledge, the information process theorists emphasise the process of retaining and retrieving this knowledge.

Gagné (9) devised a model of learning and memory. He describes a process whereby stimuli from the environment affect the receptors and then enter the nervous system via a sensory register which codes the information into a patterned representation. The information remains in this form for fractions of a second, after which it is either lost through decay, or entered into short-term memory. Once in short-term memory it is coded into a conceptual form, where it remains for only a few seconds.

The short-term memory has a limited capacity to store about seven items. Rehearsal of the information may retain it for longer, or even allow it to be encoded into long-term memory.

From short-term memory the information is either lost through decay and interference, or it is once again transformed and organised, ready to enter the long-term memory, where it is stored for later recall.

Once in long-term memory, information is categorised, and the general meaning, rather than exact details, is stored.

The DNE now looked thoroughly confused, so the candidate produced a diagram to help clarify this model.

Retrieval of information depends on how it is stored in long-term memory, that is, the representation and organisation. As discussed previously, information that is linked or coded into the appropriate conceptual or cognitive structure is more likely to be recalled efficienctly.

Although information is thought to be stored permanently once it is entered into long-term memory, retrieval can be obscured by interference. Retroactive is the term used when new information interferes with old, and proactive describes old information interfering with new.

'How can nurse teachers use this?' asked the DNE enthusiastically.

The candidate said there were many ways teachers could maximise learning and retention.

First, the teacher can help students to focus attention selectively by changing the stimulus regularly and making use of colours, movement, voice and varying teaching methods. Novelty and humour can be very useful, but may also distract attention if not used carefully. The students can be given cues as to which points are particularly important. The teacher must also be aware of fatigue, limited attention spans, and the amount of new information being introduced, to prevent information overload.

Second, the teacher can help make new information meaningful by linking it to that already known — this may involve helping learners to retrieve the relevant previous knowledge.

Third, repetition of information can aid the encoding process. The spacing of the repetition or practice can be important.

'Thank you,' said the DNE. 'I have another appointment now, so we must end. I must admit that I am not too keen on learning outcomes. They seem a little too precise and related to objectives. But I am interested in some of your learning theories. I particularly like the sound of Bruner's ideas. I think that Ausubel's advance organisers are excellent and, of course, an understanding of perception, insight and memory is imperative.

'I have one final candidate to interview, so I'll be in touch with you after that.'

References

1. Woolfolk A E, Nicolich L M (1980) *Educational Psychology for Teachers*. Prentice-Hall, Englewood Cliffs, NJ.
2. Child D (1986) *Psychology and the Teacher*, 4th edn. Cassell, London.
3. Quinn F M (1980) *The Principles and Practice of Nurse Education*. Croom Helm, London.
4. Bruner J S (1966) *Towards a Theory of Instruction*. Belknap, Cambridge, Mass.
5. Bigge M L (1982) *Learning Theories for Teachers*, 4th edn. Harper and Row, New York.
6. Myles A (1987) Psychology and the curriculum. In: P Allan, M Jolley (eds) *The Curriculum in Nursing Education*. Croom Helm, London.
7. Ausubel D P (1968) *Educational Psychology: A Cognitive View*. Holt, Rinehart and Winston, New York.
8. Bernard-Lovell R (1987) *Adult Learning*. Croom Helm, London.
9. Gagné R M (1975) *Essentials of Learning for Instruction*. Dryden Press, Hinsdale, Ill.

23. Learning Theories Made Easy: Humanism

Gilean McKenna

This is the last of three articles explaining theories of learning with particular relevance to clinical areas. In the story so far, the Director of Nursing Education at the St Elsewhere Academy of Nursing is trying to create the ultimate programme of nursing education. In order to ensure that the very highest standards of teaching and learning are achieved, the DNE has decided to employ a theorist of learning. She first interviewed the candidate representing the school of behaviourism and last week the cognitivist candidate made his presentation. The series now concludes with the humanist candidate — and the final decision.

The candidate representing the humanist theorists appeared relaxed and self-assured as he walked into the office. He shook the DNE's hand firmly, introducing himself as Bob, and asked her first name. The DNE appeared a little surprised by his lack of formality, but the man seemed pleasant and very knowledgeable as he explained his ideas for nursing education.

The humanist theory of learning is concerned with feelings and experiences, leading to personal growth and individual fulfilment. Maslow (1) made a significant contribution to the humanist approach with his theory of motivation and hierarchy of needs. In order to ascend to self-actualisation, lower level needs (that is, comfort and security), must first be partially satisfied.

The goal of education is therefore to assist the achievement of self-actualisation, and fulfil the maximum potential for personal growth. This is closely linked to the work of Carl Rogers and Malcolm Knowles.

Rogers (2), who advocated a student-centred approach to learning, identifies a continuum of meaning. At one end of the continuum is material which has no personal meaning. This learning involves only the mind and not feelings, that is, it has no relevance for the whole person and therefore becomes futile. At the opposite end of the continuum is significant, meaningful, experiential learning, which involves both thoughts and feelings.

Rogers (2) believes that significant, experiential learning has five qualities:

- It involves the whole person — both feelings and cognitive processes
- It is self-initiated, with a sense of discovery coming from within
- It is pervasive and makes a difference in the behaviour, attitudes and maybe the personality of the learner

Gilean McKenna: 'Learning Theories Made Easy: Humanism' in *NURSING STANDARD* (1995), 9 (31), pp. 29–31.

- It is evaluated by the learner, who knows if his or her needs have been met or not
- The essence of it has meaning.

The teacher is primarily concerned with permitting the students to learn by feeding their own curiosity. The students are given responsibility and freedom to learn what they wish to learn, as they wish.

'Hold on for just one minute,' said the DNE. This idea sounds all very well for school children, but I have a set curriculum that must be met in order to conform to UKCC and ENB guidelines. How can I possibly allow the students to study whatever takes their fancy?'

Pleased that this issue had been raised, Bob explained that, in order to decrease student anxiety and frustration at not being spoon-fed, there is a need for a perceived structure in the form of limits and minimal requirements. This gives enough direction for work to commence, thus ensuring that the content requirements of the curriculum are fulfilled, but the process remains free.

'Do the students like this method?' asked the DNE. 'Isn't it easier for them to simply take notes from a lecture?'

Bob smiled. He agreed that, initially, the struggle for personal growth may be painful. It may even evoke student hostility and resentment, but in the long-term, true learning will take place above and beyond the set curriculum. This learning will be remembered, utilised and valued for years to come.

'Yes, I can see that you're possibly right, but doesn't it require a rather special type of teacher to do this?' questioned the DNE. 'Some of my tutors have been giving lectures for years, and would not be best pleased to give them up!'

Bob reassured her that it did indeed require a rather special teacher, one who had been through a process of self-discovery for him/herself and was prepared to become a 'real' person to the students, sharing their own joys and disappointments, and not being a faceless embodiment of knowledge.

This teacher must also genuinely value, accept and empathically understand the students to allow a trusting relationship to develop. The role changes from that of a teacher and evaluator, to a facilitator of learning. The members of the class, including the teacher, become a community of learners.

The DNE was not quite convinced. 'I think some of my tutors would need a great deal of help to achieve that! It does sound interesting though, if not perhaps a touch idealistic. How do I know this approach will work in nursing education?'

Bob then reached for the work of Burnard, who has written extensively on the value of experiential methods and the facilitation of learning in nursing. Burnard (3) suggested that experiential knowledge is gained through direct encounter. Students learn either by direct experience in the present, or by reflecting on past experience in order to make sense of the present.

Students enter nursing as adults, bringing with them a wealth of valuable life experience. Many of the skills of nursing do not have to be taught, as they are already grounded in personal experience. A skilled facilitator is able to make use of these experiences, as well as providing new experiences. Burnard (4) believed that this is particularly relevant for the development of interpersonal skills.

'I accept that it is useful, but doesn't the facilitation of all these experiences take up much more time than the traditional methods?'

Bob then explained that much propositional knowledge — concepts, theories, models and propositions — may be gained from reading books and articles. This leaves more classroom time for experiential learning.

Referring to Burnard (4), Bob quickly added that, if teachers control the learners' educational experiences too much, they limit the amount of personal growth that can occur. Nursing education will then churn out clones of the profession, who do not question what they see, and who neither trust nor know themselves.

'Yes, well that's certainly worth thinking about, but I do think there are times when learners need specific and structured teaching, for example, just before their final exams. Do you have anything else to offer?'

The candidate continued. Knowles (5) developed the theory of andragogy, the art and science of teaching adults. He acknowledges that adults have a vast range of experience, which forms a basis for new learning. Therefore, pedagogical methods of teaching were not appropriate in adult education.

Burnard (3) summarises the major differences of androgogical learning:

- Adults need to be able to apply what they have learned
- Adults have a wealth of personal and life experiences that should be used in education
- Adult learning involves an investment of self and any new learning will affect that self-concept
- Adults are mostly self-directed and their education should accommodate this.

The relationship between teacher and student should be one of mutual respect. Eduard Lindeman highlighted this in 1926 by stating: 'None but the humble become good teachers of adults. The student's experience counts for as much as the teacher's knowledge' (5).

Knowles (5) suggests that as adults, students should help formulate the curricula, rather than adapt themselves to what is offered. Burnard (3) says that, in nursing education, even though the national boards set out a syllabus, students still have considerable scope to decide how and when various topics were learned.

The DNE nodded: 'Yes, I agree that we must acknowledge that student nurses are adults, and treat them appropriately. Thank you Bob for such an interesting and illuminating discussion. I shall be in touch to let you know of my decision.'

References

1. Maslow A (1971) *The Farther Reaches of Human Nature*. Penguin, Harmondsworth.
2. Rogers C R (1983) *Freedom to Learn for the 80's*. Merrill, Columbus, Ohio.
3. Burnard P (1987) Teaching the teachers. *Nursing Times* 83 (9): 63–65.
4. Burnard P (1988) Building on experience. *Senior Nurse* 8 (5): 12–13.
5. Knowles M (1978) *The Adult Learner: A Neglected Species*, 2nd edn. Gulf Publishing, Houston.

24. Teaching in Clinical and Community Settings

Francis M. Quinn

Nursing, midwifery and health visiting practice is carried out in a range of workplace settings, including hospital wards and departments, community health centres, GP surgeries, schools, nurseries, day centres, residential homes, and industry. It is therefore self-evident that these settings constitute important learning environments; indeed, experiential learning is based on the premise that learning gained through experience is more meaningful and relevant than that acquired in classrooms.

Some people prefer to use the term *learners* to describe individuals who are pursuing an education or training programme in the workplace, but given that everyone is now meant to be a 'lifelong learner', the term student seems a more appropriate distinction. Within a given workplace setting, there is a variety of individuals who can be classed as 'students' at one time or another:

1. *Pre-registration students.* These are students undertaking an educational programme in a higher education institution leading to an academic award and registration as a nurse or midwife. Their presence in the workplace is on the basis of a placement, i.e. they spend a given amount of time in a range of workplace settings, but are not part of the workforce of those settings.
2. *Post-registration students.* These are qualified registered nurses or midwives who are undertaking either:
   (a) an educational programme in a higher education institution leading to an additional academic and/or professional award; or
   (b) an in-house programme of professional development.

Most of these are in-service students, i.e. they are undertaking their studies on a part-time or flexible basis, whilst maintaining their responsibilities as members of the workforce in a given workplace setting. However, some post-registration programmes, such as health visiting, lead to a further professional registration and are therefore classified as being both pre-and post-registration! These programmes require full-time attendance, and the students undertake placements in a range of community workplace settings.

3. *National Vocational Qualification (NVQ) students.* These are normally health care assistants who are undertaking an NVQ programme at a college of further education leading to an NVQ award. These are part-time in-service programmes with an emphasis on workplace learning and assessment.

Francis M. Quinn: 'Teaching in Clinical and Community Settings' from *PRINCIPLES AND PRACTICE OF NURSE EDUCATION* (Stanley Thornes, 2000), pp. 413–443.

From the foregoing discussion, it can be seen that workplace settings in nursing, midwifery and health visiting provide the learning environment for a whole range of personnel, including those undertaking formal programmes, and those receiving informal, and often spontaneous, teaching as part of their day-to-day practice. Hence, this environment for learning becomes a crucial factor in the success or otherwise of the personnel involved, so it behoves nurse teachers to appreciate the social dynamics of the workplace. Selected aspects of group dynamics relating to the workplace are included below.

Group dynamics and the workplace

The workplace does not simply provide an environment for learning the knowledge and skills required for practice, it also serves as a vehicle for pre-registration students' socialization into the profession of nursing or midwifery.

Socialization

From early infancy, individuals learn the values, knowledge and patterns of behaviour that make them a member of their particular society; the process by which an individual undergoes induction into these expected behaviours or roles is termed socialization, and is a lifelong process involving transmission of culture.

Primary socialization

This begins in infancy and is mediated through the immediate family; sex roles, social class morals and manners are all part of this early socialization process.

Secondary socialization

This begins once the child commences school, and this is influenced not only by teachers but by peers; the latter exert a powerful effect as the child moves into adolescence, when peer-group pressure may result in behaviour at variance with the child's family or society.

Occupational socialization

This is a particular kind of secondary socialization, which involves the induction into specific occupational roles after leaving school. Nursing culture has a powerful influence on new members, socializing them into the role of nurse, with all its attendant values and behaviours. In the past, there was great emphasis on conformity and obedience to superiors and a very rigid code of personal and professional behaviour.

Socialization may begin in anticipation of future rules and this anticipatory socialization is important in facilitating the eventual uptake of such roles. Many girls are socialized into nursing from an early age by means of play, especially that associated with hospitals and caring. The mass media is a powerful influence on such socialization and may well be responsible for sex-role stereotyping and racism. Television, newspapers and even children's books may portray nursing as being the exclusive preserve of women; indeed, women are commonly portrayed in occupations such as nursing, teaching, domestic work and catering, rather than in engineering or medicine.

The public nature of work-based teaching

One of the major differences between classroom teaching and workplace-based teaching is that the latter is a much more public endeavour. In the classroom, the teacher is normally alone with the students; in contrast, the workplace is populated by a wide range of people including:

- nursing and medical staff;
- practitioners from the professions allied to medicine, e.g. physiotherapist, occupational therapist, medical laboratory technicians, etc.;
- support workers and administrators;
- patients, clients, relatives and friends;
- counsellors, ministers of religion.

It is very likely that much of the teaching will take place in this public arena, so it may be helpful to explore the effects of an audience on human performance. The mere presence of an audience may facilitate or hinder behaviour, the so-called 'audience effect'. For example, many actors and athletes feel that they need an audience in order to perform to their fullest ability, and this effect is supported by studies.

The effect of having someone actually performing a task with another person (i.e. co-acting) has also been studied extensively; the classic study by Allport (1924) concluded that the presence of a co-worker enhances the speed and quality of work on simple tasks. On the other hand, the presence of others can exert an inhibitory effect on behaviour and this has been demonstrated in a number of interesting studies.

Latane and Darley (1968) showed the effect of the presence of other people on an individual's reaction to emergency situations. They conclude that people are less likely to intervene in an emergency if other people are present and this can be explained by diffusion of responsibility. If a person is alone when he or she encounters an emergency, then that person is solely responsible for his or her actions. If, however, other people are present, each individual may feel that their own responsibility is reduced and this makes them less likely to become involved.

Roles and norms

Within the workplace setting, roles and norms exert a significant influence. Roles are actions within a given status, such as the leadership role of the ward manager. Norms are standards or values of behaviour, which may be formal or informal. Formal norms in a workplace setting are imposed by the organization, such as a requirement for practice to be evidence-based. Informal norms develop from within the group as a result of interaction; for example, one ward may have a norm involving a particular way of organizing the daily workload. Individuals tend to conform to the prevailing norms of the workplace, and there is evidence that norms may develop over a short period. In a classic study on group norms, Sherif (1936) demonstrated the rapid convergence to a group norm of individuals' opinions regarding the extent of apparent movement of a spot of light in a darkened room. Hence, individuals who join a workplace setting will be expected to adhere to the norms, or risk alienation or ostracism.

Labelling theory and expectancy effect

Another aspect of group dynamics that has significance for workplace settings is that of labelling and expectancy effect. In sociological terms, labelling is the assigning of an individual to a category as a means of classifying his behaviour or state. Hence, 'ill' is a label used to distinguish people who are not healthy; 'vandal' is a label that distinguishes people who exhibit antisocial behaviour involving damage to property.

Labelling, then, involves classifying people who deviate from what is considered to be normal; the term *deviance,* however, is used to indicate a negative social evaluation.

Primary deviance

This is the assigning of a label to particular behaviours or states judged by society as deviant; these behaviours are socially defined and will vary between different cultures. The behaviours that a society considers deviant may change over the course of time; in the UK, it used to be considered deviant to attempt suicide, or to live as a couple without being married, whereas nowadays these behaviours are seen in quite a different light.

Secondary deviance

Once society has assigned a label to an individual, certain consequences may occur and these are termed. When a person is labelled 'deviant' he or she becomes stigmatized or disgraced in the eyes of society; depending upon the nature of the deviance, the individual may be shunned or worse – this is particularly true for labels such as 'rapist'. Many diseases, however, can stigmatize the sufferer, especially mental illness, epilepsy, AIDS and even such problems as deafness or blindness. Indeed, it can be argued that the diagnosis of such conditions in itself constitutes labelling of primary deviance, setting in train a series of predictable social consequences.

The 'self-fulfilling prophecy'

A second major effect of labelling is that of changes in the individual's self-concept; as a result of social reactions to the original label, the affected person begins to respond in a way that is compatible with that label. In other words, he comes to believe that he is what the label says he is and produces stereotyped behaviour that accords with it. This phenomenon has been termed the 'self-fulfilling prophecy' – a prophecy that comes true solely because it has been made. For example, a ward manager labels a student nurse as 'lazy' and people begin to react to him according to his label; eventually the nurse begins to accept the label and his behaviour becomes lazy. Obviously, there must have been an initial episode that led to the label, but it may have been a 'one-off' incident entirely untypical of the individual.

The notion of self-fulfilling prophecy has been explored in education, where it is known as 'teacher-expectancy effect'. There is a good deal of evidence about the effect of people's expectations on certain outcomes; experimenters have to be cautious when interpreting results because such results may be due to the 'Hawthorne effect' – a variation in subjects simply due to the fact they are being observed. The presence of an observer may have either positive or negative effects on the performance of students that are totally unrelated to the style of teaching given.

In a classic study (Rosenthal and Jacobson, 1968), carried out in an American school, teachers were given false information about some of the children in their classes; these children were purported to have unusual academic potential and were called 'spurters', but in reality they were randomly selected from the total class. The children were given tests of non-verbal intelligence at the start of the experiment and again at four months and eight months and results showed that the 'spurters' had gained significantly more in terms of IQ than the other children. This was ascribed to the fact that teachers' expectations of the 'spurters' had acted as a self-fulfilling prophecy, which made them achieve more. The study has been criticized on methodological grounds, but there is some support from other studies that teacher-expectancy can influence learning.

The workplace learning environment

The qualified staff are a key factor influencing the learning environment in hospital placements, the role of ward manager being particularly influential. Not only do they have control of the management of the area, but also serve as role-models for nursing practice. The leadership style and personality of the ward manager are important determinants of an effective learning environment, as demonstrated in a series of classic surveys in the 1980s (Orton, 1981; Fretwell, 1983; Ogier, 1982, 1986; Pembrey, 1980).

Characteristics of a workplace environment conducive to learning

The following summarizes the main perceptions of students in these research studies with regard to the characteristics of a good clinical learning environment.

A humanistic approach to students

Qualified staff should ensure that pre-registration students are treated with kindness and understanding and should try to show interest in them as people. They should be approachable and helpful to students, providing support as necessary, and try to foster the students' self-esteem. In the case of colleagues undertaking post-registration programmes, qualified staff need to be sensitive to their study needs, a point easily overlooked when a colleague has been working in the clinical area for some time as a full-time practitioner.

Team spirit

Qualified staff should work as a team and strive to make the student feel a part of that team. They should create a good atmosphere by their relationships within the team.

Management style

This should be efficient and yet flexible in order to produce good quality care. Teaching should have its place in the overall organization and students should be given responsibility and encouraged to use initiative. Nursing practice should be consistent with that taught in the university.

Teaching and learning support

Qualified staff should be encouraged to act as supervisors, mentors, preceptors, and assessors as appropriate. Opportunities should be given for students to ask questions, attend medical staff rounds, observe new procedures and have access to patients/clients records. Non-nursing professionals such as doctors, physiotherapists, dieticians and chaplains can also contribute to the learning environment provided they are made to feel part of the total team. It is important for the ward manager to spend a little time with new non-nursing colleagues in order to explain the ethos of the ward or department in relation to learning, thus encouraging them to see themselves as a resource for student learning.

It is not always appreciated that students themselves are very much a part of the learning environment and not merely the passive recipients of its influences. An effective environment will encourage the students to take responsibility for their own learning and to actively seek out opportunities for this. Critical thinking and judgement are fostered in an atmosphere where the student can question and dissent without feeling guilty or disloyal.

An important part of the learning process is experimentation, in which the student can try to apply concepts and principles in different ways; this implies that the student will need to adopt different approaches to patients and to be innovative. There may be other students in a clinical area and this peer support can be invaluable. By planning for two students to work together, there can be substantial benefits for both, provided they take time to discuss approaches and decisions and their underlying rationale.

The learning environment in community nursing

So far we have discussed learning environments with reference to hospital settings, but the environment is equally important when students are in community placements. Prior preparation in advance of a student placement is vital to ensure that the student gains the most from it. It is good practice to establish empathy with the student many weeks before the actual placement, for example, by the mentor giving the student his or her work and home telephone numbers in order to discuss expectations, and also 'housekeeping' issues such as transport arrangements, etc.

The physical environment is clearly very different from that of a hospital, particularly when it involves domiciliary visits to patients in their own homes. Nursing staff are guests in this situation, with no right of entry and consequently, much of the teaching will occur by observation, with discussion following later after leaving the patient's home. Much of this discussion takes place in the practitioner's car in a one-to-one setting, calling for very good interpersonal skills on the part of the teacher. The practitioner needs to put the student at ease and treat him or her as an equal. The effects of a strained relationship are much more difficult to cope with when there are only two people involved.

Clinics and post-natal groups provide another community learning environment for students. When running a well-baby clinic the mentor can combine tutorials for both student and parent, since the information is common to both. In community placements, media resources tend to be less readily available than in hospital settings, and hence the mentor places greater reliance on discussion and role modelling strategies.

Stress and the workplace learning environment

The concept of work-related stress has become a major issue for employers and employees, evidenced by the increasing numbers of claims for compensation arising out of work-induced, stress-related illness. Indeed, the term has now become a normal part of our everyday experience of living, exemplified in the expression, 'I'm really stressed-out'.

There can be few work settings that have more potential for stress than hospitals or community health settings; the very nature of the work involves staff in close contact with patients who are themselves often distressed and traumatized.

The nature of stress

Stress is a difficult concept to pin down, but it is generally thought of as consisting of two components:

1. *Stressors.* These are events in our lives that threaten our physical or mental well-being.
2. *Stress responses.* These are our reactions to the stressors we encounter.

The reaction of the individual to stressors occurs in three well-defined stages termed 'the general adaptation syndrome' (Selye, 1956):

1. *The alarm reaction.* This is a short-term reaction characterized by changes in physiology such as increased heart rate, respiration, endocrine activity and sympathetic-nervous-system activity. This combination is commonly referred to as the 'fight or flight' reaction.
2. *Resistance to stress.* In this stage the body processes return to normal and the individual adapts to the stress.
3. *Exhaustion.* This rarely occurs in psychological stress, although it is common in extreme physical conditions such as severe exposure. Here, the individual has used up all the resources for coping, and death may occur.

This adaptation syndrome is non-specific, in that it occurs when the person encounters any form of stress, of whatever severity.

One approach to stress is called 'person-environment fit theory' (Caplan, 1983), in which stress is defined as either:

- demands that exceed the individual's capability to fulfil, i.e. s/he is overwhelmed;
- an individual's capability exceeds the demands upon her/him, i.e. s/he is underwhelmed. This is typified by the case of an individual whose work does not sufficiently 'stretch' her/his capabilities.

Effects of stress upon the individual

The impact of stress can be classified into two main categories: the effects of stress on students' performance in the workplace, and the effects of stress on the health of students and staff in the workplace.

Effects of stress on students' performance in the workplace

An individual's level of emotional arousal has a significant effect on her/his subsequent performance, including cognitive as well as physical performance (Hebb, 1972). Each individual has an optimal level of arousal at which they perform at their best; under-arousal or over-arousal results in a deterioration in performance of learning tasks, particularly complex ones. Figure 1 shows the Yerkes–Dodson law on the relationship between emotional arousal level and performance.

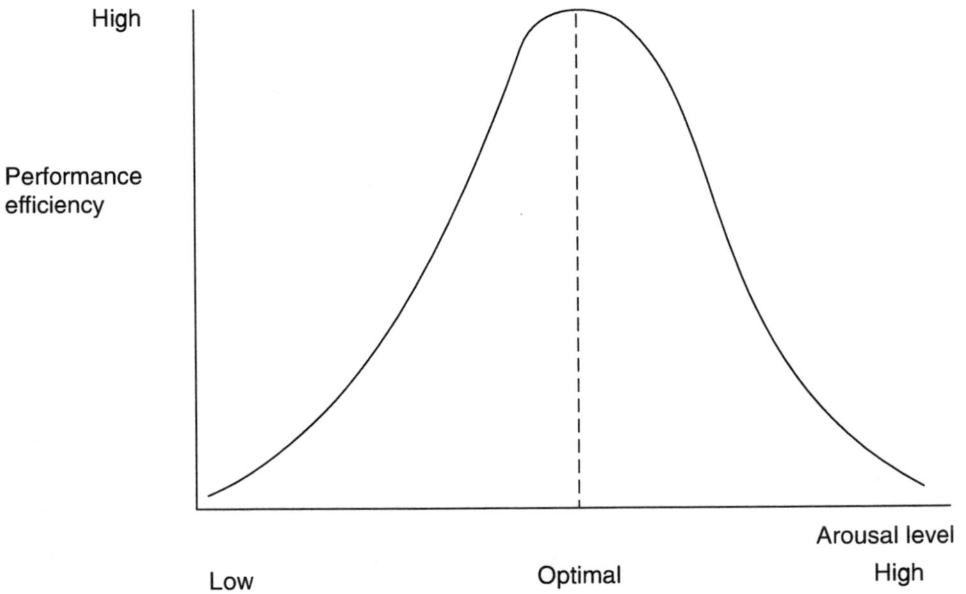

Figure 1 Yerkes-Dodson law: emotional arousal level and performance

It can be seen that arousal beyond the optimal level for a particular individual will cause a deterioration in performance. This effect is commonly observed in life-threatening situations, where individuals' behaviour often becomes disorganized and irrational, i.e. the phenomenon called panic. It is important to note that well-learned behaviours are much less likely to be disrupted by hyper-arousal than complex activities that require the integration of information, as the latter require more information-processing by the brain. So it is likely that a member of staff who is suffering from stress may be able to continue to perform many of the more routine, well-learned skills, but will be less able to cope with more complex and demanding situations in nursing practice.

Stress can also affect an individual's ability to concentrate on tasks and to retrieve information from memory, due to the intrusion of distracting thoughts about the possibility of failure. In the context of examinations, this has been termed test *anxiety*. Another aspect of stress-related behaviour is the tendency for the individual to stick to inappropriate patterns of behaviour because they are unable to consider alternatives. Atkinson *et al.* (1993) cite as an example the behaviour of some people trapped in a burning building; they died because they continued to push at doors that were designed to open inwards.

The effects of stress on the health of students and staff in the workplace

The reaction to stress will vary from individual to individual, with some experiencing feelings of anger and aggression, and others apathy and depression. Relationships can be affected, and some individuals may find solace in alcohol. Anxiety is another common symptom of stress, and there is evidence that it can impair the response of the immune system, leading to illness. There is also evidence of a link between stress and heart disease, especially in relation to the 'Type A personality'.

Sources of stress in the workplace

The categorization of sources of stress in organizations by Cooper and Marshall (1976) is adapted below to provide a framework for thinking about sources of stress in the clinical and community workplace.

1. Job-related stressors:
   - too much work to get through in the time available;
   - insufficient staff to support practitioners;
   - inadequate availability of equipment or resources;
   - little opportunity to use higher level skills.
2. Role-related stressors:
   - role ambiguity, e.g. lack of clarity about boundaries of role;
   - role-conflict, e.g. between role as practitioner and manager;
   - inadequate staff development for role;
   - role-conflict between work and family.
3. Relationship-related stressors:
   - conflict with superiors;
   - conflict with subordinates;
   - difficulties with colleagues from other health disciplines.
4. Career-related stressors:
   - pressures of continuing professional development;
   - expectations of promotion;
   - fear of redundancy.
5. Organization-related stressors:
   - inadequate communication;
   - internal politics;
   - secrecy and lack of trust.

Cooper (1999) gives a list of stressors that are specific to nurses working in outpatients departments:

- volume of patients;
- aggressive patients;
- unpredictable workloads;
- always in the public eye;
- new technology;
- lack of managerial supervision;
- fluctuating shift times;
- lack of time for training.

Coping with stress in the workplace

Many of the stressors encountered in the workplace will be beyond the individual practitioner's power to change. The organization carries a responsibility for the health and safety of its employees, and the increasing incidence of litigation on the grounds of stress-induced illness is forcing organizations to look more seriously at workplace stressors.

One of the most important elements of coping is being able to recognize the signs of stress in oneself, and to attempt to identify the main stressors involved. This enables coping strategies to be mobilized at a relatively early stage before the stress gets to a more serious level. The following coping strategies are commonly identified in the literature:

- Avoid taking on more work than you can cope with, by developing your assertive ability to say no to requests.
- Delegate jobs to other colleagues where possible.
- Always ensure that breaks are taken outside of the workplace area, e.g. go to the staff dining room for coffee, and go outside to the shops at lunch time.
- Undertake relaxation techniques at appropriate times, such as physical-relaxation techniques and meditation.
- Suggest to management that stress reduction programmes should be made available for staff.
- Try setting up a stress support group in the workplace, where colleagues can share their experiences.
- Use the individual performance review/appraisal system to bring to the attention of management the workplace stressors you have identified, e.g. lack of staff development for your role; inadequate resources, etc. This will ensure that they are formally recorded with the organization, an important point if evidence is needed at a later date.

- Report to your GP if your symptoms of stress are severe. Not only may treatment be provided, but a formal record is made which may be important evidence if needed at a later date.

Managing emotion in the workplace

Clinical and community settings are, by their very nature, places of intense emotions. These encompass positive emotions, such as excitement, joy, elation, and also negative emotions, such as anger, frustration and fear. It is interesting to note that both positive and negative emotions can equally disrupt normal functioning in an individual, including their relationships with others, and their ability to make judgements and take decisions. It may be necessary for nurses, midwives and health visitors to manage other people's disruptive emotions in the workplace, be it those of colleagues, patients or clients, and a number of principles of good practice for managing other's emotions are suggested by Ostell *et al.* (1999):

1. *Deal with the emotional reaction before attempting to resolve the problem.* The individual's disruptive level of emotion needs to be reduced so that they can begin to consider their problem rationally, and the authors' suggest two approaches to this. Apologising to the individual can be helpful if there is a justifiable grievance of some kind, e.g. a patient having to wait in the accident and emergency department for a long time, or if the recipient of the outburst is responsible in some way for the circumstances provoking the outburst. An alternative approach is to use reflective statements such as 'I can see that you are unhappy about ....', which may help defuse the emotion, but they may well have the opposite effect if perceived as stating the obvious.

2. *Avoid behaviour that heightens adverse emotional reactions.* When responding to disruptive emotional outbursts it is self-evident that one should avoid any behaviours that might exacerbate the other person's emotional state. Hence, any form of confrontation should be avoided, and it is important not to become angry when dealing with an angry person, as this will simply fuel their emotional reaction.

3. *Employ behaviours likely to dissipate adverse emotional reactions.* It seems normal to offer sympathy to individuals who demonstrate disruptive emotional reactions, but this can often reinforce the adverse emotional reaction by seeming to agree with their view of the circumstances. It is preferable to use empathy to show that the person's circumstances are understood, and this can be done by reflecting their views back to them, and by non-judgemental questioning.

4. *Recognize differences between emotions.* The authors point out that all emotional reactions should not be treated in the same way, because different emotions tend to be stimulated by different patterns of thinking, e.g. anger commonly arises when an individual's demands have been denied; anxiety when individuals anticipate unpleasant consequences that they perceive to be beyond their control.

5. *Where appropriate, attempt to find a solution to the underlying problem.* Finding a solution to the underlying problem can only occur once the disruptive emotional reaction has subsided. It is important to find a solution in order to prevent similar outbursts when the circumstances are encountered again. A counselling

approach can be useful here, but advice and instructions are also helpful in some cases.

6. *Learn to 'actively accept' reality.* There are some problems causing adverse emotional reactions that are not capable of solution, e.g. bereavement, redundancy; in such cases, the individual must learn to accept reality by letting go of these unattainable desires. However, this may take considerable time, and the help of a professional counsellor may be required.

Auditing the workplace learning environment

In order to be considered as an appropriate placement for pre-registration students, a workplace must meet the standard laid down by the relevant National Board for Nursing, Midwifery and Health Visiting. The ENB standard for practice experience is shown in Table 1.

Table 1 The ENB standard for practice experience (ENB, 1997)

Practice experience provides learning opportunities which enable the achievement of the stated learning outcomes.

Criteria

1. There is a strategy for the selection and monitoring of practice experience for the provision of learning opportunities which enable achievement of the learning outcomes of the programme
2. Practice provision reflects respect for the rights of health service users and their carers
3. The provision of care reflects respect for privacy, dignity and religious and cultural beliefs and practices
4. Care provision is based on relevant research-based and evidence-based findings
5. Pre-registration nursing and midwifery students' experience includes the 24-hour cycle of patient/client care
6. Plans for practice experience demonstrate equity of opportunity for individual students' learning experiences
7. The number and skill mix of clinical staff and the experience available support the achievement of the learning outcomes of the educational programme
8. A named person who holds effective first level registration on the Professional Register and other professional and academic qualifications and experience commensurate with the context of care delivery supervises and assesses students in health care settings
9. A named person who holds professional and academic qualifications and experience commensurate with the context of care delivery supervises and assesses students in non-health care settings
10. In non-health care settings a first level registered nurse/midwife/health visitor liaises with and supports the named person and student

Guidelines on educational audit have been produced by the English National Board for Nursing, Midwifery and Health Visiting (ENB, 1993a).

Practice placement audit focuses on six categories:

1. *Student learning experience/evaluation.* This includes provision for orientation, appropriate and accessible learning opportunities, adequate length of placement, ethos, appropriate care model, staff commitment, and mentorship system.
2. *Academic staff perspective.* This includes commitment to relationships with placement staff, maintenance of clinical competence, integration of theory and practice, monitoring of placement evaluation, and staff development of unit staff.
3. *Service provider unit staff perspective.* This includes a commitment to individualized care, team approach, multidisciplinary teamwork, communication with the college, commitment to the PREP standards by service managers, and appraisal system.
4. *Purchaser requirements.* This includes identifiable and agreed standards, and quality assurance mechanisms.
5. *Environment.* This includes adequate physical environment to deliver quality care, to facilitate development of competencies, to provide teaching and learning opportunities, space and equipment, and health and safety requirements.
6. *Quality assurance mechanisms.* This includes congruence of curriculum and placement, unit staff preparation, monitoring and annual review mechanisms, system for ensuring clinical knowledge base of academic staff, and adequate supervision of students.

Placement support systems for students and staff

Supervision

The term *supervisor* is used in a general sense to indicate someone who oversees the work of another, and this meaning is captured in the ENB's definition:

> *'an appropriately qualified and experienced first-level nurse/midwife/health visitor who has received preparation for ensuring that relevant experience is provided for students to enable learning outcomes to be achieved and for facilitating the students' developing competence in the practice of nursing/midwifery/health visiting by overseeing this practice. The role of the supervisor is a formal one and is normally included in the individual's managerial responsibilities' (ENB, 1993b).*

According to Faugier (1992), the role of the supervisor is to facilitate personal and professional growth in the supervisee, and to provide support for the latter's development of autonomy. She proposes a 'growth and support' model comprising the following elements:

1. generosity of time and spirit;
2. rewarding supervisee' abilities;
3. openness;
4. willingness to learn;

5. being thoughtful and thought-provoking;
6. humanity;
7. sensitivity;
8. uncompromising rigour and standards;
9. awareness of personal supervisory style;
10. adoption of a practical focus;
11. awareness of differences in orientation between supervisor and supervisee;
12. maintenance of distinction between supervisory and therapeutic relationship;
13. trust.

Supervision is one of a triad of concepts relating to the support of students in workplace settings, the others being mentorship and preceptorship.

Mentorship

Mentorship is perceived as an important concept by the nursing and midwifery professions, as evidenced by the considerable number of papers published in the area. The English National Board (1993a) defines a mentor as

> *'an appropriately qualified and experienced first-level nurse/ midwife/health visitor who, by example and facilitation, guides, assists and supports the student in learning new skills, adopting new behaviour and acquiring new attitudes'.*

Mentorship is seen by many writers as being a long-term relationship that extends throughout a student's programme, whereas others limit the concept to a relationship within a specific placement. In some systems, students are encouraged to choose their own mentors, and in others the mentor is assigned to the student. The former is preferable if possible, since it increases the likelihood of compatibility between mentor and student, an important factor in the relationship.

One of the controversial issues in mentoring is whether or not a mentor should also act as an assessor in relation to their students. Anforth (1992) argues that the role of mentor is incompatible with that of assessor, since it presents a moral dilemma between the guidance and counselling role and the judgemental assessment role. However, I find it difficult to understand why there should be a dilemma between these two aspects, since assessment should constitute an important teaching and learning strategy and not simply a punitive testing of achievement. If the mentor has an open, honest and friendly relationship with the student, assessment can provide a rich source of feedback and dialogue to further the student's development. At this point I should nail my colours to the mast with regard to mentorship: I use the term *mentor* to describe a qualified and experienced member of the practice-placement staff who enters into a formal arrangement to provide educational and personal support to a student throughout the period of the placement (Quinn, 1995). This support may involve a range of functions including teaching, supervision, guidance, counselling, assessment and evaluation. However, the mentor is not the only member of the practice-placement staff who carries out these functions, and other staff will undertake these according to the needs of the student and the practice area.

Preceptorship

From the foregoing discussion it is apparent that there is much overlap in the literature between the concepts of mentor and preceptor. Burke (1994) sees preceptors and students as having a short-lived, functional relationship for a specific purpose in a practice setting. Given my definition of mentorship above, I see preceptorship as a specific teaching and learning strategy rather than as a generic support system for students. My definition of a preceptor, therefore, is 'an experienced nurse, midwife or health visitor within a practice placement who acts as a role model and resource for a student who is attached to him or her for a specific time-span or experience'.

Preceptorship utilizes the principle of learning by 'sitting next to Nelly' but in a more systematic and planned way. A student is attached to the preceptor for a relatively long period of time such as a day or a week, and 'shadows' the preceptor throughout. The student's role is to observe the various interactions and decisions that the preceptor is involved with in the course of his or her work, and then time is made available for the student and preceptor to meet privately to discuss the events that have occurred. During these meetings, there is two-way dialogue about the various approaches adopted and the decisions made by the preceptor; and the student can ascertain the basis for such decisions. Clearly the person chosen to be the preceptor needs to have the confidence and interpersonal skills to be questioned about why one course of action was taken rather than another, and the system needs an equally confident student who will not be overawed by the power differential.

In management training, the preceptorship is often conducted in an institution other than the one in which the trainee works, and this has the advantage of avoiding a 'boss' relationship between preceptor and student. Preceptorship offers not only benefits to the students, but also to the preceptors, since the system helps the preceptors to clarify their reasons for making particular decisions or taking certain courses of action.

Role of the lecturer-practitioner or link-teacher

At one time in nursing, there were two types of nurse teacher: the nurse tutor, whose primary responsibility lay in classroom teaching, and the clinical teacher, whose primary responsibility was teaching in practice-placement settings. These roles have been unified under the title of lecturer/practitioner, a qualified teacher who has retained clinical competence and whose responsibilities include teaching, supervision and assessment of students.

The ENB commissioned a research project on the role of the teacher/lecturer in practice (ENB, 1998), in nursing and midwifery practice in both institutional and community contexts. The aims of the project were to map the national range and variations in the roles and responsibilities; to explore the factors promoting or inhibiting the role, and to identify the most effective model to meet criteria for clinical competence/credibility, promoting professional knowledge and scholarship. The main findings included:

- the most dominant model was that of 'link teacher';
- two thirds of respondents said there was no specific preparation for the role;
- the system is almost uniformly an un-managed system;
- students expressed a strong preference for lecturer/practitioners to work alongside them;
- practitioners felt they should continue to undertake practice assessments of students, but valued lecturer support in this activity;
- all respondent groups referred to the difficulties of being accountable to 'two masters'.

It is interesting to note that the dominant model is that of the link-teacher, whose role is to establish relationships with a small number of clinical areas for the purposes of liaison, trouble-shooting and staff development. The latter is primarily aimed at qualified staff in clinical areas, who will be acting as supervisors, mentors and preceptors to students undertaking practice placements.

Gerrish (1992) identifies three key roles for teachers in practice settings:

1. *Educational support for practice-based staff.* This includes advice about dealing with supernumerary students on pre-registration programmes, and support for staff acting as mentors to students.
2. *Tutoring students.* This includes facilitating the development of students' autonomy as students, and their skills with regard to reflective practice.
3 *Facilitating good practice.* This includes awareness of current practice, providing a resource to unit staff, promotion of research-mindedness, and fostering a critical approach to practice.

Gerrish suggests that teaching in practice placements requires a commitment by the teacher, collaboration between education and service staff, and staff development for teachers on their new role in relation to practice.

Staff development for supervisors, mentors and preceptors

The careful selection of practice-placement staff for these important roles is crucial, and Burke (1994) suggests that personal characteristics, clinical expertise, teaching skill, and motivation are important. Courses of preparation may take the form of recognized courses such as Teaching and Assessing in Clinical Practice (ENB, 1997, 1998), City and Guilds of London Course 7307, or a Certificate in Education course. On the other hand, they may be specifically designed in-house courses of preparation, and these need careful joint planning between education and service, and also ongoing monitoring and quality assurance.

Encouraging student autonomy means a 'hands-off' approach which some experienced practitioners may find uncomfortable. There is also the potential for perceived threat on the part of practitioners who qualified some time ago, when supporting DipHE or undergraduate students. This may result in barriers arising between mentor and student, to the detriment of learning.

One very useful strategy for staff development is networking between practice-placement support staff. Networking can be formal or informal, and functions in much the same way as self-help groups by providing mutual support and sharing of experiences. Jinks and Williams (1994) describe a study of the effectiveness of an educational strategy for community nurses in relation to teaching, assessing and mentoring of pre-registration students. They found that half the sample felt their preparation had been adequate and this correlated with the taking of a formal course of teaching and assessing.

Clinical supervision

Clinical supervision is a relatively recent peer-support initiative for practitioners in clinical and community settings, and is defined by the Department of Health (DoH) as:

> *'a formal process of professional support and learning which enables the individual practitioner to develop knowledge and competence, assume responsibility for their own practice and enhance consumer protection and safety of care in complex clinical situations' (DoH, 1993).*

Clinical supervision is described by the UKCC as 'an important part of strategies to promote high standards of nursing and health visiting care into the next century' (UKCC, 1996). Table 2 gives the main characteristics of clinical supervision.

Table 2 Characteristics of clinical supervision (Grant and Quinn, 1998)

Purpose
Professional support and learning
Development of knowledge and competence
Responsibility for own practice
Enhance consumer protection
Help practitioner to examine and validate her practice and feelings
Pastoral support
Formative assessment
Ensuring standard of clinical and managerial practice
Maintain and support standards of care
To help the client
Improve quality of patient care
Improve staff performance
Reduce stress and burn-out
Process
A formal process
A practice-focused professional relationship
Should be developed according to local circumstances
Every practitioner should have access
Preparation for supervisors is important, and should be included in pre- and post-registration programmes
Evaluation is needed, and should be determined locally

Clinical supervision is carried out in two main ways: one-to-one supervision and group supervision.

One-to-one clinical supervision

This is the most common form of clinical supervision, in which an experienced nurse acts as the clinical supervisor for a less-experienced colleague. Practitioners normally choose someone with whom they have a good relationship to be their clinical supervisor, usually a colleague from the same area of work.

Group clinical supervision

In this approach, one supervisor is designated for the group, and the advantages claimed are that it exposes supervisees to alternative modes of helping, and an appreciation of the widespread nature of their concerns.

Implementing one-to-one clinical supervision

The introduction of clinical supervision is a very sensitive issue, and may be regarded with scepticism or suspicion by some practitioners. For example, prospective supervisors may see it as an unnecessary, time-consuming activity that diverts resources from direct patient/client care. Supervisees may be suspicious of the motives of managers in introducing clinical supervision, seeing it as a covert means of disciplining staff for inadequate practice.

Some practitioners may consider it naive to openly and honestly disclose important aspects of their professional practice to a clinical supervisor, particularly if they feel that such disclosure might adversely affect their future employment prospects. It is also possible that some models of clinical supervision may give staff the impression that it is a counselling intervention or, at worst, some kind of amateur psychotherapy.

Hence, one of the most important aspects of clinical supervision is the relationship between supervisors and supervisees. Mutual trust is required, and this could take some time to develop, particularly if there was no choice in the selection of the supervisor.

Negotiating the supervision contract

The first meeting between the clinical supervisor and supervisee tends to be the most difficult, since both parties may be unsure about how to proceed. It is helpful if this first meeting focuses on negotiating the supervision contract, as the process of negotiation will itself help to encourage the development of rapport between the two parties. Since the contract contains tangible aspects such as practical arrangements and record-keeping, it provides a less-threatening focus for discussion in the initial phase of the meeting when the parties are at their most anxious. A supervision contract is a useful way of clarifying the working agreement, as well as making for an easier relationship, since everyone knows where they stand. Table 3 shows the components normally included in a supervision contract.

Table 3 Elements of a supervision contract (Grant and Quinn, 1998)

Practical arrangements, i.e. time, place, frequency and length of meetings
Record-keeping arrangements
What will happen in the case of missed sessions
Confidentiality
What will happen in the case of incompetent practice
What communication if any will there be between the supervisor and the supervisee's manager
What access (if any) will the supervisee have to the supervisor between sessions

Practical aspects of supervision meetings

Practical arrangements for clinical supervision may not always be straightforward. For example, offices are rarely appropriate for clinical supervision, as constant disturbance can be expected from telephones and visitors. Cowes and Wilkes (1998) report that 'all members wanted to get away from their immediate working environment in order that privacy could be ensured and distractions minimized'.

Difficulty may be experienced in finding a suitably private room that is not already booked, particularly if several clinical supervision meetings are taking place on the same day. Over-running of a previous meeting is a common occurrence, resulting in erosion of the time available for the next meeting; one hour is a reasonable time allocation but timing will vary depending on local circumstances. The problem of room bookings is further compounded where supervision for practice nurses and health visitors takes place in rooms in GP surgeries, because the use of such rooms may be chargeable and this will impact on the overall resource provision for clinical supervision.

Given that both parties to clinical supervision are busy practitioners, it is likely that one or both will arrive late from time to time. When negotiating the supervision contract, it is useful to allow a margin 'for late arrival; for example, they might agree to wait up to half an hour for the other to arrive. This margin can help reduce panic reactions, such as driving too fast to get to the meeting on time. The time of day in which the meeting takes place will vary according to local circumstances, but many supervisors and supervisees prefer the end of the day, when patient/client demand may be less. The frequency of meetings varies widely in the literature, ranging from weekly to three-monthly.

Keeping records of supervision

It is important that both supervisor and supervisee keep records of clinical supervision for their personal professional profile, as evidence of professional development. Whilst these records are confidential to the individuals concerned, it is also necessary to keep a managerial record of clinical supervision which contains the minimum amount of information required by management in order to be able to confirm that supervision has occurred, and to enable the time to be costed. This would normally be the names of the supervisor and supervisee, the dates on which it took place, and the reasons for any cancellation. In cases of litigation by patients or clients, such records can provide evidence of the ongoing professional development of the practitioner involved.

Teaching and learning strategies in the workplace

The principles of teaching and learning that have been expounded in this book are applicable to teaching and learning in the workplace. However, some teaching strategies are more appropriate for the workplace environment than others, and this section will explore a range of these.

Teaching on a one-to-one basis

Teaching on a one-to-one basis demands skills quite different from those used in the classroom setting; both teacher and student are more exposed to each other and the encounter takes place in the presence of other staff, patients and visitors. The need to appear competent and credible to all these groups, including the student, can add considerable pressure on the teacher, making it more difficult to allow the student to make decisions or to try out new approaches. On the other hand, there can be great personal satisfaction in helping to provide good quality nursing care whilst at the same time facilitating the growth of nursing skills in the student.

Much one-to-one teaching is opportunistic, i.e. the kind of spontaneous teaching that occurs as part of everyday professional practice, with either students, qualified staff, or patients and clients. Opportunistic teaching can arise in a number of ways; for example, students may ask the teacher to go through some aspect or procedure with them, or simply ask questions about the care of specific patients. On the other hand, the teacher may herself initiate teaching by asking questions or by explaining aspects or procedures.

Teaching can also be initiated by the teacher if she perceives that a student or qualified member of staff is experiencing difficulty with procedures or understanding. Within a given workplace setting there will be some concepts that most students find difficult to understand, and the teacher is asked time and time again to explain these to each new student. It is a useful strategy to prepare an explanation in advance that can be 'wheeled out' as required, preferably using some kind of visual material. Feedback on student learning is important even in spontaneous one-to-one teaching, so the teacher needs to use questioning to elicit the students' understanding of any explanations given.

Coaching

Coaching is a familiar concept in sport and athletics, where a skilled coach offers analysis and advice to help a sports-person or athlete to improve his/her performance. The term is also used in education, where it implies the offering of additional support and tutoring to help a pupil or student to prepare for examinations. Coaching can also be used as a management strategy for improving staff performance at work, and it is in this context that its relevance to clinical supervision becomes apparent.

Some NHS Trusts are using a self-study guide called the *Coaching Toolkit Programme* as part of the preparation for clinical supervision. The toolkit defines coaching as 'a person-to-person process which helps individuals to come to their own conclusions about the best way to achieve improved performance at work' (South and

'West Development Forum, 1996). This definition emphasizes the empowerment aspect of coaching; the onus is on the individual to decide how s/he will achieve improved performance. Within an organization, anyone can be a coach to anyone else, provided they have appropriate expertise and experience, and coaching is commonly used to help individuals to acquire new skills, take on new roles, apply learning gained from attendance at courses or study-days, and as part of annual individual performance review.

The key skills identified for coaching are fundamental skills that underpin any interpersonal encounter, including counselling and clinical supervision, and these are listed in Table 4.

Table 4 Coaching skills

Developing rapport and trust
Listening
Summarizing and reflecting
Self-disclosure
Questioning
Giving feedback
Using silence

The coaching toolkit uses a five-stage model with the acronym 'C.O.A.C.H.' to help make the coaching session more effective:

1. *Circumstance.* In this first stage the coach and the individual attempt to get an overall picture of the current issue for the coaching session.
2. *Objective.* The coach helps the individual to formulate the objectives s/he wishes to achieve.
3. *Alternatives.* In this stage the possible range of options and alternatives are discussed.
4. *Choice.* During this stage, both parties come to a decision about which alternative is most appropriate, given all the factors.
5. *Handover.* This final stage is about how the choice is to be implemented, and the support required to do this.

Case-conferences

Ideally these should involve all members of the nursing team in discussion and evaluation of the nursing care of a particular patient. Medical staff have long used the case presentation method as a learning tool for students and qualified doctors, and the same principles apply to the use of nursing-care conferences. There is no standard format for such a conference, but it is usual for one nurse to present the patient's case and then for the whole team to be involved in the discussion. This helps the student to feel part of the nursing team as well as providing the skills in a public presentation of 'self'. Such conferences provide a useful holistic view of the patient and his or her problems, together with an opportunity to analyse critically the care that has been received, to the mutual benefit of both nurses and patients.

Handover report

Many qualified practitioner nurses view the handover report as a valuable opportunity to do some teaching. Handover is done normally in two ways:

1. verbal handover involving the entire nursing team meeting together in a room for a reasonable period of time during the day;
2. non-verbal handover is conducted at patients' bedsides using documents.

Verbal handover can be a useful teaching strategy if the ward manager or staff nurse often take time to ask questions about aspects of patients' conditions and care, and provided that the atmosphere is relaxed and informal. There are important trade-offs from a ward report in addition to the actual report itself, namely the fostering of team spirit and the development of public speaking ability and confidence in presenting information to peers. However, there are disadvantages of verbal handover, including nurses' reliance on memory, the amount of time consumed, and the fact that nurses are often called away before the handover is complete.

Kennedy (1999) reports on a study of non-verbal bedside handover in an elderly care setting. Using non-participant observation, the study investigated the early-to-late shift handover, and the key components of handover were identified as venue, grade of nurse, documents used, patient involvement, content of handover, whether the person handing over was the care-giver, and whether unnecessary people were present. The main findings were as follows:

- handover was quicker, and staff were available on the ward for other patients if needed;
- support workers played little part in the handover;
- staff were not confident about using care plans for the handover, as these could not be relied upon.

The study recommended that all qualified nurses should attend planning workshops, that bedside handover should continue and that patients should be included wherever possible, and that the role of the support worker should be reviewed in relation to communication and documentation.

Clinical rounds

Students can gain a great deal from accompanying a doctor or nurse on a clinical round. The former is useful for gaining insight into the role of the medical team in patient care, and it is interesting to listen to the discussion with regard to treatment. Students may find it valuable to accompany a nurse teacher on a similar round and to make comparisons of the needs of patients with similar conditions, and also to look at the difference in attitudes between such patients. Examples of pathology can be pointed out, for example oedema or inflammation, and the reasons discussed at the end of the round. Students should always carry a notebook to write down any queries or observations, but single sheets of paper must not be allowed, as they can easily be lost and other patients may read the confidential details.

Reflective practice diary

Reflective diaries or records are one of the key strategies in experiential learning and consist of brief written descriptions of situations that can be used as the basis for reflection later. The following examples are from the reflective diary of a health visitor who is undergoing training as a mentor.

Situation 1: student's first day on community placement

The first day of the student's placement was spent in discussion and negotiation of her learning contract in the light of my case load requirements. Since child protection is a major facet of my work, I made it clear to the student that this aspect must by law take priority over all other matters. Before commencing their community placement students are required to complete a community profile so that they have insight into the area. However, the student in question arrived at my office having completed a community profile on a completely different area to the one in which I work. This meant that the student had no information whatsoever about the area, so we had to negotiate a series of sessions in which I could explain the key aspects of the placement community. I also contacted her personal tutor in the college of nursing to emphasize how important it is for the student to undertake a community profile which relates to their placement.

Situation 2: student's first visit to a client's home

One of the items on my student's learning contract was to visit a family with a new baby. By accompanying me on the visit, the student was able to see and understand exactly what a health visitor does in such a visit. During a prior briefing discussion I explained the official standard for a new-birth visit, and asked the student to pay particular attention during the visit to how I taught the mother to look after the baby, and to compare my performance with that of the official standard. I wanted her to focus particularly on my use of verbal and non-verbal communication with the family, since interpersonal relationships are fundamental to the health visitor role.

On arriving back at the surgery following the visit, we had a debriefing session in which I challenged the student by asking her to evaluate my performance against the official standards, and how she would now approach her next new-birth visit in the light of what she had learned.

Situation 3: developmental assessment in the clinic

At age 18 months infants come to the clinic for assessment of physical and behavioural development, and this involves a variety of tests, e.g. hearing, speech, vision, motor movements, etc. I acted as a role model for the student, in that she was asked to observe and record carefully my relationships and involvement with the clients, with particular emphasis in this case on the practical aspects of testing. One of the objectives in the student's learning contract was to develop the skills of developmental assessment of infants, so I planned the learning environment with this goal in mind. During the clinic, the student was asked to observe me performing the developmental assessment on a number of infants, and was then encouraged to participate in the assessment of a number of infants. Once I was satisfied that she had grasped the essential points, I allowed her to conduct an assessment in partnership with me, but she was asked to take the lead, and to treat me as student, showing me what to do. This was a very effective way of teaching, as it showed the student aspects which she needed to study further.

Critical incident technique

Critical incident technique (CIT) is a useful tool for identifying aspects of practice which the student felt were particularly positive or negative (Flanagan, 1954). These critical incidents can then be reflected upon and analysed to give new insights into practice. Critical incident technique was used by Benner (1984) in her study of acquisition of nursing skill, and she identified critical incidents as any of the following:

- those in which the nurse's intervention really made a difference in patient outcome;
- those that went unusually well;
- those in which there was a breakdown;
- those that were ordinary and typical;
- those that captured the essence of nursing; and
- those that were particularly demanding.

Subjects were asked to include the following information in their description of critical incidents:

- the context;
- a detailed description;
- why the incident was critical to the subject;
- what the subject's concerns were at the time;
- what they were thinking about during the incident;
- what they felt about it afterwards; and
- what they found most demanding about it.

Learning contracts

Learning contracts are an effective tool for developing student autonomy in practice placements. It is useful to meet with students prior to the placement to begin the initial contract negotiation, and this can be modified as required once the placement has commenced.

Teaching a motor skill

Although it is possible to teach some motor skills by simulation in a nursing laboratory, such learning will still need to be consolidated in the workplace setting. Teaching motor skills involves the same principles as any other form of teaching, namely, an atmosphere conducive to learning that is free from threat or stress. There must be opportunity for feedback and analysis of the performance, and teachers must appreciate that learning a skill requires time and that individual students will differ in the amount of time they require. One point to be borne in mind is that nursing procedures involve more than motor skills; Gagne (1985) classifies procedures as intellectual skills or rules for determining the sequence of actions and thus students need to learn the procedural rules as well as the motor skills aspects.

When planning to teach motor skills, the teacher will have to consider the level at which the student must learn the skill. It is obvious that students cannot achieve the highest level of proficiency for every skill they learn; indeed, experienced nurses will vary in their relative degree of skill amongst the nursing procedures they practise. There will be some motor skills that students must learn to the highest level and others where an intermediate level is acceptable. A useful point of reference for levels of skills is the notion of taxonomies of motor skills. The taxonomy has seven levels as follows:

1. perception – concerned with perception of sensory cues;
2. set – concerned with readiness to act;
3. guided response – skills performed under guidance of instructor;
4. mechanism – performance becomes habitual;
5. complex overt response – typical skilled performance;
6. adaptation – skills can be adapted to suit circumstances; and
7. origination – creation of original movement patterns.

It would seem that many nursing skills learned by students will be geared at level 3 or 4 and that the higher levels may only be reached when the student has practised as a qualified nurse for some time. Skills at level 3 are commonly taught in specialist areas, where the student is allowed to perform under guidance having first been shown how to do a procedure. For example, the skills of dialysis may be taught at this level during a student's allocation to a renal clinical area, but there is no expectation that the student nurse will achieve a highly-skilled performance during the brief allocation period. The same can be said for other clinical specialisms such as intensive-care units, neonatal units and the like.

The teaching of motor skills involves the provision of information and the opportunity for practice under supervision. Table 5 gives a checklist for teaching a motor skill, and the key points are further elaborated below.

Table 5 Checklist for teaching a motor skill

1. Provide an atmosphere conductive learning
2. Carry out a skills analysis to determine part-skills and elements
3. Determine the sequence of the procedure
4. Assess entry behaviours of students – these need not be taught again
5. Model the skill by demonstration at normal speed
6. Teach the sequence of the procedure
7. Teach the motor skill by either whole-learning or part-learning method
8. Allocate sufficient time for practice
9. Provide augmented feedback on performance
10. Prompt student to use intrinsic feedback
11. Encourage transfer of existing similar skills by pointing out similarity

The provision of an atmosphere conducive to learning has already been discussed and its importance noted. Skills analysis is a useful way of identifying the part-skills that comprise the total motor skill. Table 6 shows a task analysis for the motor aspects of the procedure of performing a surgical dressing.

Table 6 The procedure of performing a surgical dressing

Total motor skill	Part-skills (tasks)	Elements*
1.0 Preparation of work area	1.1 Clearing space	1.11 Pushing locker away
		1 12 Moving bed table
	1.2 Screening	1.21 Holding curtain and pulling it round
	1.3 Closing windows	1.31 Pulling window cord
	1.4 Positioning patient	1.41 Asking if possible to lie recumbent
		1.42 Removing pillows
		1.43 Folding bedclothes
		1.44 Loosening clothing
		1.45 Covering with blanket
2.0 Preparation of equipment and trolley	2.1 Hand-washing	
	2.2 Cleaning trolley	
	2.3 Collecting equipment	
	2.4 Setting trolley	
	2.5 Taking to bedside	
3.0 Performance of dressing	3.1 Opening bags	
	3.2 Loosening dressing	
	3.3 Hand-washing	
	3.4 Opening packs	
	3.5 Removing dressing	
	3.6 Cleaning wound	
	3.7 Applying dressing	
4.0 Organization of trolley	4.1 Closing pack	
	4.2 Closing bags	
	4.3 Securing bags	
5.0 Ensuring patient's comfort	5.1 Attending to position	

Table 6 The procedure of performing a surgical dressing

Total motor skill	Part-skills (tasks)	Elements*
6.0 Clearing of trolley and equipment	6.1 Removing from bedside	
	6.2 Disposal of soiled dressings	
	6.3 Disposal of instruments	
	6.4 Hand-washing	
	6.5 Clearing equipment	
	6.6 Cleaning trolley	
	6.7 Hand-washing	
7.0 Returning to patient	7.1 Assist with clothing	
	7.2 Assisting with position	
	7.3 Offering drink, newspaper, etc.	
	7.4 Removing screens	
	7.5 Returning tables, locker, etc.	
8.0 Recording and reporting	8.1 Writing report	
	8.2 Reporting verbally to nurse in charge	
	8.3 Comparing report with previous one	

**Elements are stated only for Section 1.0 of the total motor skills*

These motor skills are further subdivided into part-skills and elements, and it can be seen that the elements consist of many previously learned entry behaviours, such as moving the bed table and pulling curtains. Determining the sequence of the procedure is important and it may be forgotten that students must remember this as well as the motor skills. Entry behaviours need to be identified, since they are already learned and hence do not need to be taught again.

Modelling of the skill is normally done by an actual demonstration, but in the classroom setting it can also be done by video, and it gives the students an overall impression of the skill they are aiming at.

There is some controversy as to whether skills should be taught in their entirety (whole-learning), or divided into part-skills, with each part being taught separately first and then combined into a whole – part-learning. The disadvantage of whole-learning is that it may be difficult to comprehend large units of procedures if taught together. However, part-learning may waste time because the student has to learn the part-skills first and then learn to combine them together. It may also be boring for the student if the part-skills are simple. The advantages of whole-learning are that it may be:

- more meaningful, as perceived as whole;
- more efficient, as students can identify the aspects which need further practice within the whole;
- more effective for students who already have a background in the skill;
- better for highly-motivated students; and
- better for older students.

The advantages of part-learning are that it may:

- help to motivate students, as each part-skill provides immediate achievement;
- by its small-step nature act as a reinforcement for learning;
- be better for younger students;
- be better for students lacking a background in the skill; and
- help to improve specific responses for part-skills.

Another area of controversy is that of massed practice versus spaced practice; massed practice involves continuous practice until the skill is learned, whereas spaced practice may spread the practice over a period of time, with rest in between. There is no evidence that one is better than the other, but there are obvious pitfalls associated with massed practice, such as boredom and fatigue. As we have seen earlier, feedback is a crucial aspect of motor-skills learning, without which no improvement can occur. The teacher needs to encourage students to become aware of the intrinsic feedback from their own muscles and joints, which informs them about the position of limbs and the action of movements. Information gained from their own observation of their actions will also help the students to learn a skill and here again the teacher may use questioning to ascertain whether each student is able to self-evaluate outcomes.

The main role of the teacher is in providing augmented feedback in the form of verbal guidance both during and on completion of the motor performance. The nurse teacher can teach for transfer of learning by using a variety of techniques to make the student understand the principles underlying the skill. Existing skills must have been well-learned if they are to transfer positively to the new skill, and the similarities need to be pointed out to the students.

Benner's model of skill acquisition in clinical nursing practice

Patricia Benner's book *From Novice To Expert* (1984) has become one of the most frequently quoted research studies in nurse education. Benner conducted paired interviews with beginners and experienced nurses about significant nursing situations they had experienced in common, in order to identify any characteristic differences between their descriptions of the same situation. Additionally, she carried out interviews, critical incident technique, and participant observation with a sample of experienced nurses, new graduates, and senior students, to ascertain the characteristics of performance at different stages of skill acquisition.

Using an adaptation of the five-stage model of skill acquisition developed by Dreyfus and Dreyfus (1980), she described the characteristics of performance at five different levels of nursing skill: novice, advanced beginner, competent, proficient, and expert. During her passage through these stages, the student relies less upon abstract rules to govern practice, and more on past experience. Nursing situations begin to be seen as a unified whole within which only certain aspects are relevant, and the nurse becomes personally involved in situations rather than a detached observer. It is important to note that Benner uses the term *skill* in its widest sense to mean all aspects of nursing practice, and not simply psychomotor skill performance.

Stage 1: novice

This level is characterized by rule-governed behaviour, as the novice has no experience of the situation upon which to draw, and this applies to both students in training and to experienced nurses who move into an unfamiliar clinical area. Adherence to principles and rules, however, does not help the nurse to decide what is relevant in a nursing situation, and may thus lead to unsuccessful performance.

Stage 2: advanced beginner

Unlike principles and rules, aspects are overall characteristics of a situation that can only be identified by experience of that situation. For example, the skills of interviewing a patient are developed by experience of interviewing previous patients, and the advanced beginner is one who has had sufficient prior experience of a situation to deliver marginally acceptable performance. Advanced beginners need adequate support from supervisors, mentors and colleagues in the practice setting.

Stage 3: competent

This stage is characterized by conscious, deliberate planning based upon analysis and careful deliberation of situations. The competent nurse is able to identify priorities and manage their own work and Benner suggests that the competent nurse can benefit at this stage from learning activities that centre on decision-making, planning and co-ordinating patient care.

Stage 4: proficient

Unlike the competent nurse, the proficient nurse is able to perceive situations holistically and therefore can home in directly on the most relevant aspects of a problem. According to Benner, proficient performance is based upon the use of maxims, and is normally found in nurses who have worked within a specific area of nursing for several years. Inductive teaching strategies, such as case-studies, are insist useful for nurses at this stage.

Stage 5: expert

This stage is characterized by a deep understanding and intuitive grasp of the total situation; the expert nurse develops a feel for situations and a vision of the possibilities in a given situation. Benner suggests that critical incident technique is a useful way of attempting to evaluate expert practice, but considers that not all nurses are capable of becoming experts.

References

Allport E (1924) cited in J Davis (ed) (1969) *Group Performance.* Addison Wesley, Reading, MA.

Anforth P (1992) Mentors, not assessors, *Nurse Education Today* 12: 299–302.

Atkinson R L, Atkinson R, Smith E E, Bern D J (1993) *Introduction to Psychology,* 11th edn. Harcourt Brace Jovanovich, New York.

Benner P (1984) *From Novice to Expert: Excellence and Power in Clinical Nursing Practice.* Addison Wesley, London.

Burke L (1994) Preceptorship and post-registration nurse education, *Nurse Education Today* 14: 60–6.

Caplan R (1983) Person-environment fit: past, present and future. In: C Cooper (ed.) *Stress Research: Issues for the Eighties.* Wiley, Chichester.

Cooper C, Marshall J (1976) Occupational sources of stress. *Journal of Occupational Psychology* 49: 11–28.

Cooper J (1999) Managing workplace stress in outpatient nursing, *Professional Nurse* 14 (8): 540–543.

Cowes F, Wilkes C (1998) Clinical supervision for specialist nurses, *Professional Nurse* 13 (5): February.

Department of Health (1993) *Vision For The Future.* HMSO, London.

Dreyfus S, Dreyfus H (1980) A five-stage model of the mental activities involved in directed skill acquisition. Unpublished report supported by the Air Force Office of Scientific Research, University of California, Berkley.

English National Board for Nursing, Midwifery and Health Visiting (1993a) *Guidelines for Educational Audit.* ENB, London.

English National Board for Nursing, Midwifery and Health Visiting (1993b) *Regulations and Guidelines for the Approval of Institutions and Courses.* ENB, London.

English National Board for Nursing, Midwifery and Health Visiting (1997) *Standards for Approval of Higher Education Institutions and Programmes.* ENB, London.

English National Board for Nursing, Midwifery and Health Visiting (1998) *The Role of the Teacher/Lecturer in Practice. Research Highlights 31 May 1998.* ENB, London.

Faugier J (1992) In: T Butterworth, J Faugier *Clinical Supervision and Mentorship in Nursing.* Chapman and Hall, London.

Flanagan J (1954) The critical incident technique. *Psychological Bulletin* 51: 327–358.

Fretwell J (1983) Creating a ward learning environment: the sister's role. *Nursing Times Occasional Papers* 79 (21, 22).

Gagne R (1985) *The Conditions of Learning and Theory of Instruction,* 4th edn. Holt, Rinehart and Winston, New York.

Gerrish K (1992) The nurse teacher's role in the practice setting. *Nurse Education Today* 12: 227–232.

Grant P, Quinn F M (1998) Clinical supervision. In: F M Quinn (ed.) *Continuing Professional Development in Nursing: A Guide for Practitioners and Educators.* Stanley Thornes, Cheltenham.

Hebb D O (1972) *Textbook of Psychology,* 3rd edn. Saunders, Philadelphia.

Jinks A, Williams R (1994) Evaluation of a community staff preparation strategy for the teaching, assessing and mentorship of Project 2000 Diploma students. *Nurse Education Today* 14: 44–51.

Kennedy J (1999) An evaluation of non-verbal handover. *Professional Nurse* 14 (6): 391–394.

Latane B, Darley J (1968) Group inhibition of bystander intervention in emergencies. *Journal of Personality and Social Psychology* 10: 215–221.

Ogier M (1982) *An Ideal Sister.* RCN, London.

Ogier M (1986) An 'ideal' sister – seven years on. *Nursing Times Occasional Papers* 82 (2).

Orton H (1981) Ward learning climate and student nurse response. *Nursing Times Occasional Papers* 77 (17).

Ostell A, Baverstock S, Wright P (1999) Interpersonal skills of managing emotion at work. *The Psychologist* 12 (1): 30–34.

Pembrey S (1980) *The Ward Sister – Key to Care.* RCN, London.

Quinn F M (1995) *The Principles and Practice of Nurse Education,* 3rd edn. Stanley Thornes, Cheltenham.

Rosenthal R, Jacobson L (1968) *Pygmalion in The Classroom.* Holt, Rinehart and Winston, New York.

Selye H (1956) *The Stress of Life.* McGraw Hill, New York.

Sherif M (1936) *The Psychology of Social Norms.* Harper, New York.

Simpson E (1972) The classification of educational objectives in the psychomotor domain. *The Psychomotor Domain* 3. Gryphon House, Washington DC.

South and West Development Forum (1996) *The Coaching Toolkit Programme.* Foreward, Cheshire.

United Kingdom Central Council For Nursing, Midwifery and Health Visiting (1996) *Position Statement on Clinical Supervision for Nursing and Health Visiting.* UKCC, London.

25. 'Letting Go': Rationale and Strategies for Student-centred Approaches to Clinical Teaching

Elizabeth M. Rideout

To date the clinical practice portion of nursing education has tended to emphasise patient problems related to specific disease processes and the technical interventions needed to deal with those problems. Teacher-centred methods of education that place control of the process and content of learning with the teacher have seemed appropriate. However, the role and function of nursing is changing. Autonomy, independence and decision-making are more highly valued. In order that nurses develop these skills and abilities, a shift in focus in nursing education is required. This paper presents a rationale for more student-centred approaches to education. Strategies for clinical teaching will be described that emphasise collaboration between student and teacher. Suggestions designed to facilitate change in the roles of teachers and students will be offered.

Introduction

Clinical practice is an important component of any educational programme designed to prepare health professionals such as nurses, physicians and occupational therapists. The purposes of clinical experience in nursing education are similar to those for other professional groups and include enabling learners to integrate knowledge and skills associated with caring for patients and ensuring that students acquire the ability to provide nursing care (Woolley and Costello, 1988). The emphasis in clinical experience has been on the technical component of nursing practice with its focus on the performance of specific actions and skills. Traditional methods of nursing education have placed the control of the content and process of learning to nurse in the hands of the teacher. The purpose of this paper is to demonstrate that changing demands on the health care system, on the role of nursing and on approaches to teaching require that more control of the clinical practice component of nursing education be shared with students.

Rationale for change

Nursing has been described as consisting of three components: the technical with its focus on the performance of specific actions or skills; the rational which emphasises decision-making and critical thinking; and the emotive which encompasses the interpersonal or relational aspects of nursing (Bevis and Watson, 1989). Nursing education in general and the clinical practice portion in particular has tended to emphasise the technical component of nursing. The curriculum in most schools of nursing has focused on basic disease processes and the technical interventions

Elizabeth M. Rideout: '"Letting Go": Rationale and Strategies for Student-centred Approaches to Clinical Teaching' in *NURSE EDUCATION TODAY* (1994), 14(2), pp. 146–151. Reprinted by permission of the publisher Churchill Livingstone.

needed to deal with those diseases. However, the health care issues facing us are changing. The health problems associated with increasing numbers of elderly and those with chronic diseases require skills and abilities additional to the technical ones. The role of the nurse is also changing, from that of assistant to the physician where technical skills and abilities are most valued, to one of greater autonomy and independence, where the rational or decision-making component of nursing assumes greater importance (Bevis and Watson, 1989; Lindeman, 1989). Altogether the changing demands of nursing require the teaching of reflection, criticism, independence, creativity and inquiry. It is these qualities that are particularly needed for nursing in the future (Lindeman, 1989). Elements of discovery and innovation are important for nurses (and other health care professionals) to provide the care required (Schön, 1987). This dictates that the teaching–learning process be reconceptualised as a participatory process model, so students can develop the self-reliance to function in the rapidly changing situations that characterise the health care system of today and tomorrow (Lindeman, 1989). A move from traditional teacher-centred methods of nursing education to more student-centred approaches is required.

Definition of terms: student-centred and teacher-centred

To date nursing educators have relied on teacher-centred approaches to education that emphasise essential content and skills as defined by the teacher (Bevis and Watson, 1989). In this approach there is reliance on a subject or content orientation and the emphasis is on direct instructional techniques such as demonstrations and return demonstrations. The knowledge and skills to be acquired are identified by faculty and the evaluation is in relation to criteria specified by faculty (Miller and Seller, 1990; Stenhouse, 1975). A student-centred approach describes collaboration between students and faculty, where educational goals and the means to achieve the goals are determined through discussion and deliberation (Bevis and Watson, 1989). Although the faculty define the outcome objectives to be achieved, there is much opportunity for individual learning within the broad confines of the specified objectives.

Moving toward student-centred methods

Selecting clinical settings and patients

The traditional teacher-centred approaches to clinical teaching that emphasise the development of technical expertise (DeYoung, 1990; Woolley and Costello, 1988) would be familiar to most clinical nurse educators. These will be described and more learner centred strategies will be presented that should promote the development of nurses prepared to face the challenges of working in our changing health care system.

In the traditional approach to clinical teaching, students are assigned by the teacher to hospital and community practice settings and to patients within those settings. Patient assignments are made for students according to the student learning needs as identified by the teacher and based on course objectives. The choice of patients is often made in relation to the medical diagnosis of the patient and the resulting opportunity for skills practice. Information is provided by the teacher about the patient so nursing care can be planned for the 'typical' patient problems. Students then provide the care, modifying it as necessary as they learn more about individual patient needs. In the traditional teacher-centred method, placements for practice are also selected by teachers, based on the belief that students must be exposed to all clinical settings where nurses function. This is congruent with a content rather than process approach, where the focus is learning the specific knowledge and skills needed to function in diverse settings such as maternal–child, paediatrics, medicine, surgery and psychiatry.

A more student-centred strategy would promote student choice of placements for clinical practice and the selection of patients within those settings. Student input into choice of patients within settings would be encouraged in a student-centred approach. Students would select patients based on individual learning needs within the framework of course and programme objectives. In a system that allowed for student selection of clinical placements, some teacher control would be important to ensure that any statutory requirements for practice are met and a basic level of knowledge and skills is achieved while allowing individuals to pursue particular areas of interest. This approach would shift the focus from specific content to the process of nursing, from learning the nursing interventions for medical diagnoses to learning the process of care for common problems faced by patients and families, such as pain, grief and loss (Bevis and Watson, 1989).

Using clinical learning plans

Another student-centred strategy would be the use of clinical learning plans to facilitate the defining by students of individual learning objectives to be achieved in the clinical setting. Learning plans:

> 'replace a content plan with a process plan. Instead of specifying how a body of content will be transmitted (content plan), it specifies how a body of content will be acquired by the learner' (process plan). (Knowles, 1986, p. 39).

The roles of student and teacher must shift when learning plans are introduced. The teacher becomes the facilitator of self-directed learning and a content resource. The student assumes an active role in selecting objectives for learning from within the range of course and programme objectives. The outcomes for the student include expanded participation in planning learning experiences, enhanced ability for resource selection and acquisition, and increased skill in self-evaluation of current performance levels. Additional benefits are an increase in assertiveness and confidence that follows from the changed view of self and the modified relationships with teachers (Knowles, 1986).

Methods of clinical teaching

Record review

Record reviews are a useful strategy in clinical teaching (DeYoung, 1990). In the traditional, teacher-centred approach such reviews provide an opportunity to appraise the student's documentation of assessment and management of patients. The focus of the activity is the quality of the documentation; discussion of the interpretation of the data recorded is uncommon. The emphasis for the student is the meeting of teacher expectations for concise and accurate recording. In a more student-centred approach, record reviews could continue to provide a method for confirming precision of documentation while also providing an opportunity for discussion of the patient and the related care requirements (Edwards & Baptiste, 1987). In particular, the discussion could allow for a focus on the patient's particular response to illness rather than issues related to the completion of nursing care tasks. As such the record becomes a teaching tool and the educational strategy is a dialogue between teacher and student.

Pre- and post-conferences

Pre- and post-conferences are another part of the clinical practice experience of most nursing programmes. The pre-conference is held for 15–30 min prior to going to the clinical area. Traditionally it is used to question the students concerning their plans for the day; the primary purpose is to determine the degree of student preparedness to provide care for their assigned patient, and arranging times for teacher observation of skill performance. The pre-conference has been dubbed 'drill and grill' and it often resembles just that (Woolley and Costello, 1988).

The post-conference, which traditionally follows the clinical experience and lasts from 15–30 min, provides the opportunity for students to share their experiences and to learn from the approaches and interventions displayed by their classmates. The post-conference is sometimes referred to as 'facts and events' since it is used to describe within the group the events of the clinical session.

Changes in the format and use of pre- and post-conferences would provide another method of enhancing student-centred learning. For example, conferences could be student rather than teacher led. Rather than the 'drill and grill' routine, the conferences could provide the opportunity to meet individual learning objectives as outlined in student learning plans. Weekly rounds attended by students, nursing staff involved in the day to day provision of care as well as patients could replace the traditional conference. The content would shift from discussion of the day's events to mutual problem-solving around common issues of care as applied to particular patients. Opportunities for interdisciplinary conferences might also be provided, allowing for learning about the contribution of other health professionals to patient care.

The process of evaluation

Evaluation is an integral part of clinical teaching (Tower and Majewski, 1987). In the traditional approach, data for evaluation come from direct observation by the teacher of the quality of patient care provided by the student. The focus of evaluation is the extent to which the student meets the expectations of the teacher, as they reflect the course objectives (Bondy, 1984). This sets up what Bevis and Watson (1989) describe as an adversarial relationship between the student and the teacher/content:

> 'The students 'do battle' with the content, and the teacher tries to help the content to be learned' (p. 278).

In a student-centred approach to clinical teaching, evaluation would be shared with the student (Blomquist, 1985). This can be achieved in a number of ways. Any data supportive of achievement of learning objectives as specified in the student's learning plan can be incorporated into the evaluation. The use of student self-evaluation is also a student-centred strategy. To use self-evaluations effectively requires that students develop skill in self-evaluation and that teachers trust the judgements of students. Through the process of self-evaluation, students develop self-awareness, enhance self-esteem and increase their sense of professional development (Best *et al.* 1990).

Implications for faculty development

Changes in the roles of teachers and students are required if student-centred teaching strategies are to be effective. Students must be allowed and encouraged to move to self-directed learning while teachers must learn actions that facilitate independence on the part of students. Teachers need to 'let go', to see their role as assisting and facilitating the development within their students of the potential to be successful. The actions necessary for teachers are movement from roles of transmitter and authority figure to roles of model, guide and facilitator (Bevis and Watson, 1989; Grow, 1991). Faculty development is an essential feature of such a shift of focus. Strategies must be directed toward clarification and modification of the values and attitudes of the faculty as they adopt a new approach to education. They also need the knowledge and skills to assist learners to make the transition from teacher-centred to student-centred learners.

The establishment among the faculty of a philosophy of education that incorporates student-centred processes is essential if there is to be a successful transition from teacher-centred to student-centred teaching approaches. Specific faculty development activities could include reading and discussion of some of the recent literature such as that cited in this paper. In particular, reflection on personal values of education would be helpful (Miller and Seller, 1990; Schön, 1987). Workshops and training sessions on philosophy and practice of student-centred approaches should be presented (Rush *et al.* 1991).

Teachers must also learn about, and incorporate strategies that can help students become student-centred learners (see Grow, 1991; Pratt, 1988). Both Grow and Pratt identify that not all adult learners are self-directed and therefore willing and able to embrace student-centred strategies. Barrows (1984) offers a model for student development of the skills and confidence needed to increase control of their learning, and suggests that modelling is an effective first step, where the teacher models the desired behaviours. Coaching is a second activity, where students are actively engaged in dialogue about what they are observing, and how they are putting the data together. The process is more interactive with the teacher, and the learner is being coached in the processes of both patient care and interactive learning. The teacher becomes a facilitator and guide, as the student owns the ideas expressed. The teacher is also encouraging metacognition through this process: students are encouraged to think about thinking, to consider their questions and observations. The final stage suggested by Barrows is fading, where students begin to function on their own and the teacher is available to provide support and encouragement.

The support of administration is imperative (Rush *et al.* 1991). It is difficult if not impossible for teachers to make a shift from teacher-centred to student-centred approaches without the support of administration and other faculties. Changes in the administration's conception of teaching can be facilitated through discussion of teaching approaches. Often outside consultants are useful in such deliberations, since they bring a fresh perspective to a situation and may be seen as more knowledgeable (Rush *et al.* 1991).

Conclusion

This paper has presented the argument that more control of the clinical practice component of nursing education must be shared with students. Through more active participation in their learning, students would learn the skills and develop the qualities needed to function in a rapidly changing health care environment. Recent writings by experts in the field of curriculum development are encouraging such changes (Bevis and Watson, 1989; Lindeman, 1989), and schools of nursing are revising their curriculums to reflect these changing views (Programme Handbook, School of Nursing, McMaster University). Overall the need for such changes in nursing education are both feasible and essential as the expectations within nursing change, from an emphasis on the technically skilled individual whose role is to assist other members of the health care team, to that of a more independent practitioner skilled in the art as well as the science of nursing.

References

Barrows H (1984) A specific problem-based, self-directed method designed to teach problem-solving skills and enhance knowledge retention and recall. In: H G Schmidt, M L De Volder, (eds) *Tutorials in Problem-based Learning: New Directions for Training for the Health Professions.* Van Gorcum, Assen/Maastricht.

Best M, Carswell J B, Abbott S D (1990) Self-evaluation for nursing students. *Nursing Outlook* 38 (4): 172–177.

Bevis E O, Watson J (1989) *Toward a Caring Curriculum: A New Pedagogy for Nursing.* National League for Nursing, New York.

Blomquist K B (1985) Evaluation of students: Intuition is important. *Nurse Educator* 10 (6): 8–11.

Bondy K N (1984) Clinical evaluation of student performance: The effects of criteria on accuracy and reliability. *Research in Nursing and Health* 22 (9): 376–382.

DeYoung S (1990) *Teaching Nursing.* Addison-Wesley, Redwood City.

Edwards M, Baptiste S (1987) The occupational therapist as a clinical teacher. *Canadian Journal of Occupational Therapy* 54 (5): 249–255.

Grow G O (1991) Teaching learners to be self-directed. *Adult Education Quarterly* 41 (3): 125–149.

Knowles M (1986) *Using Learning Contracts.* Jossey-Bass, San Francisco.

Lindeman C A (1989) Clinical teaching: Paradoxes and paradigms. In: *Curriculum Revolution. Reconceptualising Nursing Education.* National League for Nursing, New York.

Miller J, Seller W (1990) *Curriculum: Perspectives and Practice.* Copp, Clark Pittman, Mississauga.

Pratt D D (1988) Androgogy as a relational construct. *Adult Education Quarterly* 38 (3): 160–181.

Programme Handbook, BScN Programme. McMaster University, Hamilton, Ontario.

Rush K L, Ouellet L L, Wasson D (1991) Faculty development: The essence of curriculum development. *Nurse Education Today* 11: 121–126.

Schön D A (1987) *Educating the Reflective Practitioner*. Jossey-Bass, San Francisco.

Stenhouse L (1975) *An Introduction to Curriculum Research and Development*. Heinemann, London.

Tower B, Majewski T (1987) Behaviorally based clinical evaluation. *Journal of Nursing Education* 26 (3): 120–123.

Woolley A S, Costello S E (1988) Innovations in clinical teaching. In: *Curriculum Revolution: Mandate for Change*. National League for Nursing, New York.

26. Situated Learning in the Practice Placement

Peter Cope, Philip Cuthbertson and Bernadette Stoddart

Nurses who had just completed their training in Scotland were interviewed with regard to their experiences on placements. The nurses had either completed a traditional training course or came from the first cohort of the Project 2000 diploma level course. The interviews focused on the way in which the student nurses had learned in their practice placements. The results suggest that the placement is a complex social and cognitive experience in which there are elements of situated learning. Acceptance into the community of practice is important but this can be separated, conceptually at least, into a social acceptance which might be extended to any student and a professional acceptance which relies on the display of appropriate competence. The nurses described the way in which their mentors had interacted with them in terms which suggested that cognitive apprenticeship strategies had been used to further their learning in practice. It is concluded that, in view of the central importance of the placement for training nurses, explicit use of mentoring techniques derived from situated learning and cognitive apprenticeship might be beneficial.

Introduction

Background

Critical for the maintenance of a profession such as nursing is a pre-service education programme which recognizes the complexities of professional practice. Such a programme must prepare students to operate in the face of the daily practical challenges of nursing while ensuring that the necessary skills are underpinned by a well-developed knowledge base. The problem is that it is far from clear how this can be achieved, partly because the relationship between practical skills and the so-called underpinning knowledge is not well understood. There is a basic and familiar divide, which has been made many times, in the distinction between 'knowing how' and 'knowing that'. However, the relationship between practical knowledge and higher-order knowledge is not well understood (Ohlsson 1994). In the United Kingdom (UK) the reforms of nurse education stemming from Project 2000 have sought to increase the emphasis on higher-order knowledge (United Kingdom Central Council for Nursing, Midwifery and Health Visiting 1986). Recent institutional restructuring has also meant that nurse education is now located within the higher education (HE) context. Professional education courses recognize the need for higher-order learning and require students to demonstrate its acquisition. However, difficulties in making connections between the theory, which is the focus of the higher education institution, and the practice, which takes place in clinical areas, have long been a feature of professional nurse education and training (Hislop *et al.* 1996). It is certainly the case that higher-order learning does not necessarily lead to competence

Peter Cope, Philip Cuthbertson and Bernadette Stoddart: 'Situated Learning in the Practice Placement' in *JOURNAL OF ADVANCED NURSING* (2000), 31 (4), pp. 850–856.

in practice and it has long been recognized that being knowledgeable is not, of itself, sufficient for expertise. There are many reasons why knowledge may remain 'inert' so that it does not support appropriate action in practice. Bransford *et al.* (1989) discuss some of the shortcomings which higher-order learning may display when action is required. Students may, for example, be perfectly aware that particular symptoms indicate a particular diagnosis but may be unable to recognize them in a real situation. The combination of knowledge and skill implied in Project 2000's 'knowledgeable doer' is not a trivial aspiration.

The community of practice

It is now widely accepted (Dreyfus and Dreyfus 1986, Berliner 1988) that experts do not operate by following rules derived from higher-order knowledge but rather, by using complex situational understanding, a mature and practised dexterity which comes from their breadth and depth of experience. Much of their expertise is directed to dealing with the contextually-bound demands of the situation which cannot be accounted for by context-independent technical-rational models. There has been considerable attention devoted to the tacit nature of this understanding and to the difficulty of making expert behaviour explicit, either by external observation or by introspective analysis by experts. The key to the development of skills of this nature is practice in authentic contexts. It is only in such contexts that novice practitioners can learn to interpret situations and to deal with them effectively.

Recent research (Lave and Wenger 1991) has underpinned the central place of this type of exposure but has also pointed out that becoming proficient is as much to do with joining a culture of practitioners as it is of becoming technically skilled in some fashion. Lave and Wenger emphasize that learning in practice is a matter of acculturation, of joining a community of practice, rather than the application of skills or principles which operate independently of social context. A critical part of this socialization into practice is the opportunity to make an authentic contribution to the communal enterprise. Since novices are not sufficiently skilled to play a central role, they are given tasks to complete which are peripheral but authentic to the activity. This process has been termed *legitimate peripheral participation* (Lave and Wenger, 1991) and is considered to be a crucial aspect of eventual success.

Cognitive apprenticeship

One of the features of learning in a practice context is that experts are able to guide novices through the complexities of practice. Brown *et al.* (1988) have further developed the concept of situated learning by analysing the way in which novices learn from experts. This is a form of apprenticeship which Brown *et al.* are at pains to distinguish from crude notions of 'sitting with Nellie'. By emphasizing the way in which the expert can focus the learner's attention towards the salient cognitive features of the activity in question, they conclude that learning in practice can, in some circumstances, be described as a cognitive apprenticeship. Their analysis leads them to describe strategies which can be employed to support novices as they develop their competence. These include modelling, coaching, scaffolding, fading, articulation, reflection and exploration.

Modelling involves the demonstration of particular aspects of practice by the expert, whilst drawing attention, where appropriate, to the key features of the successful completion of the activity. One of the defining characteristics of the *cognitive* apprenticeship is that it is one in which experts make their situational knowledge explicit as they coach the learner. Coaching involves the provision of feedback on the learner's performance, often making use of the Vygotskian (Tharp and Gallimore 1988) notions of scaffolding and fading by which novices are supported in the completion of tasks which they would be unable to achieve without help. As they become more competent and confident, the expert withdraws (fades) the support (scaffolding) in such a way as to transfer the responsibility for the task to the learner. As the novices increase in confidence and competence, they can be encouraged to use more advanced strategies such as articulation, reflection and exploration. Articulation requires learners to make explicit their understanding of practice while reflection is a process of comparison between their competence and that of the expert. Once the learner is operating with a secure competence, they can be asked to consider alternative approaches to the practical problems which they face in a process of exploration. Arguably it is these types of activity to which mentors might aspire when they are supervizing and instructing students on placements.

In nurse education, therefore, we might expect to see that placements involve several key processes, some of which are not emphasized by current training programmers. Practice placements represent the interface between the theoretical perspectives presented in the college components of the course and the realities of practice. Ideally they should provide students with the opportunity to place some of their learning into an appropriate context and to deepen its meaning accordingly. However, placements are complex social contexts and students have to succeed in joining and being accepted by the community of practice. Part of this process, and a crucial aspect of students' learning, is the capacity to learn from established members of the community. We might, therefore, expect students to describe features of the community of practice and their acceptance (or otherwise) within it and we might also expect them to report that their mentors used at least some of the strategies represented in the cognitive apprenticeship mode.

This study examines students' perceptions of these processes and was part of an internal research project aimed at examining the placement experiences of students trained in a Scottish college of nursing. Some of these students had completed a Project 2000 programme and others had been through the traditional version of the course which preceded Project 2000.

One of the features of the Project 2000 course is the increased emphasis on theory, with a corresponding decrease in the emphasis on placement. The pre-Project 2000 course devoted around 20% of its time to theoretical input from the college (28 weeks) and 80% to placements (118 weeks). Around 40% (58 weeks) of the Project 2000 course was spent on college input and 60% (88 weeks) on placements. Although both courses are heavily weighted towards placement, there has been a significant change in the weighting since the introduction of the new course.

The study

Methodology

The study was constructed as an analysis of the experiences of students in Scotland who had recently completed the last course established under the auspices of the 1982 curriculum (82 group) and students who were completing the first Project 2000 course 1992 curriculum (92 group). A random sample of 10% of each cohort was selected by using student registration numbers to give 11 from the 82 scheme and 19 from the Project 2000 scheme. Semi-structured interviews were carried out with the Project 2000 group during the final week before completion of the course and over a period of 4 weeks with members of the 1982 scheme. The latter was protracted because of problems with recall of the group who had qualified the previous year.

The content of the questionnaire used in the interviews was established by identifying areas of the curriculum that had significantly changed with the change in programmes. For example, the variation in practice placement, the increase in the involvement of other subject matter from an increasingly wide range of disciplines, and the perceived theory–practice gap. Interviews were carried out by two researchers who were on the lecturing staff of the college. However, the lecturers had neither pastoral nor direct teaching responsibilities for the students whom they interviewed. This paper reports on the section of the interview which dealt with the practice placement and difficulties with theory and practice. All interviews were tape-recorded and transcribed. Confidentiality was seen as vital to the process of complete disclosure and ensured by allocating numbers to students in order to ensure anonymity in transcription and analysis.

Data were examined for emerging categories which were informed by theoretical perspectives derived from situated learning theory (Brown *et al.* 1988, Lave and Wenger, 1991). To ensure inter-researcher reliability each transcript was examined by two people and the emerging categories were confirmed by comparison of findings. Each category was discussed by the team and its inclusion was confirmed by agreement upon the validity of observation and by consideration of the reliability of the data.

Results

Differences between the two courses

One of the striking aspects of the results was the similarity of the responses of each group as they described their placements. The only way in which the two groups appeared to differ was in the more frequent reporting of induction difficulties caused by short placements among the 92 group. It may be that there were fine-grained distinctions that were not picked up by this research but both groups talked about similar experiences in terms of the acceptance into the community of the placement, the way in which their learning was contextualized by the experience, and the support which they received from the practitioners with whom they worked. This is understandable since the placements were still the most significant component of each course, both in terms of time and in terms of student perception.

Three significant themes emerged from the analysis, joining the community of practice, the contexualization of learning and the support of learning in practice.

Joining the community of practice

There were clear examples of the beginnings of successful incorporation into the community of practice among both groups of students. This was most commonly expressed as being accepted as part of a team:

> Well, I think what made the difference was, you were right in there, you were one of the team, you know, you really got your work to do... (92 group)

However, it also included references to participation in authentic professional activity. For example:

> ... when I got to the ward I got on well with staff and within, you know, your settling down period and then you were given more responsibility... and it was a case of 'Well, you were getting that way because we feel you are able to deal with it'. So as the weeks went on you felt as though you were getting somewhere and that you were obviously doing a good job otherwise you would not get the responsibility. (82 group)

There was often a sense of 'earning' the acceptance by demonstrating competence where, as in this example, there is a clear indication that the community was increasing the responsibility delegated to the student as confidence in competence increased.

Although students had to earn the right to be given real responsibility, social incorporation into the team was something which could happen from the start of the placement if the staff involved felt that it was important:

> Part of the team. I felt from like day one as soon as you went in you were included in what was happening, and you were informed in everything that was going on .... (92 group)

This suggests that there is a distinction to be made between social acceptance, which is clearly important to the students, but which may be granted before competence has been demonstrated, and a sense of professional incorporation. Professional acceptance requires a basic familiarity with the context of the placement, confidence in one's own capability within the context and acceptance by the professionals themselves. This latter has to be earned by working in the community and gradually building up professional trust. In practice, however, these aspects of acceptance were often bound up with one another. Social inclusion could ease familiarization and could increase the student's confidence so that they were more likely to show the competence required for professional acceptance. If there was a personal or social difficulty at the start of the placement, it tended to be associated with professional problems. These were reported by the students as being a deficit on the part of the community itself, although it has to be borne in mind that there would be two sides to stories of this nature.

> ... one of the wards I went to in the second half of my training had a bad name amongst students in the way they were treated ... I always went into everywhere with an open mind but two or three of the staff, and it was actually those who were mentors, were like "do this, do that." If you questioned them it was like "You should know that". [82 group]

However, another reason for the lack of this sense of membership was that the placement could be too short to allow a successful induction to take place so that there was no time to build up familiarity with the context and no time to become professionally incorporated:

> ... I think you are only starting to settle in and get to know where everything is and knowing the staff, and then you were away again, you didn't really have time to learn too much. (92 group)

Although this was reported by some members of the 82 group, it was more common in the 92 group, presumably because of the greater prevalence of short placements in the early part of the training. The supernumerary status of the students may have contributed to this feeling of marginalization:

> ... placements for the university going out one day a week was a bit hard going. You could never fit in anywhere, you never felt as though you were part of the team, working with anyone. You always felt an odd carrot. (92 group)

This contrasts vividly with descriptions of the feeling of empowerment which derived from the sense of legitimate participation in authentic placement activity: 'I felt like a nurse for the first time, I was going in and getting so much experience because I had my own ten patients' (82 group).

The contextualization of learning

The inert nature of theoretical knowledge was something which many of the students felt keenly and there were many examples of students reporting that their theoretical knowledge seemed neither sufficient nor appropriate for the practicalities of placements:

> I felt [that] the academic side of things were concentrated on [in the college], and not actual nursing... I left 'Well right, I can write an essay, but don't ask me to do anything to these patients, because I haven't clue what I'm doing here'. (92)

However, one of the clear effects of the placement was to place learning into a meaningful context. This was partly because the placement often seemed to give knowledge a personal rather than, or in addition to, an objective slant:

> You could really understand, you knew that a patient was suffering from schizophrenia before but that was sort of it. As a student you had already been taught the signs and symptoms to look out for when somebody's mental state had deteriorated. You could actually see it happening and understood why and you know how to try and prevent it. (82)

However, it was also clear that the placement could have the effect of putting knowledge into a context which had powerful situating effects on its meaning:

> ... so you really felt that everything was clicking into place and you were understanding what you were doing and why you were doing it. (92)

This re-contextualization of knowledge did not appear to be a straightforward, linear process in which theory learned in the college was contextualized in the placement. Rather there was evidence that, for some students at least, there was a cyclical process in which knowledge from the theoretical components of the course was situated in a context arising from the placement. This contextualization then stimulated re-examination of the theoretical basis of the knowledge. Sometimes this cycle was encouraged by the mentor as part of a variety of strategies for learning:

> ... she showed me what to do, and I learned from that, or she would give me books or show me the right direction, or she would talk me through...'. (92)

However, sometimes this strategy was perceived as cheating in some way and as not an authentic aspect of membership of the community of practice:

> I used to hide my bag, separate from other peoples' bags, so that if necessary I could run back and refer to various books and pieces... I was expecting to be intimidated, to forget things... getting away with it [i.e. using the book] made me feel bad. (82)

It seems to us that, far from cheating, this represents a sophisticated strategy for incremental construction and contextualization of knowledge and one which could be emphasized by both the college and the practice community.

The support of learning in practice

The support for learning provided by the placement community was often described in terms which fit the cognitive apprenticeship model described by Brown *et al.* (1988). Learners were coached by mentors who modelled good practice and who provided appropriate but progressively withdrawn support. The following succinct description of how learning took place encapsulates this model:

> ... just by doing it really, watching, and then doing it myself, or after my mentor watching me, seeing that I was doing it right, and then after I had done it once or twice I was left ... . (92 group)

Scaffolding learners means providing them with sufficient support to allow them to achieve more than they would be able to without help. As the competence of the learner increases, the support is withdrawn in such a way as to pass responsibility over to the learner. In this way, learners are able to move towards independent competence in areas where they initially needed help:

> Well they showed me the ropes, expanded a little on what I learned in theory, well a large bit of what I learned in theory, let me get my hands on, as soon as they noticed I was gaining confidence, they let me build up my own confidence and work away on my own pretty quickly. (82 group)

One aspect of scaffolding provision involved being present and ready to step in should anything unexpected occur:

> I was able to do them [tasks], but whether that was because you knew there was a staff nurse there beside you, that there couldn't be any major problems because there was somebody there to take over. It might have been a different ball game if you had been on your own. (92 group)

Sometimes the mentor would take the novice through a 'dry-run' before letting them perform an authentic technique:

> There was one point that I had to do an aseptic technique at X, and the staff nurse said 'Come in with me, try it on me first before we do it to this man'. (92 group)

Scaffolding also took the form of directing the student's attention to features of the case which they had not noticed, and which enabled them to focus on the relevant theoretical knowledge:

> 'Have you had a look at his feet?' 'No, I never thought about his feet.' 'Well have a look at his feet.' You know, and you realise the guy's got circulation problems or whatever. (92 group)

There were also examples of the more advanced learning strategies described by Brown *et al.* For example, students' contextualization of knowledge often involved a conscious process of reflection:

> It wasn't till then that I thought 'This patient's got renal failure', and I had just studied renal failure, and 1 started looking for the symptoms, and sort of thinking, 'Why am I doing this, why is the patient getting this?' (92 group)

Discussion

It is unsurprising to find a strong student endorsement of the central nature of placements in their sense of becoming competent nurses. The uneasy relationship between the college and practical components of the course was also an aspect of the work which was anticipated. Students' reports provide support for the importance of recognizing placements as a social as well as a technical context and for the significance of becoming accepted into the culture of the workplace. Becoming a nurse is about joining the community of practice represented by qualified nurses as much as it is about learning the technicalities of nursing. The fact that this was a feature of both the 82 and the 92 group confirms that this has long been a priority of student nurses on placements. However, it is one which is rarely taken into account formally in course planning or curriculum development. Students require social support and reassurance when they start a new placement. There may be feelings of vulnerability associated with starting in a new social and professional context which will be amplified by novice status. Some of these are due to the problems that any newcomer would face, such as not knowing where things are, being unfamiliar with routines, having to interact with a number of strangers, etc. However, these are compounded by the lack of practical competence which characterizes novices and which is the very thing which the placement is designed to overcome.

Hay (1993) has pointed out that novices are not automatically incorporated into communities of practice and that marginalization and isolation may result when newcomers are rejected, for whatever reason. There were examples of such isolation in this study, where novices did not feel that they had been accepted as legitimate members of the community. Short placements, which are not unusual in the common foundation programme in the Project 2000 course, clearly make it difficult for students to play anything but an observer's role. It is easy to ignore the fact that such a role might be socially as well as intellectually challenging and that the lack of authenticity in the students' roles might provide an obstacle to effective learning. Although we have no evidence for it in this study, it is interesting to speculate that the supernumerary status of students might not be as unequivocally beneficial as might first appear since, theoretically at least, it may remove them one place from genuine membership of the culture of nursing. However, it is equally clear that being part of the workforce is not in itself a guarantee of an easy passage into the community. Cahill (1996), for example, describes the problems experienced by student nurses on a pre-project 2000 course where the perceived importance of fitting into the ward led them to tolerate less than ideal learning conditions. Students could end up 'doing all the work with little support' (Cahill 1996 p. 796) and feel powerless to protest for fear of provoking an unsatisfactory ward report. The need for students to join the community of practice appears to be ubiquitous. Cahill's account warns us that it may, in some circumstances, result in exploitation.

However, it is clear from the current study that mentors do provide support to students and that they use the types of strategies described by Brown *et al.* (1988). There was plenty of evidence of modelling and coaching, involving careful support which was often withdrawn in highly effective and sensitive ways so as to increase the independence and competence of the learner. Students need professional support which is geared to their competence and which provides them with appropriate scaffolding to allow them to try out techniques which are at the limits of their current capacity. However, fading is necessary to transfer the onus to them in a controlled fashion so that they move through the zone of proximal development towards independent competence. What is interesting is that most mentors are likely to be performing this type of support role in an implicit fashion. It seems improbable that mentors have an explicit strategy for such support, or at least that they are aware that in behaving in this way they are exemplifying Vygotsky's theories of learning (see, for example, Moll 1990). Studies have repeatedly referred to the problems of definition of mentoring in nurse education. Burnard (1990) suggests that in the absence of clear definitions the terms preceptor and mentor are often used interchangeably and that they may encourage a 'sitting with Nellie' approach to learning. The strategies we have reported above do, at least provide 'Nellie' with a rationale for her approach to the business of mentoring.

One of the main conclusions of this paper is that this knowledge, i.e. the contribution of the expert, can be passed on by situating knowledge in authentic contexts and by utilization of cognitive apprenticeship techniques. It is clear that placements have some of the characteristics of a community of practice as far as the students are concerned. This is recognized in other studies of mentoring. Wright (1990), for example, found that factor analysis of student nurse responses to an evaluation of their experience of mentoring produced four factors, two of which, socialization into the work role and professional role acquisition, fit well with the community of practice interpretation.

Much of the learning of the students in the current study appears to take place by the strategies described by Brown *et al.* We would argue that a step forward in the design of nurse education programmes would be to recognize these fundamental features of placements and to capitalize on them to maximize student learning. Mentors would benefit from knowing the importance of social and professional incorporation of students and the difference between them. It would also help if they were aware of the types of strategy available to them to enhance student learning, many of which they may already be employing. Whilst this would not provide a definition of mentoring as such, it would provide an opportunity to systematize and rationale mentoring practice. Students would gain from a similar knowledge of the nature of placements so that they could prepare themselves for the social induction which is necessary at the start. Placement experience and learning remain a fundamental aspect of nurse training and understanding their nature is a crucial step towards improving their effectiveness.

References

Berliner D (1988) *The Development of Expertise in Pedagogy*. American Association of Colleges for Teacher Education, Washington DC.

Brown J S, Collins A, Duguid P (1988) *Situated Cognition and the Culture of Learning*. Tech. Rep. No. IRL 88–0088. Institute for Research on Learning, Palo Alto.

Bransford J D, Franks J J, Vye N J, Sherwood R D (1989) New approaches to instruction: because wisdom can't be told. In: S Vosniadou, A Ortony (eds) *Similarity and Analogical Reasoning*, pp. 470–497. Cambridge University Press, New York.

Burnard P (1990) The student experience: adult learning and mentorship revisited. *Nurse Education Today* 10: 349–354.

Cahill H A (1996) A qualitative analysis of student nurses' experiences of rrientorship. *Journal of Advanced Nursing* 24: 791–799.

Dreyfus H L, Dreyfus S E (1986) *Mind Over Machine: The Power of Human Intuition and Expertise in the* Era *of the Computer*. Blackwell, Oxford.

Hay K (1993) Legitimate peripheral participation, instructionism, and constructivism: whose situation is it anyway? *Educational-Technology* 33: 33–38.

Hislop S, Inglis B, Cope P, Stoddart B, McIntosh C (1996) Situation theory in practice: student views of theory-practice in Project 2000. *Journal of Advanced Nursing* 23: 171–177.

Lave J, Wenger E (1991) *Situated Learning: Legitimate Peripheral Participation*. Cambridge University Press, New York.

Moll L C (1990) *Vygotsky and Education: Instructional Implications and Applications of Sociohistorical Psychology*. Cambridge University Press, Cambridge.

Ohlsson S (1994) Learning to do and learning to understand; a lesson and challenge for cognitive modelling. In: P Reimann, H Spada (eds) *Learning in Humans and Machines: Towards an Interdisciplinary Learning Science*, pp. 37–62. Elsevier Science, Oxford.

Tharp R, Gallimore R (1988) *Rousing Minds to Life: Teaching Learning and Schooling in Social Context.* Cambridge University Press, New York.

United Kingdom Central Council for Nursing, Midwifery and Health Visiting (1986) *Project 2000: A New Preparation for Practice.* UKCC, London.

Wright C M (1990) An innovation in a diploma programme: the future potential of mentorship in nursing. *Nurse Education Today* 10: 355–359.

27. A New Paradigm for Practice Education

Cynthia B. Edmond

This paper explores the complex nature of professional practice. It suggests that educating for all practice disciplines is about to undergo a paradigm shift whereby the value of practical education and experience will be better understood, more rigorously analyzed and integrated with propositional knowledge in the construction of personal professional knowledge and identity. It relates this cross-disciplinary position to the present problems of skills deficits which are evident in nurses at the point of registration and demonstrates how routinization and internalization of process and tacit knowledge can create problems for students and newly qualified staff nurses. It also suggests how this can be addressed. It discusses the present culture of 'clinical education by default', unavailability of mentors and resources, and general lack of formal collaborative structures between education and service institutions and suggests that the present system cannot sustain the complex demands, expectations and pace of the clinical context and the evolution of nursing practice. Clinical credibility is an issue as is the current heavy clinical workload of staff nurse mentors, and several collaborative clinical education models are outlined which ensure that staff nurses or resident clinical educators are available and can make clinical teaching their priority. History and the present crisis in nursing suggest that there is a case for mandatory collaborative education/service structures to ensure adequate funding and to monitor the effectiveness of selected models so that staff nurse mentors can work with lecturer colleagues to articulate and teach the complexities of clinical practice through related research. It is predicted that this collaborative approach is capable of addressing both the skills deficits and the wider intellectual challenge of developing a new paradigm of practice education and providing an integrated base for continuing professional development.

Introduction

> Practice requires integration of thinking, feeling and doing, focusing on performance and judgement in handling many variables and many levels of problem . . . Clinical work has not (yet) been seen as a practical discipline of communication; perception, strategies, judgements, decisions and actions worth studying in its own right. Practice is many orders more complex than laboratory science as it works with soft data. The intellectual challenge is to develop a new paradigm of practice as a more logically and quantitatively rigorous discipline which integrates the intuitions learned from experience using the perceptual parallel processing, 'right brain' with the logical reasoning of the verbal, numerical, sequential processing, 'left' brain. (Cox 1997, p. 268)

Cynthia B. Edmond: 'A New Paradigm for Practice Education' in *NURSE EDUCATION TODAY* (2001), 21, pp. 251–259.

In discussing the need for a more rigorous approach to practical clinical education, Cox (1997) focuses on a critical issue that impacts on medicine and other practice disciplines in which prevailing educational norms put the emphasis on academic achievement as preparation for practice. Certainly this is the case in UK nursing, where practical clinical experience has been devalued to the point that there are very few formal structures and even fewer resources devoted to it. But as the current crisis in recruitment and retention in nursing forces educators and service providers to look more critically at preparation for practice, there 'is a resurgence of interest in the educational value of practice and how 'real nursing' experience can be more effectively employed in the overall education of students at both pre- and post-registration levels' (Birchenall 1999, p. 173).

This paper takes a provocative stance in attempting to address two main issues which impact on both the student and the newly qualified staff nurse; first and foremost in exploring the nature of professional practice itself and evidence for the primacy of practical clinical education and experience; and secondly in asking where the responsibility lies for clinical nurse education and what can be done to ensure that students are provided with appropriate clinical experience.

Several studies relating to Project 2000 provide evidence of deficits in performance of practical clinical and work management skills in nurses at the point of registration (May *et al.* 1992, Luker *et al.* 1996, Runciman *et al.* 1998, Gilmour 1999). Although there are many strengths in the present system of initial education as a basis for professional practice, the indications are that students do need more and improved, practical clinical experience; a position that was confirmed by the UKCC Commission for Nursing and Midwifery Education Report and Recommendations regarding *Fitness for Practice* (1999).

Most of the studies cited above have identified the fact that staff nurse mentors and preceptors carry unrealistically heavy clinical work loads which leave them little time for teaching. This situation is compounded by lack of strategic management of the practice role of lecturer/teachers and increasing demands of academia on their time. Aston *et al.* (2000) found evidence both from the literature and their own study that lecturers placed little formal value on their clinical practice role and had difficulties in fulfilling it. They were generally unprepared, unsupported and unmonitored so that students were left largely unsupported during clinical placements.

However, the problems go beyond availability of clinical teachers and originate in a basic misunderstanding of the nature of practice itself and the knowledge, skills and performance 'know how' that make up professional practice.

The nature of professional practice

The cross-disciplinary perspective

A cross-disciplinary analysis by Eraut (1999) which looks at developing professional knowledge and competence, suggests that for most practice disciplines there is an overemphasis on theory and neglect of structures and opportunities for integrated practical experience for students 'in spite of increasing evidence that the frontloading of theory is extremely inefficient' (p. 12). Certainly there appears to be a general misunderstanding on the part of curriculum developers about the essential nature of practical education and experience, and a tendency to disregard the importance of the practice context because of an assumption that it is easily 'picked up' once the individual is qualified.

There is increasing evidence from the social and biological sciences of interactive pathways and dynamic learning capabilities being developed during immersion in practice. The study of artificial intelligence and robotics, in discovering what robots *cannot do,* continues to illuminate the intricacies, perceptual wholeness and dynamic nature of human learning and capability (Clancy 1997, Sternberg 1994).

Eraut (1999) discusses the different kinds of knowledge that make up professional expertise propositional, process and tacit – and recommends that: 'Process knowledge must be given a high priority in both academic and practice settings but without neglecting the contribution of propositional knowledge to the process' (p. 120). The complexities of process knowledge which he defines as, 'essentially knowledge of how to do things and how to get things done', relates to the social context and perceptual wholeness that characterizes a practice discipline and he emphasizes that, 'it is dangerous to cultivate the notion of disembodied skills that exist independently of context and purpose. . . (because) possessing skills . . . is only one aspect of process knowledge. One also needs to know when and how to use them' (p. 94).

This knowing 'when' and 'how' is learned through integration and application of propositional knowledge and repeated experience in interpreting practice situations, responding appropriately and reflecting on feedback, and logically can only take place in the social context of the practice setting. It also involves perceptual wholeness which uses all the bodily senses together with pre-conscious learning to create 'the habitual skilled body' with its capacity to respond to situations automatically, as described by Benner and Wrubel (1989).

The educational position is that through the perceptual wholeness of experience and feedback from each clinical interaction, every kind of knowledge is continually integrated, constructed, deconstructed and reconstructed to become personal professional expertise and to build professional identity through increasing knowledge and competence (Chaklin and Lave 1996, Clancy 1997, Birchenall 1999, Cox 1997, Eraut 1999, Jarvis 1999). Cox (1997) also emphasizes the human and social characteristics that permeate each activity in a practice discipline 'the communication, the perceptual, reasoning and management skills, and the ethical, behavioral base of professional practice. . . ' (pp. 266–267).

The nursing perspective

As both the reality of nursing practice and employers' expectations require nurses to be accountable practitioners at the point of registration, it is timely to acknowledge the importance of clinical education and to redesign pre-registration practical experience to meet both educational and service expectations.

> Learning to learn in and from practice needs to form part of the initial curriculum. Practice is the basis not only of our reflective learning, but also the basis on which we construct our own theory. Naturally this involves changing the emphasis in initial preparation and having more

> teacher/lecturer practitioners, and more mentors and preceptors . . . and placing a great deal more emphasis on their role. (Jarvis 1999, p. 272)

Context and work-based learning

Learning to interact with, and to manage the clinical context in all its complexity is a major factor in nursing practice, but one that is constantly overlooked even by nurses themselves as they master and internalize each stage of their own professional development. Benner (1984), in articulating what nurses actually 'do', illustrated some of the complex interactive skills that all too frequently go unrecognized; skills that demonstrate complete mastery of contextual and situational variables as well as technical and intellectual competence. This responsiveness to situational variables that is underpinned by ethical and human qualities is precisely what differentiates nursing from technical and procedural care that could be carried out by robots. Nursing is situational and much of the knowledge needed to practise effectively is situated in practice itself (Benner and Wrubel 1989). The ability to 'read' a particular situation whilst at the same time monitoring all other patient-related activities, and to interpret the subtle signs of psychosocial needs and know when and how to respond appropriately, can only be constructed through repeated experience in the practice setting.

A key issue, therefore, is to try to understand how best we can 'get at' the 'knowledge embedded in clinical practice' (Benner 1984). Is it enough just to provide longer practical placements in the hope that 'something will rub off' or is there more to it? We could start by questioning the degree of 'reality shock' (Kramer 1977) and skills deficits associated with the transition from student to staff nurse. Why does this continue to be so significant when students have spent 3 or 4 years preparing for the role, 50% of which time has been spent in practice placements? Birchenall (1999) suggests that, 'work-based learning . . . is intended to capture the essence of workplace activity as the principal resource for learning. . . ' (p. 173); but it would appear that, although newly qualified nurses may have strengths in other areas, the 'essence of workplace activity' has escaped a significant number of them.

The staff nurse role and the clinical context

Much of what nursing students and beginning practitioners need to know is hidden in the day-to-day activity of 'nursing'.

The newly qualified nurse must move into a complex and turbulent service context where social and economic constraints create instability, heavy workloads and stressful working conditions. Where the pace is so fast that a thorough grasp of the clinical context is essential in order to carry out normal nursing duties. Although deficits in some discrete clinical skills may cause some anxiety as indicated by the studies cited above, the author's current doctoral research indicates that by far the most overwhelming concern newly qualified nurses have, is to do with co-ordinating and managing the multiple activities of a normal shift workload and bringing the shift to a meaningful conclusion. This involves what most experienced nurses describe cryptically as 'the basics', 'putting it all together' and 'knowing the routine and getting the work done'. What appears to be missing in the newly qualified nurse is an overall ability to manage the clinical and situational context – in other words, the process and tacit knowledge which is dependent on interactive practical experience (Edmond in progress).

Managing the workload – the 'invisible' role of the staff nurse

The fact that nurses do manage and coordinate all multidisciplinary patient-related activities simultaneously, as well as performing discrete nursing procedures, is seldom acknowledged even by themselves because of the complexity and 'taken for granted nature' of its many components. Nursing is not a linear process like many other types of work, where one discrete job follows another in sequence. It is multi-linear in that there are multiple activities going on at the same time which relate to several patients and staff, and the nurse must monitor and progress them all at the same time. It is a composite skill that once it is mastered, is internalized and becomes so automatic to them, that it is invisible and usually referred to only in the most cryptic terms. Yet, it is 'what nurses do'. It also relates to what they consider to be 'the basics', 'the routine', 'putting it all together' and 'getting things done' and it is descriptive of a major part of the complex work management role of the staff nurse. The more experienced a nurse is, the more she tends to use cryptic language to communicate with colleagues, which only makes sense when they too have a range of experience and a deep understanding of the specific context in which the communication occurs, so that the meaning is mutually understood (Benner 1984, Eraut 1999).

Internalizing a theory of action

Developing routines and decision habits

The 'invisibility' of the work management role of the staff nurse is an example of the human tendency to condense and internalize complex descriptions, meanings and performance patterns in everyday life in order to avoid perceptual overload and be free to focus attention on actual situational priorities. This cross-disciplinary point is supported by Eraut (1999) who, in discussing the practice discipline of teaching, says:

> There are too many variables to take into account at once, so people develop routines and decision habits to keep mental effort at a reasonable level. This evolution and internalisation of theory of action is one aspect of learning to become a teacher and coping in the classroom. (p. 31)
>
> Eraut also explains that: . . . gradual routinization . . . is necessary for them to be able to cope with what would otherwise be a highly stressful situation with continuing 'information overload'. . . (it) is a natural process . . . responsible for increased efficiency . . . .(p. 111)

This can easily be applied to nursing where complex interactions occur at a rapid rate and where speed and accuracy must underpin situational demands. The staff nurse who has been in post for 12 months or more has completely internalized the interactive work-management role and can work quickly from that routinized base; but the novice coming into post must first be made aware of the components and activities involved in the role, then learn how to interact with the context and 'put the basics together' before her personal internalization process can begin. The ability to manage work efficiently is only conspicuous by its absence as in the case of the novice or, to a lesser extent, any newcomer to a specific clinical environment, because of the context-specific nature of the skills required to do so (Benner 1984).

Articulating and teaching the work management role

Articulating the components of the staff nurse role

The challenge is to identify and articulate the 'taken-for-granted' components of the staff nurse role so that they are visible and more easily learned. A pilot study (Edmond 1998) which used a critical pathway in order to develop the interactive work management role of the newly qualified staff nurse during orientation has shown promising results. This critical pathway provides a dynamic framework which derives from an analysis of clinical context and articulates the components of the staff nurse role. It is adaptable to different clinical contexts in that the components can be expanded by context-specific activities and criterion referenced learning contracts to provide an interactive tool for learning to coordinate and manage the staff nurse role in each clinical context (Kinkade 1992, Lohrman and Kinkade 1992, Evers *et al.* 1994).

Aston *et al.* (2000) make the point that, although lecturers could be expected to demonstrate discrete clinical procedures they would 'not be expected to manage the ward' (p. 184). This is predictable because managing and coordinating ward activities is a context-specific skill that demands peer group acceptance and intimate knowledge of context and team activities. Logically then, the staff nurse mentor is the best person to teach work-management skills through role modelling and discussion, and should be given the time and the tools to do so.

It is proposed that tools such as the critical pathway could be used with students as well as with newly qualified nurses in order to encourage early analysis of clinical context. These tools could also be used to raise awareness of the structures and processes embedded in professional practice, so that by the point of registration they have developed learning sets and have internalized dynamic theories of action for dealing with clinical reality. This should go some way to reducing the 'reality shock' of role transition. Early guided immersion in the reality of the clinical practice world would also encourage development of social and corporate responsibility and a sense of belonging, as well as personal professional identity (Eraut 1999).

Birchenall (1999) supports the idea of a 'reappraisal of the stage at which pre-registration students should be exposed to practice because there is a growing realization that people enter nursing to nurse and not necessarily to sit through interminable lectures without any extended reference points to the client group' . . . (he continues).. . 'if the work-based philosophy is rejected . . . we serve only to deny practitioners the opportunity to become truly immersed in their craft . . . thus stunting professional and personal growth and decreasing an understanding of organizational development' (p. 173).

Availability of clinically credible teachers/mentors

The pivotal issue for the majority of clinical areas though is that they cannot guarantee availability of staff nurse mentors and preceptors because of heavy workloads; and there is an urgent need to address the issue and to place a great deal more emphasis on their role (Morton-Cooper and Palmer 1993, Jarvis and Gibson 1997, Jarvis 1999). Research suggests that the staff nurse is the best person for this role, because of clinical credibility and acceptance by the clinical team. However, a staff nurse taking on this responsibility should either take a reduced work load or work 'off-line' and be temporarily seconded to the University, in order to be primarily available for teaching and working alongside students and preceptees. Such posts should ideally be funded jointly by education institutions and service providers (Davies *et al.* 1999).

The evidence is that because the acquisition of clinical skills is context dependent and the ability to apply knowledge and perform competently is dependent on familiarity with the specific clinical context, this can be achieved more easily where there is initial close linking between the mentor and the student, and optimizing of learning opportunities (Benner 1984, Steinaker and Bell 1979, Hinchliff 1992, Davies *et al.* 1999). It also relates to the perceptual wholeness of interactive learning opportunities and situated cognition, which claims that learning is occurring with every human behaviour and that human knowledge is located in physical interaction and social participation (Clancy 1997, p. 344). Therefore, the success of any approach to practical education depends on tackling the major problem of availability of mentors or clinical educators and provision of appropriate structures and resources to ensure that they have the time, the tools and the training to provide quality practical education and experience.

Collaborative education/service structures for practical education

The expressed need for more and improved practical clinical education for students

The recommendations of the *Fitness for Practice* (UKCC 1999) document and the prevailing Government strategy for an increase in nursing recruitment and for more practical experience for students, were made in response to evidence of deficits in practical and work management skills at the point of registration and student dissatisfaction with their practice placements. It is timely, therefore, to consider the current emergent interest in the value of practical education in all the practice disciplines and in light of the evidence to extend and improve student nurse practice education and experience.

Interpretation of the cross-disciplinary literature regarding the complex dimensions of professional practice, together with nurses' common lived experience, is consistent with the recommendations of the *Fitness for Practice* document, regarding the need to adopt a more comprehensive and rigorous approach to practical clinical education and review pre-registration curricula.

The report recognizes that early and extended clinical experience and active and well-supported participation in client care is vital for learning the nuances of professional practice skills, which is consistent with the literature indicating that early and extended immersion in clinical practice is important for developing situational learning sets, theories of action, personal professional knowledge and professional identity (Benner and Wrubel 1989, Eraut 1999). This debate also introduces a cautionary note regarding use of laboratory simulation which, although it has its place in the initial stages of learning psychomotor skills, cannot replace the situated knowledge, the feedback, the infinite variety and the moral and ethical elements of social responsibility that can only be experienced in the 'real world' (Cox 1999).

Unavailability of mentors/preceptors

The report recognizes that the role of the mentor is crucial for clinical guidance and role modelling. Almost by default we have come to rely on staff nurses to provide most of this, as and where they can, and it is usually the same individual who also acts as preceptor for newly qualified nurses. The evidence is that, although mentors/preceptors are nominated and most are keen to carry out their role, the teaching commitment is usually unrecognized and undervalued and it is seldom that time or other resources are allocated for teaching activities. This situation is complicated by staff shortages, erratic staffing practices, high turn-over of both staff and patients, heavy workloads and an ever-changing clinical environment. Link lecturers are seldom seen in the practice setting because academic expectations mediate against active clinical participation which results in their loss of confidence and clinical credibility, and in students being largely unsupported in the clinical setting. It is increasingly obvious from research and anecdotal evidence that the unavailability of mentors/preceptors is a major problem which continues to handicap both students and newly qualified staff nurses (Gilmore 1999).

As far as clinical credibility and peer group acceptance is concerned, staff nurse mentors are, and will remain, the most appropriate people to teach practical clinical skills and responsiveness to situational variables; however, it is also the case that the concept and practice of professional clinical education needs to be developed into a more rigorous discipline and, therefore, needs a well-integrated and powerful collaborative team approach.

Fitness for Practice, recommendation 25 states that: 'Recognising that no one individual can provide the full range of expertise required by students, service providers and HEIs should work together to develop diverse teams of practice and academic staff who will offer students expertise in practice, management, assessment and mentoring and research' (p. 48).

Therefore, if education and service institutions acknowledge a joint responsibility for clinical education, partnerships and collaborative structures can be set up to ensure a more comprehensive, rigorous and exploratory approach to practical education.

Collaborative education/service models for practical clinical education

Partnerships between Higher Education Institutions (HEIs) and service providers

The idea of collaborative schemes between service providers and education institutions has been evident for some time (Baker *et al.* 1989). Until recently, however, it has been expressed mainly in the form of joint appointments or posts which tend to be strategic, advisory and few in number. However, following recommendations arising from the *Fitness for Practice* (UKCC 1999) and *Making a Difference* (Department of Health 1999), documents, collaborative partnerships are being set up between service providers and HEIs, and newly designed pre-registration courses are currently under demonstration in selected sites across the UK (Glen 2000). These are yet to be evaluated, but are expected to have a major influence on the future development of nursing education.

Funding for dedicated time in education for practice staff and dedicated time in practice for lecturers is a vital and pivotal issue, and one that has crippled past efforts to ensure support and quality guidance for both pre-registration and newly qualified nurses. However, the report strongly recommends that funding should also be reviewed to take account of the cost involved.

It is comparatively recently that models of practical clinical education, which involve the mentor or preceptor being available for individual 'hands-on' clinical teaching, are gaining prominence and selected examples are outlined below.

Staff nurse secondment

A model piloted by Davies *et al.* (1999) describes a scheme whereby preceptors (Australian equivalent to mentors) are seconded to the University for several days each week when students are on practical placements. This frees them to concentrate on working alongside and teaching their students during those days. The University pays the Hospital for their services and the Hospital can then afford to employ a replacement staff nurse. This, in turn, means that other colleagues do not have to take an additional workload and eases tension all round. Evidence is presented which also suggests that it is important that the preceptor remains working as part of the clinical team the rest of the time in order to maintain clinical credibility and peer acceptance, both of which reflect positively on the students.

Secondment and affiliates

Another model described by Gassner *et al.* (1999) takes a different approach, whereby staff nurses spend some time teaching in the University and lecturers have affiliate roles in the clinical area of their expertise in order to supervise their students. The effectiveness of this model depends on the lecturer maintaining clinical credibility and the staff nurse gaining a qualification in education.

Resident clinical teachers

A Canadian model experienced by a colleague described each speciality unit as having a resident clinical teacher who had been appointed from senior staff nurses in that particular specialty and whose prime responsibility was to work alongside all newcomers to the unit including students of nursing and medicine, junior doctors, and newly qualified nurses. The post was funded jointly by University and Service.

Supernumerary education and support posts

The model piloted and reported by Alderman (1999) whereby vacant D grade posts were topped up and made into F grades and given supernumerary status for the purpose of being available for education and support of all staff, is also interesting. This model was funded by a special grant but could be funded equally well by HEIs and service providers.

The common denominator for all the models described above is that the main players are immersed in clinical practice, are clinically credible and are actively teaching from within the clinical setting. This is a most critical point.

Mandatory collaborative structures

The partnership structures between HEIs and service providers have the potential to raise the profile of practical clinical education and to formalize and promote it. However, history suggests that such ideals can easily be lost in the struggle for dwindling resources, and a formal requirement through legislation may be necessary to ensure that practice based models are indeed set up, and that the representative teams have a more rigorous and integrated approach to clinical education and adequate funding to carry out their purpose.

Conclusion

There is increasing evidence that educating for practice disciplines is about to undergo a paradigm shift whereby practical experience will be better understood, more rigorously analyzed and integrated, and valued as highly as academic learning. Practitioners across disciplines will regard both dimensions as being essential for the ultimate expression of professional practice. The evidence is that the different kinds of knowledge and intuitive nuances of professional practice can only be apprehended, comprehended and internalized through well-guided immersion in the reality of practice itself.

The present culture of 'clinical education by default', unavailability of resources and few formal collaborative structures between education institutions and service providers cannot sustain the complex demands and pace of the evolution of professional nursing practice. The problems have been defined and redefined over recent years and it is time now to move on.

This paper has suggested that there is overwhelming evidence for an urgent review and reorganization of nursing education; that misunderstanding and devaluing of practical clinical education is the root cause of many of the problems currently being experienced by nurses at the point of registration; that educating for professional clinical practice can be illuminated by cross-disciplinary research; that tools such as the critical pathway can be used to articulate some of the process knowledge relating to the staff nurse role; and that the collaborative partnerships between HEIs and service providers, given the necessary incentives, could be predicted to facilitate development and implementation of models of nursing education capable of recognizing the primacy of professional clinical practice. There is a case to be made for mandatory education/service structures to ensure recognition of practical clinical education as a formal, intellectually diverse component of nursing education, and organize and fund teaching models that will 'free up' staff nurse mentors/preceptors and education lecturers to carry out integrated clinical teaching and to analyze and articulate clinical process knowledge through related research. This kind of approach is capable of addressing both the skills deficits that are presently evident at the point of registration and the wider intellectual challenge of developing a new paradigm of clinical practice education.

References

Alderman C (1999) Practice makes perfect. *Nursing Standard* 13 (38): 16–17.

Aston L, Mallik M, Day C, Fraser D, *et al.* (2000) An exploration into the role of the teacher/lecturer in practice: findings from a case study in adult nursing. *Nurse Education Today* 20: 178–188.

Baker C M, Boyd N J, Staslowski S A, Simmons B J (1989) Interinstitutional collaboration for nursing excellence; Part 2, Testing the model. *JONA* 19: 8–13.

Benner P (1984) *From Novice to Expert: Excellence and Power in Clinical Nursing Practice.* Addison-Wesley, Menlo Park.

Benner P, Wrubel J (1989) *The Primacy of Caring. Stress and Coping in Health and Illness.* Addison-Wesley, Menlo Park.

Birchenall P (1999) Developing a work-based learning philosophy. Editorial. *Nurse Education Today* 19: 173–174.

Chaiklin S, Lave J (1996) Understanding practice. Perspectives on activity and context. Cambridge University Press, Cambridge.

Clancy W J (1997) *Situated Cognition. On Human Knowledge and Computer Representations.* Cambridge University Press, Cambridge.

Cox K (1997) Work-based learning. *British Journal of Hospital Medicine* 57: 265–269.

Davies E, Turner C, Osborne Y (1999) Evaluating a clinical partnership model for undergraduate nursing students. *Collegian* 6: 23–40.

del Bueno D J (1978) Competency-based education. *Nurse Education* 3: 10–14.

Department of Health (1999) *Making a Difference.* London.

Edmond C B (1998) Competency-based preceptor programme for newly employed staff nurses. Pilot study report to client group, Glasgow.

Edmond C B (in progress) Competency-based preceptor programme for newly employed staff nurses. Pilot Doctoral Thesis.

Eraut M (1999) *Developing Professional Knowledge and Competence*, 4th edn. Falmer Press, London.

Evers C, Odam S, Latulip-Gardiner J, Paul S (1994) Developing a critical pathway for orientation. *American Journal of Critical Care* 3: 217–223.

Gassner L, Wotton K, Clare J, Hofmeyer A, Buckman J (1999) Theory meets practice. *Collegian* 6: 15–21.

Gilmore A (1999) Report of the analysis of the literature evaluating pre-registration nursing and midwifery education in the United Kingdom. Commissioned by the UKCC.

Glen S (2000) Partnerships: the way forward. *Nurse Education Today* 20: 339–340.

Hinchliff S (ed) (1992) *The Practitioner as Teacher.* Scutari Press, London.

Jarvis P (1999) The way forward for practice education. *Nurse Education Today* 19: 269–273.

Jarvis P, Gibson S (1997) *The Teacher Practitioner and Mentor in Nursing, Health Visiting, Midwifery and Social Work*, 2nd edn. Stanley Thornes, Cheltenham.

Kinkade S L (1992) Competency-based orientation: concept and theory. In: J M Lohrman, S L Kinkade (eds) *Competency-based Orientation for Critical Care Nursing*. pp. 3–11. Mosby, St Louis.

Kramer M (1977) *Reality Shock: Why Nurses Leave Nursing*. Mosby, St Louis.

Lohrman J M Kinkade S L (1992) *Competency-based Orientation for Critical Care Nursing*. Mosby, St Louis.

Luker K, Carlisle C, Riley E, Stilwell J, Davies C, Wilson R (1996) *Fitness for Purpose*. Report to the Department of Health. The University of Liverpool, Warwick.

May N, Veitch L, McIntosh J B, Alexander M F (1992) *Preparation for Practice. Evaluation of Nurse and Midwife Education in Scotland*. Glasgow Caledonian University, Glasgow.

Morton-Cooper A, Palmer A (1993) *Mentoring and Preceptorship: A Guide to Support Roles in Clinical Practice*. Blackwell Science, London.

Runciman P, Dewar B, Gailbourne A (1998) *Project 2000 in Scotland. Employers' Needs and the Skills of Newly Qualified Project 20000 Staff Nurses. Final Report*. Queen Margaret College, Edinburgh.

Steinaker N, Bell R (1979) *The Experiential Taxonomy: A New Approach to Teaching and Learning*. Academic Press, London.

Sternberg R J (1994) PRSVL: an integrative framework for understanding the mind in context. In: R J Sternber, R K Wagner (eds) *Mind in Context. Interactionist Perspectives on Human Intellegence*, pp. 218–232. Cambridge University Press, Cambridge.

UKCC (1999) *Fitness for Practice. The Report of the UKCC Commission for Nursing and Midwifery Education*. UKCC, London.

28. The Clinical Environment: A Source of Stress for Undergraduate Nurses

Malcolm Elliott

The clinical area is an important learning environment for undergraduate nursing students. Unfortunately, it can also be a source of significant stress and anxiety for students and there are a number of reasons for this. Much can be done to help alleviate this stress and create a positive learning environment for students. This paper explores the literature to ascertain the common sources of stress for undergraduate students in the clinical area. It also reviews strategies for improving the quality of the learning experience.

Introduction

In the 1980s New South Wales, Australia, transferred nursing education from the hospital-based apprenticeship system to the tertiary sector. The assumption underlying this transfer was that tertiary education would prepare nurses who were better able than their hospital-based colleagues to meet the challenges of nursing in the future (Perry 1988, p.19). With this transfer universities became solely responsible for the education of student nurses and their preparation for registration. They also assumed responsibility for coordinating the education of nursing students in the clinical area.

One of the many criticisms of undergraduate nursing courses is that they do not contain sufficient clinical experience for students. It is certainly true that nursing students in tertiary programs receive fewer and briefer clinical placements than their hospital-based contemporaries (Perry 1988, p.19). However, Battersby and Hemmings (1991, p.31) suggest that the quantity of time spent in the clinical area may not be as significant as the quality of the experience and guidance the student receives.

Regardless of the amount of time students spend in the clinical area, it can be a very stressful experience. Students are often thrust into foreign surroundings, not knowing the staff, patients or the ward routine. The patients and staff may have high expectations of them, even though they are 'just a student'. The clinical facilitator may also expect them to perform to a certain level even though they are still learning. Students may be expected to be familiar with pathophysiological or pharmocological concepts they have not yet addressed in their studies.

This manuscript reviews the literature related to clinical education and focuses on sources of stress experienced by students in the clinical area. Through understanding the nature and causes of these stressors, nursing academics and clinical facilitators can improve the quality of the clinical learning experience for undergraduates. The

Malcolm Elliott: 'The Clinical Environment: A Source of Stress for Undergraduate Nurses' in *AUSTRALIAN JOURNAL OF ADVANCED NURSING* (2002), 20 (1), pp. 34–38.

areas addressed include clinical supervision, assessment and preceptorship. Recommendations are made for improving the quality of the learning experience.

Disillusionment

Beck and Srivastava (1991) surveyed 94 undergraduate nursing students to investigate their perception of level and source of stress. The data were collected using a questionnaire consisting of three instruments: one to measure general distress and psychiatric disorders; one to describe a recent stressful event as well as stressors from academic, financial, clinical and interpersonal areas; and, a profile sheet to obtain demographic and background information about selected characteristics of the environment and mediating factors (Beck and Srivastava 1991, p.128). Although this study did not focus on the clinical environment, the atmosphere created by the clinical facilitator was ranked as one of the most stressful items. The study found that the students experienced relatively high levels of stress, and quite alarmingly, that the prevalence of psychiatric symptoms was higher in undergraduate nursing students than in the general population (Beck and Srivastava 1991, p.131).

Disillusionment may also occur because of misconceptions about what the nursing role involves. Students may have chosen a nursing career because of their desire to help people but often they are not prepared to deal with the complexities of the world of nursing (Beck and Srivastava 1991, p.128). Experiencing reality shock or realising the realities of the job can make students doubt their career choice (Beck 1993, p.490). The professional education experience can be very stressful and the high incidence of distress in the educational years may lead to impairment in the practising years of the professional (Beck and Srivastava 1991, p.127).

Sources of stress

Learning in the clinical setting creates challenges that are absent from the classroom: facilitators have little control of environmental conditions; students must combine the use of cognitive, psychomotor and affective skills to respond to individual client needs; client safety must be maintained whilst he or she is cared for by a student; and, facilitators must monitor client needs as well as student needs (Windsor 1987, p.151). Beck (1993) surveyed 18 undergraduate nursing students about their initial experiences in the clinical area. The students' written descriptions were analysed and the significant statements extracted. Some of these were: anxious and nervous; afraid of hurting the patient; no self-confidence; uncomfortable with the equipment; overwhelming; felt incompetent or abandoned; confusing and shocking; felt scared and ignorant; and, felt stupid and worthless (Beck 1993, p.493). These data were clustered into six themes which were: pervading anxiety; feeling abandoned; perceiving self as incompetent; encountering reality shock; doubting nursing as a choice of career; and, uplifting consequences. Although the sample size was small, the findings are still relevant to nursing education today. Beck (1993, p.496) concluded that students need more time to reflect and verbalise their feelings; a climate needs to be created in which less than perfect behaviour at new skills is acceptable; and, faculty need to concentrate on the positive instead of the negative.

Pagana (1988) explored the initial medical-surgical nursing experience of 262 undergraduate students. The students were approached during the first week of their clinical experience and asked to participate. The survey tool contained open-ended questions which asked the respondent to describe the stresses, challenges and threats they were experiencing. The majority (77%) of students expressed feelings of inadequacy. Other stressful issues were fear of making mistakes (34%), fear of the unknown (28%), the clinical facilitator (26%), feeling scared (19%), and, the threat of failing (14%). The feelings of inadequacy were related to inexperience and lack of knowledge and were reinforced when trying to absorb large amounts of knowledge in a short time. Other sources of these feelings included the high expectations of others, being actively responsible for nursing care or being asked to perform procedures they were not familiar with. Feelings of inadequacy have much to do with the attitude and practices of ward staff (Nolan 1998, p.626). This is a contentious issue because the ward staff may not understand the undergraduate curriculum or may be reluctant to allow students to practise relevant procedures (Napthine 1996, p.22).

Sources of stress in the clinical environment

Exploitation, in which the students are used as de facto rostered staff members is not uncommon. This may occur if staff are not familiar with the curriculum or aware of the goals and roles of students. It may also occur because senior staff are more concerned about the budget than patient safety. Exploitation is a potential source of stress for students as they are trying to please the clinical facilitator, the university and the ward staff, whilst trying to 'pass' the clinical placement (Napthine 1996, p.23). This situation creates the threat of failing which causes more anxiety for students.

Harming the patient by making an error or mistake is another source of anxiety for students (Pagana 1988; Wilson 1994). This is a particular concern because of students' limited knowledge bases. Students are concerned not only about harming another human being but also about the implications for their careers. Kleehammer *et al.* (1990) also found that one of the highest levels of anxiety expressed by students concerned fear of making mistakes. They surveyed 92 nursing students over a four-year period. The survey tool addressed 16 different issues including communication and procedural aspects of patient care, interpersonal relationships with health care providers and interactions with members of faculty. Apart from making mistakes, other anxiety producing issues included clinical procedures, hospital equipment, talking with physicians, being late and being observed and assessed by a member of faculty. Other similar potential sources of anxiety identified included unfamiliar clinical procedures, hospital equipment, talking with physicians, being late and evaluation.

The 'social component' of the clinical setting also brings with it feelings of fear and anxiety, which affects the students' responses to their learning environment (Nolan 1998). This social component may include the complexities of the medical and nursing hierarchies. Unfortunately, these fears are frequently intensified by faculty demand for a near-perfect performance (Wong and Wong 1987, p.508). Being constantly watched by staff and facilitator, as well as being formally assessed is a major constraint on confidence and learning (Nolan 1998, p.625), although feeling abandoned is not an uncommon experience either (Beck 1993).

Improving the quality of the clinical learning experience

The stressful nature of the clinical environment for undergraduate nursing students has been described. Many students complain however that they do not spend enough time in the clinical area, although it is probably the quality of the experience rather than the quantity that makes the most difference. What therefore can be done to improve the quality of the clinical learning experience?

Adequate preparation by students for clinical practice has been credited with 'making all the difference in the world' (Windsor 1987, p.152). This preparation may include being familiar with assessment tasks, knowing who the clinical facilitator will be or reading the institution's policy on infection control. All these things can occur before the student arrives in the clinical area. Adequate preparation may also include teaching students priority setting and problem-solving skills early in the undergraduate program (Beck and Srivastava 1991, p.132). Students should also be encouraged to recognise the influence they exert over their own clinical learning environment and to proactively work to create the kind of environment which will best meet their learning needs (Dunn and Hansford 1997, p.1303).

Clinical supervision

The clinical facilitator has been identified as a potential threat to students (Pagana 1988). Terms used by students to describe the facilitator include intimidating, threatening, demeaning, impatient, strict and demanding (Pagana 1988, p.421). Unfortunately facilitators often lack any tertiary teaching background (Napthine 1996, p.21). As such their ability to guide, supervise, direct and teach students may be inadequate or completely absent. However the reasons such a person could be employed as a facilitator may include budgetary constraints or limited availability and thus choice of other suitable staff (Napthine 1996, p.23).

Registered Nurses (RNs) working on wards in which students undertake clinical learning experiences should be adequately prepared and supported for their role in student learning (Dunn and Hansford 1997, p.1303). For example, this may involve the RN having a reduced patient workload so that adequate time can be spent teaching and supervising the student. Students should be made to feel they are an important part of the nursing team. Students appreciate recognition for their contribution to patient care and are disappointed when their work is not acknowledged (Hart and Rotem 1994, p.28).

Wong and Wong (1987) suggest the following for improving the quality of clinical education: pairing of veteran and novice staff members in clinical instruction; utilisation of senior faculty as role models in clinical settings; faculty development programmes on clinical instruction; and, careful selection of candidates for clinical faculty appointment. Wood (1992, p.406) suggests early instructor sensitivity to possible student problems in the clinical situation. She presented the findings of a descriptive and exploratory study aimed at identifying non-traditional student nurse issues. Although the sample size was small, stress was a key factor in five of the situations studied and it actually affected the students' nursing care. She also suggests (p.406) that initial tasks in the clinical area should be relatively simple and straightforward to develop student self-confidence.

Assessment

Whilst observation and evaluation are necessary aspects of the clinical learning environment, they should be performed in a supportive, non-threatening manner and be used for formative guidance, not just summative evaluation (Kleehammer *et al.* 1990, p.186). This again emphasises the importance of utilising clinical facilitators who are competent and skilled and who know how to teach. Students should not feel that someone is looking over their shoulder waiting for the opportunity to criticise. Instead they should feel that they have immediate help and support available to guide them through difficult tasks at any time they need it. Feelings of incompetence can be decreased by creating a climate for learning where less than perfect 'behaviour' is acceptable (Beck 1993, p.494). Opportunities should be made available for students to reflect and verbalise their feelings about their clinical experiences, be they positive or negative.

Preceptorship

Preceptorships are a useful way of reducing stress in the undergraduate student and fostering their development in the clinical area. Preceptorships are a one-to-one reality-based clinical experience in which the RN supervises the learning experience of the student (Peirce 1991, p.244). The preceptor is an expert nurse who assists students to achieve predetermined clinical learning goals through the use of modelling and subsequent student practise of appropriate nursing behaviour (Perry 1988; Dilbert and Goldenberg 1995). The use of preceptors in nursing is based on the androgogical premise that a one-to-one relationship facilitates effective learning (Clayton, Broome and Ellis 1989, p.73). In the undergraduate degree, the preceptor's roles include reducing transitional stress and promoting socialisation (Beattie 1998, p.15).

Preceptorship is being used frequently in nursing education to facilitate the acquisition of clinical competence by the student (Ferguson and Calder 1993, p.32).

A clear distinction, however, must be made between preceptor and mentor because although these terms are often used interchangeably, they are not the same. Mentoring is concerned with making the most of human potential (Morton-Cooper and Palmer 1993). It focuses on the development of a deeper relationship between mentor and protégé, capable of influencing major career changes and promoting self-actualisation in both participants (Madison 1994, p.17). Preceptorship relates more closely to an educational relationship (Coates and Gormely 1997). It has a narrower emphasis on individualised teaching, learning and support in the clinical environment (Neary 2000). Burnard (1990, p.351) states the preceptor is more clinically active, more of a role model, and more concerned with the teaching and learning aspects of the relationship than a mentor. Interestingly, the English National Board (2001) defines a mentor as a nurse who facilitates learning and supervises and assesses students in the practice setting. This is similar to the definition of a preceptor.

Preceptorship is said to enhance the performance of nurses, whilst preceptors remain stimulated educationally and professionally by the experience (Bain 1996, p.105). Perry (1988, p.22) believes that preceptorships have the potential to enhance student learning in tertiary nursing courses by utilising the teaching skills of expert nurses already employed in service settings. However, the assumption being made by Perry (1988) is that if a nurse is an 'expert', he or she will possess teaching skills. Napthine (1996, p.21) says it is a myth that because one is a good clinical nurse, he or she will have knowledge of teaching and learning principles, and will be a good teacher.

The specific role or function of a preceptor, therefore, needs to be clearly defined so that the preceptee can gain the most from the experience. In one study (Coates and Gormley 1997), RNs who acted as preceptors listed their most important duties as role model, teacher and supervisor. The least important were assessor, critic and protector.

A preceptor also needs to be chosen carefully. Too rigid selection criteria will restrict selection to availability rather than ability of preceptors (Bain 1996, p.106). Preceptorships should be constructed in response to specific learning needs of the student and developed independently of learner characteristics such as age, gender and social class (Perry 1988, p.23). A situation in which RNs are chosen as preceptors because it is their turn or because there is no else more suitable, will contribute to problems with the establishment of a positive student-teacher relationship, which precedes the facilitation of meaningful learning (Beattie 1998, p.16).

The potential advantages of incorporating preceptorship programs into nursing education include their value in: transferring theory into practice; aiding in the transmission of desired nursing behaviours throughout the profession; engendering creative synthesis in nursing practice; and, initiating the basis for mentoring and future collegial networks (Perry 1988, p.20). Preceptorship also provides close supervision and allows immediate feedback on performance (Reilly and Oermann 1992). Jairath *et al.* (1991) found that a preceptor program promotes assumption of behaviours consistent with the professional nursing role and thus facilitates the transition from student to professional nurse. Packer (1994, p.412) believes that preceptorships eliminate the reality shock experienced by students. Another advantage is the cost. One-to-one instruction by faculty is prohibitive due to the expense whilst using qualified ward staff acting as preceptors is not (Clayton *et al.* 1989, p.74).

Preceptorship does, however, have its weaknesses or limitations. These may include the demands of work taking over learning; the difficulty in monitoring the progress of one student in isolation from the others; preceptors lacking educational qualifications or ability; and, preceptor burnout (Grealish and Carroll 1998, p.7).

Collaboration

Collaboration between the higher education and health care sectors is essential if the clinical learning environment is to best meet the needs of undergraduate nursing students (Dunn and Hansford 1997, p.1301). This collaboration should aim to establish creative models for clinical education which take into account current health and education socioeconomic reforms (Dunn and Hansford 1997, p.1301). For example, the nursing unit manager and clinical facilitator could cooperate in the development and implementation of strategies to enhance the acceptance of students as fully participating members of the ward team (Dunn and Hansford 1997, p.1302).

Conclusion

Exposure to the clinical environment is an important part of any undergraduate nursing curriculum. The clinical environment can, however, be a source of stress and anxiety to students. There are numerous strategies that can be used to reduce the impact of these stresses and to improve the quality of the clinical learning experience for students. The use of competent, skilled and empathic facilitators is one. Preceptorship is another.

Although nursing education has been in the university setting for many years, the use of the clinical environment as a learning or teaching experience is yet to be maximised. Academics, educators and clinicians have many options available to them to improve this situation.

References

Bain L (1996) Preceptorship: A review of the literature. *Journal of Advanced Nursing* 4 (1): 104–107.

Battersby D, Hemmings L (1991) Clinical performance of university nursing graduates. *Australian Journal of Advanced Nursing* 9 (1): 30–34.

Beattie H (1998) Clinical teaching models: A review of the role of preceptor in the undergraduate nursing program. *Australian Journal of Advanced Nursing* 15 (4): 14–19.

Beck C (1993) Nursing students' initial clinical experience: A phenomenological study. *International Journal of Nursing Studies* 30 (6): 489–497.

Beck D, Srivastava R (1991) Perceived level and sources of stress in baccalaureate nursing students. *Journal of Nursing Education* 30 (3): 127–133.

Bumard P (1990) The student experience: Adult learning and mentorship revisited. *Nurse Education Today* 10 (5): 349–354.

Clayton G, Broome M, Ellis L (1989) Relationship between a preceptorship experience and role socialization of graduate nurses. *Journal of Nursing Education* 28 (2): 72–75.

Coates V, Gormley E (1997) Learning the practice of nursing: Views about preceptorship. *Nurse Education Today* 17 (2): 91–98.

Dilbert C, Goldenberg D (1995) Preceptors' perceptions of benefits, rewards, supports and commitment to the preceptor role. *Journal of Advanced Nursing* 21 (6): 1144–1151.

Dunn S, Hansford B (1997) Undergraduate nursing students' perceptions of their clinical learning environment. *Journal of Advanced Nursing* 25 (6): 1299–1306.

English National Board (2001) *Placements in Focus: Guidance for Education in Practice for Health Care Professions.* Online: www.enb.org.uk (accessed 3 November 2001).

Ferguson L, Calder B (1993) A comparison of preceptor and educator valuing of nursing student clinical performance criteria. *Journal of Nursing Education* 32 (1): 30–36.

Grealish L, Carroll G (1998) Beyond preceptorship and supervision: A third clinical teaching model emerges for Australian nursing education. *Australian Journal of Advanced Nursing* 15 (2): 3–11.

Hart G, Rotem A (1994) The best and worst: Students' experiences of clinical education. *Australian Journal of Advanced Nursing* 11 (3): 26–33.

Jairath N, Costello J, Wallace P, Rudy L (1991) The effect of preceptorship upon diploma nursing students' transition to the professional nursing role. *Journal of Nursing Education* 30 (6): 251–255.

Kleehammer K, Hart L, Keck J (1990) Nursing students' perceptions of anxiety-producing situations in the clinical setting. *Journal of Nursing Education* 29 (4): 183–187.

Madison J (1994) The value of mentoring in nursing leadership: A descriptive study. *Nursing Forum* 29 (4): 16–23.

Morton-Cooper A, Palmer A (1993) *Mentoring and Preceptorship: A Guide to Support Roles in Clinical Practice.* Blackwell Science, London.

Napthine R (1996) Clinical education: A system under a pressure. *Australian Nursing Journal* 3 (9): 20–24.

Neary M (2000) *Teaching, Assessing and Evaluation for Clinical Competence: A Practical Guide for Practitioners and Teachers.* Stanley Thornes, Cheltenham.

Nolan C (1998) Learning on clinical placement: the experience of six Australian student nurses. *Nurse Education Today* 18 (8): 622–629.

Packer J (1994) Education for clinical practice: An alternative approach. *Journal of Nursing Education* 33 (9): 411–416.

Pagana K (1988) Stresses and threats reported by baccalaureate students in relation to an initial clinical experience. *Journal of Nursing Education* 27 (9): 418–424.

Peirce A (1991) Preceptorial students' view of their clinical experience. *Journal of Nursing Education* 30 (6): 244–250.

Perry M (1988) Preceptorship in clinical nursing education: A social learning theory approach. *Australian Journal of Advanced Nursing* 5 (3): 19–25.

Reilly D, Oermann M (1992) *Clinical Teaching in Nursing Education,* 2nd edn. National League for Nursing, New York.

Wilson M (1994) Nursing student perspective of learning in a clinical setting. *Journal of Nursing Education* 33 (2): 81–86.

Windsor A (1987) Nursing students' perceptions of clinical experience. *Journal of Nursing Education* 26 (4): 150–154.

Wong J, Wong S (1987) Towards effective clinical teaching in nursing. *Journal of Advanced Nursing* 12 (4): 505–513.

29. Developing Reflection and Expertise: Can Mentors Make the Difference?

Bruce G. Barnett

Mentors in the field of education are asked to take on a variety of roles in working with their protégés, whether they be novice teachers or administrators. The literature on mentoring is replete with definitions and illustrations of the roles and functions mentors are expected to fulfil. Schein[1] contends successful mentors must be teachers, coaches, trainers, role models, protectors, and sponsors at some point during their relationships with novices. By engaging in these roles, a mentor can be viewed as "a master at providing opportunities for the growth of others, by identifying situations and events which contribute knowledge and experience to the life of the steward"[2, p. 3].

Developing a personal relationship with a colleague who is a novice in the field is the hallmark of mentoring. For instance, Ashburn *et al.*[3, p. 1] define mentoring as the "establishment of a personal relationship for the purpose of professional instruction and guidance". Similarly, building solid relationships where mutual trust and respect develop demands that mentors possess certain qualities and skills, such as being people-oriented and respectful[4]; warm, caring, and sensitive[5]; empathetic[6]; and able to nurture and support other people[7].

Furthermore, a successful mentoring relationship is not stagnant, but is a dynamic process in which mentors and protégés move through several stages, phases, or levels. Examples of these stages include: initiation, cultivation, separation, and redefinition[8]; initiation, protégé, break up, and lasting friendship[9,10]; and initiation, sparkle, development, disillusionment, parting, and transformation[11]. Regardless of the terminology, all of these stage theories indicate that "healthy mentor/protégé relationships involve a progression from relative protégé dependence at the beginning of the relationship to autonomy and self-reliance as the protégé grows into a colleague and peer"[10, p. 12]. As these relationships develop, astute mentors must also match their support to the novices' cognitive developmental stage. For instance, protégés who solve problems at a concrete level will require more substantive, tangible feedback on their performance than novices who solve problems at a more abstract, higher order level[10]. Training programmes for mentors are beginning to acknowledge the progression of mentor/novice relationship as well as the cognitive capabilities of novices (e.g.[6,12]).

Coupled with this literature on the unfolding of the mentor/protégé relationship is the implication that over time protégés begin to solve problems similar to experts in the profession, namely their mentors. The foundation of this article, therefore, rests on three basic premisses:

Bruce G. Barnett: 'Developing Reflection and Expertise: Can Mentors Make the Difference?' in *JOURNAL OF EDUCATIONAL ADMINISTRATION* (1995), 33 (5), pp. 45–59.

(1) The most effective mentors are those who consciously move their protégés from dependent, novice problem solvers to autonomous, expert problem solvers.

(2) Reflection is the catalyst for developing protégés' autonomy and expertise in problem solving.

(3) By adhering to the principles of cognitive coaching, mentors can assist protégés in becoming more reflective and more expert-like in their problem-solving abilities.

These premisses blend some of the current thinking on expert problem solving, reflection, and cognitive coaching. For example, the ideas of Short and Rinehart[13] on the relationship between reflection and expertise, Leithwood and Steinbach's[14] notions of how expert problem solving is developed, and the work of Costa and Garmston[15] on the value of cognitive coaching as a way to develop autonomous, higher order thinkers serve as the foundation for the arguments being advanced.

To build the article's argument, it begins with a brief review of the extant literature on what is known about information processing and how experts, especially teachers and administrators, tend to solve problems. Next, how reflective practice is related to developing expertise is explored, including a discussion of how reflection can be measured and developed. Building on these concepts of expertise and reflection, attention is then directed to the promise of cognitive coaching as a means for mentors to assist novices in becoming autonomous, expert problem solvers. Practical hints for the coaching tools mentors might utilize and how they might assess protégés' mental capacities are provided. Finally, the article concludes with a discussion of the possible implications for mentors and protégés involved in such a cognitive coaching process.

Expertise in problem solving

If a key function of mentors is to assist protégés in becoming expert problem solvers, then what do we know about how experts process information? A growing body of literature exists about how experts in many professional fields think and act as compared to novices. Many of the concepts driving the study of problem solving derive from cognitive psychology and psychobiology (e.g.[16–18]). Regarding the problem-solving expertise of educators, recent research has been conducted with school teachers and administrators to determine their strategies for processing information and making decisions, especially when facing problems which are not well defined[19]. Following a brief overview of some of the principles of information processing which highlight how experts frame and solve problems, attention is directed to expert problem solving studies conducted with teachers and administrators.

Principles of information processing

Cognitive psychologists have discovered that human beings process information using four types of thought patterns. Input of information occurs through the senses and memory; learners then process these data by forming cognitive structures (referred to as schemata or mental networks) to represent relationships between pieces of information; the output of their learning occurs as learners apply these schemata in new situations; and learners experience metacognition whenever they monitor their own thought processes[15]. As information is processed, learners "call up meaningful information from storage, whether the event is commonplace or a complex learning experience"[15, p. 87]. If the stored cognitive schemata do not account for new information, learners can refine and/or expand their existing cognitive structures, acknowledge that their current understanding is not sophisticated enough to represent this novel situation, or do both[14]. Some scholars argue that only the most complex, higher order thinking results in the formation of the sophisticated mental networks which frame learners' experiences[20]. Likewise, Costa and Garmston[15, p. 87] argue that the most complex form of thinking or problem solving occurs when learners are forced to:

- draw on the greatest amount of data or structures already in storage;
- expand an already existing structure;
- develop new structures.

The information processing of expert thinkers is significantly different from that of novice thinkers. Because research indicates "expertise requires a knowledge base that is extensive and accessible"[13, p. 502], experts, as contrasted with novices, have better-developed mental models and are more adept at applying these structures in novel situations. Experts relate problems to their social contexts[21]; use principles, concepts, and theories when solving problems[17,18]; and have well-defined pattern recognition skills[21]. In contrast, novices tend to rely on surface features when solving problems and do not identify deep structures or underlying principles when analysing problems[17,18].

Educators' expert thinking

A growing body of evidence is being gathered about how expertise is displayed by teachers and principals. Many of these findings lend strong support to the previously-mentioned studies comparing expert and novice problem solvers. The mental networks of expert teachers are more complex and interconnected than the mental structures used by novices[21]. Expert teachers are much more likely to access complex, rich patterns of information, provide multiple interpretations of situations, and frame alternative solutions than novice teachers[22]. The contrast between how expert and novice teachers perform is best summarized by Sparks-Langer *et al.* [23, p. 25].

> When confronted with a problem situation or decision, experts can draw on [a] rich source of previously learned patterns and information and thus can make more appropriate decisions. Novices, in contrast, can produce fewer interpretations and possible alternatives in a given situation.

Similarly, expert principals outperform novices in many of the same ways. In their initial studies on problem-solving expertise, Leithwood and Stager[24] discovered experts use more basic principles in framing problems and are better at recognizing patterns than typical principals. As a result of these studies, Leithwood and Steinbach[14] have created a model outlining the six major areas in which the problem-solving processes between experts and typical principals differ:

(1) problem interpretation;

(2) goals for problem solving;

(3) underlying principles and values;

(4) constraints;

(5) solution processes;

(6) effect.

In general, their model indicates typical principals take into account many fewer variables when making decisions, are more likely to see constraints as insurmountable barriers to reaching goals, give less attention to planning, and are more fearful of the consequences of their actions than expert principals.

Reflection and expert thinking

One of the underlying premisses of successful mentoring stated earlier is the value reflection has for assisting protégés to become autonomous, expert thinkers. A great deal of attention has been directed to the necessity of educational practitioners becoming more reflective about their work (e.g.[23,25–30]). A host of conceptual models and theoretical frameworks have been developed to describe the reflective process. Examples include Van Mannen's[31] description of technical, practical, and critical reflection; Schon's[26] comparision of tacit knowledge, knowing in action, and reflection on/in action; Hart's[32] notion that reflective practitioners integrate theoretical, empirical, and experiential knowledge; Barnett and Brill's[28] contention that reflective practice is best represented by Kolb's[33] experiential learning theory; and Osterman and Kottkamp's[34] formulation of reflection as a means of contrasting espoused theories with theories-in-use.

In sorting through conceptual frameworks and descriptions of reflection, Ross[35] outlines the five basic components individuals engage in during the reflective process:

(1) identify the problem/issue to be resolved;

(2) respond to the problem/issue by determining similarities to other situations and unique features of the situation;

(3) frame and reframe the problem/issue;

(4) anticipate possible consequences and implications for various solutions to the problem/issue;

(5) determine whether the anticipated consequences are desired.

When conceptualized this way, reflection is viewed as an information-processing strategy which not only provides opportunities for individuals to create mental networks, but also to develop more complex interconnections and depth of thinking characteristic of expert thinkers. Therefore, if reflection is conducted in a thoughtful way so that practitioners are allowed to expand their knowledge base and improve their actions[32], then there is every reason to believe this knowledge will become more intertwined and integrated, resulting in cognitive schemata which demonstrate the thinking patterns of experts[13,36]. With appropriate practice and time, individuals can "autonomously reflect" on their thought processes by engaging in the metacognitive process of double-loop learning[14, p. 330].

> Individuals engaged in double-loop learning ...are managing their own cognitive resources and monitoring and evaluating their own intellectual performance ...Such reflection is dialectical because the learner engages in a "conversation" with the setting in an effort to understand it better, as well as the meaning that the setting has for the assumptions underlying the problem-solving activity.

If reflection is the key to facilitating higher order/expert thinking, is there any evidence that training programmes can improve individuals' capacity for reflection? In answering this question we begin by examining how to measure reflection before describing various ways in which practitioners' reflective and problem-solving capacities have been enhanced.

Measuring reflection

The mental mapping processes which occur during reflection can be ascertained in a variety of ways. Costa and Garmston[15] outline a series of measures which can be used to ascertain the complexity of individuals' reflective thought processing:

- taxonomies;
- critical incidents;
- portfolios;
- dialogues and interviews.

Taxonomies are an orderly classification of a construct (e.g. learning, moral development) and capture increasingly complex levels of growth and/or development. Examples of instruments which measure incremental levels of conceptual and reflective thought include the Hunt Paragraph Completion Method[37], the Levels of Reflectivity[31], and the Framework for Reflective Pedagogical Thinking[23]. The Framework for Reflective Pedagogical Thinking has been used in a variety of university classroom settings to determine the levels of reflective thinking of students who are using case studies[38] as well as students participating in teacher education and administrator preparation programmes which emphasize reflective thinking[13,23]. Other measures of reflectivity are somewhat more open-ended and subjective than taxonomies, relying on another person's observational and analytical skills. For instance, *critical incidents* include unexpected events and activities which provide evidence of how the learner behaves in actual situations; artifacts and written reflections in *portfolios* document the progression of the learner's growth; and verbal statements which learners express during *dialogues* and *interviews* capture their current thinking. In some cases, the taxonomies used to measure reflectivity described above might be used to assess the information collected from critical incidents, portfolios, and dialogues/interviews, determining specific levels of reflective thought being observed and/or heard.

Developing the capacity to reflect

Because reflection is considered to be a cognitive skill, we might expect that with concentrated practice and feedback individuals could improve their reflective capacities. There is emerging evidence that certain instructional conditions positively influence educators' reflective and problem-solving abilities. Illustrations include:

- The capacity of aspiring educational administrators to reflect is enhanced when they use the critical incident process to stimulate group discussions and keep reflective journals[13].
- Undergraduate students who use case study methods are more reflective about the role of classroom teachers than students experiencing traditional teaching methods[38].
- The reflective thinking of pre-service teacher education students significantly increases when they are allowed to link course content to field experiences[23].
- Problem-based instruction increases the problem-solving abilities of practising principals and vice-principals[14].

In summary, these initial investigations provide compelling evidence that if instructional strategies are intentionally designed to stimulate reflection, then prospective and practising educators do become more proficient in their ability to reflect and solve problems. Consequently, these studies lend further support to the notion that reflection is a catalyst for developing expert thinking.

Although these investigations on expertise and reflective thinking have rarely been associated with mentoring, there is no reason to believe mentors cannot use these same principles in nurturing the reflective and cognitive capacities of protégés. We now focus on how cognitive coaching can be used by mentors as a way to affect the cognitive development and expertise of protégés.

Cognitive coaching

To this point, three ideas have been advanced which directly bear on the mentor/protégé relationship:

(1) over time protégés are less dependent on mentors, eventually becoming autonomous learners;

(2) experts (mentors) think and behave differently than novices (protégés);

(3) mentors who use instructional strategies which promote reflection can enhance protégés' capacities for expert thinking and problem solving.

In examining these ideas together, an important question remains: How can mentors (the experts) assist protégés (the novices) to be more reflective and subsequently become autonomous, expert problem solvers?

The answer to this question would appear to be related to the mentor's ability to become "a skilled coach...[who] is likely to facilitate improvement in the [protégé's] guiding schema and actual performance much faster than if the [protégé] has available only his or her own analysis of discrepancies"[14, p. 324]. The literature on mentoring for novice teachers reinforces this image of the mentor being a skilled coach who has well-developed communication, observational, conferencing, and problem-solving skills[10].

The concept of cognitive coaching for principals and teachers developed and popularized by Costa and Garmston[15] fits this image of the mentor's role as a developer of a protégé's mental processing. The guiding principle of cognitive coaching is that instructional behaviours will not be affected until the inner thought processes of teachers are altered and rearranged. Although cognitive coaching has been advocated primarily as a process for educators, we believe its fundamental premisses and practices are extremely relevant for mentors to use in developing the intellectual functioning of their protégés. The goals and assumptions of cognitive coaching complement the arguments we have made about the development of intellectual expertise and autonomy. The goals of cognitive coaching include:

- establishing and maintaining a trusting relationship between coach and novice;
- developing the mental capacities and perceptions of the coach and novice;
- allowing novices to become autonomous, self-dependent learners.

These goals are supported by the basic assumptions of cognitive coaching:

> If teachers do not possess [certain] mental capacities...no amount of experience alone will create it. It is through *mediated processing* and *reflecting* upon experience that these capacities will be developed. The act of coaching engages, causes awareness of, develops, labels, and enhances these intellectual functions[15, p.107, emphasis added].

To provide a better sense of the relevance cognitive coaching has for mentors and protégés, we describe the coaching tools and practices mentors can employ and then examine the ways mentors can assess their protégés' intellectual growth and development. In making this translation, the term "mentor/coach" is substituted for "cognitive coach".

Practices of mentor/coaches

Because the cognitive coaching process is aimed at enhancing teachers' thinking about their classroom practices, the typical sequence of steps the mentor/coach and teacher engage in include:

- a planning conference (prior to observing a class);
- an observation of an instructional lesson;
- a reflecting conference.

During the planning and reflecting conferences, the general stance of the mentor/coach is to be a *mediator* of another professional's cognitive development, as opposed to being directive, critical, or evaluative of his/her performance. Although it may not be appropriate for many mentor/coaches to use this exact series of steps, especially if their protégés occupy roles other than teachers (e.g. administrators, clerical and support staff), the same stance and behaviours apply in developing the mental processing of protégés. As a mediator, the mentor/coach[15, p. 17]:

- diagnoses and envisions desired stages for (protégés);
- constructs and uses clear and precise language in the facilitation of (protégés') cognitive development;
- devises an overall strategy through which (protégés) will move themselves towards desired states;
- maintains faith in the potential for (the protégé's) continued movement towards more autonomous states of mind and behaviour;
- possesses a belief in his/her capacity to serve as an empowering catalyst of (protégés') growth.

As these mediation behaviours suggest, the mentor/coach must have well-developed communication skills, especially in forming and asking questions, clarifying and probing, and being non-judgemental[15]. First, and perhaps the most essential talent mentor/coaches must possess in order to mediate cognitive growth, is their *questioning skill*. The power of asking appropriate questions has been acknowledged outside the concept of cognitive coaching. Lee and Barnett, for example, advocate the use of *reflective questioning* as a way for "individuals to reflect aloud to be heard by one or more colleagues, and to be prompted to expand and extend thinking through follow-up questions" [39, p. 16]. Successful mentor/coaches are aware not only of the subtle messages communicated through their voice intonation, sentence structure, and use of positive presuppositions[15], but consciously formulate questions which force protégés to use different levels or types of thinking. For instance, clarifying questions allow protégés to recall events and describe their feelings, actions, and thoughts; purpose and consequence questions are aimed at stimulating protégés to determine cause and effect relationships as well as the intended and unintended consequences of their actions; and linking questions force protégés to consider possible connections between the context of a situation, personal beliefs and values, goals and aspirations, and related personal and professional experiences[39].

Second, astute mentor/coaches are capable of clarifying and probing their protégés' responses. On the one hand, clarifying entails getting protégés to "recapture the event for purposes of examination... and serve as a springboard for deeper explorations of meanings, alternatives, and conclusions"[39, p. 19]. On the other hand, probing protégés' responses forces them to be more precise and clear in describing their thoughts, feelings, and actions. Costa and Garmston[15] advocate the use of probes to help individuals define vague nouns, pronouns, and verbs (e.g. "I use several learning activities"); explain unclear comparisons (e.g. "Those parents are better than most"); justify absolute phrases (e.g. "I can't stop getting angry"); and challenge universal statements (e.g. "Everybody hates those tests").

Finally, in order for protégés to develop trust in the coaching process and reveal their innermost thoughts and feelings, mentor/coaches must strive to be non-judgemental. Evidence exists that when peer colleagues have a non-judgemental attitude toward their peers' learning, trust and higher level thinking are more likely to occur[40–42]. Mentor/coaches can take a neutral and non-judgemental stance by acknowledging the protégés' responses; paraphrasing what protégés express by rephrasing, translating, or providing examples; and empathizing with protégés' accomplishments, fears, and frustrations[15,39]. By seeking and valuing the learners' point of view, mentor/coaches are taking a constructivist view of their protégés' learning[43].

Measuring results of cognitive coaching

A variety of research studies have revealed the effects of cognitive coaching on teachers' classroom behaviours and student learning (e.g.[44,45]) teachers' cognitive development (e.g.[46,47]), and teachers' and administrators' professional relationships (e.g.[48,49]). While these accounts are promising for teacher development, what can other educators who are serving as mentor/coaches do to ascertain the progress of their protégés' cognitive development? Certainly, some of the approaches described earlier might be appropriate. For instance, by listening to the responses of protégés during informal discussions or by reviewing written reflections protégés prepare in a journal or portfolio, mentor/coaches might formally assess the level of thinking expressed using a taxonomy of reflective thought, such as the Framework for Reflective Pedagogical Thinking[23]. Over time, results from these administrations of the Framework can determine if protégés' levels of reflective thinking are increasing. Furthermore, observing how protégés solve problems during certain critical incidents can provide additional informal data for mentor/coaches to evaluate.

Another possible way to determine informally the cognitive growth of protégés is for mentor/coaches to observe the degree to which "five states of mind"[15] are being achieved. These five states are: efficacy, flexibility, craftsmanship, consciousness, and interdependence. Costa and Garmston believe these states of mind affect not only the decisions educators make about curriculum, instruction, and assessment, but "serve also as diagnostic tools, constructs through which we can assess the cognitive development of other individuals and groups and plan interventions" [15, pp. 131–2]. Therefore, astute mentor/coaches, through their observations and discussions, can determine if protégés: believe they can positively affect situations (efficacy); examine situations from different perspectives (flexibility); take pride in their work and strive to improve themselves (craftsmanship); are conscious of their own values, beliefs, and actions (consciousness); and work together with colleagues to achieve common goals (interdependence). Regardless of whether formal or informal measures are used, obtaining these data will provide mentor/coaches and protégés with a better sense if cognitive coaching is helping protégés become more expert-like in their ability to reflect, problem solve, and make important decisions.

Implications for mentoring

Mentors hold the key novices need to unlock their professional expertise. By embodying the philosophy and qualities of a "cognitive coach", mentors become the catalysts for developing expertise in reflective thinking, cognitive development, and problem solving with the protégés with whom they work. Therefore, the image of a successful mentor is that of someone who not only encourages a protégé to become a more reflective, inquiring professional[50,51], but also who "come[s] to [his/her] responsibilities with a deep sense of wanting to serve others and to provide expertise to professionals"[52, p. 27].

Leithwood and Steinbach[14] contend that on-the-job experience by itself will not produce expertise, rather novices need to receive adequate instruction and be actively engaged with professionals who can model expert problem solving. Substantial evidence exists which indicates that when potential and practising professionals are provided with a systematic, well-designed programme aimed at developing their cognitive abilities, they measurably improve their reflective and problem-solving abilities[13,14,38]. Nevertheless, the view that mentors are capable of being the catalysts for cognitive development rests on three important assumptions, which are that mentors must be:

(1) reflective practitioners who are expert problem solvers;

(2) capable of helping novices develop these same mental capacities;

(3) able to ensure protégés can become autonomous, independent problem solvers.

To believe these assumptions hold true for all educators who are asked to fulfil the mentoring role is an extremely risky proposition.

Given the complexity of mentoring[10], especially in helping protégés to develop expertise, there is reason to believe these three assumptions will not be true for most mentors. By implication, mentors who become cognitive coaches will require ongoing assistance in developing their own cognitive abilities and teaching skills. Cognitive coaching training programmes have been created (e.g.[53]) as well as mentor training programmes for teachers and administrators (e.g.[12,52]). In order to provide some sense of what a training programme might consist of for mentors who wish to develop the intellectual capacities of protégés, outlined below are the basic components of such a programme.

A training model aimed at developing and maintaining the capacity of mentors to facilitate the cognitive growth of their protégés would consist of many of the elements proposed by Daresh and Playko[52]. These components include:

- orientation to the mentoring role;
- instructional leadership skills;
- human relations skills;
- mentor process skills.

Time devoted to the first three elements provides the foundation for the most crucial component, mentor process skills. For example, during the orientation phase, the mentors' basic role of asking protégés the right questions to stimulate their thinking and helping protégés to articulate their personal and professional goals would be emphasized. Next, the instructional leadership skills associated with "structured forms of inquiry to develop a validated knowledge base which... guide the actions of successful [educators]"[52, p. 26] would be acknowledged and discussed. Finally, attention would be devoted to mentors' human relations skills, especially those which help mentors identify the cognitive development level of protégés[54,55]. Introducing the instruments identified earlier which measure the level of reflective thinking and problem solving (e.g.[13,14]) would be appropriate for this portion of the training.

Following discussion and training in these three areas, concerted attention would be directed at developing, refining, and mastering mentor process skills. Daresh and Playko[52] believe these process skills include problem finding, problem solving, and reflection. To guide mentors in this process, Leithwood and Steinbach provide a framework for the types of activities which mentors might build into their working relationships with protégés[14, p. 324]:

- models of expert performance;
- multiple opportunities for practising administrative problem solving;
- a sequence of increasingly complex task demands;
- feedback about the adequacy of performance and the sophistication of (protégés') guiding cognitive schema.

Specific activities would be introduced and practised in order to facilitate the development of these process skills. For instance, mediation skills associated with cognitive coaching would be examined[15,53]. Instructional activities would be devoted to assisting mentors in how to form reflective questions, clarify and probe protégés' responses, and ask questions non-judgementally. The materials and activities associated with peer-assisted leadership training[39,40,56] would be most helpful. Once again, the measures of reflective thinking and problem-solving capacity introduced earlier in the training could be re-examined in order to assist mentors and protégés in discovering if protégés are developing additional problem-solving expertise. Finally, by incorporating the ideas developed by Gray and Gray[12] in their Helping Relationship Model, mentors could discern ways in which to gradually relinquish their influence over protégés, encouraging them to become independent, autonomous problem solvers.

An important aspect of this training is that it be ongoing, rather than be conducted only at the beginning of the formation of the mentor-protégé relationship. To expect mentors to be able to grasp and excel in their roles as cognitive coaches without periodic debriefing, feedback, and monitoring of their progress, is to underestimate the complexity of this new mentoring role[10]. Not only will these ongoing sessions assist mentors in learning new skills and examining ways in which their protégés are becoming autonomous experts, they will also allow mentors to explore the effects these new relationships are having on their own job satisfaction and mental growth.

We suspect mentors using such a training approach will soon realize that coaching the mental development of other educators positively affects their own mental capacities and perceptions as well. And as Clutterbuck[57] suggests, it is just this type of win-win situation that can make mentoring so motivating and professionally rewarding for both parties. Undoubtedly, such training programmes will require additional time and commitment from mentors; however, if schools and communities truly want educators who can think and act as experts, then the potential of such professional development programmes for seasoned professionals and up-and-coming novices cannot be overemphasized.

References

1. Schein E (1978) *Career Dynamics: Matching Individual and Organizational Needs.* Addison-Wesley, Reading, MA.
2. Wasden D F (1988) *The Mentoring Handbook.* Brigham Young University College of Education, Provo, UT.
3. Ashburn E A, Mann M, Purdue P A (1987) Teacher mentoring: ERIC clearinghouse in teacher education. Paper presented at the Annual Meeting of the American Educational Research Association, Washington DC.
4. Clawson J (1979) Superior-subordinate relationships for managerial development. Unpublished doctoral dissertation. Harvard University, Cambridge, MA.
5. Alleman E (1982) Mentoring relationships in organizations: behavior, personality characteristics, and interpersonal perceptions. Unpublished doctoral dissertation. University of Akron, Akron, OH.
6. Thies-Sprinthall L, Sprinthall N A (1987) Experienced teachers: agents for revitalization and renewal as mentors and teacher educators. *Journal of Education* 169 (1): 65–79.
7. Kram K (1985) *Mentoring at Work: Developmental Relationships in Organizational Life.* Scott, Foresman and Company, Glenview, IL.
8. Kram K (1983) Phases of the mentor relationship. *Academy of Management Journal* 26 (4): 608–625.
9. Hunt D M, Michael C (1983) Mentorship: a career training and development tool. *Academy of Management Review* 8 (3): 475–485.
10. Head F A, Reiman A J, Thies-Sprinthall L (1992) The reality of mentoring: complexity in its process and function. In: T M Bey, C T Holmes (eds) *Mentoring: Contemporary Principles and Issues.* Association of Teacher Educators, Reston, VA.
11. Phillips L L (1977) Mentors and protégés: a study of the career development of women managers and executives in business and industry. Unpublished doctoral dissertation. University of California, Los Angeles, CA.
12. Gray W A, Gray M M (1985) Synthesis of research on mentoring beginning teachers. *Educational Leadership* 43 (3): 37–43.
13. Short P M, Rinehart J S (1993) Reflection as a means of developing expertise. *Educational Administration Quarterly* 29 (4): 501–521.
14. Leithwood K, Steinbach R (1992) Improving the problem-solving expertise of school administrators: theory and practice. *Education and Urban Society* 24 (3): 317–345.
15. Costa A L, Garmston R J (1994) *Cognitive Coaching: A Foundation for Renaissance Schools.* Christopher-Gordon Publishers, Norwood, MA.
16. Shank R, Abelson R (1977) Scripts, *Plans, Goals and Understanding.* Lawrence Erlbaum, Hillsdale, NJ.
17. Chi M T H, Feltovich P J, Glaser R (1981) Categorization and representation of physics problems by experts and novices. *Cognitive Science* 5: 121–152.
18. Hardiman P T, Dufresne R, Mestre J P (1989) The relation between problem categorization and problem solving among experts and novices. *Memory & Cognition* 17 (5): 627–638.
19. Leithwood K A, Cousins B, Smith M (1990) The principals' world from a problem solving perspective. *Canadian School Executive,* January, February, March (3 instalments).

20. Broudy H (1981) *Truth and Credibility: The Citizen's Dilemma,* Longman, New York.

21. Berliner D C (1986) In pursuit of the expert pedagogue. *Educational Researcher* 15 (3): 5–13.

22. Leinhardt G, Greeno J G (1986) The cognitive skill of teaching. *Journal of Educational* Psychology 78 (2): 75–95.

23. Sparks-Langer G M, Simmons J M, Pasch M, Colton A, Starko A (1990) Reflective pedagogical thinking: how can we promote it and measure it? *Journal of Teacher Education* 41 (5): 23–32.

24. Leithwood K A, Stager M (1989) Expertise in principals' problem solving. *Educational Administration Quarterly* 25 (2): 126–161.

25. Schon D A (1987) *Educating the Reflective Practitioner.* Jossey-Bass, San Francisco.

26. Schon D (1983) *The Refective Practitioner.* Basic Books, New York.

27. Barnett B G (1987) Using reflection as a professional development activity. In: W D Greenfield (ed.) *Instructional Leadership: Concepts, Issues, and Controversies.* Allyn & Bacon, Newton, MA.

28. Barnett BG, Brill A D (1990) Building reflection into administrative training programs. *Journal of Personnel Evaluation in Education* 3: 179–192.

29. Biehler R F, Snowman J (1993) *Psychology Applied to Teaching,* 7th edn. Houghton-Mifflin, Boston.

30. Eggen P, Kauchak D (1994) *Educational Psychology: Classroom Connections,* 2nd edn. Merrill, New York.

31. Van Mannen M (1977) Linking ways of knowing with ways of being practical. *Curriculum Inquiry* 6 (3): 205–228.

32. Hart AW (1990) Effective administration through reflective practice. *Education and Urban Society* 22 (2): 153–169.

33. Kolb D (1984) *Experiential Learning: Experience as the Source of Learning and Development.* Prentice-Hall, Englewood Cliffs, NJ.

34. Osterman K F, Kottkamp R B (1993) *Reflective Practice for Educators: Improving Schooling through Professional Development.* Corwin Press, Newbury Park, CA.

35. Ross D D (1989) First steps in developing a reflective approach. *Journal of Teacher Education* 40 (2): 22–30.

36. Glaser R (1989) Expertise and learning: how do we think about instructional processes now that we have discovered knowledge structures? In: D Klahr, K Kotovsky (eds) *Complex Information Processing: The Impact* of *Herbert A. Simon.* Lawrence Erlbaum, Hillsdale, NJ.

37. Hunt D E, Greenwood J, Noy J, Watson N (1973) *Assessment of Conceptual Level: Paragraph Completion Method.* Ontario Institute for Studies in Education, Toronto.

38. Allen J D (1995) The use of case studies to teach educational psychology: a comparison with traditional instruction. Paper presented at the Annual Meeting of the American Educational Research Association, San Francisco.

39. Lee G V, Barnett B G (1994) Using reflective questioning to promote collaborative dialogue. *Journal* of *Staff Development* 15 (1): 16–21.

40. Barnett B G (1987) Peer-assisted leadership: using peer observations and feedback as catalysts for professional growth. In: J Murphy, P Hallinger (eds) *Approaches to Administrative Training in Education.* SUNY Press, New York.

41. Lee G V (1991) Peer-assisted development of school leaders. *Journal of Staff Development* 12 (2): 14–18.

42. Blom S, Kruger M, van Roozendaal T (1995) Peer-assisted leadership: narrowing the gap between theory and practice. Paper presented at the Annual Meeting of the American Educational Research Association, San Francisco.

43. Brooks J G, Brooks M G (1993) *In Search of Understanding: The Case for Constructivist Classrooms.* Association for Supervision and Curriculum Development, Alexandria, VA.

44. Garmston R, Hyerle D (1988) *Professor's Peer Coaching Program: Report on a 1987–88 Pilot Project to Develop and Test a Staff Development Model for Improving Instruction at California State University.* California State University, Sacramento.

45. Flores J (1991) Cognitive coaching: does it help? Unpublished Master's Thesis. California State University, Sacramento.

46. Edwards J (1992) The effects of cognitive coaching on the conceptual development and reflective thinking of first year teachers. Unpublished doctoral dissertation. Fielding Institute, Santa Barbara.

47. Lipton L (1993) Transforming information into knowledge: structured reflection in administrative practice. Paper presented at the Annual Meeting of the American Educational Research Association, Atlanta, GA.

48. Naylor J (1991) The role and function of department chairpersons in the collegial peer coaching environment. Unpublished doctoral dissertation. University of Illinois, Champaign/Urbana.

49. Garmston R, Linder C, Whitaker J (1993) Reflections on cognitive coaching. *Educational Leadership* 51 (2): 57–61.

50. Howey K R (1988) Mentor-teachers as inquiring professionals. *Theory into Practice* 27 (3): 209–213.

51. Reiman A (1988) An intervention study of long-term mentor training: relationships between cognitive-developmental theory and reflection. Unpublished doctoral dissertation. North Carolina State University, Raleigh, NC.

52. Daresh J C, Playko M A (1991) Preparing mentors for school leaders. *Journal of Staff Development* 12 (4): 24–27.

53. Costa A, Garmston R (1994) *The Art of Cognitive Coaching: Foundation Seminar.* Institute for Intelligent Behavior, Berkeley.

54. Hunt D (1974) *Matching Models in Education.* Ontario Institute for Studies in Education, Toronto.

55. Thies-Sprinthall L (1984) Promoting the developmental growth of supervising teachers: theory, research programs, and implications. *Journal of Teacher Education* 35 (3): 53–60.

56. Barnett B G (1990) Peer-assisted leadership: expanding principals' knowledge through reflective practice. *Journal of Educational Administration* 28 (3): 67–76.

57. Clutterbuck (1991) *Everyone Needs a Mentor,* 2nd edn. Institute of Personnel Management, London.

Assessing and Evaluating Learning in Practice

Assessment is a key role for anyone involved in mentoring. The focus for the extracts in this section is on assessment and evaluation of learning in a workplace environment and issues of formal theoretical assessment through examinations and assignments are not addressed in any significant way in any of the extracts or articles provided.

Many definitions of assessment exist and lead to a general confusion about what it is and what it is not. Nicklin and Kenworthy (2000) provide a relatively simple yet unambiguous definition which might prove useful:

> 'Measurement that directly relates to the quality and quantity of learning and as such is concerned with student progress and attainment.' (Nicklin and Kenworthy, 2000: p. 103)

In a range of healthcare professions, continuous assessment of practice is now the required strategy to ascertain whether a learner meets certain competencies which allow him/her to progress through his/her programme of study. Continuous assessment of practice integrates formative and summative assessment strategies, which increases the chances of validity and reliability of the assessment strategy. It is a concept which embraces and integrates different assessment strategies into a unified approach and as such is arguably not an assessment strategy in its own right but rather a philosophy of assessment (Oliver and Endersby, 1994).

Rowntree (1992) and Jarvis (1997) are two key figures in the area of assessment. They suggest that the process of assessment carries with it a great deal of responsibility. Rowntree (1992) feels that assessment is about getting to know people and making judgements about their capabilities. Jarvis and Gibson (1997) contend that assessment is the gatekeeping mechanism through which people do, or do not, make progress in their chosen course or occupation.

Assessment is therefore an ethical activity (Milligan, 1996). There is a requirement to be as certain as possible about the accuracy of judgements made in assessment and to be able to actively support those judgements be they good or bad. There is an inescapable fact that, however sound the assessment strategy, the assessment of individuals in the ever changing context of the workplace requires the exercise of professional and experienced judgement.

References

Jarvis P, Gibson S (1985) *The Teacher Practitioner and Mentor in Nursing, Midwifery and Health Visiting.* Stanley Thornes, London.

Nicklin P, Kenworthy N (2000) *Teaching and Assessing in Nursing Practice,* 3rd edn. Bailliere Tindall, London.

Oliver R, Endersby C (1994) *Teaching and Asssessing Nurses: A Handbook for Preceptors*. Bailliere Tindall, London.

Rowntree D (1992) *Assessing Students – How Should we Know Them?* Harper and Row, London.

30. What is Assessment?

Derek Rowntree

If we wish to discover the truth about an educational system, we must look into its assessment procedures. What student qualities and achievements are actively valued and rewarded by the system? How are its purposes and intentions realized? To what extent are the hopes and ideals, aims and objectives professed by the system ever truly perceived, valued and striven for by those who make their way within it? The answers to such questions are to be found in what the system requires students to *do* in order to survive and prosper. The spirit and style of student assessment defines the *de facto* curriculum.

A cause for concern

I was constantly reminded of the crucial nature of assessment during the writing of a previous book on curriculum development (Rowntree, 1974). There I found that in every chapter, whatever I was writing about — aims and objectives, the design of learning experiences, the sequencing and structuring of knowledge, the evaluation and improvement of teaching — questions of assessment kept rearing their heads and threatening to dominate the discussion.

If assessment is so crucial, one might expect the subject to have an extensive literature already. So why add to it? Indeed much has been written (see, e.g. Ebel, 1972; Gronlund, 1971; Hudson, 1973; Lewis, 1974; Pidgeon and Yates, 1969; Schofield, 1972; Terwilliger, 1971; Thorndike, 1972; Thyne, 1974; etc.) But, for the most part, the literature takes for granted the present nature of assessment and seeks improvement merely through increasing its efficiency. Thus, for example, it is easy to find writers concerned with how to produce better multiple-choice questions, how to handle test-results statistically, or how to compensate for the fact that different examiners respond differently to a given piece of student work. It is much less easy to find writers questioning the purposes of assessment, asking what qualities it does or should identify, examining its effects on the relationships between teachers and learners, or attempting to relate it to such concepts as truth, fairness, trust, humanity and social justice. Writers of the former preoccupation rarely give any indication of having considered questions of the latter kind. Insofar as they appear to regard assessment as non-problematic, their writings, though often extremely valuable in their way, gloss over more fundamental questions about whether what we are doing is the right thing and offer simply a technical prescription for doing it better. This James Thyne (1974) approvingly calls 'the goodness of examinations as technical instruments'. Even then, the implications of doing it 'better' are rarely pursued very far. In short, the literature addresses itself chiefly to the question 'How?' rather than the question 'Why?'. In this [book] I shall try to adjust the emphasis.

Derek Rowntree: 'What is Assessment?' from *ASSESSING STUDENTS: HOW SHALL WE KNOW THEM?* (Kogan Page Ltd, 1977; 1987), pp. 1–13.

The discontinuity between technical and philosophical considerations in assessment is not new and has long been recognized. Here is Kandel (1936) saying of examinations what I would wish to say of all forms of assessment:

> '. . . the problem of examinations is not primarily one of discovering more accurate scientific and technical methods of constructing and scoring examinations. The problem of examinations strikes at the very roots of the whole meaning and significance of education in society. . . . The essence of the problem is the validity of education.' (p. 151)

My hope is that this book will encourage colleagues in education (by which I mean students as well as teachers) to bring together the technical and the philosophical, and to examine assessment anew from a broader perspective. Teachers tend to be trapped in a time-vortex that inhibits them from giving too much thought to assessment that has happened previously, or will happen later, to their students in institutions other than their own. Awareness is greatest near the gateways between two stages in a student's career, e.g. top juniors, or 6th form, or first year at college. But, even then, attention tends to be restricted to the last or next gateway. My contention is that we can all learn much by considering how assessment operates in learning mileux other than the ones with which we are directly concerned. Thus the university teacher may gain substantial insights from thinking about assessment in the primary school, and so may the primary school teacher from thinking about assessment in higher education. Similarly, teachers in one country can learn from the practices of those in another country or another time. Hence I make no apology for including examples from all levels of education, and from other countries (especially the U.S.A.) and other times. Further, we should at least be aware that educational assessment has more than a family resemblance to many other forms of assessment prevalent in our society. To name but a few:

everyday conversational dialogue;
medical and psychiatric diagnosis;
the writing of biography;
forensic cross-examination;
job-interviews and promotion appraisals;
criticism of art and literature;
'refereeing' of books and of papers submitted for publication in scholarly journals.

Such forms of assessment will sometimes offer revealing parallels and contrasts with those common in education.

In recent years, writings and conferences debating basic aspects of student assessment have begun to occur more frequently. Extreme positions get taken up. People may be passionate apologists for the system as it is now held to exist. Or they may be equally passionate denouncers of assessment as a tyrannical means of persuasion, coercion and social control, enhancing the power of one group of people (the teachers, together perhaps with whatever others they may believe themselves to be representing — 'the discipline' or profession, parents, employers, 'society') over another group (the students). Not surprisingly then, debates on assessment can raise strong feelings. The clash of ideologies — in the Marxian sense of ideas being used as weapons in a struggle for dominance between groups with conflicting interests — can be more in evidence than honest reflection and rational analysis. Consequently, assessment debate is awash with hidden assumptions, unstated values, partial truths, confusions of ideas, false distinctions, and irrelevant emphases. It is also flooded with specialist terminology — jargon, even — which we will have to find our way around in the following pages.

The nature of assessment

Some of the confusions and false distinctions will become apparent as we begin exploring a working definition of assessment. Dictionary definitions tend to agree that to assess is to put a value on something, usually in financial terms. Such definitions are clearly not centred on educational assessment, although it is true that certain outcomes of educational assessment, e.g. a student's degree class, may well determine the salary he can expect. Again, such valuational definitions do chime in with what many teachers think of (erroneously, I would say) as essential components of assessment, *viz* the assigning of numerical marks or letter grades, and the ranking of students in order of preference or relative achievement.

More basically, assessment in education can be thought of as occurring whenever one person, in some kind of interaction, direct or indirect, with another, is conscious of obtaining and interpreting information about the knowledge and understanding, or abilities and attitudes of that other person. To some extent or other it is an attempt to *know* that person. In this light, assessment can be seen as human encounter. In education we are mainly conscious of this 'encounter' in the shape of teachers finding out about their students. But we must not forget that students also assess one another, especially when working together as co-operative teams. They also assess their teachers (see Miller, 1972; Page, 1974). Mutual assessment is perhaps what Nell Keddie (1971) has in mind when she refers to 'the ways in which teachers and pupils scan each other's activities in the classroom and attribute meaning to them' (see also Downey, 1977). Nor should we hesitate to turn the definition in upon itself and think of the person (student or teacher) finding out about *himself* —self-assessment.

Despite one of the assumptions commonly made in the literature, assessment is not obtained only, or even necessarily mainly, through tests and examinations. Finding out about a student's abilities and so on may not involve testing him or measuring his performance in any formal way. We can imagine a spectrum of assessment situations ranging from the very informal, almost casual, to the highly formal, perhaps even ritualistic. At the informal end of the spectrum we have, for instance, the continuous but unself-conscious assessment that takes place between partners in an everyday conversation where each is constantly responding to what he takes to be the emerging attitudes and understandings of the other as he decides what to say next in consequence. Compare this with the monologue of a platform speaker or with the programmed patter of the kind of door-to-door evangelist who steadfastly ignores all responses that might suggest he should depart from his 'script'.

In a classroom conversation, however, where the intentions of the participants may be rather more directed to specific tasks and goals, the assessment may be slightly more formal, or at least more self-conscious. When assessment becomes the purpose, even if unstated, of initiating a conversation, e.g. in asking the student what he knows or feels about an issue, the formality becomes yet greater. So too, as far as the teacher at least is concerned, when he unobtrusively observes the student in action in order to assess. The ultimate in formality, for both teacher and student, is reached when the student is required to perform in what is patently a test-situation — quiz, interview, practical test, written examination, or whatever.

But it is worth noting here that, despite another common confusion, all these shades of assessment can be practised without any kind of measurement that implies absolute standards; it may be enough simply to observe whether, for each student, some personal, even idiosyncratic, trait or ability appears discernible to greater or lesser extent than hitherto. There need be no requirement to compare the findings for one student with those for another, let alone arrange students in some kind of order as a result of any such comparisons. Joan Tough (1976, p. 32) makes the point very well in distinguishing between testing and 'appraisal':

> 'How does the child walk and run? What is the quality of his movement? What kind of control does the child have of fine and intricate manipulation and of movement that needs concentration of strength and effort? What is the child's general co-ordination of movements like? Is he awkward and ungainly or does he move easily and smoothly without apparent effort? Many of these qualities would defy measurement, and many would defy comparison with other children. But all could be appraised, i.e. described in terms which build up a picture of what the child is like.'

Again, despite many assumptions to the contrary, assessment is not the same thing as grading or marking. If you 'grade' or 'mark' a student (or his work — the distinction is often unclear both to students and teachers) you are attaching a letter or number that is meant somehow to symbolize the quality of the work and allow comparison with the work of other students. Such grading cannot take place without prior assessment — the nature and quality of the student's work must be determined before it can be labelled with a suitable symbol. But assessment can, and perhaps usually does, take place without being followed by grading. Assessment can be *descriptive* (e.g. 'Bob knows all his number bonds up to 20') without becoming *judgemental* (e.g. 'Bob is good at number bonds'). It may be that in secondary and higher education the only assessments that count are those which are, in fact, followed by grading. But in infant schools and, to a large extent, in junior schools (with the exception of those still preparing children for the 11-plus exam) developing skills are constantly being assessed without any apparent compulsion to label them with letter grades or numerical marks. Odd, then, that a colleague of mine, admittedly in higher education, should rebuff a suggestion that we abandon the grading of essays by saying 'No, we can't claim to be teaching properly unless we know how our students are progressing.'

Just as tests and examinations are possible means of assessment, so grades and marks are possible outcomes. But they are not the only ones possible. Assessment is also a necessary precondition for *diagnostic appraisal* — ascertaining the student's strengths and weaknesses, and identifying his emerging needs and interests. In truth it is the practice of diagnostic appraisal (not grading) that enables us to claim we are teaching. Given that the student has reached such-and-such a state, what can he or should he aim for next? What implications does this have for the ensuing learning experiences? Diagnostic appraisal does not involve grading. Nor need it necessarily be based on formal tests and measurements. It is dependent on some kind of assessment having taken place, however, together with pedagogic judgements as to what new learning experiences are possible, and value-judgements (the student's perhaps, as well as the teacher's) as to which are desirable.

There is a further useful distinction we can make between two words which, in everyday parlance, and indeed in most dictionaries, seem virtual synonyms — assessment and evaluation. In education, though, it is common in Britain to use the two words to refer to two rather different, though closely-related activities. If assessment tries to discover what the student is becoming or has accomplished, then evaluation tries to do the same for a course or learning experience or episode of teaching. Evaluation is an attempt to identify and explain the effects (and effectiveness) of the teaching. In such an attempt, assessment is clearly a necessary component. Assessment, whether formal or informal, reveals to us the most important class of 'effects' — the changes brought about in the knowledge and understanding, abilities and attitudes of our students. If students have not changed or have somehow changed for the worse, e.g. they may have learned to solve simultaneous equations but also to detest algebra, we suspect something is wrong with the teaching. But student assessment is only part of evaluation. A full evaluation will also need, for example, to consider the effects of the course on people other than students — on the teachers participating, on other teachers who have contact with the students, on parents, on employers, on other people in the community, and so on. Thus, data additional to the assessment data — gained perhaps through participant observation, discussions, interviewing, reading of local newspapers, internal memoranda, etc. — will be needed. Incidentally, in the U.S.A. the word 'assessment' is rarely used in this context at all; instead, the word 'evaluation' usually has to do duty for both the concepts described above. In scanning the American literature, one must know whether one is looking for evaluation (of students) or evaluation (of courses).

The American literature (Scriven, 1967) has, however, developed a distinction between types of evaluation (of courses) that is equally useful in thinking about assessment. Thus, *formative* evaluation is intended to develop and improve a piece of teaching until it is as effective as it possibly can be —a well-tested programmed textbook would be a prime example. *Summative* evaluation, on the other hand, is intended to establish the effectiveness of the teaching once it is fully developed and in regular use. The distinction is, in fact, rather hard to preserve in considering the evaluation of most kinds of teaching; but it is very descriptive of what goes on in student assessment. Diagnostic appraisal, directed towards developing the student and contributing to his growth, can be thought of as formative assessment. Summative assessment, on the other hand, is clearly represented by terminal tests and examinations coming at the end of the student's course, or indeed by any attempt to reach an overall description or judgement of the student (e.g. in an end-of-term report or a grade or class-rank). Peter Vandome and his colleagues (1973) recognize this distinction and remind us that each is generally used (though it need not be) for a different purpose, by labelling the former 'pedagogic' and the latter 'classificatory'. In formative (pedagogic) assessment the emphasis is on potential, while in summative (classificatory) assessment it is on actual achievement.

The dynamics of assessment

In Rowntree (1974) I considered how the concepts we have been talking about flow together in a teaching situation. Figure 1 illustrates the dynamic relationships between formative assessment, formative evaluation and summative assessment. At each stage in his teaching (T) the teacher makes an assessment (A) of the student's learning which, together perhaps with non-assessment data on the effects of the teaching (N), enables him to evaluate how successfully he has taught so far (E). The assessment also helps him to diagnose (D) the new needs of the student, and diagnosis and evaluation together go to determine the purpose and nature of the next stage of the teaching (T). This 'teachmg', which may be of a few seconds' or a few weeks' duration continues until further assessment gives rise to more evaluation and diagnostic appraisal. If these essentially formative assessments are translated into grades (G) for the student and some or all of these grades are to count towards an overall summative assessment, the system may be called 'continuous assessment'. Strictly speaking it might better be described as 'continuous grading'. The student may, in addition, be given a final summative assessment (big A), perhaps taking account of some or all of the previous formative assessments as well as a special end-of-course examination assessing what he has learned over the course as a whole. He may also be given a final, overall grade (big G), made up out of some or all the grades awarded so far.

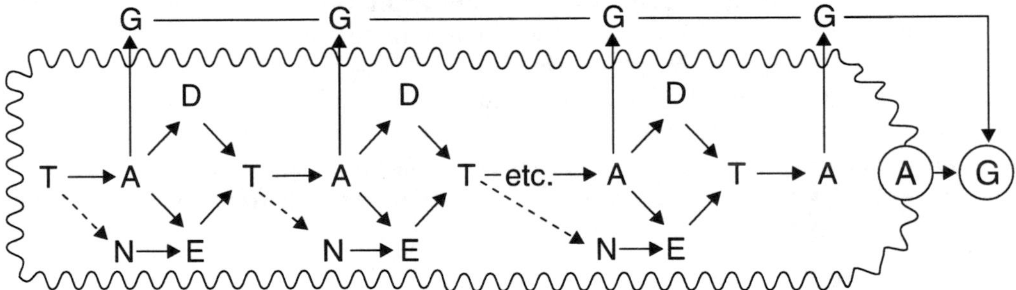

Key:
T = Teaching; A = Assessment of what the student has learned (essentially formative); N = Other data on effects of teaching; E = Evaluation of teaching effectiveness; D = Diagnostic appraisal of student's needs; G = Grade based on A; Ⓐ= Assessment of what the student has learned overall (summative); Ⓖ= Grade based on Ⓐ and previous Gs.

Figure 1 Assessment, evaluation, diagnosis, and grading

Clearly, then, the field of assessment is full of conceptual quagmires and terminological traps for the unwary or short-sighted. Further specimens will be identified later. But already we see the need for considerable circumspection when approaching the literature. We must keep asking ourselves, for instance, whether an author is talking about evaluation or assessment, informal assessment or formal, formative or summative, pedagogic or classificatory. And, if it is possible to tell which kind of assessment he is talking of, we must ask whether what he says really applies to that kind and to that kind only.

Questions of responsibility

Nor should we overlook, at a practical level, the conflict and ambivalence of purpose that can arise in a teacher as he decides what to do about the result of an assessment. Especially, he may be troubled as to how sensible it is both to evaluate the effectiveness of his own teaching and to grade the students according to what they have learned from it. Who or what is on trial? Who deserves the grade — the teacher or the student? If, in an extreme case, the teacher 'fails' his student, has the course indeed failed him or has the student failed the course? (Note, as a grim parallel, that many a terminally ill patient feels that he has 'failed' his surgeon.) Of course, when a student has been openly uninterested and has made no effort to learn, then it may be only in a weak sense that the responsibility can be laid upon the teacher rather than the student. But suppose the student has shown great interest and worked conscientiously, perhaps even learned a great deal, though not entirely what the teacher wanted him to learn, and gained personal satisfaction from his progress? Then the teacher who sees fit to penalize the student for having failed to satisfy teacher's requirements may in quite a strong sense be asked to consider that he has failed his student.

Does it matter who is 'to blame' for ineffective learning? Not much when assessment is used privately for diagnostic appraisal or evaluation and therefore benefits the student. More so, however, when assessment is done with public grading in view; for this is often not so much for the student's benefit (through discovering his learning needs and improving the teaching) as for the benefit of other people who will use it (with no thought of shared 'blame') to determine what the student's life-chances are to be.

The most casual browse through the literature of assessment is enough to establish that the vast bulk is concerned with how to use assessment for purposes of grading and ranking. Only a minuscule proportion considers how to use it to enhance the student's educational growth. This bias in the literature faithfully reflects the priorities of the education industry. As Donald McIntyre (1970) forthrightly says:

> '. . . although we spend an enormous amount of time and money on assessment, very little is obtained which helps teachers to teach. Instead, we give pupils marks or grades, that is, we concentrate on *judging* them, on saying how 'good' or 'bad' they are, on putting them in an 'order of merit'. Assessment of this . . . sort can make no contribution to effective teaching. Its function is to select pupils, gradually as they pass through our schools, for different positions in the socio-economic hierarchy of our society, positions for which we then proceed to train them.'

Such ideological interpretations can easily be attached to the grading decisions that arise out of assessment, but not so easily to diagnostic and evaluational decisions. Assessment itself can be a reasonably objective gathering of information; though, of course, some kind of subjective preference will inevitably be directing the assessor's attention to some things rather than others. But the form assessment takes, and the uses to which the gathered information is put, may vary with the assumptions that are being made about the division of responsibility in teaching and learning. Thus, 'grading' assumes that the teaching is essentially beyond reproach, and that the student is to be rewarded according to how well he has discharged his responsibility to learn from it, and that this will be revealed objectively and reliably by assessment. 'Diagnostic appraisal' makes no assumptions about the responsibility for teaching and learning; and its value-judgements about the student's apparent strengths and weaknesses and needs are not published as objective truths about the student. 'Evaluation' does tend to make assumptions about responsibility, however, and they may be quite the opposite of those made by 'grading'. Evaluation assumes that weaknesses in the student's learning may well be explicable by weaknesses in the teaching and that it is the responsibility of the teaching to change in such a way as to optimize the student's learning.

In educational practice, of course, these three attitudes to assessment often operate together. Clearly, different teachers within a teaching team may take up different stances. But even the teacher who is assessing with a view to ranking his students according to how much they have learned may be shocked into an evaluational stance if he discovers that scarcely any of them have learned anything. And, of course, a given teacher may intentionally operate with different assumptions at different times. If he slips unwittingly from one set of assumptions to another, or if he needs to co-operate with people whose assumptions he fails to recognize as being different from his, then confusion can arise.

Five dimensions of assessment

To provide a framework for our exploration of assessment, I have chosen to identify within it five dimensions. These five dimensions refer to five different kinds of mental activity among people who undertake assessment. Each kind of mental activity results in decisions being made and actions being taken. Naturally, the five dimensions correspond to what seem to me to be the key activities in the process of assessment. The questions underlying these five dimensions are as follows:

> *Why assess?* Deciding why assessment is to be carried out; what effects or outcomes it is expected to produce.
>
> *What to assess?* Deciding, realizing, or otherwise coming to an awareness of what one is looking for, or remarking upon, in the people one is assessing.
>
> *How to assess?* Selecting, from among all the means we have at our disposal for learning about people, those we regard as being most truthful and fair for various sorts of valued knowledge.
>
> *How to interpret?* Making sense of the outcomes of whatever observations or measurements or impressions we gather through whatever means we employ; explaining, appreciating, and attaching meaning to the raw 'events' of assessment.

How to respond? Finding appropriate ways of expressing our response to whatever has been assessed and of communicating it to the person concerned (and other people).

To put some flesh on that austere framework, let me give a couple of examples. An infants' teacher may wish to assess the developing self-confidence of a new child in her class with a view to helping him settle in; she may do this by observing the child in situations that he might see as threatening; she may interpret the behaviour she observes by comparing it with behaviour in similar situations in the past and considering what experiences have contributed to the child's growth; she may respond by encouraging the child, providing some 'growth experiences' for him, and perhaps by writing some brief diary comment. On the other hand, a secondary school mathematics teacher may wish to predict his students' chances in a public examination; he may therefore assess their ability to solve a range of problems under 'mock' examination conditions; he may interpret their performance by comparison with what he believes to be the standards of the examiners; he may respond by giving each student a grade for the examination as a whole and giving extra tuition to those students he feels are not yet ready to enter for the public examination. (He may also notice areas in which his previous teaching might have been improved.)

Some words of warning. I am not suggesting that the five dimensions will all be present in any given assessment situation — certainly not all consciously, or all in the mind of any one individual. Nor am I suggesting that those that do enter a person's mind will or should arrive in the sequence I followed in my list and examples. Nor, yet again, am I suggesting that the dimensions are clearly separable from one another or that any one of the mental activities can be carried out and 'completed' without either reference to one of the others or the need to return to it later with 'second thoughts'. In fact, as in most human information-processing, we start where our situation demands, putting the emphasis where we feel it is wanted and pursuing each activity as far as we need, returning if necessary more than once to re-cycle our earlier decisions. Thus, if a teacher is limited as to the assessment techniques he can choose among (as in the Open University where he cannot easily meet his students face-to-face), his decisions about what to assess will be highly dependent on prior decisions (and not necessarily his) about what techniques are available, rather than vice versa. But any teacher, once he has engaged with the problems of how to assess, how to interpret the outcomes and how to respond to them, is likely to see development in his views as to what should be assessed and why.

Interestingly, for the parallels between teaching and doctoring are always illuminating, the How to Assess / Interpret / Respond dimensions are very similar to what Michael Balint (1964, Preface) described as the successive phases of the *diagnostic* process in medicine — listening, understanding, and using the understanding so that it should have a therapeutic effect. That is, '"listening" provides the material which is then ordered into "understanding" . . . "using the understanding so that it should have a therapeutic effect" is tantamout to a demand for a more exacting form of diagnosis; the therapist is expected to predict with a fair amount of accuracy what sort of effect his envisaged interventions will have.' So too is the teacher.

But before we consider further the dynamics of assessment, we must consider why it is done at all. In the [next chapter] we'll examine some functions and purposes commonly ascribed to assessment. And in [the chapter after that] we'll consider some outcomes that are not so generally ascribed, or even admitted.

References

Balint M (1964) *The Doctor, his Patient and the Illness.* Pitman, London. (First published 1957.)

Downey M E (1977) *Interpersonal Judgements in Education.* Harper and Row, London.

Ebel R (1972) *Essentials of Educational Measurement.* Prentice-Hall, Englewood Cliffs, New Jersey.

Gronlund N E (1971) *Measurement and Evaluation in Teaching.* Macmillan, London.

Hudson B B (1973) *Assessment Techniques.* Methuen, London.

Kandel I (1936) *Examinations and their Substitutes in the United States.* Carnegie Foundation for the Advancement of Teaching, Bulletin 28, New York.

Keddie N (1971) Classroom knowledge. In: M F D Young (ed.) *Knowledge and Control.* Collier-Macmillan, London.

Lewis D G (1974) *Assessment in Education.* University of London Press, London.

McIntyre D (1970) Assessment and teaching. In: D Rubinstein and C Stoneman (eds) *Education for Democracy*, 2nd edn. Penguin, London.

Miller R (1972) *Evaluating Faculty Performance.* Jossey-Bass, San Francisco.

Page C F (1974) *Student Evaluation of Teaching: The American Experience.* Society for Research into Higher Education, London.

Pidgeon D, Yates A (1969) *An Introduction to Educational Measurement.* Routledge and Kegan Paul, London.

Rowntree D (1974) *Educational Technology in Curriculum Development.* Harper and Row, London. (Second edition published 1982.)

Schofield H (1972) *Assessment and Testing: An Introduction.* Allen and Unwin, London.

Scriven M (1967) The methodology of evaluation. In: R W Tyler *et al.* (eds) *Perspectives of Curriculum Evaluation.* Rand McNally, Chicago.

Terwilliger J S (1971) *Assigning Grades to Students.* Scott, Foresman, Glenview, Illinois.

Thorndike R L (ed.) (1972) *Educational Measurement,* 2nd edn. American Council on Education, Washington DC.

Thyne J M (1974) *Principles of Examining.* University of London Press, London.

Tough J (1976) *Listening to Children Talking.* Ward Lock, London.

Vandome P *et al.* (1973) Why assessment? A paper given limited circulation in the University of Edinburgh.

31. The Purposes of Assessment

Derek Rowntree

Already we have seen that assessment has several purposes — diagnosis, evaluation, grading. But these are not ends in themselves, of course. They are means towards further ends. What are those over-arching purposes? In this chapter we shall consider why assessment is carried out at all. How is it justified? (Later we must ask what else is achieved that may not be explicitly claimed for it or even welcomed by the people involved.) More ominously, we can ask the question so often posed by the sleuth in old-fashioned crime-stories when considering whom to suspect of the murder: 'Who benefits?'

In general, the beneficiaries can be seen to be the student, his teacher and 'other people' (often referred to as 'society' — chiefly comprising parents, teachers and administrators in other educational institutions, and employers). Who benefits in particular instances depends on the nature and purpose of the assessment, e.g. formal or informal, formative or summative, pedagogic or classificatory, etc. Brian Klug (1974, p. 5), in what he says 'is undoubtedly an incomplete list', has gathered together thirty-two reasons for formal assessment. Here I shall concentrate on what I see as the six main reasons commonly advanced.

1. Selection by assessment

One very common purpose of assessment is the *selection* of candidates for various kinds of educational opportunity or career. In some parts of Britain, children are still assessed at the age of '11-plus' to decide for them whether they should have a grammar school education aiming towards university and the professional life, or some other sort. Again, at 16-plus, another batch of examinations or other assessment devices acts effectively to select some students for 6th-form education, some for other less prestigious further education, and some for the world of work. The '18-plus' controls entry to university and the professions and, of course, the universities and professional bodies have their own tests to select those students who are to be awarded degrees or professional standing. Even when he is well into his working life, a person's progress is still dependent on assessment. Whether by formal interviews or less formal observation and reporting by his boss, or by the appraisal of his peers, he is selected for advancement or redundancy. Such assessment always involves some kind of grading and the putting of people into categories, even if 'Pass' and 'Fail' are the only two used.

Selection tests are probably what most people think of when they talk about assessment. Actually, it is often somewhat euphemistic to call them 'selection' tests. For the majority of candidates many such tests function rather as *rejection* tests. Thus, the 11-plus rarely selected more than 20% of the children in an area to attend the local grammar school, and thereby rejected 80%. In the U.S.A., where selection testing, especially for college entrance, is big business and heavily bureaucraticized,

Derek Rowntree: 'The Purposes of Assessment' from *ASSESSING STUDENTS: HOW SHALL WE KNOW THEM?* (Kogan Page Ltd, 1977; 1987), pp. 15–33.

Hillell Black (1963) minced no words when he called his book on the subject *They Shall Not Pass.*

Selection (and rejection) is necessary because no country believes it can afford to give every citizen all he might desire in the way of education. A basic minimum may be available for everyone, e.g. ten years of normal schooling; but anyone who wants access to additional resources may have to prove that his need, or ability to benefit, is greater than that of others. We usually identify this competition for extra resources with the scramble for places in college and university. But, at the other end of the age-range, places in 'special schools' for children with learning difficulties are also limited: not every child whose parents and teachers believe he could profit from their more costly facilities will be selected. In many developing countries, places are in short supply even for secondary education and most children will fail to be selected.

One of the assumptions implicit in selection tests for advanced education is that only the brightest, most promising, and patently talented should be funded to continue. Now it is not logically obvious that extra educational resources should go to students who are already highly accomplished rather than to those with more ground to make up. However, advanced education is largely financed in the expectation that it will produce sufficient numbers of people capable of carrying out complex tasks in society — doctors, lawyers, engineers, etc. — and with the minimum investment of resources. To select students by lottery from among all interested candidates would clearly be egalitarian, and many students might gain entry and do well who would, at present, be considered too weak for selection. But such students might also make disproportionate demands on the teaching resources available, causing a reduction in the total number of 'capable persons' that could be produced.

Selection of 'students most likely to succeed' usually depends on public examinations. Since the Chinese invented them (before Europe had even evolved the feudal system) they have done something (though far less than as is usually assumed) to preserve some opportunities for talented children from poor families that might otherwise go to less promising children from richer homes. Essentially, selectors assume that the students who perform best in current examinations are those who would become most capable as a result of further educational investment. This is open to question, however: 'Correlation between GCE examinations and University examinations are, in general, low. . . . Whatever may be the value of the GCE 'A'-level examination as a school-leaving examination, as a basis for student selection for the University it has serious shortcomings' (Nicholson and Galambos, 1960). Comparisons of 'A'-level grades and degree class have rarely shown much of a correlation: see, for example, Petch (1961), Barnett and Lewis (1963), Nisbet and Welsh (1966), and UCCA (1969) which reports correlation coefficients between final degree and three 'A'-level results of between r=0.33 (engineering) and r=0.17 (social sciences). Such low correlations would suggest that less than 11% of the variation in university success can be 'explained' by variation in academic attainment at the time of entry. Perhaps such factors as personality and motivation may have as much or more influence on success in higher education (see Holland, 1960; Wankowski, 1970). For instance, medical students with poorer entry qualifications but with concern and empathy for ordinary people may emerge as better general practitioners than academic high-fliers who may feel they have failed if they do not get to be specialists or researchers. Of course every profession needs some reasonable level of academic performance from its would-be entrants. But there is little doubt that this level could, without detriment, be significantly lower than it is today if more serious attempts were made to assess interests and motivation and other personal qualities in applicants.

Assessment results are also used in selection for job and career opportunities. This is especially true of summative assessments at the end of a student's school or college career, or at the end of a period of professional training. In the absence of any thorough research, our knowledge of how employers actually use this assessment data is patchy and impressionistic (see Cox and Collins, 1975). Clearly, many use it as a screening device. That is, a candidate won't be looked at or even encouraged to apply unless he can offer a degree, or two 'A'-levels, or five 'O'-levels (including maths and English), or whatever is the going rate. This may be administratively convenient in cutting down the number of applicants. Again there may be a superstitious belief that the required qualifications betoken some kind of general quality of mind or spirit that will be useful to the employer. He may unconsciously be echoing the assumptions made by Lord Macaulay in defending the use of academic examinations to select administrators for the India Civil Service:

> 'Whatever be the languages — whatever be the sciences, which it is, in any age or country, the fashion to teach, those who become the greatest proficients in those languages and those sciences, will generally be the flower of youth — the most acute — the most industrious — the most ambitious of honourable distinctions.' (quoted in Keith, 1961, pp. 252–3)

Admittedly, a reverse tendency may sometimes operate here among many employers, perhaps based on more than superstition, to view 'the flower of youth' as being *less* useful in that they may think they 'know it all' and so object to undergoing further training.

As a pamphlet produced jointly by Army personnel staff and British Airways Staff College points out, there is a tendency to use examination results, so conveniently and effortlessly available, 'without due regard to their relevance. It is a safe bet that most entry qualifications expressed in terms of exam performance are the result of armchair deliberations rather than empirical investigation' (Kilcross and Bates, 1975). Even within education itself the respect paid by employers to qualifications (and other previous experience) is arbitrary and often capricious. Thus English schoolteachers start higher up the salary scale and enjoy better promotion prospects if they have a degree, regardless of the subject studied and whether or not it has any bearing on their work with children.

Again, too, universities are sometimes accused of encouraging 'qualifications for qualifications' sake' — perhaps as a means of ensuring a continuing market for their 'product'. Here the critic might point at the 'academic inflation' that results when universities begin to encourage their graduates to take up work that was not formerly done by graduates, and then infiltrate more and more graduates into that area until it eventually becomes spoken of as a 'graduate profession' and a degree becomes an *essential* entry qualification. Business management and accountancy and law appear to be heading in this direction. Ronald Dore (1976) gives many further examples. Having examined numerous career guides published since the beginning of the century, he sees their emphasis 'slowly shifting from personal aptitudes to quantitatively measurable educational achievement' (p. 24). The 'institutionalizing' of professional education has resulted in fewer and fewer opportunities for young people to work their way up from artisan to professional status (e.g. as an engineer) by 'learning on the job'. Consequently, employers are having to put more and more faith in certificates and diplomas awarded on the basis of other people's assessments.

Clearly there is no way of comparing the success in a job of people with qualifications and people without them if, in fact, the latter group were rejected as candidates. However, there is little evidence of a close connection between high educational qualifications and success in later life. In the U.S.A., for example, Donald Hoyt (1965) reviewed 46 studies of the relationship between college grades and subsequent achievement, only to conclude that 'present evidence strongly suggests that college grades bear little or no relationship to any measures of adult achievement'. Even medical school grades appear not to predict future proficiency as a general practitioner (see Taylor *et al*, 1965). The statistical investigations of Ivar Berg (1973) confirm that the variety of academic achievement among people doing the same job and earning the same rewards is as great as it is between people doing different jobs; and in some cases, selling insurance for instance, people with least education but most experience perform best. Fewer such studies have been carried out in Britain, but Liam Hudson (1966a) examined the degree-class gained by each of a large sample of distinguished scientists, politicians and judges, concluding that 'there was evidence of some slight relation between eminence and degree-class, but it was far from clear-cut and there were many striking exceptions'. For instance, more than half of High Court judges, and a third of Fellows of the Royal Society, had gained only second-, third- or fourth-class degrees. Is it the case that a person's job experience and achievements *since* gaining his qualifications generally assume far more relevance and significance in selection for later career opportunities? The suggestion made in recent years that a degree should carry an expiry-date, with the warning that its validity is not guaranteed beyond that time, would then be almost superfluous.

Nevertheless, most people still do need the ritual assessment 'qualifications' if they are to get started at all. It is not their fault if selectors place more trust than is justified in such credentials and then ludicrously over-generalize in ascribing qualities and special status to the possessor. Although Dave and Hill (1974)are talking about effects of school-leaving examinations in a developing country, India, are things so different in the West?

> 'A person's standing in the examinations affects many aspects of his life. Not only is it a basis of his economic success, but it affects his prestige in his family and his (or her) value in the 'marriage market'. The examinations thus form the basis of a kind of educational caste system, superimposed on the traditional caste system of the country.'

2. Maintaining standards

Closely related to the selection-purpose is this second purpose, but it has a life of its own. Teachers would probably still feel obliged to assess for this purpose even if they thought it immoral or impolitic to disclose individual results to outsiders. The clientele is broadly the same — employers and the 'invisible college' of academics in other institutions who must be assured that some form of 'quality-control' is in operation and that the people being certified this year are of pretty much the same standard as those certified last year and five years ago, and so on. Standards-oriented assessment can also be of interest to any administrators who want to 'keep tabs' on teachers.

As with purpose 1, the student is a secondary beneficiary insofar as he wants to be assured of the acceptability, almost literally 'the value' of his certificate. As one science student put it, rather more extremely than most would, in a debate reported by Ellsworth-Jones (1974): 'What matters to me is the job I get when I leave here. When I get a degree I want to know that employers will think it's worth something.'

Many difficulties attend the attempt to maintain standards. It is difficult enough to get teachers to agree on what the standard is or should be — whether, for example, the criterion is to be content covered, skills acquired, original knowledge created, attitudes expressed, none of these, or some of these and others in variously contested proportions. Discussions of standards easily degenerate into cliches, stereotypes and confident half-truths like 'the first-class mind proclaims itself'. Certainly one cannot judge the standard of, say, an examination paper simply by looking at the questions. One also needs to know what the markers accept as a satisfactory response. (For example, the spoof question-paper printed on [p. 136] may appear quite stiff; but for all we know the candidate has merely to write his name correctly on the answer-paper to score the 85% pass-mark). When the argument does come down to cases, in the analysis of a student's work, there is typically considerable disagreement (though surmountable by consent) among any group of assessors as to just what standard the student has attained.

The difficulties are compounded when the content of the curriculum is changing. This year's students may be assessed on areas of knowledge quite different from those of a year or so ago, even though the 'subject' is nominally the same. Inevitably then, it is quite impossible to establish the equivalence of standards between subjects and institutions. It makes no sense to ask whether the standard reached by physicists labelled 'second-class' in a given university or school is 'really' the same as that reached by 'second-class' historians, mathematicians and musicologists in the same institution in the same year, let alone in other institutions in other years. In fact, one simply has to take it as axiomatic that the 'quality-controllers' in various subject areas will be equally stringent in bestowing their approval on students. (Though one might still speculate as to what happens in universities to result in subjects like law and mathematics 'approving' (i.e. producing) a much smaller proportion of 'good' degrees than subjects like psychology and zoology, despite the fact that they start off with a far higher proportion of students entering with particularly high 'A'-level grades.) Whatever it means in terms of standards, the approval bestowed tends to operate, as Jonathan Warren (1971) has suggested, 'like a set of recommendations to an exclusive club written by long-term members who know the kind of people the other club-members prefer'.

Even within a subject, the standards being maintained are more probably standard assessment procedures rather than standard attainments. Indeed, there is a distinct possibility that standard procedures — especially if they include awarding a *fixed* proportion of As, Bs, etc. — may fail to acknowledge changes in level of attainment. Stuart Miller (1967) quotes statistics showing that even though the quality of students entering the University of California at Berkeley increased considerably between 1947 and 1960 (as measured by three different pre-entry criteria) their grade-point-averages in university remained precisely the same. Nearer home, in a letter to *The Times* (October 9th, 1972), Professor I. H. Mills argues that 'what we demand for "A"-level examinations in many subjects today is the same standard that was expected for final degree examinations thirty years ago'. Nor have the higher standards required of entrants to British universities in recent years been reflected in a proportionate increase in the 'good degrees' awarded. The standard of 'output' is maintained *despite* an apparent improvement in the standard of 'input'.

3. Motivation of students

After two assessment purposes whose benefits appear to be mainly administrative and go chiefly to people outside the immediate teacher-student relationship, this third purpose seems to be more educational and more related to the present needs of the student. With motivation we are talking of using assessment — e.g. homework assignments, weekly quizzes, classroom questioning, project reports, examinations, etc. — in order to encourage the student to learn. Many students would endorse this purpose. For instance, the male undergraduate quoted by Gerda Siann and Kate French (1975):

> 'The idea of Edinburgh University becoming a three-year holiday camp, all expenses paid, galls me, and I am reactionary enough to believe that the 'threat' of exams (i.e. the inherent threat of failure and becoming an outcast) is the only reason that the library doormats are cleaned.'

Though it must be noted that for every student who confesses himself in need of a constant prod from assessment there will be another who claims to be distracted and enervated by it. Whether we believe that such students are to be confirmed in these attitudes — or whether the former should be 'educated' to get on by himself without such constant stimulus and the latter 'educated' to come to terms with the need to periodically review his progress through others' eyes — may affect how we classify the use of assessment in particular cases.

However, we must also recognize that 'motivational' assessment could be used to benefit the teacher rather than the student. In effect, by structuring the student's allocation of time and effort, by legitimizing certain kinds of activity and outlawing others, by indicating what is to count as knowledge worth having and what is not, 'motivational assessment' can define the reality of academic life for the student and give the teacher control over his perceptions and behaviour. To be blunt, assessment can be used as an instrument of coercion, as a means of getting students to do something they might not otherwise be inclined to do — especially if unfavourable assessments can have unpleasant consequences. Thus, R. L. Bowley (1967) gives teachers a tip for a practice that sounds alarmingly like extortion:

> 'Occasionally it may be desirable to ask a class to make an especially hard effort when tackling a set piece of work. A simple but useful device to encourage this is to raise the total out of which the work is to be

> marked and inform the class accordingly beforehand. For example, if it is customary to mark out of a total of twenty, the raising of this figure to thirty will often have the desired effect.' (p. 116)

Some teachers consider it as much a necessary part of their duties to supply students with motivation as it is to supply them with objectives and structured lessons. Even though they may believe it to be in the students' long-term interest to achieve the objectives, they believe the students cannot be expected to recognize this and so provide self-motivation. Thus, assessment (in the form of quizzes, exams, etc.) may be used as one side of a carrot-stick inducement-system (the other side being represented by 'trying to make it as interesting as possible', audio-visual 'treats', etc.). The fervour with which this particular stick is waved can perhaps be seen as gradually increasing after the student's infant school years and reaching its peak in his later secondary school and college years.

But the line between coercion and encouragement is hard to draw. Much must depend on the intentions and perceptions of teacher and student and the relationship between them. Consider the teacher whose aim is for the student to become autonomous enough to develop his *own* goals and learning strategies. Even he may feel that the student's motivation will be all the better for some external stimulus from assessment. After all, many such a teacher, while valuing his own freedom to decide how he spends his time, will admit how the occasional deadline or external stimulus, like the imminent need to deliver a lecture, or prepare a report for a committee, or finish the next chapter of a book he is writing with a colleague, can concentrate and energize his activities. So too he is likely to encourage his students to work towards targets and deadlines, and public commitments — preferably ones they have identified and thought through themselves before agreeing them in discussion with him.

4. Feedback to students

It is necessary to distinguish between the motivating effect of knowing that you are to be assessed and the quite different sort of motivation resulting from knowing how you performed on the assessment exercise. The latter is much more clearly perceivable by students as being meant to help them learn. The student stands to benefit educationally from his tutor's response to what he has produced. In his study of the reactions of San Francisco teenage gang members to assessment, Carl Werthman (1963) quotes a student describing how he worked at getting more helpful feedback than is contained in a grade:

> 'After we got our compositions back I went up to him you know. I asked him about my composition. I got a D over F and I ask him what I did wrong. He told me that he could tell by the way I write that I could do better than what I did. And he explained it to me and he showed me what I need to improve. And he showed me, if I correct my paper, I would get a D, a straight D instead of that F. O.K. And I got the D for half the work. But any way he showed me how I could get a regular D and pass his class. I mean I feel like that teacher was helping me.'

Feedback, or 'knowledge of results', is the life-blood of learning. Having said or done something of significance — whether a physical action, a comment in conversation, or an essay in an examination — the student wants to know how it is received. He wishes to know whether he communicated what he intended to communicate, whether what he said seemed right or wrong, appropriate or inappropriate, useful or irrelevant to his audience. And he may need a response fairly rapidly if it is to confirm or modify his present understanding or approach. Effective feedback enables the student to identify his strengths and weaknesses and shows him how to improve where weak or build upon what he does best.

Feedback from assessment comes in many forms, of varying degrees of usefulness (see Sassenrath and Garverick, 1965). In its least useful form it comes as a mark or grade. The student may be told his work has earned a C or 55% or 6 out of 10. This may give him some hint as to whether or not his teacher thinks he is making progress. That is, he may be able to compare this grade or mark with those he has earned on similar assessment previously. But, of course, it is very non-specific. It tells him neither what he has done to merit such a mark nor what he could do to earn a better one. Such non-specific feedback becomes increasingly useless to the student as the size and diversity of the performance being assessed increases. Thus a grade for a single essay gives little enough information, but to be given merely an overall grade for, say, an examination in which several essays were written leaves the student uncertain even whether he did equally well on all essays or whether some were thought atrocious and some brilliant.

Institutions often find it administratively convenient not to give students feedback about individual answers in an examination. Very often the marked papers are not even returned to students. Only a few years ago, Hilda Himmelweit (1967) reported that 'In the University of London, the teacher is even *forbidden* to inform the student of his performance in the different subjects in Part I, at the very time when he has to select his major subjects for Part II.' This may save a lot of arguments about the fairness or otherwise of the marking, but it is also to neglect a valuable educational opportunity. Even in continuous assessment, feedback on answers may be withheld, as sometimes happens in the Open University, so as to economize on question-writing by using the same questions again on subsequent students. Inadequate feedback can indicate that the assessment is serving the interests of people other than the students.

Another kind of feedback the student may obtain, sometimes instead of a grade or mark, is knowledge of whether he has passed or failed. Or, more widely, whether or not he has reached some standard. If he has some conception of what knowledge or skill is required to meet this standard, then a pass will tell him that he has achieved them. It will not tell him how or in what way he may have over-achieved, of course. Similarly, to be told he has failed will not tell him what particular aspects of the required performance he is deficient in. Interestingly enough, people who fail a driving test are given more information about their faults and where improvement is needed than are students who do poorly in the educational examinations (CSE or GCE) at the end of their school careers.

Again, whether instead of marks or grades or as well as, a student may be given a rank. He may be told that his performance puts him third from top of the class or into the bottom 10% of his age group. The student can gain little from this sort of feedback: unless he knows what sort of performance the reference group has put up, he won't be able to judge his own either. Is he third-best of a bad bunch or is he in the bottom 10% of an excelling group? More generally, merely to be told he is better or worse than certain others tells him nothing at all about whether he is better or worse than he himself has been or would wish to be, let alone in which particulars.

Feedback from assessment only begins to be useful when it includes *verbal comments*. The teacher who has made the assessment needs to verbalize his reactions to the student's performance, saying which aspects strike him as strong, weak, or simply interesting. Ideally, he should give whatever suggestions he can to help the student improve. This kind of feedback flows out from diagnostic appraisal. Even the briefest of comments, e.g. 'A well-argued essay in the main, but what evidence are your third and fourth conclusions based on?', can be more helpful to the student than a C or a 65% if we want him to learn from considering his performance again in the light of our reaction. Research has confirmed (see Page, 1958) that students who are given individualized verbal comments on their work, incorporating suggestions for improvement, do tend to 'improve' significantly more than students who are given standard comments (e.g. 'poor', 'average', 'good, 'excellent') or grades.

Robert Birney (1964) found that college students were agreeable to frequent assessment — so long as it was 'in language they understand'. That is, not in grades or marks, which told them nothing specific about their strengths and weaknesses, but in detailed verbal commentary. If the information fed back is really intended to contribute to the student's growth it must tell him either that he has already achieved what he was trying to achieve or else must enable him to take some further action towards achieving it. Even in the former case it may be able to indicate possible *new* objectives and ways of approaching them. Useful feedback then is more to be expected from formative assessment than from summative. However, apart from the demands of common courtesy, any examiners who subscribe to the ideal of 'continuing education' should ponder the waste of not giving the student a detailed analysis of how he has performed at the climax of his formal education. They might consider also the ethics of involving the student in what may be a nerve-racking assessment experience that yet leaves him no wiser as to who he is and what he can do. It is in such a milieu that the student can be asked, 'What did you get out of this course?', and reply in all seriousness, 'I got a B' (see Kirchenbaum *et al.*, 1971).

Of course, feedback need not be supplied directly by a teacher. For many students, their first experience of sustained feedback has come from programmed texts. In such texts, the author can weave into his line of argument occasional questions requiring the student to use the ideas that have been introduced so far. Having come up with his own answer to these self-assessment questions, the student reads on to compare it with the answer given and explained by the author. Thus the student is constantly informed as to how well he is learning and the assessment comes frequently enough for him to correct any significant misunderstandings as soon as they occur.

But nor does feedback have to be verbal. The teacher's smiles or scowls, the colleague's mirth or laudatory silences can have a shaping influence on the student's behaviour. Sometimes the student will get his feedback from pictures, e.g. when drawing graphs or envisaging the landscape depicted by a map. Sometimes real events will provide the feedback, e.g. when the screaming of his car's gears tells the driver that he has not got the feel of the clutch or when the smell from the test-tube indicates that the student has applied too much heat.

Such indirect kinds of assessment can be seen as steps towards *self*-assessment. Increasingly, if the student is to become capable of learning to work for his own satisfaction rather than for the approval of his teacher, he must assume responsibility for providing his own feedback. He must be weaned off dependence on others for knowledge of how well he is doing. This demands that he be encouraged to recognize and internalize rules and standards and strategies whereby he may test the validity of his own responses.

5. Feedback to the teacher

Just as assessment may give the student feedback as to how well he has learned, so too it may give the teacher feedback as to how well he has taught. This is how assessment contributes to course evaluation. Insofar as the assessment data reveal strengths and weaknesses in the student's learning, the teacher may be able to identify where he has failed to explain a new concept, confused an issue, given insufficient practice, and so on. Knowing where and how his students have had difficulty may enable him now to teach so as to remedy the situation.

At times, however, e.g. in end-of-course examinations, the teacher may get this feedback too late for him to be able to use it for the educational benefit of the students who provided it. He may use it, instead, to report on their achievements. He may also use it to modify his teaching for the benefit of *subsequent* students. Thus, some assessment can have as its purpose feedback to the teacher but without feedback to the student also being intended.

One of the great weaknesses of externally marked examinations like GCE is that the teacher normally gets no feedback as to the strengths and weaknesses demonstrated by his students. He thus has no means of knowing which of his prior teaching interventions have borne fruit and which have not. Were this evidence available, it might enable him to improve as a teacher.

6. Preparation for life

Some teachers would wish to justify assessment on the grounds that it reflects, and therefore prepares students for, 'real life'. Let us note, in passing, how odd it is to imply a distinction between the student's educational career and his real life. Education is *part* of his life, and an increasingly large part. Unavoidably, it may also in some sense prepare him for that part of real life which it is not. But this does not imply that education, or, to be exact, the people who control aims and objectives in education, should take the predicted real life for granted and merely train the student to 'cope'. Educationally, it would be equally valid, perhaps more so, to provide a counter-curriculum that might enable the student to challenge or ignore the pressures of 'real life'. Such an argument can be heard, for example, from teachers concerned about the power of commercial pop-culture.

How far is educational assessment a preparation? Certainly much of the *informal* assessment that goes on in school and college is related to the mainly informal assessment that goes on in the rest of life. Approbation and criticism (verbal or non-verbal) from teachers and fellow-students are not dissimilar to what the student will meet from parents, workmates and friends. But it is probably not this informal kind of assessment that teachers see as the life-preparer. Those who do see assessment as a preparation are most likely thinking of the competitive system of public examination, grading, and ranking. Such experience is thought to prepare students for the life-struggle in general and career advancement in particular. The thoughts of Luther Evans (1942, p. 59) are representative: 'A student who completes a programme of higher education without facing the rigorous evaluations of a grading system has missed one great chance to learn the helpful lesson that life is full of tests and trials.' An even more emphatic statement has been made by the 'Black Papers' author, Brian Cox (1971): 'All life depends on passing exams. . . . To create an education system without examinations is to fail to prepare children and students for the realities of adult life.' Let's hope they are not thinking of the 'rigorous evaluations' and 'realities' evoked by Norman Russell's poem:

End of a Semester

This is the week of tests the season of fear
everywhere the running the typing the scritch scratch
shuffling of papers the door and the people
coming going looking for the symbols
looking for the little symbols written on the papers
stuck with tape to doors and walls
this is the week of the fearhope swallowed in the stomach
a time of livingdying a time of cominggoing
a time of inbetween the things one cannot grasp
too fast too fast we never sleep
we only keep ongoing.

and somewhere someone in a great office
pushing buttons marking papers calling telephones
we think a devil who we cannot see is laughing

and all the things we knew were true
will never do will never do
we all are weak we all are strong
the days are long the days are long

this is the week of tests the season of fear
somewhere we think a devil who we cannot see is laughing.

Norman Russell (1966)

Fortunately, life outside education is not really like that. With the exception perhaps of the civil service and the armed forces, most people seldom ever again meet the experience of being tested or examined on prescribed syllabuses for the purpose of being graded and ranked and chosen. Assessment in industry and the professions is generally informal, diffuse, *ad hoc* and continuous. It is based largely on the person's 'track record' over a *period* of time and in fulfilling his duties rather than on what he can write about something at a given *point* in time. Nor is such assessment quantitative in any simple way. The candidate for, say, a high academic post may be chagrined to find that his thirty published papers do not win him preferment over another candidate whose output is thought more significant even though his papers number only three!

As things are now, competitive public assessment does prepare for future job-competition — in the sense that success in previous competitions is normally demanded as an entry qualification for further competition. But this is an artefact of the system and, even if such competition were regarded as reasonable (e.g. on the grounds of greater efficiency, maximization of output, etc.), we have no means of knowing whether people excluded at earlier stages might not have proved 'winners' if allowed to 'work their way up' through the lower reaches of their chosen profession (see Dore, 1976). There is, of course, enough evidence of 'late developers', and of people unexpectedly 'finding themselves' in a situation where they were called upon to draw on unsuspected powers and grow into the job, to make us suspect the efficiency as well as the ethics of competitive elimination from further competition. But even if such people are held to be exceptions, there is still reason to doubt whether any but the winners benefit from preparation. The losers, through loss of self-respect and reduced optimism may be *less* prepared to face up confidently to subsequent life-struggles. Even with dogs, as Scott (1972) observes: 'In a test set up so that one dog can do it and another can barely succeed, the initial difference in hereditary ability may not be great. However, the dog which fails soon stops trying, while the one which succeeds becomes more highly motivated with each success. It keeps on trying and succeeding at more and more complicated problems so that in the end the hereditary difference has been immensely magnified' (p. 132).

There is a growing feeling among teachers that education should no longer meekly accept that society must necessarily be competitive. Many recognize the emerging need for people to share and collaborate rather than seek maximum personal and material advantage. They would not see eliminative assessment as a preparation for this kind of co-operative living. Nevertheless, it might still be argued that people will always be competing, if not with somebody then with some*thing* — the soil, the weather, disease, poor housing — and so on. Some such competition, together with the attendant storm and stress, might widely be agreed to be an inescapable component of 'real life'. But one could accept that education could reasonably be expected to help students prepare for it, without accepting that the appropriate means must be to promote interpersonal competition in school.

Naturally, teachers who see the student's future in terms of his being externally assessed in competition with others rarely extol the preparatory virtues of *self*-assessment. Insofar as schooling does give the student opportunities to develop criteria for assessing himself and encourages him to take decisions based on his assessments, it will be 'preparing' him for a life in which he expects to have some control over his own destiny. There is considerable lip-service paid to the ideal of self-assessment, but the practice very often belies or trivializes the intent. Students may, for example, be 'trusted' to mark their own work — but using teacher's criteria as to what counts as 'good' work. They may be asked to assess their own progress during a term or over a course using whatever criteria seem appropriate to them — but their assessments are not allowed to influence the overall report that is given them. They are asked to choose which subjects to specialize in (e.g. Arts vs. Sciences) at an early age, without ever having been helped to develop relevant criteria for assessing their own strengths and weakness in relation to the various courses of action open to them. Obviously, self-assessment cannot be a preparation for anything, not even for further self-assessment, unless it is supported by open access to relevant information, unless the results of the assessment are regarded as significant and actionable, and unless the person assessing himself is to be allowed responsibility for the outcomes of his own judgements and decisions.

Balancing the purposes

I have outlined six broad categories of purpose in educational assessment. They are not entirely without overlap and we might possibly need a seventh 'miscellaneous' category to catch a few more purposes that are less commonly spoken of. Even so, we have seen more than enough to suggest that the teacher who pauses to ask why he is assessing has plenty to think about. How does he, in fact, thread his way through the various potentially conflicting purposes and what determines his personal intentions?

The teacher's use of assessment will be heavily influenced by the expectations of the teaching system within which he is working. But his attitudes to assessment will largely depend on his ideas as to what teaching and learning and knowledge and education are all about. That is, on his professional world-view, or what some sociologists (see Esland, 1972) call his *pedagogic paradigm*. Different teachers can be seen, for instance, as taking up different positions along a continuum whose opposite extremes are labelled by writers using such terms as closed vs. open (Bernstein, 1971); manipulative vs. facilitative (Rowntree, 1975); or transmission vs. interpretation (Barnes, 1976).

To put it crudely, one end of the continuum tends to attract the teacher whose first loyalty is to a public corpus of pre-existing knowledge on expertise (which he knows everyone ought to acquire) and the need to 'get it across' to a succession of students who learn, as far as their limited capacity and motivation will allow, by absorbing and reproducing the products of other people's experience. The other end of the continuum attracts the teacher who distrusts generalizations about what everyone ought to know, and who, believing people to have unlimited potential for growth unless 'discouraged', gives his first loyalty to individual students and encourages them to exercise their own developing motivation and sense of purpose in mastering cognitive and affective capacities, making their own meaning and creating new knowledge out of their own ideas and experiences. The paradigm with which a particular teacher operates will rarely be so extreme, of course. Although most of his or her paradigm may consist of beliefs and assumptions from one end of the continuum, it is likely to be tempered with more moderate beliefs. Of the two extreme paradigms indicated, the former is more likely to be found in secondary schools, the latter in infant schools; perhaps also the latter paradigm is more typical of arts-based subjects than science-based subjects, and more typical of women than men.

In the paragraph above, I mentioned only a few of the kinds of belief and assumption that go to make up a teacher's pedagogic paradigm. What if we go on to consider beliefs relevant to student assessment? We may decide that teachers attracted towards one end of the continuum may be more inclined to see assessment as an objective and accurate means of determining a student's present achievement and future potential, thus legitimizing selection and special treatment; and, insofar as students are aware that many are called but few are chosen, as a powerful device for reinforcing teacher's control over the wayward and idle. Conversely, teachers attracted to the other end of the continuum may tend to see assessment primarily as a means of developing the relationship between the student, themselves and the subject matter, by giving both the student and themselves more information about the present state of the student's understandings; but as incapable of providing valid information about the student to outside parties or about his long-term potential to anyone at all. Various belief-systems and attitudes will emerge as we push deep into the undergrowth of assessment. As I have indicated, we can look for them to tie in and be consistent with other aspects of the way the teacher sees education — his pedagogic paradigm.

Looking back over this chapter, it would appear that the 'purposes' I have discussed are those ascribed to assessment by the actions of *teachers*. Perhaps this is not surprising. It is, after all, teachers rather than students who develop the rules of the game and tell us what it is supposed to be achieving. Maybe in the [next chapter], where we look at some of the *unintended* effects of assessment, we shall catch a glimpse of the purposes that *students* ascribe to assessment by the ways they use it.

References

Barnes D (1976) *From Communication to Curriculum*. Penguin, London.

Barnett V D, Lewis T (1963) A study of the relationship between GCE and degree results. In: *Journal of the Royal Statistical Society* 126: Series A (General): 187–226.

Berg I (1973) *Education and Jobs: The Great Training Robbery*. (First published 1970.) Penguin, London.

Bernstein B (1971) Open schools, open society. In: Cosin B R *et al.* (eds) *School and Society: A Sociological Reader*. Routledge and Kegan Paul, London.

Black H (1963) *They Shall Not Pass*. Morrow. New York.

Bowley R L (1967) *Teaching Without Tears*. Centaur, London.

Cox C B (1971) In praise of examinations. In: C B Cox and A E Dyson (eds) *The Black Papers on Education*, pp. 71–77. Davis-Poynter, London.

Cox G, Collins H (1975) Arts assessment: who cheats and who cares? *Assessment in Higher Education* 1 (1): 13–34.

Dave R H, Hill W H (1974) Educational and social dynamics of the examination system in India. *Comparative Education Review* 18 (1): 24–38.

Dore R (1976) *The Diploma Disease*. Allen and Unwin, London.

Ellsworth-Jones W (1974) How to fail an exam and become a martyr. *The Sunday Times*, 3 November 1974.

Esland G *et al.* (1972) *The Social Organization of Teaching and Learning*, Units 5–8 in Course E282. Open University Press, Bletchley.

Evans L D (1942) *The Essentials of Liberal Education*. Ginn, Boston.

Himmelweit H (1967) Towards a rationalization of examination procedures. *Universities Quarterly* June: 359–372.

Holland J L (1960) The prediction of college grades from personality and aptitude variables. *Journal of Educational Psychology* 51: 245–254.

Hoyt D P (1965) *The Relationship Between College Grades and Adult Achievement*. American College Testing Program, Iowa City.

Hudson I (1970) *Frames of Mind*. Penguin, London.

Keith A B (1961) *Speeches and Documents on Indian Policy 1750–1921*. Oxford University Press, Oxford.

Kilcross M C, Bates W T G (1975) *Selecting the Younger Trainee*. HMSO, London.

Kirchenbaum H, Napier R, Simon S (1971) *Wad-ja-get? The Grading Game in American Education*. Hart, New York.

Klug B (1974) *Pro Profiles*. NUS Publications, London.

Miller S (1967) *Measure, Number and Weight: A Polemical Statement of the College Grading Problem*. Learning Research Center, University of Tennessee.

Nicholson R J, Galambos P (1960) *Performance in GCE A-Level Exams and University Exams*. Occasional papers of the Institute of Education, University of Hull.

Nisbet J, Welsh J (1966) Predicting student performance. *Universities Quarterly* 20 September.

Petch J A (1961) *GCE and Degree*. Joint Matriculation Board, Manchester.

Rowntree D (1975) Two styles of communication and their implications for learning. In: J Baggaley *et al.* (eds) *Aspects of Educational Technology*, VIII, pp. 281–293, Pitman, London.

Russell N H (1966) End of a semester. *American Association of University Professors Bulletin* Winter: 414.

Sassenrath J M, Garverick C M (1965) Effects of differential feedback from examinations on retention and transfer. *Journal of Educational Psychology* 56 (5): 259–263.

Siann G, French K (1975) Edinburgh students' views on continuous assessment. *Durham Research Review* 7 Autumn: 1064–1070.

Taylor C G, Price P B, Richards J M, Jacobsen T L (1965) An investigation of the criterion problem for a group of medical general practitioners. *Journal of Applied Psychology* 49 (6): 399–406.

UCCA (1969) *The Sixth Report: Statistical Supplement 1967–68*. Universities Central Council on Admissions, Cheltenham.

Wankowski J A (1920) *GCEs and Degrees*. University of Birmingham.

Warren E J (1971) *College Grading Practices: An Overview*. ERIC Clearing House on Higher Education, Washington DC.

Werthman C (1963) Delinquents in schools: a test for the legitimacy of authority. Reprinted in Cosin B R *et al.* (1971) *School and Society*. Routledge and Kegan Paul, London.

32. Using Assessment to Promote Student Learning

Sandra Robertson, Joan Rosenthal and Vickie Dawson

Postcard 6

> Dear All
>
> Well I'm half way through my visit here, I can't believe how quickly the time has gone. This is the time during a normal placement that I would be assessed by my clinical educator. It's great not to have that stress around! I have decided though, to take some time this week and evaluate my own performance so far and set come personal goals for the remainder of my stay. I already know that I need to do some more work on the content and manner in which I'm giving feedback to the CBR workers. I've also decided to ask the CBR workers for feedback about how they think I'm going and also the paediatrician on the team. I'll let you know what they say.
>
> Love Sally

Chapter overview

This chapter discusses some of the issues surrounding the complex area of student assessment within the clinical setting. Specific methods of clinical assessment such as viva voce and case studies are not discussed. Rather, concepts and processes which underlie assessment are analyzed. Assessment within the context of adult learning is examined and some fundamental questions are addressed with regard to the why? and how? of the assessment process. Some insights into students' views of clinical assessment are considered, together with thoughts on peer assessment. Finally, some examples will illustrate the wide variety of assessment methods. Some of these are well-tried and proven, while others describe innovative pilot studies in progress.

Assessment: what does it mean?

The *Concise Oxford Dictionary of Word Origins* (1989) informs us that the term 'assessment' is derived from the verb 'to assess' whose original meaning was linked with the settling of amounts of taxation and has come to mean also the determining of the value of something. The Old French and Latin origins also carry the idea of 'to sit by' and hence the 'doer', the 'assessor' is someone who 'sits as assistant or adviser ... with a judge or magistrate to give advice on technical matters'. The dictionary also highlights the relation to the adjective 'assiduous', meaning 'attend or apply oneself; persevering, diligent'.

Sandra Robertson, Joan Rosenthal and Vickie Dawson: 'Using Assessment to Promote Student Learning' from *FACILITATING LEARNING IN CLINICAL SETTINGS* (Stanley Thornes, 1997), pp. 154–184.

For all those involved in the process of assessing students in the clinical setting, there is a fascinating link in the definitions above. There is, firstly, the idea of determining value, but it is for the reader to decide whether this refers to the student or the 'outcome' or the 'product' of the education process. This issue will be considered later in the chapter.

Secondly, in relation to our definition, the 'doer', the person who 'assesses', may be considered as an assistant or adviser. There is no apparent hierarchy in the definition of 'assessor'; no implicit 'superior' person who must assess, no authoritarian figure with the automatic right to assess. Within the clinical setting, therefore, it is an open question as to whether the role of 'assessor' is fulfilled by the clinical educator, university staff, an external examiner or a fellow student or colleague.

Thirdly, the adjective 'assiduous' can be applied to both students and clinical educators. The word conjures up a picture of hardworking, conscientious students, diligently applying themselves to their clinical education. However, the adjective might also be applied to the 'assessor', and such an application carries with it the charge to perform the task of assessing with diligence and integrity.

Assessment in the context of adult learning

In a statement summarizing the outcomes of a national study in the UK funded by the Council for National Academic Awards (Oxford Centre for Staff Development, 1992), the observation was made that the assessment system is the most significant influence on the quality of student learning and that without changes to assessment, changes in a student learning will not be reinforced. Pletts (1981) makes a similar observation, specifically within the context of clinical education: 'the evaluation of the student is also a vital part of the whole teaching process. It is useful, when setting out on a journey, to know the destination; to plan the route, and finally, be able to recognize when one has arrived' (p. 131).

It is clear, then, that when considering facilitating students' clinical learning, it is necessary to take a long hard look at the whole area of assessment and to consider its place within the sphere of adult learning philosophy and practice. Indeed, one of the indicators of 'good' teaching is that an explanation is given early in the course of how learning will be tested. Further, assessment must be congruent with, and must reflect, teaching and learning objectives. These indicators follow naturally on the heels of two others – good course organization and a clear definition of what has to be learned (Eastcott and Farmer, 1991).

Reference has already been made in this book to Kolb's learning cycle involving experimentation, experience, reflection and conceptualization (Kolb, 1984). Nowhere is this cycle more applicable than within clinical education; the phases implied in Kolb's model help move the student from one stage to the next in a sequential spiral. Each spiral represents a stage in clinical development which, it could be argued, can be assessed before the student moves to the next stage.

For example, the student might plan an intervention session for a client (experimentation), then implement this plan while being observed by a clinical educator (experience). The third stage would be the student's self-evaluation of the session (reflection) and the fourth stage would be making sense of what occurred in the light of the clinical educator's feedback and his or her own theoretical knowledge (conceptualization). The student then proceeds to the next 'loop' in the developmental spiral and plans the following session with accumulated wisdom and constructive criticisms from this most recent assessment. This example may be regarded as an over-simplification of the whole process, but it serves to underline the principle that the assessment procedure is an integral part of the learning experience and can be absorbed naturally within the whole process.

Learning styles

Within the context of adult learning it is important to consider not only the stages and processes involved, as described in Kolb's learning cycle, but also the learning styles of individual students. Different learning styles will affect the way in which students learn within the clinical situation, but they also affect the way in which students anticipate assessment, respond to criticism, react to failure and benefit from feedback. It is important for clinical educators to be aware of the varied reactions which the assessment process might arouse. Indeed, it could be argued that the better acquainted clinical educators are with students, the more sensitive they will be able to be to that individual's learning style, and the more easily they will be able to adapt the feedback to ensure maximum benefit and progress, as opposed to increasing anxiety, anger and frustration.

For example, 'activist' learners (Honey and Mumford, 1986) may respond in a very positive manner to assessment and welcome suggestions for a change of approach, perhaps without reflecting enough on the rationale behind the criticism; 'reflectors' may prefer to think through the implications of specific criticisms and produce their own solutions; 'theorists' may feel threatened and wounded initially by criticism, but after further consideration may think through to a logical conclusion and a new approach; 'pragmatists' may not feel personally implicated by the critical comments and may greet with enthusiasm new ideas for future management.

Student growth

As students grow in their clinical skills and professional competence, what is assessed and how it is assessed should change. Beginning level students have been found to be anxious about their ability to perform basic clinical procedures, such as writing session plans for therapy with clients (Chan, Carter and McAllister, 1994). Students at this stage are often self-focused as they concentrate their attention on developing clinical skills. Assessment of such students would appropriately focus on their mastery of basic clinical procedures. Beginning students may need feedback designed to prompt them to think of the client holistically and to build self-confidence to enable the shift of focus to the client. Advanced level students have been shown to feel confident about their clinical skills but anxious about their emergent professional personae (Chan, Carter and McAllister, 1994). Such students would benefit from assessment and feedback designed to promote the growth of professionalism and confidence in their professional selves. As well as end-point assessment needed for certification or licensure, self-assessment and peer assessment should be emphasized, in preparation for the real world of evaluation in professional practice.

Why assess?

According to Harris and Bell (1994) the rationales for assessing students are seven-fold:

- mastery
- increasing the motivation of learners
- prediction of an individual's potential
- diagnosis of learning
- diagnosis of teaching
- evidence of competence or attainment
- accreditation, classification and comparison with other learners.

These reasons for assessment apply in the clinical setting within various health professions.

The student's mastery of the clinical situation is an obvious target and reason for assessment to take place. This mastery will require evaluation at various stages throughout the educational programme. Early assessments provide opportunities to identify learning needs and to support the growth of clinical skills, while exit point assessment ensures that professional standards have been attained.

Motivation of the student is an essential element of assessment. Positive reinforcement, reassurance that progress is being made and encouragement that further development will occur are key reasons behind the assessment process. In relation to formative assessment (i.e. assessment for the purpose of providing feedback), the nature and mechanism of the feedback following assessment is vitally important to the continuing motivation of the student. Prediction of the individual student's potential is primarily the responsibility of the clinical educator and is an integral part of that role. However, students also must be able to view their potential in an objective way through the process. Occasionally, an appropriately-timed assessment may give a negative prognosis for developing as a clinician, and in the ideal world it should be the student who recognizes this and with guidance from the clinical educator perhaps makes the decision to withdraw from further clinical education. On the other hand, a well-timed assessment with positive reassurance of good clinical potential at a time when the student's morale is flagging will provide motivation.

Assessment will undoubtedly focus to some extent on what has been learned. This is a major reason for periodic testing of theory and skills. The use of the term 'diagnostic' implies that the student and the assessor will recognize the strengths and weakness of the knowledge and skill base and plan future study and practice accordingly.

It is not only the student's learning which is the focus of assessment. Directly or indirectly, the assessment process should also help to identify and review the amount, nature and effectiveness of the teaching which has taken place. Further, changes in content, style or emphasis of teaching may be a desirable outcome of assessment.

When a student reaches the end of a period of study and clinical education, it becomes essential that evidence of competence is presented. Implicit in this aspect of the rationale is an understanding of the concept of competence which should be explicitly defined for both students and clinical educators.

The final reason for assessment on the Harris and Bell list is the need to certify that students are fit for practice – that they are eligible for the awards of the educational establishment and the professional body, and that they compare satisfactorily to other graduating students within the same field. Thus assessment provides students, clinical educators and the educational programme with evidence that the defined end-point standards have been met; and that a required level of professional competence has been attained.

Assess for whom?

Implicit within the question 'Why assess?' is a second question 'For whom is the assessment?' As implied above, several people are directly affected by, or involved in the assessment process.

Firstly, consider the students. They are the major focus of this collaboration. The system exists to facilitate their development. As the focus of this collaboration they are subject to some extent to the whims and demands of the other participants – the clinical educator, university staff and perhaps also at some point, an external assessor. In many programmes this triad of assessors writes the regulations, defines the standards and, at least to some extent, dictates the procedures. On the other hand, students can demonstrate knowledge, skills and mastery of the clinical situation through, perhaps, choice of client, assessment procedure or treatment technique, or the setting of achievable sessional goals. It is important that the assessment process provides some degree of choice, so that students retain some control.

Secondly, consider the clinical educator, either as external assessor from the university or as on-site clinical educator. However much they may appear to be 'in control' in the assessment process, there is an element of self-assessment which they themselves bring to the process. Their teaching standards are exposed to scrutiny; they have to recognize and adhere to the demands of external assessors and statutory bodies. They must be the gatekeepers to the profession, which means that they have the burden of decision-making and justifying such decisions to both external bodies and students alike. Theirs also is the responsibility of judging fairly and without prejudice.

Finally, consider the external forces involved in the assessment process. To a great extent they can be regarded as the 'overlords' of the whole system. These external forces to be reckoned with are the overseers of the educational system, the outside adjudicators checking comparability of standards, and the awarders and rubber stampers of certificates to practise. They too must be regarded as collaborators in the assessment system. As bodies which award credentials to programmes, they can at most only 'sample' the assessment process – they can observe, examine and/or evaluate a small proportion of the students, the clinical educators, the teaching, the techniques, the competencies or the standards. They uphold the standards of the profession or an institution and yet they cannot assess every professional. Accreditation of an individual, a course or an institution must always, to some extent, be taken on trust.

The student's view of assessment

It is probably true to say that most of the decision-making regarding methods, timing and feedback mechanisms of student clinical assessment is undertaken by the academic or academic plus clinical team designing the course. Students, in most instances, would have very little input into such planning, yet they are central to the whole exercise. Their perceptions of the validity and fairness of the assessment process are vital to their valuing of the results of the assessment. If the assessment outcome matches what students feel inwardly, it will give them confidence to take upon themselves the role of self-assessor. On the other hand, if the mismatch is too great or if students do not trust the assessment system, they may be seriously hindered in their professional career, lacking the confidence to monitor their own performance.

Stackhouse and Furnham (1983) suggest that students need to develop a confidence within themselves and not just meet external criteria in order to feel an inward competence with which to meet the world of clients: 'The recognition that clinical competence is as much dependent on inner satisfaction (Ward and Webster, 1965), self-awareness (Kaplan and Dreyer, 1974), and interpersonal skills (Klevans and Volz, 1978), as on meeting prescribed academic standards has resulted in self-awareness as well as sensitivity to others being important goals in clinical teaching' (p. 171). Stackhouse and Furnham further observe that: 'unilateral assessment, i.e. by supervisors alone, will result in extrinsic based learning, such as for examination purposes or attempting to please supervisors, rather than more intrinsically motivated factors such as curiosity, discovery, and personal satisfaction' (p. 172). If it is agreed that the ultimate goal of clinical supervision is to produce a clinician capable of self-supervision (Dowling and Shank, 1981) then the balance must be struck between a supervisory 'stranglehold' on assessment (Heron, 1988) and a student-dominated system which is equally undesirable.

In a survey of final-year speech therapy students in the United Kingdom, one author sought their views on the clinical assessment procedures they had experienced during their course (Robertson, 1995). Fifty per cent of the respondents (n = 212) felt very positive about the methods of clinical assessment used; 35 per cent were non-committal and 15 per cent felt their clinical assessment was unsatisfactory and inappropriate. The optimist might interpret this data as indicating that students were reasonably happy with the assessment process. However, the more critical reader would recognize that approximately half of the students had some misgivings about the fairness of the system.

Further analysis of the methods of clinical assessment reviewed in the Robertson survey indicates that 95 per cent of the students had experienced assessment by visiting university staff and, of this number, 64 per cent found the visits to be very/extremely valuable. Thirteen per cent did not find these visits valuable and 23 per cent were non-committal. Clinical educators' report forms, a nationwide method of evaluating students, were considered by 79 per cent of the students to be a very/extremely valued method of assessment.

A definite trend emerged from this data which was confirmed by a question which asked how valuable was the contribution of university staff, clinical educator and combined university staff/clinical educator to the assessment of students' clinical work. The responses are displayed in Table 1. Students perceived clinical educators' input to assessment as important, adding value and fairness to the whole procedure. In any model of clinical assessment, therefore, it is important to ensure that the clinician with whom the student has been working over a period of time is an integral part of the assessment process.

Table 1 Students' perceptions of the contribution to the assessment of students' clinical work by university tutor, clinical educator and combined university tutor/clinical educator (Robertson, 1995)

Tutor	Very valuable	57%
	Non-committal	28%
	Not valuable	15%
Clinical educator	Very valuable	91%
	Non-committal	8%
	Not valuable	1 %
Tutor/Clinical educator	Very valuable	82%
	Non-committal	14%
	Not valuable	4%

What is to be assessed?

In Chapter 1 reference was made to the goals of clinical education as being much broader than discipline-specific clinical skills. The need to develop competence and capability for professional practice were emphasized. If these broader goals are to be pursued, the focus of assessment will need to change.

Clinical or professional competence?

In her development of a model of professional practice, Stengelhofen (1993) commented: 'If we are to prepare students adequately for professional work then we need to consider what is involved in the practice of the profession' (p. 11). She suggests that professionals typically recognize three elements of professional practice, which are knowledge, skills and attitudes. Stengelhofen considers that what is important is not simply to see these as individual elements of professionalism, but rather to consider their inter-relationship. She proposes a model (see Table 2) which shows the gradual integration of the elements of knowledge and attitudes with skills to produce a whole, which is professional competence.

Table 2 A model of the elements of professional competence (Stengelhofen, 1993)

Surface level	Techniques and procedures	
First deep level	Knowledge and Relationship with understanding employing authority and Knowledge awareness	All levels are influenced by: Life experiences Pre-registration learning Work experience Continuing education Work context (e.g., hospital, school, clinic, private practice, etc.)
Second deep level	Attitudes Giving meaning to what is done and influencing use of knowledge, technique and procedures	

At the surface level, it may be possible for students to pick up skills through practice and at this level to appear to be clinically able. However, for students to prove that they are professionally competent, then the deeper levels of knowledge and understanding as well as professional attitude must also be evident. It is not sufficient to assess only the knowledge base of students. Nor is it enough to view the acquisition and demonstration of clinical techniques as an indication of competence, since these may be utilized at an efficient but mechanical and superficial level.

The third attribute at the deepest level of professionalism is the most difficult to define, the most elusive to address within a course of study and the most intangible to assess, yet *attitude* is at the very heart of professionalism and we neglect it at our peril. Stengelhofen (1993) describes attitude as 'the driving force for effective practice'. It certainly encompasses notions of ethical, moral and considerate behaviour towards clients and colleagues, seeing clients holistically and working with colleagues to achieve holistic management of clients. It is in these aspects of professional practice that marginal students often experience greatest difficulty.

Genuinely mature professional practitioners will recognize that the knowledge, clinical skills and professional attitude discussed above must continue to develop throughout their professional career. However, these elements must begin to show integration at the student education stage so that the idea of competence becomes holistic and internally conceptualized, leading to professional maturity. It is this holistic integration of knowledge, skills and attributes which allows for the inclusion of educationally as well as professionally sound, competency-based curricula in higher education and for competency-based assessment, which is discussed further later in this chapter. Graduation and certification or licensure are the first rungs of the professional ladder. However, progression from ground level to that first rung is an enormously important step and each of the three elements must already be showing definite signs of growth and internalization. These elements must be viable and capable of surviving with minimal support once the student graduates.

If the most important outcome of the clinical learning experience is that students demonstrate 'professional competence', then competency-based assessment is an appropriate method of assessment in clinical education.

Competency-based assessment

'Competency-based assessment is the assessment of a person's competence against prescribed standards of performance' (Gonczi, Hager and Athanasou, 1993, p. 5). It contrasts with norm-referenced assessment in that it is based on prescribed standards rather than on a set of norms or the normal distribution. It is based on the inference of competence from performance with consideration being given to the context of the performance. Characteristically, it uses a variety of assessment methods in order to gather adequate evidence of competence. Competency-based assessment is a form of judgemental assessment rather than scientific measurement. That is not to say that it is any less valid or reliable than traditional scientific measurement techniques, but it is based on cognitive theories of human functioning which reflect the complex combinations of abilities, skills and knowledge that are not fixed and finite.

Competency-based assessment, as is made clear by Gonczi, Hager and Athanasou (1993), can use all existing forms of assessment such as questioning, direct observation and evidence of prior learning, The difference lies in how the forms of assessment are used and interpreted. A competency-based approach to assessment needs to have an emphasis on performance and on integrated or holistic methods of assessment if it is to be valid and effective. Ideally, assessment is carried out in the workplace by direct observation, but in practice this is not always practical nor possible because of time constraints.

At present, competency-based assessments are used in some tertiary and further education institutions, but there is potential for far greater use of this type of assessment especially in undergraduate and postgraduate education of health professionals (see Appendix 1). Case Study 1 describes the structure of the competency-based occupational standards developed by the speech therapy profession in Australia, to be used to assess overseas applicants for membership of the Speech Pathology Association of Australia.[1]

[1] Formerly known as the Australian Association of Speech and Hearing (AASH).

Case Study 1

Competency-based occupational standards: An example from the speech therapy profession in Australia

In 1994 the Speech Pathology Association of Australia, then known as the Australian Association of Speech and Hearing (RASH), published the Competency-based Occupational Standards for entry level speech pathologists in Australia, now commonly known as the C-BOS. This provided the profession with the criteria against which to assess candidates for entry to the profession using a competency-based assessment (see Appendix 1).

Briefly these standards describe the skills, knowledge and attitudes of speech therapists in terms of units, elements and performance criteria. They start with a key purpose statement for the profession. It also includes a range indicator statement that outlines the contexts and areas of responsibility covered by the profession at entry level. An example is the first range indicator which states that 'if requested, the speech pathologist must be able to demonstrate competence in any unit in both paediatric and adult practice in the areas of speech, language, swallowing, voice and fluency' (p. 7).

To facilitate the description of the complex total competency of the entry level speech therapist, the standards are divided into seven units which describe broad areas of professional activity:

Unit 1: Assessment of the client
Unit 2: Description and/or diagnosis of the client's communication and/or swallowing problem and determination of the likely outcome or prognosis
Unit 3: Planning client management
Unit 4: Implementation of speech pathology management of the client
Unit 5: Planning, maintaining and developing speech pathology service
Unit 6: Professional, group and community education
Unit 7: Professional development.

Each unit is further broken down into *elements* that describe specific activities carried out to achieve the unit. For example, Unit 1, Assessment of the client, contains six elements, which are:

1.1 Interviews and takes case history
1.2 Identifies the speech pathology areas requiring investigation and the most suitable manner in which to do this
1.3 Administers the speech pathology assessment to obtain the information required
1.4 Analyzes and interprets speech pathology assessment data
1.5 Provides feedback on results of speech pathology assessments to the client and/or significant other and referral sources, and discusses management
1.6 Writes report.

Case Study 1 cont/d

Each element is elaborated by *performance criteria* that specify the evidence that is required for the element to be carried out competently. As an example from Unit 1, the five performance criteria for Element 1, Interviews and takes case history, are:

1.1a The clients and/or significant other's description and perception of the communication and/or swallowing difficulty is identified so that the nature of the problem is clarified and its impact established

1.1b Information required for speech pathology assessment, diagnosis and intervention is elicited by using an appropriate interview process and collection of data

1.1c Information that is pertinent to the communication and/or swallowing problem is identified to ensure that the necessary information for speech pathology management is gathered

1.1d Information gathered is not released without the informed consent of the client or guardian, and every effort is made to maintain confidentiality at all times in accordance with the Australian Association of Speech and Hearing Code of Ethics and Freedom of Information Acts

1.1e Information is recorded accurately, systematically and in English, according to speech pathology and the service provider's requirements.

Further information on what is required for some performance criteria is supplied in the cues for assessors. These are examples or illustrations of the behaviour or items referred to within the performance criterion to which they are attached and are neither inclusive nor exclusive.

How do we assess?

'We believe that decisions relating to assessing can make or break a learning situation'. This is the strongly held view of Harris and Bell (1994, p.96) 'who outline many routes through the minefield of assessment. They suggest that there are many types of assessment available, from informal and casual observations, through teacher organized and marked questions, standardized tests, to assessment of criteria devised and used by students. They suggest that each mode of assessing can be located within bipolar continua (see Figure 1). Although these constructs are listed as bipolar, it is not necessary to assume that a given mode of assessing contains elements of only one pole. Indeed, in the clinical situation, it is quite possible, for example, that we could utilize assessments which contain both formative and summative elements. Nor should we regard the selection of one of these constructs, for example, process/product, to preclude application of any of the other constructs.

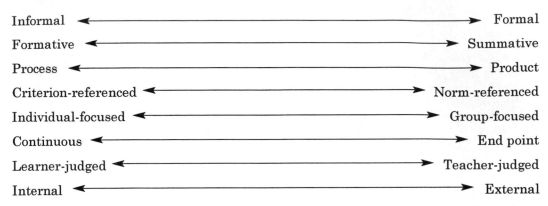

Figure 1 Bipolar continua for each mode of assessment (Harris and Bell, 1994)

Pletts (1981) reminds us that 'when attempting to measure clinical skills the number of variables that must be accounted for makes the task daunting. Even more difficult to measure are the attitudes and interpersonal skills so essential to successful clinical work' (p. 131). This comment reminds us once again of the necessity to assess the three major components – knowledge, skills and attitudes. Each of these components probably requires a different method of assessment. For instance, although it may be possible to link a test of skills with a test of knowledge, it is difficult to conceive that this could also incorporate an evaluation of attitude. Therefore, the methods of assessment must vary in accordance with the focus of the component to be assessed. Let us briefly consider the Harris and Bell aspects of assessment and note their relevance to clinical assessment.

Informal-formal

It is impossible to imagine a clinical situation in which informal assessment does not take place. Clinical educators are constantly observing a wide range of student behaviours every time they watch students in action in the clinic. Similarly, students are also making constant informal judgements of the clinician and of themselves. To reinforce the value of such observations, it is probably helpful to introduce a more formal element to the proceedings. For instance, at the end of each therapy session or clinical day, it is important to hold a debriefing period. In this way, students and clinical educators may be encouraged to focus on specific areas which can be varied from session to session, so that learning can be enhanced over a period of time.

Formative-summative

Stengelhofen (1993) describes 'formative assessment' as the 'feedback process' and encourages us to view 'summative assessment' as developing naturally from this process. 'The student's self assessment, together with assessment by clinical tutors preceded by and followed by setting objectives and working towards achieving them, again receiving feedback and making further progress, is all part of continuous assessment' (p. 180).

The concept of summative assessment and a discussion of its relevance assessment within clinically-based courses is crucial to our subject. The term 'summative assessment' describes an appraisal of various aspects of student clinical performance; numeric values are assigned to each of these aspects, and the values are added together to provide an overall rating of current clinical skill. Note that in summative assessment there is an implicit assumption that the parts add up to the whole – that is, the component aspects which are assessed do indeed comprise a rounded picture of clinical performance. An example of a summative assessment tool is found in Figure 2 and discussion of its development is found in Case Study 2.

The University of Sydney
Faculty of Health Sciences

CLINICAL EDUCATION: MARKING GRID
School of Communication Disorders
Speech Pathology Clinical Subjects

Name of Student: ______________________ Clinical Educator: ______________________

Period of Training: Year of Course ________ Clinic: ______________________
Semester ________
Mid or End (Circle one)
Adult or Child (Circle one)

Weightings*		Shows no skill in this area	Shows a little skill in this area	Shows some skill in this area but not to expected level	Satis-factory	Shows above average skill in this area	Shows consistent excellence in this area
	Rapport with client						
	Rapport with relative/caregiver						
	Rapport with other clinicians, staff and outside agencies						
	Knowledge of Clinical Procedure: Preparation						
	Investigation and evaluation speech and language						
	Investigation and evaluation of contributing factors						
	Therapeutic procedure						
	Theoretical background						
	Writing up and reporting						
	Clinical management						
	Clinical behaviour as demonstrated in: Awareness of factors influencing client's behaviour						
	Adaptability						
	Interest in client's total rehabilitation needs						

Recommendation & Comments

____

____

____

Year 2: Number of client contacts:
Year 3/4: No of days present: Signature: ______________
Year 3/4: No of days absent:
Year 3/4: No of absent days made up: Date: ______________
Year 4: No of on-campus client contacts:

* Assign each behaviour item a weighting between 0 and 25. Only one weighting of 0 and 25 may be assigned. Weightings must total 100.

Figure 2 The Grid: A summative assessment protocol devised in the School of Communication Disorders, The University of Sydney (see Case Study 2)

Case Study 2 The Grid: An example of a summative assessment tool

For our explanation and discussion of summative assessment we use as an example a summative assessment protocol which was devised in the School of Communication Disorders at The University of Sydney. This assessment protocol, which is shown in Figure 2, became familiarly known among staff and students as *The Grid*. The Grid was developed over a number of years with input from the many clinical educators and students who used it, found its problems, and made suggestions as to how it could work better. In basing our discussion of summative assessment on the Grid we in no way suggest that it is the ideal summative instrument for all programmes. However, consideration of aspects of the Grid will help the reader to appreciate the decisions to be made in developing a summative instrument.

Parameters to be assessed

One axis of a summative assessment protocol lists the parameters of student clinical performance which are assessed. In the Grid these parameters are listed on the left side, beginning with 'Rapport with client'. How, it may be asked, are these parameters determined? How can the user be sure that all important aspects of clinical performance are included? How can overlap between parameters be avoided?

Developers of assessment protocols do not reinvent their particular wheel! Published protocols and protocols used in similar settings provide multiple resources for selecting suitable parameter descriptors. In the case of the Grid, initially 14 parameters were chosen: in addition to those shown, a category 'Self confidence in therapeutic role' was included. After some time of trial use of the Grid in a variety of settings, clinical educators were asked to evaluate its parameters. In a brainstorming session clinical educators reported comfort with assessing all parameters except this 'self confidence...'; they believed it overlapped with other parameters and was indeed to a certain extent an outcome of performance in other parameters. As a result of these considerations 'self confidence ...' was dropped as a parameter, to the evident satisfaction of users.

Brainstorming sessions among experienced clinical educators, as mentioned above, are an important tool in development of a summative assessment protocol. Consultation with users, both clinical educators and students, can provide an impetus for changes leading to improvements in validity and reliability of the instrument. An example will demonstrate the use of brainstorming sessions to improve reliability of the Grid.

During the years of use of the Grid it became evident that, not surprisingly, all clinical educators did not necessarily consider the same behaviours in assessing a particular parameter. Further, less experienced clinical educators expressed lack of confidence in their evaluation of particular parameters, such as 'Rapport with relative/caregiver'. Students expressed a wish for a clearer delineation of what was being assessed. It thus became apparent that the parameter labels alone did not provide sufficient information for users. Several brainstorming

Case Study 2 cont/d

sessions held with clinical educators were used to develop lists of behaviours to be considered within each parameter. Some of the more than 50 behaviours listed for 'Rapport with relative/caregiver' included:

- respects caregiver's privacy rights and maintains confidentiality
- explains purposes of tests used
- checks out that 'messages' are received, re-explains where necessary
- responds appropriately to verbal and behavioural cues provided by caregiver
- maintains caregiver's optimal involvement in therapy.

Clearly, not all the listed behaviours would be expected of a beginning student. Therefore, again by a process of consultation with clinical educators, the behaviours were assigned to levels of the education programme at which they should be expected. Some behaviours, like 'smiles, uses friendly voice' would be expected at early stages of student practicum; other behaviours would be expected only of students near to graduation. In addition, certain behaviours, such as those involving confidentiality were highlighted as prerequisites for passing any clinical placement.

Since each parameter on the Grid was now associated with two or more explanatory pages of component behaviours, a booklet of these guidelines was printed for use with the instrument. The booklet was provided to all clinical educators, with the aim of maximizing uniformity and hence reliability in the use of the instrument.

Method of assigning marks

The second axis of a summative assessment protocol provides the skill level descriptors to be used by the assessing clinical educator. It is possible simply to use a numerical range such as 1–7, or a percentage scale, or verbal descriptors, or a combination of these. In developing the Grid, the decision was made to use verbal descriptors, which could subsequently be converted to numerical marks by administrative staff. This decision was based on the consideration that there would be more agreement among users if asked to rate performance on a particular parameter with a verbal description such as 'shows some skill in this area but not to expected level' than if asked to rate it with a numerical mark such as 4 out of 10. The actual values assigned to the verbal descriptors were, however, made known to both clinical educators and students (they were a numerical range 0–10).

An additional essential consideration in assigning marks is the relative weighting to be given to each parameter in the total. It is unlikely that each parameter will be of equal importance in the overall picture of clinical performance. In the case of the Grid, it could be argued that 'therapeutic procedure' is more important to overall clinical performance than is 'rapport with other clinicians, staff and outside agencies'. Admittedly, the converse could also be argued – fuel for an interesting debate on clinical effectiveness! The first

Case Study 2 cont/d

to this problem in the case of the Grid was to allocate weightings to each parameter. (For information for the mathematically inclined, the weightings totalled 100, and the assigned mark for each parameter became one tenth of the allocated weighting for that parameter, producing a total mark out of 100 which could be converted to a grade.)

This solution had its own problems, however, in that the fixed weightings allocated to parameters were not necessarily appropriate in diverse clinical settings. Some clinical settings, for example, provided relatively little opportunity for interaction with clients' relatives or caregivers; in other settings such interaction was an important part of the clinical process. This particular problem was highlighted by student input to discussions of the Grid. It was resolved by requiring clinical educators at each placement to allocate their own weightings to each parameter, based on their knowledge of the demands and nature of the setting. The weightings were still to total 100, with parameters allocated a weighting between 0 and 25, although each extreme weighting could be applied to no more than one parameter. Student and clinical educator response indicated perceptions that this 'individualized weighting system system increased the validity of the Grid as a summative instrument.

It is clear that a summative assessment instrument, such as the one described, needs flexibility in its development. It is unlikely to remain unchanged. It benefits from contributions both from those who use it and from those whose performance is assessed. In addition, those who are to use it benefit from induction into its use.

Process-product

On first consideration it would appear that clinical performance is more amenable to process assessment than product assessment. In most clinical situations students will be judged on a sequence of events, such as the preparation, management and evaluation of a therapy session, or the gradual development of a relationship with a new client. However, on further consideration, it is possible to select specific 'products', to isolate target tasks to judge the result. This 'product assessment' could apply to evaluation of a student's ability to score a standardized test, or to write a report or letter for a particular purpose, or to design and produce a piece of equipment for a client.

Criterion referenced-norm referenced

According to Harris and Bell (1994) 'norm-referenced assessing aims to compare the achievements of the learner with those of other learners' (p.101). While it may be helpful to students during their clinical education to have some indication of their progress clinically in comparison with their peers, ultimately it is imperative that their work is measured against clearly defined standards for entry into the profession. Thus we must aim for criterion-referenced assessment which assesses the learner by comparison with some predetermined or negotiated criteria. Most clinical education programmes will provide for students a detailed list of expected professional competencies developed according to established criteria, which must be met by the time students are due to graduate. Intermediate criteria should be set at various key points throughout the programme, so that students have a useful and achievable reference point. Consistent with adult learning approaches, the ultimate goals and criteria must be communicated to the students early in the programme.

Individual focused-group focused

Within a clinical education programme leading to a professional qualification it is clearly inappropriate to consider anything other than an individual-focused assessment. An assessment of group performance, although having its uses perhaps in some areas of the learning process, is not relevant to the acquisition of clinical skills and techniques, since learning in this area must take account of individual needs, strengths and weaknesses. However, a compilation of clinical assessment profiles of a cohort of students may be of value to the educational institution. Such a compilation could indicate deficits in the educational programme which prepares students for and supports their clinical practice. Or it might reveal areas of clinical practice to which students have inadequate exposure. A responsive educational institution would seek to make appropriate curriculum changes.

Continuous-end point

Continuous assessment is a two-edged sword. On the one hand, it would seem to be the ideal learning situation for the student in a clinical education programme since it allows for immediate and constant feedback by the clinical educator who is able to monitor each stage in development. This may also relax the tension normally associated with assessment. On the other hand, some students report that they feel constantly under scrutiny and pressure and feel they are never able to make mistakes in private.

Continuous assessment is most suitable for the clinical educator responsible for the day-to-day practicum of a student placement. As Stengelhofen (1993) suggests, this situation is conducive to the use of continuous assessment, which may be the least invasive in relation to the ongoing work of the student. This will have benefits for client care as well as student learning. However, it should be recognized that objectivity in assessment is sometimes compromised because of the personal interactions between clinical educator and student in the clinical setting.

A valuable type of assessment which captures both the concept of continuous assessment by the clinical educator and regular self-evaluation by the student is the checklist. Figure 3 provides an example of a checklist adapted from one originally designed to be used by a teacher after a teaching session.

	Very well	Satisfactory	Not very well	Not applicable
How well did I ...				
plan this session?	......	......	......	......
introduce this session?	......	......	......	......
make the aims clear to the client?	......	......	......	......
present the materials?	......	......	......	......
pace the session?	......	......	......	......
interact with the client?	......	......	......	......
use reinforcement?	......	......	......	......
handle problems of inattention/distraction?	......	......	......	......
handle the client's questions?	......	......	......	......
record the client's questions?	......	......	......	......
build up the client's confidence?	......	......	......	......
round off the session?	......	......	......	......

Figure 3 Example of a self-evaluation checklist to be used after a therapy session by the student, which could also be completed by the tutor and used as a basis for discussion (adapted from Eastcott and Farmer, 1991)

At the opposite pole of this aspect of assessment is 'end point' assessment. While it is probably important to assess students within a clinical setting just prior to their qualifying, it would seem to be extremely bad practice to judge the whole of a student's clinical work on one final clinical examination. It may be felt necessary to have an 'end point' assessment for the purpose of certification or licensing, but where this exists it surely must be part of a wider assessment package.

Learner judged-teacher judged

A major metamorphosis that must occur in the student clinician is the transformation from dependent, non-skilled, apprenticed technician into an independent, responsible, skilled, self-evaluating professional. The ability to evaluate oneself is a skill which individuals need in everyday professional life, so it must be nurtured during the embryonic stages of clinical education. Students must learn to recognize their strengths, and weaknesses, abilities and limitations, since recognition of these will be important throughout their working life. By learning to use effectively some of the self-assessing procedures already mentioned, (for example, the sessional checklist in Figure 3), students will eventually become skilled, reflective practitioners.

In the clinical situation, of course, assessment by the clinical educator is clearly necessary, but within the context of deep approaches to learning, this should not be a unilateral judgement. As previously discussed in the Robertson (1995) study, students value particularly the judgement of the clinical educator.

Internal-external

Internal assessing is widely accepted in higher education. It involves all those participating in the learning/teaching process having control over the assessment – student, peer group, university staff and clinical educator. They should all be involved and utilize the relevant forms of assessment already discussed.

In addition, however, in an education process leading to a professional qualification, it is entirely appropriate, and may even be a statutory requirement, that an external examiner is also involved. It is normally not possible for the external examiner to assess each student individually, so the role of this external person may be to scrutinize the assessment process and possibly to examine a sample of the students in order to evaluate and moderate the fairness of the internal judgements made.

In preparation for future professional work, the involvement of internal and external judges is important, since the work of the clinician on a daily basis is constantly under scrutiny. As a professional, the clinician is accountable to the clients and to the employing body to maintain high standards of client care.

Student self-assessment

The discussion above of the various continua in assessment has referred a number of times to self-assessment. What is the role of the student self-assessment in the evaluation of clinical skills? Falchikov and Boud (1989), highlighting the need for students to take more responsibility for their own learning, state: 'Life-long learning requires that individuals be able not only to work independently, but also to assess their own performance and progress (p. 395). Woolliscroft, Tentlaken, Smith and Calhonn (1993), describing the use and value of self-assessment in the training of medical students, underline the view that 'self-evaluation is central to the function of the clinician' (p. 290). They further suggest that individuals' views of themselves are 'constructed from repeated feedback from others as well as through introspection' (p. 290) and that it is multidimensional, combining the actual self, the potential self and the ideal self.

Students, therefore, who engage in self-assessment are not only looking at themselves as they are, but are trying to judge realistically what they could become, while at the same time holding in mind the vision of how they would like to be, perhaps modelled on observations of more experienced practitioners. Students are aware of the standards against which to measure themselves, or, as Woolliscroft *et al.* (1993) summarize, 'accurate professional self-assessment requires a self-representation of actual performance that is congruent with reality as it would be judged by other individuals using appropriately developed performance monitoring systems' (p. 290).

It is possible for discrepancies to exist between some students' views of themselves and the way they are viewed by clinical educators. Woolliscroft *et al.* (1993) were able to identify such cases by the administration of the questionnaire shown below to third-year medical students within the University of Michigan Medical School, comparing the responses with those of clinical educators. Early identification of students whose self-assessment is unrealistic may permit the introduction of remedial strategies, such as placement with clinical educators who could become strong clinical role models.

Boud (1992) considers the use of self-assessment schedules like the one devised by Woolliscroft *et al.* (1993) to be of great value, because schedules appear to prompt students 'to reflect on their learning and think about the application of ideas in their own situations' (p. 191). The self-assessment schedule which Boud himself describes incorporates four main headings: goals, criteria, judgements, and further action. He reports that 'although the exercise appears at first sight to be an intellectual one, it drew a number of students into their personal experiences, emotions and feelings' (p. 192). Students found the task both 'excruciating' and 'challenging', as well useful. As one student reported: 'It highlighted the need to improve my discipline of keeping a portfolio regularly'; and another reported: 'What it added to my understanding and to my awareness of what learning had taken place was a sense of form' (p. 192).

Self-assessment by students: Questionnaire used in the Internal Medicine Clerkship, University of Michigan Medical School, USA, 1988-89 (Woolliscroft *et al.,* 1993)

Medical history/interview

1 I elicit an appropriate medical history.

Physical examination

2 I am able to detect the important physical findings.

3 I accurately interpret the significance of the physical findings.

Initial patient write-ups

4 I accurately document appropriate data in my initial patient write-ups, including all major and minor problems.

Daily patient progress

5 I am aware of my patients' daily developments.

6 I accurately document all patient developments in my daily progress notes.

Oral presentations

7 My oral presentations are logical and well organized.

Application of knowledge

8 I apply my knowledge base in a well-integrated manner to patient problems.

Problem list, assessment, and plan

9 I develop appropriate problem lists.

10 I develop complete differential diagnosis.

11 My diagnostic and therapeutic plans are well organized.

Self-education

12 I use independent self-learning to extend my medical knowledge base.

13 I require little direction to perform my patient care responsibilities.

Interpersonal interactions

14 I interact with patients and their families in a professional manner.

15 I interact with other members of the health care team in a professional manner.

(a) Limits to self-assessment

Should we assume that students are the best judges of their own performance and that, in appreciation of reflective learning, ultimately students should be their own assessors? Whilst it is an admirable aim that developing professionals should become responsible and well-equipped to monitor their work, we must remember that this, like many other skills students are developing, needs practice and training. The observations of Falchikov and Boud (1989) suggest that students at a more advanced stage of their studies are more accurate assessors than those in the beginning stages.

A further indication that students' untrained self-assessment may lack validity is provided by Stackhouse and Furnham (1983), who compared the ratings of speech therapy students' clinical skills by students themselves, clinical educators and university staff. The clinical educators tended to give the highest ratings of the students' skills, while the students gave themselves the lowest ratings. Stackhouse and Furnham (1983, p. 176) commented:

> 'Observations have shown high anxiety levels in students entering their first clinical placement and this, coupled with inexperience, results in unrealistic goals being set for themselves ... Another reason for students' harsh ratings of themselves may be artefactual. It is well known that self-raters may conform to social desirability factors and succumb to pressures of humility ... As the student's role as "learner" is clearly defined they may be unwilling to score high ratings as this would be inappropriate for their role at this time'.

Over the years a number of studies of student self-assessment have indicated that when evaluating themselves, students not only use different criteria to university staff or clinical educators, but when, for example, they view themselves on video they will look at and comment on different aspects of their own and the client's behaviour. This observation was nade clearly by McGovern and colleagues in a series of studies of speech therapy students in Scotland in the early 1980s (McGovern and Davidson, 1982; 1983; McGovern, 1985; McGovern and Dean, 1991).

Three groups (students, university staff and clinical educators) watched video-taped recordings of other students' treatment sessions and made comments which were later transcribed and grouped into various categories: viewer orientation, therapist behaviour, content presentation, content stimuli, interaction, management of space, client behaviour and generalizations. The trends can be described as follows. The clinical educators as a group looked mainly at content presentation and rarely at client behaviour. The students as a group looked mostly at content presentation but also at client behaviour. They made few comments about therapist behaviour or management of space. The university staff as a group most frequently commented on interaction or content presentation, rarely on client behaviour and management of space.

The studies revealed wide discrepancies in the way that the three groups commented on the video. The authors therefore urge that clinical educators become aware of their own biases in allocating importance to different aspects of the clinical situation. Case Study 3 contrasts students' self-assessment before and after viewing a video of their treatment session.

The observation has been made that educational assessing is traditionally a unilateral activity controlled by the educators (Harris and Bell, 1994). They set the criteria, mark students' work and provide the feedback. A contrasting picture is that of independent learners who decide their own goals and criteria, manage their learning and monitor their progress wards the final outcome. These are the two poles of the continuum representing learner autonomy.

Case Study 3 Student self-evaluation: The usefulness of video replay (McGovern, 1985)

Eight beginning speech therapy students were videoed for a minimum of 15 minutes during an ongoing therapy session with a client. At the end of the session the students were asked to comment on their session. These comments were recorded. The students then viewed the video of their performance and were again asked to comment on the session and a tape recording of their comments was again made. The two tape recordings were transcribed and analyzed for the number, range and focus of comments made.

Comments made by students immediately following the session mainly related to the success or otherwise of the session plan they had prepared and their perceptions of their performance, for example, 'I'll need to spend a bit more time explaining how to do that'; 'He got all the words and he seemed to enjoy finding them' (p. 298). When the students were asked to comment on the same session after viewing a video of it, their observations were much broader and could be subdivided into three headings:

1 *Observations on personal factors affecting interaction*, for example, 'My voice wasn't particularly clear at times'; 'I wondered if I could possibly make more use of gestures' (p. 298)

2 *Criticisms of student therapist's response to client's performance*, for example, 'The task might have been too long. I should have changed to something else'; 'I could have got his attention more before trying to do certain things' (p. 298);

3 *New observations on client's performance*, for example, 'I was interested in the difference between his reading rate and his conversational rate'; 'She didn't understand "yours" and "mine" ... gives me a new lead into therapy' (p. 298).

Within the context of healthcare clinical education, neither of these extremes is appropriate. The first is undesirable because it is important for students to develop the skills of monitoring their own performance and taking responsibility for it in preparation for professional life. The other extreme is also inappropriate since there is a statutory duty on the part of the educational institution setting up and managing a professionally accredited course to examine the student and judge their fitness to practise. A balance between the two poles of assessment must therefore be found and such a model will no doubt contain elements of assessment which reflect several stages between *teacher-controlled assessment* and *learner-controlled assessment.* We conclude this discussion with an apt comment by Boud (1990): 'The challenge for all of us is to find meaningful ways of incorporating aspects of self-assessment within courses so that learning within the course is enhanced and students gain confidence in judging their own performance. This is most likely to occur when self-assessment is an integral part of learning activities and not an appendage or afterthought' (p.110).

Peer assessment

With the growth of programmes leading to a speech therapy qualification, there has been a corresponding trend for placement of more than one student at a time in clinical settings. Taking advantage of this situation, clinical educators have 'paired' students in clinical roles and functions which facilitate learning. Probably the most frequent mode of peer placement is one in which members of the pair treat a client together, alternating between being clinician and observer (Stengelhofen, 1993). This practice provides opportunity for students to give each other feedback. In the Robertson study (1995) cited earlier in this chapter, speech therapy students were asked for their views on peer placements. Sixty-nine per cent of students who had experienced paired placements considered them to be very valuable.

While the concept of peer or collaborative placements has been well documented (for example, Callan, O' Neill and McAllister 1993; Lincoln and McAllister, 1993; McFarlane and Hagler, 1993), less has been recorded about the processes and results of peer assessment in clinical practice. Informal discussions with students confirm the impression that when carrying out clinical peer assessment students are supportive of each other, giving positive reinforcement and praise as well as honest, constructive criticism. The benefits of such a method of assessment are best experienced when the students concerned have worked closely with each other, probably during a joint placement, for some time. This allows them to build mutual trust, potentially leading to an evaluation which is both open and rigorous.

Harris and Bell (1994) propose that peer and self assessment are closely related. They point out that judgements made during self-assessment are responsive to feedback from peers, particularly when those peers are co-learners in the same educational situation. Peer assessment is in all senses a collaborative activity making equal demands on each student involved in the process. It not only allows the assessed partner to learn constructively from a colleague, but the requirement that students watch, question, criticize, praise and instruct their fellow students demands a high level of concentration, knowledge and skill on their parts.

Conclusion

Throughout this chapter we have emphasized our belief that assessment in clinical education can be congruent with the approaches and characteristics of adult learning. To achieve this congruence clinical educators need to be clear about the reasons for assessment and the constructs which underlie assessment procedures. For this reason, this chapter has discussed the topics of why assess?, what to assess?, who should be involved in assessment? and how might we choose or construct assessment procedures?

Appendix 1: Development of competency-based assessment strategies (Vickie Dawson)

The Competency Based Occupational Standards (C-BOS) is a detailed, accurate and powerful document which has been developed with considerable consultation with the profession and is widely accepted as a valid reflection of the desired standards for entry level practice of speech pathology in Australia. Accordingly the profession desired to base the assessment of overseas-educated speech pathologists who wish to practise in Australia on the C-BOS. In order to do this it was necessary for the Speech Pathology Association of Australia[1] to set about developing competency-based strategies that could be used with the document.

In principle the project steering committee felt that the assessment of overseas-educated candidates for membership to the profession should be similar to, and no more stringent than, that imposed on Australian university graduates. It was therefore proposed that the professional association would work with the six Australian universities that provide undergraduate education for speech pathologists to achieve parity between the university assessments and the competency-based assessment strategies to be applied to overseas candidates.

Although, ideally, competency-based assessment takes place through direct observation in the workplace, in this case it was not a practical possibility. It is frequently found that such direct workplace involvement is impractical or impossible, and indirect observation using, for example, simulations, standardized cases and video, is used as a substitute. Many of the university departments use video presentation for various forms of assessment and it seemed appropriate that videoed performance in a student's final placement clinic or in the overseas-educated candidate's current clinic might well be an acceptable way to view and assess the competency of the candidate.

With this in mind, the first draft of the assessment strategies included as the forms and methods of assessment, indirect observation via video, pen and paper questioning through a modified essay and extended multiple-choice examination and recognition of prior learning through presentation of a portfolio. There was also some provision for areas of the standards, which are not easily evaluated outside the workplace, to be covered by a mentoring system of support rather than assessment.

Pilot project

Because so little is known about using video as an assessment tool, it was decided to carry out a pilot study on this method of assessment. As stated, the indirect observation method initially adopted was observation and assessment of videoed performance in clinic. The videos were to be made of the candidate working in clinic situations in his or her native country. For the pilot study, video tapes of a simulated candidate carrying out one assessment session and one treatment session in clinic were shown to panels of assessors. Documentation covering the plans, goals, results and conclusions of the candidate in relation to the two sessions was also given to the panels. The panels included university staff and non-university practising speech pathologists who were all asked to view the videos and review the documentation to assess the competence of the simulated candidate. Half of the panels had been given some training in assessment using the C-BOS and half had not.

There were four levels on which panel members were to assess the candidate's performance. These were: overall competency, competence in each of the two sessions (one assessment and one treatment), competence at the element level of the C-BOS and competence at the performance criteria level of the C-BOS. In order to achieve overall competency, the candidate had to be judged competent in both assessment

[1] Formerly known as the Australian Association of Speech and Hearing.

and treatment. The hypotheses were that the videoed clinical performances and accompanying documentation submitted by the simulated candidate could be reliably evaluated using the C-BOS, that the university assessors would be more reliable than non-university assessors and that trained assessors would be more reliable than untrained assessors.

Inter-rater reliability analysis on the four levels demonstrated that the reliability of assessment was not adequate using video extracts of performance even though all assessors came to the same conclusion about the overall competency of the candidate (i.e. that competency had not yet been achieved). Many of the assessors felt that the possibility of cheating in the production of the videos, for example by scripting and editing, made video unsuitable as an assessment method for overseas candidates. Problems also arose with the difficulty of standardizing the assessment when considering the enormous variety of clinic situations which could be presented. There were also major difficulties with candidates in their native countries having access to clients with whom they could work in English. With such a level of dissatisfaction it was necessary for the reference group to review their recommendations and make far reaching changes.

Consultation has been carried out throughout the project not only with the speech pathology profession but also with representatives of government employing bodies, unions, the Government's National Office of Overseas Skills Recognition and the universities, all of whom provided feedback which was used in the revision of the assessment strategies.

The assessment strategies

In the final form of the assessment strategies, the reference group maintained the pen and paper questioning and the portfolio for the recognition of prior learning, but adopted a much modified video section in two parts. The first part of the section involves standard video presentations made by the Association and viewed by the candidate, followed by a telephone interview between the assessor and the candidate based on the clinical situations presented on the videos. Because the areas of responsibility are so broad in speech pathology and the Association wished to sample the candidate's competency in a variety of areas, it was decided that a number of different videos were to be made by the Association. The videos would cover both adult and paediatric cases, and those involving speech, voice, language, fluency and swallowing problems. It was agreed that the candidate would be presented with the list of scenarios on video and be permitted to choose the first one, but the Association would choose the second one to ensure a variety of situations for assessment. A certain amount of documentation about each of the videos would also be given to the candidate who, following the interview, would be asked to write a report or letter about the clinical situation presented.

The reference group worked out that this method would cover many of the same elements of the C-BOS that had been the target of the previous video presentations. However, there were some elements that referred to the establishment of rapport and the manner in which a client is approached that were still not covered by any assessment. In a second part of the video section therefore, it was decided to ask the candidate to present a video of him or herself interacting with a client and to present a summary of the case. for the assessors. This video would not be used for the assessment of clinical decision-making but purely to evaluate the interactive skills, attitudes and manner of the candidate with a client.

In the assessment strategies devised by this project, clinical decision-making, client management, planning and report-writing are assessed using the standard video cases with interviews and reports or letters. Interactive skills are assessed through observation of a video of interaction with a client and through the telephone interview. More extensive assessment of the knowledge base and its application to the management of speech pathology services, community education and professional development is carried out in the pen and paper examination. Extra qualifications and initial education are reviewed in the portfolio for the recognition of prior learning. In covering such a wide variety of assessment methods the assessment strategies comply with the principles of competency-based assessment and have face validity in that assessors should have considerable exposure to the various skill areas of the candidate.

Conclusion

The assessment strategies described are as yet untested as the Association is still developing the materials to be used in them. The Speech Pathology Association of Australia plans to use the new assessment concurrently with the existing assessment for a period before switching entirely to the new competency-based strategies. This will provide an opportunity to compare the performance of the new with the old, and allow for the fine tuning of the more extensive competency-based assessment. Following the results of the pilot study, it is thought it will be essential to train the assessors in the use of competency-based assessments and in the C-BOS before being able to rely on the strategies for accepting or rejecting candidates for membership to the profession.

Competency-based assessment is claimed to be a fairer and more realistic assessment of skills, knowledge and attitudes. It is not a quick and easy alternative to examinations of knowledge, but is thorough, time-consuming and requires a broader evaluation of performance within context. It is essentially a summative type of assessment, evaluating whether or not competency within a complex professional activity has been achieved.

References

Australian Association of Speech and Hearing (1994). *Competency-based Occupational Standards for Speech Pathologists (1) Entry Level, (2) Basic Grade Practising Level.* Australian Association of Speech and Hearing, Melbourne.

Boud D (1990) Assessment and the promotion of academic values. *Studies in Higher Education* 15 (1): 101–111.

Boud D (1992) The use of self-assessment schedules in negotiated learning. *Studies in Higher Education* 17 (2): 185–200.

Callan C, O'Neill D, McAllister L (1993) Adventures in two to one supervision: Two students can be better than one. *Supervision* 18 (1).

Chan J, Carter S, McAllister L (1994) Sources of anxiety related to clinical education in undergraduate speech-language pathology students. *Australian Journal of Human Communication Disorders* 22 (1): 57–73.

Dowling S, Shank K (1981) A comparison of the effects of two supervising styles, conventional and teaching clinic, in the training of speech and language pathologists. *Journal of Communication Disorders* 14: 51–58.

Eastcott D, Farmer S (1991) Planning teaching for active learning. *Effective Learning in Higher Education,* Module 3. CVCP, London.

Falchikov N, Boud D (1989) Student self-assessment in higher education: A meta-analysis. *Review of Educational Research* 59 (4): 395–430.

Gonczi A, Hager P, Athanasou J (1993) *The Development of Competency-based Assessment Strategies for the Professions.* National Office of Overseas Skills Recognition, Research Paper No. 8. Australian Government Publishing Service, Canberra.

Harris D, Bell C (1994) *Evaluating and Assessing for Learning,* rev. edn. Kogan Page, London.

Heron J (1988) Assessment revisited. In: D. Boud (ed.) *Developing Student Autonomy in Learning,* 2nd edn, pp. 77–90. Kogan Page, London.

Honey P, Mumford A (1986) *The Manual of Learning Styles.* author, Berkshire.

Kaplan N, Dreyer D (1974) The effect of self-awareness training on student speech pathologist-client relationships. *Journal of Communication Disorders* 7: 329–342.

Klevens D R, Volz H B (1978) Interpersonal skill development for speech clinicians. *Journal of National Studies, Speech and Hearing Association* December: 63–69.

Kolb D (1984) *Experimental Learning.* Prentice Hall, New Jersey.

Lincoln M A, McAllister L (1993) Peer learning in clinical education. *Medical Teacher* 15: 17–25.

Maxwell M (1995) Problems associated with the clinical education of physiotherapy students: A Delphi study. *Physiotherapy* 81: 582–587.

McFarlane L, Hagler P (1993) Collaborative treatment and learning in a university clinic. *Supervision* 18: 13–14.

McGovern M, Davidson J (1982) Appraisal of therapeutic performance. *British Journal of Disorders of Communication* 17: 23–31.

McGovern M, Davidson J (1983) Student perception of performance. *British Journal of Disorders of Communication* 18: 181–185.

McGovern M (1985) The use of video in the self evaluation of speech therapy students. *British Journal of Disorders of Communication* 30: 297–300.

McGovern M, Dean E C (1991) Clinical education: The supervisory process. *British Journal of Communication Disorders* 26: 373–381.

Oxford Centre for Staff Development (1992). *Improving Student Learning: Project Report.* 1–4 March. Oxford Polytechnic/CNAA, Oxford.

Pletts M (1981) Principles and practice of clinical teaching. *British Journal of Disorders of Communication* 16: 129–134.

Robertson S J (1995) Clinical Education in Speech and Language Therapy. Unpublished data.

Stackhouse J, Furnham A (1983) A student-centred approach to the evaluation of clinical skills. *British Journal of Disorders of Communication* 18: 171–179.

Stengelhofen J (1993) *Teaching Students in Clinical Settings.* Stanley Thornes, Cheltenham.

Ward L M, Webster E S (1965) The training of clinical personnel I: Issues in conceptualisation. *Asha* 7: 38–40.

Woolliscroft J O, Tentlaken J, Smith J, Calhonn J G (1993) Medical student's clinical self-assessments: Comparisons with external measures of performance and the students' self-assessments of overall performance and effort. *Academic Medicine* 68: 285–294.

33. Evaluation
How can we tell . . . ?
Alan Rogers

The need for evaluation

Like earlier sections of this book, this chapter is intended to raise questions rather than to propose firm answers. The approach to evaluation here is a practical one; the intention is to make conscious what most of us do much of the time as part of the process of teaching. It is often assumed that the need for and the means of evaluation are self-evident, but if it were, teachers would be better at doing it and would be able to see themselves doing it, more often and more effectively. Evaluation is one of the more difficult skills required of the teacher, and we need to work at it consciously. There are different possible strategies involved, and our task is to choose between them, to decide for ourselves our own preferred way of working.

Along with this should go a willingness to change what we (and our student participants) are doing. There is no point in evaluating the teaching–learning situation if we are unwilling to change course. Evaluation will be effective only if we are prepared to alter or even scrap our existing programme when we detect something wrong and begin again.

A distinction also needs to be drawn between evaluation and assessment. *Assessment* is the collection of data on which we base our evaluation. It is descriptive and objective; if anyone else were to do it, they would come up with much the same findings. *Evaluation* on the other hand is a process of making personalised judgements, decisions about achievements, about expectations, about the effectiveness and value of what we are doing. It involves notions of 'good' and 'bad' teaching and learning, of worth. It is based on our own ideology.

Why evaluate?

Evaluation is necessary for at least three reasons:

- To improve our performance as teachers. Questions of quality, of accountability, of protecting our 'customers', of being effective are important not just for the providers and organisers but also for our student participants and for ourselves. We must believe in what we are doing and that we are doing it well, in order to do it well.
- To plan new strategies, make choices, establish priorities; to determine where we are in the teaching–learning process at present and what to do next; to identify helps and hindrances and decide what to do about them.
- To learn: to assess how much progress has been made, in which direction and how much farther there is to go. Evaluation is an essential part of learning.

Alan Rogers: 'Evaluation: How can we tell . . .?' from *TEACHING ADULTS* (Open University Press, 1996; 2nd edn), pp. 220–233.

Two main forms of evaluation have been identified by writers on this subject: *formative* — the ongoing evaluation that is inherent in the learning process itself and leads to learning changes; and *summative* — evaluation that takes place at different times, particularly at the end of the programme of learning, to see how far we have got. But these are not in fact two distinct processes, only one. If a summative evaluation undertaken at the end of a course (a teacher's report, for instance) is used to plan new programmes and new approaches, then it becomes a formative one. It is the way evaluation is used that distinguishes it. If it looks only backwards and reviews what has been done, it is summative; if in addition it looks forward to, and influences, new procedures, it is formative. The latter is more productive; evaluation judgements should lead to change. But there is also a time for the former.

Who evaluates?

We can also distinguish between *external* and occasional evaluation, practised by the organiser of the programme or some inspector or external validating body, and *internal*, more regular evaluation, practised by the teacher in the course of the teaching programme.

The *organiser* will be assessing how the programme objectives are being met. Are we getting in our groups the right kind of student-learners, the ones the programme is primarily intended for, those we feel to be in most need? Are they learning the right things? Are the courses meeting their needs and intentions? Are the programmes on offer reflecting the selectivity-, competitiveness- and competency-based criteria of the existing educational system, or are they offering a different (non-selective, non-competitive and effort-based) ethos? In addition, at a time of static or dwindling resources, the providers' concern will be with matters of quality control. They need to determine whether the resources they have at their disposal are being used most effectively and, in certain circumstances, to establish priorities. To do all this, they will need criteria to determine whether some courses are better than others and to plan accordingly.

The *teachers* also evaluate their work in order to plan. They are concerned with whether they are being effective as teachers; whether the objectives they have set are the right ones and at the right level, as well as whether they are being met. They need to assess progress, match between intentions (objectives) and outcomes (the results of the teaching–learning process), to measure change, appraise efforts, identify new needs and assess strengths and weaknesses. They will wish to learn whether the short-term goals and the tasks they have laid before the group have been achieved and whether they are of the kind that will contribute towards the desired learning changes. They need to test whether the learners are ready to move on to the next stage or not. They will want to see clearly the *intended* programme of learning, the *implemented* programme (which may be different from what was intended for various reasons) and whether that again differs from the *received* programme.

Both organiser and teacher, then, evaluate for much the same reason, for their own learning and to plan changes. But teachers also build evaluation into the teaching–learning process for the learners' sake. They use evaluation for (extrinsic) motivation (although not all of the participants need this). What is more, an ongoing programme of evaluation is a necessary part of the learning process and becomes part of the work of the whole group.

So thirdly the *learners* themselves evaluate in the course of learning. Evaluation is an essential tool for developing new skills, knowledge and understanding. Hitting a tennis ball against a line on a wall in a practice session brings about no learning changes by itself (though it may strengthen the muscles). What is needed is a series of judgements: 'That was too high'; modification; 'That was too low'; modification; 'That was about right'; repetition; 'That was good'; once more; and so on. Only by such an evaluative process will learning changes take place. Trial-and-error learning particularly is based on evaluation, but most other kinds of learning also rely on this process for effective changes. The learners then engage in formative evaluation in order to learn. They will also pursue summative self-evaluation for motivation: assessing their own progress and performance, rekindling their enthusiasm for the learning goals in the light of their achievements (what is called ipsative evaluation).

It is likely — though not inevitable and probably not desirable — that the evaluation by the teacher and by the outside body (usually organiser) will not be the same, for their objectives differ to a certain degree (even though those of the organiser are subsumed in those of the teacher). It is also likely — and almost certainly undesirable — that the evaluation by the teacher and by the learner will be different. A hierarchy of evaluation thus emerges and should be developed more consciously, the organisers and inspectors (where they exist) should encourage the teachers to evaluate, and they in their turn should encourage the student participants to engage in evaluation. Since evaluation is largely a skill, the teachers need to teach the learners how to evaluate; they should demonstrate the process. Evaluation is one of those exercises that need to be practised jointly between teacher and student participant rather than be taught by exhortation.

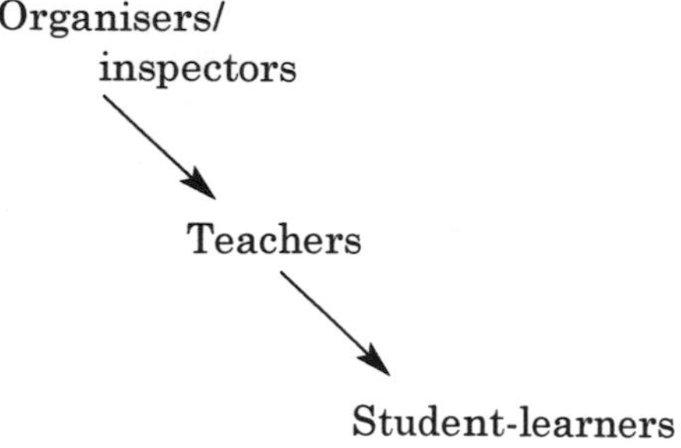

Evaluate what?

There are many different tools of evaluation. One of the more useful ones which may be used for any formative evaluation of adult learning programmes is the appropriately named SWOT approach: to assess the *strengths* and the *weaknesses* of the programme or class and to assess the *opportunities* which it opens and which may or may not have been taken up, also the *threats* which will hamper the effectiveness of the programme and which need to be addressed if the goals of the learning programme are to be achieved. This approach has specific advantages in that it encourages us to look beyond the normal assessment of strengths and weaknesses to explore other possibilities and the risks faced in the programme.

In evaluating our adult education activities, there is one overriding concern — whether the learners are learning or not. That must be the eventual standard by which our programmes need to be judged. In order to assess this, we may look at three main elements: goal achievement, teaching processes, and student attainments.

1. Goal achievement

The learning objectives need to be submitted to evaluation in two main ways: Are they the right ones? How far are they being met? We need to identify clearly the intentions of the programme of learning and to submit these to some form of judgement. Perhaps we take for granted that the objectives of our courses — to learn a craft or other skill, to study literature and so on are the right ones, self-justifying. But these assumptions need to be examined in depth. Is the learning primarily concerned with personal growth, or with socialisation and social change, or with vocational advancement? Whose goals are they, ours or those of the student participants? We also need to assess how far these intentions are being achieved, whether the programme of learning is proving effective. Throughout, we must ask whether the student participants are learning in a particular area, even when this learning is seen as a means of achieving some goal that lies behind the learning. Even if the goal is to pass an examination or to create a work of art for oneself, the means to the satisfactory attainment of these goals is student learning.

2. Teaching processes

The entire process by which the teacher creates the learning opportunity (planning skills as well as powers of exposition) needs to be evaluated. Once again the main concern is with the learner rather than the teacher; the purpose of effective teaching is student learning. The question is less whether we are teaching well than whether the student has been well motivated. There is not much point, as we have remarked before, in the teacher teaching if the learner isn't learning. Evaluation of our own teaching thus includes the process of feedback.

3. Student-learner attainments

At the heart of the evaluation process there lies the question of student learning. Are the learners learning? How much and what are they learning? What form of learning are they engaged in: is it product or process, to handle tools or to produce a table to a set standard? What is the quality and level of their learning? How well is the material learned? Have their skills of learning increased during the programme? These and many other similar questions occur in the process of thinking about the evaluation of our work as teachers of adults.

One of the issues here lies with the concept of progress in learning. If ignorance is seen to be deprivation, then progress will be seen in terms of acquisition — of new skills, knowledge, understanding and attitudes. 'Progress' is usually viewed as advancement along a straight line of development. But there is not always a straight line of progress in learning.

An essential part of this evaluation will be with the attitudinal development of the student participants — with how much additional confidence, how much increased motivation have arisen from the teaching–learning programme. This aspect is often omitted from the evaluation process which concentrates more on increased knowledge and more highly developed skills; but the assurance and enhanced self-image of the students, their willingness to continue to study, their increased interest are all outcomes which need to be evaluated.

And finally we will need to look for the unexpected outcomes, the impact of our teaching–learning programmes. Some of this may have to be done some time after the course has finished — what is sometimes called *post hoc* or postscript evaluation. Experience indicates that at times, whereas the learning objectives of a programme may have been achieved, the longer-term impact of one or other course could be negative (Rogers, 1992).

Evaluation methods

Exercise

Before starting this section, look at the course which you are taking as your case study and try to determine how you plan to evaluate it — what indicators will you look for. I suggest that you write them down here:

How to evaluate?

Student learning is the main focus of our process of evaluation. But there is no single right way of evaluating this; we have to decide for ourselves how to do it. Obviously we need to ask a series of questions, and determining what some of these should be is relatively simple. It is more difficult to come to some agreement on the criteria by which to judge the answers.

Over the years, organisers and providers have used a number of criteria to assess the effectiveness of their programmes and to establish the relative merits of their courses. Some argue (on *a priori* grounds) that longer courses are better than shorter ones (by no means always true) or that those taught by well-qualified teachers are better than those taught by less well-qualified staff (again not always true). They thus judge their programmes in terms of the numbers of longer courses or by the qualifications of the teachers used.

1. Satisfaction indicators

Others rely more heavily on satisfaction indicators such as

- indicated demand — requests from prospective student participants, individually or through organisations, on which the programme is built and which are taken to indicate that it must be meeting needs;

- effective demand — the numbers of student-learners attracted to particular classes; the size of the group is sometimes taken as a means of assessing the value of a course;
- follow-on — whether an extension of the learning situation is requested and taken up; a course is deemed successful if the learners request more of the same;
- follow-up — whether the learners continue to study on their own or pass into new programmes, whether they practise their new skills, read more, etc.;
- attendance figures — in terms of both regularity of attendance and low numbers of drop-outs;
- verbal or written comments by the student participants — both approval and complaints, indicating the learners' sense of success or dissatisfaction.

Teachers, too, often use such popularity or satisfaction indicators to help evaluate their work. But we need to examine them more closely to see whether such popularity signals truly indicate that effective learning is taking place.

2. Contextual preconditions

Among the factors that contribute towards the effectiveness of the learning process are those relating to the context within which the teaching takes place. These too are the concern of evaluation by both organiser and teacher. Since part of the task of evaluation is the identification of the good and bad influences that affect the results of our teaching, we need to consider carefully the *setting* (the room, furniture, temperature, lighting, teaching aids) to see whether it is conducive to the student participants' learning and to remedy any hindrances it contains. The *climate* also needs examination, both that of the institution within which the course is set and that of the learning group itself. There is little hope of creating effective learning changes in the direction of greater self-confidence and self-determination if the whole ethos of the institution is opposed to this or if the class denies the learner any opportunity to exercise such qualities. Overt and covert pressures for or against the goals are important elements in the process of teaching adults, and need evaluation.

3. Criteria from teaching

These two elements in the evaluative process, satisfaction indicators and signs of a conducive context, although valuable, say little about whether the student participants are learning or not. For this, other ranges of criteria can be drawn up, both by organisers concerned with the quality of the programmes they provide and teachers concerned about the effectiveness of their work. These criteria are based on what happens during the teaching–learning experience, and sometimes consist of a description of what happens, moment by moment, an analysis in terms of events and learning episodes. Some attempts have gone beyond this, trying to identify those processes that need to be reinforced and those needing to be corrected or nullified.

1. Some evaluators have looked to the *emotional climate* and *management controls* of the class for their indicators. These are perhaps more properly the preconditions of learning; they do not necessarily indicate whether learning is

taking place. However they should contribute to the criteria by which we can assess teaching–learning effectiveness.

2. Another kind of evaluation is based on an analysis of what educational events occur during any teaching session. Thus some have recorded the number of *learning events* taking place and of what kind they are. (One such scheme divides these events into acts of memorisation, acts of divergent and convergent thinking, and acts of evaluative thinking.) Others have concentrated on the logic of teaching and of the language used in teaching; episodes have been listed such as defining, reporting and designating. These techniques however are more readily practised by others than by the teachers themselves; you cannot easily use them on your own group except by watching yourself teach with the use of a video-recorder. (It is well worth doing this, if you can get hold of the equipment; but if not, you can visit other classes and see other teachers at work, and in this case it is valuable to have in mind what you are looking for.)

3. More useful for the practising teacher is the analysis of the number and kinds of *transactions* that take place during any teaching session: transactions between teacher and learner, and between learner and learner. The participation of the student-learner in the work (activities) of the group is seen as one indicator that learning is taking place. If the teacher talks for a long time, only one kind of transaction is taking place; questions on the other hand comprise more transactions. The most frequently cited analysis of these transactions is that by Flanders, which records events every three seconds, but once again teachers usually need to rely on what they can deduce from their own teaching, and sophisticated techniques are probably not appropriate.

4. Others have concentrated on *types of method* used in the class and the involvement of the student participants in their own learning. The use of 'approved' teaching–learning methods such as demonstration or discussion is frequently felt to lead inevitably to learning. But it is not always easy to see how the teacher can test, at the end of each such occasion, how much and what kind of learning has taken place by the use of these methods. A substantial amount of subjective impression will add itself to our evaluation; we will *feel* good about the teaching session. But a reliance on particular teaching methods will not always lead to learning and may introduce an element of artificiality into the experience.

4. Teacher and learner

An analysis of what goes on during the teaching session can tell us about ourselves and about the learners, and may throw light on whether learning is taking place.

The first part of this analysis relates to our *performance* as teacher. Such an analysis will centre upon our subject expertise and skills of presentation and communication. Evidence of preparation, both of the subject-matter and of the modes of teaching; awareness of the student-learners; the clarity with which the goals of learning are defined; the structure of the learning episode — its level, pace of learning, relevance to the learner and to the task in hand — and the clear signposting of each step of the learning process are all capable of assessment. Our personal style of teaching (self-projection, confidence, voice level, powers of organisation, the rapport built up with the learners, the development of interaction and feedback), the methods used, the involvement of the learners in the processes, and the creation of feedback and evaluation procedures can all be recorded on a positive–negative scale. Positive recordings are those which it is believed will produce an occasion conducive to learning. This is perhaps as far as we can go along this line of enquiry.

Secondly the range and nature of *student activity* can be recorded as part of the evaluative process. The nature of the group, the kinds of interaction between members, the range of expectations and intentions they declare and the clarity of their goals, the kind of work they do in each session and between sessions, the questions they ask (as signs that they are grappling with the new material), the involvement of the learners in evaluating themselves — positive recordings in each of these areas are thought to be indicators that learning is taking place. At each stage, judgements need to be made: as to whether the activity in which the participant is engaged really aims 'at the *improvement* and development of knowledge, understanding and skill and not merely at its exercise'. In the end a description of the programme of work is not in itself an adequate means of assessing effectiveness, but a programme in which the learners are active is more likely to lead to learning changes than one in which they are passive recipients of information and instruction.

5. Performance testing

Involvement by the learners in the learning activities does not always reveal the kind of learning taking place, even if it can be relied upon to indicate that some form of learning changes are taking place. We noted [earlier] the two types of learning (inner learning and the behavioural expressions of that learning, the distinction expressed in the terms 'public' and 'private' effects of our teaching) and the discussion as to whether all 'private' outcomes can and should express themselves in behavioural (performance) terms. *Behavioural changes* and performance targets are easier to assess than inner changes in understanding, values and attitudes, and this fact will influence the procedures of assessment and evaluation we adopt. Part of the process of evaluation then is to interpret behavioural patterns and to create a range of performance situations in order to see how the more private learning changes are expressed.

We need to identify or create certain activities (making something, or writing, or speaking, say) that in themselves express the desired learning, in order to assess whether progress is being made and what kind of learning change is being achieved. But once again we need to remind ourselves of a number of caveats:

- These situations should be real ones, not artificial; there is little point in asking adult student-learners to engage in false activities that they will never engage in again once the course is over.
- The primary purpose is to evaluate the hidden depths (expressive objectives) that lie beneath these competency-based activities.
- Outside influences may hinder or prevent the exercise of the desired function. Activities (including words) do not always reflect inner learning changes and

they rarely reflect their nature. But they are often the only way we can evaluate the learning changes of others.

6. Examinations

Despite the hesitations of many teachers in adult education, examinations are used with adults to evaluate student learning, and there are signs that their use is increasing. The variety of such so-called objective tests (usually subject based) is also increasing. They range from the very formal (standardised testing) to the very informal: written examinations (unseen, open-book, pre-set or home based), tests, essays (whether structured or subjective; that is, devoted to whatever the learner wishes to write about), practicals, observation of exercises, oral tests, questions, discussion, assignments, projects and so on. They tend to test the end product of the learning, the competencies attained; and their effect on the learning process is usually short-term.

The problems of marking examinations, of norm and criterion referencing (that is, whether each exam is to be marked against a 'normal' distribution pattern of success and failure, say 5 per cent top grade, 20 per cent second, 50 per cent third, etc.; or against an objective standard of competence that is supposed to exist somewhere outside of the examiner) and of whether the learners are thinking for themselves are well known. Their accompaniments — the prejudices of the examiners in relation to particular learners, the problem of extrinsic rewards rather than intrinsic motivation, the increase in competitiveness and selectivity, feelings of anxiety, failure and injustice, the distortion of the curriculum and of the pace of learning, the fact that many exams are set and marked by people unknown to the learners so that the aim comes to be to defeat the examiner rather than to learn — are again well known. They have led to a widespread concern to seek ways to replace élitist and selective examinations with other forms of evaluation; to replace prizes with goals that all may achieve. One of the most significant modern developments is the marathon run, which all may enter and all may win in their own terms because the participants choose their own standard and determine their own attainments; frequently they set themselves against themselves alone and assess their own attainments. Modern processes of evaluation are seeking similar ways of helping student participants to assess their own learning progress.

Nevertheless we may not dismiss such formal methods of evaluation entirely, for they can be formative as well as summative in their nature. Internal tests may be as much a means of new learning as of assessment. Sometimes they are intended to be solely summative, leading to the evaluation of attainment levels and on occasion to the award of certificates of competency. There may be a place for these in some forms of adult education, but a number of factors limit their usefulness:

- The problem of how to evaluate progress made as distinct from levels of attainment. Some adult learners, starting from a base lower than that of others in their group, make more rapid progress but remain well behind the attainment levels of the rest. The way to reward such effort and advances while retaining the prescribed or desired attainment levels is problematic.

- Adult learners not only start at very different points; they also choose different goals for themselves. The ends and intentions of adult learners are not homogeneous.
- There are no age-related criteria for adult learners as there are for many younger people.

7. End product

It remains a fact that the most frequent means of assessment and evaluation in adult education is the quality of the end product, be it a piece of writing, the ability to engage in a series of exercises, a fabricated article or role-play exercise completed to the satisfaction of the teacher, who is for this purpose the assessor. These, as we have seen, are not to be judged solely on their own but according to certain criteria attached to the performance of behavioural objectives: the level, the purpose for which it is being done, the conditions under which the actions are being performed, and so on. Any evaluation will need to include some clarification of these conditions as well as a definition of the activity itself.

The only fully satisfactory mode of assessment as to whether the learners are learning the right things and at the right level is the performance of the student participants after the end of each stage of the learning programme. Do they act in such a way as to reveal increased confidence, in whatever field of learning they are engaged in? Do they exercise the new skills better and/or more often? Do they reveal new understandings and new knowledge in what they say and do? Are they continuing to learn in directions of their own choice? Do they show signs of being satisfied with their own performance in their chosen field or of striving towards further improvement? The ultimate evaluation of the success or failure of our teaching will be seen in the exercise of the new skills, knowledge and understandings and of new attitudes towards themselves and the world around them. It is a question of whether our adult students reveal in their behaviour signs of increased adulthood and maturity, of development of their talents, greater autonomy and a sounder sense of perspective.

This is not easy, especially as most teachers of adults lose contact with their student participants soon after the end of the course or programme. The possibility of delayed learning (we know that it takes time for feelings, creative approaches and understandings to emerge) means that we can never be sure, in the case of seeming failures, that our work will not eventually bear fruit. Nor can we be sure that the learning of those with whom we seem to have been most successful will be permanent. For true evaluation ought to address itself not only to what the learners *can* do but to what they *do* do subsequently.

Does this mean that summative evaluation is impossible for the teacher of adults? The answer must be no. But it does mean

- that formative evaluation is more important in teaching adults than summative;
- that our summative evaluation will always be tentative; we can never know for sure.

Some teachers of adults will find this unsatisfactory; but we will often have to be content to cast our bread upon the waters in the expectation that it will (may?) return to us after many days. Perhaps the most rewarding aspect of the evaluation of adult learning are those signs of satisfaction that so many adults reveal in their relations with their teachers. The student participants are after all the best judges of whether they are getting what they feel they need.

Objectives • their nature • the clarity with which they are perceived
Context • the milieu/setting • the climate
Teacher • subject competency • performance as teacher • materials used
Student learners • activities in group • activities as individual learners
Level of performance • the finished product
Unexpected outcome • positive • negative
Indicators of satisfaction • whether goals have been/are being attained
Assessment of success or failure • and reasons

Figure 1 An evaluation schedule: suggested headings

Further reading

Charnley A H, Jones H A (1979) *Concept of Success in Adult Literacy*. Cambridge, Huntington.

Clark N, McCaffrey J (1979) *Demystifying Evaluation*. World Education, New York.

Flanders N A (1970) *Analyzing Teaching Behavior*. Addison-Wesley, Reading, MA.

Guba E, Lincoln E S (1981) *Effective Evaluation*. Jossey-Bass, San Francisco.

Rowntree D (1987) *Assessing Students*. Kogan Page, London.

Ruddock R (1981) *Evaluation: A Consideration of Principles and Methods*. Manchester University Press, Manchester.

34. Perspectives on Competence

Auldeen Alsop

Competence is a notoriously difficult concept to define, yet the public expects health professionals to be competent. An exploration of perspectives on competence should help promote a better understanding of the term and how to remain competent to practise. Developing competence is an individual responsibility both for self-development and for advancing the profession.

This article explores the nature of competence and its relationship with practice. Competence has to be developed and sustained for continuing state registration and in the light of changing contexts of practice. Professionals must develop critical powers to advance their own practice and to transform their profession. Lifelong learning is now a familiar concept to those working in health and social care. The formal, structured process of professional education is the early stage of a continuum of learning for a career.

The journey to competence

Students of the allied health professions initially undertake a programme leading to qualification and eligibility to apply for state registration. The learning journey first entails becoming competent, then maintaining that competence at a safe and sufficient level for current practice and, from there, improving competence in order to enhance practice and to prepare for career moves. Continuing professional development is the process by which practitioners might normally be expected to remain competent for state registration and develop competence for professional growth.

Qualification is the first landmark. It is what Eraut (1994) calls the climax of rule-guided learning. It can be seen as a rite of passage into a profession and assumes the status of competence at that point. It also confers a status on the individual and places a responsibility on the professional for maintaining that competence to practise over time in order to safeguard the quality of practice and its relevance to client care. This responsibility is reinforced by expectations detailed in many professional codes of ethics and professional conduct.

Qualification, however, does not denote competence for life. Nor can it be assumed that competence naturally becomes enhanced through years of practice. The number of years of being qualified may only reflect a level of seniority within the profession and not a higher level of competence. As Brookfield (1995) remarked, length of experience does not automatically confer insight and wisdom. Professionals use critical reflection to question assumptions about practice. The learning that results from critical reflection and inquiry contributes to competence maintenance and

Auldeen Alsop: 'Perspectives on Competence' in *BRITISH JOURNAL OF THERAPY AND REHABILITATION* (2001), 8 (7), pp. 258–264.

development. Personal aspirations for career development beyond the job should also be seen as integral to any plan for developing competence.

Definitions of competence

Dictionary definitions provide assistance in understanding a term such as 'competence' and its relevance to practice. For example, words and phrases such as suitability, sufficiently good, sufficient for the purpose, legally qualified, fitness, capacity or the condition of being capable can be found in dictionaries to describe the state of competence. These remind us of such terms as fitness for purpose, fitness for practice and fitness for award, which are now commonly perceived as goals of a professional programme leading to state registration.

More formally, the consultation document (NHS Executive, 2000) about modernizing the regulation of the allied health professions proposed definitions of competence and continuing professional development as follows:

Competence: '...having the skills and abilities required for the lawful, safe and effective practice of the profession without supervision'.

Continuing professional development: '...such training or experience, or both, as may be required to attest to the continuing competence of a registrant or former registrant'.

If these definitions are ultimately adopted by the Health Professions Council (HPC), they will be the ones against which the activity of state registered practitioners in the allied health professions will be judged. 'Lawful', 'safe' and 'effective' suggest the ultimate standards for practice. These have arguably always been the measure, but now, as explicit statements, they could become the standards for judging practice at both the entry level and in continuity.

Where a practitioner's fitness to practise is called into question because of lack of competence, it will fall within the remit of the new HPC and its committees (Department of Health, 2001). Additionally, from a legal perspective, Dimond (1997) claimed that competent staff must practise 'to the current accepted, approved practice of reasonable practitioners in that field'. A description of practice that falls outside of the currently accepted and approved practice of reasonable practitioners could therefore be adjudged in law as not competent practice, an issue that could be debated for litigation purposes. So knowledge and understanding of these definitions are important for practitioners, who must take steps to retain the competence required for practice.

Competence in practice

Eraut (1998) offered a definition of competence as 'the ability to perform tasks and roles to the expected standard', but this begs some further questions. For example, who sets the standard the profession, the employer or the HPC, and who will say whether the expected standard has been met? These are important questions for practitioners if their livelihood is to depend on assessment of continuing competence for state registration.

Eraut (1994) also remarked on the binary nature of competence. A practitioner, he proposed, is either competent or not competent, with no gradations in between. He offered two descriptions of a competent person, the first as someone who was 'capable of getting the job done', the second as someone who was 'adequate but less than excellent'. This latter statement, however, does infer that there could be levels of competence beyond a given minimum standard. It reminds us of the levels suggested by Dreyfus and Dreyfus (1986), often referred to as novice, advanced practitioner, competent practitioner, proficient practitioner and expert. But even here there seems to be no consensus about how the levels are applied in practice.

Arguably, it was never intended that 'competent' on this continuum should equate to the standard expected at the time of qualification, although some professional programmes err towards matching the two. Students of a profession might be thought to move from a novice state through the state of advanced beginner to attain a state of competence at the time of qualification. However, the view offered by Hodkinson (1995) was that the novice-to-expert continuum describes the quality of performance of a practitioner.

Practitioners at the point of qualification are thus deemed novices who then progress through the various levels as they gain greater situational understanding. So no assumptions can be made about the interpretation of these terms in practice.

Difficulties with terminology and definition do not end there, however.

Metacompetence, competence and competency

Metacompetence, competence and competency are terms often used to denote some form of competence. They are often used inconsistently and in ways that do not hold across cultural boundaries.

According to Bowden and Marton (1998), the terms competence and competency can both imply, first, sets of independent, observable units of behaviour in the workplace and, second, the capability of seeing and handling novel situations and integrating disciplinary and professional knowledge. Some might label the first as competency and the second as competence. Eraut (1998) described competency as an underlying characteristic or a combination of attributes. Competence, he maintained, integrates attributes with performance. Hager and Gonczi (1996) described competency as a single attribute, whereas many attributes comprise competence. Competence, they suggested, is conceived as complex structuring of attributes needed for intelligent performance in specific situations incorporating the idea of professional judgement. Competence is therefore the integration of attributes and their application within practice. Competence embraces professional judgement where competency does not.

Despite these differences many authors agree that competency is a reductionist term, denoting technical rational performance, whereas competence is a term that integrates decision-making and professional judgement. Issitt and Hodkinson (1995) suggested that trying to measure competency attributes separately could trivialize professional practice. Competence that demonstrates integration of knowledge, attributes and professional judgement is what should ultimately be judged in education pre-qualification and thereafter for continuing competence to practise.

However, more recently the term metacompetence has been introduced into professional language to denote overarching aspects of competence, e.g. communication, creativity, the skills of analysis, problem-solving and self-development (Cheetham and Chivers, 1999). It would certainly be difficult to exclude these dimensions from an assessment of competence. If it should be agreed that these aspects of competence constitute metacompetence, it is possible to view the three terms in a hierarchical way from competency through competence to metacompetence. What seems to be important, however, is to adopt definitions that distinguish clearly between the different terms and that can be used consistently in practice. Only then can judgements be made about competence, or lack of it, in a professional context.

A model of professional competence

Cheetham and Chivers (1999) offered a provisional model of professional competence that separates the three terms of metacompetence, competence and competency yet integrates them into a comprehensive whole.

The metacompetencies of competent performance are:

- Communication
- Creativity
- Skills of analysis
- Skills of problem-solving
- Self-development.

These are common across professions. The four core components of competence are:

- Knowledge/cognitive competence
- Functional competence
- Personal behavioural competence
- Values and ethical competence.

Some of these would necessarily vary from profession to profession.

Each core component of competence then comprises groups of competencies as a set of attributes. These are extensive – Cheetham and Chivers' work gives more detail.

It could be suggested that a judgement about professional competence ought to draw on an integrated model that comprises knowledge (formal, informal and tacit), values and behaviour as well as its practical use for effective performance, demonstrated in context. But there also needs to be a recognition that competence in a situation is not static but dynamic and subject to change.

Situational competence

Hollis (1997) maintained that competence had a situational component, as it was necessarily about the ability to perform roles in the workplace. If competence was context-specific, it could not be static, as the nature of the workplace is constantly changing. Change in the form of new developments, shifts in thinking and moves into new contexts of practice can affect the way in which professionals are expected to work and can therefore challenge a state of competence (Alsop, 2001).

Barnett (1997) pointed out that knowledge is an open-ended commodity, liable to be superseded by new knowledge at any time. This has to be acknowledged by professionals, as much of a professional's knowledge at the time of qualification could be out of date within 5 years (Haines, 1997). Building on existing knowledge and developing new knowledge is crucial to remaining competent. Retaining obsolete knowledge is impractical (Eraut, 1994). Discarding outdated knowledge and embracing new concepts is essential for accommodating change (Barnett, 1997). Failing to keep abreast of change or even to prepare for change can lead to an inability to fulfil professional and organizational expectations and may ultimately present a risk to service users (Alsop, 2001).

Learning skills for competent practice

A crucial and integral feature of competence is a professional's capacity to learn, because this is needed for working with change and for continuing to develop professionally (Alsop, 2000).

Crist *et al.* (1998) considered professional competence to be the outcome of thoughtful, self-directed professional development activities that are shaped through careful evaluation of one's current knowledge, skills, abilities and individual learning needs in relation to future career and employment responsibilities. In effect, this covers both pre-qualifying and post-qualifying education and professional development. The development of skills of independent learning was also seen as essential to lifelong learning.

Competence to learn

Competence covers a range of behaviour and skills, first and foremost the ability to know and work within one's limit of competence. A self-assessment of knowledge and skills and the capacity to perform within the context of practice should help determine how competence levels might be changing in the light of changing external factors. This should highlight professional development needs. Second, the attributes of competence also include the willingness and ability to take steps to develop competence, primarily as a requirement to keep up to date and secondarily as a responsibility to enhance and advance practice. Having the competence to learn is integral to competence to practise and involves:

- Having a positive attitude to learning
- Recognizing learning needs
- Taking initiative to learn
- Knowing how to find and use learning resources
- Seizing learning opportunities as they occur
- Being open to new approaches to practice
- Working with new ideas and concepts

- Knowing how to reflect on, analyse and critique practice
- Evaluating progress and future needs.

The use of these attitudes and skills is fundamental to ensuring ongoing learning and continuing professional development.

Lack of competence

It is necessary to acknowledge that there may be times when competence cannot legitimately be demonstrated fully. Students of a profession might justly be regarded as 'not yet competent'. This is acceptable in the early stages of a professional programme when students aspire to attaining competence to practise in their chosen profession. At the point of qualification, it is assumed that a state of competence has been attained and that the newly qualified professional will thereafter take responsibility to maintain this competence, particularly in the context of his or her employment.

However, the consequences of not maintaining competence must also be considered. For example, lack of competence might be an acceptable state in some circumstances provided that it is recognized as such and efforts are being made to rectify the situation. For example, those moving from one field of employment to another or those returning to practise after a career break may not be recognized as wholly competent in the new context in the first instance.

It may be possible to use skills transferred from one environment to another, but if competence is context-specific, then a time of adjustment to the new environment may be necessary to reassess how skills should be used for effective performance in the new situation. A clearly defined, agreed and explicit education and development programme designed to bring knowledge, skills and attributes to an acceptable level of competence may be required in these circumstances. The limits of competence that affect any aspect of practice should be acknowledged and steps should be taken to ensure that no member of the public is put at risk.

Deficiency in competence or the state of incompetence may be a different matter, especially if it is not recognized by the practitioner being in such a state. Measures such as those afforded by clinical governance may need to be drawn upon in order to manage the situation. It needs to be raised in performance review or another formal situation where proceedings are documented. An action plan for addressing the issues would be required and plans made for a further review of progress. Persistent failings may need to be referred to the statutory body.

Demonstrating competence

Anyone who is qualified as a health professional is duty-bound to maintain competence as a bare minimum requirement. Those who are claiming to be competent must therefore be able to:

- Profile their own competence
- Demonstrate that competence to others
- Justify that claim to competence

- Be prepared to be judged on that claim to competence.

The new HPC will determine the way in which registrants must demonstrate their ongoing competence. Registered professionals will be required to undertake continuing professional development and present evidence of such continuing professional development in portfolio form (Department of Health, 2001). Responsibility for managing the process is likely to be devolved to the professional bodies, but details of the process have yet to be agreed. Guidance on portfolio preparation can be found elsewhere (Alsop, 2000).

Competence analysis

Given that the minimum obligation on each member of the allied health professions is to remain competent to practise, there must be some way in which competence can be assessed and education and training needs determined so that efforts can be made to maintain a state of competence for practice. Performance review with a line manager can help to determine learning needs in the light of changing practice and service developments. However, it is also useful personally to be able to identify areas where knowledge or skills might be lacking and affect competence.

The first practical step might be for the practitioner to list those roles that form part of his or her current remit. The practitioner might also be, for example, an educator, mentor, supervisor, manager, researcher, leader or consultant as well as a clinician. Each of these roles will demand a level of competence in different skills and abilities, such as technical, supervisory, leadership, facilitation, teaching and/or organizational skills. The domain of practice is also important. Some practitioners may be specialists in a particular area of practice, others may carry mixed caseloads across the domains of health care. They may work with a mixed group comprising children, adults and older people or be specialist practitioners with one group. Each domain makes different demands and needs to be assessed separately.

It is possible for a practitioner to build up a profile of responsibilities within his or her current sphere of employment and assess the level of competence in each aspect of practice. In some areas, the practitioner might be an expert and in others might be just competent or have only a novice level of competence. Gaps in knowledge can thus be determined and an action plan formulated to address the deficiencies. The analysis should be shown in the personal portfolio to demonstrate that efforts have been made to review and enhance competence.

Competence to advance one's profession

Barnett (1994) argued that professional responsibilities extend beyond those that advance clinical competence to those that advance the profession itself. In his view, professional competence is about competence in sub-roles and the whole role and involves:

- Being knowledgeable, skilful and ethical
- Developing critical powers
- Offering insightful thoughts about practice
- Developing and transforming practice over time

- Embracing new practice and discarding out-dated practices
- Creating knowledge through one's own practice
- Learning not only from one's own practice but from that of other people
- Examining society's changing demands
- Having a vision and not just being responsive
- Forming views about the profession's needs
- Taking steps to shape change.

These attributes should advance the profession as well as the professional. They are higher-order responsibilities of a competent professional that require the development and effective use of the ability to think and practise critically and to take a critical stand in the context and changing world of practice.

Some may argue that these qualities are beyond those required to remain on the register. Yet essentially, this competence draws on the same skills that are required to make critical professional judgements. The way in which these skills are applied may be different and beyond those concerned with the immediacy of one's practice environment. Nevertheless, they should come within a professional's responsibility and domain of concern. These were arguments also advanced by Eraut (1998). He described a capable practitioner as requiring practice knowledge, a critical approach to practice, a flexible mind with the capacity to adapt to change and the capacity to generate new professional knowledge. These may be the qualities of those seeking not just to remain competent but also to advance practice.

Conclusions

There may be many definitions of competence and many terms used to describe it. But one thing is certain: competence is not, and cannot be, a fixed concept (Issett and Hodkinson, 1995). Practitioners must therefore be able and willing to adapt to change, particularly to changing contexts. Steps must be taken to ensure continuing competence, minimally to satisfy legal requirements and thereafter to satisfy personal aspirations for professional growth and for transforming practice over time.

References

Alsop A (2000) *Continuing Professional Development: A Guide for Therapists.* Blackwell Science, Oxford.

Alsop A (2001) Competence unfurled: developing portfolio practice. *Occupational Therapy Int* 8: (in press).

Barnett R (1994) *The Limits* of *Competence.* Society for Research into Higher Education and Open University Press, Buckingham.

Barnett R (1997) *Higher Education: A Critical Business.* Society for Research into Higher Education and Open University Press, Buckingham.

Bowden J, Marton F (1998) *The University of Learning, Beyond Quality and Competence in Higher Education.* Kogan Page, London.

Brookfield S (1995) *Becoming a Critically Reflective Teacher.* Jossey-Bass, San Francisco.

Cheetham G, Chivers G (1999) Professional competence: harmonizing reflective practitioner and competence-based approaches. In: D O'Reilly, L Cunningham, S Lester (eds) *Developing the Capable Practitioner; Professional Capability through Higher Education,* pp. 215–228. Kogan Page, London.

Crist P, Wilcox B L, McCarron K (1998) Transitional portfolios: orchestrating our professional competence. *American Journal of Occupational Therapy* 52: 729–736.

Department of Health (2001) *Establishing the new Health Professions Council.* Department of Health, Leeds.

Dimond B (1997) *Legal Aspects of Occupational Therapy.* Blackwell Science, Oxford.

Dreyfus H L, Dreyfus S E (1986) *Mind over Machine: The Power of Human Intuition and Expertise in the Era of the Computer.* Blackwell, Oxford.

Eraut M (1994) *Developing Professional Knowledge and Competence.* Falmer Press, London.

Eraut M (1998) Concepts of Competence. *Journal of Interprofessional Care* 12: 127–139.

Hager P, Gonczi A (1996) Professions and competencies. In: R Edwards, A Hanson, P Raggatt (eds) *Boundaries of Adult Learning,* pp. 246–260. Routledge, London, in association with The Open University.

Haines P (1997) Professionalization through CPD: is it realistic for achieving our goals? *British Journal of Therapy and Rehabilitation* 4: 428–447.

Hodkinson P (1995) Professionalism and competence. In: P Hodkinson, M Issitt (eds) *The Challenge of Competence, Professionalism through Vocational Education and Training,* pp. 58–69. Cassell, London.

Hollis V (1997) Practice portrayed: an exploration of occupational therapy clinical skills and their development. Unpublished PhD thesis. University of Exeter, Exeter.

Issitt M, Hodkinson P (1995) Competence, professionalism and vocational education and training. In: P Hodkinson, M Issitt (eds) *The Challenge of Competence, Professionalism through Vocational Education and Training,* pp. 146–156. Cassell, London.

NHS Executive (2000) *Modernising Regulation – The New Health Professions Council.* A consultation document. NHS Executive, Leeds.

35. Responsive Assessment: Assessing Student Nurses' Clinical Competence

Mary Neary

This paper argues for a new approach to continuous assessment of students of nursing clinical competence, which I call responsive assessment. Its argument for this is based on a research study highlighting the problems and concerns students and practitioners identified in relation to the assessment of their nursing practice and clinical competence.

It puts forward a case for challenging role boundaries by implementing contract assignments: as an integral part of adult learning and continuous assessment (Neary 1992a, 1998) and for developing a conceptual model called responsive assessment, in which the students' readiness for assessment and their response to patient/client needs is identified.

The arguments are developed against the background of Benner's movement from novice to expert (Benner 1984) and Stake's (Stake 1977) three stages of antecedents, transaction and outcome as a process for professional students development.

Introduction – the study

The study aimed to establish what has happened in nursing practice in relation to assessing the clinical competence of nursing students during their Nurse Education Programme. It was based upon the perceptions of skilled practitioners and students of their own experiences, set against information gathered from other significant practitioners, the historical and changing policy contexts of nurse education. The general literature on assessment and competence was interrogated, with particular reference to attempts to develop clinical assessment tools.

Factors shaping and influencing methodology

From the start, the strongly debated issue of quantitative versus qualitative methodology in nursing research stood high on my list of considerations. Historically, a quantitative approach takes its rationale from the physical and natural sciences, by privileging measurement of operational features of representative properties of a phenomenon. From such data, conclusions have often been drawn that have influenced action and formed the basis for policy making. Nurses have favoured such approaches and for a long time seemed reluctant to adopt qualitative approaches. The latter tend not to place so much emphasis on the testing/prediction, but rather favour. 'understanding' behaviour. Qualitative research is usually conducted in naturalistic settings so that the context in which the phenomenon occurs is considered to be part of the phenomenon itself. The researcher attempts neither to place experimental controls upon the phenomenon being studied nor to control the extraneous variables.

Mary Neary: 'Responsive Assessment: Assessing Student Nurses' Clinical Competence' in *NURSE EDUCATION TODAY* (2001), 21, pp. 3–17.

As many aspects as possible of the problem are explored, and variables arising from the context are considered as part of the problem.

A qualitative approach to understanding, explaining and developing theory is an inductive one. Inductive theory is directed towards bringing knowledge into view. It is generally descriptive, naming phenomena and positioning relationship. Subjectivity is always a problem. The amount and quality of data and depth of analysis are highly dependent upon the ability of the researcher as active participant, coordinator or empathizer in the relationship and context which constitute the data. The qualitative researcher is in no way absolved from seeking appropriate generalization, concept development and relationship with literatures.

Given my interest in how students and practitioners described what they really thought and believed about the nature of continuous assessment of clinical competence and their role in relation to the assessment process, I was led naturally toward consideration of an initial, qualitative approach. My first need was to clarify the understanding of assessors and students of their roles in the assessment process, as well as their perceived preparation for it. Semi-structured focused interviews were devised. Facts, conditions and concepts emerging from data gathered from the initial interviews with assessors were used to construct a list of context-specific factors and context-free issues for the final questionnaire.

However, taken as a whole, my methods included both the qualitative and quantitative, employing interviews, questionnaires and non-participant observation. Questionnaires were designed to yield both qualitative and quantitative data having 'closed' and 'open' responses which, on the other hand, provided data which lent itself to numerical coding for statistical manipulation, some items being rated on a Likert-type scale and, on the other, data retaining some meaningful configuration of individual response.

Interviews with 70 students and 80 assessors were conducted in a manner which allowed freedom to modify the sequence of questions, change their wording, or to explain or add to them, according to the situation that I found myself in. This method helped to created a more relaxed atmosphere. Interviews with both students and assessors helped not only to gather information having direct bearing on the research objectives, measure respondent knowledge and information, values and preferences, attitudes and beliefs, but helped to design the main questionnaire. Follow-up interviews to questionnaire results allowed me to go deeper into the motivations of respondents and the reasons for their responses.

Main findings

Data was collected from questionnaires at various stages throughout the Common Foundation Programme (first 18 months of a 3 year course) from 300 student nurses, 155 nurse practitioners and interviews with 70 students and 80 assessors at three colleges of nursing, codenamed Hillside, Roseside and Brookside. Throughout this study the data indicated that students tended to favour the use of criteria referenced assessment, but with some flexibility and it should not depend solely on pre-set objectives, which they found restrictive, and seldom reflected real life situations. Assessors often found themselves trying to fit the objective to the students' performance and claimed that assessment strategies were too 'objective bound' to suit the college academic requirements. Assessors and students welcomed written comments on their progress reports regardless of the grade awarded, or ticks given in the appropriate boxes. Students appeared to be sceptical about assessors having access to previously written assessment documents and the results. Students acknowledged their exposure to stress caused by continuous assessment but assessors did not, believing that students were protected from most stressful situations. Most students were given time to read and discuss the outcome of their assessment of progress. Students considered that time should always be allowed to discuss progress during and at the end of practical experience and that both the discussions and outcomes should relate to the reality of the situation and experience at the time of the assessment. Assessors argued that they preferred to respond to students' performance and reaction to patient/client nursing care needs during the assessment that related to the changing circumstances of their patient/client health needs. As one assessor explained:

> Students come with their assessment books which need filling in, I have problems with this. I find I am trying to fit the day-to-day nursing care needs of my patients to the criteria in the book, it's just impossible. All I end up doing is filling in the book to keep the college staff happy. I prefer to assess students' performance related to patient's requirements.

They appreciated the need for continuous assessment but favoured a change in the way the continuous assessment booklets were designed and used. Both assessors and students tended to have some knowledge of the range of purposes for which the completed continuous assessment booklet was used, and the purposes of continuous assessment itself. As part of their preparation some students suggested that a pre-allocation visit to the practice placement might help them and their assessors to identify their learning needs and to agree learning outcomes which related to patient/client nursing needs. Student perceptions of the learning programmes in practice settings were mainly positive. However, students and assessors rarely knew the detail of the assessment criteria, or how to interpret them. Assessors were also concerned about 'unassessable qualities'. There were some assessors who fostered student competition rather than collaboration. It appeared that team work was not a principle readily adopted in practical assessment strategies.

Students moved between what they regarded as practice reality and college ideals. They learned to live with their differing perspectives without obvious difficulty. Such differences were more of a stumbling block for curriculum planners, tutors and practitioners. The reality of practice was highly valued as a learning resource. Students quickly learned to use assessment documents to their advantage. The stress that they experienced was related to the method of assessment rather than the assessment tool itself.

Students experienced variation within practice placements concerning both what assessment criteria should be and what should be assessed. Students and practitioners developed strategies to cope with the 'messy' problem of assessment of clinical competence by negotiating their own objectives, often rejecting college set objectives, while 'ticking in the boxes' to 'keep the college happy'.

Potential abuse

Throughout the study many comments, both written and voiced by students and assessors indicated. that they saw the value and necessity of as well as the problems with continuous assessment, or as some students called it, 'progressive assessment'. Students appreciated constructive comments in support of grades given or boxes ticked and considered that assessors needed to devote more time to the actual assessment and feedback process. Some students and assessors advocated the use of a 'team approach' when compiling final written comments and had misgivings about the usefulness of only one person giving feedback (Neary 1996). They identified potential abuse of the system if care was not taken. The process might become no more than:

> ...filling in the forms to keep the college staff happy...
> (Roseside, CFP student, 6 months into course)

where

> ...assessors were afraid to give adverse comments because it could cause problems with college staff...
> (Brookside, CFP student, 4 months into course)

and which

> ...creates too much paperwork if a student is reported because of failing to achieve.
> (Hillside, CFP student, 2 months into course)

Most assessors were aware of the more academic thrust of the new nurse education course and some still displayed anxiety about dealing with and relating to the new breed of 'academic students'. A few found themselves avoiding them in case they were asked 'academic' questions to which they did not have the answers. This avoidance was also practised by some when it came to assessing student progress and competence, as illustrated by one assessor during my last meeting with the group:

> I work well with the student all day, but I avoid asking him about his assessment booklet which I know must be completed before he leaves the department. The truth of the matter ... even after nearly 2 years, I still have problems with the wording and the forms, ... I feel so foolish at times like these. (Roseside Staff Nurse, 4.5 years qualified)

For some students, failure to match up to the expectations of the ward staff regarding basic nursing skills was a major problem. University nurse tutor encouragement to be critical and analytical contrasted sharply with the dismissal that they sometimes felt they met from practitioners when they tried to follow such injunctions. Rapidly discovering that practice assessments depended on their relationship with assessors and other ward staff, they soon learned the benefit of 'getting on with your assessor or mentor' as a means of getting through the programme and getting qualified, even if this was at the expense of developing qualities that the scheme set out to nurture. One might argue how little has changed, for Melia (1987) informed us 13 years ago of the same 'games' in her study of student nurses.

The effectiveness of the assessment system was seen by practitioners to be very much related to the quality of mentorship and the adequacy of mentor and assessor preparation reinforcing the findings of Davies *et al.* (1994). There was general concern that the system could work unfairly. Inconsistencies in how grades were awarded, for example, in never giving an 'A' on principle, the use of arbitrary criteria and inappropriate personal opinions were mentioned during group interviews. Some students in Roseside criticized the assessment booklets as being 'burdensome' with insufficient scope to reflect student performance accurately and helpfully. Continuous assessment was created to evaluate performance over time, so as to ensure acceptable standards. Not only was defining a standard difficult but Colleges inevitably required assessment by grades. The College grading systems varied from 'A–D', 'satisfactory–poor', 'pass–fail' and 'achieved–not achieved' and it was not clear that all who were involved were fully aware of the meaning or value of the particular grading scheme used.

Influence of position and power

The data highlighted that most assessors saw control as being one of the responsibilities of their position. They tended to feel that it was up to them to establish the ground rules for a relationship that included monitoring student performance and, if necessary, carrying out disciplinary action. Their position required that they act as a student's manager and this was seen as legitimate by teachers. However, very few students perceived such 'position power' as legitimate, though the majority accepted the roles of the assessors as manager, monitor and disciplinarians as legitimate. The data suggest that they also felt that such roles should be exercised in virtue of either charismatic (person) or rational (expert) power, no doubt reflecting their relative innocence of the realities of nursing relationships. Typically they described their assessors as being assertive, keeping control over what they 'do and cannot do' in a 'nice' way, respecting them as 'people' not just 'another Project 2000 student' or just a 'CFP student'.

Assessors and students made clear acknowledgement that while nurse lecturers/ tutors (teachers) may have control over the educational process, the students had control over the outcome of that process and a power of veto over learning, while assessors had control of the assessment process and its outcomes. While outcomes were dependent on a teacher and assessor controlled educational process and students could not choose to be successful 'on their own', they could refuse to learn either from discrete teaching sessions or modules or from individual teachers and/or assessors. It was strongly claimed by students that it was up to the individual to take responsibility for their own learning over which assessors, in making decisions on progress, had more control than teachers. If this was the reality, they believed that assessment of their performance in the practice placement must be patient care related.

Comments received during interviews with students revealed that they preferred to be assessed on their day-to-day nursing care delivery and not just on the set learning objectives which were agreed by college staff. Most students talked about 'the real world of nursing practice', for example:

> ...on the wards the mentor can judge my level of competence more realistically, because it is the real world of work.

Another student talked about 'responding to patients actual health needs'. She continued:

> In the community I have learned to respond to the patient's needs, my community mentor and assessor focused on how I responded...

One mature student echoed that which many students said should happen:

> The learning objectives can be used as a general guideline but the assessments of clinical competence must be based on students' performance on a continuous basis.

In the context of the patient's nursing care needs, one male student identified what he believed to be the main problem with assessments of nursing practice as:

> Qualified staff stick rigidly to college set objectives even when these do not match the real world of practice.

Not all practitioners agreed with the above as illustrated by one experienced ward manager:

> I always respond to students performance, against patients health status and nursing needs. If I didn't it would lack value and credibility.

Another practitioner expressed the importance of 'worth':

> Assessing students in context always responding to the worth of the nursing care given to an individual.

A case for responsive assessment

The data showed that while assessors agreed that it was necessary to assess student performance in the practice setting, trying to categorize it by using a list of learning objectives that aimed to match the various stages and levels at which the students were expected to achieve was a problematic undertaking for both college staff and practitioners. Nurse Education Programme innovations attempted to move assessment away from the more artificial to more real life situations. One assumption underlying this approach was as problematic as it had been when underlying more traditional modes of assessment; successful performance on one day is no guarantee of it on another (Jarvis 1995). Even more problematic was the process of trying to subdivide professional action into those competencies which would meet the requirements of National Boards and UKCC for registration, thereby arriving at a complete list upon which there was general agreement (Neary 2000).

Assessment of student clinical performance was viewed by some assessors as a 'technical process' whose emphasis should be on practical rather than academic skills, somewhat overlooking that such assessment involves human beings in specialized environments. As a challenge to such a tradition, Stake (1977) put forward a 'countenance model', producing a framework he hoped anyone might utilize. He proposed that a programme should be looked at in terms of antecedents, transactions and outcomes. Antecedents are the conditions obtaining before teaching or learning has occurred, e.g. individual ability and willingness to learn. The request by students to visit their practice placement before being allocated their placement would satisfy this aspect of the responsive assessment (see Figure 1). Transactions represent all the teaching and learning processes that are engaged in, for example, teaching methods, contract assignments, assessments or tests and dialogue between student and assessor. Outcomes represent the product of the antecedents and transactions and are characterized inter alia by ability and achievement. Stake placed these terms in two matrices, one representing judgement and the other description, linking them together through contingency and congruence, reasoning that:

> For any one educational programme there are two principal ways of processing data: finding the contingencies among antecedents, transactions and outcomes and finding the congruence between intents and observations. (Stake 1977, p. 152)

Critics of Stake's model (Whitely 1990) argued that as a framework it was rather complex to operationalize and, for some, too difficult even to comprehend. However, it is my contention that, even with such weaknesses, this model can be developed through a well defined assessment strategy of student potentiality in the real world of clinical practice and contract assignments which assess both theory and practice (Neary 1997a). This would allow assessors the opportunity to deal with unintended and unexpected outcomes in a positive way, i.e. turn them into 'learning opportunities' for both students and themselves (Neary 1992b). This can only be done if both students and assessors recognize the importance of unintended and unexpected outcomes as part of the learning process and the development of competence in patient/client care. The focus of nursing care is the client/patient; therefore teaching and learning cannot be assessed within a void. Unanticipated events occur during clinical practice; these events alter the original situations that were intended to give students the chance to demonstrate behaviour specified in the learning objectives. To be fair to students, situational events need to be considered during the assessment process. It is this consideration that turns the assessment of students' nursing care practice into a 'responsive assessment'. Here continuous assessment can come into its own in allowing for such dynamism (see Figure 1).

It seems logical to argue that feedback on performance resulting from both intended and unintended outcomes and adequate time for reflection upon them, helps the student to develop to full potential. The more immediate this feedback and reflection, the greater the potential learning and the greater the possibility that the student will gain in confidence and increase personal autonomy. As illustrated by one 1st year student:

> I was nervous because [Named Assessor] worked with me all week and right away she told me where I went wrong. She responded quickly by helping me to understand what I needed to learn. [Name] did not waste any time in telling me how and what to do. I like that, I know where I need to improve ... I can respond to this level of feedback. I feel more confident now, I can get on with the job.

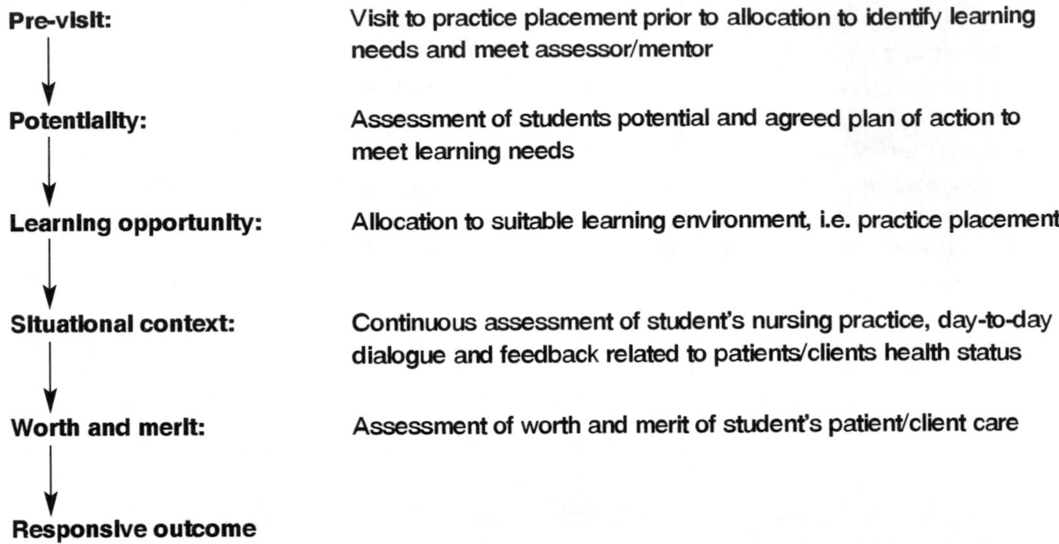

Pre-visit:
Visit to practice placement prior to allocation to identify learning needs and meet assessor/mentor
Potentiality:
Assessment of students potential and agreed plan of action to meet learning needs
Learning opportunity:
Allocation to suitable learning environment, i.e. practice placement
Situational context:
Continuous assessment of student's nursing practice, day-to-day dialogue and feedback related to patients/clients health status
Worth and merit:
Assessment of worth and merit of student's patient/client care
Responsive outcome

Adopting teaching and assessing in response to patient/client needs and student's performance. Identify learning outcome to be developed and achieved.

Figure 1 Responsive assessment process

Assessment takes a very central role in any scheme of learning but:

> ...building on strengths and correcting weakness, is not possible if competence-data is the only information available. (Ashworth and Saxton 1990, p. 24)

Students need the opportunity to learn from skilled practitioners who are experts in responding and reacting effectively to the unintended and unexpected outcomes they face each day in their clinical placements and such a process would seem to enhance the opportunity for formative assessment. What is important in this context is not only the frequency of the feedback and reflection but its nature and quality.

Stake (1986) recommends that learning objective be used as part of the instructional, rather than the assessment, plan. A clear specification of objectives makes measurement of learning possible and helps to establish the relationship between theory and practice. However, the premise from which objectives are designed and used often determines their effectiveness.

In the real world practice changes constantly, sometimes very quickly. It is at times like these that the skilled practitioner acts not according to the rules or text book procedures but to needs of the individual patient/client and 'knows', in that situation, what is necessary. As illustrated by one first year student:

> ...My assessor took one look at me and right away she told me, 'Mr X is not well, keep an eye on him, watch his colour, take his B/P' ... he could get worse...

Student continues:

> How did she know?

It was to such situations typically that students were exposed on practice placements, where the preset objectives that they bore with them from college proved not very relevant. The data showed assessment strategies to be full of such pre-set objectives. Students and assessors argued that such objectives restricted learning opportunities. Most students expressed the need to consider the affective as well as cognitive and psychomotor domains of learning as well as to receiving 'useful' feedback. We would argue that these entirely reasonable aspirations should be met within an assessment framework that allows for consideration of creativity and the emergent along with student, teacher and assessor satisfaction in the teaching-learning process. Clinical learning objectives and learning opportunities could be used as realistic measures of growth in assessment of individual need, rather than for determination of student weakness, in a model for assessment of clinical competence that is dynamic and flexible, rather than linear and prescriptive. As highlighted by one student when she said:

> Each day is different on this ward ... new patients ... new conditions,... and sometimes patients get poorly not better. I have to abandon my learning objectives for now so that I can concentrate on the day-to-day needs of my patients.

Stake put it that educational evaluation (in our sense, assessment) of this type:

> ...responds to audience requirements for information... (Stake 1986, p. 14)

It is important to note that Stake cautioned assessment away from the presumption that only measurable outcomes testify to the worth of a programme. What about the opinions of the clients/patients who are at the receiving end – I would argue that they too should be involved in the assessment process as they can and do respond within a situational context, as illustrated by Table 1 and field notes.

Very few eluded to the patient's involvement in assessing students' clinical and nursing competence. However when prompted the assessors and students thought it was a 'good idea' to ask patients for their view on students' ability to give high standards of care. There was evidence that patients/clients did assess students informally, which the following field notes illustrate.

Field notes

One patient, now looking comfortable after having his dressing changed, and the student asks 'Is there anything else I can do to make you more comfortable Mr Jones'. Patient replies 'Oh nurse, you could just move my locker closer, I need a drink,' which the student promptly does. Patient Jones turns to the staff nurse who is observing the student and says 'You got a good 'un there Sister, she is gentle and cares, I feel much better now. She'll go far that one will, indeed she will'. Staff Nurse nods and smiles, then turns to the student and says 'Well done [Name], let's discuss your progress now that we have time'.

Another patient turns to researcher and proceeds to tell the story of how:

'Nurse [Name] took me for a bath today, I feel safe with her, the way she encouraged me into the bath, my first after the op. you know, I was frightened I'd fall, old pegs not so steady any more you see, not since the fall, that's why I'm in the hospital. Nurse [Name] never left my side, gave me confidence, she did, good lass that she is'. The assessor for this student had an in-depth discussion about the patient's care.

The above are two of many examples observed during this study of 'responsive assessment' by patients and of the assessor responding to the situation.

Description and judgement

A primary reason for suggesting a responsive assessment model is that responsive assessment changes the assessor role by requiring two actions, description and judgement. Description is the process of providing necessary information about the student. Judgement involves a value component. The assessor is assumed to be qualified to decide the relative value of a student performance. Assessments become a process for both describing students and judging the merit and worth of their performance. Clinical learning objectives are one source of input for determination of the merit of student work, whereas judgement of the worth of that work depends on the interactions between students and patients/clients in selected situational contexts as illustrated above. The use of a 'responsive' model would encourage this judgement. Objective criteria for performance would not then be the sole measure for comprehensive practical assessment.

Another rationale for adopting responsive assessment lies, arguably, in the style/method of verbal and written reports of student progress to which it gives rise. Instead of reporting specific changes in student behaviour, responsive assessment records performance within a situational context. Each report identifies progress and provides stimulus for the student to develop personal reflection and adjust learning and personal objectives for successive clinical/practical experiences. Such a model (see Figure 1) might satisfy the assessors who, in response to the main questionnaire, said that they would prefer to write or report on student performance on a blank page alongside the pre-set college objectives, rather than tick boxes or simply use scales. This study and others (Powell *et al.* 1992, O'Neill *et al.* 1993, Davies *et al.* 1994, Jowett *et al.* 1994, Phillips 1994, Phillips *et al.* 1994, Neary 1996) have shown that it is common practice for colleges to identify which objectives have and which have not been met, omitting additional experiences that have occurred. Much of this is encapsulated by a student with 8 years experience as a ward clerk prior to entering nursing who said:

> The learning objectives set for my second placement were the same as for the first placement, I had already achieved these, but I was not credited with this when allocated to my next placement. No allowance was made for my new achievements. It is very frustrating, my progress is bound-up by the same set of objectives for the whole of the Common Foundation Programme.

These supplemental experiences, often unplanned, may provide the stimulus for enhanced personal development and opportunities for practice over and above simply behavioural objectives.

Table 1 Assessors and students' interviews

Comments/issues highlighted during interviews	Situational Context Students (n = 70) Frequency	Assessors (n = 80) Frequency
Assessment strategies need to include the following:		
Student readiness for assessment	70	73
*Patient orientated assessment	70	73
*Responding to patient/client needs	69	78
*Unpredictable outcomes	68	70
*The worth and merit of care given	62	71
*Dialogue between student and patients	62	75
*Patients' day-to-day health status	60	69
Link College academic requirements with day-to-day patient care	58	61
College set objectives combined with client/patient care needs	42	59
*Patients/clients involvement in assessing students	30	20

*These comments strongly support the need for a responsive assessment, i.e. that which is patient/client orientated and allows for the dynamic and shifting sands of day-to-day patient/client care.

Merit and worth

With responsive assessment, assessors and students will be responding to the situational context, which leads to the assessment of the merit and worth of the nursing care being given to patient/client health needs. As illustrated by one second year student:

> ...the patient I was caring for last week became very poorly, it was my last week on this ward, so my assessment had to be completed. Staff Nurse [Name], my mentor, assessed me. She was great, she took the patient's condition into account [Name], explained to me the care I gave had worth and merit because I responded to the patient's altered health status and gave the appropriate nursing care...

In nursing practice, assessing the 'merit' of the intervention can rarely be treated as totally independent of other conditions and desired outcomes. A good example, based on student experience, was related on a study day. It concerned a student carrying out 'total patient care', including positioning, lifting, moving and handling that in turn required precision and safety for both the patient/client and herself. While it was made clear that assessment of 'merit' of this sequence of action would be positive if the student had followed the correct procedure, assessment of the 'worth' of the interventions to the patient/client, with respect to his/her feelings and student attitudes towards the patient, e.g. having an awareness of discomfort, pain and emotional need, may be different. An assessor ought to consider student–patient interactions before, during and after such an episode when the patient/client may have been in pain and frightened. Should the student fail to minimize pain and fear by explaining the procedure, or provide emotional support, the actions are not of great 'worth' to the patient/client. Yet on the other hand, even if the student had minimized pain, explained the procedure and provided emotional support but failed to maintain 'safety procedures', the 'merit' when lifting and handling the patient/client and consideration of the action's 'worth' to the patient and herself, are irrelevant. By not adhering to safety procedures, the student may have compromised the safety of them both, as well as patient progress. A good assessment decision could not be made without simultaneous consideration of both merit and worth. In this context, while 'merit' can be assessed using agreed college and placement learning objectives and competencies, 'worth' consists of the unpredicted, unexpected, and unintended learning outcomes which require to be assessed 'responsively', so as to allow assessors to enact the two components of this process, description and judgement.

Conceptual framework

I offer a diagrammatic outline of my conceptual framework for a responsive assessment model in Table 2. It juxtaposes Stake's (1997) three stages of antecedents, transactions and outcomes against Benner's (1984) movement from novice to expert, (Figure 3) the skills development required of the reflective practitioner (Schön 1983, 1987) and Steinaker and Bell's (1979) taxonomy of levels (Figure 2).

(Benner (1984, p.13) pointed out that:

> ...in acquisition and development of a skill, a student passes through five levels of proficiency; novice, advanced beginner, competent, proficient and expert, and that these different levels reflect changes in the three general aspects of skilled performance. One is a movement from reliance on abstract principles to the use of past concrete experience as paradigms. The second is a change in the student's perception of the demand situation, in which the situation is seen less and less as a compilation of equally relevant bits, and more and more as a complete whole in which only certain parts are relevant and the third is a passage from detached observer to involved performer.

Responsive assessment assesses students competence in a situational context, feedback from the assessor is immediate, thus helping students to move through Benner's stages of development quickly and effectively. Benner's five stages, incorporated in Table 2 and detailed in Figure 3 are probably the shiniest worn steps in the nurse curriculum pathway. The individual is seen as moving from being little more than a bundle of antecedents at the beginning of the nurse education programme to being in continuous education at the beginning of professional life. Over these steps and stages, the assessment focus moves from initial 'survival kit' issue (Neary 1997a), through assessment of potentiality and responsive assessment

Table 2 A model for the future: developmental assessment model

Stage of training (Neary 1996)	Knowledge of student (Stake 1997)	Assessment process (Neary 2000)	Level (Steinaker and Bell taxonomy 1979)	Progress (Benner 1984)
CFP entry				
Introductory Induction period	Antecedence Transaction	Survival kit: practice in safe environment Assessment of student potentiality (ASP)	Exposure	NOVICE ↓
Observation and orientation period	Antecedence Transaction	Aims and intentions identified Action plan agreed	Participation Identification	BEGINNER ↓
Full participation in practice setting	Transaction	Responsive assessment (RA) Contract assignments (student set aims, objectives, intentions)	Identification Internalization	COMPETENT ↓
End of CFP				↓
Entry to Branch Programme				↓
	Transaction	ASP and RA in branch specific areas	Participation Identification Internalization	COMPETENT ↓

Table 2 Cont/d

Stage of training (Neary 1996)	Knowledge of student (Stake 1997)	Assessment process (Neary 2000)	Level (Steinaker and Bell taxonomy 1979)	Progress (Benner 1984)
End of Branch Programme				↓
	Outcome	Competent practitioner (has ability and has achieved UKCC requirement to become a 1st Level Registered Nurse)	Dissemination	PROFICIENT ↓
Req. to remain on Register				↓
	Continuous education	Post-registration education and practice (consolidation and development as expert)	Dissemination continues	EXPERT AND REFLECTIVE PRACTITIONER

of both CFP and Branch experience, to competence and consolidation as expert. Exposure, participation and identification lead on to internalization and then dissemination (Figure 2), as novice works through to expertise and reflection.

Exposure	Observing student reaction to the initial activities to determine attention; understanding of terms, scenes, and purpose; and readiness and/or willingness to proceed
Participation	Examining student choices; signals of understanding or of lack of understanding; replications; discussions; questioning to determine understanding; ability to succeed and, where appropriate, explanation of how the learner 'would do it' if given the opportunity
Identification	Using criteria, teacher-developed tests or assignments, and mental or actual checklists to assess student progress and teaching or unit effectiveness
Internalization	Using projective measures such as open-ended, anonymous response questionnaires and/or direct measures such as rating scales and interviews; using a post- and retest method in which a different test form or assignment is given at a later date and is compared with the original test or assignment to determine retention
Dissemination	Using student self-assessment instruments; assessing the time devoted to tasks, the variety of techniques employed to use or to promote the learning, and/or the degree of influence achieved

Figure 2 Experiential taxonomy: assessment methods. After Steinaker and Bell (1979) modified by Kenworthy and Nicklin (1989)

Stage 1	Novice	Beginners have had no experience of the situation in which they are expected to perform
Stage 2	Advanced beginner	Students can demonstrate marginally acceptable performance
Stage 3	Competent	Competence, typified by the student who has been on the job in the same or similar situations develops when the student begins to see his/her actions in terms of long-range goals and are consciously aware
Stage 4	Proficient	The proficient performer perceives situations as whole rather than in terms of aspects, and performance is guided by maxims. Perception is the key word here
Stage 5	Expert	The expert performer no longer relies on the analytic principle (rule, guideline) to connect his/her understanding of the situation to an appropriate action

Figure 3 Novice to expert

Analyzing practitioner descriptions of their experience was a central method in Benner's work. In her view, nursing had failed to articulate the uniqueness and richness of the knowledge embedded in expert clinical practice. She utilized the Dreyfus (1980) model of skill acquisition to frame the movement from novice to expert:

> ...a movement from a reliance on abstract principles and rules to use of past, concrete experience...

During interviews throughout the study, practitioners claimed to base their actions on previous experience that became progressively more significant as they developed expertise and appeared to support the argument that continuing education and staff development programmes should be designed to help them use such experience in developing their assessor role, and that of mentor if required.

Benner (1984) asserted that nursing practice had been studied primarily from a sociological perspective, and that the profession had learned much about role relationships, socialization and acculturation in nursing practice. She argued that we have learned less about the knowledge embodied in actual nursing practice, the knowledge that accrues over time in the practice of an applied discipline. Carper (1978) echoed the same sentiments when she stated that such knowledge has gone uncharted and unstudied because the differences between practical and theoretical knowledge have been misunderstood. Benner (1984) also relied on the writings of Polanyi (1958), who developed Ryle's (1949) distinction observed that 'knowing what' and 'knowing how' were two kinds of knowledge. They pointed out that we have many skills (know-how) that are acquired without 'knowing what' and further, that we cannot always theoretically account for own know-how in many common activities.

> ...some practical knowledge may elude scientific formulation of 'knowing what' and 'know how' that may challenge or extend current theory, can be developed ahead of such scientific formulation Benner (1984, p. 2)

It is my belief that responsive assessment would help students to develop the 'know how' and the 'know what' in a more effective, efficient and realistic way and one way to develop this process could be through adequate preparation of both students and practitioners (Neary 1999) and through the process of a partnership model (Neary 1998).

Partnership model

The data suggested that the way forward may best be achieved in developing a responsive assessment scheme which assesses student professional and personal growth through teaching, learning, assessing and evaluating, as illustrated in Figure 4. However, for this to be carried out effectively, more effective communication will need to be developed between student, teacher, assessor and significant others as the basis of a more 'balanced partnership'. During interviews students highlighted what they believed to be an unfair system because:

> Only one mentor assessed me and I did not agree with her assessment of me. If there were more people involved we could discuss my progress and come to a more 'realistic' assessment of my performance. I think the tutors should also be involved.

Questionnaires from both students and assessors identified that it was rare for more than one person to be involved in the assessment of students clinical competence on each placement.

Figure 4 illustrates how a partnership model might present itself and shows the functional role of each player, as follows:

- Formal and informal teaching and learning by tutors, assessors and significant others
- Assessors responding to situational events experienced by students (responsive assessment)
- Learning opportunities identified for students to enable them to apply theory to practice
- Assessing student potential by teachers, assessors, significant others, and student self-assessment during the formative and summative stages of continuous assessment
- Final outcome of students progress by summative assessments.

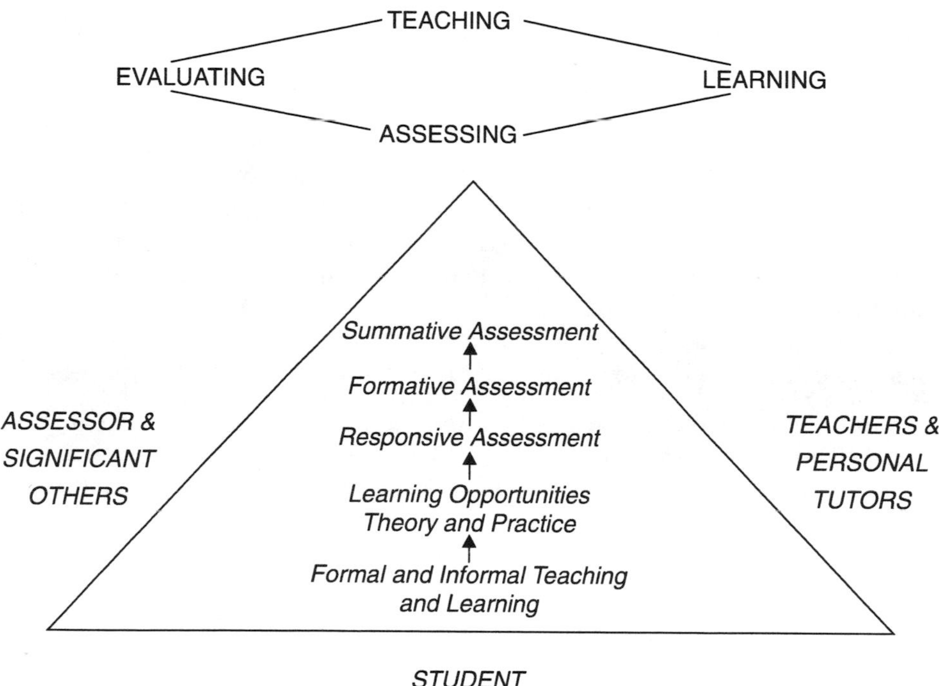

Figure 4 Partnership model

One practitioner was very much in favour of the partnership approach, when she said:

> I feel that students should participate in their own planning and identifying their own learning needs, but as an assessor and mentor I am

> a 'partner' in the planning, teaching, assessing and evaluating process. I need to respond to the real situation of practice. I also believe that University tutors and significant others must also become partners in the assessment process.

The data suggests that this model would satisfy those assessors and students who claimed they needed more help and support from college staff and would also help all staff to carry out their twin roles as assessors and mentors. It would also become a vital component in a responsive assessment.

Conclusion: tension between education and assessment

Students and assessors at all stages of the study, and in many other studies (Davies *et al.* 1994, Neary 1998, Jowett 1995), agreed that nursing is an action discipline and nurses learn by doing. According to Craddock (1993) the true test for the nurse from the patient perspective is not her espoused theory but rather her clinical expertise. The latter has to be associated with theory to fulfil the nurse's:

> ...regard to the environment of care and its physical, psychological and social effects on patients/clients, and also to the adequacy of resources, and make known to appropriate persons or authorities any circumstances which could place patients/clients in jeopardy or which militate against safe standards of practice. (UKCC Code of Practice Clause 10, 1992)

The data which I have presented here, alongside that of many others to whom I have made reference, would suggest that if the New Nurse Education Reforms are to fulfil their vision, i.e. to develop a competent, reflective practitioner who is able to make clinical judgements which will improve patient/client care and is a result of evidence based practice, the assessment of student clinical competence and the support needed by students, be it by the mentor, preceptor, supervisor, personal tutor, assessors or significant others in the form of a skilled practitioner (Neary 1997a, 1997b, 1997c, Phillips 1994), will need to develop along the lines suggested in this paper.

Assessment of clinical competence in nursing continues to be a source of difficulty for education. The main assessment technique used was direct observation of clinical skills. Both the validity and reliability of this method have been questioned in terms of the subjectivity of the assessor, the small and varied behaviours which are observed, lack of uniformity and control of behaviour observed. No single procedure is adequate for assessing clinical competence.

Continuous assessment is a complex process and much of the tension between educating and assessing arose from conflict between the humanistic concerns of educators and the bureaucratic concerns of assessments. Non-participant observation during this study demonstrated teacher belief that this bureaucratic aspect of assessment/examination might be reduced by effective use of responsive assessment.

Drawing my professional and researcher intentions together in framing the characteristics of a possible new approach to assessing clinical competence through responsive assessment, its components would include learning contracts and contract assignments intended to lead students to a type of self-directed behaviour which gives structure for a more effective support and guidance system for both students and assessors in a 'partnership model'. One assumes that students may develop from novice to competent practitioner status within a structured framework that allows for practical skills, underpinning knowledge and professional attitudes to be assessed with less confusion, ambiguity, and anxiety than is currently experienced. I freely acknowledge that this sketch of responsive assessment constitutes thinking in progress. Its claim is that it is rooted in the realities – both strengths and weaknesses – of what I have seen in the field, conceptualized through what I believe are the leading edges of nursing education theory. It is, of necessity, untried and if I have learned only one thing in the course of my research experience, then it is that what is best planned is rarely what is neatly delivered. Indeed, it is for this very reason that we must aim for a system which is 'responsive'.

References

Ashworth P, Saxton J (1990) On competence. *Journal of Further and Higher Education* 14 (2): 3–25.

Benner P (1984) *From Novice to Expert: Excellence and Power in Clinical Nursing Practice.* Addison Wesley, Henlo Park.

Carper B (1978) Fundamental patterns of knowledge in nursing. *Advances in Nursing Science* 1 (5): 13–23.

Craddock E 1993 Developing the facilitator role in the clinical area. *Nurse Education Today* 13: 217–224.

Davies B, Neary M, Philips R (1994) *Final Report. The Practitioner-teacher. A Study in the Introduction of Mentors in the Pre-registration Nurse Education Programme in Wales.* UWCC, School of Education, Cardiff.

Dreyfus S E, Dreyfus H L (1980) A Five Stage Model of the Mental Activities Involved in Directed Skill Acquisition. Unpublished report supported by the Air Force Office of Scientific Research (AFSC). USAF, University of California, Berkeley.

Jarvis P (1995) *Adult and Continuing Education: Theory and Practice*, 2nd edn. Routledge, London.

Jowett S (1995) A longitudinal study with Project 2000 students: their views and experiences during and after the course. Unpublished PhD thesis. Kings College, University of London, London.

Jowett S, Payne S, Walton (1994) *Project 2000. The Final Report.* NFER, Slough.

Kenworthy N, Nicklin P (1989) *Teaching and Assessing in Nursing Practice: An Experiential Approach*, p 32. Scutari, London.

May K (1982) Mentorship for scholarliness. *Nursing Outlook* 32: 22–26.

Melia K (1987) *Learning and Working: The Occupational Socialization of Nurses.* Tavistock Institute, London.

Neary M (1992a) Contract assignments: an integral part of adult learning and continuous assessments. *Senior Nurse* 12 (4): 14–17.

Neary M (1992b) Planning, designing and developing an assessment tool. *Nurse Education Today* 12: 357–367.

Neary M (1994) Teaching practical skills in college. *Nursing Standard* 8 (March 30): 35–38.

Neary M (1996) Continuous assessment of clinical competence: an investigation. Unpublished PhD thesis. School of Education, University of Wales, Cardiff.

Neary M 1997a Project 2000 students survival kit: a return to the practical room nursing skills laboratory. *Nurse Education Today* 17: 46–52.

Neary M (1997b) Defining the role of assessors, mentors and supervisors Part 1. *Nursing Standard* 11 (42): 34–39.

Neary M (1997c) Defining the role of assessors, mentors and supervisors Part 2. *Nursing Standard* 11 (43): 34–38.

Neary M (1998) Contract assignments and change in teaching, learning and assessment strategies. *Educational Practice and Theory* 20 (1): 43–58.

Neary M (1999) Preparing practitioners for continuous assessments. *Nursing Standard* 13 (18): 141.

Neary M (2000) *Teaching, Assessing and Evaluation for Clinical Competence. A Guide for Practitioners and Teachers.* Stanley Thornes, Cheltenham.

O'Neill E, Morrison H, McEwen A (1993) *Professional Socialisation and Nurse Education: An Evaluation.* Queen's University, Belfast.

Philips R (1994) Providing student support systems in Project 2000 nurse education programmes – the personal tutor role of nurse teachers. *Nurse Education Today* 14: 216–222.

Phillips R M, Davies W B, Neary M (1996a) The practioner-teacher: a study in the introduction of mentors and the pre-registration nurse education programme in Wales Part 1. *Journal of Advanced Nursing* 23: 1037–1044.

Phillips R M, Davies W B, Neary M (1996b) The pracitioner-teacher: a study in the introduction of mentors and the pre-registration nurse education programme in Wales Part 2. *Journal of Advanced Nursing* 23: 1080–1088.

Polanyi M (1958) *Personal Knowledge.* Routledge and Kegan Paul, London.

Powell A, Owen L, Hatton N (1992) *Learning in Clinical Settings. Perceptions of Students in Nursing.* University of Western Sydney, Sydney.

Ryle G (1949) *The Concept of Mind.* Hutchinson, London.

Schön D A (1983) *The Reflective Practitioner: How Professionals Think in Action.* Maurie Tample Smith, UK.

Schön D A (1987) *Educating the Reflective Practitioner.* Jossey-Bass, London.

36. Supporting Students' Learning and Professional Development Through the Process of Continuous Assessment and Mentorship

Mary Neary

This paper is based on the results of two studies carried out by the writer, over a period of 6 years (1991–1996), aimed to establish what happens in nursing practice in relation to assessing clinical competence of nursing students and the support they receive during their Nurse Education Programme.

Study number one (1991–1995) was based upon the experiences and perceptions of 155 skilled practitioners and 300 students from three Colleges of Nursing and 45 interested practitioners, who volunteered to join the research at a later date because they were experienced assessors and mentors. Many themes and categories emerged. One in particular was that of the role of the practitioner who has been charged with the responsibility of assessing student performance on practice placement. Initial interviews with 155 practitioners of varying experience as assessors were used to design a questionnaire containing both context-free and context-specific items. Subsequent follow-up interviews were undertaken with both students and practitioners and non-participant observation of practitioners working with students were carried out.

The majority of students accepted the dual role and at times, even the triple role of assessors, mentors and/or supervisors forced upon practitioners, provided that the practitioners assessing them were well prepared and 'trained' as assessors, were perceived to be 'fair', 'competent', 'skilful' and 'knowledgeable' (Neary 1997a).

Study two (1992–1994) aimed to establish the process and outcomes of practitioner-teachers and mentorship in Wales, and was based on the data from a much extended period of semi-structured interviews with policy makers, managers, teachers and nurse practitioners (n = 360, 330 analyzed in detail) spanning 10 months, which gave an invaluable picture of ongoing changes in the placement areas and the basis from which to construct a widely administered questionnaire (n = 1332) dealing with context-free and context-specific factors underpinning the definition of the mentor role, selection and relationship with students. Similar logic lay behind the use of reflective semi-structured diaries which asked 138 students and 133 practitioners to keep during practice placements. This study showed the practitioners readily adopted the term 'mentor' to describe their role in their relationship with students in clinical practice. How they were selected for this role proved to be more complex (Davies et al. 1994), for the purpose of this paper the data from both studies is merged to give a stronger and more focused picture of how both students and

---

Mary Neary: 'Supporting Students' Learning and Professional Development Through the Process of Continuous Assessment and Mentorship' in *NURSE EDUCATION TODAY* (2000), 20, pp. 463–474.

practitioners perceived their roles in the assessment and support systems which were in action at the time of the studies.

Methodology and data analysis: a brief overview

For both studies the methodology involved qualitative and quantitative methods and data triangulation. The multi-method approach contrasts with the ubiquitous, but generally more vulnerable, single method approach that characterizes so much of research in the social sciences. It permitted mapping and explanation of some richness and complexity. Such triangulation enabled the validity of themes and theories developed from one set of data, such as interviews, to be measured against another, for example the questionnaires, diaries and observations.

The questionnaires were analyzed and statistically tested using the SPSS package, with open-ended items allowing respondents freedom to answer in their own way. Given the large number of respondents the text was subjected to analysis using OCP (Oxford Concordance Programme) which provides, concordances, indexes and word lists from texts in a variety of languages and alphabets. It was used for text analysis, application and frequency of responses to the same category. Micro-OCP offers a wide variety of methods of choosing the context and specifying the format of the themes, categories and references.

Interviews were conducted in a manner which allowed freedom to modify the sequence of questions, to explain, or add to them according to the situation that we found ourselves in. Follow-up interviews to questionnaire results allowed for in-depth analysis of responses. Interview transcripts were read and re-read and tapes revisited alongside the finally agreed list of themes, categories and sub-categories to establish the degree to which they covered all aspects of the interviews. A coding system was developed which helped to identify frequencies of the categories.

Given the emphasis of the interviews and questionnaire data, the observations were focused on the practitioner's day through their perspective, particularly with respect to the interaction which took place between students and practitioners using the tools of 'watching', asking questions and attending opportunistic meetings with practitioners and students. Field notes were written at the time and revisited and analyzed immediately after the event.

Introduction: reforming the system

The UKCC Report, *Project 2000, A New Preparation for Practice* (UKCC 1986), argued that the reforms proposed for nurse education would result in a new autonomous 'knowledgeable doer' who would organize and deliver nursing care in hospital and community settings. The UKCC outlined the outcomes which were incorporated into assessment documents that identified students' requirements in order for them to meet in order to become registered competent practitioners by the three colleges in the main study and code named Brookside, Hillside and Roseside.

Focus on the role of the nurse as an autonomous practitioner raised several problems for those developing the curriculum and the assessment strategies within it. Students and assessors must understand how their respective roles differ from the nurses' traditional role. The new role implies that the key skills required to practice are those related to clinical decision-making and professional judgement. These, in turn, suggest to me that nursing theory and practice lie at the heart of the curriculum, if students are to be placed in specific practice settings to enable them to develop clinical competence and those skills required to become safe, competent practitioners. It is against this background of proposed and required change in structure, process and outcomes of nurse education that the two studies were carried out.

The manner in which students are taught, supervised and assessed during clinical practice has been steeped with assumptions for many years. Since the mid 1970s many studies have emerged which sought to examine clinical learning environments and how they were orientated towards students and the assessment of student performance (Neary 1996). Supervision and assessment of students has traditionally been in the form of distant supervision because of the expediency and pressure of workloads and students hitherto being part of the work force, with the consequence that assessment of skills development has been largely by inference. The new curriculum aimed to provide an experience which enables professional growth and the development of competent, independent practitioners. The reorganization of the clinical experience was concerned with making the theoretical component come alive making it meaningful so that students might relate their studies in a way which informed their practice, and allow for continuous assessment of their performance. The overriding concern is that since time available for practice experience has reduced considerably in comparison with conventional courses, the need to re-examine the criteria for students' clinical nursing skill development has become evident together with an investigation of how practitioners can be best helped to develop their role as assessors (Neary 1999). Watts (1992, p.175) argued that there was a need for sound and effective preparation in relation to the practice component of Project 2000 courses. More time, not less time needs to be spent with staff charged with the responsibilities of supervising, mentoring and assessing.

What are we – assessors, mentors or supervisors?

This section title stems from the question practitioners frequently asked themselves. It highlights the perceived interrelationships, or lack of them, that exist among practitioners with respect to their roles as mentor, assessor and supervisor. They encompass issues of preparation for these roles, concerns about the value of assessment of clinical competence and its management in the new system of nurse education.

The question of the preparation of practitioners raises the obvious issues of 'preparation for what?'. The role of the 'first level nurse' in the mentoring, teaching and assessing of students has received regular attention, and the trend towards continuous assessment on many courses has placed increasing emphasis on the importance of the clinical staff. It is argued that present courses should not involve the students in significantly less practical experience than traditional courses, but that the nature of the experience should be different, not least because of the change of status of the student from employee to supernumerary student. At all three colleges much time and energy was devoted to devising systems of support for students during their practice placements to help the transition from academic to student nurse. Morle (1990) expressed concern at the increase in new terminology or jargon which bombards the nursing profession and even more worried by the seeming readiness to adopt such terminology without an adequate understanding of what is entailed. Burnard (1990) went so far as to say 'nurses can now talk at length without saying anything'. Much of the discussion of mentorship, assessors and supervisors appear to exemplify these concerns.

It was evident during my observation that there seemed to be no common agreement as to the precise roles and functions attached to these terms. How then can we be sure that we are all talking about the same thing? How can we have an effective, let alone unified system of preparing assessors and mentors unless we are clear what it is they do and ought to do. Is the role of the assessor to make professional judgement on the ability of the students to learn, to develop nursing skills, apply knowledge to practice and to form and maintain healthy attitudes towards their work and colleagues? Three statements were put to 200 practitioners (Box 1). These consisted of the 155 respondents (Study 1) and the 45 who joined in as interested subjects later in the same study.

Box 1 Three statements put to assessors (*n* = 200)

Please respond to each of the following:

A. In my capacity as a Mentor to student nurses my responsibilities are:

B. In my capacity as a Supervisor to student nurses, my responsibilities are:

C. In my capacity as a Named Assessor my responsibilities are:

THANK YOU FOR HELPING WITH THIS RESEARCH

MARY NEARY

Mentor, assessor, supervisor responsibilities

Responses were grouped under 'key words' in search of their 'attributes'. As attributes emerged it became clear that they fell into three 'support' themes, educational, psychological and managerial. As can be seen in Table 1 below, these were arranged in descending order of frequency to highlight the most common attributes regarding the role of practitioners as mentors, supervisors and or assessors to the students during their practice placement experiences.

As mentors, respondents saw themselves as offering educational support, offering to assess and give feedback on student progress while at the same time being facilitators. However, they mainly saw themselves as giving psychological support, being a friend, advisor with element of counselling and motivating and, for some, being approachable. They saw their management input as offering to liaise with appropriate staff, creating a learning environment that is safe and being resource agents, managing placement allocation and when (and for a few) necessary to reprimand students which they see as a lesser function.

Table 1 Mentor responsibilities

Educational Support	Frequency	Psychological Support	Frequency	Managerial Support	Frequency
Assessor/ assessing	82	Student support	96	Liaise with staff	40
Facilitation	80	Friend	80	Identify learning opps	15
Teaching	77	Advisor	78	Resource agent	15
Narrowing T/P gap	20	Guidance	15	Create safe environment	8
Role model allocations	8	Motivation	8	Management of placement	7
Achieving learning objective	7	Counselling/ listen	8	Reprimand	4
Feedback/ progress	5	Personal development	8		
Demonstrate skills	2	Approachable	4		
		Protector of student	2		
	281		307		89

Although there was some overlap of the practitioner's definition of their responsibility as mentor and as supervisor, there was clear evidence that staff acting as supervisors did not see themselves as teachers, role models or facilitators. They mainly saw themselves as assessors (Table 2), who were approachable and had a managerial responsibility as supervisor and observer. Here we see that the educational and management support appeared to be of greater importance to the practitioner who had supervisory responsibility.

It was not surprising to discover that the assessors mainly saw themselves as giving educational support in the form of teaching, monitoring and assessing (Table 3). What was surprising, was the low number of those who saw their responsibility as working with students. It is difficult to know how these respondents intended to assess student progress if they did not work with them.

Table 2 Supervisor responsibilities

Educational Support	Frequency	Psychological Support	Frequency	Managerial Support	Frequency
Assessing etc.	180	Approachable/ available	60	Supervisor	160
Learning fun experience	160	Be responsible for student	60	Acting as observer	150
Helping to achieve objective	155	Student support	20	Arrange/plan for learning	145
Monitor progress	65	Personal development	5	Report student progress to others	125
Act as assessor: when absent	48			Maintain standards	50
Give feedback/ correct	35			Create safe environment	40
Demonstrate correct practice	35				
Offer knowledge	20				
Facilitation	5				
Teaching	5				
Role model	2				
Mentoring	2				

Table 3 Named assessor responsibility

Educational Support	Frequency	Psychological Support	Frequency	Managerial Support	Frequency
Mentoring	80	Friend	30	Liaising with others	35
Teaching	60	Counselling	2	Preparing students	10
Assessing and student self-assess	36	Professional Development	2	Safe environment/ standards	8
Monitoring progress	32			Feedback to others	3
Identifying strengths/ weaknesses	12				
Evaluating	2				
Work with students	2				

Role overlap

Analysis of the response, suggested that there was continuing confusion and misunderstanding over being an assessor, which overlapped with the responsibilities of mentor and/or supervisor. There was clear evidence that all staff identifying themselves as mentors saw as their main task 'to support the students during their clinical/practice placements', echoed in study two by Davies *et al.* (1994).

The debates with these groups highlighted that the terms 'mentor' and 'assessor' were regularly interchanged and adding 'supervisor' created further anxiety and misunderstanding. One assessor commented:

> ...to me there is no difference. These are just words that teachers play around with to make themselves sound like academics. (Brookside, Staff Nurse, 6 months qualified)

Another stated:

> According to my learning package on Mentorship, I need to possess the following qualities: empathy, energy, enthusiasm, experience and excellence. Some of these qualities I already have but I would need at least three years' post-qualification experience to have 'experience' and 'excellence'. I am without preparation as a named Assessor to P2000 students with only three months post-qualification experience. My anxiety levels are so high, I am afraid for those students. (Brookside, Sister, 3 months in post)

One experienced assessor stated, and received cheers from the others present:

> The function of the assessor is the same as that of the mentor or supervisor, so why have so many names? I would be happier if teachers spent more time helping me to assess the students rather than spending time arguing over 'what name to give me'. Just call me 'Sister'. One who has responsibility for training students. Perhaps you could call me 'Training Sister' or 'Teaching Sister'. (Hillside, Sister, 15 years qualified)

I may have helped create the phenomenon by requiring response to an instrument that suggested that they might be assessor, mentor and supervisor, as illustrated by this assessor at the end of the study day:

> All of these roles, responsibilities are interchangeable. They are part of our every working day. Why do we need to be called 'mentor', 'assessor' or 'supervisor'? I am a 'supervisor' by the sheer fact that I am a first level nurse with responsibility for the safe delivery of care to my patients which is often given by unqualified staff – that makes me a 'supervisor'. (Roseside, Staff Nurse, 4 years' qualified)

Another stated:

> ...we know that students' clinical competence must be assessed as directed by the National Boards and other national examination bodies. Just teach us how and what to do. Too much time is spent on the theory

> of teaching and assessing and not enough is spent on the practicalities of 'how'. (Brookside, Staff Nurse, 1 1/2 years qualified)

A 'good' mentor

Many descriptions illustrated the importance that the mentor attached to the learning needs of the student and his/her actual commitment to teaching and supporting them. They were keen to discuss the characteristics of good mentorship as they perceived it, which was someone who planned the duty rota to give students wide experience and made a point of knowing the stage of training of the new arrivals. The study by Davies *et al.* (1994) showed that a 'good' mentor was confident of his/her ability to teach and devoted a considerable amount of time to this activity. The overall picture presented by the students' comments was of a happy, purposeful learning environment guided and regulated by a confident, considerate mentor who made students feel part of the ward team, and was concerned for the well-being and development of all students in his/her charge. A 'good' mentor utilized every opening to create and maximize learning opportunities (a good mentorship relationship is a dialogue between two people committed to 'improvement' (Neary 1997)) and had no hesitation in accepting the role of student assessor.

The newly qualified staff saw the value of not having the 'traditional' experience of their 'older' colleagues, and suggested that:

> ...as newly qualified staff, we are not bogged down with traditional methods of training and assessing students. (Roseside, Staff Nurse, 6 months qualified)

This staff nurse spoke for the others:

> Our experience has been with CFP students only. We are familiar with the new programme and the role conflict potentially inherent (in the 146 week course) in the learner/worker. Dichotomy was not experienced by us or the students. We no longer regard them [students] as workers, therefore we attach great importance to their learning needs. It makes the role of assessor more effective and reliable when combined with the role of mentor in the new world of supernumerary students because students are not charged with the responsibility for patient care.
>
> They [students] no longer feel they have to keep busy merely for the sake of appearance which was common practice in the old days. Students are now freer to approach us if they need guidance and/or have personal problems. It makes the role of assessors easier because we get to know the students well.

Students perceptions of mentorship were expressed during interview as someone to emulate:

> Someone whose ideas, opinions and experience are of benefit to me as a student nurse. Someone I can emulate. (Brookside, student, end of CFP)

A contact person:

> The person I shall have most contact with on wards regarding learning experiences and any problems I may come across. They're there to help me. (Roseside, student, end of CFP)

Someone to have a chat with:

> Someone to talk to on an informal basis about my experiences and problems. Just someone to chat with. (Hillside, student, end of CFP)

A teacher and guide:

> Mentor is the person who guides me on the ward. She teaches me and is responsible for me while out on the wards. (Brookside, student, end of CFP)

An assessor/supervisor:

> A kind of supervisor who takes you under their wing, someone you will be working with and who gives feedback on your progress. (Hillside, student, end of CFP)

The question may well be asked whether mentors, as envisaged by nurse education programmes, are really mentors in the generally accepted sense of the word. Morle (1990) believes that preceptorship would be a more appropriate model to follow. However, a revisit of Phillips' writings helps to highlight some of the confusion.

Preceptor

Phillips (1994) argued that the terms 'mentor', 'preceptor' and 'supervisor' are sometimes used synonymously, so there may well be confusion of roles in the use of this terminology. In addition, elements of a teacher's role, such as pastoral functions and personal tutor responsibilities, overlap with some of these other supportive positions. Indeed, a teacher may be a supervisor, mentor and personal tutor to the same student at any one time. Most authors, however, draw a distinction between 'mentor' and 'preceptor' in the manner of Armitage and Burnard (1991); mentorship being seen as a broader, longer-term relationship aimed at guiding the student towards an established place in a profession (Zwolski 1982), while the emphasis with preceptorship remains on individualized teaching and support.

Supervisor

Phillips (1994) suggested that there are many similarities between the role of the academic supervisor and the personal tutor, however, the term 'supervisor' is usually applied when a teacher is assigned to a student undertaking a research project, although there are exceptions. Jarvis (1984) for example, described a supervisor in much the same manner as others describe a preceptor (Chickerella and Lutz 1981, Donius 1988) or a mentor (CNAA 1985). In describing the role of the supervisor, Jarvis (1984, p.126) stated: 'Hence the new recruit to the profession, or the new entrant to the organisation/hospital/community, is allocated to the senior person with whom she will work and who will assist her to develop her skills and abilities within the work context.'

Practitioner-teachers and teacher-practitioners

The extension of mentorship designed to support and facilitate student learning in the practice placements may not so much diminish as alter the established role of nurse teachers in the clinical area. Clinically originating mentors themselves require support, which Wright (1990) saw as the role of nurse educationalists. Morle (1990) also described a situation where nurse teachers, in providing support to the ward manager, may be seen to be taking on a mentoring function for clinical staff. With the implementation of new programmes, the subsequent change in emphasis, time involved in preparation and the advent of mentorship of students by clinical staff, the degree to which the nurse teacher will teach nursing in the clinical area and, indeed, whether this is a feasible proposition, may well be questioned. Bidwell and Brasler (1989) stated that students see their clinical instructor as the most important person to portray and teach the nursing role. There is still an opportunity for nurse teachers to develop a clinically orientated role, but it seems more likely that the current move towards a clinical career structure will develop advanced practitioners (Welsh Office 1991), who will wish to fulfil the clinically-based teaching role and provide the role model for the student nurse.

Personal tutor

Phillips (1994) argued that a personal tutor may be described as a designated teacher who has been assigned the responsibility of guiding a student towards meeting objectives. The objectives may be formal, as dictated by. the course curriculum, but also covert and personal to the student to help them achieve their own maximum potential. The personal tutor-student relationship is formalized in the sense that it is a teaching/learning strategy initiated and implemented by the curriculum team. The relationship need not be formal in nature, however, with each student/personal tutor pair allowed to negotiate the parameters of the partnership which best suit their individual needs. Although the key purpose of the relationship is 'academic', an element of pastoral care in the form of friendship and support is desirable if an individual learner's potential is to be realized. While the personal tutor may draw upon counselling skills (Quinn 1988), the degree to which pastoral care involves counselling per se, should be approached with caution by the teacher (Hamblin 1978).

With respect to adult learners, which student nurses are, Phillips (1994) goes on to say what seems clear, emerging from the maze of descriptions and definitions of titles given to teachers in various supportive situations, is that despite the variety of terminology, there is considerable similarity and overlap in the functions that mentors/preceptors/supervisors/personal tutors perform. Essentially, each has a 'teaching' and 'support' role within an overall framework of androgogy, which facilitates student-centred learning, and maximizes the learning potential and personal development of each adult learner. Equally, one could argue that adult learners are best supported through a system of academic supervision or alternatively, allocation to a personal tutor. The distinction is largely one of semantics and of limited value. It is more important that all those involved in supporting adults in a learning situation and the students themselves, working together at a local level – be it school, college or clinical/work-based setting – reach a common understanding of what is expected from a student support system and specifically the teacher and student responsibilities, rather than to arrive at a universal definition of the designation of the teacher pivotal to the support provision.

From the perspective of the Welsh Office (1994) study by Davies *et al.* (1994), the students were viewed as the bridge between two changing social systems, the clinical area and the education centre. In a changing organization, the role of the student is inevitably subject to negotiation and re-negotiation as she/he proceeds through the education programme and becomes involved in the acquisition of knowledge and skills in different clinical settings. In order to create experiences through which the student integrates the theory of nursing taught in the classroom with the practice of nursing in the clinical area, nurse teachers and clinical nurses need to understand their individual roles, and the tasks and relationships associated with them with some clarity.

Problems and concerns of practitioners enacting the role of assessors and supporting students

During interviews both assessors and students cited a variety of problems and constraints associated with the assessment process, ranging from the impact of professional socialization and personality factors to the 'real demands' of nursing events and the constant pressure of time (O'Neill *et al.* 1993, Jowett *et al.* 1994, Davies *et al.* 1994, Neary 1996, Le van 1996, Carlisle *et al.* 1997).

Recent research has regarded the socialization of nurses as beginning with the way in which, as students, they acquire the behaviour of a 'nurse' (O'Neill *et al.* 1993, Mead 1993). While traditional students would readily abandon college-based instruction when confronted with the ward method, for Project 2000 students:

> This constant 'battle' between their college-based 'thinking' and their clinical 'doing' effectively 'retards' the socialisation process. (ONeill *et al.* 1993, p. 309).

While no more than a couple of our assessors offered evidence that a few students clung to interpretations offered by tutors, sometimes even in the face of uncompromising ward routine and assessors' opinions, the data showed overwhelmingly that most of them also readily abandoned college instructions relating to clinical assessment in favour of agreed ward objectives. Assessors suggested that when confronted with mismatch between college set objectives and clinical placement reality, the majority of students followed the advice of ward staff, for example:

> ...the student came with a book of unrealistic objectives to be achieved on this ward, we (staff and student) tried to make sense of them but in the end I told the student what she would be assessed on while she was on my ward. (Brookside, assessor with 18 years' experience)

A student, 3 months into the programme, and on her third placement, confirmed the above to be common practice:

> The competencies in our booklet do not relate to this department. My supervisor agreed to make the experience fit the college assessment. (Brookside, student, 3 months into CFP)

Across all three colleges, assessors negotiated learning opportunities with the students. Students readily came to perceive and make a difference between 'to meet' and 'to achieve' learning needs in contexts where less than 5% of their assessors worked alongside college staff in setting learning objectives, but 100% of them were required to create the conditions for their pursuit. The value of the knowledge gained from the college-based curriculum either could not or was not always fully utilized in the clinical area. An assessor stated:

> I noticed the students leave a lot of their knowledge behind when they come to the ward, they are so eager to have hands-on care. However they (student) do remember when I ask questions of them on A & P. (Hillside, an ex-tutor now working part time on the wards)

More often than not, students admitted to 'falling into the routine of the ward', preferring to be involved in and assessed on nursing care rather than via a list of objectives and competencies identified in their assessment booklets. A student on her first placement said:

> I think about what the tutor said in class, but it does not always fit in with what you are doing to patients, it would be fairer if I was assessed on what I do here (ward). (Hillside, CFP, 2 months into course)

Another felt that:

> You learn more things on the wards because you saw things every day. The tutors should watch us doing real care on the ward and assess our progress. (Brookside, CFP, 5 months into course)

No doubt such views had their origin, at least in part, in working with staff who believed that:

> Although I am an experienced assessor and supervisor and understand the need for education reform, I still hold my possibly ideological view of nursing as a practical based, all caring profession in which students should be learning and be assessed on their ability to give safe, effective, professional care. (Brookside, Sister, 18 years as assessor)

Neary (1996) underlined the need to recognize the individual's expectation of nursing. The extent to which expectations were met in the initial stage of the nurse education programme shaped students' views of the practice placement and the role of assessors. One student spoke for many in stating her expectation as:

> For me nursing is about looking after the sick and helping patients to be restored to health. To implement the plan of care. My supervisor should assess that I am able to follow the planned care. My expectations to date have not been fulfilled.

'In charge' but not assessing

Both interviews and questionnaires revealed that most practitioners were available and able to teach and assess students during allocations. Traditionally, the ward sister/charge nurse/ward manager had been the most important person in this respect in hospital settings. Standards of care, ward atmosphere and the promotion of a good learning environment have been found consistently to depend largely on the managers and their leadership styles (Pembrey 1980, Fretwell 1982, Davies *et al.* 1994). However, our data suggested that administrative and managerial functions have inhibited direct teaching and assessing by those 'in charge' of practice areas. Ward managers have remained influential, but the day-to-day teaching and assessing of students in all practice placements has largely developed to staff nurses of D and E grades, the most junior in the nursing Team. Studies by Davies *et al.* (1994) and Payne *et al.* (1991) support these findings and note that they have occurred at a time when nurse teachers no longer assess students or provide nursing care. Some students were left to carry out new nursing procedures when trained staff were not always available to supervise or instruct, causing some students anxiety and unpleasantness from practitioners when they did not get it 'quite right'. Many comments, both written and voiced by students and assessors, indicated that they saw the value and necessity of as well as the problems with continuous assessment, or as some students called it, 'progressive assessment'. Students appreciated constructive comments in support of grades given or boxes ticked and considered that assessors needed to devote more time to the actual assessment and feedback process. Some students and assessors advocated the use of a 'team approach' when compiling final written comments and had misgivings about the usefulness of the booklet/form, believing that they needed to be more clearly written and less 'jargonistic'. They identified potential abuse of the system if care was not taken. The process might become no more than:

> ...filling in the forms to keep the college staff happy. (Roseside, CFP student, 6 months into course)

where:

> ... assessors were afraid to give adverse comments because it could cause problems with college staff. (Brookside, CFP student, 4 months into course)

and which:

> ...creates too much paperwork if a student is reported because of failing to achieve. (Hillside, CFP student, 2 months into course)

According to some students, some assessors were paying 'lip-service' when carrying out their role as assessors, with one student echoing:

> ...they lacked 'professional pride' and were 'professionally incompetent' to take on the role of assessor or supervisor. (Brookside, CFP student, ex-teacher, 3 months into course)

Most assessors were aware of the more academic thrust of the new course and some still displayed anxiety about dealing with and relating to the new breed of 'academic students'. A few found themselves avoiding them in case they were asked 'academic' questions to which they did not have the answers. This avoidance was also practised by some when it came to assessing student progress and competence, as illustrated by one assessor:

> I work well with the student all day, but I avoid asking him about his assessment booklet which I know must be completed before he leaves the department. The truth of the matter ... even after nearly two years, I still have problems with the wording and the forms, ... I feel so foolish at times like these. (Roseside Staff Nurse, 4 1/2 years' qualified)

For some students, failure to match up to the expectations of the ward staff regarding basic nursing skills was a major problem. Tutor encouragement to be critical and analytical contrasted sharply with the dismissal that they sometimes felt they met from practitioners when they tried to follow such injunctions. Rapidly discovering that practice assessments depended on their relationships with assessors and other ward staff, they soon learned the benefit of 'getting on with your assessor or mentor' as a means of getting from the Common Foundation Programme (CFP) to the Branch programme and getting qualified, even if this was at the expense of developing qualities that the scheme set out to nurture. One might argue how little has changed, for Melia (1987) informed us years ago of the same 'games' in her study of student nurses.

Conclusion

Policy-makers, practitioner and teachers must collectively find ways to make visible improvements to the methods for defining:

1. who becomes a mentor and who becomes an assessor
2. for creating standards of teaching nursing practice
3. for assessing the outcomes which are intended to develop students competence as a critical, reflective practitioner and ensure fitness for practice (UKCC, 1999).

The statutory bodies' failure to define and distinguish the terms mentor, preceptor, assessor and supervisor has exercised academics for some time. However, this study showed that practitioners fulfilling these roles were less concerned about what to call themselves, their concern lay in the 'how' to do the job of teaching, assessing and supporting students more effectively.

The wider literature cautions against imposing mentors and assessor roles simultaneously on one person. Some NVQs schemes have managed to avoid this potential role conflict, e.g. operating Department Practice. However, if the organization insists on the same practitioners being the mentor and assessor with responsibility for the management of patient/client care, then a new organizational structure within the practice area will need to be developed and with it the opportunity for staff to come to terms with the changes. The substantial pressures on practice-based staff to gain further qualifications, supervise students, increase their management responsibilities, and direct and deliver patient/client care in a dynamic NHS make it increasingly unrealistic to expect mentorship and student assessment of clinical competence to be just another activity to be tagged on to an already overburdened staff requirement. I would suggest a model whereby the 'named practitioner' be supernumerary to the nursing team and given the status of teacher, supervisor, assessor with responsibility for student taught practice. I would also suggest that this named practitioner be given recognition by creating a new, clearly defined role, and that a new teaching, assessing and evaluating course for assessors be developed which also pays attention to change theories and coping strategies. The named practitioner would work with student, mentor and significant others, further enhancing a partnership model between students, practitioners, nurse lecturers and significant others, built on mutual responsibility for teaching, assessing and evaluating and ensure that all aspects of student progress were taken into consideration when writing a final report on the student.

All this may be best regarded in words used by Schon (1994) when referring to new managers:

> ...managers are making constructive attempts to deal with the chaos and to create teams within their organisations capable of responding to it ... Most of them are new managers coming into key and sensitive positions in the middle of a new game where rules are not yet clear. (Schon, 4 Oct. 1994, King's Fund, London).

References

Armitage P, Burnard P (1991) Mentors or preceptors? Narrowing the theory-practice gap. *Nurse Education Today* 11: 225–229.

Bidwell A, Brasler M (1989) Role modeling versus mentoring in nursing education. *Journal of Nursing Scholarship* 21: 23–25.

Burnard P (1990) The student experience: Adult learning and mentorship revisited. *Nurse Education Today* 10: 349–354.

Chickerella B, Lutz W (1981) Professional nurturance: preceptorships for undergraduate nursing students. *American Journal of Nursing*: 107–109.

Carlisle K, Kirk S, Lukar K (1997) The clinical role of nurse teachers within a Project 2000 course framework. *Journal of Advanced Nursing* 25: 386–395.

CNAA (1985) Circular 2f/27.

Davies W B, Neary M, Philips R (1994) *Final Report. The Practitioner-teacher. A Study in the Introduction of Mentors in the Pre-registration Nurse Education Programme in Wales.* UWCC, School of Education, Cardiff.

Donius M (1988) The Columbia Precepting Program: building a bridge with clinical faculty. *Journal of Professional Nursing*: 17–22.

Fretwell J E (1982) *Ward Teaching and Learning: Sister and the Learning Environment.* Royal College of Nursing, London.

Hamblin D (1978) *The Teacher and Counselling.* Blackwell, London.

Jarvis P (1984) The educational role of the supervisor in the tutorial relationship. *Nurse Education Today* 3: 126–129.

Jowett S, Payne S, Walton I (1994) *Project 2000. Final Report.* NFER, Slough.

Le Var R (1996) *NVQs in Nursing and Midwifery: A Question of Assessment and Learning.*

Mead D (1993) *Primary Nursing in Wales. Nursing Research and Development.* Department of Health. Research Management Executive. Welsh Office, Cardiff.

Melia K A (1987) *Learning and Working: The Occupational Socialization of Nurses.* Tavistock Institute, London.

Morle K (1990) Mentorship – is it a case of the emperors new clothes or a rose by any other name? *Nurse Education Today* 10: 66–69.

Neary M (1996) An investigation: continuous assessment of clinical competence. Unpublished PhD thesis. School of Education, University of Wales, Cardiff.

Neary M (1997a) Defining the role of assessors, mentors, supervisors. Part 2. *Nursing Standard* 11: 34–38.

Neary M (1999) Preparing assessors for continuous assessment. *Nursing Standard* 13: 41–47.

O'Neill E, Morrison H, McEwen A (1993) *Professional Socialisation and Nurse Education: An Evaluation.* Queen's University, Belfast.

Payne S, Jowett S, Walton I (1991) *Nurse Teachers in Project 2000: The Experiences of Planning and Initial Implementation.* NFER, Slough.

Pembrev S (1980) *The Ward Sister – Key to Nursing.* Royal College of Nursing, London.

Phillips R M (1994) Providing students support systems in Project 2000, nurse education programme. The personal tutor role of nurse teachers. *Nurse Education Today* 14: 216–222.

Quinn F (1988) *The Principles and Practice of Nurse Education,* 2nd edn. Croom Helm, London.

UKCC (1986) *Project 2000: A New Preparation for Practice.* United Kingdom Central Council, London.

37. Clinical Competence Assessment in Nursing: A Systematic Review of the Literature

Roger Watson, Anne Stimpson, Annie Topping and Davina Porock

Background. *The assessment of clinical competence has returned to centre stage of nurse education. However, there is little evidence to support the use of clinical competence and a wide variety of methods for its use.*

Research question. *The present study was designed to investigate the evidence for the use of clinical competence assessment in nursing.*

Design. *A review using systematic methods of literature pertaining to clinical competence in nursing was conducted using defined dates, databases and search terms.*

Results. *There is still considerable confusion about the definition of clinical competence and most of the methods in use to define or measure competence have not been developed systematically and issues of reliability and validity have barely been addressed.*

Conclusion. *The assessment of clinical competence remains almost universally accepted in the nurse education literature as a laudable pursuit yet there are aspects of it that remain at odds with the higher education of nurses.*

Introduction

The assessment of clinical competence has become central to nurse education which, in the United Kingdom (UK), has moved completely into the higher education sector in the last decade. Alongside theoretical assessment, assessment of practice (clinical competence assessment) forms 50 per cent of the overall volume of assessment of individual students. Both the theoretical and practice assessments have to be passed in order to register as a nurse. Clinical competence also plays a part in the assessment process of postregistration programmes but this is not uniformly undertaken across the sector. Some postregistration programmes are entirely theoretical, with only theoretical assessment as an outcome.

However, many courses leading to qualifications that can be recorded on the professional register, such as former English National Board for Nursing, Midwifery and Health Visiting courses in cancer and palliative care, include clinical components and assessment of clinical competence as an outcome.

Roger Watson, Anne Stimpson, Annie Topping and Davina Porock: 'Clinical Competence Assessment in Nursing: A Systematic Review of the Literature' in *JOURNAL OF ADVANCED NURSING* (2002), 39 (5), pp. 421–431.

At the end of the last decade, a new programme of nurse education was introduced by the UK government (Department of Health 1999 [DoH]) and endorsed by the United Kingdom Central Council for Nursing, Midwifery and Health Visiting (UKCC 1999) in which clinical skill development was given greater emphasis. Indeed, it has been argued that clinical competence was given greater emphasis than theoretical (academic) competence and this was demonstrated by the shortening of the common foundation programme – ostensibly the academic part of the programme – from 18 to 12 months (Watson and Thompson 2000). Moreover, the overriding imperative of clinical competence is symbolically emphasized in the shortened common foundation programme and greater emphasis on skills acquisition through training.

The roots of clinical competence

Clinical competence is not unique to nursing and arose in North America as an alternative to intelligence testing for jobs where a high level of intelligence was not deemed necessary (McClelland 1973). These jobs tended to be manual and not professional and the argument was that instead of subjecting people to rigorous specific academic or general intelligence testing, they could be tested for sets of skills specific to occupations that required them (Winter and Maisch 1996). Such notions have been very influential and underlie, for example in the UK, City and Guilds and National Vocational Qualifications which are competence – in contrast to academically – based (Ashworth 1992). Clearly, there are occupations where competence rather than high academic ability is appropriate. However the notion of competence is now firmly rooted in the professions, for example teaching and nursing, and this makes the issue of competence – specifically clinical competence in nursing – a controversial issue. This is especially the case where clinical competence and educational preparation for nursing appear to be in conflict (Barnett 1994). An argument regularly aired is that all that is required to be a nurse is a 'good heart' and that the educational preparation of nurses – especially in universities – is an unnecessary burden on a mainly female occupational group who simply want to provide care (Watson 2001). From whatever perspective competence is viewed it is not, as Eraut (1994, p. 159) says, 'value neutral'. In Eraut's view it is detectable among the general public 'that competence in practical matters must be preserved against the encroachments of the intellectuals' (p. 159). Competence may be tantamount to 'faint praise' but 'competence might be preferred to excellence if it resulted in quicker and cheaper service' (Eraut 1994, p. 166). The language of competence iterated within recent policy and often linked with anti-intellectual rhetoric concerning nursing may have more to do with the chronic shortage of nurses in the UK national health service and competition for recruits to a profession that could be deemed as hard work, substandard education (non-graduate) and poorly paid.

Controversies in clinical competence

One of the major difficulties with clinical competence assessment is the definition of the term 'competence'. In fact, competence is a nebulous concept which is defined in different ways by different people. As Short (1984) explains, competence usually refers to a quality possessed by someone without specifying all that they can do in a given set of circumstances: 'Mastering particular *things is* not the same as possessing certain *qualities'* (p. 201). However, the definitions of competence have become synonymous leading to further confusion between competence and performance. Moreover, its relationship to other concepts such as capability and expertise is also unclear (Eraut 1994). For example, there is no consensus on whether competence represents a greater degree of ability than capability or *vice versa* (Eraut 1998). Performance and competence also have a confused relationship. Performance is clearly concerned with demonstrated ability to do something (Eraut 1994). However, whether this demonstrates competence or not and whether performance is required in order to demonstrate competence – meaning that competence merely represents the potential to perform – also lacks consensus (Eraut 1998).

Gonczi (1994) describes three ways of conceptualizing competence: (1) as task-based or behaviourist, which depends upon 'direct observation of performance' (p. 28) for evidence; (2) as pertaining to the 'general attributes of the practitioner that are crucial to effective performance' (p. 29) and this approach relies on generic competencies being instilled in practitioners; (3) as bringing together a range of general attributes, such as knowledge, skills and attitudes, in such a way that these specifically address the needs of the practitioner. The first two conceptualizations are problematic in that, as described below, on the one hand, the direct observation and measurement of performance is itself problematic and, on the other, there is no guarantee that generic competencies exist or are sufficient across the board. The third, more integrated and holistic approach, addresses some of the criticism of the competence approach but the problematic issue of measurement remains.

No discussion of competence would be complete without reference to occupational standards. In one way they are the flipside of a coin with competence on the other. Instead of specifying what a person is deemed competent to do, occupational standards specify what the public can expect from a practitioner. As Eraut (1994, p. 211) states 'All professions should have public statements about what their qualified members are competent to do and what people can reasonably expect from them'. Occupational standards 'define the level of performance required for the successful achievement of work expectations', according to Storey (1998, p. 3). Some schools of nursing in the UK are adopting occupational standards for postregistration education of nurses in addition or as an alternative to competence-based approaches. This will soon be reflected in preregistration nurse education, in common with all of the UK higher education sector, with the move towards benchmarking statements for health care programmes (Quality Assurance Agency for Higher Education 2001). However, as Eraut (1994) indicates, instead of very general statements about competence – with all the inherent problems that competence entails – this may lead to 'cumbersome standards' (p. 212) which take too long to read and an over-zealous hunt for perfection. Eraut (1994) addresses this by saying that 'trying too hard to produce a foolproof system will only make intelligent people feel that they are being treated like fools' (p. 212).

To summarize, competence may be achieved merely by undergoing a period of education or training in a particular aspect of nursing without performance being assessed. On the other hand, competence may be achieved by a general level of performance being assessed or it may be achieved by having a number of component parts of competence, so called competencies, being performed. Lack of consensus on whether competence equates to potential or actual ability leads to a broad spectrum of ways in which competence is defined, operationalized and, of course, assessed (Eraut 1998). According to Howard *et al.* (1990, p. 31) 'There are as many evaluative measures as there are approaches to clinical instruction' leading to 'ambiguity, inaccuracy, and subjectivity' in assessing competence'.

Assessment of competence

Even where agreement has been reached about the definition of competence and whether or not performance is necessary in order to demonstrate it, there are major issues regarding the assessment of competence. Assessment of competence invariably involves some form of measurement by one person of another. The person making the assessment has to indicate the level of competence attained by the person being assessed or, at least, has to indicate that they have attained a particular threshold for competence. According to Rossel and Kakta (1990, p. 17) 'Prior to the 1960s, clinical evaluations were based on a general impression derived from repeated student–teacher interactions' but the process has become more specific.

Reliability (the extent to which an instrument measures consistently) and validity (the extent to which an instrument measures the construct of interest) are fundamental issues in the use of measurement and should be applied rigorously to the measurement of clinical competence (Benett 1993). However, it is very rarely the case that these issues have been addressed in the measurement of clinical competence in nursing (Norman *et al.* 2000). There are several dimensions to the validity of a measurement, all of which contribute to the ultimate concept of construct validity. The construct validity of an instrument encompasses its content validity, face validity, convergent validity and discriminant validity, and is underpinned by the authenticity and directness of the items which the instrument contains (Messick 1994). Authenticity means that concepts relevant to the construct of interest are included in the instrument. The inclusion of too many irrelevant concepts will undermine the directness (and sensitivity) of the instrument. Given the lack of consensus about the definition of clinical competence and the means by which it should be measured, the likelihood that vital concepts are excluded and irrelevant concepts are included in existing clinical competence assessment instruments is very high. Nursing is not alone in this, as Cox and Ewan (1988) demonstrate in relation to medicine.

Even if reliable and valid instruments for the measurement of clinical competence are developed, there remains the issue of what level of performance indicates competence and therefore at what level a student can be deemed incompetent. There is likely to be less disagreement on incompetence than on levels of competence (Eraut 1998). If someone is 90% competent, as judged by a series of tasks or observations, are they competent to practise or do they have to achieve 100%? Are some competencies, comprising a level of competence more important than others, do they receive a weighting or do they indicate failure if not achieved? The question also arises of whether competence can be assessed by addressing several individual competencies, each of which may be performed well, when it is the interaction between competencies that is of greater importance (Messick 1994). Clearly, some of these questions will be task- or competency-specific, if competence is being judged by observing and measuring performance. On the other hand, someone could be deemed competent through a display of knowledge, as in an examination, where the pass mark is likely to be considerably less than 100%. Lack of agreement on what competence means compounds these issues.

Whether or not competence is measured using an instrument – however, reliable and valid – or assessors simply make a judgement about the achievement of clinical competence in individual students, the problems of subjectivity and socialization arise (McGaghie 1991). According to Howard (1990, p. 31) 'a myriad of circumstances are created that impede the objective evaluation of students' performance'. One person's judgement, without explicit criteria, is likely to be biased and the judgement may be biased even further – in either direction – by the assessor getting to know the student. This raises the issue of who should carry out clinical competence assessment, as discussed by Toohey *et al.* (1996). If the assessment is carried out, possibly over a significant length of time, by a preceptor, mentor or other individual who works with the student then a socialization process will take place which may bias the assessment. If, on the other hand, an external assessor – a lecturer or person who has not worked with the student – carries out the assessment, then on what basis do they make the assessment? The preceptor or mentor may have had the opportunity to become familiar with the work of the student over a significant period of time, albeit that socialization will take place. However, the external or unfamiliar assessor will have to make a judgement based on a very short observation, which may not be representative of the competence of the student, particularly as demonstration of competence may be impeded by a range of extraneous influences such as 'stage fright', local circumstances and resource deficiencies.

The above methods refer to the assessment of competence as a result either of observation of clinical practice or on the basis of knowledge tests related to clinical practice. An alternative to the above is the objective structured clinical examination (OSCE) which was developed for the training of medical students (Harden *et al.* 1975) and which remains in use (Dupras and Li 1995). The OSCE, where students demonstrate their competence under a variety of simulated conditions, has advantages in that an element of objectivity can be introduced by using observers or examiners who do not know the students and who may even come from other institutions. Another advantage of simulation is that all of the clinical situations which could be tested can be tested; in real life students are unlikely to meet a full range of clinical situations in a clinical setting. However, simulated conditions are artificial and in terms of validity, according to Eraut (1994), are 'second-best'. McKinley *et al.* (2001) strongly recommend that competence he assessed through direct observation of practice. Furthermore, due to the examination nature of the OSCE, some students may perform less well than they would in clinical practice.

This review of methods of clinical competence assessment is by no means comprehensive. For example, self-assessment and the use of portfolios have not been considered but these have been reviewed recently elsewhere (Gannon *et al.* 2001, Redfern *et al.* 2002). Self-assessment is now part of the requirements of UK nurses in terms of professional development and the use of portfolios is one way of achieving this. Clearly, the issue of subjectivity is paramount in self-assessment and the reliability and validity of portfolios is questionable. However, self-assessment of clinical competence could form part of a multimethod approach, as recently advocated (Norman *et al.* 2000), where simulation, clinical assessment and educational assessments relevant to clinical practice are used in a combined approach to assessment of clinical competence.

In summary, the assessment of clinical competence is problematic due to difficulties in deciding what to assess, whether competence should be assessed globally or through multiple competencies, and issues around the lack of objectivity of assessment methods where socialization processes may take place. Simulation overcomes some of these problems but raises others, such as lack of validity. Self-assessment, which is widely encouraged, may be a useful adjunct to other methods of clinical competence assessment.

The study

The present study was conducted in order to answer the research question:

What is the research evidence for the use of clinical competence assessment in nursing?

Method

The research question was addressed by systematic review of the literature relating to clinical competence in cancer nursing, palliative care and clinical competence in nursing. The present paper reports only on the literature on clinical competence in nursing; the literature review on cancer nursing and palliative care will be reported elsewhere.

The literature review was carried out between 1980 and 2000 inclusive using the following search terms: nurse, nursing, nurses and competence, competencies, competences, competency, cancer, palliative care, oncology. The following databases were consulted: Medline, CINAHL, ENB, BIDS, IBSS, ERIC, Web of Science, Nesli, OMNI, ABI, Cochrane Information, EMBase and Psychlit. Only papers in English were reviewed.

The literature review initially identified 245 papers, of which 212 were relevant to the study because they were explicitly and solely concerned with clinical competence assessment generally or in nursing, or with clinical competence assessment in cancer nursing and palliative care. Papers concerned solely with cancer nursing or palliative care were set aside for a separate review which will be published in a separate paper leaving 107 papers. Sixty-one papers were retained as being appropriate for the study because they were solely concerned with clinical competence in nursing, as opposed to medicine or non-nursing education and were not letters, editorials or other opinion pieces that did not make reference to any other literature in the field.

The papers were classified in two ways to produce the matrix shown in Table 1. First, they were read and a classification system derived which categorized them on the grounds of whether they were considering primarily (i) concept clarification of competence (ii) the assessment of competence or (iii) the tensions inherent in competence based approaches to nurse education. Second, the papers were read and classified according to the main method or characteristics described by the authors used to study competence and this produced the following categories: unclassified, reviews, correlation, qualitative, experimental. In order to confirm the categorization of papers a random selection of papers in each category was checked by two of the research team (RW & AT).

Table 1 Classification of papers from systematized review

	Concept clarification	Assessment	Tensions	Total
Unclassified	9	10	1	22
Reviews	6	8	5	17
Correlation	–	13	2	16
Qualitative	3	2	–	5
Experimental	–	2	–	2
Total	18	35	8	61

Results

A review, using systematic review methods, was conducted of literature pertaining to the assessment of clinical competence in nursing. This fell into three categories: concept clarification, assessment of competence and tension between competence and other educational approaches. According to subject classification, the majority of papers were concerned with assessment of competence (35) and a small number were concerned with the tensions between competence assessment and education (8). According to the methodological classification, the majority of papers fell into the 'uncertain' category (22): no identifiable method had been used to study competence in nursing. 'Reviews' was the next largest category (17) but none of these took a systematic approach by identifying search term, database or date parameters for the review although some attempted a more research-based approach toward systematically examining the literature (Coates and Chambers 1992, Fitzpatrick *et al.* 1994). The smallest number of papers was concerned with experimental or quasi-experimental studies of competence in nursing education (2). The papers are categorized in Table 2. There is an obvious bias in the literature reviewed towards UK, as opposed to North American literature. This can be explained perhaps by the point that clinical competence may have become more of a 'movement' in North America. The outcome is that there is a considerable North American literature on clinical competence which would not be uncovered by the present review methods due to the fact that it may precede the date parameters set, in other words, it precedes 1980. In addition, taking Benner *et al.*'s work (Benner 1984, Benner *et al.* 1996) and Waltz and Strickland (1990) as examples, some of the most significant work is published in textbooks that were not included in the present review but some of which were referred to as background literature.

Table 2 Classification of papers from systematized review

Paper	Category	Method
Aggleton *et al.* (1987) Developing a system for the continuous assessment of practical nursing skills. *Nurse Education Today* 7, 159–164	A	C
Alspach (1992) Concern and confusion over competence. *Critical Care Nurse* 12, 9–11	D	U
Andre (2000) Grading student clinical performance: the Australian perspective. *Nurse Education Today* 20, 672–679	A	U
Arthur (1999) Assessing nursing students' basic communication skills: the development and testing of a rating scàle. *Journal of Advanced Nursing* 29, 658–665	A	C
Ashworth *et al.* (1999) 'Levels' of attainment in nursing: reality or illusion? *Journal of Advanced Nursing* 30, 159–168	A	C
Ashworth and Morrison (1991) Problems of competence-based nurse education. *Nurse Education Today* 11, 256–260	D	U
Bechtel *et al.* (1999) Problem-based learning in a competency-based world. *Nurse Education Today* 19, 182–187	T	R
Benner (1982) Issues in competency-based testing. *Nursing Outlook* 30, 303–309	A	Q
Bondy (1983) Criterion-referenced definitions for rating scales in clinical evaluation. *Journal of Nursing Education* 22, 376–382	A	U
Bondy (1984) Clinical evaluation of student performance: the effects of criteria on accuracy and reliability. *Research in Nursing and Health* 7, 24–33	A	E
Bondy *et al.* (1997) The development and testing of a competency-focused psychiatric nursing clinical evaluation instrument. *Archives of Psychiatric Nursing* 11, 66–73	A	C
Bradshaw (1997) Defining 'competency' in nursing Part 1: a policy review. *Journal of Clinical Nursing* 6, 347–354	D	U
Bradshaw (1998) Defining 'competency' in nursing Part II: an analytical review. *Journal of Clinical Nursing* 7, 103–111	D	U
Bradshaw (2000) Competence and British nursing: a view from history. *Journal of Clinical Nursing* 9, 321–329	T	R
Bujack *et al.* (1991a) Assessing comprehensive nursing performance: the Objective Structured Clinical Assessment (OSCA) Part 1 – development of the assessment strategy. *Nurse Education Today* 11, 179–184	A	U
Bujack *et al.* (1991b) Assessing comprehensive nursing performance: the Objective Structured Clinical Assessment (OSCA) Part 2 – report of the evaluation project. *Nurse Education Today* 11, 248–255	A	C
Carlisle *et al.* (1999) Skills competency in nurse education: nurse managers' perceptions of diploma level preparation. *Journal of Advanced Nursing* 29, 1256–1264	D	Q

Table 2 Continued

Paper	Category	Method
Cattini and Knowles (1999) Core competencies for clinical nurse specialists: a usable framework. *Journal of Clinical Nursing* 8, 505–511	D	U
Chapman (1999) Some important limitations of competency-based education with respect to nurse education: an Australian perspective *Nurse Education Today* 19, 129–135	T	R
Clafin (1997) A practical approach to competency. *Journal of Healthcare Quality* 19, 12–18	A	U
Coates (1992) Evaluation of tools to assess clinical competence. *Nurse Education Today* 12, 122–129	A	R
Davies and Hughes (1995) Clarification of advanced nursing practice: characteristics and competencies. *Clinical Nurse Specialist* 9, 156–160	D	R
Donoghue and Pelletier (1991) An empirical analysis of a clinical assessment tool. *Nurse Education Today* 11, 354–362	A	C
Dozier (1998) Professional standards: linking care, competence and quality. *Journal of Nursing Care Quality* 12, 22–29	D	U
Dunn *et al.* (2000) The development of competency standards for specialist critical care nurses. *Journal of Advanced Nursing* 31, 339–346	D	Q
English (1993) Intuition as a function of the expert nurse: a critique of Benner's novice to expert model. *Journal of Advanced Nursing* 18, 387–393	D	R
Eichelberger and Hewlett (1999) Competency Model 101: the process of developing core competencies. *Nursing and Health Care Perspectives* 20, 204–208	A	U
Fitzpatrick *et al.* (1994) The measurement of nurse performance and its differentiation by course preparation. *Journal of Advanced Nursing* 20, 761–768	A	R
Fitzpatrick *et al.* (1996) Operationalization of an observation instrument to explore nurse performance. *International Journal of Nursing Studies* 33, 349–360	A	C
Fitzpatrick *et al.* (1997) Measuring clinical performance: development of the King's Nurse Performance Scale. *International Journal of Nursing Studies* 34, 222–230	A	C
Fosbinder (1994) Patient perceptions of nursing care: an emerging theory of interpersonal competence. *Journal of Advanced Nursing* 20, 1085–1093	A	Q
Friedman and Mart (1995) A supervisory model of professional competence: a joint service/education initiative *Nurse Education Today* 15, 239–244	D	U
Girot EA (1993a) Assessment of competence in clinical practice: a phenomenological approach. *Journal of Advanced Nursing* 18, 114–119	D	Q

Table 2 Continued

Paper	Category	Method
Girot (1993b) Assessment of competence in clinical practice – a review of the literature *Nurse Education Today* 13, 83–90	A	R
Girot (2000) Assessment of graduates and diplomates in practice in the UK – are we measuring the same level of competence? *Journal of Clinical Nursing* 9, 330–337	A	R
Greenhaigh and Macfarlane (1997) Towards a competency grid for evidence-based practice. *Journal of Evaluation in Clinical Practice* 3, 161–165	D	U
Gurvis (1995) The anatomy of a competency. *Journal of Nursing Staff Development* 11, 247–252	A	R
Hardcastle (1999) Assessment of mental health nursing using level 11 academic marking criteria: the Eastbourne assessment of practice scale. *Nurse Education Today* 19 89–92	A	U
Hogston (1993) From competent novice to competent expert: a discussion of competence in the light of the post registration and practice project (PREPP). *Nurse Education Today* 13, 167–171	D	U
Holzemer, Resnik and Slichter (1986) Criterion-related validity of a clinical simulation *Journal of Nursing Education* 25, 286–290	A	C
Houge and Deines (1987) Verifying clinical competence in critical care. *Dimensions of Critical Care Nursing* 6, 102–109	D	U
Inman and Haugen (1991) Six criteria to evaluate skill competency documentation. *Dimensions of Critical Care Nursing* 10, 238–245	A	U
Krichbaum *et al.* (1994) The clinical evaluation tool: a measure of the quality of clinical performance of baccalaureate nursing students. *Journal of Nursing Education* 33, 395–404	A	C
Lofmark *et al.* (1999) A summative evaluation of clinical competence: students' and nurses' perceptions of inpatients' individual physical and emotional needs. *Journal of Advanced Nursing* 29, 942–949	A	C
Manley and Garbett (2000) Paying Peter and Paul: reconciling concepts of expertise with competency for a clinical career structure. *Journal of Clinical Nursing* 9, 347–359	T	R
May *et al.* (1999) Critical thinking and clinical competence: a study of their relationship in BSN Seniors. *Journal of Nursing Education* 38, 100–110	T	C
Maynard (1997) Relationship of critical thinking ability to professional nursing competence. *Journal of Nursing Education* 35, 12–18	T	C
Milligan (1998) Defining and assessing competence: the distraction of outcomes and the importance of educational process. *Nurse Education Today* 18, 273–280	T	R
Nicol *et al.* (1996) Assessment of clinical and communication skills: operationalizing Benner's model. *Nurse Education Today* 16, 175–179	D	U

Table 2 Continued

Paper	Category	Method
Nicol and Freeth (1998) Assessment of clinical skills: a new approach to an old problem. *Nurse Education Today* 18, 601–609	A	U
O'Connor *et al.* (1999) Monitoring the quality of preregistration education: development, validation and piloting of competency based performance indicators for newly qualified nurses. *Nurse Education Today* 19, 334–341	A	C
O'Neill and McCall (1996) Objectively assessing nursing practices: a curricular development. *Nurse Education Today* 16, 121–126	A	U
Roberts *et al.* (1992) Simulation: current status in nurse education. *Nurse Education Today* 12, 405–415	A	R
Roberts and Brown (1990) Testing the OSCE: a reliable measurement of clinical nursing skills. *Canadian Journal of Nursing Research* 22, 51–59	A	C
Ross *et al.* (1988) Using the OSCE to measure clinical skills performance in nursing. *Journal of Advanced Nursing* 13, 45–46	A	E
Stephens (1999) Development of standards for differentiated competencies of the nursing workforce at time of entry/advanced beginner. *Journal of Nursing Education* 38, 298–300	A	U
Sutton and Arbon (1994) Australian nursing – moving forward? Competencies and the nursing profession. *Nurse Education Today* 14, 388–393	T	U
While (1991) The problem of clinical evaluation – a review. *Nurse Education Today* 11, 448–453	A	R
While (1994) Competence vs. performance: which is more important? *Journal of Advanced Nursing* 20, 525–531	D	R
Woolley (1977) The long and tortured history of clinical evaluation. *Nursing Outlook* 25, 308–315	A	R
Worth-Butler *et al.* (1994) Towards an integrated model of competence in midwifery. *Midwifery* 10, 225–231	D	R

Classification code: D, concept of clinical competence; A, assessment of clinical competence; T, tensions between clinical competence and other educational approaches.
Methodological code: U, uncertain method; R, review (not systematic); C, correlational study (quantitative); Q, qualitative; E, experimental.

Discussion

Clinical competence has returned to centre stage in nurse education since 1999; it 'is back and it appears to be back to stay' (Girot 2000, p. 331). However, the concept suffers from a lack of definition, it is difficult to measure and methods claiming to measure it have rarely been tested for reliability and validity. The present review of the literature on clinical competence in nursing, spanning the last 20 years of the 20th century appears to support this view. Generally speaking there are very few papers in this field which have sufficient rigour to inform the debate about clinical competence, many papers are hard to classify on the basis of method and very few address the measurement of clinical competence rigorously.

Concept clarification of clinical competence

The confusion between competence and competency is evident in nursing (Ashworth and Morrison 1991, Alspach 1992), as is the confusion between competence and performance (While 1994). Bradshaw (1997, 1998) gave the issue of competency in nursing thorough consideration, pointing to its lack of definition by the statutory nursing bodies in the UK, and concluded that the lack of definition and 'haphazard' approach to training constituted a threat to the safety of patients. The problem of lack of definition is not unique to preregistration nursing but also applies to specialist and advanced practice (English 1993, Davies and Hughes 1995, Cattini and Knowles 1999, Dunn *et al.* 2000) and to midwifery (Worth-Butler *et al.* 1994). Girot (1993, p. 115) states, in relation to clinical competence that the 'literature appears confusing and contradictory, the term being described as overdefined rather than ill defined'. Notwithstanding some publications outlining models for drawing up competence frameworks and competencies (Houge and Deines 1987, Friedman and Mart 1995, Nicol *et al.* 1996, Greenhaigh and Macfarlane 1997), it would appear that the search for competence is a bottomless pit. Despite several years of competence-based education in nursing, health service managers remain unsatisfied with what nurses are able to do in practice (Carlisle *et al.* 1999).

Assessment of competence

Some authors report favourably on work which claims to measure clinical competence in nursing (Aggleton *et al.* 1987, Inman and Haugen 1991, Krichbaum *et al.* 1994, Gurvis 1995, Clafin 1997, Nicol and Freeth 1998, Arthur 1999, Eichelberger and Hewlett 1999, Hardcastle 1999, Lofmark *et al.* 1999, O'Connor *et al.* 1999, Stephens 1999, Andre 2000). However, very few of these studies address reliability and validity. There are some more rigorous studies which do address the issue of reliability (Bondy 1984, Fitzpatrick *et al.* 1994, 1997, Bondy *et al.* 1997, 2000) but few which have directly addressed validity (Bujack *et al.* 1991a,b). Nevertheless, much of the literature which addresses assessment refers to lack of reliability and validity of methods for measuring competence. For example, Girot (2000) – who has addressed the issues of reliability and validity in clinical competence assessment (1993) – points out that we are unable to articulate different levels of competence, for example between diplomate and graduate. If this is the case, then it is hard to imagine how purported levels could be measured and this is supported by Ashworth *et al.* (1999) who demonstrated that lecturers were, indeed, unable to distinguish between supposed diploma and degree competencies when presented out of context. Research has already been referred to (Norman *et al.* 2000), which demonstrated the lack of reliability and validity in current assessment instruments for clinical competence assessment and thus was underpinned by the work of Coates and Chambers (1992), who earlier demonstrated the lack of any systematic approach to the development of clinical competence assessment instruments.

Tensions between competence and education

As indicated in the Introduction, the concept of competence arose in the 1970s and has not been universally accepted in any field of professional education. In other fields, such as education and medicine, where a sound educational background amongst practitioners is assumed, the issue has perhaps not been felt as much as in nursing. In education and medicine, competence training has been used as a way of making educated people better at their jobs. In nursing, which in the UK has moved rapidly from hospital-based schools of nursing through colleges of nursing into higher education, the issue has been more related to whether or not nurses require education at all and whether being competent is not all that should be aspired to. In fact, according to Bechtel *et al.* (1999, p. 182) 'two camps have been formed, one theory-based and one practice-based'. In light of the changes in nurse education of the past decade, Bradshaw (2000, p. 321) asks 'What is the purpose of the modern nurse?' given that the training patterns of the past were clearly aimed at producing competent bedside nurses. She claims that the purpose of nursing in the UK has become 'clouded' and that this has led to the UK government asking for clarification about which common core competencies nurses should have, as articulated recently (Department of Health 1999). On the other hand, some see competency-based education as being limited (Chapman 1999) and offering little to nurse education (Milligan 1998) and only a limited view of nursing practice (Sutton and Arbon 1994).

Conclusion

This systematic review of the literature on clinical competence in nursing was conducted against a background of considerable non-nursing literature on competency based training in other professions. The background literature demonstrated that there was conflict between competency-based and educational-based approaches to training and that competence remained a poorly defined term. Moreover, assessment of competence remains problematic due to lack of rigour in the instruments and methods used for assessment. Nursing, which has adopted a competence-based training system and which has affirmed its affinity for this approach to producing nurses, has apparently learned little from the other areas in which competence has been tried, tested and to a large extent failed. All of the problems of definition, lack of rigour in assessment and tension between competence-based training and other educational approaches are apparent in the nursing literature. There are some notable examples where rigorous approaches have been adopted, as in the use of simulated situations, but the validity of these as a way of preparing nurses for the real world of work are also questionable. In conclusion, it is certainly possible to say that the nursing literature reviewed between 1980 and 2000 does not support the use of competency based approaches to nurse training. This is not the same as saying that competency-based approaches to the preparation of nurses are wrong. However, if a reliable and valid method of competency-based training has been produced then it has not, at the time of reporting, been published.

Acknowledgements

This work was funded by a research grant from the English National Board for Nursing, Midwifery and Health Visiting. The views expressed are those of the authors and not the sponsoring organization.

Contributions

Study design: AT, DP, RW; Literature retrieval: AS; Systematic review: RW; Manuscript preparation: RW, AT.

References

Aggleton P, Allen M, Montgomery S (1987) Developing a system for the continuous assessment of practical nursing skills. *Nurse Education Today* 7: 159–164.

Alspach J G (1992) Concern and confusion over competence. *Critical Care Nurse* 12: 9–11.

Andre K (2000) Grading student clinical performance: the Australian perspective. *Nurse Education Today* 20: 672–679.

Arthur D (1999) Assessing nursing students' basic communication skills: the development and testing of a rating scale. *Journal of Advanced Nursing* 29: 658–665.

Ashworth P (1992) Being competent and having 'competencies'. *Journal of Further and Higher Education* 16: 8–17.

Ashworth P, Morrison P (1991) Problems of competence-based nurse education. *Nurse Education Today* 11: 256–260.

Ashworth P D, Gerrish K, Hargreaves J, McManus M (1999) Levels' of attainment in nursing: reality or illusion? *Journal of Advanced Nursing* 30: 159–168.

Barnett R (1994) *The Limits of Competence, Knowledge, Higher Education and Society.* Open University Press, Buckingham.

Bechtel G A, Davidhizar R, Bradshaw M J (1999) Problem-based learning in a competency-based world. *Nurse Education Today* 19: 182–187.

Benett Y (1993) The validity and reliability of assessment and self-assessment of work-based learning. *Assessment and Evaluation in Higher Education* 18: 83–94.

Benner P. (1984) *From Novice to Expert.* Addison-Wesley, Menlo Park, CA.

Benner P. (1982) Issues in competency-based testing. *Nursing Outlook* 30: 303–309.

Benner P, Tanner C A, Chesla C A (1996) *Expertise in Nursing Practice.* Springer, New York.

Bondy K N (1983) Criterion-referenced definitions for rating scales in clinical evaluation. *Journal of Nursing Education* 22: 376–382.

Bondy K N (1984) Clinical evaluation of student performance: the effects of criteria on accuracy and reliability. *Research in Nursing and Health* 7: 24–33.

Bondy K N, Jenkins K, Seymour L, Lancaster R, Ishee J (1997) The development and testing of a competency-focused psychiatric nursing clinical evaluation instrument. *Archives of Psychiatric Nursing* 11: 66–73.

Bradshaw A (1997) Defining 'competency' in nursing Part 1: a policy review. *Journal of Clinical Nursing* 6: 347–354.

Bradshaw A (1998) Defining 'competency' in nursing Part 11: an analytical review. *Journal of Clinical Nursing* 7: 103–111.

Bradshaw A (2000) Competence and British nursing: a view from history. *Journal of Clinical Nursing* 9: 321–329.

Bujack L, McMillan M, Dwyer J, Hazelton M (1991a) Assessing comprehensive nursing performance: the Objective Structured Clinical Assessment (OSCA) Part 1 – development of the assessment strategy. *Nurse Education Today* 11: 179–184.

Bujack L, McMillan M, Dwyer J, Hazelton M (1991b) Assessing comprehensive nursing performance: the Objective Structured Clinical Assessment (OSCA) Part 2 – Report of the evaluation project. *Nurse Education Today* 11: 248–255.

Carlisle C, Luker K A, Davies C, Stilwell J, Wilson R (1999) Skills competency in nurse education: nurse managers' perceptions of diploma level preparation. *Journal of Advanced Nursing* 29: 1256–1264.

Cattini P, Knowles V (1999) Core competencies for clinical nurse specialists: a usable framework. *Journal of Clinical Nursing* 8: 505–511.

Chipman H (1999) Some important limitations of competency-based education with respect to nurse education: an Australian perspective. *Nurse Education Today* 19: 129–135.

Clafin N (1997) A practical approach to competency. *Journal of Healthcare Quality* 19: 12–18.

Coates V E, Chambers M (1992) Evaluation of tools to assess clinical competence. *Nurse Education Today* 12: 122–129.

Cox K C, Ewan C E (1988) *The Medical Teacher*, 2nd edn. Longman, London.

Davies B, Hughes A M (1995) Clarification of advanced nursing practice: characteristics and competencies. *Clinical Nurse Specialist* 9: 156–160.

Department of Health (1999) *Making a Difference.* DoH, London.

Donoghue J, Pelletier S D (1991) An empirical analysis of a clinical assessment tool. *Nurse Education Today* 11: 354–362.

Dozier A M (1998) Professional standards: linking care, competence and quality. *Journal of Nursing Care Quality* 12 (4): 22–29.

Dunn S, Lawson D, Robertson S, Underwood M, Clark R, Valentine T, Walker N, Wilson-Row C, Crowder K, Herewane D (2000) The development of competency standards for specialist critical care nurses. *Journal of Advanced Nursing* 31: 339–346.

Dupras D.M., Li J.T.C. (1995) Use of an objective structured clinical examination to determine clinical competence. *Academic Medicine* 70, 1029–1034.

Eichelberger L W, Hewlett P O (1999) Competency Model 101: the process of developing core competencies. *Nursing and Health. Care Perspectives* 20: 204–208.

English I (1993) Intuition as a function of the expert nurse: a critique of Benner's novice to expert model. *Journal of Advanced Nursing* 18: 387–393.

Eraut M (1994) *Developing Professional Knowledge and Competence.* Falmer Press, London.

Eraut M (1998) Concepts of competence. *Journal of Interprofessional Care* 12: 127–139.

Fitzpatrick J M, While A E, Roberts J D (1994) The measurement of nurse performance and its differentiation by course preparation. *Journal of Advanced Nursing* 20: 761–768.

Fitzpatrick J M, While A E, Roberts J D (1996) Operationalisation of an observation instrument to explore nurse performance. *International Journal of Nursing Studies* 33: 349–360.

Fitzpatrick J M, While A E, Roberts J D (1997) Measuring clinical performance: development of the King's Nurse Performance Scale. *International Journal of Nursing Studies* 34: 222–230.

Fosbinder D (1994) Patient perceptions of nursing care: an emerging theory of interpersonal competence. *Journal of Advanced Nursing* 20: 1085–1093.

Friedman S, Marr J (1995) A supervisory model of professional competence: a joint service/education initiative. *Nurse Education Today* 15: 239–244.

Gannon F T, Draper P R, Watson R, Proctor S, Norman I J (2001) Putting portfolios in their place. *Nurse Education Today* 2: 534–540.

Girot E A (1993a) Assessment of competence in clinical practice: a phenomenological approach. *Journal of Advanced Nursing* 18: 114–119.

Girot E A (1993b) Assessment of competence in clinical practice – a review of the literature. *Nurse Education Today* 13: 83–90.

Girot E A (2000) Assessment of graduates and diplomates in practice in the UK – are we measuring the same level of competence? *Journal of Clinical Nursing* 9: 330–337.

Gonczi A (1994) Competency based assessment in the professions in Australia. *Assessment in Education* 1: 27–44.

Greenhaigh T, Macfarlane F (1997) Towards a competency grid for evidence-based practice. *Journal of Evaluation in Clinical Practice* 3: 161–165.

Gurvis J P (1995) The anatomy of a competency. *Journal of Nursing Staff Development* 11: 247–252.

Hardcastle .M (1999) Assessment of mental health nursing using level 11 academic marking criteria: the Eastbourne assessment of practice scale. *Nurse Education Today* 19: 89–92.

Harden R McG, Stevenson M, Wilson Downie W, Wilson G M (1975) Assessment of clinical competence using objective structured examination. *British Medical Journal* 1: 447–151.

Hogston R (1993) From competent novice to competent expert: a discussion of competence in the light of the post registration and practice project (PREPP). *Nurse Education Today* 13: 167–171.

Holzemer W, Resnik B, Slichter M (1986) Criterion-related validity of a clinical simulation. *Journal of Nursing Education* 25: 286–290.

Houge M, Deities E (1987) Verifying clinical competence in critical care. *Dimensions of Critical Care Nursing* 6: 102–109.

Howard E P (1990) Measurement of student clinical performance. In: C F Waltz, O L Strickland (eds) *Measurement of Nursing Outcomes*, Vol. 3, pp. 31–43. Springer, New York.

Inman L, Haugen C (1991) Six criteria to evaluate skill competency documentation. *Dimensions of Critical Care Nursing* 10: 238–245.

Krichbaurn K, Rowan M, Duckett L, Ryden M B, Savik K (1994) 'The clinical evaluation tool: a measure of the quality of clinical performance of baccalaureate nursing students. *Journal of Nursing Education* 33: 395–404.

Lofmark A, Hannersjo S, Wikblad K (1999) A summative evaluation of clinical competence: students' and nurses' perceptions of inpatients' individual physical and emotional needs. *Journal of Advanced Nursing* 29: 942–949.

Manley K, Garbett R (2000) Paying Peter and Paul: reconciling concepts of expertise with competency for a clinical career structure. *Journal of Clinical Nursing* 9: 347–359.

May B A, Edell V, Butell S, Doughty J, Langford C (1999) Critical thinking and clinical competence: a study of their relationship in BSN Seniors. *Journal of Nursing Education* 38: 100–110.

Maynard C (1996) Relationship of critical thinking ability to professional nursing competence. *Journal of Nursing Education* 35: 12–18.

McClelland D C (1973) Testing for competence rather than for 'intelligence. *American Psychologist* 28: 1–14.

McGaghie W C (1991) Professional competence evaluation. *Educational Researcher* 20: 3–9.

McKinley R K, Fraser R C, Baker R (2001) Model for directly assessing and improving competence and performance in revalidation of clinicians. *British Medical Journal* 322: 712–715.

Messick S (1994) The interplay of evidence and consequences in the validation of performance exercises. *Educational Researcher* 36: 13–23.

Milligan F (1998) Defining and assessing competence: the distraction of outcomes and the importance of educational process. *Nurse Education Today* 18: 273–280.

Nicol M J, Fox-Hiley A, Bavin C J, Sheng R (1996) Assessment of clinical and communication skills: operationalizing Benner's model. *Nurse Education Today* 16: 175–179.

Nicol M, Freeth D (1998) Assessment of clinical skills: a new approach to an old problem. *Nurse Education Today* 18: 601–609.

Norman L, Watson R, Calman L, Redfern S, Murrells T (2000) *Evaluation of the Validity and Reliability of Methods to Assess the Competence to Practise of Pre-registration Nursing and Midwifery Students in Scotland.* National Board for Nursing, Midwifery and Health Visiting for Scotland, Edinburgh.

O'Connor S E, Pearce R L, Smith D, Vogeli D, Walton P (1999) Monitoring the quality of pre-registration education: development, validation and piloting of competency based performance indicators for newly qualified nurses. *Nurse Education Today* 19: 334–341.

O'Neill A, McCall J M (1996) Objectively assessing nursing practices: a curricular development. *Nurse Education Today* 16: 121–126.

Quality Assurance Agency for Higher Education (2001) *Benchmark Statement: Health Care Programmes.* QAA, London.

Redfern S, Norman L, Calman L, Watson R, Murrells T (2002) Assessing competence to practise in nursing: a review of the literature. *Research Papers in Education* 17: 51–77.

Roberts J, Brown B (1990) Testing the OSCE: a reliable measurement of clinical nursing skills. *Canadian Journal of Nursing Research* 22: 51–59.

Roberts J D, While A E, Fitzpatrick J M (1992) Simulation: current status in nurse education. *Nurse Education Today* 12: 405–415.

Ross M, Garroll G, Knight J, Chamberlain M, Fothergill-Bourbonnais F, Linton J (1988) Using the OSCE to measure clinical skills performance in nursing. *Journal of Advanced Nursing* 13: 45–46.

Rossel C L, Kakta B A (1990) Clinical evaluation of nursing students: a criterion-referenced approach to clinical evaluation based on terminal characteristics. In: C F Waltz, O L Strickland (eds) *Measurement of Nursing Outcomes*, Vol. 3, pp. 17–30. Springer, New York.

Short E C (1984) Competence reexamined. *Educational Theory* 34: 201–207.

Stephens P (1999) Development of standards for differentiated competencies of the nursing workforce at time of entry/advanced beginner. *Journal of Nursing Education* 38: 298–300.

Storey L (1998) Functional analysis and occupational standards: their role in curriculum development. *Nurse Education Today* 18: 3–11.

Sutton F A, Arbon P A (1994) Australian nursing – moving forward? Competencies and the nursing profession. *Nurse Education Today* 14: 388–393.

Toohey S, Ryan G, Hughes C (1996) Assessing the practicum. *Assessment and Evaluation in Higher Education* 21: 215–227.

United Kingdom Central Council for Nursing Midwifery and Health Visiting (1999) *Fitness for Practice.* UKCC, London.

Waltz C F, Strickland O L (1990) *Measuring Nursing Outcomes.* Springer, New York.

Watson R (2001) Elitism, advanced practice and the Charge of the Light Brigade. *NTresearch* 6: 791–796.

Watson R, Thompson D R (2000) Recent developments in UK nurse education: horses for courses or courses for horses? *Journal of Advanced Nursing* 32: 1041–1042.

While A E (1991) The problem of clinical evaluation – a review. *Nurse Education Today* 11: 448–453.

While A E (1994) Competence versus performance: which is more important? *Journal of Advanced Nursing* 20: 525–531.

Winter R, Maisch M (1996) *Professional Competence and Higher Education: the Assett Programme.* Falmer Press, London.

Woolley A S (1977) The long and tortured history of clinical evaluation. *Nursing Outlook* 25: 308–315.

Worth-Butler M, Murphy R J, Fraser D M (1994) Towards an integrated model of competence in midwifery. *Midwifery* 10: 225–231.